PROTECTED CELL COMPANIES:

a guide to their implementation and use

Second edition

AF755293

NIGEL FEETHAM

LLB, LLM, Barrister-at-Law (Gibraltar)

GRANT JONES

LLB, LLM, FCA, FCCA, FCIArb, Solicitor (England and Wales) New York Attorney and Licensed Insolvency Practitioner (UK) and Special Professor of Law at Nottingham University

Hassans

COOPER • PARRY

Published by Spiramus Press Ltd,
102 Blandford Street, London, W1U 8AG.

First published 2008

Second edition March 2010

© Spiramus Press Ltd 2010

ISBN 978 1904905 92 9

British Library Cataloguing-in-Publication Data.

A catalogue record for this book is available from the British Library.

The right of Nigel Feetham and Grant Jones to be identified as the authors of this work has been asserted by them in accordance with the Copyright, Designs and Patents Act, 1988.

All rights reserved. No part of this publication may be reproduced, stored in a retrieval system or transmitted, in any form or by any means, electronic, mechanical, photocopying, recording and/or otherwise without the prior written permission of the Publishers. This book may not be lent, resold, hired out or otherwise disposed of by way of trade in any form, binding or cover other than that in which it is published without the prior written consent of the publishers.

Note from the authors and publisher: This book is not intended to offer legal, tax or regulatory advice. No liability is accepted by the authors, publishers or their servants or agents for the use of information contained herein in any circumstances. Nor are the authors, publishers or their servants or agents responsible for any errors or omissions within the book. The documents provided in the Appendices to this book are for guidance purposes only and should not be treated as definitive. No resemblance to any company or entity is intended nor should be inferred from any documentation. Where statutory or legal references are cited anywhere in the book, the primary sources should be checked before they are even relied upon.

This publication is based upon the law as at 19 February 2010.

Typeset by: Spiramus Press Ltd Printed and bound by CPI Group (UK) Ltd, Croydon, CR0 4YY

To our Mothers, without whom
nothing ever was possible

Acknowledgments

When we first embarked on the task of creating the 'PCC book' we were treading on unploughed land where no one had gone before. However, since the first edition, academic interest has grown.

We would like to acknowledge all those who have assisted with this second edition. In particular we are very grateful to our respective associated firms, Hassans, Squire Sanders Dempsey London ("SSD") and Cooper Parry LLP; more especially at Hassans Yvonne Chu-Feetham (for her unflinching support) and at Cooper Parry LLP, Michelle Murray.

Tribute should also be paid to those who have reviewed the second edition draft material at some stage, more especially, Thomas J. Salerno of SSD, Professor Larry Ribstein, Jonathan Drake of Ashursts and Gabriel Moss QC. We also re-iterate our thanks to those who helped with the first edition.

Also, a debt of gratitude to all those who have given us encouragement and/or help with the second edition of this book: Robin Amos, John Steven De Lara (John Stephen completed his LLM thesis at Nottingham University on the subject of PCCs after reading the first edition of the book), Jack Husbands, Srećko Vujaković, Raffaela Rametta, Edward Rands, Philip Rogers, Belen Valarino, Freddie White, Adrian Hogg, John Rowson, Peter Cottrell, Matthew J. O'Toole, Steve Quinn, Dr Paul Woehrmann, Mike Harvey and Peter Abbott. In particular, we are deeply appreciative of the time so willingly given by Robin (an authority on the Cell Captive in his own right); so too for the help from James Oton.

We would thank our publisher, Spiramus, especially Carl Upsall for his proof reading and skillful editing. Finally we owe a debt of gratitude to our families. We acknowledge too the debt of gratitude we owe to our clients without whom we would never have gained the experience to write this book.

Special thanks also to Shannon, Matthew, Nancy and Margaret for being so understanding.

All views expressed in this book are entirely the authors' own and we therefore remain solely responsible for any errors and/or omissions.

About the Authors

Nigel Feetham is a partner at Hassans International Law Firm. His area of practice includes insurance, funds, and structured finance including tax work. He has been a leading figure in the local financial community for a number of years and has played a major part in some of the most significant developments in the Gibraltar finance sector. He has advised the Government on the implementation of specific legislation including the Protected Cell Companies Act and the modernisation of Gibraltar's funds legislation. Nigel is also a non-executive member of the Gibraltar Financial Services Commission. He graduated with a First Class Honours degree from Manchester Metropolitan University, and was awarded a Masters degree in law with Distinction at Manchester Victoria University. He serves as a non-executive director in a number of Gibraltar insurance company Boards.

Grant Jones first practised as a chartered accountant before realising the law was easier. He practises as an attorney with Squire Sanders Dempsey London. But accountancy could not keep him away. He is a partner with the London office of Cooper Parry LLP, a UK medium sized accounatcy practice. His professional practice encompasses insolvency, finance, pensions, arbitration, and of course, PCCs. He is a member of the Governing Council of the Institute of Chartered Accountants in England and Wales, and a Special Professor of Law at Nottingham University.

Preface to the Second Edition

The first edition of this book was based on the law as at 24 January 2008. We pointed out back then that there was a dearth of legal authority and detailed commentary on the subject of the protected cell company. Since then there have been developments on different aspects of this subject.

On the judicial front, the proposed amalgamation of a PCC with a conventional company was the subject of judicial decision in Guernsey (the original home domicile of the PCC), whilst a decision of the tax appellant tribunal in India found in favour of a foreign taxpayer incorporated as a PCC. There has also been a helpful tax ruling issued by the Australian Tax Office recognising the PCC structure and the existence of the PCC as a legal entity within the territory of the EU was recognised for the first time in the draft European Commission proposal for the Savings Directive of 24 April 2009.

The first redomiciliation (migration) of a PCC between EU Member States took place in 2008 and many new cell companies have been set up over the last two years. Also, the PCC has been involved in several cross border litigation cases. Finally, in the context of a non-EU insolvency, the House of Lords unanimous decision in *McGrath v Riddell [2008] UKHL 21* has come to the aid of the PCC.

In the insurance industry, the major project of the moment is Solvency II, due to become operational in late 2012. The full implications of this are beginning to be widely recognised since the EU Framework Directive was published. We discuss how the PCC structure is particularly well-suited to a risk-based solvency regime such as Solvency II.

We have also added new chapters on US 'Series LLCs' (a business form analogous to the PCC first introduced in Delaware in 1996) and taxation. This second edition has therefore drawn heavily from the experience in the US.

In this second edition, chapters have been updated to take account of these and other developments whilst retaining the practical emphasis of the first edition. Writing the first edition of the book (with its many imperfections as we acknowledged at the time) was not easy. But we expected it would be easier to update future editions of the book as materials became available and in particular as we drew from our professional experience in areas of interest to the book.

There is still a great deal of misconception on what a PCC is. Even today, some people refer to the PCC as a 'fund' and a cell as a 'nominee' for the relevant cell shareholder.

The extraordinary events in the international financial markets since the summer of 2007 affected every financial domicile, and generated a huge amount of scepticism of financial innovation, amongst the general public, and with governments and regulators alike. A full treatment of this subject is unfortunately beyond the scope of this book.

Although the PCC is not a commonly used business form and still tends to be restricted to specialist areas, the technology under which it operates has been widely used. There are also numerous structures across many jurisdictions that share the essential features of the PCC including the ICC and the Series LLC. A positive trend is that more and more lawyers, accountants and institutions are now making these entities available to their clients. In many ways, the subject discussed in this book is no longer just about 'the PCC'. It is about 'segregated business structures' and in future years the PCC will likely become part of this wider subject-matter as what was once seen as a relatively new business form receives international acceptance from professionals, lawmakers, and of course, the judiciary.

Among the many articles and materials we have read when compiling this new edition the words of Professor Ribstein are worth repeating and echo as true today as when they were written in 2003: *"The recent past shows that our "laboratory" of state laws can develop and refine business forms when the business need arises, notwithstanding seeming tax or theoretical impediments. We can promote this laboratory by keeping the road to the future as free as possible of regulatory and tax potholes. There are also ways to encourage evolution. In particular, the future, like the past, owes to the work of lawyers in the trenches, both on behalf of clients in individual cases and at the bar and law-reform level. Preserving this dynamic system is a key to this country's continued prosperity" (LLCs: Is the future here? Business Law Today, Vol 13, Number 2, November 2003).*

As we pointed out in the Preface to the first edition, due to the international nature of this book we accept that in writing about specific statutory provisions or legal principles in other jurisdictions, we may have erred in some instances. Notwithstanding this, the book is not intended to offer legal advice of any kind or in respect of any jurisdiction (including Gibraltar or England).

Finally, we apologise! PCCs are a worldwide phenomenon. Perforce, we are two Euro-centric authors and if our non-European readers, especially US readers, think we have overstated matters, we acknowledge that in future editions, we will need to pay more heed to non-European developments.

Request for Information

With a view to improving future editions of the book, we continue to ask readers to send us your comments and/or materials on any of the subjects covered by this edition.

Foreword to the Second Edition
By Professor Larry Ribstein, Illinois, USA

This Second Edition of *Protected Cell Companies* is not only a valuable resource for practitioners who work with this important new business form, but also an insightful look at the dynamic processes of business innovation. I am particularly interested in this book because it demonstrates the importance of two phenomena I have studied in two recent books – the role of jurisdictional competition in business development – what Erin O'Hara and I call *The Law Market* – and the increasing importance of non-corporate or alternative business forms, which I have referred to as *The Rise of the Uncorporation.*

Nigel Feetham and Grant Jones show us how PCCs began, as is typical of business innovation, with contracts that "ring-fenced" sets of assets from creditors' claims against related assets. However, only a statute could provide the necessary certainty and predictability. It is therefore not surprising that the next step was the enactment of "protected cell company" statutes, first in the early 1980s in Bermuda, and then in 1997 in Guernsey. The statutes helped provide a foundation for the all-important bankruptcy protection of the individual cells. The enactment of these statutes was encouraged by the flexibility inherent in unincorporated business forms.

The enactment of the Guernsey statute gave rise to the First Edition of this book, which itself provides the legal analysis essential to further use and development. The book provides comprehensive guidance on such complex issues as insolvency, veil-piercing, tax, accounting and even Shariah law issues. As lawyers and business people came to understand the PCC its uses spread from its origins in captive insurance companies to providing a bankruptcy remote vehicle for special purpose vehicles, credit derivatives, and open-end investment companies. The authors show that PCCs are now widely used by insurers, insurance brokers, banks, investment and fund managers and international tax planning advisers. They also describe the use of PCCs and related devices not only in their originating jurisdictions but in the EU, the US and around the world.

The next step in the development of new business forms is their spread in the "law market" beyond the originating jurisdiction. Feetham and Jones insightfully analyze how the contractual origins of the PCC support cross-jurisdictional enforcement along the lines of other commercial contracts.

As an American I was particularly interested in the authors' analysis of recent developments in the "Series LLC" in the US, beginning in Delaware in 1996, around the time of the enactment of the Guernsey statute. The authors accurately spot a critical distinction between the Series LLC and the PCC in the former's more complete separation of the cells. This illustrates jurisdictional competition's laboratory for experimentation with new business forms. The opportunity for further experimentation in the 51 US jurisdictions arguably counterbalances what Feetham and Jones call the "missed opportunity" of the US refusal to propose a uniform Series LLC provision. Further development in the US will continue to proceed on a state-by-state basis. This is perhaps slower than if the Series LLC had been accorded official recognition through a uniform law, but surer because of the opportunity for testing new approaches.

Feetham and Jones note that while Delaware enacted PCC legislation aimed at the captive insurance market, Guernsey is likely to remain the gold standard for such legislation because it has already attracted significant support, and because Delaware's LLC-based series concept cannot easily be exported outside the US. However, I am not sure that we have yet seen the end of the multi-jurisdictional evolutionary process, and the Series LLC may yet prove to be globally influential. One reason for this is the greater separation it offers between cells, as discussed further below.

The authors insightfully discuss several issues that may determine the future of the PCC/Series LLC concept. First, there is so far little illuminating case law either in the US or around the world clarifying the application of these concepts in their home jurisdictions and in other states and countries, particularly regarding enforcement of the cells' internal firewalls. This clarification is a necessary prerequisite for the further expansion and development of the concept. But it is likely that the use of these devices has spread widely enough that judicial clarification is an inevitable next step.

Second, the authors wonder if the PCC is likely in the long run to be more accepted across US jurisdictions than the Series LLC. They cite several factors supporting this conclusion, including the fact that the US PCC is limited to insurance, supported by the powerful insurance sector and endorsed by state regulators, has been used throughout the world, and originated in contractual arrangements that have been used for many years. However, another plausible scenario is the Series LLC will become widely accepted in the US for a variety of purposes while the PCC remains a niche vehicle for captive insurers.

Third, there is a question concerning whether the PCC might be superseded by a later development, the Incorporated Cell Company, or ICC, which permits cells to be incorporated into separate entities. As the authors note, the ICC can be seen as a creation of the "legal laboratory." The authors observe that this may aid recognition of cell separation by foreign jurisdictions, which already recognize corporations as separate entities for liability purposes. However, as the authors note, courts may see no substantial difference between the two types of firms, or may at least pierce the veil. It is worth noting that the ICC is actually similar to the US Series LLC because of the separation between the cells. If the Series LLC becomes widely accepted and the internal firewall enforced across jurisdictions, the Series LLC ultimately may replace the ICC.

Fourth, there is a question of how the development of the PCC may be affected by hostility toward financial innovation that has arisen in the wake of turmoil in financial markets and the Madoff scandal and PCCs' association with offshore financial centers. The authors note that the suspicion and risk may increase as PCC deals increase in size and complexity and used for new purposes. They suggest that PCCs should be enforced if properly structured, marketed and managed and kept within the current legislative bounds. Surely this book will serve as an essential guide to accomplishing these goals. In the long run, as the authors suggest, there is a strong argument for protecting the PCC through an international convention.

In short, this book, particularly in its new edition, is both a valuable tool for the practitioner and important grist for the academic. It is certainly rare in combining these features and should enjoy great success.

Larry E. Ribstein, University of Illinois College of Law, Champaign, Illinois, USA

February 2, 2010

Foreword to the First Edition

By Steve Butterworth, Guernsey

It is fairly well known that the PCC was introduced under my stewardship as an insurance regulator in Guernsey 10 years ago. What is less well known is that the concept was conceived (at least intellectually) much earlier, during my time in the Cayman Islands.

There was certainly a Eureka moment! It happened in the Cayman Islands in 1983 or 1984, I forget which year.

There were several events which influenced the way that I was thinking. They were mainly tax-related and concerned US-owned, single-parent captive insurance companies.

Premiums paid to a captive insurer could be disallowed by the authorities as a tax deduction in the parent's tax computation because the insurance company (the captive) was in the same economic family as the policyholder (the parent).

Most tax systems can be unfair, but this one seemed to unfairly penalise those companies having their own insurance companies. Cost savings and dividends from the captive, and better and more efficient risk management, made the parent financially stronger, and able to make a greater contribution to the parent company and thus to the US economy.

There were some exemptions to the "economic family" principle, one of which was used or (from my regulatory perspective) abused extensively! This was for the captive to write more than a prescribed percentage of third party business. It was just what an insurance regulator did not want to see, namely, a captive, which knew its parent risks inside out, starting to write 'other' ill-considered risks, purely driven by tax considerations at parent company level. There were some notable casualties, particularly amongst captives owned by some major companies, as unexpected and substantial claims soon started to materialise from the unrelated business.

There must be another way I thought to myself! The obvious solution was for the premiums to be paid to an insurer that was not considered part of the happy economic family, but for the parent to still be able to benefit from any profits made from its insurance arrangements.

The Eureka moment came a year or so later sitting in my office in the "glasshouse" (local knowledge needed), reflecting upon a drinks reception following the first annual general meeting of a group of US-based podiatrists, who were very pleased, even though they told me they had made quite a high initial loss. There were several firms of podiatrists owning and participating in the association captive insurer. As podiatry skills varied throughout the association, those with better loss prevention methods were fearful that the losses of their lesser brethren would eat into their own profits. Thus they all separately engaged lawyers whose task it was to protect their client's assets as far as they were able to.

The thought was of a company that had separate parts, with statutory force, each protecting a block of assets from the liabilities of the other parts, whilst still being a single legal entity.

The main single purpose in my mind was the protection (or ring-fencing) of assets but I have to admit, as a Chartered Tax Advisor by background, I also thought of this as a way of solving the problem that US-owned single parent captives were facing. This latter would be the icing on the cake – if it worked of course! It seemed to me to be just an extension of the limited company concept, albeit with some concerns on creditor protection and on international recognition.

It was perhaps a bit too radical for the time and was also too early for Guernsey to consider when I took up my regulatory position there in 1986. I must admit to not being as forceful as I should have been in promoting the idea. Even the insurance sector, which was later to be one of the principal beneficiaries, was only partly in favour. It was, however, in 1994 when the fund sector, which recognised the structure as ideal for an umbrella fund, supported the concept, that we were able to make progress.

The first drafting of the legislation was unsuccessful and a senior lawyer in the local private sector, Advocate Nik van Leuven (who is now HM Procureur to the States of Guernsey) offered to start from scratch and to produce the PCC legislation. When I read his draft, I was delighted, as it was very user-friendly and very much how I had imagined the concept, with one remarkable exception. I had not envisaged that individual cells would be able to issue 'cell shares'. Was this consistent with concept of the 'single legal entity'? I had always considered that the cell participants would receive their profits back by way of return premiums or even by way of loans, but I was thinking only of insurance operations and was persuaded that having the ability to have cell shares, and thus pay dividends, was the only way that the legislation would be acceptable to potential participants.

Before I saw the draft legislation, I could see numerous insurance uses – rent-a-captives, association captives, life companies for high net worth individuals, composites, joint ventures and securitisations etc., but once I realised that the legislation was an extension of company law, as an ex-practitioner in offshore company management, I could envisage myriads of opportunities, especially in the asset management sector. Of course, whether or not there would be rapid growth in PCCs would depend on several factors, not least of which would be the industry (and especially their international legal advisors) acceptance, as well as its recognition world-wide.

Because it was a new concept (although I later found out that there was private legislation in Bermuda that performed similar functions) it was decided to restrict the uses to insurance companies and collective investment funds, when it made its debut in Guernsey on 1 February 1997.

I was delighted when the Cayman Islands followed with their own version reasonably quickly, although despite my plea to the contrary, they called their version a 'segregated portfolio company'. Later Bermuda would call their version a 'segregated accounts company' – as if a poor old prospective policyholder needed any more confusion!

It was also very encouraging to see certain States in the US introducing their own versions as this would help achieve international recognition we so much hoped for.

The last 10 years has witnessed the rapid evolution and growth of the PCC and also the recent development of incorporated cell companies (ICCs), of which I thoroughly approve. As I write this foreword in early 2008 I believe that there are over 300 such entities with literally thousands of cells. For the future, I really believe that we have only scratched the surface and that cell companies will become a very common vehicle in many structures.

Against this background, I welcome this book on the subject. I am very surprised that it has taken 10 years! The book is written by professionals with extensive experience of the Protected Cell Company. Their insight on a wide array of topics related to the PCC should prove beneficial to the understanding, development process and advancement of the industry.

Good luck with future innovation!

Steve Butterworth,
Guernsey, February 2008.

Contents

Tables of Authorities

Cases

Statutes

Rules and Statutory Instruments

EU Directives /Regulations

Statutes and Regulations of other Authorities

Accounting Rules

Introduction

In January 1998 the Home Office appointed Mr. Andrew Edwards, a former HM Treasury official, to conduct a review of the laws, systems and practices in Guernsey, Jersey and the Isle of Man, specifically in respect of regulating banking, insurance and financial services business, combating money laundering and registering companies.

The review was conducted with the authorities in each of the islands and led to the publication of a report on 19 November 1998, *Review of Financial Regulation in the Crown Dependencies* (the "Edwards Report").

The report made the following observations under the heading "Protected Cell Companies", a type of company which had first been introduced a year earlier (1997) in Guernsey:

"*9.9.5 A critical question, which has prompted considerable debate, is whether the protection of the cells would stand up in the event of legal challenge. If one of the cells became insolvent, and the PCC's common capital was insufficient to pay the debts, the liquidator or others would doubtless seek to realise assets from the other cells to pay the creditors. Depending on the scale of the debts, the other cells too could be put at risk.*

9.9.6 In the view of the lawyers I have consulted, Courts in all the major jurisdictions would consider ineffective protected cell structures established by means of contracts within an ordinary company (that is, not within a PCC). Such contracts would be seen as an attempt to put shareholders above creditors. The other cells would be deemed liable, pari passu, if the company's capital was insufficient.

9.9.7 The question, therefore, is whether the Guernsey law would give the other cells protection where a contractual agreement would not.

9.9.8 If the case were heard in Guernsey and the assets were in Guernsey, the structure would doubtless be effective.

9.9.9 As the Guernsey authorities themselves have been the first to acknowledge, however, there is no knowing whether Courts in other jurisdictions would accept the structure or set it aside, especially in cases concerning PCC debts and assets in other jurisdictions.

9.9.10 This issue arose soon after the original legislation was introduced. After consultation with a leading UK QC[1]*, therefore, the Guernsey authorities have amended the legislation to make clear that the provisions as to limitation of liability are, under the rules of international law, substantive and not merely procedural. The authorities believe that the legislation, as amended, will be effective in protecting the assets of individual cells from the liabilities of other cells.*

9.9.11 The uncertainty over how overseas Courts would regard the legislation is clearly a factor which any potential participant in a protected cell structure needs to weigh carefully. The Guernsey authorities have rightly, therefore, been scrupulous in making clear that the legislation has not been tested in the Courts. They should continue to ensure that firms offering such structures are similarly scrupulous."

The legal issues surrounding the PCC are too complex to have expected a more considered response. The observations in the Edwards Report although broadly accurate, were incomplete. Almost 12 years later, this second edition of the book attempts to revisit and discuss these very same issues in a manner which it is hoped is both meaningful and practical. In particular, it will consider the legal framework within which the PCC operates and the main legal (including insolvency) issues which arise in relation to them.

---

[1] The QC was Gabriel Moss QC, the leading UK legal commentator on protected cell companies, who also subsequently advised the Government of Gibraltar on its implementation of PCC legislation.

1. RING FENCING AND THE EVOLUTION OF THE CELL COMPANY

One of the risks of the globalisation of trade and commerce is the introduction of legal concepts emanating from one jurisdiction into another. These new concepts may not necessarily be upheld in the new jurisdiction. This is particularly so in respect of insolvency legislation. Against this background, there are, essentially, two views of the Protected Cell Company[2] (PCC). One view is that the segregated cell (or segregated portfolio *et al*) is an efficient way of executing business activity using the corporate medium and that its use should not be restricted. The alternative view is that this is an innovation that is relatively untested in any court and therefore best avoided. The answer surely lies somewhere in the middle of these two extremes, namely limiting, at least initially, the use of the PCC to defined business activities. Most policy makers and regulators in legislating in this area have preferred this approach.

Protected Cell Company legislation is, of course, a fairly recent creation in offshore jurisdictions including Bermuda, the Cayman Islands, Guernsey and in the 'onshore jurisdictions' of many US States. Some jurisdictions are only now taking the initial necessary steps to implement PCC legislation (e.g. Labuan and the UK). The most common use so far for this type of company is captive insurance. The legal structure has also been used for collective investment schemes and in more recent times in other areas such as 'repackaging'. Interestingly, Gibraltar was the first EU jurisdiction that implemented PCC legislation. Malta followed Gibraltar's lead when it joined the European Community.

Although it is not possible to state the value of assets held through such companies or indeed the corresponding liabilities, given the proliferation of the PCC worldwide, this cannot be insignificant. The number of domiciles with PCC legislation has been estimated to now stand at 39, with an approximate total of 300 cell companies and an estimated 3000 cells worldwide (Cell Company Handbook 2009) (see table 1 below).

---

[2] There are many other terms used throughout the world, including Segregated Portfolio Company (SPC) and Segregated Account Company (SAC). For the sake of simplicity, this book shall refer throughout to the 'PCC'.

Territory	Total number of cell companies	Total number of individual active cells
EUROPE		
Gibraltar	5	29
Guernsey	72	344
Isle Of Man	3	7
Malta	4	10
Jersey	8	-
CARRIBEAN & BERMUDA		
Anguilla	8	-
Cayman Islands	126	514
Barbados	14	9
Bermuda	271	-
BVI	9	18
NORTH AMERICA		
Arizona	1	-
District of Columbia	10	12
Hawaii	1	1
Montana	1	2
Nevada	5	1
Oklahoma	1	1
South Carolina	2	27
Vermont	17	67
MIDDLE EAST & AFRICA		
Dubai	1	-
ASIA PACIFIC		
Vanuatu	1	6

Source: Cell Company Handbook 2009, a Captive Review Publication

Table 1: Cell Company activity by region

However, it would be a mistake to think that the idea of one corporate entity representing a number of different economic interests is something new or that such companies can only operate under a legislative regime for protected cell companies. This is not the case. The concept of a statutory regime for such companies may be relatively new, but the basic mechanics by which they perform their function have been widely used by the banking, insurance and fund sectors over many years.

In the insurance sector, in particular, cell captive type vehicles have been a feature in the market long before PCC legislation was ever introduced. In Gibraltar, for example, the first cell captive facility was set up in 1996, although the concept was previously developed and used extensively in a number of jurisdictions over many years (e.g. South Africa). Such structures rely on contractual arrangements between the various participants. It is therefore common to refer to them as 'contractual cell companies'. In truth, as we will see, contractual cell companies and protected cell companies within the statutory regime can (and do) co-exist side by side. The objective of cell-segregation can therefore be achieved through common law contractual principles without the need for legislation, as it had for many years before the PCC came into the scene. Despite the common ignorance today of what a PCC is, as we will see it is no different in its intended effect from the tools already widely used in markets of all kinds.

It is not just the modern financial markets that have sought segregation of assets and liabilities through innovative solutions. An early historical example of an attempt to segregate assets and liabilities as between separate operations of a single business dates as far back as the 15th century and to the most pre-eminent of banking families, the Medici of Florence. Previous leading banks had collapsed when branches of the business amassed huge debtors who could not, or in the case of Edward III of England, would not repay their debts. The shrewd Medici family is credited with the innovation of establishing a holding company structure and separate entity for each branch of the Medici Bank, thereby protecting the holding company from the bankruptcy of separate branches situated in major European cities of the time.

As Tim Parks writes in his highly readable book '*Medici Money: Banking, Metaphysics, and Art in Fifteenth-Century Florence*', "*The relationship of these branches to each other and to the central office in Florence was to be crucial. The Bardi and Peruzzi banks that had preceded the Medici collapsed in part because there was no juridical distinction between its operations in different countries. The bank as a whole was liable for the debts of each of its outlets. [The Medici] resolved these difficulties with a simple structural correction.... Each branch was to be a separate company. The shareholders were: the branch director ... and the Medici Bank .... Not the Medici family personally, and not the Florence branch, which had the same status as other branches, but rather a separate holding company located in a separate office in Florence."* Such risk management innovation intended to offer legal protection to an international banking business from bankruptcy following the failure of separate branches, predated modern banking regulation and supervision, but judging by the successful growth of the Medici's banking activities during the 15th century must have achieved acceptance without geographical limitation.

1.1. The Cell Captive

The relative ease with which large and medium sized corporate entities could set up their own insurance company and underwrite (and control) their own insurance programme, retaining those layers of risk that they considered were predictable and reinsuring what risk they chose not to retain, developed the captive industry into a multi-billion dollar global industry. The cell captive itself is an evolution of the captive insurance market and has been used as a risk management tool for over 30 years. Such facilities allow the users to enter a captive both as owner and insured with the same benefits as a wholly owned captive. It is crucial to the structure that the business underwritten for separate insured is segregated (ring-fenced) and accounted for individually - thus why each is referred to as a 'cell'. The term cell in this context, of course, has no statutory basis. It is a market term used to describe the separation of business (and economic interests) within the company in respect of different participants. Having said this, the "protected cell company" legislation was undoubtedly first conceived specifically in response to the needs of the captive insurance market.[3]

What is interesting is that Bermuda has legislated since 1992[4] for the segregation of assets and liabilities for individual reinsurance companies through private Acts of the legislature and therefore did so before Guernsey introduced its PCC Ordinance (public legislation). These were established in Bermuda through statute and the legal regime applied specifically to individual companies rather than to all companies as in the case of public legislation. In no small measure this application of Bermuda private Acts as a means of providing for legal segregation of assets and liabilities enhanced the reputation of the island as a base for leading the world in the evolution of insurance and reinsurance products.

---

[3] See the introduction to this issue in Steve Butterworth's Foreword to the first edition of this book.

[4] The first private Act was the Universal International Reinsurance Limited Private Act 1992.

In 2000, however, Bermuda followed Guernsey in enacting public legislation (which it preferred to call the Segregated Accounts Companies Act rather than Protected Cell Companies Act) and companies seeking to operate segregated accounts would now apply to be registered as a 'SAC'. Some commentators consider that the Segregated Accounts Companies Act strengthens the cell arrangements on the basis that the legislation establishes substantive law whereas private Acts which preceded this legislation were largely procedural law provisions.

1.2. The Cell Captive structure: how does it work?

In a contractual cell captive the objective of cell segregation is achieved by contract based on principles of contract law governing limitation of liability. The corporate structure suitable for this purpose is the company limited by shares and the procedure for incorporation is the same as that of any such company. The company is not, therefore, afforded under the companies legislation a distinct corporate status. There is consequently no need for the constituting document or its corporate name to include the expression either "Protected Cell Company" or "PCC". It follows from this that the 'protection' of assets in a cell company is not effected by anything in the companies or insolvency legislation. It is achieved via contract law.

Under the typical cell captive structure the corporate promoters will hold the ordinary voting shares. The subscription monies for such shares will constitute the general assets of the company. The company then allows equity participation by cell participants in the form of non-voting redeemable preference shares. The proceeds of such issue represent the 'cellular' assets in a PCC structure. The purpose of this is so that each preference shareholder can have risks underwritten though the company with respect to the insurance business undertaken by the company; and also by reference to the value of that shareholders equity capital and retained earnings. This allows each preference shareholder to receive dividends and participate in the earnings allocated from segregated funds supporting the underwriting activities of the respective preference shareholder.

Each preference shareholder will also enter into an insurance contract with the company. In addition to the subscription of shares, each insured will therefore pay premiums under the insurance policy.

The basic structure of a cell captive involves the insured at group level having an ownership interest in the company (along with other insured).

The preference shareholder will therefore be dealing with the company in two capacities; his capacity as shareholder, and, as insured. The separate relationship between the company and the shareholders, and the insured in the first instance, and between the shareholders *inter se*, in the second instance, is the basis for the contractual relationship between the parties. This has several consequences.

First, the Articles of Association constitute the agreement between the members to abide by the internal regulations of the company. Thus, where the company is incorporated in a jurisdiction based on English company law the rights of a member *qua* member can usually (in the absence of a shareholders agreement) only be enforced against other members through the medium of the company.

Second, just as liabilities imposed upon a member are limited to liabilities incurred by him in this capacity, so are the rights that he has against the company limited to rights *qua* member. Consequently, no rights given by the articles in a capacity other than as a member (e.g. as policyholder) can be enforceable as such in that capacity.

Third, since the Articles of Association govern the rights and obligations of members in their capacity as members, any provision in the articles or other contractual provision to which it is a party to, which purports to limit the claims of creditors generally against specific assets of the company for the purpose of making other assets available to meet the liabilities of a particular class of unsecured creditors only, is unenforceable as against those creditors. This is both as a matter of law (i.e. they are not parties to this contract), and as a matter of public policy. The public policy is that of offending the statutory rule of law which provides that a company's assets in winding up shall be realised and applied in satisfaction of the company's debts and liabilities *pari passu*.

In order to enforce and protect rights of shareholders in some other capacity (e.g. as policyholder) or validly agree to the limiting of claims in that other capacity, the shareholder must enter into a contract outside the articles. The preference shareholders in a cell captive will therefore usually enter into a shareholders agreement in similar terms setting out in full the method of calculation, and further, the value of each class fund on which a particular claim under any insurance policy will be limited. Moreover, where in any particular case the insured is not the same person as the preference shareholder, in order to apply the required limited liability, the insurance policy (itself a stand-alone document) should also contain claims limitation language.

In the US case of *Pemaquid Underwriting Brokerage, Inc. v. Mutual Holdings (Bermuda) Ltd No. Civ.A. 02-4691(JAP) June 3, 2003*, involving a Bermudan cell captive, the United States District Court of New Jersey had to consider a choice of venue of a dispute between parties to a cell arrangement. As is typical in such arrangements (and explained above) there was a shareholders agreement which explicitly provided that Bermuda was the choice of forum and Bermuda law applicable to any disputes between the parties. After considering the arguments of the plaintiffs the court held that Bermuda was the appropriate forum for the litigation stating:

"Plaintiffs have not rebutted the presumption of validity that forum selection clauses enjoy. This provision was one clause within an agreement between savvy business individuals. Plaintiffs have offered no proof that their ability to negotiate for a fair agreement was compromised in any way or that they ever objected to the choice of law/choice of forum provision."

1.3. Claims Limitation

The limiting of claims to a prescribed and defined fund, which is the underlying principle of cell-segregation, is therefore achieved by the inclusion of a properly drafted claims limitation clause in the shareholders agreement and insurance policy. Most jurisdictions recognise the principle of freedom of contract and consequently, the right of parties to enforce an agreement in respect of their limitation of liability in given circumstances. Subject to any specific mandatory rules of law on the extent to which liability may be limited, these contractual arrangements are regarded as enforceable in accordance with the relevant contract.

The claims limitation clause inserted in the shareholders agreement for a contractual cell company could read as follows:

"The preference shareholder acknowledges that, notwithstanding anything to the contrary in any agreement, policy, document or notice of the company or in the articles, it shall have no claim against the company whatsoever nor shall the company be in any way liable in respect of or arising out of or in connection with its insurance policies or in respect of any return of capital as a preference shareholder or in respect of any other claim, whether in contract or in tort or otherwise, which the preference shareholder may have against the company, and whether in its capacity as shareholder or as a policyholder or otherwise save to the extent of the amount of the preference shareholder's fund after deducting therefrom all income or amounts accrued but not yet received by the company (if positive). The enforcement of, and all rights and remedies in respect of, all such

claims and liabilities described above is and shall be limited as stated above and the company shall have no further obligation or liability or responsibility in respect thereof. The preference shareholder may not take proceedings or enforce judgment against the company or any assets of, or prove as a secured or unsecured creditor in the liquidation of, the company other than in accordance with this clause. The preference shareholder acknowledges that no claim may be made or enforced against the company by it or on its behalf to the extent that such a claim would have to be satisfied out of funds allocated to other holders of preference shares or to any policyholder, whether such allocation arises pursuant to any agreement between any of the shareholders or policyolders and the company or pursuant to the articles or otherwise. The preference shareholder acknowledges and agrees that any shortfall shall be extinguished and, in particular, that the preference shareholder shall not take any steps to wind-up the company; and

It is agreed that, if the preference shareholder shall succeed in seizing or attaching by any means or otherwise levying execution against any assets attributable to any funds allocated to other holders of preference shares or to any of the ordinary shareholders, the preference shareholder shall hold those assets or their proceeds on trust for the company and keep those assets or proceeds separate and identifiable as such trust property; and

It is further agreed that if the preference shareholder succeeds by any means whatsoever or wheresoever in a claim that would have to be satisfied out of funds allocated to other holders of preference shares or other assets of the company, the preference shareholder shall be liable to the company to pay a sum equal to the value of the benefit thereby obtained by him."

1.4. Unfair Contract Terms Directive

The question will sometimes arise as to whether such contractual provisions conflict with consumer protection legislation. In a European Community context, an example of this is the Unfair Contract Terms Directive.

Council Directive 93/13/EEC provides for unfair terms included in a contract with a consumer (being any natural person who, in contracts covered by the Directive, is acting for purposes which are outside his trade, business of profession)[5] by a seller or supplier being (any natural or legal person who, in contracts covered by the Directive, is acting for purposes relating to his trade, business or profession, whether publicly or

[5] Article 2(b)

privately owned)[6] concluded after 31 December 1994, not to be binding on the consumer. This does embrace insurance contracts. A contract term which has not been individually negotiated is to be regarded as unfair if, contrary to the requirement of good faith, it causes a significant imbalance in the parties' rights and obligations arising under the contract to the detriment of the consumer.

The Directive specifically provides that assessment of the unfair nature of terms shall not relate to the definition of the main subject matter of the contract. Further, nor should it relate to the adequacy of the price and remuneration on the one hand, as against the services or goods supplied in exchange on the other.

It should further be noted that the Directive does not apply to commercial contracts. It would be open to an individual, however, to challenge a limitation clause in an insurance contract as contrary to the Directive. It could be challenged if he could claim that such a clause had not been individually negotiated. However, it would seem unlikely that a court would uphold such a claim where the parties had willingly entered into the contract and the individual was independently advised.

Indeed, the limitation of claims in insurance contracts has been a feature of the market over many years and has generally been recognised and upheld at least in English law. The limiting of claims to a certain amount is an extension of the general principle that the parties to an insurance contract can agree between them that the insurer should limit its liability for claims. Clearly there must be no ambiguity in the contract as any limitation clause will be interpreted strictly in accordance with its terms. It will not necessarily be interpreted by what the parties may or may not have intended. Moreover, if on its proper construction, the clause is interpreted as blocking remedies, rather than limiting liability (i.e. the value of the claim) then such a clause may not be enforced by a court.

Despite the fact that third party claims and liabilities arising outside the shareholder/insured relationship cannot be limited, other than contractual liabilities arising in the ordinary course of its insurance business, a cell captive company (underwriting captive type business) is not expected to be exposed to such claims, and is therefore in a position to control these. It is also worth emphasising that the principle of segregation within the company has to be strictly observed. The assets

[6] Article 2(c)

attributable to a contractual 'cell' have to be segregated in order to be able to determine a valuation for the purposes of redemption *qua* shareholder.

Not surprisingly, the jurisdictions that have historically been the home for cell captives are those with a common law background; their laws having been based on English equivalent legislation. The prevalence of the use of English law as the governing law of certain types of insurance policies even where the risk is not situated in the UK has also historically attracted cell companies looking for contract certainty to the English legal system. Therefore it is common for a contractual cell captive to be incorporated in one jurisdiction (say, Guernsey or Gibraltar) but for the contracts between the parties (including the shareholders agreement) to be governed by English law. The one document governed by local law would have to be the Articles and Memorandum of Association (or equivalent constitutional document). This is because the company would be subject to the overall supervision of the local Registrar of Companies in relation to company law matters. Such matters include its incorporation, administration and other matters so prescribed by its company law such as shareholder disputes, issues of new shares, transfer and redemption of shares, dividends, reductions of capital, reorganisation, receivership and liquidation. Insofar as local company legislation prescribes any mandatory provisions or procedure (including the matters which are subject to supervision of the Registrar of Companies or the courts), local law will govern such matters. In relation to matters not so prescribed or subject to such supervision, effect will be given to the choice of the law as the governing law (e.g. English law in respect of the shareholders agreement).

To avoid any conflict of law issues, a typical shareholder's agreement expressed to be governed by a foreign law states that in the event of conflict with local company legislation or the Memorandum or Articles of Association in relation to a matter prescribed by such legislation, which cannot be modified by the agreement of the parties (as expressed in the shareholder's agreement), then the companies legislation should prevail, but otherwise the shareholders agreement shall prevail.

Although English law is accepted as the choice of law for very many insurance contracts, where it is not possible for the parties to apply English law as the governing law of an insurance policy (e.g. where the territory where the risk is situated applies local law) it would be prudent to consider whether there are any local mandatory rules of law, which cannot be a contracted out of, or mandatory rules which might conflict with the claims limitation clause.

As already pointed out, and notwithstanding where the application of English law is fully recognised by a foreign court, there can be a number of potential claims and liabilities in respect of which the liability of a contractual cell company cannot be limited. The liability of the company to persons who are not a party to the 'contract' logically cannot be limited. Examples of this are liabilities to taxation authorities (including social security) and liability for torts (other than tortious liability to contracting parties). Such liabilities are referred to as 'involuntary creditors' in this book. As a matter of public policy any provisions limiting recourse against a company for claims such as these would be unenforceable.

1.5. Why the need for the protected cell?

The obvious question is: if such contractual structures worked, why did we need PCC legislation? This is the question that all jurisdictions seeking to implement PCC legislation have had to consider. Undoubtedly, the potential weakness of a contractual cell captive structure is that all the liabilities of the company (whether or not referable to particular assets or limited by contract) can, in principle, be sued for or executed upon against the company and its assets. Moreover, whilst the insurer is carrying on business, the contractual arrangements are in essence accounting provisions. However, on insolvency the mandatory *pari passu* distribution rule will take precedence and contractual provisions may not necessarily be respected in all cases. This may be particularly relevant where what the parties propose is for the rights of the policyholders under individual insurance contracts not to be limited in value, but limited to specified assets. Once the insurer is subject to insolvency, of course, the focus is on the actual assets that are available to meet its liabilities as they are valued.

In some jurisdictions, creditors are permitted to limit their rights in this way. For example, the decision of the English High Court in *Maxwell Communications Corporation plc (No 3) [1993] BCC 369* confirmed that an insolvent liquidation does not disturb a contractual agreement by creditors to limit their rights by way of subordination. As a matter of English contract law, it therefore appears that a contractual commitment by policyholders, limiting their rights to certain specified assets, would be enforceable such that they would not be able to claim against the assets supporting the rights of other policyholders. This would be subject, among other things, to those assets being clearly identified. The position is, of course, not free from doubt. Moreover, parties who had not entered into the contractual arrangements would not be bound by such limitations; as we have seen, as a matter of general law such third parties could therefore claim on assets allocated between the contracting parties.

A way of minimizing this risk therefore is to create security interest over such assets. The ring fencing through the creation of a security interest over specific assets is, in essence, similar to the creation of a statutory cell under a PCC. The insurance contracts would therefore all stipulate that the liability of the company would be satisfied from identifiable (secured) assets and to the extent that there was a shortfall, the balance of the claim would be extinguished. In essence, it provides the additional mechanism to allow the company to achieve the objective of segregation of assets and liabilities. The legal effect of this is that the policyholders would only have recourse to these specified (secured) assets to satisfy their claim under their individual policies. The security document would therefore grant them security over 'their' particular assets. Clear identification of those assets is essential. To the extent that such measures are not practicable and the jurisdiction of incorporation has PCC legislation, it is most likely that the company will consider converting into a PCC instead.

However, as we will see, the two regimes (contractual and statutory) can co-exist even within the same structure – therefore contractual provisions can and do reinforce the legislative regime. It is, in fact, common in a PCC to retain contractual provisions (e.g. claims limitation, paid as paid clauses) as these can serve to give the PCC cellular concept contractual force. Care should obviously be taken for any contractual provisions to be consistent with the legislative regime and careful drafting is required. We will also see elsewhere in this book that there may be circumstances where security arrangements are in fact an available option even in the context of a PCC.

One pioneer of the contractual cell company that deserve some mention in this book is Guardrisk of the Republic of South Africa[7]. Guardrisk has used cell captives in a number of jurisdictions over many years. In 1996 it helped to establish a cell captive facility in Gibraltar under the name of Euroguard Insurance Company Limited. That company has been very successfully involved in cell captive business since then and in 2007 converted into a PCC under the statutory regime. This was the first conversion of a cell captive in Gibraltar to a PCC. The first conversion within the EU of a company to a PCC took place in Malta a couple of

[7] Surprisingly, South Africa has yet to implement PCC legislation. See National Treasury Discussion Paper of 7 April 2008 *"The Future of Micro-insurance Regulation in South Africa"*.

months before (1 November 2006) and the company concerned was Atlas Insurance PCC Limited of Malta.

Another corporate example of the cell captive structure being successfully used, this time for the annuities (pensions) business, is London & Colonial Assurance plc, which also has its home in Gibraltar. The use of a captive type vehicle for the pensions sector may not have been new, but the product itself was.

It would be a mistake to think, however, that the contractual arrangements for segregating assets and liabilities within an insurer have only existed in a captive (or single policy) context. They have also in recent years been put in place to support underwriting arrangements by some small direct writers operating under the EU passport regime. Typically, the promoters of such insurers will have their own core insurance business, but may also provide an underwriting facility for third parties (typically broker business) which could not be available through the medium of a PCC under the statutory regime (e.g. motor). This is not the typical captive situation and although fronting and profit share arrangements have been available in the tradional broker-insurance market for many years, this type of structure allows the introducer of business (typically a broker) to participate in the profitability of its book of business as shareholder without having to set up its own insurer. This participation can be structured via a separate class of redeemable preference shares to ensure the benefits of ownership (i.e. dividends and return of capital).

Broadly speaking, in a jurisdiction that followed English company law the relevant clause in the Articles of Association could read:

"The rights, preferences and limitations of the preference shares are:

(a) The preference shares shall only be redeemed at the option of the Company and with the prior consent of the holders of the said shares and the Regulatory Authority. The Company shall reserve the balance of the preference shares of the Class issued and allotted to the preference shareholder for issue at a future date to the preference shareholder, and the Company shall not to issue such shares to any other person.

(b) Each outstanding preference share shall entitle the registered holder of record of such preference share to dividends and participation in the profits of the Company in accordance with the provisions of this clause, or as the case may be, any shareholders agreement entered into between the shareholders and the Company.

(c) *The holders of preference shares shall not be entitled to vote at meetings of the Company.*

(d) *The amount payable by the holder of any preference share upon the issue of such shares shall be the aggregate of the nominal value of such shares and such premium as the Board in its discretion shall decide. The consideration received by the Company upon the issuance of the preference share will be allocated to a segregated fund supporting the capacity to write the insurance business which may from time to time be introduced by the preference shareholder and accepted by the Company, in its absolute discretion. The Directors will allocate to such fund all premiums received by the Company in relation to the insurance business introduced by the preference shareholder together with any interest and investment income and gains accruing thereon and with all re-insurance recoveries and re-insurance commissions received by the Company, deducting such claims settled, reinsurance premiums paid, any investment losses and all other liabilities, fees and expenditure attributable thereto (including taxation) as the Directors in their absolute discretion shall think fit. The Company shall manage and maintain all the assets, liabilities, income and expenses and costs attributable to the fund segregated and separate from all other assets, liabilities, income and expenses and costs of any other business underwritten by the Company. For the avoidance of doubt, such assets form part of the assets of the Company and accordingly are available to the creditors of the Company as prescribed by law, whether in winding up or otherwise.*

(e) *Dividends with respect to the preference shares may be paid only out of profits attributable to the said fund, subject to all statutory or regulatory requirements concerning solvency margins and reserves with respect to the Company. For the avoidance of doubt, no dividends shall be declared or payable if the Company, after giving effect to the dividend, will not have sufficient net assets to meet the general business solvency margins prescribed by law and required of the Company.*

(f) *The Company shall keep separate accounts for the purposes of the business underwritten by the Company pursuant to this clause.*

(g) *Notwithstanding any other provision of these Articles, in the event of any voluntary liquidation, dissolution or winding up of the affairs of the Company, after payment of all liabilities of the Company and before any distribution of the assets of the Company shall be made to the holders of the Ordinary Shares, the holder of the preference shares shall be entitled to receive a return on capital (including share premium) on their preference shares, plus an entitlement to an amount equal to the value determined by the Directors in their absolute discretion of all the assets, less all the liabilities (actual, contingent and prospective so far as the same can be quantified), comprised within the relevant fund calculated in accordance with the provisions of this clause.*

(h) *The holders of the preference shares shall not be entitled to transfer their shares or assign their rights as shareholders of the Company without the prior written consent of the Directors. The Directors shall have an absolute discretion to refuse registration of any transfer of preference shares. Any transfer without the consent of the Directors shall constitute a breach of these Articles and the shares shall carry no rights whatsoever.*

(i) *Except as otherwise set out in these Articles, the preference shares shall not confer on their holders any further right to participate in the profits of the Company."*

It should be noted from the above that liability is unsegregated as far as insurance creditors are concerned. In other words, in the absence of appropriate claims limitation clauses in the policy, the insurance liabilities of the preference shareholder's insurance fund could be met out of the assets of the company's other insurance business because as far as insurance creditors are concerned there is common pool of assets and no limitation of liability. The segregration of 'funds' as between separate books of business are no more than accounting provisions to enable the insurer to calculate relevant values. The insurer is therefore required to maintain a margin of solvency for *the company as a whole.*

Those practitioners who are familiar with the funds industry will be familiar with many of the concepts described above. The basic mechanics of a cell captive is indeed similar to that of an umbrella fund. Today it is typical to find umbrella funds established as protected cell companies, but their not too distant relatives have been around for many years and are still commonly used. Moreover, the use of special purpose vehicles in the financial markets by banks as a means of spreading risk to investors has been widespread since at least the 1990s and the basic legal environment under which these transactions (known as repackaging) operate is also similar. So when PCC legislation was first introduced, their use to 'ring-fence' repackaging transactions was quickly spotted by investment banks. Funds and repackaging therefore deserve specific attention in this book.

1.6. Repackaging

The last decades have seen an explosion in the range and volume of derivative products available in the financial markets. The reasons for this dramatic expansion are attributable principally to the enormous liquidity of the markets in the 1990s and before 2007. This was led in many cases by the unprecedented growth in pension and mutual funds, the enhanced investment and risk management opportunities which derivatives were perceived to offer, and the flexibility provided by derivatives for regulatory arbitrage. The result was the creation of a global derivatives industry worth trillions of dollars. Within the derivatives industry, one of the fastest growing segments was the market for repackaged notes. These repackaging trades are still arranged only by the large investment banks and repackaged notes (which may be listed in a stock exchange) are usually sold only to institutional investors such as other banks, insurance companies and pension funds. The Cayman's Islands, Luxembourg, Dublin and Gibraltar created an entire industry to service the needs of this market.

1.6.1. What is a repackaging?

A repackaging can be described as a form of securitisation that allows institutional investors to purchase bonds of their choice (whether listed or rated) that comply with their internal regulatory requirements and also meet their investment objectives.

The flexibility offered by a repackaged note can best be demonstrated by a simple comparison with an asset swap transaction.

1.6.2. Asset Swap

An asset swap could allow an investor to purchase a bond and take a credit exposure on the bond issuer, whilst at the same time hedging the cash flows into the desired interest rate and currency. The rationale for this may be, for example, that the investor wanted the bond issuer's credit exposure, but it did not want it in the currency in which the issuer's debt is expressed. The hedging arrangement would be achieved by entering into a swap with a swap counterparty under which cash flows between the parties were exchanged. Thus the investor may have purchased a sovereign bond of his choice, but if one simply follows the cash flows in the transaction, the swap would 'transform' this into say a bond payable in US currency.

One of the obstacles that gave rise to the demand for the repackaged note was that certain investors were not permitted to enter into ISDA swaps for regulatory reasons. Therefore, the hedging opportunities of an asset swap were simply not available to them. The market's answer to this was the development of the repackaged (or structured) note.

1.6.3. The Special Purpose Vehicle

A repackaging transaction involves the setting up of a 'bankruptcy remote'[8] Special Purpose Vehicle (SPV), where typically the institutional investor will purchase notes issued by the SPV which, following on from the example given above, in turn uses the proceeds of issuance to purchase the underlying bonds the investor wants to obtain a credit exposure to. The SPV notes are issued at an interest rate and currency which satisfies the investor's investment objectives or internal regulations. This is achieved by the SPV, itself, entering into the swap with the swap counterparty under which the cash flows are exchanged in the same way as under an asset swap transaction. To secure the obligations of the SPV under the notes and swap, the SPV will grant security over the underlying bonds to the investor and the swap counterparty. The SPV also grants security over the swap to the investor. The SPV can therefore perform the same transformation as an asset swap. Thus allowing the investor to repackage an asset class into a tailor-made bond issued by a company specifically set up for the purpose. Under English law this achieves an effective 'ring-fence' because there would be few assets available to unsecured creditors in a liquidation of the company.

It is worth noting that the 'SPV' was not the exclusive domain of 'offshore' jurisdictions and that whether onshore or offshore, these entities were largely, if not, universally unregulated. They did not fall within the banking or collective investment scheme legislation and in securitisation transactions (e.g. mortgage backed securities) SPVs have now typically been set up 'onshore'. In the UK, for example, before the liquidity crisis of 2007, domestic securitisations were a crucial source of funding for lenders in the mortgage industry.[9]

---

[8] The SPV is owned and controlled by a charitable trust set up for the purpose.

[9] The financial crisis in the global markets saw a very significant decline in the sale of mortgage backed securities.

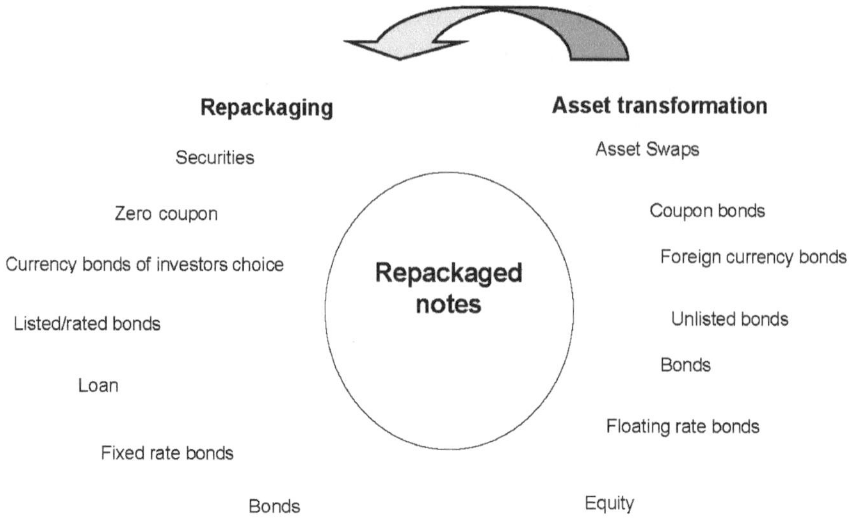

Diagram 1: Transformation made possible by repackaging

1.6.4. Credit-linked Notes

Repackaging is also used in conjunction with credit derivatives. A 'credit derivative' is a general term used to describe various swap and option contracts designed to lay off credit risk on loans, debt securities or other assets, or in relation to a particular reference entity or country, in return for either swap payments or payment of premium. One party is therefore referred to as the buyer of protection/seller of risk and the other party can be referred to as the seller of protection/buyer of risk. In a typical repackaging transaction, the notes issued by the SPV are credit-linked notes, under which the redemption amount payable by the issuer is determined or varied by reference to the credit performance of one or more selected reference entities and/or debt obligations, or by reference to a country or convertibility risk. The cash-flows coming to and from the SPV will therefore depend on specified credit-related events. These structures have revolutionised the financial markets in a number of ways. First, credit-linked notes are a particularly useful tool in permitting financial institutions to transfer to investors part of their exposure to a particular reference entity in exchange for giving up part of their return. Alternatively, an investor may not be able to purchase debt from the reference entity because of internal constraints and therefore the credit-linked note permits the investor to simulate this investment.

The flexibility of these repackaged transactions is such that the investor will not only get the credit risk of his choice, but also do so in the form of a structured product that complies with its investment requirement and any documentation format which the investor's regulations may dictate.

The large banks have helped to set up very many of these companies worldwide and the location will invariably be dictated by tax, legal or regulatory considerations. The primary consideration for most transactions is based on the need for tax neutrality and also in ensuring that the legal structure of the documentation is secure within the legal system and regulatory framework of the jurisdiction concerned.

Most repackaging trades are not issued as a single issue of bonds but rather as multi-issuance under programme documents pursuant to which the SPV will issue as many bonds as investors wish to purchase. Each series of notes issued will have their own separate terms and conditions with regards to currency, interest rate, underlying assets etc. This is often known as a 'Note Programme'. The documentation for such programmes has become standardised with the parties applying and disapplying programme documents and specific provisions for particular trades. It is a cheaper alternative to the stand-alone note issue. Under its Note Programme the notes issued by the SPV are backed-up by a specified pool of assets and a specific swap entered into with the arranger bank. It is essential therefore that each transaction is 'ring-fenced' so that the investors of a specific series of repackaged notes only have a claim to those assets and no claim on the assets held by the SPV to back up any other note series. It should be noted how in substance this is no different from a cell captive situation with each policyholder's class fund. The need for 'ring-fencing' is just the same i.e. the protection of specific assets in respect of multiple transactions in a single corporate entity.

Thus the structure can fall apart if investors of a particular note issue (having received diminished returns from their own investment, or even upon early termination, seeing the underlying assets reduced to worthless securities) attempted to have recourse to the assets intended only to be available to other investors.[10] This is the key concern in any of these transactions and the market's initial answer to this was to protect the pool of assets in repackaging transactions through the creation of security interests in favour of separate investors over 'their' assets and through the contract between the parties limiting their claim under the notes to those assets only (known as 'limited recourse' provisions). In

---

[10] For an amusing anecdote see *Traders, Guns & Money* by Satyajit Das, pages 234-236

addition, the parties would be prohibited contractually from commencing winding-up or similar action against the SPV.

- **"Limited Recourse" through separation of each series and creation of security interests.**
- **The liquidity of a specific Repackaged Note issue will depend on the liquidity of the assets comprising the underlying collateral**
- **Investor's credit exposure is to the Swap Counterparty and the Underlying Assets**
- **Wide range of Notes can be issued by the SPV**
- **Wide range of Assets can be purchased by the SPV**

Diagram 2: Multi Issue Vehicle

Once again it is no surprise that the standard legal environment for these structures is English law. The use of security interests and claims limitation clauses as a means of ring-fencing one transaction in a single corporate entity from any other transactions of the company has already been discussed above. These structures have been around for many years. But when the PCC found its way into the statute books of offshore jurisdictions as a tool for cell captives, it did not escape those involved in the repackaging industry that its uses were not just confined to insurance, and that some of the similar risks faced by cell captives were also potentially avoided by registering the special purpose vehicle as a PCC.

This was a view held not just by those involved in offshore transactions. It has been held also by lawmakers and practitioners in onshore jurisdictions, as 'securitisation' became a common feature of the financial markets worldwide.

Interestingly, an early example of securitisation legislation providing for segregation of assets and liabilities within a single entity is Chile. In 1994

Chile introduced Law 19301[11] (amending the Securities Market Law no. 18.045) Title XVIII relating to securitisation companies ('sociedades securitizadoras'). The legislation is analogous to PCC legislation but came into existence three years before Guernsey's PCC Ordinance. Article 132 stated: *"Las sociedades a que se refiere este título, se constituirán como anónimas especiales y su objeto excluviso será la adquisición de los créditos a que se refiere el artículo 135 y la emisión de títulos de deuda, de corto o largo plazo. Cada emisión originará la formación de patrimonios separados del patrimonio común de la emisora. Estas sociedades deberán incluir en su nombre la expresión 'securitizadora'."* Roughly translated - the companies shall be constituted as special companies with the sole purpose of acquiring credits and issuance of long term or short term debt securities and the assets backing each issue of debt securities shall be kept separate from the general assets of the company. The name of company shall include the word 'securitisation company'. The law then contained a number of articles providing for the segregation of assets and liabilities in similar manner to PCC legislation.

1.7. Funds

Similar structures have also been adapted for use by open-ended investment companies and umbrella funds over many years. Whereas the market in repackaged debt instruments has been largely the domain of institutional investors, private investors (in particular High Net Worth Individuals – "HNWI") have been able to gain access to wider investment opportunities as alternatives to cash deposits, money market instruments, bonds, etc, through fund related structures. This lead to an explosion in the 1990s and early 2000s in both institutionally and privately managed funds. For tax, legal and regulatory reasons, most of these vehicles are domiciled in Dublin, Luxembourg, BVI, Channel Islands, and in more recent times, Gibraltar. It is in the context of the discussion on the segregation and protection of assets within a single corporate entity by different parties wishing to pool assets that the 'umbrella fund' is of particular relevance.

The so-called umbrella fund usually exists in corporate form; as a private or public company. It is no different from any other corporate investment vehicle except that it is intended to facilitate the ease of establishment and administration of potentially unlimited 'sub-funds' within the same corporate entity (or umbrella). This enables fund managers to offer a

[11] http://www.leychile.cl/Navegar?idNorma=30668

large range of funds to their international clients. There are a number of variations to such a structure. But the basic mechanics are not much different from the cell captive. The Articles of Association (in respect of a company incorporated in an English law-based jurisdiction) will constitute the contract of membership between the various investor shareholders and sets out how each sub-fund is constituted, valued etc. The investors will usually be offered non-voting redeemable preference shares with sole economic rights attached to the shares. The promoters of the fund, on the other hand, will retain the voting and management (but no economic) rights; typically through the issuance of voting ordinary shares. Some umbrella funds also allow each sub-fund to be set up with separate custodian, investment adviser and manager. The use of such flexible, professionally managed investment vehicles, has offered private investors (both the HNWI segment and retail clients) exposure to asset classes and investment strategies that have not been typically available in the traditional equity markets.

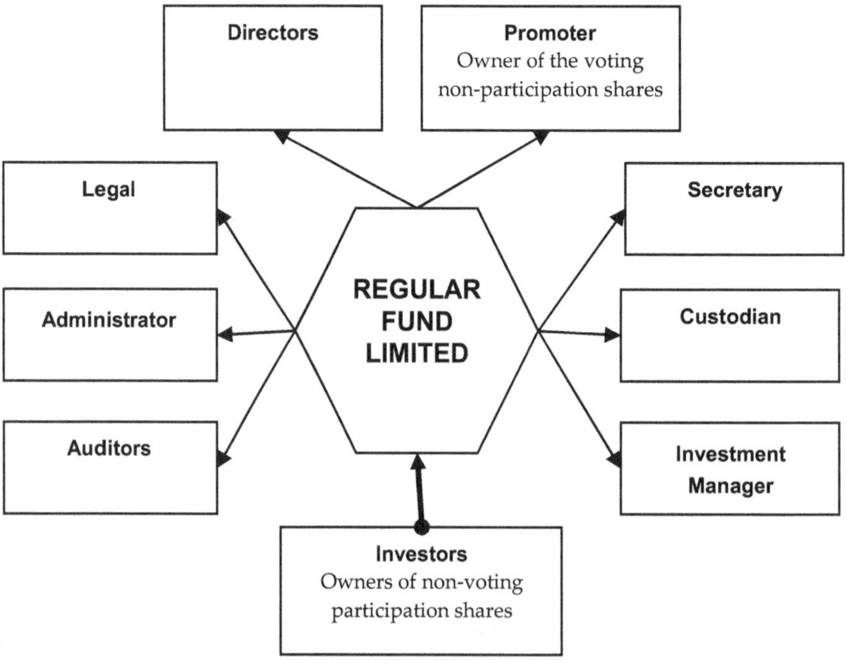

Diagram 3: A Regular Fund

Again, it is important to emphasise that the protection of assets within the traditional umbrella structure is achieved by strict observance of its Articles of Association. Although shareholder investors in a fund (registered as a limited company) are protected by limited liability, the liability of the company itself is unlimited and therefore all its assets are available to creditors subject to the applicable laws on preferential and security rights. Each sub-fund in an umbrella structure is therefore potentially at risk from third party liabilities. The obvious weakness of such a structure is that unless an investment by the company is fully funded in advance, or such liability suitably limited by contract, all assets of the company will be at risk. Examples of this would be where the company undertakes short selling of securities or buys securities on margin for obtaining leverage. Due to such limitations, investment advisers of these vehicles have to be extremely careful in the management of the company's assets to ensure that the investment strategy of any particular sub-fund does not undermine the contractual segregation of assets and liabilities within the structure. It is usual therefore to find numerous investment restrictions set out in the offer documents (prospectuses and private placement memoranda). As a last resort shareholders would be required to subscribe for additional funds, but the company would obviously be exposed to the risk of any shortfall in shareholder funds.

The umbrella fund can also be constituted within a trust (known in the industry as a 'unit trust scheme'). Generally, the investors in the unit trust scheme will subscribe cash in return for 'units' (rather than shares) in the unit trust scheme. The unit trust scheme is constituted by a 'trust deed' (with a trustee) and the typical declaration of trust clause could read as follows:

"The Trustee shall stand possessed of the Trust Fund during the Trust Period and until the termination thereof upon trust for the holders of the Units of the relevant class from time to time outstanding pari passu according to the number of undivided shares in the Class Fund represented by the Units of the class held by each such holder, upon the terms of this Deed but so that no unit shall confer any interest or share in any particular part of a Class Fund. The number of Units to be issued in relation to any Class Fund shall be unlimited and as the Trustee shall determine. Units shall be without par value. All monies forming part of a Class Fund shall from time to time be held or invested by the Trustee in accordance with the provisions of this Deed and the Offering Memorandum."

The characteristics of units in the 'Fund' is that each 'unit' represents one undivided share in the 'Sub-Fund' to which that 'unit' relates and its dividend income (if any).

Units of the 'Fund' are therefore divided into classes relating to each of the 'Sub-Funds' according to the investment policy applicable to them. In respect of each sub-fund separate and segregated investment portfolios are maintained in which the assets and liabilities and income and expenditure attributable or allocated to each sub-fund are applied or charged. The relevant clause in the trust deed may read as follows:

"(a) *The proceeds from the issue of each class of Units shall be applied by the Trustee in the books of the Trust to the Class Fund established for Units of that class and the Investments and the liabilities and Income and expenditure attributable thereto shall be applied to or charged against such Class Fund.*

(b) *Where any Investment is derived from another Investment (whether cash or otherwise) such derivative Investment shall be applied in the books of the Trust to the same Class Fund as the Investment from which it was derived and on each revaluation of an Investment the increase or decrease in value shall be applied to or deducted from the relevant Class Fund.*

(c) *Save as otherwise provided herein the Investments and Income of each Class Fund shall be applied solely to the type or class of Investments specified by the Trustee for each particular Class Fund and the Investments so held in or for each Class Fund shall be applied solely in respect of Units of the class to which such Class Fund relates and, subject to the provisions of the Law, the Trustee shall be entitled to treat the Units of any particular class as if they were units in a separate unit trust and as if that particular Class Fund constituted assets and liabilities of a separate unit trust.*

(d) *Any Investment held by the Trust for the account of a Class Fund may, at any time, be realised in order to provide funds in cash which are properly required for the purpose of the relevant Class Fund or in order to retain the proceeds of sale in cash or on current or deposit account or partly for one of such purposes and partly for another."*

In the above, for 'Class Fund' read 'cell'; for 'Units' read 'cell shares'; and it will be appreciated that the legal characteristics of a 'unit trust scheme' are not very different from those of a PCC. Clearly the availability of the PCC provided the promoters of both corporate based funds and unit trust schemes with an excellent opportunity to establish a more robust 'ring-fence' than was available through traditional contractual and trust arrangements. The use of the PCC has therefore increased over the last few years and has now become the tool of choice for promoters of funds (and funds of funds) in many jurisdictions.[12]

---

[12] Today promoters of funds even include international banks.

Fund managers in jurisdictions that do not have a protected cell regime have sometimes had difficulty in marketing their fund products because of the concern with regards to the unsegregated nature of liabilities between sub-funds.

Although the ring-fencing protection that can be obtained through the use of a PCC is undoubtedly greater, it would be a mistake to think that the statutory route presents no risk at all. In an ideal world this would be the case, but as we will see elsewhere in this book, risks do still exist. It is for those who manage such companies to also manage those risks.

2. THE ADVENT OF THE PCC

The intended effect of the PCC statutory regime is to restrict the ability of a cell participant to enforce his claim against all the assets of the PCC. When PCC legislation was first introduced, it was sometimes customary to speak of cells as if they were separate legal entities; in fact they were not. Guernsey has, however, introduced legislation to do precisely that – the so called, Incorporated Cell Company (ICC). But typically, PCC legislation, whilst recognising that there is only one legal person, legislates the effect of 'the contract' between the parties by providing for the segregation of cell assets and liabilities and restricting creditor enforcement to cell assets. This applies to both voluntary and involuntary creditors. The economic (not the legal) effect of a cell is therefore broadly similar for the counterparty to the taking of a security interest over particular assets.

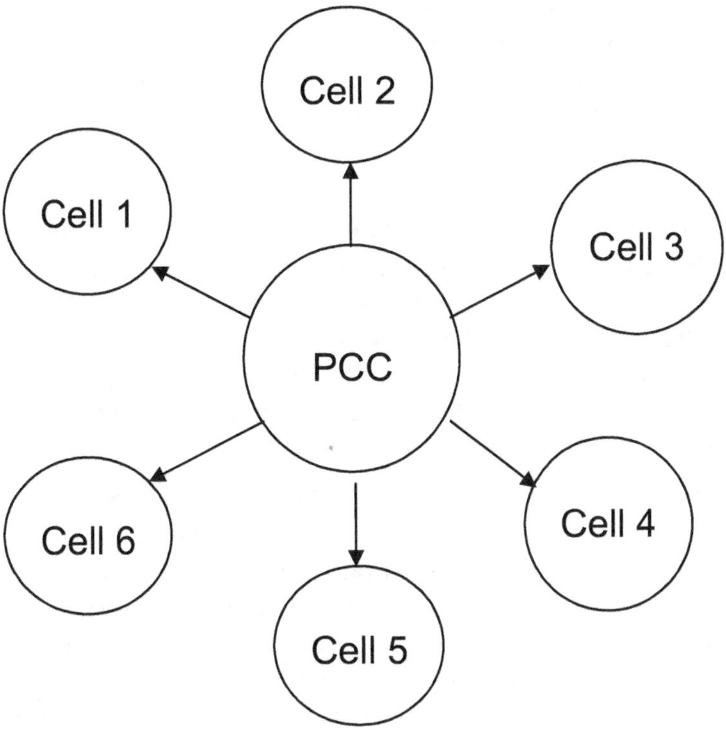

Diagram 4: PCC structure

The legal nature of a PCC is a company with particular legal characteristics, which are described below.

There are usually three ways of establishing a PCC: by incorporation, by conversion and by redomiciliation. In many jurisdictions a PCC will adopt the legal form of a company limited by shares for the purposes of the companies legislation. Thus, although a PCC is subject to the provisions of the PCC regime with regards to the segregation of assets and liabilities, it is a 'company' incorporated under local company legislation like any other.

Examples of this can be seen in:

Guernsey's PCC Ordinance 1997 – Section 1(3): *"The provisions of the 1994 Law shall, subject to the provisions of this Ordinance, and unless the context requires otherwise, apply in relation to a protected cell company."*

Gibraltar's PCC Act 2001 – Section 3(3): *"The provisions of the Companies Act shall, subject to the provisions of this Act, and unless the context requires otherwise, apply in relation to a protected cell company."*

Isle of Man's PCC Act 2004 – Section 1(4): *"The Companies Act shall apply in respect of a company that is a PCC as they apply in respect of any other company" and Section 36(1): "This Act may be cited as the Protected Cell Companies Act 2004 and shall be construed as one with the Companies Act, and those Acts together with this Act may be cited as the Companies Act 1931 to 2004."*

It is important in terms of international recognition for the concept of the PCC, that a PCC will usually take the legal form of a limited company with shares. Typically a certificate of incorporation of a PCC would certify that, "[ABC PCC Limited] is this day incorporated under the [Companies Act] subject to the provisions of the [Protected Cell Companies Act] as a Protected Cell Company and the Company is Limited."

Given the nature of these companies, they necessarily, however, attract special consideration. There can be no doubt that the critical test of a PCC will come where there is a cross-frontier element (including insolvency) and the company has assets abroad. It is clearly impossible to give a complete global picture of the integrity of such structures. Whilst contract law, driven by the needs of international commerce, tends to harmonise over time, insolvency laws do not easily do so. Even the EU insolvency regime is not a harmonising regime, but recognises the radically different approaches taken by Members States to insolvency.

We can turn to the PCC regime for guidance as to what it means for creditors. In the case of a cell captive registered as a PCC, for example, the usual creditors are insurance creditors (policyholders) making a claim under a policy issued by the company as insurer.

The first point to make in looking at a PCC is that the operating legislation's effectiveness is dependent upon a number of factors. The PCC must be established as a PCC in accordance with the terms of the PCC legislation. Typically the rules require that the affairs of the PCC must be organised such that the assets and liabilities of each cell are physically separated and kept separately identifiable. The directors usually also have a duty to inform third parties dealing with the company that they are contracting with a protected cell company and that the transaction in respect of which they are contracting is attributable to a particular cell. The benefits of the statutory ring-fence will not occur automatically simply because a company is incorporated as a PCC. The company must also be managed and conduct its affairs in accordance with the terms of the operating legislation.

Although the concept of a PCC has not been judicially tested (save tangentially) in a cross border situation, the statutory segregation of assets and liabilities is intended to ensure that creditors of particular cells do not have recourse to the assets of other cells wherever the creditors or assets may be. To do otherwise would obviously defeat the 'ring-fence'.

As we have seen (Chapter 1) outside of PCC legislation, under the general insolvency laws of countries based on the English legal system, on a liquidation of a company, its property is usually applied in satisfaction of its liabilities *pari passu;* that is without preferring any one creditor over another (subject to security arrangements, certain statutorily preferred debts and the mandatory set-off provisions applicable in a liquidation). Similar rules apply in most other jurisdictions. In legislating for the PCC statutory regime, PCC legislation has therefore departed from the general (but fundamental) principle that all creditors should be treated equally on liquidation. It is worth noting, however, that in the context of an insurance insolvency, EU and other legislation had already modified the *pari passu* principle.

2.1. The Challenge

The basic starting point of any discussion on the PCC is that a distinction needs to be drawn between the application of PCC legislation by a local court, and the likely interpretation of the legislation under rules of private international law by a foreign court i.e. if proceedings were instituted against the PCC in such a forum. In any action instituted in the courts of the jurisdiction of incorporation of the PCC, there cannot be any doubt that PCC legislation would be given effect to. Such a court (other than a court in an EU Member State obliged to give effect to conflicting EU legislation) would naturally apply local law. The concern is that the protection afforded to cell assets may be lost were an action to be instituted in a foreign court and these assets are situated within that jurisdiction. This however is not a new concern. Even before Guernsey introduced PCC legislation in 1996, those involved in the discussion around the concept of the PCC identified this as an issue; but it was not felt by the Guernsey Financial Services Commission as a good enough reason for not implementing such legislation. Regulators in other jurisdictions (initially at least) took a more cautionary approach. The Isle of Man Government, for example, at first decided against introducing PCC legislation and did not do so until 31 March 2004 - even so, the use of the PCC was restricted initially to the carrying on of insurance business. This prevarication resulted in Guernsey having a head start over all its 'offshore' competitors, although this was not without its challenges. Twelve months into its legislative life, PCC legislation in Guernsey came under the scrutiny of leading UK Counsel instructed by a potential PCC user[13] regarding the likely interpretation of the legislation by the English courts.

An exception to the rule that a local court could be expected to apply domestic law is where the matter is subject to international treaty obligations, which a local court is required to give effect. An example would be EU Directives. Member State courts are required to interpret local law implementing a Directive as far as possible in comformity with the wording and purpose of the relevant Directive.[14] In certain circumstances, where the provisions of a Directive are unconditional and sufficiently precise, the European Court of Justice (ECJ) has said that they may be relied upon against any contrary national provision.[15] The local courts must therefore not apply domestic law incompatible with EU legislation.

A possible example of this in the context of a PCC would be a provision in the PCC regime that was inconsistent with Directive 2002/47/EC of the

---

[13] *"The Euroguard Commentary"* issue June 1998.

[14] *Case 14/83 Von Colson and Kamann v Land Nordrhein –Westfalen [1984] ECR 1891*

[15] *Francovich [1991] ECR I-05357*

European Parliament and Council of 6 June 2002 on financial collateral arrangements (the Collateral Directive).[16]

2.2. Substantive versus procedural

Would PCC legislation be given effect to by a foreign court? The answer to the question may depend on whether the provisions of limitation of liability under PCC legislation would be classed as 'procedural' rather than 'substantive'. Clearly, the intention of PCC legislation is to accord substantive rather than procedural status to the concept of a protected cell company. Assuming that they are effective, the legislation should (in common law jurisdictions or jurisdictions based on the UK system of law) require, at least in theory, the foreign court, under rules of international law, to apply PCC legislation to the issue rather than the local law.

The distinction is not always an easy one to draw, but the issue seems to be this. If a foreign court were to regard PCC legislation as being procedural in nature (that is to say, that the effect of the legislation was to *block remedies*) then the courts would likely not give effect to PCC legislation. Where, however, the legislation is construed as *substantive* (that is to say, that its effect was to reduce liabilities in any transaction of the company) then under principles of international conflicts of laws, a court applying English principles of law should apply PCC legislation in very much the same way as under contractual arrangements that purported to achieve a similar result. In drafting PCC legislation the intention of the draftsman therefore has to be to ensure that provisions of the law are classified as substantive and not merely procedural in nature. Of course, this is easier said than done.

Other than perhaps on insolvency (which is considered separately), the concept of a PCC should not be offensive to a foreign jurisdiction if we simply take a PCC as being a statutory limitation of liability of a company in a particular transaction. It is no different from a contractual limitation of liability clause; except that instead of the liability of the company being limited to a specific amount, the liability is limited to specific assets. In fact, as we have seen (Chapter 1) the concept of 'limited recourse' (where a company contracts to limit its liability to specific charged assets) is not one that is unfamiliar to foreign jurisdictions. Indeed, limited recourse arrangements are widespread in financial transactions of all kinds. Assuming that a foreign court does view PCC legislation as an attempt to

---

16 A provision preventing the enforcement of security as a result of administration proceedings.

limit liability rather than an attempt to block remedies, or as a mechanism used to deprive creditors of statutory protection or rights otherwise afforded to them, there is no reason why they should find it offensive.

In particular, a foreign court should not have much sympathy for a claim put forward by a voluntary user of a cell against the assets of another cell. After all, he has willingly participated in the company on the basis that it was a PCC. Accordingly any attempt to litigate outside the jurisdiction of incorporation of the PCC could be viewed simply as an attempt to evade the application of the 'statutory contract' he has freely entered into and itself may be regarded as an abuse of process. The underlying principle of PCC legislation is that persons who transact with the PCC transact at their peril and on an informed basis as to their rights (in the same way as for an ordinary 'limited company').

Interestingly, prior to 1931 Californian law did not embrace the principle of limited liability of members. Under the then law of California every shareholder of a company, whether incorporated in California or elsewhere trading within that State was personally liable for such proportion of the company's debts as the amount of his shares bore to the whole of the subscribed capital of the company. This led to a potential conflict of laws between the application of foreign company law where this limited the liability of members to the subscription amounts (a principle almost universally embraced by that time), and Californian law, which did not confer such preferential treatment. In a case where litigation was commenced in England, the Court of Appeal resolved this obvious conflict in favour of English law and held that Californian law could not impose personal liability on a shareholder of an English company without his assent: *Risdon Iron and Locomotive Works v. Furness, [1906] 1 K.B. 49 (C.A.)*. This can be contrasted with the decision of the US Supreme Court in *232 US 221 Frank Thomas v. Conrad H Matthiessen* where the shareholder authorised the business of the company in California and was essentially held to have given his assent to the statutory contract by virtue of which he had assumed liability. In a PCC, voluntary creditors with notice of cellular/hub liability should therefore similarly be considered to be bound by PCC legislation.

Still, the directors of the PCC would be well advised to continue to reinforce the statutory ring-fence through the inclusion of a limited recourse acknowledgement in the contract between the parties. Such a 'limited recourse' provision could read:

"The [contracting party] acknowledges that, notwithstanding any other provisions hereof or of anything to the contrary in any agreement, document or notice of the PCC, all payments to be made by the PCC pursuant to this agreement will be payable only from, and to the extent of, the sums paid to, or net proceeds recovered by or on behalf of, the PCC in respect of [Cell A] and the liability of the PCC shall therefore be limited to the assets attributable to [Cell A] and there shall be no liability on the part of any other assets of the PCC or any other Cell of the PCC, and any outstanding claims which cannot be satisfied from the sums paid to, or net proceeds recovered by or on behalf of, the PCC in respect of [Cell A] shall be extinguished. The [contracting party] will look solely to such sums and proceeds and the rights of the PCC in respect of the relevant Cell for payments to be made by the PCC under this agreement. This provision shall survive any termination of this agreement."

Above, we have avoided the use of the words "will have no recourse to or against" and instead made reference to the liability being limited to the assets of the relevant cell.

The parties may also wish to consider the inclusion of a non-petition clause:

"Notwithstanding any other provisions herein or of anything to the contrary in any agreement, document or notice of the PCC, the [contracting party] shall not be entitled at any time to institute against the PCC, or join in any institution against the PCC of, any bankruptcy, administration, moratorium, reorganisation, arrangement, insolvency, winding-up or liquidation proceedings or similar insolvency proceedings or other proceedings under any applicable bankruptcy or similar law in connection with any obligations of the PCC, this agreement or otherwise owed to the [contracting party], save for lodging a claim in the liquidation of the PCC which is initiated by another party or taking proceedings to obtain a declaration or judgment as to the obligations of the PCC."

Despite the novelty of the PCC concept, it would be wrong to assume that such statutory segregation was entirely new. The UK, for example, did already have its own segregation of assets and matching liabilities in the context of an insurance company insolvency; that is, where part of the business of an insurance company being wound up was long term business.[17] It could be argued that a PCC structure is no more offensive than this segregation of 'funds' within a life insurance company. This now reflects the requirement in Article 19 of the Consolidated Life

[17] Rule 5 of the Insurance Companies (Winding up) Rules 1985

Directive (2002/83/EC) that an insurer offering life assurance and non-life insurance business is required to manage them separately (implemented both in Gibraltar and in the UK).

In fact, in the context of EU law, it is also arguable that if the intended purpose of the Insurance Directives is the protection of policyholders (as it undoubtedly is), and policyholders have 'agreed' to participate within the special statutory framework of a PCC (intended to ensure the maintenance of separate insurance funds of assets to meet specific liabilities), it would be inconsistent with (and indeed defeat) that purpose for a Court in the EU to undermine the segregation of assets and liabilities within that regime to the detriment of any policyholder.

Although PCC legislation was not immediately universally embraced, Gibraltar followed Guernsey in implementing PCC legislation in 2001.[18] A consultation process within the industry, which resulted in general support for PCC legislation, preceded this. The Government of Gibraltar took its own legal opinion from leading UK Counsel[19] and it is no secret that Gibraltar adopted the Guernsey legislative model. In contrast, in other jurisidictions (e.g. Bermuda), companies were initially registered as PCCs by private Acts of the local legislature. Today, of course, the PCC has wide acceptance within the insurance industry – for example, Pool Re accepts reinsurance risks from a PCC provided it is supported with an acceptable legal opinion; but warns that a *"PCC may be required, depending on their legal structure, to enter into [certain additional] documentation"* and undertakes to *"advise on the form of any additional documentation required to be entered into by Protected Cell Companies on a case-by-case basis"*.[20]

In summary, there should not be any doubt, that in general, if an order of a court were obtained in a foreign country which was clearly contrary to the provisions of PCC legislation; and in which the PCC had no assets, and which therefore needed to be enforced against assets of the PCC situated in its jurisdiction of incorporation, that in any proceedings brought before the local courts to enforce that foreign judgment there would be a strong likelihood that such a court would not recognise the foreign judgment. Non-recognition would be on the grounds of public policy on the basis that it conflicts with its own domestic law.

---

[18] The US National Association of Insurance Commissioners (NAIC) also published a PCC Model Act.

[19] Gabriel Moss QC.

[20] Pool Re "Explanatory Memorandum", February 2005, page 17.

The critical test for a PCC will come in the event of an insolvency of a cell (or the company as a whole) where there is a cross-frontier element and the company has assets abroad. The directors of the company can properly minimise such risks by not having assets (e.g. investments) abroad[21], adopting local choice of law clauses (e.g. in insurance contracts) and through the contractual arrangements that back-up the statutory provisions. In this respect, as we will see in this book, the matter may therefore have more theoretical than practical importance.

2.3. Location of assets, custodian and Collateral Directive

When considering whether, and if so, how a third party may attempt to undermine the cell structure it is necessary to look at the nature, location and transferability of the relevant cell assets. This can give rise to difficult theoretical and practical legal issues.

Private international law tends to make a distinction between assets of two broad types, immovable and movable (or real and personal property). An immovable asset or real property is essentially land or buildings. Movable assets or personal property is essentially everything else and includes intangibles, such as contractual rights to payment. The location of movable or personal property will normally depend on the type of asset in question.

Although the holding of securities can be different than what is suggested below, this may serve as a useful point for illustration purposes.

If the cell assets are comprised of dematerialised[22] or bearer securities[23], the securities will likely be held in one or more settlement or clearing systems each of which is set up differently and under each of which the depositor of the securities gets differing rights. Where the securities, however, are held by a custodian through a securities account with the relevant settlement system it will be the custodian which has the co-proprietary interest in the securities. The company will have no direct proprietary rights *vis-à-vis* the settlement system. As a practical matter, there should be little doubt as to where a custodian is located (as opposed

[21] Or securities can be held via a local custodian.

[22] No physical certificates representing the securities are issued and an electronic recording system replaces the register.

[23] The issuer, instead of maintaining a register of owners of its securities (in physical or dematerialised form), issues the securities in the form of a global note that may or may not be replaced after a period of time has elapsed post-issuance by definitive securities in physical form.

to where the underlying assets are located) where it operates from a single place of business.

As a consequence of this, where a PCC uses a local custodian, the protection afforded by PCC legislation would apply and this should minimise the potential risk of having assets outside the jurisdiction.[24]The expectation is that the the location of the custodian in the PCC jurisdiction would protect the contractual rights from attack by a non-cellular creditor seeking to attach the custodian's interest in the securities. The contractual issues as between the PCC and the custodian would be made subject to the laws of the PCC jurisdiction. Proprietary issues, including ownership and the rights of third parties, would also be governed by such law.

If a creditor litigates in the jurisdiction of location of the relevant securities (for example, in dematerialised form) and seeks to attach the PCC's alleged interest in the securities in that location, the local court should arguably refer the question of the ownership of the assets or rights of the creditor to the jurisdiction of the custodian which is also the jurisdiction of the PCC. The attack would presumably therefore fail.

Thus whilst there is a theoretical risk for a PCC where assets are located outside the PCC jurisdiction (namely, in a jurisdiction that did not recognise the segregated cell structure), the appointment of a local custodian can in practice alleviate this risk.

It is worth noting, too, that the EU Collateral Directive[25] has, indirectly, come to the aid of the PCC. Among the principal effects of the Collateral Directive in relation to security financial collateral arrangements are the elimination of the need to register as security a financial collateral arrangement as a charge under domestic legislation. There is also the disapplication of any statutory freeze on enforcement of security. The practical consequence of this for a PCC is that it minimises any issues around registration of security in respect of cell assets as well as the uncertainty with regards to administration proceedings and its potential effect on the provision of cell security.

---

[24] Where the assets are held in cash this would also avoid any difficulty since the cash can be deposited with a bank in the PCC jurisdiction: the location of the asset would be the location of the relevant office (head office or branch) at which the account is maintained in which the debt representing the cash deposit is recorded.

[25] 2002/47/EC

2.4. Beware of claims that may not be limited! Especially involuntary creditors

But even in foreign proceedings, the likely view of a foreign court may depend on who is initiating legal action. For example, a liability in respect of environmental risks could be such as to elicit little sympathy from a foreign court. This is particularly relevant where a PCC is set up as an investment vehicle to invest in separate property (real estate) portfolios. If the PCC was in breach of local legislation (e.g. planning laws or damage to third parties), there is no guarantee that in any local legal proceedings against the company (e.g. where a hefty fine would be imposed) the only recourse would be to specific cell assets in the manner prescribed by the operating legislation. Notwithstanding such risk, property investment protected cell companies do exist. In addition, the laws of a jurisdiction may provide, as a mandatory rule of law, that the legal liability of an insurer to third parties is unlimited. In these circumstances the third party may be able to argue successfully in a court of law in his jurisdiction that, as far as his claim is concerned, the liability of a PCC is unlimited and therefore that all the assets of the company are available to satisfy his insurance claim. The principal example here is motor third party liability and there must be a risk of such a claim being successfully upheld. In this respect the insurance market has tended to be more cautious in its approach than the property investment market. Another example is the use of a cell in a PCC to underwrite risk which would be considered manifestly contrary to public policy so as to render the contract of insurance not only void but which gives rise to civil liability against the PCC. It would be difficult to speculate as to the kind of activity concerned and it would have to be a serious criminal offence or tort. But nevertheless if the matter came before a foreign court, the exercise of judicial discretion and public policy considerations may result in the courts challenging the cell structure.[26] Arguably, however, this situation is no more offensive than the conduct of the same business through the medium of a limited liability company.

Captive managers therefore generally recognise that in assessing a particular line of insurance business in the context of a cell, it is necessary to consider whether the use of a PCC is *"fit for purpose"*.

---

[26] Although the authors are not aware of any such company, the use of a PCC to carry on segregrated international gaming operations may not be appropriate presently.

Any discussion on PCC legislation requires mention of specific statutory provisions. However, given the impossibility of reviewing the legislation of all jurisdictions with PCC legislation, the best we can do is choose one as the reference point for further discussion. That model for a large part of this book is Gibraltar (and indirectly Guernsey[27], since Gibraltar's PCC regime, when first implemented, was substantially based on the Guernsey model). Gibraltar is the home for numerous protected cell companies and the first European jurisdiction to have introduced PCC legislation for cell captives, funds and repackaging. We have, however, wherever possible also sought to consider other jurisdictions.

2.5. Provisions of Gibraltar (and Guernsey) PCC legislation

As the cells of a PCC do not have separate legal personality, any legal action would be commenced against the company in respect of a cell (not against a cell itself). Thus if the PCC fails for any reason to meet the obligations attributable to any one or more of its cells or its non-cellular assets, a creditor may make an application for the winding up of the company. The commencement of such winding up proceedings may result in the company being dissolved and the assets of the relevant cells being realised and applied to pay off the liabilities attributable to those cells respectively. A consequence of this is that proceedings may be issued against the PCC in respect of one cell failing to have sufficient assets to meet its obligations, while the other cells continue to have sufficient assets to discharge their respective liabilities. In other words, the failure of the company in respect of discharging the obligations of one cell would have an adverse impact on the PCC as a whole notwithstanding that other cells are otherwise solvent in the event winding-up proceedings are commenced.

2.5.1. Requirements on incorporation/conversion

A PCC must state that it is a PCC in its company name (for example, incorporating the terms PCC or Protected Cell). The PCC's Memorandum of Association must also state that the company is a protected cell company. Each cell must also have its own distinctive name or designation.

---

[27] Most jurisdictions will, in fact, have a variation of the Guernsey model.

2.5.2. Duty to inform third parties

The directors of protected cell companies have a duty to inform third parties dealing with that company that they are contracting with a protected cell company and that the transaction is attributable to a particular cell. The directors of the PCC are personally liable for any failure to do so.

2.5.3. Separation of assets

The cellular assets of each cell must be kept separately identifiable from assets attributable to other cells of the protected cell company and all non-cellular assets.[28] However, directors of PCCs may permit the assets of a cell to be held by or through a nominee or a company whose shares and capital interests may be a combination of cellular assets and non-cellular assets.

The assets may be collectively managed by an investment manager provided that the assets remain identifiable. Provided the requirements of the legislation are complied with, the rights of creditors are limited to the assets of the cell of which they are a creditor(s) (the cellular assets will primarily be used to satisfy any liability and non-cellular assets will only be used once the cellular assets have been exhausted).

This requirement in a PCC to keep the assets separately identifiable is a consequence of the cellular structure and the question sometimes arises as to whether it is permissible to pool investments. One simple example of where it is permissible is a deposit held with a broker or custodian bank. The cash would be separately identifiable to the extent of the respective amounts. So, if Cell A places £50,000, Cell B £30,000 and Cell C £20,000 in the account, the percentage ownership will be Cell A 50%, Cell B 30% and Cell C 20%. There is clearly an obligation on the broker and custodian to keep and maintain separate records and these will be produced with the appropriate designation ("ABC PCC Limited Cell A: £50,000"). Where the asset class is the same (for example, units in a fund, or even same series bonds or equities) the assets will, again, be separately identifiable by keeping an electronic record of how many units are attributable to each cell. Sometimes brokers and custodians also open

---

[28] In the context of life insurance, even before the implementation of PCC legislation, Gibraltar insurance laws (following the then UK legislation) required (and still does) an insurer to maintain one or more separate funds of assets to meet the liabilities of its long term business, segregated from other funds: sections 75, 75A and 83 Financial Services (Insurance Companies) Act 1987. These were essentially "accounting" provisions.

sub-accounts for individual cells (although it would be much simpler to open a separate bank account per cell).

Therefore, where a manager manages a pool of assets held in a custodian bank in respect of a number of cells (in terms of units), the PCC must be able to periodically determine a valuation (NAV) of the assets and thereby the entitlement of each cell to share in the value of the assets.

Clearly the directors must ensure that they notify the investment managers of the investment guidelines together with the applicable restrictions for each cell and that they accept that there is no right of recovery against the other (cell) accounts (as implied by PCC legislation). Such a clause in the relevant contract could read:

"Notwithstanding any other provision of this Agreement, all persons claiming under or with respect to or seeking to effect this Agreement agree and acknowledge that the extent of the liability of the PCC is limited to the assets attributable to [Cell A] (the PCC's protected cell) and that in the event of the exhaustion of the assets attributable to [Cell A], there shall be no liability on the part of any other Cell established by the PCC or the non-cellular assets of the PCC and that the PCC has no obligation whatsoever to use any of its property or assets, other than the assets attributable to [Cell A], to satisfy any claim or liability in the event of the exhaustion of the assets attributable to [Cell A]."

This is intended to give the counterparty notice of the effect of the cell structure and get them to agree to it.

Clearly, the key problem for a PCC is poor governance and internal controls whereby transactions are not properly identified and assets and liabilities not segregated in accordance with the PCC regime (e.g. intermingling of cell assets).

As a corollary of the cell structure and segregation of assets and liabilities, the PCC must attribute liabilities to specific cell assets or assets of the core/hub. A fundamental requirement in a PCC is, therefore, attribution, namely the liabilities arising from a transaction must be attributable to a particular cell or core/hub. Once a liability is so attributed, it can be accounted for separately in the books of the company as such and the liability is limited to the relevant assets, which must be kept separate and separately identifiable at all times. Any liability that cannot be attributed to a cell must fall on the core/hub. The legislative intention is fairly simple, namely each cell is legally protected and must operate as a separate business from other cells within a single entity. In practice, complex questions as to whether certain liabilities are (or even can be) attributable to cells, do sometimes arises.

It is nevertheless important to note that the PCC is not the only business form that requires the segregation and protection of assets. There are other examples used in many commercial transactions including the use of trusts, custody and broker accounts as well as security arrangements of all kinds.

2.5.4. Share capital

PCCs may create and issue shares in respect of any of its cells (known as 'cell shares') and the proceeds of any issue of shares are comprised in the assets attributable to that cell. PCCs may pay dividends.

2.5.5. Administration

The legislation makes provision for administration orders in respect of a PCC or cells. This is typically the case in the PCC legislation of other jurisdictions and therefore the discussion below is of general relevance. Administration is discussed in detail elsewhere within this book. Suffice to say here that it is a UK based system similar to the US Chapter 11; a system designed to protect a company from its creditors.

"Administration" as a concept is generally an anathema to offshore jurisdictions that rely on international business transactions. Banks and secured creditors are sometimes wary of the administration process to the extent that they can freeze the enforcement of their security, or prevent the commencing or continuing proceedings without the leave of the court. Athough security is not lost on administration, the concern is that the ability to realise it may be delayed.

Theoretically, a PCC could become the subject of an administration process if its non-cellular liabilities exceeded its non-cellular assets or if the liabilities of any cell exceeded the assets of such cell.

It is accepted by insolvency practitioners (IPs) that in the context of a PCC, administration (and by parity of reasoning, receivership orders) should generally only be available as a shield (protection of cell assets against non-cellular creditors) rather than a sword (allow non-cellular creditors to disrupt the cell structure). Equally, a creditor should not be able to petition for an Administration Order in respect of a cell of which he was not a creditor. A company director or shareholder of a PCC would have to persuade the court that one of the purposes of administration would be achieved, namely, the survival as a going concern of the cell or as the case may be of the company; or the more advantageous realisation of the business and assets of or attributable to the cell or (as the case may be) the business and assets of the company than would be achieved by receivership of the cell or (as the case may be) by the liquidation of the company. The primary emphasis under an administration procedure is therefore on rescuing the company or achieving a more advantageous realisation of the company's assets than would be effected in a winding up or a receivership of a cell.

Clearly, an administration is not an end in itself, but an interim step, ending with the company re-emerging as a going concern or, perhaps more often, in a voluntary arrangement or insolvent winding up.

In the case of a PCC where a cell is established for defined business transactions with the agreement of specific parties (creditors), the courts should, in exercising their discretion, have to consider the purpose for which PCC legislation was enacted (i.e. the protection or ring-fencing of cell assets). It would be strange and undesirable if a court would grant an administration order in respect of a cell with a single creditor whose assets were not in need of protection from third parties. In the opinion of the authors, the court would also be extremely unlikely to exercise its discretion to make an administration order in respect of a PCC or a cell in circumstances where it would defeat the rights of secured cellular creditors to enforce their security. It is therefore likely that even if an Administration Order were made, the court would grant leave to allow a secured creditor to enforce their security. There is also an argument that the statutory prohibition preventing enforcement of security would not apply to security constituting financial collateral arrangements under the Collateral Directive.

Further, the generally accepted view is that the prohibition of commencement or continued legal proceedings against the PCC would not stay the exercise of netting or set-off rights. Netting and set-off provisions should not be considered a "proceedings", "execution" or "legal process" within the meaning of the PCC regime, since they do not involve court or arbitral process.

The possibility of an Administration Order being granted in respect of a cell to defeat the rights of secured creditors where the relevant cell has been established specifically for the purpose is not, in the authors' view, therefore, a serious practical concern.

It should be noted that the PCC legislation was amended in Gibraltar to allow special purpose vehicles in relation to capital markets transactions (repackaging) to opt out of these moratorium provisions by express exclusion in the Memorandum of Association.

2.5.6. Cells are not legal entities

A PCC is a single legal person and the creation of a cell of a PCC does not, in respect of that cell, create a legal person separate from the company. This has several legal consequences:

(1) The assets of a PCC are owned by the PCC itself (as a corporate entity) and not by individual cells.

(2) Cells cannot contract with each other nor can they contract with the core/hub.[29] This would be analogous to a person contracting with himself.

2.6. Entrenchment

A typical PCC structure will involve a number of parties, including shareholders and counterparties to various contracts. To ensure that future decisions by those who control the PCC do not prejudice the rights of these parties (e.g. the non-voting cell shareholder's exclusive rights to dividends), the promoters should consider whether it is possible under local law to entrench certain rights and/or obligations in the company's Articles or Memorandum of Association so that such rights and obligations cannot be altered (e.g. to entrench the dividend rights against future alteration).

In overseas British territories that have largely adopted the Companies Act 1929 ('CA29') and the Companies Act 1948 ('CA48') of England and continue to do so, it may be possible, although case-law is far from clear on this point.[30]

Section 4 of CA29 prohibited the alteration of conditions contained in a company's Memorandum except to the extent provided for in that Act.

Like section 4 of CA29, section 4 of CA48 prohibited the alteration of conditions contained in a company's Memorandum except to the extent provided for in the legislation itself. Section 23(1) of CA48 specifically allowed any condition in a company's Memorandum which could lawfully have been contained in its Articles to be altered by special resolution. Nevertheless, section 23(2) of CA48 allowed the alteration right set out in section 23(1) to be expressly disapplied in the Memorandum itself.

---

[29] Inter-cell transactions are permissible in some jurisdictions. Guernsey, for example, has introduced the "incorporated cell company" (ICC).

[30] See *Re Scientific Poultry Breeders' Association Limited [1933] Ch 227* and *Re RAC Motoring Services Ltd [2000] 1 BCLC 307.*

2.7. Market acceptance and respecting the intention of the parties

As we have seen there is wide market acceptance for the use of PCCs for numerous transactions. In the authors' view there is an interesting analogy worth noting between the debate about the PCC concept and the historical debate on whether credit derivatives were contracts of insurance.

The credit derivative market is one of the largest in the international financial markets. Anyone who has structured these (admittedly complex) instruments will also know that sometimes the credit derivative will be embedded into another instrument such as a credit-linked note (in many cases issued by a Special Purpose Vehicle – see Chapter 1). The question that has vexed everyone ever since these products came to market was, are credit derivatives 'contracts of insurance'? If so, all such transactions (worth many billions in financial terms) would be at risk since only licensed insurance companies can undertake insurance business.

It is not necessary for the purposes of this book to address this question. Suffice to say that the arguments for and against are well documented elsewhere.[31] Numerous legal opinions have also been sought in support of the validity of credit derivatives and the authors of this book are not about to challenge that analysis.

But we could be forgiven for discerning that the market's approach to the regulatory uncertainty was as much to rely on legal counsel as it was on an expectation (perhaps convenient and pragmatic?) that a Court would be unlikely to upset the documentation and structure. To upset the documentation and structure of the contract would be to characterise the transaction into what the parties had not intended it to be. It would thereby defeat the underlying commercial objectives of the parties.

More recently, in the case of *Re Colt Telecom Group plc [2002] EWHC 2815 (Ch)* Jacob J considered whether a non-petition clause was valid under English law as an attempt to oust the jurisdiction of the Courts. Jacob J was reluctant to engage in judicial activism of the sort that would have destabilised the international bond market. Therefore, in response to submissions by counsel that public policy overrode the non-petition

---

[31] See, for example, *The Law on Financial Derivatives*, 4th Edition, Prof. Alastair Hudson, Sweet & Maxwell.

clause, the judge rejected this assertion and stated that if counsel was right:

"... the effect is startling. It would mean that English companies could not readily issue bonds with no-action clauses -whatever the terms of the bond, and whether pre- or post default, they would be exposed to the potentiality of a single bondholder bringing an administration petition. It is not self-apparent why that should be so. Certainly such bonds are regarded as enforceable under New York law with no harm to public policy. Nor is there any evidence of harm to the public by the enforceability of these clauses so far as this country or any other country is concerned [Paragraph 62]".

It may also be worth noting the words of Staughton LJ in the *Welsh Development Agency v Export Finance Co. Ltd [1992] BCLC 148* case (at page 189):

"It can be said that Exfinco have adopted their method of business because their customers wished to avoid the registration provisions of the Companies Act, and the appearance of loans in their balance sheets. But one should not, from sympathy for creditors or rather for a debenture holder, overthrow both established law and recognised methods of providing finance for trade and industry."

Due to the globalisation of business, it is possible for a number of PCCs to all be connected in a financial chain of transactions ('upstream' or 'downstream' or both). To illustrate the point consider the following examples:

A.

(a). A PCC insurer domiciled in an EU jurisdiction invests in a UCITS (Undertaking for Collective Investment in Transferable Securities) established pursuant to the relevant EU Directive.

(b). The UCITS is afforded statutory segregration of assets and liabilities in its home jurisdiction.

(c). The UCITS, in turn, invests, within the investment restrictions and available limits, in listed bonds issued in respect of a cell of a PCC investment vehicle (as issuer).

B.

A PCC umbrella fund invests via a cell (on behalf of hedge fund investors) in cell shares of a PCC insurance company attributable to particular insurance cell.

C.

An EU PCC insurer reinsures 100% of its obligations in respect of a cell with a non-EU PCC reinsurer.

D.

An EU PCC insurer issues rated debt finance to a PCC umbrella fund treated for regulatory purposes as Tier 2 capital to support the underwriting activities (solvency) of a particular cell. The insurance company (a PCC) would therefore be borrowing from the PCC umbrella fund through the issuance of a subordinated loan note.

E.

A PCC repackaging vehicle issues bonds to international investors and uses the proceeds to invest in cell shares (as underlying collateral) issued by a PCC umbrella fund.

F.

A PCC life company issues a cell policy unit-linked to the performance of an underlying asset, being a cell of a PCC umbrella fund.

As can be seen from the above examples, the PCC has access to the capital markets, would have recognition from regulatory, listing or rating agencies in various jurisdictions, would segregate assets and liabilities at different levels (and in different territories) and could execute transactions via any type of financial instrument (debt or equity or hybrid) and with any number of counterparties.

A consequence of globalisation is that the world has become 'smaller' as global markets become accessible to capital, goods and services. Key to this has been financial and legislative innovation. In the words of former US Treasury Under Secretary, Robert K. Steel in early 2008, "*Globalization and technological developments have led to innovations in financial products and forever changed our economy and the capital markets. As a result, some have suggested the world has flattened. At the very least, today's world has unquestionably become more compressed. And I believe this compression will increase with the passage of time.*[32]" Nevertheless, the extraordinary events in the international financial markets of the last 18 months have created a huge amount of scepticism of innovation. It would be wrong to blame innovation for the virtual collapse of the global financial system in 2008 and the massive bailout of financial institutions that followed. Much of the problem lay with excessive risk taking and inadequate internal controls and governance. There is a danger, nevertheless, that legislators and regulators will in future stifle the development and legitimate use of new products.

---

[32] February 5, 2008, Las Vegas

3. SERIES LLC: AN ANALOGOUS BUSINESS FORM TO THE PCC

In researching for this second edition we came across new information that caused some initial excitement. Being the pioneer in something, in whatever field, not only gives a competitive advantage in the market place, but allows the pioneer's name to be associated with it into the future. So it was with Guernsey and the PCC. Since Guernsey enacted the Protected Cell Company Ordinance in February 1997, the perceived wisdom is that Guernsey was the birthplace of the concept of statutory segregation for different business activities and economic interests within the same legal entity. This does not appear to be entirely correct. In 1996 Delaware introduced the "Series LLC" into law (6 Del. Code § 18-215). The LLC is a business form that provides limited liability for members within a form of partnership. It is therefore important to note that an LLC is an unincorporated entity. The Delaware LLC Series legislation was, in fact, pre-dated by, and based on, series provisions in the Delaware Business Trust Act 1988, now known as the Delaware Statutory Trust Act. Since the enactment of the Delaware Business Trust Act, other States in the US also adopted business (or statutory) trust legislation based on the Delaware legislation.

We recognise that the short discussion in this chapter cannot do justice to the considerable (and indeed thorough) commentary on the subject among US practictioners[33] and academics.

3.1. Delaware

The first US State to introduce the "Series LLC" was Delaware[34]. Looking at this business form, for 'series' read 'cell' and no doubt readers will appreciate why this caused us such excitement. Under a Series LLC, an LLC can have individual 'series', each with a separate business purpose or investment objective and with their own separate assets and liabilities (just like a cell of a PCC). According to the sypnosis that accompanied the Delaware legislation implementing Series LLCs: *"upon compliance with the requirements of new § 18-215(b), a limited liability company may provide that such series shall be treated in many important respects as if the series were a separate limited liability company, including limiting the recourse of creditors*

---

[33] See Symonds & O'Toole on *"Delaware Limited Liability Companies"* (Wolters Kluwer).

[34] The US has Federal and provincial or State law. There is no such thing as 'US law'. It would be Delaware, Iowa, Nevada law etc.

with respect to liabilities of the series to the assets associated with the series, and not the assets of the limited liability company generally or the assets of any other series."

Thus under § 18-215 (b): *"the debts, liabilities, obligations and expenses incurred, contracted for or otherwise existing with respect to a particular series shall be enforceable against the assets of such series only, and not against the assets of the limited liability company generally or any other series thereof, and, unless otherwise provided in the limited liability company agreement, none of the debts, liabilities, obligations and expenses incurred, contracted for or otherwise existing with respect to the limited liability company generally or any other series thereof shall be enforceable against the assets of such series."*

But what was the rationale for this new statutory provision? Why not just set up new LLCs in the same way as one would set up separate corporate entities? A possible answer as Professor Ribstein explains in his book *The Rise of the Uncorporation*[35] is *"that using commonly managed and operated LLCs presents a risk that the courts will pierce the veil and attribute the liabilities of one of the commonly managed firms to the 'sister' LLC. A Series LLC statute effectively instructs the courts to keep the liabilities separate as long as the members have followed the formalities and record-keeping rules."* If so, it was conceived for a different reason to the Guernsey PCC.

What was surprising on further examination is that the Delaware Series LLC has not been more widely used[36]. Why?

In the US, the Series LLC has had some powerful detractors and the view that it was a new and judicially untested concept appears to have prevailed. The National Conference of Commissioners on Uniform State Laws produced a revised uniform Limited Liability Company Act (4 December 2006) approved and recommended for enactment in all States but Series LLC were noticeable for their absence. The Report stated:

"The new Act also has a very noteworthy omission; it does not authorize 'series LLCs.' Under a series approach, a single limited liability company may establish and contain within itself separate series. Each series is treated as an enterprise separate from each other and from the LLC itself. Each series has associated with it specified members, assets, and obligations, and – due to what have been called 'internal shields' – the obligations of one series are not the obligation of any other

---

[35] p.147

[36] The authors are reliably informed there were 5,780 Delaware series LLCs as of October 2009. We are also informed that the total number of Delaware LLCs in 2008 was 501,670.

series or of the LLC. Delaware pioneered the series concept, and the concept has apparently been quite useful in structuring certain types of investment funds and in arranging complex financing. Other States have followed Delaware's lead, but a number of difficult and substantial questions remain unanswered."

The unanswered questions, according to the Report, include those familiar to any practitioner of the PCC and were not new, namely:

"bankruptcy – Bankruptcy law has not recognized the series as a separate legal person. If a series becomes insolvent, will the entire LLC and the other series become part of the bankruptcy proceedings? Will a bankruptcy court consolidate the assets and liabilities of the separate series?

efficacy of the internal shields in the courts of other States – Will the internal shields be respected in the courts of States whose LLC statutes do not recognize series? Most LLC statutes provide that "foreign law governs" the liability of members of a foreign LLC. However, those provisions do not apply to the series question, because those provisions pertain to the liability of a member for the obligations of the LLC. For a series LLC, the pivotal question is entirely different – namely, whether some assets of an LLC should be immune from some of the creditors of the LLC."

There was a clear rejection on the part the Drafting Committee of the series proposal: The Report noted that *"after serious discussion, no one was willing to urge adoption of the proposal, even for the limited purposes of further discussion"*.

This surely was a missed opportunity. As Bruce H. Kobayashi and Professor Larry Ribstein write: *"Here, action by NCCUSL might have had a significant effect in leading States toward uniformity in a still-developing area in which there are several disparate statutes. Even if NCCUSL did not want to adopt a specific provision, it could have clarified that adopting States should enforce the series law of the state in which a foreign LLC is organized. Instead, NCCUSL not only explicitly declined to adopt a provision, but took a position in the comments against enforcing organization State law."*[37]

Whilst it is possible to view the Series LLC narrowly in terms of an internal shield against courts piercing the veil and holding an entity or entities liable for debts incurred by sister entities or subsidiaries, in trying to solve a potential problem it could also be said to have stretched the boundaries of innovation too far by providing virtually unrestricted

---

[37] *The Non-Uniformity of Uniform Laws*: Bruce H. Kobayashi & Larry E. Ribstein

business use for this new business form[38]. This was bound to be controversial and something that legislators of the PCC concept have avoided. In Guernsey's case, the PCC was introduced principally as a response to the needs of the captive insurance industry. In other words, it was not intended to be available for all business activities. On the other hand, the Delaware Series LLC run the risk of being marketed by formation agents as a cheap alternative to setting up separate LLCs (due to the single formation cost involved and ability to have separate ownership interests in the same structure).

Interestingly, the term 'series' had long been used in financing arrangements where a single issuer issued debt or other securities, with each individual financing designated as a different 'Series' (e.g. Series 1, 2, 3, 4 etc). It is easy to see a use for the Series LLC in financing transactions of this kind and its application and promotion in these areas would be uncontroversial. So too where an entrepreneur owned an LLC and wished to hold his private investments under separate series to avoid the setting up multiple LLCs. The potential problems arise where different owners of assets use the Series LLC as a means of achieving cost efficiency for separate trading businesses operated through each series as a means of limiting liability (e.g. manufacturing).

Delaware introduced its own separate PCC legislation on the 1 January 2005 aimed at the captive insurance sector. Perhaps had Guernsey not introduced PCC legislation in 1997, had Delaware extended the 'series' provisions to other corporate forms, and had this attracted the support of global captive insurance managers (as in the case of Guernsey and the PCC), Delaware could have been the birthplace for the 'series captive' (now known as the protected cell captive). The Delaware code would also have become the gold plate legislation for other jurisdictions and we would today be talking about 'series' rather than 'cells'. But it did not. Nor could the Series LLC law be easily 'exported' outside the US since it was a by-product of the LLC legislation widely used in the US but not outside those shores.

The Delaware Series LLC recently received a significant boast when Delaware Insurance Commissioner Karen Weldin Stewart, CIR-ML, licensed the world's first series entity captive. A news press release dated 25 January 2010 states: *"This is a break-through in the captive insurance world with the first captive of this type… A series captive entity provides greater*

---

[38] Except for banking

flexibility and advantage than other traditional structures, including protected cell structures. The licensing of this serial captive insurance company reflects my initiative to build Delaware's captive insurance industry. Since my staff began informing the insurance industry of the opportunity offered by Delaware of serial entities as an alternative risk solution less than six months ago, my office has had numerous inquiries about how a captive can be formed under Delaware law. What delights me is the number of inquiries arising not only from within Delaware as well as from across the country, but also from outside the United States…"[39].

The table below compares the main features of the Delaware Series LLC with PCC legislation.

Key Issues	Delaware Series LLC Code – as amended in 2007	Gibraltar/Malta/Guernsey PCC Act
Core/Master LLC creditors have recourse to Cell/Series LLC? (downstream liability)	No, but otherwise yes if specifically allowed for in the LLC agreement.	No, according to the Act.
Cell/Series LLC creditors have recourse to the Core/Master LLC? (upstream liability)	No – excluded explicitly in section (b) of the Code.	Yes for involuntary creditors. For other creditors – no – but only if there is a "cell limitation" or similar limited recourse provision. Note Guernsey have now reversed this, and recourse to the core is not given to anyone, unless this is provided for by contract.
Can Cell/Series hold title to assets?	Yes, according to the Code.	Not exactly, since only the PCC is a legal entity, but the title would be "in respect of" the cell.

[39]See http://delawareinsurance.gov/departments/news/012510-Press-FirstCaptiveCompany.shtml

Can Cell/Series contract in its own name?	Yes, according to the Code.	Not exactly, since only the PCC is a legal entity, but the contract would be "in respect of" the cell.
Can Cell/Series sue and be sued?	Yes, according to the Code.	Not exactly, since only the PCC is a legal entity, but the proceedings would be "in respect of" the cell.
Can Cell/Series grant security interests?	Yes, according to the Code.	Not exactly, since only the PCC is a legal entity, but the security interest would be "in respect of" the cell.
Can Cells/Series contract with each other in the same umbrella company?	No prohibition in the Code.	This is not allowed.
Can a Cell/Series merge with another equivalent entity?	No explicit provision in the Code.	No explicit provision in the PCC statute but amalgamation has been upheld by the Guernsey Courts.
Can an entity convert to a PCC or Series form?	Yes, this is possible.	Yes, and there are examples where this has happened.
Cell/Series LLC - Legal Entity?	No – but many features of a legal entity are in place. Unclear how the concept would withstand insolvency and recognition by other states of the USA – or foreign jurisdictions.	No – this has always been the key feature of the PCC.

Clear identification to Third Parties Required?	No explicit requirement in the Code.	Yes – directors are personally liable if the business is not attributed to a cell.
Typical Applications	Investment funds	Primarily captive insurance and investment funds.
Recognition by other jurisdictions	Limited	In the context of insolvency, the EU regime requires mutual recognition between EU states, and the EU regime is itself likely to be recognized or persuasive in other countries. Note Guernsey is not in the EU so it may have less recognition from other jurisdictions.
Adjustable structure?	Members of a Series may or may not have voting rights in the master LLC. See above also re downstream liability.	The structure is prescribed such that there is only one board of directors. Nothing precludes Board sub-committees, however, on a cell by cell basis.
Relocation/ Migration?	Yes, this is possible.	Yes, between domiciles that recognise each other's PCC laws and allow for redomiciliation.

Table 2: Comparison of the Delaware Series LLC with PCC legislation

Series LLC legislation has been enacted in other States of the US apart from Delaware. Questions still remain unanswered with regards to their use, but whatever the future may hold for the Series LLC, Delaware does deserve some recognition for introducing the concept of segregated business within a single legal form before Guernsey's PCC Ordinance. The 'some recognition' qualification is necessary because, as we have seen, this sort of statute providing segregation of assets and liabilities within 'special' entities was not unique to Delaware either (other examples, as we have seen, is Chile's Law 19301 of 1994 (*sociedad securitizadoras*) and Bermuda private Acts establishing reinsurance companies with segregated accounts, both in existence before 1997).

The point is also worth making that a number of States in the US have introduced both PCC and Series LLC legislation[40] and that those States who have permitted PCCs have done so in an insurance context. The fact that the 'series' regime already existed (both for LLCs and trusts) was probably a catalyst to the introduction of PCC legislation in the US since the technology is not conceptually and legally different.

The table below shows which States in the US have introduced PCC legislation, Series LLCs or both.

USA States	Protected Cell Companies Legislation	Series LLC Legislation
Arizona	Legislation passed in 2005	None
Delaware	Legislation passed 1 January 2005	Passed in 1996 - Delaware Code §18-215, and amended 2007
District of Colombia	Legislation passed 25 October 2000	None
Hawaii	Captive insurance legislation amended in 2008 to give effect to PCCs	None
Illinois	None	Effective in 2007, per 805 ILCS 180/37-40
Iowa	None	From 1 January 2009 - Iowa Code Ann. § 489.1201
Kentucky	Sponsored Protected Cell (SPC) legislation passed in 2000	None
Montana	Protected cell captive legislation passed in April 2003	None

[40] Some states also provide for the creation of series trusts.

Nevada	Sponsored captive law passed in 2005	Nev.Rev.Stat. Ann. § 86.296 (2005)
Oklahoma	Legislation passed on 25 May 2001	18 Okla. Stat. § 18-2054.4B
South Carolina	Protected cell company law passed in 2000	None
Tennessee	None	Tenn. Code Ann. § 48-249-309 (2006)
Texas	None	Effective 1st September 2009. S.B. No. 1442
Utah	Sponsored captive law passed in July 2003	Utah Code Ann. § 48-2c-606 (2006)
Vermont	Sponsored Captive Insurance Companies law passed in 1999	None

Table 3: PCC and Series LLC legislation in the US

3.2. US Case-law

Surprisingly, there appear to be few 'intrastate' judicial authorities in the US on the Series LLC. Two reported authorities worth mentioning are *GxG Management LLC v. Young Brothers and Co., Inc., 2007 WL 551761 (D. Me. 2007)* and *GxG Management LLC v. Young Brothers and Co., Inc., 2007 WL 1702872 (D. Me. 2007)*. The latter court report states:

"In this case GxG Management LLC purchased a custom-built vessel from Young Brothers. Thereafter, pursuant to Delaware law, 6 Del.Code Ann. § 18-215(a), GxG Management formed a "series" of "limited liability company interest" for the purpose of holding title to and operating the vessel in question. Subsequently, GxG Management brought suit against Young Brothers [in the courts of Maine] asserting contract and tort law claims based on allegations of poor workmanship and misrepresentation. ... Young Brothers, ... asserted ... that GxG Management was not competent to maintain contract and tort claims against Young Brothers because it had transferred the vessel to its Series B interest. ... the unique relationship between a Delaware LLC and its series does not create a truly separate legal entity capable of independently pursuing its own legal claims. ... Series B is not a legal entity at all but merely a "series of interest" maintained by the LLC, and ... by taking advantage of the limited liability offered under Delaware law by transferring the vessel to Series B and operating the

vessel through the "vehicle" of Series B, the LLC did not forfeit rights obtained under contract or tort law in relation to the vessel[41]*."*

There were two important facts in this decision: that the contract for the construction of the vessel was entered into by GxG Management LLC and that title of the boat was held in the name of "GxG Management LLC (Series B)". We are told that *"GxG exist[ed] to manage the household affairs and the financial investments of the ... family, including their family residence ... and the vessel ...*[42]*"* and that Series B was formed *"for the purpose of holding the assets/liabilities associated with the [boat] including the [boat] itself*[43]*"*.

Similar facts could arise in a PCC contractual dispute and in substance the legal analysis would remain largely valid. This is because PCC legislation will typically provide that a cell does not create a distinct legal entity from the company. All rights of action and ownership are vested in the PCC (albeit for the benefit of an individual cell or core/hub). It is rights of enforcement against the PCC that are limited in recourse against specified assets (again, of a cell or core/hub).

Accordingly:

(1) The records of ownership of cell assets (eg held by brokers/custodians/managers acting for a PCC) would (as in the case of GxG) be in the name of the company bearing the cell name or designation eg 'ABC PCC Limited (Cell A)'.

(2) The contract would identify the assets which would satisfy any obligations that are incurred by the PCC by reference to a cell or core/hub.

Although some practitioners still refer to a contract/transaction being entered into by a PCC as being "on behalf of" a cell, this is not strictly correct. An obligation cannot be "on behalf of" since the cell lacks the necessary juridical existence. It is an obligation by the PCC "in respect of" the cell. Interestingly, Section 500.4715 of the Insurance Code of 1956 (Excerpt) Act 218 of 1956 of the US State of Michigan permitting the formation of Special Purpose Financial Captives expressly addresses this issue by acknowleding that *"(4) Although the protected cell is not a separate legal person, the property of an SPFC in a protected cell is subject to orders of a*

---

[41] 2007 WL 1702872 (D. Me. 2007) at page 2

[42] 2007 WL 551761 (D. Me. 2007) at page 1

[43] 2007 WL 551761 (D. Me. 2007) at page 2

court by name as it would have been if the protected cell were a separate legal person" and *"(5) The property of an SPFC in a protected cell shall be served in its own name with process in all civil actions or proceedings involving or relating to the activities of that protected cell ...".*

In the absence of a uniform LLC code recognized by all States, some States have expressly legislated for the recognition of foreign LLCs.

There is one reported case of an LLC (not a Series LLC) where the Federal District Court for the Northern District of California had to interpret a foreign LLC recognition provision of California law in the context of a third party claim (in tort): *Butler v. Adoption Media, LL, 2005 WL 2077484 (N.D.Cal. 2005).* It did so and denied a motion to apply Arizona law:

"Defendants argue that Arizona law applies because the Beverly-Killea Limited Liability Company Act, Cal. Corp.Code § 17000, et seq., provides for the application of the law of the state of organization (here, Arizona) to issues of liability between an LLC and its management and officers as well as to issues concerning the organization of the LLC. Cal. Corp.Code § 17450(a) ("The laws of the state ... under which a foreign limited liability company is organized shall govern its organization and internal affairs and the liability and authority of its managers and members."). The court finds, however, that § 17450(a) simply codifies the internal affairs doctrine, as applied to LLCs. In other words, § 17450(a) does not apply to disputes that include people or entities that are not part of the LLC."

In this case the choice of law was between the court applying local California law or applying Arizona law. California had a 'foreign law recognition' provision: section 17450(a). This clearly required the courts to recognise the application of Arizona law under which the LLC was formed to *"govern its organization and internal affairs and the liability and authority of its managers and members"* and the judge so held applying the 'internal affairs doctrine'. But the section was silent with regards to the choice of law governing matters external to the LLC such as rights of third parties. It was therefore open to the court to apply Californian law to the dispute. The Butler case did not have to decide and therefore there was no discussion about whether applying the law of California (which did not permit Series LLCs) a third party creditor could enforce an action against all the assets of a Series LLC in proceedings under California law. What the court did do was reject the argument that Section 17450(a) required Arizona law to be applied to disputes between an LLC and 'outsiders'. However, the court deferred the issue of whether California law should be applied for consideration and resolution on summary judgment, once discovery was closed in the matter.

Some US commentators consider that the principle in this case can be extended to draw a distinction between recognition of the limited liability of members of a foreign LLC under the 'internal affairs' doctrine (whereby a court would apply foreign law) and the recognition of the statutory segregation of the assets and liability of each series ('internal shield') in a foreign Series LLC whereby local law would be applied. This remains judicially untested.

What value does the case have for a PCC? Probably little is the answer apart from highlighting the judicial reluctance (even in a federal legal system) to apply a 'foreign' law to disputes between foreign entities and non-contracting parties. Nevertheless, unlike in a Series LLC where a series can engage in all types of business activities (except for banking), in a PCC context where the activities of the company are usually restricted to insurance, fund or securitisation business, the PCC is unlikely to face litigation from third parties. They will generally be parties that have willingly entered into a transaction with the PCC. To use the words of Judge Hamilton, they are "not part of the" [in this case] PCC in the sense that directors, shareholders and managers are, but they have accepted the 'statutory contract' that defines the rights and obligations of both sides: on the one side the PCC is required to identify the cell in respect of which an obligation is entered into and must keeps the asset of the cell separate from the assets of other cells, and on the other, the rights of the party facing the PCC are limited in recourse to those assets. The principal extraneous creditor would be tax authorities (and we deal with tax in Chapter 15).

Whilst many commentators among the US legal community continue to write about the legal uncertainty regarding the recognition of the limitation of liability provision of a Series LLC (or 'internal shield') in foreign state proceedings (obviously because of the lack of case-law), there seems to be less hostility for the PCC and indeed there is little adverse commentary directly on the question, 'will a foreign state recognise the internal fire-walls (or shields) within a PCC'? Why is this?

We could make at least some observations:

(1) The use of the PCC in the US is limited to insurance.

(2) The PCC in this context is an evolutionary next step in the development of existing structures set up by lawyers (albeit via contractual and security arrangements) and used over many years. It

was therefore technology that was previously available through other legal means.

(3) The PCC regime enjoys the support of the powerful US insurance sector. It has also been introduced successfully in many overseas jurisdictions (before it was enacted in the US) where it was already used by US groups.

(4) Insurance is a highly regulated industry and through the adoption of PCC laws state regulators have endorsed their use. In fact, the failure by the National Conference of Commissioners on Uniform State Laws to approve Series LLCs can be contrasted with the adoption of a model PCC law by the National Association of Insurance Commissioners in 2001.

More recently, in July 2009, the National Conference of Commissioners on Uniform State Laws approved and recommended for enactment in all States the *Uniform Statutory Trust Entity Act*[44]. The statutory trust form has been commonly used for special purpose vehicles in securitisation, mutual fund and real estate (REIT) transactions. The Act was therefore intended to *"bring clarity and uniformity to the law pertaining to statutory trusts"*. It is modelled on the Delaware legislation and also makes provision for series trusts (Article 4). The Act clearly validates the use of statutory trust (with one or more series) as a business form for interstate transactions. It contains the typical formulations with regards to identifying the property of the relevant series, the giving of notice in the certificate of trust, a series not being a separate entity from the statutory trust and, of course, recourse limitations for liabilities of each series. The Act also makes it clear that a statutory trust (unlike a common law trust) can sue and be sued in its own name. The American Bar Association has since approved the Act as an appropriate Act for those states desiring the specific substantive law suggested therein[45]. Why a 'Series Trust' should be more deserving of uniform business recognition than a 'Series LLC' is not entirely clear and if anything the argument for recognition of 'Series LLC' is probably now stronger than ever.

3.3. SEC Prouncement

Whilst the Series LLC has had some apparent success in investment type structures, there is one reported case of the Securities Exchange Commission (SEC) ruling that it was inconsistent with SEC regulations.

---

[44] http://www.nccusl.org/Update/Docs/Finals_NC/USTEA_FinalNC_Nov09.doc

[45] http://www.abanet.org/leadership/2010/midyear/summary_of_recommendations/111D.doc

The ruling[46], dated 1 September 2009 related to broker-dealers hoping to use the Series LLC in multiple structures and was delivered in reply to a ruling request from the Financial Industry Regulatory Authority.

It was proposed that the broker-dealer would structure the Series LLC so that the Master LLC would have no business operations. One series would operate a retail broker-dealer and the second series institutional activities. Each series would have separate assets and liabilities, and liabilities of one series would not be enforceable against the other series, but the assets and liabilities of the two series would be reported in one consolidated financial statement when filing financial reports with the SEC.

In its reply the SEC indicated that the first problem related to the capital position of the firm. Applying the net capital rule, assets of the firm have to be available to meet all of the firm's obligations; whilst at the same time all liabilities of the firm must be recognized. This was therefore inconsistent with a Series LLC structure.

Another problem was that if the firm reported its financial statements on a consolidated basis, the SEC would not be able to determine the financial position of the firm without substantial effort. Lastly, applying the customer protection rule and equal treatment of customers in liquidation, the segregation of assets and liabilities in a Series LLC was said to be inconsistent with regulations.

The fundamental difference between a Series LLC and a PCC in this respect is that a PCC is an incorporated (as opposed to an unincorporated) entity, and also separately from the cell assets, has a 'core' (non-cellular assets) which can count as fully admissible regulatory capital. Otherwise, the reasons for rejecting the use of the example structure above could equally be put forward in a cell captive context! Of course, in jurisdictions with PCC legislation this would not happen because the cell captive regime will have been introduced with the full support, if not at the request, of the local insurance regulator.

Before we end this chapter we should ask whether there are any European (Civil Law) jurisdictions with a similar concept to the PCC and the Series LLC, outside that is of securitisation (securitisation laws being common to many jurisdictions)? It would be impossible to trawl the laws

---

[46] Available in http://www.sec.gov/divisions/marketreg/mr-noaction/2009/finra090109.pdf

of every jurisdiction in the world, but in search for the answer, the authors found one such jurisdiction.

3.4. Statutory segregation under Italian law

A European country that provides for the statutory segregation (ring-fencing) of assets and liabilities within a single legal entity is Italy.[47] The relevant legislation was introduced by the Italian corporate reforms of 2004 and has the characteristics of the PCC.

It is therefore worth setting out the translated provisions of the Italian regime:

SECTION XI[48]

Of Dedicated Assets to a Specified Activity

2447-bis. Allocation of dedicated assets to specific business activities. *The company may:*

- *a) create one or more pools of business assets each of which is allocated in priority and exclusively to a specified business activity;*
- *b) agree in any agreement relating to the financing of a specified business activity, that all or part of the cash flows generated from such specified business activity shall be allocated in priority to the repayment of all or any part of such financing.*

Except to the extent provided for under special laws, dedicated assets constituted pursuant to (a) above cannot be established in an aggregate amount exceeding 10 per cent of the company's net assets and in any case cannot be established for the exercise of businesses pertaining to activities reserved by special laws.

2447-ter. Resolution constituting dedicated assets. *The resolution by which pool of business assets is allocated to a specified business activity, pursuant to letter a) first paragraph of Article 2447-bis, shall set out:*

- *a) the business activity to which a pool of business assets is to be dedicated;*
- *b) the rights and assets comprised in such pool of business assets;*
- *c) an economic/financial plan [...];*

---

[47]See Raffaella Rametta *"History and dogma behind the doctrine of the indivisibility of property in the civil law jurisdictions"*, published in "Studi in onore di Giuseppe Benedetti", Edizioni Scientifiche Italiane, Napoli, 2008.

[48]*The Italian Civil Code and Complementary Legislation,* translated by Mario Beltramo, Giovanni E. Longo, John H. Merryman, Published by Dobbs Ferry, N.Y. : Oceana, c1991.

d) any contributions to be made by third parties, and the framework for the controls on the management and the allocation of profits and losses arising from the business activity;

e) any issues of financial instruments for investing in the specific business activity, specifying rights attached to such instruments;

f) the appointment of an auditing firm [...];

g) the reporting requirements applicable to the specified business activity.

[...]

2447-quarter. Publicity for the creation of dedicated assets. *The resolution provided in the preceding article shall be deposited and registered in accordance with Article 2436.*

Within sixty days of registration of the resolution in the companies register, creditors of the company who were creditors before the registration of such resolution may apply to the court for an order preventing the creation of the dedicated assets. Notwithstanding any such application, the court may order that the resolution be implemented, subject to the company providing adequate guarantees.

2447-quinquies. Creditors' rights. *Once the two-month period mentioned in Article 2447-quarter has elapsed, or following the registration of a court order made pursuant to Article 2447-quarter in the companies register, the company's creditors will not be permitted to assert any claim against the pool of business assets dedicated to the specified business activity nor against the proceeds and income arising from the business activity.*

If the pool of business assets includes immovable or movable assets subject to registration in a public register, the provisions of the preceding paragraph shall not apply until the allocation of the pool of business assets to the specified business activity is recorded in the relevant registers.

Except as provided otherwise in the resolution made pursuant to Article 2447-ter, the liability of the company for the liabilities incurred in relation to the specified business activity is limited to the pool of business assets allocated to such activity. Notwithstanding the foregoing, the company shall in all events be liable without limitation for its unlawful acts.

All agreement entered into in relation to the specified business activity shall expressly make reference to the destination; in the absence of such express reference, the company is liable pursuant to such agreement to the extent of its other business assets.

2447-sexies. Statutory books and other account books. *With respect to the specified business activity to which a pool of business asset has been dedicated pursuant to Article 2447-bis letter a) of the first paragraph, the directors shall keep a separate set of books and accounts [...].*

2447-septies. Annual accounts. *The rights and assets included in the dedicated assets constituted pursuant the Article 2447-bis a) shall be recorded as separate item in the profit and loss account of the company.*

For each dedicated assets constituted pursuant to Article 2423 and the following, the directors shall prepare a separate report to be attached to the company's annual accounts.

In the explanatory note to the annual accounts of the company, the directors shall set out the value and the description of the assets and the rights comprised in each pool of dedicated assets; including those contributed by third parties, the criteria adopted to allocate the common items of expenses and income and the corresponding regime applicable to the liabilities.

[...]

2447-decies. Financing allocated to a specific business activity. *Any agreement relating to the financing of a specified business activity pursuant to letter b) of the first paragraph Article 2447-bis, may provide that all or part of the cash flows generated from that specified business activity shall be exclusively destined to the repayment of all or any part of such financing.*

The relevant agreement shall contain:

- *a) description of the transaction that allows the identification of the main object of the transaction; the timing and the framework for its implementation; the expected costs and revenues;*
- *b) the financial plan of the transaction, showing the share of the funding provided by the company and that provided under the financing arrangement;*
- *c) the key assets necessary for the implementation of the transaction;*
- *d) the terms of the guarantees provided by the company in relation to the performance of the agreement and the timely and proper implementation of the transaction;*
- *e) the extent to which the lender, or its agent, may control the transaction;*
- *f) the portion of the revenues allocated to the repayment of the financing and the method of determining that amount;*
- *g) any guarantees given by the company in respect of the repayment of any part of the financing;*

h) the final maturity date, following which no further amounts will be due to the lender.

The revenues of the transaction shall constitute assets segregated from the other assets of the company, and from assets relating to other financings entered into in accordance with the provisions of this article, provided that:

a) a copy of the agreement is deposited with the register of enterprises;

b) the company adopts collections and accounting systems such that the revenues of the business activity may be separately identified at all times and are held separately from the other company's assets.

Subject to the conditions of the preceding paragraph, the company's creditors shall not be entitled to claim against the revenues and proceeds of the investments made pending the repayment to the lender; subject to the same conditions, the liability of the company against the lender is limited to the segregated pool of business assets, unless a partial guarantee has been provided pursuant to g) above.

Until the repayment of the financing, or until the date specified in h) above, the company's creditors may only exercise preventative measures in relation to the assets destined for the performance of the transaction, in order to protect their rights.

If the insolvency of the company prevents the completion or the continuance of the transaction, the limitations set out in the above paragraph shall cease to apply and the lender will be able to claim in the insolvency for the amount owed to it less the amounts referred to in the third and fourth paragraphs above.

Except for securitizations governed by laws into force, the financing cannot take the form of instruments destined to circulation.

The section of the integrative note to the items of the annual accounts statements relating to the revenues described in the third paragraph above, and the assets described in the fourth paragraph above, shall set out the allocation of such revenues and any lien applicable to the relevant assets."

It will be noted that there are two forms of segregation here: one relating to the *"allocation of dedicated assets to specified business activities"* and the other *"financing allocated to a specific business activity"*.

3.4.1. "Allocation of dedicated assets to specified business activities"

Like a PCC, an Italian joint stock company may therefore separate one or more pools of assets for specified business activities with the legal consequence under Italian law that the liabilities incurred in relation to those activities are limited to assets allocated for the purpose and that those assets and their proceeds are not available to meet the claims of third party creditors. This obviates the need for (a) security over specific assets and/or (b) establishing a new company to pursue the business activities separately. As can be seen from the relevant statutory provisions, certain formalities have to be satisfied including keeping separate books and accounts in respect of each pool of dedicated assets.

3.4.2. "Financing allocated to a specific business activity"

The segregation of assets under this statutory provision is created by agreement between the company and a lender who finances a specified business activity. The assets segregated for the purposes of this financing are the revenues of the transaction and must be "separately identified" at all times and "held separately from the other company's assets."

It should be noted that in addition to these provisions of the Italian Civil Code, Italy also has securitisation legislation: Law 30 April 1999, No 130 and, as is typical of such legislation, also permits the ring-fencing of assets and liabilities within a special purpose vehicle. So the legal concept of the ring-fencing was not new in Italy in 2004. What the provisions introduced by section 2447 did was extend the concept outside securitization for specific business projects of a company.

This raises the question, if a foreign PCC was involved in litigation in Italy would the Italian courts recognize the statutory ring-fencing of assets between cells and limit a creditor's ability to claim over all the assets of the PCC? An Italian judge looking at this should not find the PCC regime to be fundamentally different from existing structures provided for under the Italian Civil Code. In that sense it should augur well for the recognition of a PCC's priority in Italian legal proceedings.

Interestingly, similar legal issues as examined in this book could arise in relation to the recognition of the Italian regime itself in a cross border transaction involving foreign legal proceedings. There does not, however, appear to have been any judicial authorities on this or any commentary on the subject.

Finally, it is also worth pointing out that the principle of limitation of liability of ship owners in maritime law existed in early modern Europe (with some writers suggesting it actually originated in the Middle Ages) whereby the liability of shipowners was limited to the value of the ship and its freight. The principle was accepted by European maritime countries including Holland and codified in France as early as 1681. The limitation upon the liability of English shipowners was also enacted by the British Parliament through a series of statutes beginning in 1734. A similar principle was adopted by the legislatures in Massachusetts and Maine in 1818 and 1821 and finally by US Congress in 1851 (See the decision of the Supreme Court of the United States in *Norwich & N. Y. Trans. Co. v. Wright, 80 U. S. 104, 20 Law.* ed. 585, 589-590 for an account of the history of this principle). Further, it was held to extend to both contract and tort losses. Thus, if a shipowner had several vessels, looked at from this perspective his liability seems no different to the liability of a PCC in respect of separate cells.

The legal principle is also an early historical example of preferential treatment for particular creditors against a particular fund, preferred to the right of general creditors. This was not lost on Judge Ware in his insightful 1831 Opinion in *The Rebecca, Case No 11,619, District Court, D. Maine, "The maritime law... has, on principles of general policy, restricted him [a creditor] to a particular fund, it not only permits him to proceed directly against it in specie, but gives him a privilege against it over the general creditors of his debtor [shipowner]. This privilege, so far from being dangerous and embarrassing to commerce, as it was represented at the argument, appears to me to be perfectly natural and just, and entirely in harmony with the general spirit of maritime law."* In essence, our 1831 claimant run the now familiar argument (and failed) that to limit liability to a particular fund was contrary to public policy. The deployment of capital at a large scale (and therefore the very advent of capitalism) had its origins in this one fundamental principle, namely, that a trader or investor would not lose more than the capital and assets he had chosen to put at risk in respect of a particular business or investment. Maritime law applied this principle long before limited liability under general incorporation law was introduced.

4. THE INSURANCE COMPANY PCC: WITH A FOCUS ON THE EU

As we have explained, the advent of the PCC was primarily a direct response to the needs of the offshore captive insurance industry ('rent-a-captives' in particular). To a large extent the PCC sector is still dominated today by insurance companies. Guernsey was undoubtedly at the forefront of this development. Small territories such as Guernsey have exploited financial services and international business opportunities in a manner totally out of proportion to their size. Among all the ingredients that have contributed to the success of the financial sectors in these small territories, the role of the local government and regulators must be high on the list. A jurisdiction can have sound reputation, a good legislative regime, excellent telecommunications, and reliable professional infrastructure. However, without responsive local authorities attuned to the needs of business, the recipe for success would not be complete.

The opposite perhaps seems to be the truth elsewhere - the experience in the large countries is for authorities to become less and less responsive and indeed accessible to business. When asked why, it is doubtful any one knows why or why it has become necessary. It has just happened. It is no co-incidence that smaller territories have benefited to the extent that they have. Global business opportunities, when they arise, need to be seized quickly and the advent of the PCC is an example of this. Whilst larger territories debated implementation of similar legislation over many years, Guernsey was quick to spot the commercial opportunities and quickly initiated the legislative process in 1996.[49] Implementation resulted in immediate success for the local captive insurance sector.[50]

The Government of Gibraltar, prompted by local lawyers (of which the co-author of this book was at the forefront), followed the events in Guernsey with enormous interest. After a period of consultation and following legal advice, the Government of Gibraltar implemented PCC legislation of its own closely modelled on that of Guernsey. It was felt that it was unnecessary to re-engineer legislation if a successful model already existed elsewhere. In Gibraltar, as in other jurisdictions, a policy

[49] See Foreword to the First Edition by Steve Butterworth.

[50] The use of the Guernsey PCC as a captive vehicle has grown significantly over the last 12 years. Guernsey, Bermuda and the Caymans today have more PCC captives than any other jurisdiction.

decision was also taken that PCC legislation would be restricted (at least initially) to the insurance, repackaging and investment sectors. In other words, it would not be open to all and sundry.

Although the legislation was not immediately put to use, the local financial regulators had to consider the policy considerations around the potential use of the PCC in those areas which they were responsible for (principally insurance). Should a PCC be available without limitation? Was it necessary to limit its use to captive type arrangements or could a PCC be used to sell, for example, motor insurance, on behalf of many different promoters, each operating separate underwriting cells? These policy issues were probably more important to Gibraltar than they were to Guernsey. Why? Gibraltar, unlike Guernsey, is part of the EU. Thus not only had Gibraltar to consider potential EU legislation, but also a PCC licensed in Gibraltar would be able to operate the EU passport in insurance, in very much the same way as any other EU insurance company could. Therefore, a failure in the market prompted by the insolvency of a cell could do irreparable damage not only to the reputation of the jurisdiction, but also to the credibility of the statutory regime if third parties attempted to challenge the segregation of assets and liabilities within the PCC. So, the financial regulators adopted the cautious (and in the authors' view correct) approach and, initially at least, limiting the use of a PCC to 'captive' type risks. Personal lines brokers who may have seen the segregated cell as the Holy Grail, it being a cheaper alternative to setting up their own insurance company, would have been disappointed.

On the other hand, and this point is worth making again, if the intended purpose of the Insurance Directives was the protection of policyholders (as it undoubtedly is), and policyholders in a captive situation have freely and willingly agreed to participate within the special statutory framework of a PCC, it would be inconsistent with that purpose for a Court in the EU to undermine the segregation of assets and liabilities within that regime.

4.1. What is a captive?

This begs the question, what is a captive? There is no precise definition of a 'captive' but it may be defined as an insurance company whose insurance business is primarily introduced, and controlled, by its parent, and who primarily insures the risks of the group. The word 'primarily' is an intentional qualification. Whilst the parent ultimately controls the captive's operation *qua* shareholder, and policyholders are invariably group entities, the beneficiaries may also include third parties. A captive, like any other insurance vehicle, will therefore issue insurance policies and receive premium in respect of the risks it covers. Wherever the captive is established, it is likely that it will be subject to local insurance regulations. Invariably a licence to conduct insurance business would be required and local rules will make provision for capital solvency (i.e. the financial resources that must be available to underwrite particular risks) and admissibility (i.e. the assets that can be invested by the company to support its capital solvency requirements). Moreover, the captive will develop underwriting, claims and investment policies through its Board of Directors, whether or not day-to-day management operations are delegated to a management services team (usually an insurance manager) based in the jurisdiction of incorporation. Clearly, the advantage of the PCC was that the single legal entity was able to provide a captive facility to any number of cell users performing the same functions as a stand-alone insurance company could do. As we have seen, the structure was not much different from a contractual cell company, except that it had the benefit of the statutory ring-fence.

4.2. Application of the PCC concept

Whilst non-EU jurisdictions such as Guernsey used the PCC for both reinsurance and insurance risks, they were constrained by their inability to write risks across the EU on the passport principle. In respect of non-EU risks the ability to write business depended on local regulations in each territory. Gibraltar (and latterly Malta), on the other hand, has access to the European market by virtue of its status in the EU and the PCC facility could potentially take off in a major way (Gibraltar was, in fact, the first EU territory to incorporate protected cell companies for insurance). Regulatory arbitrage therefore played a dominant role in the growth of the captive sector in Gibraltar through its first PCC facility, established by local captive managers Aon.[51] The Gibraltar captive sector undoubtedly received a significant boost from PCC legislation.

In its early years, the generally held view was that a PCC should not retain risk ("no risk gap in a cell"). Thus protection afforded by PCC legislation was best preserved through 100% reinsurance of the insurance risk underwritten by each cell. This meant that each cell was effectively established as a fronting facility whereby the insurance risk at the front

[51] The Aon White Rock companies are now established in Bermuda, Guernsey, Gibraltar, Luxembourg and Malta.

end was 100% reinsured outwards (normally to a non-EU based sister re-insurer). No net exposure was therefore retained in the cell. Whilst the insurance risk obviously sat with the cell, the reinsurance in respect of each cell protected the cell structure in the event of a claim on the relevant insurance policy. It was also quickly realised that additional protection (in line with the statutory ring-fence mechanism) could be afforded by the inclusion of limited recourse provisions such as 'pay as paid' clauses. Under a pay as paid clause the insured agrees that his claim is limited to available assets in the cell and to that extent the obligation to pay under the policy is dependent on the cell receiving an equivalent payment in respect of the reinsurance. A more recent technique in single policy cells involves the PCC giving the policyholder security. This typically is by way of assignment over the individual reinsurance contracts (including reinsurance recoveries). When cell policies are backed up in this way, the PCC can offer its cell users far more protection than a conventional insurance arrangement. Individual cells, in this context, not only enjoy statutory 'ring-fencing', but also the benefits of contractual segregation. Whilst there are those who will argue that this obviates the need for a PCC in the first place, it is ultimately the end user who will dictate what its requirements are. This may mean a request for more rather than less cell 'protection'.

Insuring third party risk was not encouraged in the early development of the PCC in Gibraltar. However, it was realised that such a policy was unduly restrictive. Thus, the regulators were prepared to consider short tail open-market business, particularly for warranty business to be underwritten by a PCC. This was extended to other classes such as professional indemnity. The one class that remained elusive was motor insurance. In the space of three years, Gibraltar was to become the insurance domicile of choice for UK promoters looking at underwriting niche motor business back into the UK. By 2005 the Gibraltar motor market was estimated to represent 5% of the UK market total, while Lloyd's was 6%[52]. The general view prevailed that whilst a captive policy could indeed cover motor incidental to the main group risk it chose to underwrite, the PCC should not be allowed to face the consumer (as policyholder). Whilst the large majority of motor policyholders would not necessarily care whether their policy was underwritten by a UK or Gibraltar insurer, nevertheless the use of a PCC could present more of a challenge. It was thought (rightly) that it was too early in its evolution to

[52] Deloitte & Touche LLP

test the structure in this way. Could a consumer be able to understand the legal implications for him in buying a policy from an entity identified in policy documents as a "PCC", rather than a PLC (public company) or Ltd (private company)? Moreover, should third parties be bound by statutory segregation and how would a UK court respond to a PCC when faced with such claims? Captive managers based in Gibraltar were not about to find out and the debate subsided into general acceptance that certain insurance risks were best avoided within a PCC structure.

This position did not inhibit growth of the number of protected cells established in Gibraltar. Neither did it inhibit the growth of such companies. In fact, taking into account the fact that the concept of the PCC was also novel within the EU, this level of growth was not insignificant. Whether we will see much more growth over the coming few years is not easy to predict. This may depend on a number of factors including their continued acceptance within the insurance industry as well as judicial and legal developments (both at domestic and EU level). Unsurprisingly, the PCC structure has not been widely marketed in Europe. This is because the existing companies established in Guernsey cannot write direct into the EU (passport) whilst it is only in more recent times that Gibraltar (as the then only European PCC domicile) began to actively engage the market, with Malta following closely behind after it joined the EU. There seems little doubt however that whatever the success or otherwise of the PCC within the EU, their use for captives in offshore jurisdictions outside the EU is an established part of the international insurance market and will continue.

It should perhaps also be noted that in capital terms, Guernsey had significant advantages over EU carriers (outside Lloyds of London) in that it historically allowed capital to be supported by letters of credit and also imposed lower solvency requirements than the EU. The typical structure was for a primary risk carrier in the EU to use a Guernsey PCC to write reinsurance business whilst also claiming credit for solvency purposes up to the EU allowable maximum (50%).

It may be worth setting out the examples of the potential uses of PCCs for captive insurance cited by the *International Association of Insurance Supervisors* in their issues paper *'Issues Paper on the Regulation and Supervision of Captive Insurance Companies, October 2006'*:

"• *Rental captives - The PCC structure relieves the cell user from the expense associated with establishing and sustaining a traditional captive insurer.*

- *Association captives - A PCC can be economically used by associations or similar groups to provide a cell for each individual member, capitalised as necessary, with legal separation of assets and liabilities, whilst providing a homogeneous insurance programme which can be reinsured more efficiently than through placing individual insurances for individual members.*
- *Multi-national companies and joint ventures – A PCC allows large economic groups to allocate individual cells to different parts of the group; each cell can operate independently under a common group structure. Separate cells may be established for joint ventures with another economic group.*
- *Mixed life and non-life insurers – If legislation so permits, a PCC can allow both life and non-life business to be written in the same legal entity, whilst ensuring that the assets and liabilities of each business are legally ring-fenced.*
- *Life assurance - Utilising a PCC structure, life assurance companies can legally segregate the assets and liabilities of life, pension and individual policyholder funds. In the latter case, a cell for each individual policyholder may be created which can provide robust security and greater investment flexibility to individual investors, particularly high net worth individuals.*
- *Reinsurance Pool – A PCC cell may pool business of common class from unrelated parties before retroceding a share of the overall pool to individual captives."*

4.3. Lloyd's of London and the PCC

Conceptually (but not legally), the conduct of business at Lloyd's of London has some similarities with a segregated business structure akin to a PCC.

Lloyd's of London (one of the pillars of global capitalism) underwrites risks in many countries and has done so for over 100 years. The "Society of Lloyd's" was incorporated (as a body corporate) by the Lloyd's Act 1871. The Act was amended by subsequent Acts of Parliament but otherwise remains in force. Under the 1871 Act the objects of the Society were declared, inter alia, to be the carrying on of the business of marine insurance by members of the Society. Section 40 of the 1871 Act (as amended), although providing for unlimited liability of members, contains an early example of a statutory firewall: *"Nothing in this Act shall... make any member of the Society as such responsible in any manner for any of the undertakings, debts or liabilities of any other member of the Society as such...".*

Lloyd's is therefore not an insurance company but a market for insurance. Insurance at Lloyd's is undertaken through underwriting 'syndicates'. Syndicates (like protected cells) are not legal entities. They are a group of 'members'. Members provide the capital to support the underwriting capacity of the syndicate (usually in the form of a letter of credit or funds charged in favour of Lloyd's known as Funds at Lloyd's, held with financial institutions around the world). Syndicates are managed by managing agents.

In theory, a syndicate could be comprised of a single member. In the case of a corporate member enjoying limited liability, the member would only be liable to the extent of its assets. Where a syndicate exhausts its available assets in meeting claims, Lloyd's has a right to call upon the Central Fund (which is funded by members contribution annually) to satisfy any excess liability. But otherwise the business of each syndicate is (as in the case of a cell) separate and distinct from other syndicates and one member is not responsible for the liabilities (or losses) of other members. Looked at from such perspective, a cell structure is no more offensive than this.

Lloyd's prides itself in its security structure. Substantial capital has flowed into Lloyd's from around the world and companies have also placed reinsurance business in the London market on this basis.

Lloyd's syndicates are regularly in dispute concerning insurance risks and disputes arising from policy cover placed at Lloyd's, as is normal in any insurance context. Some of these end up in foreign courts and there is nothing unusual in this.

However, Lloyd's success could be seriously threatened by foreign litigation that puts at risk its security structure or if a foreign court attributed the liabilities of one syndicate to others (not entirely dissimilar to the concerns about the cellular structure). On the contractual front, Lloyd's has therefore been particularly careful to ensure that agreements with members contain express English governing law and jurisdiction clauses to avoid foreign court intervention. This has been largely successful. For example, in 1996 a multi-billion action by US members of Lloyd's on the grounds that US securities legislation avoided the relevant agreements (and therefore the English law and jurisdiction clause), was dismissed by the US Court of Appeals for the Fourth Circuit on the basis, inter alias, that US securities laws did not apply *(Allen v Lloyd's of London, 94 F.3d 923, 1996)*. The potential damage of this to the domestic insurance market, putting at risk billions of dollars of insurance coverage for US citizens because American members of Lloyd's could demand rescission on the ground that their syndicates did not comply with US securities requirements, was not lost on the court.

Also, historically, the wording of Lloyd's policies subscribed for proportionately by more than one syndicate underpins the separate liability of insurance cover: *"the Underwriters are hereby bound each for his own part and not one for another"*. The liability under such a policy is intended to be several, not joint, and for each syndicate to be only liable in proportion to its share.

The risk of attribution of liability of one syndicate to others is less of a practical concern given that any losses that cannot be met by a syndicate would be covered by the Central Fund to the extent that there are sufficient assets in it to pay the claims. However, in an uncertain world where the cost of multiple natural disasters can run into the many billions, there is always a risk (however small it may seem) that funds will not be available to satisfy claims in full. Indeed, witness the global bail-out of banks in 2009!

A tort class action in say, the US, from our proverbial involuntary creditor, could be an even more serious threat to Lloyd's if it attached to assets held within the jurisdiction of the foreign courts. An example of this was the class action instituted in 2005 against Lloyd's (and other parties) in the US by the descendants of slaves, although the action was dismissed on constitutional and limitation principles, among other grounds *(In re African-Amercian Slave Descendants Litigation, United States District Court, N.D Illinois, Eastern Division, MDL No 1491. No. 02 C 7764).*

The point to make must surely be that although Lloyd's has been in existence as an incorporated entity since 1871, and enjoyed unprecedented success and international recognition, it still faces some theoretical challenges of its own as does a PCC (or ICC or Series LCC for that matter).

It is to be expected that PCCs around the world, both, insure UK policyholders and place reinsurance with Lloyd's. In the authors' view if a third party tried to disregard the cellular structure through the forum of the English courts, this ought to fail not just on applicable principles of private international law, but an English court is no less likely to ignore the fact that those creditors who seek to litigate in the English courts may be putting UK policyholders' and 'their' cellular assets (the security of Lloyd's reinsurance) at risk. Lord Hoffman's statement in *Re HIH Casualty and General Insurance [2008] 3 ALL ER at p 882-883* appears to underpin judicial concerns about potential damage to the London insurance market: *"The fact that there are assets in England is principally the result of the companies having placed their reinsurance business in the London market. For the purposes of deciding how the assets should be distributed, that seems to me an entirely adventitious circumstance. Indeed, it may not be to the advantage of London as a reinsurance market if the distribution of the assets of insolvent foreign reinsurance companies is affected by whether they have placed their reinsurance business in London rather than somewhere else."* Equally, Lord Collins duly noted in his opening statement in *Lexington Insurance Company v Wasa International Insurance Company [2009] UKHL 40* the importance of the London market to the UK's economy thus: *"After banking, insurance is the United Kingdom's largest invisible export, of which reinsurance forms a large part, and amounted to at least £1.2 billion in 2007: Office for National Statistics, United Kingdom Balance of Payments: The Pink Book, 2008, p 52."*

Finally, an English court may well ask itself, why should the PCC structure be any less acceptable than Lloyd's and would permitting a third party to 'attack' the integrity of the PCC cellular structure in the English courts be an unwelcome invitation to a foreign court to similarly undermine the rules that the UK itself has established for the operation and segregation of Lloyd's business?

4.4. Fronting versus Risk Bearing Cell

It is not difficult to give examples of the typical cell used within a PCC. Where the class of insurance is non-statutory and/or there is no restriction on writing the business in the territory where the risk is situated and/or the policyholder is resident, the cell is usually either separately capitalised or the risk is 100% reinsured with no net risk carried by the cell. Given that most EU countries carry restrictions in respect of at least certain classes of risks (the so-called statutory classes) and require the insurer carrying such risks to either be a local insurance company or one based within the European Union, there are two options available.

The first option is to write the business through a fronting insurer (based in the EU). The risk is then 100% reinsured into a cell created by a PCC in an offshore jurisdiction (say Guernsey or the BVI). The disadvantage of doing this is that it can be expensive and may incur not just fronting fees but also letters of credit cost in support of the fronting insurer.[53]

The second option is less expensive: using a cell of a PCC established in a European domicile (benefiting from the EU passport arrangements) and writing the business direct (with 100% reinsurance outwards). Thus

[53] Or the fronting insurer may ask for a floating charge over the assets of the cell, or trust or collateral arrangement.

effectively the PCC is a pass-through vehicle. No net exposure is retained by the cell. Where the cell is purely fronting business, the promoters will not generally be required to introduce capital into their cell ('cell share capital') but they may if they wish to do so (normally as non-voting redeemable preference shares). Therefore the 'core' capital (the term 'core' and 'hub' are interchangeably used in this book) belonging to those who establish the PCC (normally introduced via voting ordinary shares) satisfies the minimum capital and solvency requirements for writing the cell business. The cost of using the capital for this purpose is met by the cell. Whilst there is normally no regulatory requirement for the cell to retain risk, there may be reasons (tax or otherwise) why the promoters of individual cells may seek the establishment of risk-bearing cells. In such cases, cell share capital would normally be introduced to cover own risk rather than expose the core capital.

Where the cell is a fronting cell, its liabilities for its insurance obligations under the cell policy would be met solely from funds held by the PCC on account of the business of that cell and from the reinsurance recoveries under the reinsurance policy entered into for the benefit of the cell. The coverage provided under the cell policy should therefore be 'back-to-back' with the coverage provided under the reinsurance policy, otherwise there would be a mismatch between the potential liability at the front-end (cell policy) and recovery at the back-end (reinsurance). The cell policyholder would typically be asked to agree to undertake that his entitlement to claim under a policy is limited in recourse. It would be limited in recourse to the available assets of, and the benefit of any reinsurance claims attributable to, the specific cell in respect of the cell policy. The policyholder would therefore accept that any claims under the cell policy would only be paid to the extent and in so far as the respective amount had been received by the PCC under the reinsurance made in respect of the cell. Thus if amounts received from the re-insurer in respect of such a claim was less than the amount claimed by the insured, the maximum amount payable by the PCC would be limited to the amount received from the re-insurer. Since ultimately the security of the cell policy will depend on the security of the reinsurance, the onus is on the managers of the PCC to ensure that the re-insurer meets acceptable security criteria.

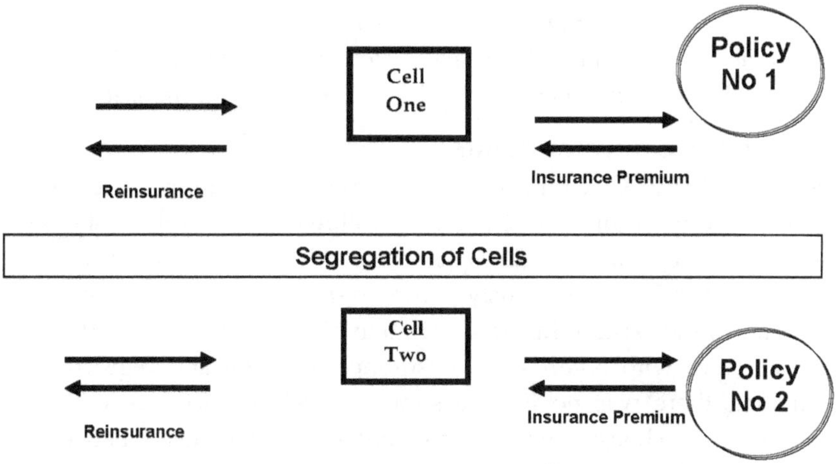

Diagram 5: Mechanics of protected cell company

Interestingly, some banking groups also have their own PCC captives as part of their insurance division and offering to their clients. For example, *"HSBC Insurance Management offers [the PCC] facility to its clients"* in Bermuda (HSBC Insurance SAC Limited), Cayman Islands (HSBC Insurance SPC) and Guernsey (HSBC Insurance PCC Limited). This is taken from the HSBC Insurance website[54] which also has a webpage entitled "Our Cell Companies" setting out information about each of its PCCs. In respect of the Guernsey PCC it says:

"HSBC Insurance PCC Limited ("HSBC PCC") is an insurance company formed in Guernsey under the Protected Cell Companies Ordinance 1997. It is a member of the HSBC Group and is owned and managed by HSBC Insurance Management (Guernsey) Limited. HSBC PCC has an authorised capital of £5 million, with a current issued core capital of £125,000. Clients may subscribe for redeemable preference shares and/or provide a letter of credit to ensure that the necessary solvency and risk gap requirements are met. Retained profits can be returned back to the cell owner by way of dividends, profit commission or return premiums. All dividend payments must be agreed by the Board of Directors of HSBC PCC. Generally, clients have no involvement in the day-to-day management of HSBC PCC. On termination of the arrangements (by novation, commutation or other extinguishment of the insurance contracts agreed by HSBC PCC), the cell owner will receive a return of the surplus assets of the cell by means of dividend declarations or the redemption of the shares. HSBC PCC

[54] http://www.insurancemanagement.hsbc.com/1/2/3/home

currently has a licence from the Guernsey Financial Services Commission to underwrite all classes of non-life business. However, it is envisaged that this will be extended in due course to permit HSBC PCC to underwrite life business".

4.5. Future developments

The use of the PCC within the EU for fronting reinsurance presents an interesting opportunity for the market following the implementation of the Reinsurance Directive (2005/68) by all Member States (its due date was December 2007). Previously "pure" re-insurers were not covered by the terms of the existing Insurance Directives and each Member State had its own rules with regards to reinsurance licensing and regulation. In particular, there was no EU 'passport' for reinsurance business (with some countries choosing not even to regulate the relationship between re-insurers and insurers). The Reinsurance Directive therefore established the appropriate regulatory framework for licensing and prudential supervision of re-insurers with their head-office within the EU. A number of Member States (principally Ireland) have tried (successfully) to position themselves in the market through early implementation of the Directive. It is not yet clear whether the Reinsurance Directive may result in Member State regulators placing restrictions on non-admitted reinsurance from outside the EU. If this were to happen, the use of the PCC cell to front reinsurance business for re-insurers currently writing EU based business from offshore domiciles, such Bermuda, will grow. Fortunately, most re-insurers operating from such offshore domiciles would already be familiar with the concept of the PCC. Therefore their use should not present much of an intellectual challenge for them.

On the 19 September 2007 Brit Insurance Holdings PLC announced[55] that it *"was to put in place a small team of senior underwriters to work in Gibraltar. Subject to approvals they will develop the reinsurance business of a dedicated cell in a newly formed and independently owned protected cell company, to be known as Rockhampton Insurance PCC Limited."* The press release concluded *"Gibraltar is an attractive location with numerous advantages, including the availability of PCC legislation, EU licensing, a favourable taxation regime and good access to London."* This was the first PCC reinsurer in the EU.

Another likely growth area is the use of PCC reinsurance captives as a means for transferring risk into the capital markets. The use of such vehicles already exists (e.g. in Bermuda). Banks, together with their

---

[55]http://www.britinsurance.com/NewsArticle/_/4518/brit_insurance_gibraltar_based_reinsurer.html

insurance clients, have helped to structure products for sophisticated investors in this way. One vehicle is known as the 'transformer', whereby (re)insurance risk (via (re)insurance paper issued by the (re)insurer) is laid off in the form of credit risk to the capital markets by the (re)insurer as an issuer. We will see in more detail elsewhere in this book how investment banks have embraced the PCC in developing capital markets products. These are therefore not new concepts for them but it is interesting to note how the PCC has also helped to bridge the needs of the insurance industry with the demands of the capital markets. This stems from the fact that where there is arbitrage (a tax or regulatory advantage to be obtained) someone will bridge the gap. The transformer does exactly that.[56] Whilst an (re)insurer issues (re)insurance policies and must usually demonstrate the risk of loss, banks enter into ISDA Credit Default Swaps and rely on a credit event. An (re)insurance company can therefore help to pass on risk in the form of insurance paper acceptable to the buyer of (re)insurance through an ISDA default swap (or embedded instrument) into the financial markets.

The use of transformers was discussed in a detailed discussion paper by the Financial Services Authority (FSA) back in 2002[57]. Interestingly, there is reference to one market participant, being an insurer who had told the FSA that they *"had done a deal through a Protected Cell Company but [were] not wholly comfortable with the structure from a regulatory perspective; they argued that they would prefer to write credit derivatives directly."* Note the concern was from a *"regulatory"*, not a *"legal"* perspective.

The Reinsurance Directive itself allows for potential growth of this sector within the EU by recognising that a special regime for special purpose vehicles should apply to allow easier access to the capital markets.

The Reinsurance Directive defines an insurance special purpose vehicle as:

"any undertaking whether incorporated or not, other than an existing insurance or reinsurance undertaking, which assumes risks from insurance or reinsurance undertakings and which fully funds its exposure to such risks through the proceeds of a debt issuance or some other financial mechanism where the repayment rights of the providers of such debt or other financing mechanism are subordinated to the reinsurance obligations of such a vehicle".

[56] An example of a transformer is the PCC, Drummonds Insurance Company PCC Limited.

[57] FSA Discussion Paper "Cross -sector Risk Transfers", May 2002.

The PCC obviously lends itself very well to this type of transformer structure. Thus it may well be the incentive needed for legislators in individual Member States introducing the PCC concept into their own insurance sectors. Time will tell.

An additional potential use for the PCC is the market for the purchase of bulk annuities (or helping to take pensions liabilities 'off balance sheet'). When the insurance and banking sectors first started to look into different pension deficit solutions, an ingredient in the structuring of such products was thought to include Special Purpose Vehicles with an offshore dimension. The PCC is an ideal structure for the segregation of such assets and liabilities although currently no such insurance company PCC vehicle exists in the EU.

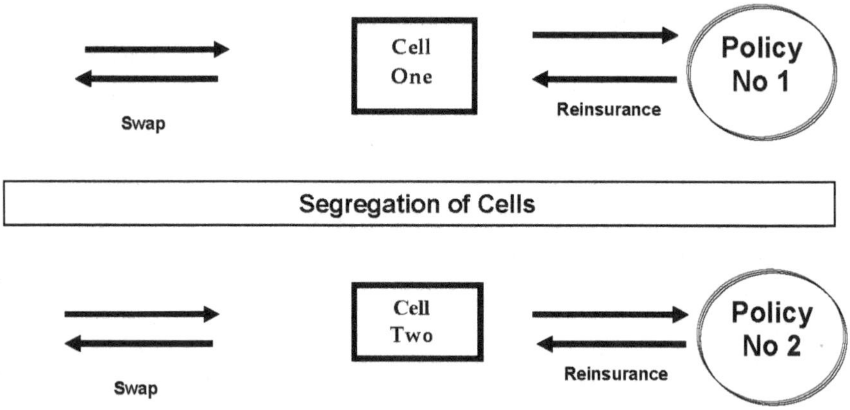

Diagram 6: A PCC transformer

4.6. Solvency II

This EU-wide project is progressing towards its planned implementation in October 2012. The aim, like Basel II for banks, is to introduce a risk based solvency regime for all insurers in the EU. Such a fundamental change to solvency regulation will have specific consequence for EU based PCCs.

Whilst some detailed aspects of the Directive are not yet settled, it is inevitable that there will be increased capital requirements for many companies, particularly the smaller insurers that do not have a well-diversified portfolio of business.

The question arises, how would we apply the risk-based capital regime of the Solvency II Directive to the cellular structure of the PCC? As we have seen earlier, the cells are not legal entities. The essence of the cell structure is that each cell is legally protected and therefore offers segregation of assets and liabilities as between separate cells. In this scenario, is it the PCC as a whole that needs to satisfy the risk-based capital requirements of Solvency II or the individual cells?

Robin Amos explained his view to the co-author *"At one level it could be said that the solvency credit under Solvency II will depend on the extent of diversification across all cells of the PCC. Simply put, the extra business from a new cell could reduce the average solvency requirement that may be attributed to the existing cells and the benefit thus shared between all cells. This benefit is perhaps more significant for small insurers that cannot otherwise meet the Minimum Guarantee Fund requirements under the current Solvency I regime. The simplified example below shows the potential capital requirement difference for the PCC under Solvency I and Solvency II. Here we can see that the solvency requirement of the PCC under Solvency I is the sum of the cell requirements, and the benefit of using a PCC is that the cells combined help to meet the Minimum Guarantee Fund (which varies but let us assume it is £2,430,000 in this example). However, under Solvency II, the overall solvency requirement of the PCC is less than the sum of each cell's Solvency II requirement. The exact amount of the discount applied will depend on a number of factors. This is known as a diversification benefit and its value is equal to £1,012,500 in the example where a 20% discount is applied. The financial benefit will increase as more cells are established."*

Cells	Premium	Solvency I Requirement	Solvency II Requirement
Cell A	£2,000,000	£360,000	£750,000
Cell B	£10,000,000	£1,800,000	£3,750,000
Cell C	£1,500,000	£270,000	£562,500
Overall PCC	**£13,500,000**	**£2,430,000**	**£4,050,000**

Table 4: Solvency requirements

Solvency II is expected to create significant increases in solvency capital requirements for insurers that are not well diversified. Also, insurers that are based outside the EU may find themselves subject to equivalent requirements to Solvency II as these jurisdictions seek to match EU regulatory standards. If the potential economic gains from this solvency-sharing in an EU PCC are large enough, it is possible that existing captives may consider whether to reconstitute themselves as a cell in a PCC.

4.7. Summary

Captives are undoubtedly an efficient risk management tool and have been around for very many years. A captive is not subject to the fluctuations of the external insurance market, it allows a group to manage risk (whilst controlling the claims settlement process) and access the reinsurance (wholesale) market for cover above its retentions. In the conventional insurance market the same insured would pay a premium in return for cover. However, it would have no control of the claims settlement process or pricing (premium rates may fluctuate from year to year). With a captive the insured is the master of his own destiny. The PCC is a step further in that evolution by allowing the insured to enter the captive market through its own protected cell without the need for a stand-alone, wholly owned, insurance subsidiary. Having said that, the benefits of the 'protected cell' are only secure if the proper management of cell structure is observed at all times.

4.8. Documentation

The documentation associated with an insurance captive constituted as a PCC is in essence no different to what one can expect to see in the conventional insurance market; except for the Articles and Memorandum of Association of such a company. Appendix 1 and 2 show a specimen of Articles and Memorandum of Association of a PCC and Articles for a contractual cell company. The name "ABC" is entirely fictious. It will be observed that in the case of a PCC, the creation of cells and the rights of shareholders are clearly designated within these documents in line with relevant PCC legislation. Appendix 5 also sets out a specimen Assignment of Reinsurance Agreement that could be adopted for use by a PCC to reinforce the statutory 'ring-fence'[58].

---

[58] In particular, see clause 9(5).

5. MANAGING A PCC CAPTIVE

The proper management of a PCC is crucial to the veracity of the cell structure. The managers of a PCC will need to be capable of understanding the statutory regime under which they operate and have relevant experience in at least underwriting and company administration. It could be fatal to a PCC if those who manage the company do not do so in accordance with statutory requirements or ignoring professional advice. As we have seen, a PCC is a very special creature and such companies therefore require special attention. We have already made the point that the benefits of statutory segregation of liabilities in a PCC will not occur automatically simply because a company is incorporated as a PCC. It must also be managed and conduct its affairs in accordance with the terms of the operating legislation. We have noted that taxation is one area that poses a risk for a PCC. This chapter discusses the issues involved in the management of a PCC in context of an insurance company although the same general principles apply to other type of PCCs.

An insurance company will usually have a number of committees, distinct from the main Board of Directors. These committees will be mainly comprised of executive directors e.g. an Underwriting and Claims Committee and an Investment Committee, and for mid-sized insurers, an Audit Committee too. Clearly every insurance company will have an underwriting and claims policy. The main Board is responsible for policy. The individual committees will ordinarily be responsible for policy implementation and overview under the guiding principle that the duty to manage a business falls upon the senior management of that business. In the case of a PCC, it is advisable to also have a Compliance Committee to review compliance with relevant legislation, in particular PCC legislation. The skills required to manage a PCC extend beyond underwriting skill to relevant experience in company administration, legal, accounting and tax related issues. The risks associated with the PCC structure can only be mitigated by ensuring proper compliance procedures are in place in respect of:

- Adequacy of documentation and identification of separate cells.
- Standard protection clauses (i.e. claims limitation and 'pay as paid' clauses) appearing in all relevant documentation.
- Reinsurance placements.
- Evaluation of risk retention levels by each cell.

- Correct filings at the Companies Registry (e.g. evidencing the allotment of cell shares and thereby creation of cells) and proper filings with the insurance regulator.
- Separate accounting of each cell.
- Physical segregation of assets and liabilities.

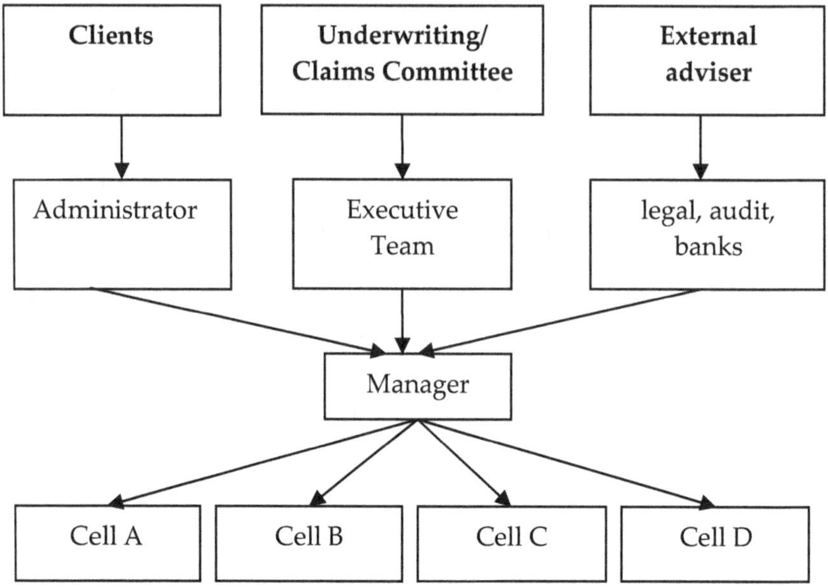

Diagram 7: Overview of governance

The administration (rather than underwriting) skills required to manage a PCC captive are not entirely different from the administration skills required of a non-insurance PCC (e.g. corporate or funds). This has led to a number of very successful service providers working pre-dominantly in the offshore financial services sector offering both captive management and fund administration services through separate operations to their clients.[59]

The driving operating principle has to be no cross contamination between cells. All controls within the company have to ensure that the directors do not expose any particular cell to underwriting or financial risk without prior written approval of the Board and without obtaining relevant regulatory consent. Each underwriting risk in a cell has to be reviewed separately by the Board or committee. This is to ensure that the risk falls within the company's risk profile and with sufficient capital (and/or reinsurance placement) to cover the exposure. The directors should have

[59] For example, the Heritage Group in Guernsey

sufficient information before them to allow them to take such decisions. In addition, the directors have to consider what claims handling arrangements should be put in place to support the underwriting activities of each cell. Because exposure to large claims in a cell could leave that cell with insufficient assets to meet its obligations to the cell policyholder, it is important that the company understands the risk that it is underwriting. Further that the company also retains adequate control of claims within the claims settlement criteria set by the company and in accordance with the terms and conditions of the policies. The delegation of unlimited claims settlement authority to the cell promoter or any other party outside the company should therefore be avoided. The directors should always retain final authority in respect of claims.

In every captive environment it is accepted practice for certain management services to be delegated to a local insurance manager who is responsible for day-to-day administration and regulatory compliance. The manager also acts as local liaison with the regulators and in some cases with the Registrar of Companies in respect of secretarial filings. This ensures that there is a second layer of responsibility for compliance. It is normal procedure in a cell captive for a policy to incept only when premiums are paid to the company. Cells should not be at risk in the absence of receipt of premiums (whether or not invoices have been issued). All invoices should be issued in the name of the company but identifying the cell in respect of which the underwriting relates ("ABC Insurance Company PCC in respect of Cell A") and proper books and accounts kept. Premiums for different cells should be paid into separate bank accounts, separately identifiable as such. Where premium tax is due and payable, the PCC should promptly settle these with the relevant taxing authorities. As the PCC may be exposed to tax penalties like any other company, care must be taken to ensure that each cell accepts responsibility for their respective liabilities. Accounting reconciliation systems (including completion of the bordereaux) is also crucial in this process. Unless transactions are properly and separately accounted and supported with appropriately worded documentation, the cell structure would be at risk.

Each promoter of a cell would be required to comply with relevant internal procedures for the creation of the individual cells. After the cell application process (KYC etc), if the directors accept to issue insurance and the regulators have approved the individual cell business plan, the board of directors will procure the allotment of the cell shares, issuance of the cell share certificate and ensure that proceeds of share capital are deposited in a separate bank account.

In order to minimise the risks inherent in a cell structure, the PCC would be well advised to require the insured to acknowledge in writing that:

1. The company is a PCC and its obligations to the insured are incurred under policies it will write for the account of the relevant 'cell'. The insured should be left in no doubt that he is dealing with a PCC in respect of a particular named 'cell'.
2. The company's liabilities under the insurance will be met solely from funds held by the company for the designated business of the relevant 'cell' and from the benefit of any reinsurance claims it may have under any reinsurance policies entered into for the benefit of that 'cell'.
3. The ability and entitlement of the insured to claim under its policy will be limited in recourse to the available assets of, and the benefit of any reinsurance claims attributable to the specific 'cell' in respect of which any policy is written.
4. The insured therefore will have no claim to the assets of other 'cells'.

At the other end of the spectrum, professional advisers for the insured should correspondingly request (as appropriate) an undertaking from the PCC and independently from the external managers, that:

1. It will not write or issue any insurance that are not risks, liabilities or exposures of the relevant introducer of the 'cell's' business.
2. Create any security interest in any of the 'cell' assets without prior approval.
3. Consolidate or merge itself or the relevant 'cell' with any person or other 'cell' or convey or transfer its properties or assets substantially or in their entirety to any person.
4. Change the domicile of the company.
5. It will not amend or alter its Memorandum or Articles of Association.
6. It will defend the 'cell' assets against claims and demands of all third persons.
7. It will not make any substantial alteration to the nature of the business of the PCC or the 'cell'.
8. It will not permit commingling of any 'cell' assets with any other property or assets of any other 'cell' of the PCC.

Given the special considerations attaching to the PCC, it is also important that the company's sole tax and business establishment should be in the jurisdiction of incorporation (the home jurisdiction). There are obvious reasons for this. Whilst authorities (tax or regulatory) in the home jurisdiction would be expected to respect PCC legislation in their dealings with the company (and its cells), there is no guarantee that a foreign authority would. This therefore remains one of the most critical challenges for a PCC. If the captive were to acquire tax residence in another jurisdiction or establish a branch there, it may become subject to the jurisdiction of a foreign tax and regulatory authority.

5.1. Regulatory

We have seen how some territories place restrictions on foreign insurers. Generally only admitted insurers are permitted to underwrite risks within particular territories. This presents an interesting challenge for a PCC given the risk of regulatory sanction and its potential impact on the cell structure. Insurers licensed in the EU, however, are able to use the EU passport without such concerns. This is because the conduct of insurance business is regulated in the EU by the relevant Insurance Directives which are required to be implemented into local law by each Member State and are therefore intended to harmonise standards. Under the Directives insurance business is divided into:

(a) Long term business[60] (also referred to as life or assurance business).

(b) General business[61] (also referred to as non-life business).

A licensed insurer is able to operate an insurance business in the European Union using one of two defined routes:

(a) Freedom of Services: This route allows any licensed insurer in a Member State to passport into any other Member State without establishing a branch or the need for obtaining regulatory approval in the host territory.

(b) Freedom of Establishment: This allows any licensed insurer in a Member State to establish a branch in any other Member State after a notification process in respect of the intention to establish such a branch to the host regulator.

Therefore under the passport system introduced by the relevant Insurance Directives, an insurer with its head-office in the home State may carry on insurance business in more than one place within the EU on a Freedom of Services or Establishment basis provided the correct procedure set out in the Insurance Directives is followed. In this respect it

---

[60] Consolidated Life Directive (2002/83/EC) of 5 November 2002.

[61] Governed by a number of Directives since the First Non-Life Directive (73/239/EEC).

should be noted that whilst Gibraltar, Malta and Dublin are in the EU, Guernsey, Jersey and the Isle of Man are not.

It is important that the insurer, exercising its right of passport, is not a brass plate. That would not be permissible. The company must be able to point to a physical office in the home jurisdiction from where it operates. That office could be within the office of its locally appointed manager.

It is not uncommon for certain administrative services to be delegated by insurance companies outside their home jurisdiction. An insurance company should be able to do so under the principle of 'Freedom of Services' provided it takes all important decisions affecting the conduct of its business, in the home jurisdiction. In a day and age where outsourcing of administration is easily available, particularly in respect of overseas customers, it is accepted that this does not undermine the competence or duties of the directors. The point is worth making because an insurance company licensed in one Member State may passport into another Member State in accordance with the relevant EU Insurance Directives. Thus there is no merit in an argument that the company had deliberately organised its affairs so as to operate in this way.

For a PCC exercising its European passport, however, it is important that it structures its affairs so that it operates under Freedom of Services (rather than Establishment). This is a factual question depending upon the circumstances at the time it falls to be considered.

There is clearly some uncertainty in this area of EU law. This is unavoidable as the only real guidance available is a European Commission Interpretative Communication[62] which is not itself legally binding. The European Commission has attempted to set out guidelines that must be satisfied in order for an intermediary to be treated as a branch of an insurer in another Member State, rather than a provider of services. Accordingly, the intermediary must meet all of the following criteria:

(i) it must be subject to the direction and control of the insurer;

(ii) it must be able to commit the insurer; and

(iii) it must have received a permanent brief.

---

[62] Freedom to provide services and the general good in the insurance sector: 2000/C 43/03, 16/02/2000 p. 0005 – 0027.

These are also the criteria that local regulators tend to look to when determining whether an undertaking is providing services or has established a branch.

5.2. Branch or Services?

Certainly, there are some important parameters to work with. With regards to the underwriting function, a major factor pointing towards rights of 'Freedom of Services' rather than 'Rights of Establishment' is where the insurance policies are only issued exclusively by the insurer (even if printed by an intermediary in the host jurisdiction on its behalf), with the pricing and underwriting decisions being taken in the home jurisdiction and with the insurer retaining power to amend or change the underwriting authority at any time or decline or reject any policy proposal that does not meet the underwriting criteria. Also, in determining whether or not the intermediary is subject to the control and direction of the insurer, the prime factor to be considered is their freedom in relation to the organisation of their activities. In particular, whether they can represent other insurers at the same time (even if in competition). The issue here is whether the intermediary's operation is in substance an extension of the insurer.

Further, if the relevant service agreement is for a definite period of time (e.g. 12 months) and not automatically renewable, it would be arguable that there is lacking the degree of permanence necessary to support a finding of an establishment (the third condition in the European Commission Interpretative Communication). The relationship should be that of independent commercial parties.

Having said this, there could be an argument that the permanence condition is satisfied where there is common or group ownership. In such a case (all things being equal) it could be argued that the intermediary and insurer are intended to have a permanent and interdependent business relationship. Conversely, an EU insurer who structured its business relationship with an independent intermediary over a long and permanent basis could eventually on account of that fact, lose its status as a service provider and fall within the scope of 'Right of Establishment'.

The appropriate drafting of the services agreement will also be crucial to this conclusion. The EC Interpretative Communication has made it clear that all three conditions must be satisfied in order for the activities of the intermediary to be covered by the rules of Establishment rather than the rules regarding Freedom of Services. This being the case we should consider each condition specifically in relation to a PCC EU insurer operating on a cross border basis.

5.3. Will the intermediary/service provider be subject to the direction and control of the Insurer?

This is a rather metaphysical concept. The issue here is whether the intermediary is in substance an extension of the insurer. It does not need to be owned by the insurer. It does not need to have common employees. Even an independent intermediary could fulfil all the necessary elements of an establishment (branch). Clearly in terms of regulator comfort the more that could be done out of the home jurisdiction the better, and what is important is also the degree of independence of the overseas operation. It would, for example, be easier to say that the intermediary was subject to the direction and control of the insurer if they shared a common Board of directors. With a PCC structure, of course, it is far more difficult to succeed in this argument for the purposes of satisfying the relevant condition given the separate cells and users.

5.4. Is the intermediary able to commit the Insurer?

If the intermediary will have binding authority to conclude policies on behalf of the insurer, it would be difficult to deny that this condition was not met. If an intermediary can make an offer on behalf of an insurance company containing all the essential elements of the proposed policy but the insurer can still reject the policy proposal submitted by the intermediary, arguably the condition of the ability to commit will not be met. If this view is correct, it would be possible to construct the contractual arrangements between the parties so that the insurer would download all policy proposals transacted on a daily basis by the intermediary, and review them against the rating criteria and underwriting rules. This function could easily be performed through appropriate computer systems. In these circumstances, the intermediary would have no authority to commit the insurer to any insurance if rejected or unless accepted. The insurer would at all times therefore retain the power to reject or accept proposals. In real time transactions, this underwriting process is usually assisted through use of automated (IT) systems such that when an underwriting proposal is submitted via the system, the computer will check whether the underwriting matrix and management controls have been satisfied and the system would then issue an electronic acceptance allowing the intermediary to print out and confirm the insurance cover. Strictly speaking, here, acceptance is effected by the insurer in its home jurisdiction. This sort of system can be adopted by an insurer for cross border business under Freedom of Services provided the underwriting controls remain with the Board of Directors (and its local employees) at all times, the server is based in the home jurisdiction and can only be amended from there.

5.5. Has the intermediary received a permanent brief from the Insurer?

Where there is a common group ownership structure, it could clearly be argued that the parties intend to have a permanent and dependent business relationship. But, assuming as follows:

(1) that the intermediary has other clients, and the relationship with the insurer, while important, is not the only relationship they have in the market,

(2) that the proposed agreement is concluded at arms length under normal commercial terms,

(3) that the insurer would be free to contract with other parties for the provision of administration services if after the duration of the agreement they do not provide them with the level of commitment and service levels they require, then this is consistent with the conduct of business by means of Freedom of Services and not by the establishment of a branch.

5.6. Freedom of Services

The European Commission Interpretative Communication accepts that an insurance undertaking that decides to transact insurance business under the freedom to provide services must be able to use certain services either upstream or downstream of the transaction in the Member State of provision. For example, an insurance undertaking should be able to use for its business under the freedom to provide services:

- a local expert to assess the risks to be covered under the freedom to provide services,
- a local expert to assess damage caused under risks covered by insurance policies negotiated under the freedom to provide services,
- canvassers who do not conclude insurance policies and whose activity is limited to sending insurance proposals received from potential policyholders to the insurance undertaking for acceptance,
- local legal services, medical or actuarial services established in the Member State of provision,

- a permanent structure for collecting the premiums for insurance policies entered into under the freedom to provide services (e.g. a credit institution or a factoring company),
- a permanent structure for receiving notices of claims relating to policies concluded under the freedom to provide services for transmission to the insurance undertaking for a decision to accept or refuse each claim,
- a permanent structure for managing files relating to claims (this may include, where appropriate, the payment of indemnities pursuant to the instructions given by the insurer himself).

In the final analysis, a protected cell company writing captive group risks of a cell user should be able to discharge its responsibilities to policyholders in Board and management meetings held in the home jurisdiction whilst operating on a Freedom of Services basis because:

(1) the cell will invariably underwrite a finite number of risks,

(2) it can clearly discharge the pricing function when the cover incepts (invariably simultaneously),

(3) the claims process and policy issuance can easily be referred to the directors in its home jurisdiction, and

(4) investment management decisions can be delegated to a bank/investment manager in the home state and performance monitored by the Board.

In a cell structure writing captive group risks the task of ensuring and demonstrating that 'mind and management' is exercised in the home jurisdiction is therefore lessened. It is easier than it would be for an open market insurer underwriting a multitude of policies and dealing with claims handling on a day-to-day basis.

The best advice possible when operating on a Freedom of Services basis is for the contractual arrangements with the intermediary to be made subject to formal review, rather than passive renewal. The directors of the insurer should also positively evaluate the performance of their functions on an arm's length basis. This is so as to avoid any implication that the service agreement is simply being renewed at the end of its term without scrutiny.

Whilst it is advisable for a PCC to maintain local bank accounts for the reasons we have discussed in previous Chapters, it may well be that this is not always commercially the best decision and the directors may wish to look elsewhere for banking support. If that is the case, careful consideration should be given to whether the relevant jurisdiction would likely recognise the cell structure. The question also sometimes arises as to whether the mere holding of a bank account 'abroad' undermines the regulatory principle of 'mind and management'. Strictly speaking, holding a bank account outside the insurer's domicile is no different from holding any other financial asset abroad. In essence, 'mind and management' relates to strategic decisions[63] about the company's business as a whole rather than day to day administration of business transactions. This, of course, may in turn raise another question: whether the company has established a place of business abroad for tax purposes and is one of fact; very broadly, whether the company is trading 'in' a jurisdiction (via itself or an independent agent), rather 'with' an entity in that jursidiction. Admittedly, the first question is for the home regulator, whilst the second question is principally (but not exclusively) one for the tax laws in the relevant foreign jurisdiction. The answer to the first question surely must be that maintaining a bank account abroad should not itself cause the home regulator any concerns as long as the decision to open the account was taken in the home jurisdiction by the Board of Directors. With regards to the second question, the issuing of payments drawn on a foreign bank account should not, of its own, be regarded as 'trading in' a jurisdiction as long instructions with regards to the operation of the account (e.g. transfer of funds) and administration thereof (i.e. where bank statements are sent and maintained) takes place in the home jurisdiction.[64] As long as the decision concerning the opening of the bank account is therefore taken by the directors in the home jurisdiction and payment instructions (and monitoring activity on behalf of the company), takes place from there, the insurer should be able to satisfy its regulator that it was exercising its mind and management and trading 'from' the foreign jurisdiction.

5.7. Governing law and jurisdiction clauses

Although a PCC should strive to ensure that any contracts it enters into are governed by local (rather than a foreign) law, this may not always be possible. In some instances there may be mandatory provisions of law that provide that the law of another country applies to the contract in question. The regime described below applies (except in Denmark) to insurance contracts entered into before 17 December 2009. The new Rome

[63] Of which opening a bank account with any particular financial institution is one since it concerns an investment decision.

[64] Such an expectation is obviously best checked with appropriate local tax advisers.

I Regulation (EEC 593/2008) applies after that date (although it does not substantially change the substance of the law set out in the Directives).

In the case of life insurance policies sold in accordance with the relevant European Directives governing the EU principle of Freedom of Services to residents of a Member State of the European Economic Area (EEA), in principle, the policy is governed by the laws of the policyholder's habitual country of residence. The general aim is to ensure that the policy is governed by a law with which the policyholder is familiar and which provides adequate safeguards for policyholders who require special protection.

The governing law provision concerning life assurance in an EU context is found in article 32 of Directive 2002/83/EC:

"CONTRACT LAW AND CONDITIONS OF ASSURANCE

Article 32

Law applicable

1. The law applicable to contracts relating to the activities referred to in this Directive shall be the law of the Member State of the commitment. However, where the law of that State so allows, the parties may choose the law of another country.

2. Where the policy holder is a natural person and has his/ her habitual residence in a Member State other than that of which he/she is a national, the parties may choose the law of the Member State of which he/she is a national.

3. Where a State includes several territorial units, each of which has its own rules of law concerning contractual obligations, each unit shall be considered a country for the purposes of identifying the law applicable under this Directive.

A Member State in which various territorial units have their own rules of law concerning contractual obligations shall not be bound to apply the provisions of this Directive to conflicts which arise between the laws of those units.

4. Nothing in this Article shall restrict the application of the rules of the law of the forum in a situation where they are mandatory, irrespective of the law otherwise applicable to the contract.

If the law of a Member State so stipulates, the mandatory rules of the law of the Member State of the commitment may be applied if and in so far as, under the law of that Member State, those rules must be applied whatever the law applicable to the contract.

5. Subject to paragraphs 1 to 4, the Member States shall apply to the assurance contracts referred to in this Directive their general rules of private international law concerning contractual obligations...."[65]

Potentially this could create a mismatch between any substantive provisions of the foreign law and the PCC regime.

This situation would not normally arise in the case of large insurance groups with separately licensed insurance operations in each Member State. In those cases the local insurance subsidiary would issue a local policy governed by local law. So where an EU PCC insurer is conducting cross border business, it must either sell local policies that conform with local laws in the jurisdiction where the policies are sold or, if permitted, issue the policies so that the company operates exclusively within the PCC jurisdiction and not on a cross border basis using the European passport in insurance.

In so far as general insurance business is concerned, Directive 92/49/EEC of 18 June 1992 on the coordination of laws, regulations and administrative provisions relating to direct insurance other than life insurance and amending Directives 73/239/EEC and 88/357/EEC, applies.

Where a "large risk" is being insured, the parties may choose any appropriate law as the governing law of the insurance policy. In the context of a cell captive it is to be assumed that substantially all the company's business is likely to involve "large risks" as so defined. Where this is so, an express choice of law as the governing law of the insurance policy would be upheld. However, in the situation where the risk being insured is not a "large risk" the choice of law is limited.

The relevant Directive will apply wherever the risk insured under an insurance policy of an insurance company is situated in a Member State irrespective of whether the policyholder has his habitual residence or central administration in that or indeed in any Member State. In enacting the Third Directive it is expected that there will be slight variations between the different Member States.

It is a general principle of these 'choice of law' rules that where the law of the Member State where the risk is situated prescribes any mandatory rules of law which parties are not permitted to contract out of under that

---

[65]http://eurlex.europa.eu/LexUriServ/LexUriServ.do?uri=OJ:L:2002:345:0001: 0051:EN:PDF

law, those mandatory rules will be given effect, even if the parties choose another law as the governing law.

In order to mitigate the potential mismatch it is advisable for the governing law and jurisdiction clause to distinguish between the application of foreign law and any mandatory provisions of local law including PCC legislation. Thus such a clause could read:

"This insurance policy shall be governed by and construed in accordance with the laws of [Member State concerned], except as may otherwise be required by any mandatory provisions of [PCC jurisdiction] law, and provided that it is expressly agreed that all matters relating to the establishment, operation and dissolution of the Insurer shall be governed by and construed in accordance with [PCC jurisdiction] law and in particular, the Protected Cell Companies legislation".

Separately, Article 9(1) of the EU (Jurisdictional Regulations) / Council Regulation EC No 44/2001 of 22nd December 2000 enable a policyholder to commence proceedings in the State of its domicile or in the state of the insurer's domicile.

The further complication from a mismatch of choice of law/jurisdiction are obvious when a reinsurer is involved. In a typical fronting arrangement, the PCC will be the insurer, and reinsure 100%, back-to-back, to the selected reinsurer.

In any potential dispute there are at least three parties: the PCC as insurer, the policyholder as insured and the reinsurer. So the contractual arrangements are: insurer enters into a contract of insurance with policyholder and reinsures its obligations under that policy by entering into a separate contract of reinsurance with the reinsurer.

In a typical fronting arrangement where the insurance and reinsurance terms are identical, there is unlikely to be a dispute between the parties. Indeed, the policyholder under the underlying policy would have consented to the reinsurance placement. In the event that a claim is properly payable under the insurance policy, the PCC, in turn, would claim under the reinsurance. Given the fronting nature of the insurance, it would be expected that the reinsurance policy would include a clause giving the reinsurer the right to control claims in respect of the underlying policy. Although the reinsurer and the PCC would have a common interest, potential disputes can arise, particularly on complex insurance programmes with multiple lawyers/reinsurers/insureds. Where a dispute under a policy sold on a cross border basis does happen, one of the questions to be considered includes, which law would govern the dispute and which court would hear and determine it? Let us assume the following:

A PCC in Malta sells an insurance policy exercising its rights under Freedom of Services to a policyholder in Germany (the insured is a large industrial group). The insurance covers liability (group) risk and although the parties have freedom to choose the applicable law, the policy is expressly governed by German law, but is silent about jurisdiction. The PCC reinsurance contract is with a UK insurer and is governed by English law and jurisdiction. If the coverage under the underlying and reinsurance policies are not indentical (i.e. on the same terms), and the insured brought a claim under its policy which the reinsurer said was not covered under the terms of the reinsurance contract, or was not properly payable under the underlying policy, or was subject to a material non-disclosure when original cover was sought, such a dispute could result in court proceedings being issued in multiple jurisdictions whereby the parties may not have the same rights as a matter of German law as under English (or indeed Maltese law). The ideal situation would have been for the underlying and reinsurance contracts to have both been expressly subject to Maltese law and jurisdiction! Indeed, what happens if an unsympathetic judge in Germany enters a judgment in favour of the claimant under the underlying policy whilst an English judge decides in favour of the reinsurer under the terms of the reinsurance contract? In such a situation, the first line of defence for our PCC may be to rely on the 'pay as paid clause' (namely, it is only required to pay the insured under the terms of the policy subject to first having received payment from the reinsurer). The final defence after that may well be the cellular structure.

The potential to produce different outcomes under the different contracts by applying different law to the same facts arose in the recent English case of *Lexington Insurance Company v Wasa International Insurance Company [2009] 4 All ER 909*. This case did not involve a PCC. Lexington Insurance was exposed to substantial claims under Pennsylvanian law including losses that occurred outside the policy period and sought to recover from its reinsurers, including Wasa. Wasa declined to pay in respect of losses occurring outside the policy period relying on the more limited exposure under English law, on the basis that the reinsurance contract was governed by English law. In the lead judgment, Lord Collins concluded by stating:-

"At the beginning and end of these appeals remains the question whether the provision for the policy period in the reinsurance is to be given the effect it has under English law, or whether the parties must be taken to have meant that the reinsurance was to respond to all claims irrespective of when the damage occurred and irrespective of the period which the losses related. There is, in my judgment, no principled basis for a conclusion in the latter sense. [Paragraph 116]"

5.8. Should the PCC structure be offensive to a regulator?

It is the authors' contention that where a PCC is properly managed (as would be the case with any other insurer), it does not present any greater regulatory challenge. Overall, there can be a high level of reassurance that the PCC structure is sufficiently robust and creates no significant issues of concern from a regulatory perspective. The important test is ensuring that the PCC is properly managed and fit for purpose. There are captive managers (Willis, Aon and Marsh) in most of the major captive centres with the specialist knowledge required to manage a PCC. In fact, they are likely to have established their own PCC in at least one jurisdiction, which they would then manage, with individual cells created and offered to clients.

It is advisable for the PCC to document, as part of its corporate governance, how it mitigates the legal and regulatory risks arising from the company's operations including:

1. Monitor third party service providers and assess their competence and experience on an ongoing basis (including insurance managers and intermediaries).
2. Assess that an insurance proposal is fit for purpose in the context of a protected cell.
3. Ensure that management information is adequate and available in a timely manner to the Board of Directors.
4. Review service agreements and insurance documentation for regulatory and legal compliance; including, in the case of EU insurers, compliance with the relevant rules in respect of carrying out passported activities.
5. Ensure that underwriting (including reinsurance) and claims settlement decisions are taken only by the Board and monitor insurance performance (including claims experience).

Regulators would be right to express concern if the level of control exercised by the Board of Directors was not adequate. The fundamental regulatory principle has to be that the customer should not suffer on account of lack of appropriate systems and controls. There must, therefore, be a proven commitment to compliance and to this end a PCC must be able to demonstrate to its regulatory authority (either acting through its Board of Directors or an external manager) that it has a clear understanding of its responsibilities under the PCC legislation. The PCC must be able, on an ongoing basis, to monitor and ensure that its activities are carried on in a compliant manner.

It is of note that where a PCC insurer is licensed in Gibraltar or Malta under the EU passport, under European legislation home State regulators (in this case the regulator of Gibraltar or Malta) reserve prudential regulation to themselves, so that the prudential regulation requirements are those of the home State. Notwithstanding this, host States are free to impose conduct of business/marketing rules in addition to those of the home State on incoming EEA firms where these are in the *"general good"* (i.e. they do not affect the single market in insurance by being discriminatory or unduly restrictive). This is recognised by the European Commission in its Interpretative Communication.

Best practice in this area is for the PCC (through its manager) to prepare a compliance manual setting out in detail its compliance procedures, in particular reflecting the status of the insurer as a PCC.

5.9. Who should perform the compliance function?

Clearly the PCC is a special type of entity. It has to therefore be assumed that the insurance manager based in the home jurisdiction would have necessary expertise in assisting PCC insurers with their compliance responsibilities. But, as we have seen, managing a PCC requires more than just insurance management experience. The key is for the compliance function to be carried out specifically *for a PCC*. This, of course, does not absolve the Directors of their statutory responsibilities in ensuring that the company complies with all other legal and regulatory requirements.

5.10. Cell Management Contract

Given the separation of assets and liabilities within each cell, it is not uncommon for each cell user to enter into a management agreement with the PCC to ensure proper governance and management of the cell structure. It is also advisable for such an agreement to be a three party contract to include the external manager.

The usual undertakings and confirmations would include:

1. Keeping such separate books of account, records and bank accounts as shall enable the company to identify all policies, premiums, fees and claim payments arising from the business of the particular cell.
2. Ensure confidentiality so that such separate books, records etc as relate exclusively to the particular cell shall be open to inspection only by (except as otherwise required by the regulator) directors, officers and employees of the company, the relevant cell shareholder, the auditors and by any other person duly authorised in writing for such purpose by the cell shareholder (including its own appointed auditor).
3. Responsibility for preparation and filing of regulatory returns and compliance generally.
4. An undertaking by the company that it shall at all times in the conduct of the insurance business of the cell and in all transactions entered into or effected by it for the account of the cell inform the persons with whom it transacts that the company is a 'PCC' and for the purposes of each such transaction properly identify the relevant 'cell'.
5. A prohibition against the delegation of duties and responsibilities.
6. An undertaking that the 'PCC' will not establish any place of business or hold any board meetings outside the jurisdiction of incorporation.

The list is not exhaustive.

5.11. Directors' Duties

All legal systems impose duties on directors of companies. Under English common law, directors of a company are, among other duties, under a duty to act bona fide in the best interests of the company. Where the company is a PCC, directors have additional statutory duties (e.g. PCC laws impose a duty on directors to disclose to counter-parties which cell they are transacting business with). Given that a PCC will group together different economic interests (including the core/hub), a PCC director should have a clear understanding of risk as between each part of the company and consider what his relevant fiduciary duties are. The cellular structure of a PCC therefore raises an interesting dilemma for a director: in the case of a PCC, is the duty of the director to act in the best interest of the company as a whole qualified by the cellular structure?

Separate cells within a PCC may have entirely different risk appetite for their own business. Ordinarily, PCC directors transacting high risk insurance business in respect of a particular cell should not owe a duty to other cells of the company. This is because liabilities are after all intended to be ring-fenced. They may breach their fidudicary duties as far as that cell is concerned but that duty should not extend to other cells in the absence of a contract between the shareholders and the company, restrictions in the Articles of Association or rules defining the investment/business limitations on the company. The situation is not dissimilar to business transacted through Lloyd's of London – a syndicate at Lloyd's does not owe duties to other syndicates.

But there may be exceptions to this general principle. First, the situation is likely to be different where a number of cells depend upon the attribution of core capital to be able to conduct business. If the core capital is deficient as a result of liabilities incurred by one cell and other cells risk trading whilst insolvent, the directors may well be in breach of their fiduciary duties if they do not take into account the interest of all the cells and indeed the company as a whole. Second, where the PCC is an insurance company, its directors must discharge their duties in accordance with applicable insurance legislation (not just PCC legislation) and that may require directors to consider the interests of the rest of the cells if, in an extreme case, the decisions of the directors in relation to one cell adversely affects the interests of policyholders of other cells. An unlikely scenario would be where the directors of an insurance PCC choose to accept risks for a cell which they know is wholly unprofitable, where there is no market for the policyholders insurance requirements, where there is no reinsurance outwards and where the cell was undercapitalised. Clearly, here, the directors would be in breach of their fiduciary duties but one could not look at such a duty narrowly and the directors' actions could be open to challenge if they damaged the interests of other cells.

5.12. Checklist of Dos and Don'ts

As we have seen, it is important to ensure that the PCC remains tax resident only in the jurisdiction of incorporation. Thus there is no branch or establishment for regulatory purposes elsewhere.

The checklist below is not intended to be exhaustive but as a summary guideline.

1. No decisions should be taken by any director or manager of the PCC whilst outside the jurisdiction of incorporation (which for our purpose we assume is the same as the jurisdiction of the home regulator). It is permissible, however, for recommendations to be

made to the Board of Directors (or manager to whom the day-to-day management function may be delegated).

2. Where any recommendations are made to the Board of Directors or manager this must be properly documented.
3. If the 'PCC' appoints a foreign services company or administrator, the appointment itself must be properly documented. Parameters for any authority must be clearly set out in the agreement. Underwriting guidelines and claims settlement criteria must be strictly limited and observed. If there is such adherence it is acceptable to delegate such services since the services company or administrator would be implementing decisions taken by the Board of Directors in its home jurisdiction.
4. No Board Meetings should be convened outside the home jurisdiction.
5. Every agreement with the 'PCC' should set out the terms of the arrangement between the parties, including an acknowledgement that the company is a 'PCC' and identifying the 'cell' in respect of which the the parties are contracting.

6. GROWING MARKET FOR THE PCC

PCC-type structures have proliferated in recent years in many jurisdictions. They have become increasingly accepted in international transactions both in structured finance and investment funds. The market for these structures is no longer the exclusive domain of captive insurers or the large banks and we are likely to see an increase in the numbers of PCCs being set up as well as their acceptance into corporate life by pension trustees, multi-national companies and HNWIs. The growth in numbers is proof that small domiciles that are prepared to embrace innovation can obtain a competitive advantage and capture significant market share in niche industries (captives, funds etc). Whilst the use of the PCC is obviously not new, the way they could be used over the coming years to help solve problems may see some innovative structures being established.

6.1. The PCC and the Investment Fund

The use of investment funds, as a tool for raising and investing capital, is now widely used in the international markets the world over. The large majority of such vehicles are established in nil tax jurisdictions guaranteeing a tax-free return on its investments. Over recent years investment funds have been the catalyst for the growth in the number of PCCs. They include hedge funds[66] and property investment companies. Whilst larger funds will invariably be set up as single vehicles (in the same way as multinationals would set up their own insurance captives), there are undoubtedly gains in smaller funds pooling together under a PCC. Such structures are also fairly easy to establish. As in multi-issue Note Programmes, the documentation has become very standardised and easy to produce.

In the EU, Luxembourg[67] and Dublin[68] have both made provision for segregated cell type structures for use by investment funds. A number of

[66] Equity research by Dresdner Kleinwort likened hedge funds to banks (6 February 2007). Although probably too innovative for regulators in the present global financial climate, in future will we see a PCC bank?

[67] A Luxembourg fund can be set up as an open-end investment company with multiple compartments ("société d'investissement à capital variable" (SICAV) à compartiments multiples) governed by Luxembourg law and, in particular, the provisions of Part I of the Luxembourg law of 20 December 2002 relating to undertakings for collective investment. The assets of each fund are ring-fenced and as a matter of Luxembourg law, the assets of

jurisdictions have also implemented experienced investor (otherwise also known in some jurisdictions as, qualified investor) funds legislation aimed at streamlining and relaxing the burden of regulation in funds sold only to experienced investors. Such investors are not deemed to require the same protection as retail investors who invest in such funds informed as to the risks that they take. In general, this relies on a system of self-certification by relevant industry professionals, with local lawyers and fund administrators in particular assuming the central role of ensuring statutory requirements are satisfied (via a process of registration with the local regulatory body).

The typical fund is established as a bespoke PCC to raise money for specified investments.[69] The investment criteria would be predefined by the promoters and made clear within the Fund documentation (for example, Cell Particulars, or in the Articles of Association). A cell is then created within the PCC for each sub-class of investment. In turn, each cell will have different share classes allowing the investor to invest in that cell. The cell will benefit from its assets and liabilities being ring-fenced from the assets and liabilities of any other cell. Each class of cell share thereby entitles its owner (the cell shareholder) in liquidation to the net assets held by the PCC in respect of the relevant cell, but not to net assets attributable to any other class of cell share. Cell shares hold the equity interest of the cell owners.

---

one fund will not be available to meet the liabilities of another. The Company is also a single legal entity.

[68] Investment Funds, Companies and Miscellaneous Provisions Act 2005

[69] They are also used by family offices where different members of the same family may wish to participate via separate cells within the PCC.

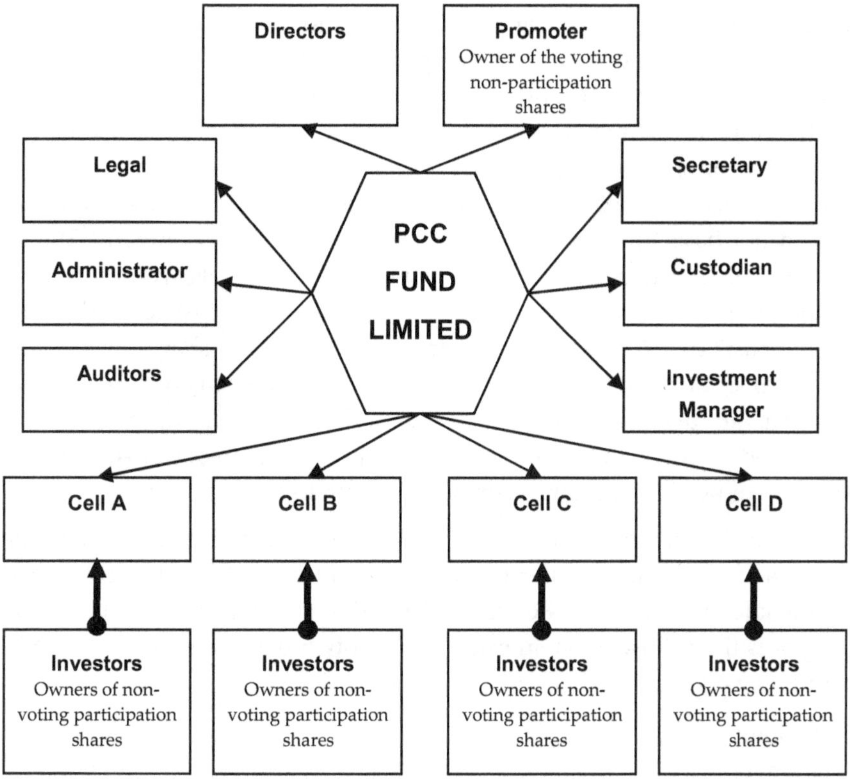

Diagram 8: A PCC Fund

A PCC Fund operates in very much the same way as an umbrella fund would in its non-statutory form. The PCC will act through its Board of Directors in the normal way and will normally appoint an investment adviser/manager and fund administrator.

The typical structure is well known. The company's ordinary shares (usually known as 'Founder' or 'Management' shares) would be held by the investment manager or any other controlling party. The holder of such shares would not have economic rights, but would usually have exculsive right to vote at meetings of the fund. The investors would subscribe for redeemable preference shares. The holders of the redeemable preference shares would have the right to participate in the risks and rewards of the cells but would (typically) not have voting rights. An investor wishing to invest in a PCC may either opt between investing in an existing sub-fund and creating their own new sub-fund. The difference is that if an investor chooses to invest in an existing sub-fund the investment criteria would have previously been established by the Board and documented as such. Whereas if a single investor desired to create his own cell, the company would resolve to allot the new class of share to activate the cell and determine and document the currency, eligible asset classes, volatility/risk appetite of the investor. Investors who invest in the same sub-fund will naturally share in the exposure to the underlying investments and their monies will be co-mingled. The obligation of such a shareholder is to contribute and pay the cell share capital. Once the cell share capital has been paid, the cell shareholder would not have any further financial obligation to the company. Where investors desire to realise their investment, withdrawals would occur as redemptions of shares (assuming redeemable shares are issued), normally on the basis of a Net Asset Value calculation. The cell shares in the PCC are an asset of the relevant shareholder and the proceeds of subscription, in turn, an asset attributable to the individual cell. In principle, if permitted by local laws, there is no reason why the holder of such shares should not be able to grant security over them to a third party.

The financial statements of a PCC Fund would be presented to state the assets and liabilities and income and expenditure of the cells of the fund and would state the net asset value in relation to the same. For illustrative purposes the following is an example of how a balance sheet of the PCC Fund may be presented:

PCC Fund

Balance sheet

	PCC Fund Total € '000	Cell A € '000	Cell B € '000	Cell C € '000	Cell D € '000
Current Assets					
Financial assets at fair value through profit or loss	142,500	10,000	120,000	8,000	4,500
Due from brokers	835	500	-	-	335
Other receivables and prepayments	90	10	50	5	25
Margin accounts	407	200	101	50	56
Cash at bank	270	100	50	70	50
Total assets	144,102	10,810	120,201	8,125	4,966
Current Liabilities					
Financial liabilities at fair value through profit and loss	40	25	5	10	-
Amounts payable on redemptions	15	10	5	-	-

Investment management fees	600	200	100	200	100
Administration fees	100	20	50	20	10
Custody fees	10	2	4	2	2
Other liabilities	40	5	10	15	10
Total liabilities	805	262	174	247	122
Net assets attributable to holders of redeemable preference shares	143,297	10,548	120,027	7,878	4,844
Redeemable preference shares in issue		**Number** 85,000	**Number** 950,000	**Number** 70,000	**Number** 33,500
Net asset value per redeemable preference share		**€124.09**	**€126.34**	**€112.54**	**€144.60**

The Income Statement of the PCC Fund would be produced based on the transactions undertaken at the cell level (in accordance with the balance sheet as shown above). An illustrative Profit and Loss Account is not included in this book.

Where the purpose of a cell is to establish a highly leveraged fund, there is the risk that a cell may be left in negative asset value. Thus the protection afforded by PCC legislation could be put to the test, particularly, where the assets are located or held on its behalf abroad and legal proceedings are commenced in a foreign court.

The investor documentation for a PCC will typically carry a health warning[70] under "Risk Factors" about the special nature of the company by virtue of its protected cell status. This may say something along the lines of: "*The Protected Cell Company is a single legal entity which may have assets held on its behalf or be subject to claims in other jurisdictions which may not necessarily recognise such ring-fencing and, in such circumstances, the assets of one cell may be exposed to the liabilities of another. There is, therefore, some concern that, the protection afforded to cell assets may be lost where an action is constituted in a foreign court and the relevant assets are situated in that foreign jurisdiction.*" There obviously remains the risk that some investors may not fully understand the risk of contagion on insolvency. In practice, this is more relevant to retail investors (UCITS) rather than schemes for

[70] Regulators will normally require such a disclosure.

professional or experienced investors and comfort may be obtained from the fact that UCITS have fairly strict investment restrictions (e.g. in respest of borrowing) which minimises the risk of insolvency but admittedly does not eliminate it entirely. UCITS with segregrated liability between funds have already been set up in Dublin.

Given the cross border nature of funds, the other risk is the possibility that one or more regulator outside the jurisdiction of incorporation may subject the PCC to its own securities laws and therefore attempt to assert jurisdiction over the company. Whilst the sale or marketing of the relevant securities may have related to only one particular sub-fund the foreign regulator may attempt to wind up the company, thereby not only putting the cell structure at risk but forcing the company to defend itself at some expense. This could have considerable consequences for the PCC and its ability to continue to meet its obligations to both investors and creditors. One of the key points for regulators with responsibility for supervision of a PCC is therefore to ensure that the company's management documents all material aspects of the establishment and operation of the fund including in respect of subscriptions and marketing. Management must be able to demonstrate a detailed degree of understanding that the company can be operated in accordance with its stated objectives and that key service providers will be engaged with adequate experience in all relevant areas (including valuation of assets and liabilities, day to day administration and in respect of all regulatory compliance). Although there is no doubt that a PCC offers a high degree of protection, its key sensitivity remains operational and compliance risk.

In principle, there is no reason why a PCC could not reinforce the statutory segregation of assets and liabilities within the company by creating security interests which would give creditors of a particular cell proprietary rights ranking ahead of all unsecured rights. Such security arrangement (which could be held via a security trustee) would provide additional ring fencing under the umbrella of a single corporate entity i.e. the PCC. Obviously the security would be subject, among other things, to those secured assets being clearly identified. In these circumstances, the protection afforded by PCC legislation would be more, not less, than if PCC legislation was not used. This seems to be the crux of the matter.

The PCC structure can clearly be a very useful tool in international transactions where investing in a single corporate entity, via separate classes of shares with differing investment objectives and to which specific assets are attributed, is essential. Fund managers in particular have set up PCCs to introduce the platform to their clients. For each separate investment a new protected cell is set up. The promoters can in fact use the PCC for any business transaction based on the investment objectives of its investors. The investment management role can be delegated and performed by the fund manager. The investors have the economic rights over the cell and are also exposed to the risk of loss in respect of the activities of the cell. The promoters, on the other hand, retain the ownership risk related to the SPV and its core assets in order to obtain the benefits of the PCC's management.

Martin Farnworth, speaking to the co-author of the book, summarised the decision to launch a PCC fund as follows: *"The setting up as a PCC was the way forward following the decision to launch our umbrella fund because of the protection afforded by the cell structure. The PCC is now accepted in many jurisdictions for international business transactions. It was therefore the obvious vehicle of choice. Gibraltar became the location due to the wealth of knowledge and experience of the professional advisers there, who we found to be proactive and helpful in bring our PCC to life."*

The PCC structure can also be used as a platform for proprietary futures trading via membership of an electronic derivatives exchange. Serial entrepreneur Pino Curcio of Arb Asset Management was the first to set up a PCC and apply for membership of Eurex. He told the co-author of the book: *"The corporate vehicle (including fund structures) had traded on exchanges over many years. Our venture was an evolutionary next step into proprietary trading using the medium of a PCC."*

Banks, custodians and investment managers have all wanted a slice of the business generated by such companies and any potential legal limitations have tended to be more theoretical than real. The Protected Cell Company is here to stay.

There is clearly a significant case in favour of the Protected Cell Company as a means of raising and segregating funds within a single vehicle. In the UK, this was acknowledged by HM Treasury in its consultation paper (May 2007) "*Consultation on Better Regulation Measures for the Asset Management Sectior*" seeking views on the introduction of a protected cell regime for open ended investment companies. Per HM Treasury *"[An] advantage of allowing protected cell OEIC sub funds in the UK would be improving international competiveness. Protected cells have been introduced in several other jurisdictions and have become an expected feature of a corporate fund vehicle. [...] The Government would therefore like to consider developing a protected cell regime for UK OEICs."* If PCC legislation were introduced in the UK (albeit for umbrella funds) it would be a major recognition for the PCC regime in the international arena.

The UK Investment Management Association commissioned a Working Group of senior industry practictioners to review the impact of the events of 2007 and 2008 on UK Authorised Collective Investment Schemes. The Working Group reported in May 2009 (*"The Credit Crunch: a stress test for UK authorised funds"*) and noted:

"FSMA and the OEIC Regulations do not currently allow for a "protected cell regime". Without such a regime, there would be possible contagion of sub-funds within an umbrella if a sub-fund was to fail and owed more than its assets. Heightened concerns and misinformation about the security of assets in CIS has led to renewed questions about the lack of a protected cell regime in the UK.

The probability of contagion within an OEIC is very small, but such a regime should be available and would be a source of comfort for some conservative, institutional investors. Furthermore, the absence of a protected cell regime is a barrier to registration in some countries. HMT is working on the introduction of such a regime and IMA is actively involved in this work. HMT has confirmed that it will be issuing a public consultation document on the regime this summer."

In July 2009 HM Treasury published a 51 page consultation document setting out its proposals for introduing a protected cell regime for Open-Ended Investment Companies (OEICs). This was in response to the support received for the earlier proposal in the "Better Regulation" consultation (above). The response to that consultation *"was unanimously in favour of developing a protected cell regime"*.

The consultation document sets out the concerns with regards to how OEICs are currently structured: *"Under current law there is no segregation of liabilities between different sub-funds. For example, if an umbrella fund contained one cautious UK bond fund and one high-risk Far-east equity fund and the Far-East equity fund collapsed with liabilities exceeding its assets, creditors could have a claim on the assets of the UK bond fund. Investors in the cautious fund therefore bear some of the risk of the riskier fund."*

While acknowledging that *"In practice the probability of an OEIC collapse is small"*, given that OEICs must comply with borrowing limits imposed by the FSA, it indicates that it is *"not zero"* and concludes that *"provided adequate protection of existing creditors can also be achieved, segregating liabilities so that the liabilities of any one sub-fund could only be met out of the assets of that sub-fund appeared desirable."*

The document refers to the *"Increased risk-aversion of investors"* as a result of "recent events" (the global downturn of 2008/2009) seeing *"any possible risk of contagion as a reason not to invest, or at least to invest elsewhere."*

The UK is not the only jurisdiction moving towards allowing the PCC structure to be used for Umbrella funds. In its recent report (30 September 2009) to the Dubai Financial Services Authority ("DFSA") a panel established to make recommendations as to how the DFSA could support the growth of the local funds industry included a similar recommendation. But unlike in the UK, the PCC is already available in Dubai for insurance and securitisation. As the panel noted in its report, in terms of 'bench-marking', *"PCC regimes or separate legal status and liability for different sub-classes of funds are now accepted practice in many well-known fund jurisdictions"*. It should be noted that in the UK and Dubai the underlying motivation for the introduction of PCC legislation for funds is the same - increasing the jurisdiction's competitiveness whilst also giving investors the comfort of knowing that the PCC regime provides for legal segregation of assets and liability (i.e. underpinning investor protection). Even more recently, Liechtenstein has been exploring introducing PCC legislation. Statistics also show that in many PCC jurisdictions, the number of PCCs set up as funds now exceed the number of PCCs set up for insurance (e.g. see Gibraltar FSC website).

Annex 1 shows a specimen Articles and Memorandum of Association of a PCC Umbrella Fund and Private Information Memorandum. The name "ABC" is entirely fictious. Readers should note that underpinning the successful operation of a PCC Fund are the same governance and management principles discussed in Chapter 5.

6.2. The PCC in the world of Structured Finance

We have seen elsewhere in the book how the issue of tailor-made securities to large international investors by companies established specifically for that purpose has proliferated over the last few decades, where the securities are secured on one or more underlying assets owned by the special purpose vehicle.[71] All the major banks have been involved in transactions of this kind, with companies set up as multi-issue vehicles (several issues under one programme) or as single-issue vehicles.[72] The

[71] SPVs are usually set up with acronyms.

[72] Every international bank has a Structured Finance (sometimes known as Structured Products) department. Since the global financial crisis some banks prefer to use other terms.

reasons why such companies (normally owned by charitable trusts to keep them 'off the balance sheet' of the arrangers) are used include:

- They enable arrangers to dispose of and repackage assets into more attractive assets for the investors(s).
- They allow access to the credit derivatives market – allowing banks to lay off credit risk and investors to buy into risk.
- Permit documentation, tax or regulatory arbitrage.
- They may also allow for more liquidity than asset swaps – there may be a secondary market if the investor wishes to sell.

Given the basic structure is not entirely dissimilar from that of an umbrella fund, the use of the PCC has become a common feature for the investment bankers who act as the arrangers in structured finance transactions. The market is entirely driven by the investment, regulatory and tax needs of the investors, although these products have been traditionally offered only to institutional markets and sophisticated counter-parties.

It is possible to structure a product in capital market transactions which uses a PCC at both ends of the product (distribution and execution). Every transaction is unique and will be driven principally by investment objectives or constraints and the regulatory and tax environment of the investor/arranger.

The establishment of PCCs by investment banks is certainly in the ascendancy and this trend is likely to continue over the coming years. The protected cell structure provides an additional level of asset protection, which is not available in the traditional contractual architecture for SPVs. Banks and institutional investors in such structures, however, are unlikely to abandon security arrangements used in SPVs, even where the medium of the PCC is adopted. In the context, for example, of a repackaging issuer established as a PCC, each series of notes would be issued in respect of individual cells and the repackaged assets would comprise the cellular assets attributable to the relevant cells. The issuer would continue to provide security interests over cellular assets with respect to each series, whilst the use of limited recourse provisions would ensure that traditional ring-fencing was also adopted within the new statutory framework. This can only mean more, not less protection for the structure.

It is also worth mentioning that a number of onshore jurisdictions have given effect to statutory forms of ring-fencing to facilitate domestic securitisations. Repackaging is itself a form of securitisation. Broadly, the difference between a repackaging and a securitisation is that in the former the nature of the underlying assets are bonds or notes (i.e. securities), and in the case of securitisation, receivables[73] (hence, the term 'securitisation'). An example of such jurisdiction is France. The *fonds communs de créances* (FCC) is a French special purpose vehicle dedicated to securitisation transactions but does not have separate legal personality. The FCC has the key feature of an umbrella fund PCC whereby the FCC can be divided into separate sub-funds. Ring-fencing as between the various sub-funds was implemented by Monetary and Financial Code, Article L214-43. More specifically, the fund may have two or more compartments if its rules so provide and each compartment gives rise to the issuance of units which represent the assets of the fund which are allocated to it. Unless otherwise stipulated in the fund's constituting documents, the assets of a given compartment may only be used to meet that compartment's debts, commitments and obligations and only benefit from that compartment's receivables. Luxembourg is another example of a European jurisdiction which allows securitisation undertakings, namely under the law of 22 March 2004 on securitisation pursuant to which a company is entitled to hold assets in compartments which effectively segregate those assets from any of its other assets.

Arguably, there is, in substance, no difference between this and the PCC regime. A practictioner arguing for acceptance of the cellular structure of a foreign PCC before a judge in France could therefore direct the court to 'equivalent' French legislation as a reason why it should be respected.

It should further be noted that securitisations have been very popular over many years and that such transactions are structured across multiple jurisdictions. Prior to the 'credit crunch', there was no shortage of investor appetite for these debt securities, many of which have also been listed and/or rated.[74]

6.3. Portfolio transfers and the potential use of the PCC

We have seen how the insurance passport allows an insurer licensed in one Member State to sell insurance across the EU on the basis of its home State regulation and supervision. Whilst the use of cell captives will continue over the coming years, one potential growth area for the PCC is

---

[73] e.g. insurance and mortgages

[74] Securities are sometimes listed and/or rated because some investors can only invest in rated securities or to increase marketability.

its use in portfolio transfers and insurance run-off sector within the framework of EU Directives. To date this has not happened although there remains significant interest both from established insurers seeking to transfer portfolios and specialist run off companies looking at running them off. In the UK such transfers are known as Part VII transfers (under the Financial Services and Markets Act 2000); a court approved mechanism whereby the reinsurance asset is also transferred.

A PCC (exercising its rights under the EU insurance passport) is the natural home for transferring separate insurance portfolios into a single vehicle with statutory segregation of assets and liabilities, thus taking advantage of the pooling together of administration (including regulatory compliance) and potentially reducing capital requirements under the cell structure. In substance, there is not much difference between a bank transferring segregated portfolios of assets into a PCC and transactions involving run-off of insurance portfolios. The cell structure is simply the mechanism for protecting assets within a single entity.

As Steve Quinn and Peter Abbott of Quest Group (Gibraltar) point out: *"The PCC structure offers unique flexibility for portfolio transfers with a range of options available from capitalisation and management of individual cells, through to management but no ownership, to cell rental only with outsourced management."*

6.4. Is the use of the PCC a possible solution for the UK pensions problem?

The purchase of bulk annuities has received significant UK media attention over the last year or so. Under such arrangements, a pension trustee will pay an insurer a premium (typically handing over assets) for taking on their pension liabilities; thereby removing all pension obligations from its books and substituting this with an admissible asset (an insurance policy). In the UK there have been a number of traditional players involved in this market such as Prudential and Aviva. But in recent years the market has seen start-up insurers supported by private equity (e.g. Paternoster and Synesis). It seems to the authors that the protected cell structure provides a regime well suited for this sort of business. There are two ways of providing solutions to pension scheme deficits. One is a buy out of assets and liabilities for a premium. The other is an insurance based solution.

Currently, as far as the authors are aware there is no PCC in any jurisdiction providing an insurance solution to pension trustees, even though the PCC offers a level of ring-fencing not otherwise available through a traditional company.

A scheme sponsor has to ensure it has adequate funding to meet the financial obligations under a scheme. Scheme trustees typically manage their pension assets on a day to day basis through outsourced investment managing arrangements.

An insurance offering which, for example, guaranteed the funding position of a scheme at, say its current level, throughout the life of the policy would sit as an asset (an insurance policy) in the books of the pension trustee. It would avoid the volatility for pension funds by replacing the uncertainty of day-to-day pension fund management to maintain asset/liability matching from scheme trustees and their sponsors. The required cash-flows of the scheme would be backed by payments under the policy and in particular the return of assets equal to a certain value at maturity of the policy.

No doubt, the serious global financial crisis of 2007 and 2008 could have had a severe impact on an insurer guaranteeing any pension fund liabilities. This is because of the substantial fall in the value of investments and of investment income. But at least the use of a PCC and separation of cells would have offered some protection and pension scheme policyholders would have been in a more secure position with the PCC structure than without it. Within a PCC, the obligations under individual cell policies could also be secured against cell assets.

6.5. Shariah law and the PCC

Shariah (the Arabic word for Islamic law) principles require the separation, within an insurance entity ("*Takaful*"), of different lines of business. Whilst the Lloyd's syndicate structure has been used for Takaful insurance,[75] arguably the protected cell provides a readily available Shariah compliant structure of its own. In the authors' view not only should a PCC meet the structural requirements of Shariah law but the policyholders themselves are buying insurance clearly on the premise that they will only have recourse to the assets of the relevant cell – the insurance policy would, in fact, not be Shariah compliant otherwise. That is precisely why such a policyholder would wish to purchase insurance from the PCC (and not from the conventional insurance market). Unlike conventional insurance, the demand for a Shariah compliant structure

[75] Creechurch

would therefore be the driver for the use of a PCC. The same is also true for other types of shariah compliant products and services (funds).

6.6. The PCC Life Company

The PCC is an efficient vehicle through which to execute life policies for the account of separate cells supported by segregated cell assets. The PCC structure is sufficiently flexible to also permit cell assets to be managed by separate investment managers selected by individual policyholders (mainly HNWIs). There are some life policies which are structured with the underlying portfolio being units in a fund of funds or even a fund linked 'Note'. In this structure, in essence, the HNWI obtains exposure to the underlying portfolio through a life policy.

This type of company looks similar and performs a similar function to an 'investment fund'. The big difference is that the product offering for regulatory purposes constitutes insurance, even if it has some of the characteristics of an investment 'wrapper'.

This raises the question, what is 'insurance' for this purpose? The starting point is that as a matter of English law, there is no UK statutory definition of insurance either for tax or regulatory purposes.[76]

The essential characteristics of an insurance contract are described in *Prudential Insurance Co. v Inland Revenue Commissioners [1904] 2 KB 658.* This case has been approved and cited by various English courts including the Court of Appeal in *Fuji Finance Inc. v Aetna Insurance Co. Ltd. [1997] Ch. 173.*

According to the judgment in *Prudential,* a contract of insurance has the following three characteristics:

(1) it is a contract whereby one party as the insurer promises in return for a money consideration to pay to the other as the insured (usually but not necessarily) a sum of money, upon the occurrence of a certain event;

(2) the specified event must involve some amount of uncertainty; and

(3) the insured has an interest in the subject matter of the contract (in other words, there is an insurable interest).

To qualify as life assurance, it is sufficient if there is a right to benefit which is related to life or death (*Fuji Finance,* particularly per Morritt LJ at 188F). As a consequence, investment products that include provision to

[76] The authors understand that the Law Commission is looking at this issue.

pay out a benefit on death or survival to a certain age should qualify as assurance.

Such a structure (which is essentially a hybrid between an Umbrella Fund and a Life Company) allow HNWIs to organise their personal, tax and financial affairs through the medium of a bespoke life assurance company. The bespoke company would be established as a PCC, where in return for the payment of premium (for example, handing over investments) an 'insurance policy' replaces the investment portfolio which in turn sits in a segregated cell. Each segregated life sub-fund is then invested using asset managers arranged for and approved by the PCC. Through the use of separate protected cells the assets are linked or tailored to the cashflows of each individual policy. An alternative to a 'life wrapper' in the UK is to use a SIPP as a 'pensions wrapper'.

Linked life policies in particular lend themselves well to concept of the PCC given that policy benefits are highly correlated to the value of a defined pool of assets. For linked policies, generally, there is no need to encourage diversification. If asset values decrease, then the policy values decrease. This correlation eliminates an important source of risk for an insurance company. The contract language in such a life policy could read:

"The PCC has established a protected cell (the "Cell") under the laws of [Gibraltar/Malta] for the purposes of and which is linked to this insurance policy (the "Policy"). The PCC owns the assets of the Cell. The assets arising out of or in respect of the Policy shall at all times be linked to the Cell and shall be kept segregated for the purposes of the [relevant PCC legislation] and separate and distinct from all other cellular and non-cellular assets of the Company."

In addition, as we have seen throughout this book, the parties would be well advised to adopt a belt and braces approach:

"The Policyholder agrees, confirms and acknowledges that the Company's liability and obligations under this Policy are limited to the assets attributable to the Cell. The Policyholder further agrees, confirms and acknowledges that the Company has no obligation whatsoever to use any of it assets, other than the assets attributable to the Cell, to satisfy any claim."

Bermuda has been the home of a number of segregated life companies. These companies are registered under the Segregated Accounts Companies Act 2000 and may establish segregated accounts (the equivalent of cells) under Bermuda law to support the benefits payable under specified policies. A segregated account is an account established by the company as evidenced by the opening of a separate ledger pursuant to the powers conferred on such company under the operating legislation. Each segregated account is legally segregated for all purposes from other segregated accounts and from the general account. The segregated accounts and the assets placed therein or allocated thereto are not intended to be available to meet the general liabilities of the company, in winding up of the company or be available to the general creditors of the company and are not chargeable with liabilities arising out of other business of the company and not intended to be subject to or affected by any other segregated accounts. On commencement of winding up proceedings in Bermuda, a liquidator is bound to recognise the separate nature of the segregated accounts and should not apply the property identified as the property of the segregated account to pay the claims of creditors of the company or policyholders other than policyholders to which the segregated account relates to.

Typically, these are bespoke policies with the following characteristics: the policies are single (or large regular) premiums, policyholders are experienced investors, they are professionally advised and bear the risk of loss of value in the underlying investment including in the event of a sale. In order to mitigate the risk that there may not be a liquid market for the assets (because the assets are not readily realisable) the policy will usually provide that the PCC reserves a right to make payments of cellular assets in specie (in kind) to the policyholder. In this situation the only risk is the operational risk of the business. Clearly these high networth policyholders do not require the same degree of protection as retail policyholders against investment risk and in theory regulators should permit a wider range of investments. The important point is to ensure that investments do not place a liability on the cell that might ultimately fall on the insurance company.

In a European context, the first PCC life companies seeking to operate the European passport were set up in Gibraltar, among them PEL Altraplan (Gibraltar) PCC Limited.

The press release on the establishment of the company read:

"NewPEL Group announces that it has been granted a license by the Gibraltar Financial Services Commission to distribute life products. This represents an important further step in the Group`s strategy, as it expands its portfolio of wealth management products available to clients across the European Union. NewPEL Group has made use of a new legal structure that has recently been introduced in the European Union, called a Protected Cell Company (PCC).

Gibraltar has taken a lead in supporting the development of these products." (30 March 2009).

A PCC-based product offering via the medium of a protected cell can be used in a number of other scenarios. It is possible for products to have different classification for regulatory and tax purposes depending on whether they are deemed to constitute insurance, a derivative, other financial instrument or a gaming contract (all of which share some characteristics). Certain transactions can also be structured and executed as gaming, insurance or derivative contracts at one end and reversed through the other. This can create an arbitrage in the market. We have already seen an example of this in Chapter 4 (i.e. transformers). A PCC can be used to capture multiple opportunities in all these areas.

6.7. The Credit Crunch and Madoff

In 2007 as the turmoil in the global financial system began to take shape there was a lot of media attention around banks' use of SPVs and structured finance, in particular their exposure to the US sub-prime. It is not entirely clear whether any PCCs were caught out in the credit turmoil.

Assuming they were, the key question for such companies was, would the ring-fence hold? All the indications (or at least the lack of public evidence to the contrary) is that it will. However, it is very difficult to make this judgment because the large majority of these transactions were private deals, involving large private investors and the massive bail out of banks on both sides of the Atlantic since the summer of 2007 meant (without exaggeration) that collapse of the global financial system was averted.

What we can say is that if properly structured (including via security interests), marketed and managed, there is no reason to believe that a PCC is any more at risk than the firewalls created in any other non-PCC structure. On the contrary, it should offer more (not less) protection. The risk may arise as deals become larger, more complex and promoters extend the frontiers of innovation driven primarily by investor appetite and commercial considerations beyond what may be prudent in a cross border scenario given, as we have seen, the legal uncertainty. This is more likely to result in a potential mismatch in legislation and therefore a failure in the statutory ring-fence.

In addition to the global banking liquidity issues throughout 2007, the Madoff case created a secondary shock wave for the stability of financial markets worldwide. This impacted on UCITS and among them investment vehicles with segregated liability between funds (the protected cell company equivalent).

Thema International Fund plc's publicly available prospectus dated 31 December 2007 described it as *"an open-ended investment company with variable capital and having segregated liability between its Funds organised under the laws of Ireland"*. The *"Risk Factors"* included the general risk disclosure that *"The Company is structured as an umbrella fund with segregated liability between its Funds. As a matter of Irish law, the assets of one Fund will not be available to meet the liabilities of another. However, the Company is a single legal entity that may operate or have assets held on its behalf or be subject to claims in another jurisdiction that may not necessarily recognise such segregation."* In an announcement on 2 January 2007 the company stated that *"with effect from 31 December 2006, the Company has converted to UCITS III status"* and as a consequence the Prospectus was amended including *"A paragraph relating to the segregation of liability between sub-funds of the Company has been deleted and corresponding amendments have been made throughout the Prospectus."*

It seems that the company launched only one sub-fund (the Thema Fund) with separate US$ and Euro denominated classes of shares; hence why there appears to have been no requirement for statutory segregation. The Thema International Fund plc has since become involved in extensive civil litigation in the aftermath of Madoff. Given the single sub-fund, the true test of ring-fencing within a segregated liability company does not appear to arise.

Another company caught up in Madoff related civil litigation was Herald Fund SPC. Herald Fund SPC is a segregated portfolio company organized under the laws of the Cayman Islands, but for our purposes, it also appears only to have had one segregated portfolio (Herald USA Segregated Portfolio One).

In respect of a third fund, Herald (Lux) SICAV (which had invested in Bernard Madoff Investment Securities LLC), on 2 April 2009, the Luxembourg District Court (*Tribunal d'Arrondissement*) ordered the dissolution and winding-up of Herald (Lux) SICAV pursuant to article 104(1) of the Luxembourg law of 20 December 2002 relating to undertakings for collective investments, as amended from time to time.

It should be noted that although an investment fund may have the protection of statutory segregation, its prime broker who may be responsible for securities transactions may not. Thus where investments by an investment fund are held by the relevant prime broker as collateral, they may not be segregated by such prime broker from its own investments. As a result of this counter-party exposure, such investments may be available to the creditors of such a prime broker in the event of its insolvency and the relevant investment fund may lose some or all of its interest in such investments.

With a UCITS III fund, however, the fund would employ a custodian to hold the assets of the fund but the assets are "ring fenced" from the custodian's own funds and assets; hence safeguarding the investors in the event of failure of the custodian.

Where assets are held by a custodian on behalf of an investor, a clause in the custody agreement to watch out for is one that would allow the custodian to 'borrow' the assets (stock lending), replacing the obligation with a debt; hence creating a counterparty risk. Stock lending is normally associated with equity holdings and these clauses have given considerable cause for concern since the financial crisis of 2008.

6.8. Could a PCC redomicile between jurisdictions or amalgamate?

Assuming the protected cell regime achieves international recognition not only on a cross border situation, but also with regards to their ability to change domicile, there is no fundamental reason why not. However, since currently those countries that permit both PCCs and redomiciliation are in a minority, it is unlikely to become a regular occurence in the corporate scene. This raises the question, what is redomiciliation (also known as migration)?

The word 'domicile' when applied to a company has been defined as referring to the country the law of which is the proper law of the company governing its constitution and powers[77] or the country under whose law it is incorporated[78]. A company may transfer its 'domicile' (or place of incorporation) from one country to another provided that their respective internal laws permit it. This process is generally referred to as 'redomiciliation' and is a concept that is recognised in many jurisdictions (e.g. Jersey, Bermuda, Malta, Luxembourg and Gibraltar) but not in others (e.g. the UK).

There have been numerous instances of redomiciliation between various offshore and even some onshore jurisdictions (including of captive

---

[77] *Carl Zeiss Stiftung v. Rayner & Keeler (No 3) (1970)* Ch. 506 at 544

[78] Dicey, *Conflict of Laws*

insurance companies). In an insurance context there is an obvious benefit in this process - the alternative would be to put the insurance company in run-off and transfer the portfolio to a newly incorporated company. This can be expensive and time-consuming.

A company re-domiciling to another jurisdiction remains the same legal entity. It is treated as having continued its corporate existence in the relevant state.

A PCC redomiciliation may present an interesting challenge given the special nature of such a company. In theory, there is no reason why a PCC established in one jurisdiction should not be able to redomicile to another PCC jurisdiction provided that both recognised the continued existence of the company as a PCC *in the context of cell segregation*. Of course, in most jurisdictions, redomiciliation legislation would have preceded PCC legislation (and that may present a challenge).

It would seem unlikely that the cell owners and creditors of a PCC would oppose a redomicilation, since provided that the legislation in both jurisdictions recognises the protected cell status on identical terms, they would not be prejudiced by the change of domicile. However, ensuring that this is the case would be important to the integrity of the cell structure.

The first reported case of a PCC redomiciliation appears to be that of a protected cell company called, Jubilee Absolute Return Fund PCC Limited. This involved one of the few cases of a reported judgment involving a PCC (Judgement 5/2006, Royal Court (Company File 44327) – 10th February, 2006).

The facts were relatively straight-forward. The company was originally incorporated in Bermuda as a 'segregated cell company' (the Bermudian equivalent of a protected cell company) and it wished to redomicile (migrate) to Guernsey whilst maintaining its legal form as a protected cell company. The question arose as to whether as a matter of Guernsey law, the company could continue in Guernsey as a PCC or whether it had to first register as a company under the companies legislation before converting into a PCC in accordance with the PCC Ordinance.

Section 1(1) of the PCC Ordinance of Guernsey stated:

"it shall be lawful, subject to the provisions of this Ordinance:-

(a) To incorporate a company which shall be a protected cell company;

(b) To convert an existing company, if so authorised by its articles, into a protected cell company."

The definition of a protected cell company in Section 27 of the Ordinance was:

"a company incorporated as, or converted into, a protected cell company in accordance with the provisions of this Ordinance."

Thus in a decision delivered in open court granting consent to the application, it was reasoned:

"Advocate Moore argued that, following the enactment of the Migration Ordinance, the word "incorporation" is to be given a broad meaning. The natural meaning of the word "incorporated" suggests that a Company which was initially incorporated in a foreign jurisdiction cannot be said to have been incorporated in Guernsey. That interpretation, in my view, is confirmed by the wording of Section 6(1) of the Law of 1994 quoted above. A foreign company which migrates to Guernsey will be registered in Guernsey under the provisions of the Law of 1994, but it will never be considered to have been incorporated in Guernsey.

I therefore conclude that a foreign company can only become a protected cell company if it so converts in accordance with the requirements of the PCC Ordinance which include obtaining the consent of the Commission. Whether to grant such consent is, as I have said, a matter for the Commission and not one which requires the approval of the Royal Court.

In conclusion, if the Commission is able to grant, and does grant, consent for the conversion under Section 8 of the PCC Ordinance and if the Commission also grants consent to the migration of the company under the provisions of Section 5 of the Migration Ordinance, application may be made to the Royal Court for the company to be registered as a company under the Law of 1994. If so registered, it will then be a protected cell company in accordance with the provisions of the PCC Ordinance.

I should add that I accepted, without hearing from the Commission, that it would grant permission for this company to convert to a PCC. On a first reading of Section 8 of the PCC Ordinance I had assumed that the Commission could only grant a consent to an existing Guernsey company. Advocate Moore argued otherwise. Since I heard from Advocate Moore in Chambers, the Commission have granted consent for the company to convert into a protected cell company upon its migration.

An application has now been tabled for the Court to consent to the company's registration as a Guernsey protected cell company called Jubilee Absolute Return Fund PCC Ltd. The application is supported by the necessary consents (referred to above) from the Commission under the Migration Ordinance and the PCC

Ordinance. I am advised that all formalities had been complied with and I duly give the Court's consent."

More recently, Aon redomiciled one of of its two existing protected cell companies from Gibraltar to Malta. Its media statement on the subject read:

"White Rock, a unique group of insurance and reinsurance vehicles with operations in key domiciles including Bermuda, Gibraltar, Guernsey and Luxembourg, has today redomiciled White Rock Insurance (Europe) PCC Ltd (White Rock Europe) to Malta. This move further enhances White Rock's ability to meet the exacting needs of clients, broadening their domicile options for Protected Cell activities.

Owned by Aon, the White Rock companies offer clients a diverse suite of insurance solutions through utilisation of Protected Cell, Segregated Account and Rent-a-Captive facilities. Aon's leadership in this field is demonstrated in its innovative approach to these structures and our tight control framework, which ensures that clients' assets are well protected.

White Rock had two licensed PCCs in Gibraltar - White Rock Insurance (Gibraltar) PCC Ltd and White Rock Insurance (Europe) PCC Ltd.

White Rock Europe is able to provide private and multinational companies alike with fronting and/or retention facilities at competitive rates. It was formed in June 2005 responding to a specific need by clients for a PCC which was not a member of the terrorism pools in the EU. Since then, the company has enjoyed a high degree of success and today has six active cells writing annual premiums in excess of €30m with gross assets of over €47m." (24 October 2008).

This raises the next question: can a PCC amalgamate with another PCC or a non-PCC company? Here too, we have the benefit of a recent judicial decision in Guernsey: *In the proposed amalgamation of AB International Fund PCC Limited with AB Asia Pacific Growth Fund Limited – Royal Court (Civil Action File 1182) – 3 July 2008*

The facts and the decision are set out in the Guernsey Law Reports 2007–08 GLR 347:

"A Guernsey-registered protected cell company sought a ruling from the court as to whether it was able to amalgamate with a non-cellular company registered abroad, to be followed by the transfer of the assets and liabilities of that company to the new entity.

AB PCC, a Guernsey protected cell company, wished to amalgamate with AB Ltd., a non-cellular company registered in the British Virgin Islands. It proposed that the amalgamated company would be a protected cell company but with a new cell (the AD Cell) to which it would attribute the pre-amalgamation assets of AB Ltd.

The Guernsey Financial Services Commission required clarification before giving its consent to the proposals under s.2 of the Amalgamation of Companies Ordinance 1997. Consent was needed because AB PCC was a "supervised company" as defined in s.14 of that Ordinance, and neither the Amalgamation of Companies Ordinance nor the Protected Cell Companies Ordinance 1997, as amended, made express provision for the amalgamation of a protected cell company with any other company, whether cellular or non-cellular. The Commission required confirmation that the proposals would operate fairly both in respect of existing members of the amalgamating companies and also in relation to their creditors."

*"**Held,** approving the proposals:*

(1) Both AB PCC and AB Ltd. fell within the terms of the Amalgamation of Companies Ordinance and there was therefore no apparent legal objection to their amalgamating. Nothing in the policy documentation preceding the 1997 Ordinances indicated that the States intended to impose restrictions which would prevent the amalgamation of a protected cell company with another company — indeed, it was the intention to provide the finance industry with additional means of furthering its interests. It followed that it was permissible for PCC to amalgamate with AB Ltd. (para. 6; paras. 8–9).

(2) Since it was proposed that in the amalgamated company the assets of AB Ltd. be attributed to the AD Cell, it was only sensible that AB Ltd.'s pre-amalgamation liabilities should also attach to that cell, as it would be prejudicial to creditors if they were to attach to the non-cellular assets, or to the assets of other cells within the amalgamated company. If they were to attach to the AD Cell, creditors of AB Ltd. would be able to follow the assets into that cell and enforce their liabilities against the same assets previously available to them. Similarly, the assets and liabilities of pre-existing cells in AB PCC would remain unaffected by the amalgamation. Although s.8(d) of the Amalgamation of Companies Ordinance made it clear that the amalgamated company would be liable for the liabilities of the amalgamating companies, though did not state whether they were to attach to its cellular or non-cellular assets, the only fair way to give effect to the merger was to attach them to the new cell as proposed. This would be of major assistance in preventing prejudice to any party as a result of the amalgamation (paras. 12–14; para. 20).

(3) Since an amalgamation proposal was within the wide definition of "transaction" in the Protected Cell Companies Ordinance 1997, s.27, it followed that s.11 of that Ordinance would require the amalgamated company to identify

to the members and creditors of AB PCC and AB Ltd. the cells involved in the amalgamation, and thus ensure that AB Ltd.'s liabilities were properly attributed to the AD Cell (paras. 15–17).

(4) Once the Companies (Guernsey) Law 2008, s.61(1) came into force, an arrangement as authorized in the present case would become slightly more complicated, since a Guernsey protected cell company would then only be able to amalgamate with another such company or a foreign "body corporate of the same type." In the absence of any provision in that Law as to how such an amalgamation would be effected, however, it appeared fair and sensible to follow the pattern established in the present case and require each of the cells of the amalgamating companies to retain their separate identity and their separate assets and liabilities in the amalgamated company, so that the integrity of each cell would be unaffected by the merger (para. 9; para. 19)."

6.8.1. Why should a PCC be objectionable to a foreign jurisdiction?

"Owing to the ease with which companies can be formed in this country and owing to the rigidity with which the courts have applied the corporate entity doctrine ever since the calamitous decision in Salomon v. Salomon a single trader or group of traders are almost tempted by law to conduct their business in the form of a limited liability company even when no particular business risk is involved and where no outside credit is required.... The courts have failed to give that protection to the business creditors which should be the corollary of the privilege of limited liability."

(O Khahn Freud *"Some reflections on company law reform"*: 1944 7 MLR 54-66).

Is it surprising that many years after the House of Lords decision in *Salomon v. Salomon [1897] A.C. 22* the principle of limited liability was still the subject of such strong sentiments? Possibly not - few legal principles have aroused as much debate as limited liability has.

In this respect it is interesting to note that the legal consequence of a limited liability company is not that the company's liability is limited in any way. The company's liability is unlimited. It is the liability of the members that is limited. It is limited to the amount of paid up capital. The protected cell regime is an extension of this legal principle and limits the liability of a cell within a PCC to the assets attributable to that particular cell. The liability of the cell is similarly unlimited but the only recourse is to the assets of *that* cell, and in the event of a shortfall, the creditors have no recourse to the assets of any other cell. Other than in the case of involuntary creditors, this is no more objectionable than the principle of limited liability itself. Indeed, for every cell created by a PCC, the promoters could have achieved the same level of protection by incorporating a separate subsidiary of the main operating company with limited liability and conducting the relevant business activity through a separate limited company.

This allocation of capital and assets to specific cells can, in substance, be seen as a capital and creditor protection rule. The creditors and the shareholders who hold cell shares have rights only in respect of the assets, the capital and the profits of the respective cell. During liquidation creditors are exclusively satisfied by the assets of the respective cell except in a case where certain assets have not been attributed to any cell (the non-cellular assets). In those cases, the non-cellular assets will satisfy the debts of a non-cellular creditor.

In recent years Guernsey (and other jurisdictions) have implemented legislation allowing for the incorporation of cells. Under Incorporated Cell Company (ICC) legislation an incorporated cell (unlike a cell in a PCC) is therefore a separate legal entity (and as such, inter-cell contracts are permitted). The 'Certificate of Registration' of a Guernsey incorporated cell would certify that *"that the Memorandum and Articles of Association of [IC [ABC] Limited] were registered on the Records of the Island of Guernsey.... pursuant to an Act of the Royal Court of the said Island ....".*

Clearly an ICC performs the same function as a PCC but is intended to address the perceived legal uncertainty of whether a foreign jurisdiction, which does not have PCC legislation, will recognise the cell structure. So the argument goes: the cell is incorporated, its members have limited liability, it can be liquidated like an ordinary company, and all assets attributable to the incorporated cell are available to meet the claims of creditors of that cell; therefore a foreign jurisdiction should treat it as it would any other incorporated company with limited liability and not as segregating assets in the same company for particular creditors to the exclusion of others. The argument is not without its conceptual difficulties. A foreign court may also not take this at face value. In essence, it is being told to look at the separate legal status of the cell and not to look 'through it'.

An involuntary creditor could feel justifiably that there is no difference in substance between a PCC and an ICC. In substance, the structure remains the same as a PCC. The distinction the ICC seeks to draw is the incorporation and separate legal existence of each cell. It is still intended to achieve the segregation of assets and liabilities within a single business form but through the medium of multiple 'incorporated' cells.

A foreign court would be expected under rules of private international law to recognise the cell's incorporated status as conferring the legal attributes of a stand-alone company especially as far as creditors are concerned. Although the 'incorporated cell' is not a corporate form which a foreign court would likely be familiar with under local law, in any foreign proceedings it would be asked to rule that any question of liability of the cell is governed by the law of the state of 'incorporation', notwithstanding that a court in a legal system based on English or US law, would still have inherent power to lift the corporate veil as between cells.

If a foreign court accepts without legal or conceptual difficulty that the incorporated cell's liability is a matter for the law of incorporation, it should be no less inclined under private international law to apply foreign substantive law and hence foreign PCC legislation to the same issue rather than local law.

The ICC was therefore conceived in Guernsey in order to try to strengthen the argument in favour of the foreign recognition for the cell structure. The PCC was in effect put into a legal laboratory and the ICC came out. According to its creation theory, it may look like a PCC, and may perform the same function as a PCC, but it is a different legal animal. The danger with this is that, by implication, the suggestion may be that the PCC is defective. The fact that the PCC has not been judicially tested, does not make it any more defective than the ICC or any other new corporate form for that matter. Even so, the ICC raises a potential legal problem of its own that a PCC does not, namely the risk of a foreign court lifting the 'corporate veil' as between incorporated cells.

It is also important to point out as we will see in the insolvency chapters of the book that a PCC established in the EU would enjoy the protection of the EU insolvency regime and in this respect neither Gibraltar nor Malta should face the same uncertainty as a Guernsey PCC would in EU insolvency proceedings. Consequently, a PCC jurisdiction in the EU does not need ICC legislation. In fact, the contrary view prevails: an EU PCC is established in a corporate form which is recognised across the EU, namely a 'limited company with shares', whereas an incorporated cell of an ICC does not.

The EU territory aside, the next leading trading nation is the US. Save for the risk of lifting the veil, would an ICC offer significantly more protection in US court proceedings than a PCC would? Many US states already have PCC or Series LLC legislation or both and recognition of a foreign regime also known to local law should not be an issue in any legal proceedings in those states.

It should further be noted that PCC legislation is by no means the only example of laws passed in one jurisdiction with potential extraterritorial application.

In the 1980s and 1990s, for example, banking mergers were facilitated in a number of jurisdictions by private Acts of the local legislature. The alternative would have been to effect a transfer of all the assets and liabilities separately from one bank to another (including seeking third party consents where contractually bound to do so). That would have been cumbersome and costly. A private Act of the local parliament, on the other hand, gave effect to the merger as a legislative measure. Given the international nature of the banking system, it is very likely that certain assets and liabilities would have been situated outside the jurisdiction and that such assets and liabilities would ordinarily have had to be transfered separately in accordance with local laws. Assuming, however, that certain residual assets and liabilities were not transfered (e.g. they remained unidentified or not transfered by the appropriate instrument of transfer), it is unlikely that this would have stood in the way of the merger in the home jurisdiction.

According to one view a legislative measure in one jurisdiction concerning an entity which owed its existence and supervision to local law (and therefore governing the rights and obligations of third parties) would have extraterritorial operation and should be given effect to by a foreign court provided it was not penal in nature. More so if the relevant legislation made express provision for extraterritorial application:

"7(1) So far as—

(a) the legislative power of the Legislative Assembly permits; and

(b) is consistent with the object of this Act; it is intended that regulations made for section 5 should apply in relation to—

(c) land and things situated outside the ACT, whether within or outside Australia; and

(d) acts done, transactions entered into, events occurring and matters arising outside the ACT, whether within or outside Australia; and

(e) things, acts, transactions, events and matters that would, but for this Act, be governed or otherwise affected by the law of a foreign country."[79]

Nevertheless, in the authors' view jurisdictions need to continue to jealously guard their reputation and avoid being accused of abusing the extraterritorial legislative powers of the State. This tension between advancing the commercial interests of PCC promoters and safeguarding the reputation of the jurisdiction is echoed in Section 6(3) of the Bermudan Segregated Accounts Companies Act 2000 (as amended): *"The Registrar may (a) impose such conditions on the registration of a company as he may consider necessary to ensure the reputation of Bermuda and in particular, to vet the account owners of segregated accounts and to ensure compliance with the Act; (b) require the company to take certain steps or refrain from adopting or pursuing a particular course of action or to restrict the scope of its segregated accounts business in a particular way."*

To conclude, the PCC offers significant opportunities and has been widely used by:

(a) Insurance brokers and insurers

(b) Banks

(c) Investment and fund managers

(d) International tax planning professional advisers.

There may be a tendency to dismiss PCCs as an offshore innovation that has no place in the mainstream financial markets. The reality, as the co-authors hope we have seen, is very different. PCC legislation now exists in many jurisdictions. There is certainly now a strong argument in favour of recognition for the protected cell regime thorough an international convention.

In the next chapters we will consider the insolvency principles relevant to PCCs.

---

[79] The Bank Mergers Act 1997 (Australian Capital Territory)

7. BASIC INSOLVENCY PRINCIPLES RELEVANT TO PCCs

It is important to know basic insolvency principles and terms, to see whether a PCC conflicts with those basic principles. These include:

- *Pari Passu* – the process whereby creditors' claims are weighted;
- Hotch pot – protection for creditors from an individual creditor making several claims in different jurisdictions in order to increase his share; and
- Insolvency Practitioner ("IP").

These, and other terms and concepts relating to insolvency, are discussed in the section below.

7.1. Pari Passu

As will be noted throughout this book, the fundamental PCC problem is its apparent abrogation of the *pari passu* principle. The *pari passu* principle depends on the notion of *"collective insolvency"*, as referred to in various international insolvency regimes. Under collective insolvency, a previous bilateral relationship between a single creditor and now insolvent debtor becomes a multi-lateral relationship between the creditors (or a class of them) and the debtor; thus resulting in a 'common pool' approach to the insolvent debtor. The common pool approach has chronological significance. Regardless (usually) of when the debt was incurred prior to insolvency, the debt now shares in the common pool. Debts incurred after this common pooling will rank ahead of debts which were incurred before the common pooling. The common pooling is the formal insolvency process, whatever its form (administration, liquidation, etc). *Pari passu* follows from collectivity. *Pari passu* requires that all debts of equivalent ranking arithmetically abate. This is based upon their proportionate share of the common pool of assets available. Their return on this abatement is their dividend. In short *"par est condicio omniun creditorum"* or *"the conditions of all creditors is equal"*.

7.1.1. Pari Passu and PCCs internationally

The core doubt as to a PCC is that it apparently abandons the universally accepted notions of *pari passu* and collectivity. Hence the enforcement of the PCC cellular priority via an insolvency process, particularly outside of the PCC home jurisdiction, may not be recognised. Consequently, PCC promoters advise that a PCC: (a) should hold all its assets within a PCC jurisdiction, ideally its incorporation home jurisdiction; (b) should manage its affairs entirely within the jurisdiction; and (c) subject all its contracts to that jurisdiction's law. To which the authors would add, "and choose a PCC jurisdiction, that in the event of PCC cellular priority being called into account in a non-PCC jurisdiction through an insolvency, will have the advantage of international recognition, most notably the EU Regulation[80] (the Regulations as implementing the Directives in the member states)."

7.2. Hotch pot

Hotch pot is the process designed to preclude an individual creditor from increasing their dividend from the common pool by exploiting multi-jurisdictional insolvency processes. A debtor may have 'several common pools'. This would stem from several jurisdictions and creditors can claim (for whatever reason) in those several pools. Thus this creditor has a comparative advantage over a creditor who cannot so claim. The several common pools usually stem from several insolvency processes taking place with regard to several sets of local assets (the several common pools). This is compounded by the lack of co-ordination between the several sets of insolvencies. Hotch pot therefore requires that account be taken of the claimant creditor who can advance these several claims. The PCC hotch pot problem, however, is even more complicated than the usual hotch pot problem. Why? Because the *raison d'être* of the PCC is to create 'several common pools' within one PCC. So, does a cell creditor of (say) cell X of ABC PCC Ltd (established according to the PCC legislation of its home incorporation State, jurisdiction 123) have a claim against (say) cell Y in an insolvency 'relating to' ABC PCC Ltd in jurisdiction 345; and if so, how is it to be calculated, if it is not to be recognised in any insolvency in jurisdiction 123?

7.3. 'Pro-Creditor' v 'Pro-Debtor'

In their treatment of insolvency, jurisdictions have traditionally been regarded as existing on a spectrum; a spectrum from extremely pro-creditor through to moderately pro-creditor, thence to moderately pro-debtor and thence to extremely pro-debtor. Internationally, there has been a movement to the centre ground. In pro-creditor jurisdictions, as the epithet suggests, creditors' rights are paramount. In pro-debtor jurisdictions, the rights of the insolvent entity are paramount. Insolvency processes are a sword in pro-creditor jurisdictions: the creditor attacks the insolvent entity to ensure it pays its debts (or rather a proportion) without

---

[80] "The EU Regulation" includes the Directive which has direct effect, and implementing Regulations of the member states. It is for this reason we have used the term "Regulation".

further delay. In pro-debtor jurisdictions, a debtor seeks protection from its creditors, through an insolvency process: it's a shield, therefore.

The UK and English law influenced jurisdictions (save for the US) have traditionally been seen as pro-creditor. However, particularly with the growth of the Administration Order since 1986 within the UK, as with most jurisdictions, the UK is moving to the centre ground. The UK Administration Order is seen as pro-debtor because one of its goals is the *"rescuing the company as a going concern [see 7.6.1"Rescue Culture" below]* [s.8(3)(a) Insolvency Act 1986 as amended by the Enterprise Act 2002]". The majority of the PCC jurisdictions are Common Law (whether totally or partially) and are, therefore, heavily influenced by English law. As such, with the very notable exception of the US, they have been perceived as pro-creditor jurisdictions. Most of the PCC jurisdictions have moved with the 'Mother Country' towards a more centre-grounded, less pro-creditor stance. This is especially if they are connected to the UK, such as the Crown Dependencies (i.e. the Isle of Man and the Channel Islands) or Overseas Territories (such as Gibraltar, BVI, Cayman Islands and Bermuda *et al*). This move has often been achieved by introducing a process modelled on the UK Administration Order. Strangely, these Administration Orders are often only introduced in respect of PCCs. There could be a variety of reasons for this:

1. The introduction of PCCs has been relatively new. There may not therefore have been a chance to review the jurisdiction's insolvency legislation wholeheartedly. Thus there is just a partial revamping via the PCC legislation.
2. Possibly, because of the need to have so many terms to distinguish between cellular and hub/core (in this book the terms are used interchangeably) insolvencies.

Alternatively, the rationale may simply be: Administration Orders were brought in to allow for specific naming. 'This is a new style of company. So let us have an updated insolvency regime at the same time as creating the new (i.e. PCC) regime'.

How, if at all, does the interplay between pro-creditor and pro-debtor stances affect PCCs? Before analysing this, it is necessary to consider who are a PCC's stakeholders. For this analysis the stakeholders are limited to creditors, debtors, shareholders, and shareholders are also often debtors and/or creditors. Shareholders can be debtors or creditors at either the hub or cellular level. A PCC's *raison d'être* is creditor protection i.e. creditors cannot attack the whole of the company's assets, but rather only those attributed to the relevant cell and/or for hub. This is achieved by firewalling (also called ring-fencing) cells from unconnected creditor attack. However, this is only half of the story. Cell creditors are likely to be, in the main, connected creditors. The normal pro-debtor analysis as being pro-non-creditor stakeholders, notably the shareholders, is misplaced within a PCC. Cellular creditors tend to be (in the case of an insurance PCC, the insured) stakeholder. Indeed, in those jurisdictions that allow for cells to have separate shareholding, the cell shareholders and majority creditors are often one. Thus, whilst the majority of the PCC jurisdictions are pro-creditor, this pro-creditor stance, also assists the otherwise competing stakeholder; the otherwise competing stakeholding being the shareholder or quasi-shareholder in each cell. Consequently, even if a PCC insolvency occurred in a non-PCC pro-debtor jurisdiction, under pro-debtor rules, it may not have such a deleterious effect on the creditors; that is provided those creditors were also shareholders.

7.4. The Insolvency Practitioner

The Insolvency Practitioner (IP) is a term used in this book to describe an individual (or in some jurisdictions a body) responsible for administering an insolvency. The majority of PCC jurisdictions (with the possible exception of the US with its debtor-in-possession) require that after a formal insolvency has been declared, an individual independent of the insolvent entity is appointed over the insolvent entity. This individual may be in private practice or may be a public official. This book often uses the term "IP" to avoid terms such as administrator, liquidator, etc, which may have specific procedural implications in any given jurisdiction. For the purpose of this book therefore, an IP could be appointed over a cell and/or the hub.

7.5. Internationalism v Nationalism

It is beyond our remit to discuss cross-border insolvency theories in detail. However, a basic understanding of international insolvency theory is necessary in order to understand the concerns arising from a PCC insolvency. Two competing theories offer different explanations of cross-border insolvency: internationalism (or the 'unity theory') versus nationalism (or the 'territoriality theory'). Unity theory expounds a single co-ordinated insolvency regime. Territorial theory expands local control over local assets. The world is moving towards internationalism with the Model Law and EU Regulation, which are discussed in this book. The PCC mantra of 'keep PCC assets within the PCC jurisdiction' accepts the territorial theory. Unless a PCC can take advantage of international codes (especially in this context as we will see, the jurisdiction of Gibraltar) it is best to observe the above mantra. Despite internationalism, even in internationalist regimes (i.e. those that have adopted the Model Law) and internationally open jurisdictions (namely, the US and the UK, both of which have adopted the Model Law and are major open trading nations), the local jurisdiction can still become territorial; this is especially if the insolvency consequences of accepting 'internationalism' are *"contrary to public policy"* (a term taken from the Model Law and the EU Regulation). As we shall see the apparent PCC abandonment of *pari passu* may be classed as *"contrary to public policy"*. As we shall see internationalism requires a *"main insolvency proceeding"* and *"secondary"* (being the EU Regulation terminology) or *"non-main proceedings"* (being the Model Law terminology). The object of a PCC IP (i.e. an IP in control of a PCC insolvency) who wishes to maintain cellular integrity is to get the main proceedings in a PCC friendly (ideally the home) jurisdiction. Further, for the secondary (and hopefully, therefore, subservient proceedings) to be subsumed into the main proceedings. In order to do this, ideally the *"secondary"* or *"non-main proceedings"* should be in an internationalist State (i.e. a Model Law enacting State) that would not regard a PCC's apparent abrogation of *pari passu* as *"contrary to public policy"*.

States have traditionally enforced territoriality in insolvency proceedings. International enforcement conventions (i.e. the Brussels and Lugano Conventions) have traditionally excluded insolvency. Nationalist outlooks have predominated. The view has been 'local assets for local creditors'. Only recently has internationalism grown. This book will concentrate inevitability on internationalism and the international or transnational insolvency regimes. This is because the book looks to how a PCC structure can be enforced internationally. However, this international focus should not lead the reader astray. Internationalism does not dominate the world of insolvency. The authors suspect that internationalism may well be tested when it comes to PCCs.

7.6. Seat Theory v Centre of Main Interest (COMI)

Given the internationalist (or, in the case of the EU Regulation, trans-nationalist) outlook of many jurisdictions, the major question becomes: 'how is the location of main proceedings ascertained?' Two competing theories explain this process.

The seat theory states that the insolvency of a legal person (we are here not concerned with natural persons) should be conducted by the locals of the incorporation jurisdiction. Thus if (say) a Manx PCC became insolvent, the insolvency should be governed by the laws of The Isle of

Man. The rationale for this theory is contractual. The entity established itself in that jurisdiction. Thus, its rights and obligations are settled by that jurisdiction. Further, 'this choice of law' adds certainty.

The competing theory is the Centre of Main Interest ("COMI") theory. The COMI theory states that the insolvency should be concluded where the entity did its primary business and had its most impact. International regimes (in this context we primarily refer to the EU Regulation and the Model Law) refer to both the seat and COMI theories. However, the EU Insurance Insolvency Regulations refer to the incorporation jurisdiction only (i.e. the seat theory). In the case of highly regulated companies, such as insurance companies, it is best that the local regulator governs any unfortunate insolvency, because the seat theory is the most relevant. In regulated industries, the rights and obligations of the company are far greater than those in unregulated industries. It is for this reason, as we shall see that for PCCs operating in regulated industries, the promoters should eschew Offshore Financial Centres ('OFCs') that preclude their corporate vehicles from operating in their own jurisdiction. In such an OFC jurisdiction, the COMI could therefore be in a PCC unfriendly jurisdiction, that is, it would not be in the home jurisdiction. One of the problems with COMI is its vagueness. There can only ever be one seat. But there can be competing COMIs. Regulated industries need to know their regulator at the outset.

In both the Model Law and the EU Regulation regimes the incorporation jurisdiction is presumed to be the COMI. However, this is a rebuttable presumption. Given the preponderance of insurance PCCs, a PCC established in a reputable jurisdiction, especially one governed by a mandatory insolvency regime (such as the EU Insolvency Insurance Regulation more especially, Gibraltar and Malta) should have its priority regime (i.e. its cellular regime) recognised extra-territorially. As to the rebuttable presumption (for non-insurance companies within the EU, i.e. companies under the EU Regulation and/or outside of the EU, and/or the UNCITRAL Model Law) the ever present mantra of keeping PCC assets within the PCC jurisdiction is extended to, 'and keep the management of the PCC in the PCC jurisdiction'.

7.6.1. Rescue Culture

The term 'rescue culture' has become a fashionable epithet in international insolvency circles. It represents a belief that the insolvency process should be seen as a value-added commercial process rather than a merely legalistic burial of the business. Its practical ramifications are to move previously pro-debtor jurisdictions to a more pro-creditor stance. In that sense it augurs well for the recognition of a PCC's priority.

7.6.2. Transnational and International Insolvency Regimes

A distinction is sometimes drawn between transnational and international regimes. The contrast can be seen in the difference between the EU Regulation and the Model Law. The EU Regulation has a final overarching judicial process (the European Court of Justice or "ECJ") which transcends national boundaries. Contrariwise the implementation of the Model Law relies entirely upon national courts. Transnational regimes therefore have greater clout than international regimes.

A general theme of this book is that PCCs should operate wherever possible within an international or transnational regime. Why? Provided that the COMI of the PCC is within its incorporation jurisdiction, then provided its other or 'secondary' activities occur within internationalist jurisdictions (i.e. those jurisdictions which recognise the COMI) these other or 'secondary jurisdictions' will follow *'the main proceedings'*. Consequently there will be a greater tendency to recognise the PCC priority structure.

A related concept is 'extraterritoriality' whereby a national jurisdiction claims that its jurisdiction extends beyond the relevant national boundaries. This book will consider extra-territorial regimes. More especially within the UK context, section 426 and Part V of the Insolvency Act 1986.

We will concentrate on two sets of international or transnational regimes; the EU (more especially, the EU Regulation and the EU Insurance Insolvency Regulations) and the Model Law regimes. Mention is also made of the UK section 426 Insolvency Act 1986 (and other Commonwealth counterparts) and Part V of the Insolvency Act 1986. The possible over-representation of UK procedures is explained by: the over-representation of PCC jurisdictions based upon English law; the internationalism of the UK insolvency process in both admitting foreign insolvency law (i.e. but not limited to the Model Law) and its willingness to export its own insolvency law (in its Part V claim to extraterritoriality); and finally, we admit it, the authors' joint training in English law.

Some international conventions and regimes, to the extent that they can be said to even exist, are overlooked. The Latin American regime[81] is ignored because there are no PCC jurisdictions in Latin America.[82] The Nordic insolvency regime[83] is ignored because there are no PCC states in the Nordic countries and two of the Nordic countries (Sweden and Finland) are in any event bound by the EU Regulation. Whilst Denmark is part of the Nordic Convention and part of the EU, as we shall see, it is excluded from the EU Regulation. As to the North American Free Trade Area ("NAFTA") and its *"principles of cooperation amongst NAFTA countries"*, and its nascent transnational regime, whilst there are a large number of US states with PCC legislation, all three NAFTA members (Mexico, US and Canada) members have adopted the UNCITRAL Model Law. Therefore it is the Model Law, not any NAFTA arrangement which is of importance. Finally, the Council of Europe (via the Istanbul Conference of 1990) transnational regime is ignored because, despite being in existence for nearly two decades, it remains unratified. Having said that, the Istanbul Conference has some background significance in that it serves as the basis for the EU Regulation.

7.6.3. Preferential or priority creditors and involuntary creditors

The rights both of these classes of creditor (to the extent that they are different classes) will impact dramatically upon the rights of a PCC. More especially the PCC's right in insolvency to enforce its own segregated priority structure.

Internationally there are two accepted historical deviations from *pari passu*: (i) preferential or priority creditors (we shall tend to use the term 'preferential creditors' in this book) and (ii) secured or *in rem* creditors (we shall tend to use the term '*in rem* creditors' in this book) and as to (ii) see below. The term 'involuntary creditor' is not an exception to the *pari passu* principle. However many preferential creditors are often claimed to be involuntary creditors. Preferential creditors are in the main State creditors (i.e. for taxes, imposts, fines, etc) and/or employee creditors (wages, redundancy, holiday pay, pensions, etc); or indeed a combination of both, such as payroll taxes, national insurance contributions, State guarantee funds and the like.

---

[81] Based on the Montevideo Conventions of 1889 and 1940, and the Bustamante Code of the 1928 Havana Conference.

[82] Apart from Belize possibly, which is not a signatory in any event.

[83] The Nordic Bankruptcy Convention of 1933.

Preferential creditors are granted priority in an insolvency. Consequently they do not abate rateably with other creditors. They are paid off first and then *pari passu* is applied to remaining creditors. However, the extent of their priority is often capped both chronologically (i.e. the liability must have occurred before a certain date before insolvency) or financially (i.e. the amount claimed cannot exceed a certain limit). If there are insufficient assets to pay the full extent of the priority of the preferential creditors, then the preferential creditors tend to abate rateably amongst themselves, i.e. a separate *pari passu* calculation applies to the preferential creditors.

This UK prioritisation of preferential debts is set out (by way of example) in section 175 of the Insolvency Act 1986:

"175 (1) [payment in priority] In a winding up the company's preferential debts shall be paid in priority to all other debts.

175 (2) [ranking in priority] Preferential debts –

(a) rank equally amongst themselves after the expenses of the winding up and shall be paid in full, unless the assets are insufficient to meet them, in which case they abate in equal proportions."

State creditors and to a lesser extent perhaps employee creditors did not choose to be creditors. In many cases the relationship between the State and the insolvent entity was that of a trust relationship, whereby the insolvent held money (such as in the case of value-added taxes) as a trustee for the beneficiary State.

An involuntary creditor is not limited to the apocryphal tortious claimant (e.g. a driver of a van of the insolvent entity hit the claimant creditor and obviously he had no choice in the matter of becoming a creditor of the insolvent entity); but is claimed to extend to other claimants, more especially preferential creditors. As can be seen the apocryphal involuntary (but not preferential) creditor is often protected by cut-through provisions (see the Rights of Third Parties Act 1932) whereby a claimant creditor can claim directly against the insurance policy of the insolvent entity.

What problems are posed for a PCC by the existence of preferential and/or involuntary creditors?

As to the preferential creditor, the obvious question is: Does the priority accorded to the preferential creditor apply to the PCC as a whole, and thereby abrogating its particular cellular priority structure, or does it recognise the PCC priority structure and therefore apply, as attributed, on a cell by cell or hub basis? Supplemental questions exist, notably given that the priority structure accorded to preferential creditors is a national policy decision, to what extent can national policy be overridden by the priority structure of a PCC without becoming contrary to national public policy? Further, the obvious supplemental real politick aspect: Would the existence of preferential creditors in large numbers affect judicial sympathy in a non-PCC jurisdiction? Finally, when considering transnational and international regimes, there are various carve-out clauses whereby COMI law is overridden by local law. Two important carve-out exceptions exist: preferential and *in rem* creditors.

As to the involuntary creditor, to the extent that the involuntary creditor is not otherwise protected, it is obvious that judicial sympathy will lie with the same. Commentators generally recognise that the involuntary creditor is perhaps the greatest threat to the international enforcement of a PCC priority in an insolvency. The rationale is easy. The voluntary creditors knew what they were doing. The involuntary creditor did not and therefore should not suffer because of this novel format.

7.6.4. Secured or *in rem* creditors

The second historically internationally accepted exception to *pari passu* is the secured or *in rem* (this book will tend to use the term "*in rem*") creditor. An *in rem* creditor should be contrasted with an *in personam* creditor. An *in rem* creditor has a claim against an asset, i.e. his claim is secured as against that asset. Contrariwise an *in personam* creditor has a claim against an entity and not an asset, i.e. his claim is unsecured. International regimes (more especially the EU Regulation and the UNCITRAL Model Law) allow for local (i.e. *'secondary'* or *non-main proceedings'*) law to dictate *in rem* outcomes, as opposed to the COMI law. One rationale for this carve-out is that *in rem* rights often need to be registered, i.e. it would have to be registered in the local appropriate registry. Failure to register a claimed or purported *in rem* right often leads to it being forfeited.

For PCCs, there are two major *in rem* considerations; one practical and one theoretical. Practically, if the *in rem* right has to be registered, how is it to be registered, when the local non-PCC jurisdiction registry will not take account of a cellular structure? Theoretically, is a creditor's claim to have a right to the prior satisfaction of his claims from a specific nominated group of assets (i.e. the assets attributable to a given cell) an *in rem* right; and if so what follows?

7.6.5. Antecedent transactions or detrimental acts

'Antecedent transactions' is the term used in UK law and 'detrimental acts' is the term used in the EU Regulation and UNCITRAL Model Law (in this book the terms are used interchangeably) to describe nefarious actions in the run-up to the formal insolvency which disturb the collective insolvency process. Examples of such transactions are sales or gifts of property at an undervalue, especially to a connected party and paying off a creditor, especially a connected creditor, before other creditors. International insolvency regimes, such as the EU Regulation and the UNCITRAL Model Law, tend to provide that such transactions will be dealt under local (i.e. *'secondary'* or *'non-main proceedings'*) law as opposed to COMI law. A PCC must tend to complicate antecedent transaction considerations. Various questions can be posed. For instance, is the mere creation of a PCC an antecedent transaction, and/or can antecedent transactions exist *inter ce* cells?

8. EU REGIMES: AN INTRODUCTION

8.1. Background

There is a natural reluctance of States to enforce a foreign insolvency law within their own jurisdiction. This is even more especially a foreign insolvency law that may seem to eschew *pari passu* principles. It is for that reason that most commentators recommend that a PCC is subject only to the laws of its home jurisdiction. Thus, in the event of its insolvency, its assets (and for that matter its liabilities) are held within the incorporation jurisdiction. Further, all of its contracts should be subject to the law of the incorporation jurisdiction. However, that may not always be possible. So, we need to look at international conventions and the like to consider the international enforceability of the cellular structure of a PCC in the event of its insolvency.

Arguably the most important transnational insolvency regime is that of the EU. This is for four reasons:

1. the EU trading bloc is enormous and consequently so will be the demand by end-users for PCCs;
2. the EU insolvency regime is the most integrationist of the transnational regimes. Consequently if a PCC is recognised within an EU insolvency, then respect for the cellular structure is likely to be accorded throughout the EU;
3. the truly international regime (that of the UN and its UNCITRAL Model Law) share many characteristics, including general concepts and specific language, with the EU regime: there will inevitably therefore be substantial cross-fertilisation; and
4. whilst other EU states may allow for contractual PCCs, there are two statutory avowedly PCC regimes within the EU, Gibraltar and Malta. This is in addition to regimes in France and Luxembourg which are not avowedly PCC regimes, but certainly look to the authors like PCCs. Given the existence of these two statutory PCC regimes, it is probable that EU end-users will therefore tend to use a statutory regime (with its claimed greater certainty) henceforth. Further it is hoped that the existence of the EU insolvency regime would allow for intra-EU enforcement of Gibraltar and Malta PCC statutory derogations from the normal (i.e. non-cellular) *pari passu* principle.

This chapter will therefore consider in detail the EU insolvency regime and the PCC regimes of Gibraltar and Malta, and the interaction between these regimes. As can be seen all these regimes (both at the EU and State level) are novel and in the case of *"investment undertakings"* at the EU level merely nascent.

Much of what we have to say is necessarily conjecture. There has been no intra-EU PCC insolvency, to date. There have been very few instances worldwide where the Courts have addressed a PCC insolvency. One case is the Messenger Case. Whilst based in Europe (Guernsey and the UK) the Messenger Case was not directly subject to the EU insolvency regime as Guernsey is not within the EU. Whilst it could have been based on the 'Commonwealth insolvency regime' (i.e. see section 426 of the UK Insolvency Act 1986), it appears to have been settled without recourse to internationalist regimes. As to PCCs generally, there is a developing EU insolvency jurisprudence, which can be of assistance in commenting on PCCs. This is more especially as to the recognition of COMI.

8.2. Relevant EU Directives and Regulations; an introduction

The EU insolvency regime segregates five types of institution:

(i) "insurance undertakings";[84]
(ii) "credit institutions";[85]
(iii) "investment undertakings" which provide services involving the holding of funds or securities for third parties (a Directive has yet to be promulgated, although one is promised);
(iv) "collective investment undertakings" (a Directive has yet to be promulgated, although one is promised); and
(v) 'everybody else' not covered by the above.[86]

Each has or will have its own separate sub-regime.

Initial PCC development was spurred by insurance industry demands and the use of PCCs for captive insurance continues unabated. Consequently the EU Insolvency Insurance Directive is of paramount importance. Whilst PCC uses continue to develop, there has been negligible use of PCCs to create banks, or credit institutions, or indeed institutions however described that would fall under the auspices of the EU Insolvency Banking Directive. Thus the EU Insolvency Banking Directive is not further considered.

---

[84] Directive 2001/17/EC, *et al*, *"the EU Insolvency Insurance Regulation"*

[85] Directive 2001/24/EC, *et al*, *"the EU Insolvency Banking Directive"*

[86] Council Regulation 1346/2000, *"the EU Regulation"*

Whilst the initial development of PCCs involved insurance, currently asset management presents some very exciting PCC development. Thus any discussion of EU insolvency law and its recognition of PCCs should ideally consider both *'investmemt undertaking'* and *'collective investment undertakings'*. Unfortunately the EU Insolvency Insurance Directive, the EU Insolvency Banking Directive and the EU Regulation all specifically exclude from their ambit, *"investment undertakings"* and *"collective investment undertakings"*, and the EU has yet to promulgate *"investment undertakings"* and *"collective investment undertakings"* directives. Consequently the insolvency of such undertakings (regardless of whether they involve a PCC) falls into an EU black hole. Whilst some residual EU (or EU inspired) law and intra-EU judicial cooperation may apply, the insolvency of such undertakings will primarily be governed national law; and if applicable non-EU transnational law, i.e. the UNCITRAL Model Law.

Whilst it is correct to say that PCC development has been driven by insurance and asset management requirements, PCCs have a number of other uses which would fall under the EU Regulation. Indeed because there is some doubt as to reinsurance, (i.e. does it fall within the EU Insolvency Insurance Directive), insurance companies (and thereby insurance PCCs) may fall under the EU Regulation; that is if they are involved with re-insurance. The EU Regulation should be the starting point for any intra-EU PCC insolvency analysis. Indeed, because the EU Regulation's language and concepts show great similarity to the UNCITRAL Model Law, it should be analysed in detail for that reason alone. Whilst the language and concepts of the EU Regulation and the EU Insolvency Insurance Regulation are similar, there are some important differences (such as "the Centre of Main Interest" or "COMI" and EU harmonisation). An explanation of both the EU Regulation and the EU Insolvency Insurance Regulation, is ideally served by a comparison between them.

The EU allows for three principal forms of EU law[87], excluding constituting treaties which give rise to law:

- Regulations;
- Directives; and
- Decisions.

[87] See Article 249 of the EC Treaty.

All three forms of EU law have a different legal impact and this different legal impact needs to be addressed in any analysis. Whilst legal impact may differ, generally EU law is supreme over national law (see section 2 of the European Communities Act 1972). In interpreting EU law member State courts are bound by principles laid down by the European Court of Justice ("ECJ", see Section 3 of the European Communities Act 1972).

9. THE EU REGULATION: AN OVERVIEW

9.1. The EU Regulation: a detailed analysis of its PCC relevant provisions

9.1.1. Introduction

The EU Regulation consists of the EU Regulation proper and an accompanying guide, the Virgos-Schmit Report.

9.1.2. Article 1. Ambit

9.1.3. The initial question

Article 1(1) states positively the ambit: *"This Regulation shall apply to collective insolvency proceedings which entail the partial or total divestment of a debtor and the appointment of a liquidator"*. There is thus a cumulative fourfold test for inclusion. This quote gives rise to the most important EU Regulation PCC question: Does a PCC insolvency (whether of a cell or of the hub) give rise to *"collective insolvency proceedings"*, involving a *"partial or total divestment"* through a *"liquidator"* (however defined) of a *"debtor"* (however defined) within the (and at the time of writing it can only be within the perceived) ambit of Article 1 (1)? Initially each word within the phrase *"collective insolvency proceedings"* (and the other emphasised words or phrases) needs to be analysed. Guidance can be obtained from both the Recital and the accompanying official Virgos-Schmit Report.

Are *"the debtor"* and *"legal person"* the same?

Recital 9 commences: *"This Regulation should apply to* ***insolvency proceedings****, whether the* ***debtor*** *is a natural person or a* ***legal person****, a trader or an individual"*. The Virgos-Schmit Report comment on *"debtor"* (paragraph 53) commences: *"Finally, Article 1(1) does not require that a debtor have a particular status"*. Consequently *"debtor"* could include a cell. However it continues: *"The Convention applies equally to all proceedings, whether these involve a natural person or a legal person, a trader or individual"*. A cell is arguably neither of these descriptions.

The vast majority of PCC statutes worldwide (including in this context, the two most relevant, Gibraltar and Malta) specifically state that a cell does not have a separate legal identity. Consequently a cell is therefore not a *"legal person"*. Obviously a cell cannot be a natural person. The reference to *"a trader or an individual"* is to cover those jurisdictions (such as Italy) that may not allow for personal consumer insolvencies (and the like) and consequently would not apply to a cell insolvency. Given that a *"legal person"* is essentially the same as a *"debtor"* (within Article 1(1)) it would seem that a cell is also not a *"debtor"* within Article 1(1). In virtually every other type of *"legal person"*, the *"debtor"* and the *"legal person"* are the same. What makes a PCC different is the fact that the *"legal person"* (i.e. as most obviously represented by the hub) is not necessarily the same as the *"debtor"* (i.e. the cell). There are two ways of anaylsing the PCC debtor conundrum. Both ways give rise to issues. First is to say that the cell is the debtor. The alternative second view is to say the PCC is the debtor, but the debtor only has rights as against the relevant cell assets. Both views represent deviations from the normal company debtor relationship. The EU Regulation preceded the introduction of PCC legislation by Member States, but given this PCC divergence from the legal norm it would be understandable if the EU Regulation draftsmen failed to take account of the same. At first sight, therefore, a cell insolvency (as opposed to a hub insolvency) or indeed a hub insolvency (involving a concomitant insolvency of a cell) possibly does not fall within the EU Regulation. Such a conclusion would be unfortunate for intra-EU enforcement of EU-based PCCs. Indirectly the Virgos-Schmit Report (paragraph 49) may also support this conclusion: *"Article 1 (1) defines the proceedings to which this Convention applies on the basis of [inter alia]... the proceedings must be based on the* ***debtor's insolvency****"*. This comment is made in respect of what constitutes an *"insolvency"*. However, the fact that it is preceded by the term *"debtor's"*, given the above assumption that a *"debtor"* and *"legal person"* must be the same proceedings, suggests that a cell insolvency would not constitute an insolvency for the purposes of the Convention and/or the EU Regulation.

"insolvency proceedings" of the "debtor" and "legal person"

Recital 9 may reinforce the conclusion above: *"The insolvency proceedings to which this Regulation applies are listed in the Annexes"*. These cross-refer and define *"liquidator"* and exclude the term 'receiver': a more detailed analysis of the term 'receiver' is given below. Thus there is obvious doubt as to whether a cell insolvency, utilising in Gibraltar 'a receiver' are *"insolvency proceedings"* to which the Regulations apply, because the term *"liquidator"* does not encompass 'a receiver' in Gibraltar. To avoid these pitfalls Gibraltar may seek amendment of the EU Regulation. According to the Virgos-Schmit Report (at paragraph 48) amendment *per se* should not be difficult because: *"In short, Article 1(1) lays down the conditions which enable proceedings to be added to the lists in the Convention by Contracting States, and only when the proceedings are included in the appropriate list will the Convention be applicable (see article 2(a) and (c))"*; and (at paragraph 62) further states: *"Contracting States may amend the list of their proceedings by using the revision mechanism laid down in article 54"*. Pending amendment, the Gibraltar authorities need to ensure that a cell insolvency never exists without a concomitant hub insolvency, i.e. the insolvency of the legal person, the PCC. However, the safeguard of concomitant insolvency proceedings (that of the hub and of the cell) still presents a textual problem for both Gibraltar and Malta. If the *"legal person"* (i.e. the PCC in the form of the hub) is not also the *'debtor'* (because the debtor is the cell) then, because the text of the EU Regulation assumes that the terms *"legal person"* and *"debtor"* are the same, it would also seem implicit in Article 1(1) that concomitant insolvency proceedings (i.e. of the cell and of the hub) would, at first sight, fail to solve the problem. However, many PCC statutes (including Gibraltar and Malta) require that a cellular deficiency is made good by the hub capital. Consequently a cellular insolvency should also give rise to a hub debtor, if not a hub insolvency. It follows that given concomitant hub and cell insolvencies, the hub is also a debtor.

"collective"

The term *"**collective** insolvency proceedings"* is not defined in either the Recital, or the definitions section or the Virgos-Schmit Report. A PCC's *raison d'être* could be said to be that it is not *"collective"* and consequently nor are its *"insolvency proceedings"*. It is not *"collective"* because the cells are firewalled against creditor action; therefore defeating the normal *"collective"* principle of *pari passu*. The alternative argument would state that regardless of the firewalling a cell insolvency is *"collective"*; its *"collective"* nature is merely limited to the cell. Each cell can be regarded as a *"collective"*, if the *"insolvency proceedings"* are themselves of a *"collective"* nature.

Indirect supporting evidence for both counter-arguments can be found within the Recital and the Virgos-Schmit Report. According to the Report (paragraph 49): *"Article 1 (1) defines the proceedings to which the Convention applies on the basis of [inter alia] ... proceedings must be "collective", i.e. all creditors concerned may seek satisfaction only through the insolvency proceedings, as individual action will be precluded"*. This is emphasised in paragraph 52: *"The creditors must seek payment of their debts through these collective proceedings*[88]*, even if they are not conducted by the courts"*. In the case of a cell insolvency, the majority of PCC statutes worldwide (and especially relevant here in the case of Gibraltar and Malta) provide that, *"all creditors concerned [i.e. of the cell] may seek satisfaction only through the insolvency proceedings [of the cell]"*.

---

[88] i.e. it is the proceedings which are collective not the outcome by way of *pari passu*.

The use of the term *"collective"* is designed to ensure *"that the procedures should not be regarded as remedies (self-help or otherwise) which are instigated by individual creditors to protect individual creditors"*. Consequently *"collective"* refers to the *'collectivity'* of the procedure and not necessarily the *'collectivity'* of the outcome, i.e. abrogating *pari passu*. There is a tension between the principle of *pari passu* and that of cellular firewalling. However, the authors believe that the correct view is that a PCC formed in either Gibraltar or Malta should not be excluded from the EU Regulation coverage on the grounds that it is not a *"collective"* procedure.

"divestment"

As noted above, Article 1 (1) requires a *"partial or total divestment of a debtor"*. Ignoring the other issues noted above concerning whether a PCC falls within the ambit of Article 1, the Virgos-Schmit Report commentary is clear, a PCC or indeed cell insolvency would fall within Article 1(1). Paragraph 49 of the Virgos-Schmit Report states: *"the proceedings must entail a total or partial divestment of the debtor, that is to say the transfer to another person, the Liquidator, of the powers of administration and of disposal over all or part of his assets, or the limitation of these powers through the intervention and control of his actions. It should be remembered that partial divestment, whether of his assets or his powers of administration, is sufficient. The legal nature that such divestment may take, depending on the national legislation applicable, has no bearing on the application of the Convention to the proceedings in question"*. Whichever view of a PCC is taken, it would appear that at the very least a *"partial divestment"* has occurred. If you take the view that the hub is the debtor; then the removal of the cell from the control of the hub by way (or indeed the whole of the PCC) of a cellular insolvency, must be a *"partial divestment"*. If you take the view that the debtor is the cell, then in a cellular insolvency, there has been a *"total divestment"*.

"liquidator"

Annex A of the EU Regulations lists the EU liquidation procedures that fall within the EU Regulation. This may cause problems for PCCs if a specific procedure is not noted within Annex A. A common feature of PCCs worldwide is that the establishment of a PCC involves specific approval from a non-judicial officer (i.e. an IP) to take certain actions. Indeed that non-judicial officer may well be intimately involved with any insolvency. This does not seem to present a problem. The Virgos-Schmit Report notes at paragraph 52: *"The Convention is drawn up on the basis of insolvency proceedings conducted by the courts. This will be the general rule. However, Article 1 does not require the proceedings necessarily to involve the intervention of a judicial authority (or of an authority with an equivalent role). They must be proceedings (comprising a minimum number of acts and formalities as set down in law) which are officially recognised and legally effective in the State in which the proceedings are opened and which fulfil the four [cumulative] conditions set out in Article 1(1)"*.

Excluded undertakings

Article 1(2) excludes: *"insolvency proceedings concerning insurance undertakings, credit institutions, investment undertakings which provide services involving the holding of funds or securities for third parties, or to collective investment undertakings"*. The Virgos-Schmit Report notes the rationale for this exclusion at paragraph 54: *"Contracting States subject these entities to prudential supervision through national regulatory authorities in order to minimize the risk to the relevant industries and to the financial system as a whole"*. Of particular concern to PCCs is the *"insurance undertaking"* exclusion. *"An 'insurance undertaking' is any entity covered by the First Council Directive 73/239/EE. of 24 July 1973 ... relating to... the business of direct insurance other than life assurance"*: paragraph 57 of the Virgos-Schmit Report. What is *"the business of direct insurance other than life assurance"*? The problem is that many EU Member States do not include reinsurance as direct insurance. Whether an EU-based insurance PCC is a direct insurance vehicle or not will often be a difficult question of fact and law.

9.1.4. Article 3 - international jurisdiction - the centre of main interest or COMI.

The concepts of *"main proceedings"*, *"secondary proceedings"* and *"territorial proceedings"* set the context for article 3.

Article 3(1) is at first sight clear and supportive of EU registered PCC intra-EU enforcement: *"The courts of the Member State within the territory of which the centre of the debtor's main interest is situated shall have jurisdiction to open [the main] insolvency proceedings"*. More importantly it follows: *"In the case of a company or legal person, the place of the registered office shall be presumed to be [its COMI] in the absence of proof to the contrary"*. In short, it is a rebuttable presumption that the COMI and the registered office are the same. There has been a developing case law (at both national and ECJ level) as to what constitutes a 'letterbox company' (i.e. where COMI would not equate to the registered office): more especially and where there could possibly be two competing COMIs. This is because (say) of the existence of operations in more than one jurisdiction. It is not the intention of this book to consider in detail this developing case law. In distillation however certain threads can be discerned. In order not to be a 'letterbox company' the following should be in existence:

(a) the directors should (in the main) be local to the registered office jurisdiction;
(b) these local directors should exercise considerable control, but need not micro-manage; and
(c) creditors should be aware that control is exercised from this local jurisdiction.

Save for possible involuntary creditors, which will always present a problem to PCCs, it is suspected that by the very nature of establishing European PCC conditions (a) - (c) are likely to apply. Thus a PCC (at the hub level) is unlikely to be considered to be a 'letterbox company'.

The Virgos-Schmit Report (at paragraph 73) is further supportive of EU registered PCC intra-EU enforcement. Paragraph 73 states: "*Article 3(1) enables main insolvency* ***universal*** *proceedings to be opened in the Contracting State where the debtor has his [COMI]... Main insolvency proceedings have* ***universal scope****. They aim at* ***encompassing all the debtor's assets on a world-wide basis and at affecting all creditors, wherever located***". As can be seen the EU Regulation is thoroughly extra-territorial. Consequently, given that one of the concerns surrounding PCCs is whether the concept would be recognised outside of the home jurisdiction, the authors would always recommend utilising an EU-based (i.e. Gibraltar or Malta) PCC; this is rather than one based and registered outside of the EU.

A question however remains: Could it be possible to argue that the hub and a cell have different COMIs? Interestingly Article 3(1) states: "*In the case of a company* ***or*** *legal person*". Surely a "*legal person*" encompasses "*a company*"? This leaves open the possibility that a cell possessing all the indices of a company, such as share capital, together with its own assets and liabilities, can be presumed to be a company: especially in a jurisdiction which does not recognise or is indeed positively antithetical to PCCs. This is despite the fact that the relevant PCC legislation may categorically state that a cell is not a "*legal person*". Unfortunately the Virgos-Schmit Report further confuses matters by introducing yet another term, which is not used in the EU Regulation itself: "*legal entities*". See paragraph 74 in the phrase: "*Which persons or* ***legal entities*** *may be subject to insolvency proceedings is determined by national law. Where the international jurisdiction rule mentions the debtor, this means the natural persons or legal entity (whether a legal person or not) concerned*". Could a cell be a "*legal entity*", i.e. having a separate legal identity, although not obviously a natural person or indeed a legal person? In the authors' opinion, the answer is 'yes, a cell, whilst not being a legal person has a legal identity'.

Already the EU Regulation has spawned competing COMI claims, such as the Parmalat [89] case where both Irish and Italian courts claimed COMI over the same entity. Given the novelty of PCCs, such a competing claim between the cell and the hub cannot be ruled out. However even if an EU Member State (more especially an EU member State court antithetical to the notion of PCCs) did accept the notion that the cell was separate (i.e. there were two companies if not two legal persons) to the hub (and consequently there could be two COMIs) that would not be the end of the matter. The mere existence of two claimed separate legal identities, both of which could be COMIs, would not necessarily give rise to two COMIs. There would have to be a degree of separate and identifiable control over the cell. Otherwise, the cell could be claimed to be merely a 'letterbox company'.

Some EU jurisdictions (notably England and Wales) have developed a notion of a group company insolvency based upon the EU Regulation.[90] Under this notion group companies are group controlled. Hence a group has a group COMI. Thus even if the cell is considered to have all the indices of a company (and hence as separate *"legal identity"*, if not being a separate *"legal person"*) it will not have necessarily a separate COMI. However this does not mean that the EU Regulation introduces the US concept of 'substantive consolidation', which offers a form of 'group insolvency'. Rather the notion of a group insolvency under the EU Regulation may run counter to the Virgos-Schmit Report which states (at paragraph 76): *"The Convention offers no rule for groups of affiliated companies (parent - subsidiary schemes)"*. Interestingly, yet another new term is thus introduced which does not appear in the EU Regulation itself, namely, *"subsidiary schemes"* and not the more obvious 'subsidiary companies'. Does the use of the word *"schemes"* import something wider than 'subsidiary companies', such as 'subsidiary cells'?

9.1.5. Article 4 - law applicable - Renvoi

This article is integral to the intra-EU enforcement of cellular insolvency priority rules of EU-registered PCCs. The Virgos-Schmit Report explains:

---

[89] *Eurofood IFSC Ltd, Re (C341/04) [2006] ECR I -3813 (ECJ)*

[90] See *Daisytek – ISA Ltd, Re [2003] BCC 562 (ChD)*

"The Convention sets out... uniform rules on conflict of laws [Renvoi] which replace national rules on private international law.... Article 4 lays down the basic rule on conflict of laws [paragraph 87].... This Article determines the law applicable to the insolvency proceedings, the conduct thereof and their material effects: unless otherwise stated by this Convention, the law of the Contracting State of the opening of the proceedings is applicable (lex concurus).[paragraph 88]. This rule... is valid for... on the main proceedings [paragraph 89]... and secondary or territorial proceedings ... The law of the [COMI] State...determines all the effects of the insolvency proceedings, both procedural and substantive[91]*, the persons and legal relations concerned .... It stipulates... who may be subject to insolvency proceedings, the requirements to open them and who may present the petition; it determines the nature and the extent of the debtors divestment and the assets covered by it; it outlines the organisation of the administration of the estate and regulates the designation of the liquidator and his powers; it decides the admissibility of claims and the rules on distribution and preferences; it governs the closure of the proceedings and its consequences, etc [paragraph 90]"*.

This is generally supportive of recognising the special priority rules of a PCC. Consequently the authors' again recommend that an EU-based (i.e. Gibraltar or Malta) PCC should be considered over and above non-EU-based PCCs. There are two exceptions:

(a) secondary proceedings to Article 4; which whilst not a specific exception may become an effective exception; and

(b) the specific exemptions noted in Articles 5-15.

As regards (b) not all of these specific exemptions would have a specific relevance to PCCs. Hence this chapter will only consider those exceptions that are considered specifically relevant.

9.1.6. Article 5 - third parties rights *in rem*, i.e. secured rights of third parties.

Article 5(1) states: *"The opening of insolvency proceedings shall not affect the rights in rem of creditors of third parties in respect of tangible or intangible, moveable or immovable assets - both specific assets and the collection of indefinite assets as a whole which change from time to time - belonging to the debtor which are situated within the territory of another Member State at the time of the opening of the proceedings"*.

As the Virgos-Schmit Report states (at paragraph 95): *"The creation, validity and scope of these rights in rem are governed by their own applicable law*

[91] See the discussion on whether PCC priority rules are procedural or substantive.

(in general the"lex rei sitae" at the relevant time) and cannot be affected by the opening of insolvency proceedings", and continues (at paragraph 102): *"... the rationale of Article 5 imposes certain limits to the national qualification of a right in rem. It must be borne in mind that Article 5 represents an important exception as regards the application of the law of the State of the opening and the universal effect of the main proceedings. It must be equally be remembered that secondary proceedings [which are a precursor to this exception] are only possible if the debtor has an establishment in that Contracting State. The mere presence of assets is not enough in order to open such proceedings"*.

It should be noted that PCCs are not likely to be standard trading entities. Consequently it is unlikely that a PCC *"debtor [however defined] has an establishment in [another] ... Contracting State"*. Nevertheless the possibility should be considered.

This is relevant to the position of PCCs because Article 5 is an exception to the general rule that COMI *"decides the admissibility of claims and the rules on distribution"*. Thus if the COMI of an EU-registered PCC is with the home jurisdiction (i.e. Gibraltar or Malta) then subject to this exception, PCC priority rules as to the *"distribution"* will apply. Two issues could arise:

(a) is the debtor the PCC hub, (or the PCC itself), or is it the cell; and

(b) what constitutes a right *in rem*?

The question of what or who constitutes the debtor has been discussed above.

As to what constitutes a right *in rem*, the existence of a PCC may cause difficulties. Given that a cell's liabilities are firewalled, there is no theoretical objection to having cellular security, i.e. creating security which only attaches to assets within that cell in respect of a liability of that cell. This has already been discussed. Indeed, as we have noted, the EU Collateral Directive is of assistance to PCCs granting security. Ordinarily the creation of rights *in rem* requires a three-stage process:

(a) the 'creation of the security', say by way of contract;

(b) 'attachment', i.e. the rights *in rem* refer specifically to an asset. If they do not refer specifically to an asset (such as a floating charge) then they will do at some point in the future by way of crystallisation; and

(c) 'perfection', whereby third parties are made aware of the right *in rem*. Perfection is often by way of registration. Save for the EU Collateral Directive which minimises perfection requirements, perfection may be difficult for a PCC.

Certain PCC jurisdictions allow for registration on the company register of cellular security as against the company. This is by way of a notice in the register noting that, whilst the security is registered against a company (i.e. the PCC) the security only impacts the cell. Given that the cell is not a separate legal person, registration can only be against the PCC; this is even in a PCC jurisdiction. The problem here, however, will be that of an EU non-PCC jurisdiction, where it is probable that there will be no formal method of registering a security against the cell alone. Thus even if the non-PCC jurisdiction recognises that the cell is the debtor (or more technically that the debtor can only go against the cells assest), there may not have been perfection of the security as against the cell. So, wherever possible, whenever registering any cell security as against the company, always make reference somehow to the cell in the registration documents. This is all more so because of Article 5(3) which states: "*The right, recorded in the public register and enforceable against third parties, under which a right in rem within the meaning of paragraph 1 may be obtained, shall be considered a right in rem*".

What constitutes a right *in rem* under the EU Regulation? More especially would the cellular firewalled structure of a PCC constitute a right *in rem*? According to Article 5(2): "*[in rem] rights... shall in particular mean:*

a) the right to dispose of assets or have them disposed of and to obtain satisfaction from the proceeds of or income from those assets, in particular by virtue of a lien or mortgage;
b) the exclusive right to have a claim met, in particular a right guaranteed by a lien in respect of the claim or by assignment of the claim by way of guarantee;
c) the right to demand the assets from, and/or to require restitution by, anyone having possession or use of them contrary to the wishes of the party so entitled;
d) a right in rem to the beneficial use of assets".

The Virgos-Schmit Report counsels against: "*An unreasonably wide interpretation of the national concept of a right in rem*" (paragraph 102). Consequently it is assumed that novel and developing forms of *in rem* rights may have difficulty in obtaining recognition. However, it should also be recognised that recognition depends on local national law. It is not the purpose of this book to consider the security law of all the Member States. A cellular structure does create: "*the exclusive right to have a claim met*", from the cellular assets. However this "*exclusive right*" does not necessarily constitute "*a right guaranteed by a lien in respect of the claim or by assignment of the claim by way of guarantee*". Although it need not so constitute because Article 5(2)(b) merely states: *"in particular a right guaranteed..."*. Certainly most PCC regimes give: *"the right to demand the assets from, and/or to require restitution by, anyone having possession or use of them contrary to the wishes of the party so entitled"*. This right is given if its assets are incorrectly moved from one cell to another or indeed outside of the cell.

The Virgos-Schmit Report comment (paragraphs 103 and 104) on Article 5(2) is understandably not particularly helpful: *"... a right in rem basically has two characteristics... (a) its direct and immediate relationship with the asset it covers, which remains linked to its satisfaction, without depending on the asset belonging to a person's estate or on the relationship between the holder of the right in rem and another person; (b) the absolute nature of the allocation of the right to the holder. This means that the person who holds a right in rem can enforce it against anyone who breaches or harms his right without his assent (e.g. such rights are typically protected by actions to recover): that the right can resist the alienation of the assets to a third party (it can be claimed erga omnes, with the restrictions characteristic of the protection of the bona fide purchaser); and that the right can thus resist individual enforcement by third parties and in collective insolvency proceedings (by its separation or individual satisfaction)...A right in rem may not only be established with regard to specific assets but also with regard to assets as a whole"*.

It should be remembered that Article 5 is an exception to Article 4. Article 4 applies the EU universality principle. Thus Article 5 focuses on the local law, i.e. in our case the local law of a non-PCC Member State in which secondary proceedings occur. Consequently the law of Gibraltar or Malta would not ordinarily be relevant. It would only be relevant if a Gibraltar PCC insolvency resulted in secondary proceedings in Malta or vice-versa. Nevertheless it is useful to look at the PCC legislation of Gibraltar and Malta in relation to what could constitute a security under Article 5 as these laws may impact upon any local definition of security. Section 6(6) of the Gibraltar PCC Act is standard: *"In the event of any cellular assets attributable to a cell...being taken...the [PCC] shall...transfer...to the cell, from the cellular or non-cellular assets...sufficient to [so] restore"*. Is such a right in *"the absolute nature of the allocation of the right to the holder"?* Perhaps, but only case law will tell.

9.1.7. Article 6 - set-off

Article 6 states: *"The opening of insolvency proceedings shall not affect the right of creditors to demand the set-off of their claims against the claims of the debtor, where such a set-off is permitted by the law applicable to the insolvent debtor's claim"*. Some difficulties follow from the debtor not always being the legal person. Two particular issues can occur: intra-PCC set-off and 'normal' set-off. As to the intra-PCC set-off, cells and indeed the hub may have liabilities to and from each other. Most jurisdictions will always allow set-off between legal entities. Therefore the question of the legal standing of the cell viz a debtor will always be raised. As to normal set-off a similar question is raised. The liability may be that of the cell as far as the PCC jurisdiction is concerned, but that of the hub (or the PCC itself) as far as the local non-PCC jurisdiction is concerned. Given the variety of ways in which Member States approach set-off, we cannot determine the likely outcomes of such a scenario.

9.1.8. Article 11 - effects on rights subject to registration

Article 11 states: "*The effects of insolvency proceedings on the rights of the debtor in immoveable property, a ship or an aircraft subject to registration in a public register shall be determined by the law of the Member State under the authority of which the register is kept*". The logic of this exception is explained at paragraph 130 of the Virgos-Schmit Report: "*The systems for the registration of property play a significant role in protecting trade and legal certainty. General confidence in its contents and consequences should be protected under the same conditions, whether the insolvency proceedings are opened in the State of registration or in another Contracting State*". It appears that Article 11 was drafted to preclude rights which may be alien to the local registration jurisdiction, being registered. If that is the case, is cellular ownership *per se* alien to the local jurisdiction? Article 11 bears some resemblance to the Article 5 (*in rem* rights) exception. If registration is required (and registration can only be in the name of the company, i.e. the legal person) then, wherever possible, some reference in the registration should be made to the cell.

9.1.9. Article 13 - detrimental acts (or "antecedent transactions")

Article 13 states: "*Article 4(2)(m) shall not apply where the person who benefited from an act detrimental to all the creditors provides proof that: the said act is subject to the law of a Member State other than that of the State of the opening of proceedings; and that law does not allow any means of challenging that act in the relevant case*". In a nutshell: "*It acts as a 'veto' against the invalidity of the act decreed by the law of the State of the opening [i.e. the COMI state]*" (Virgos-Schmit Report paragraph 136). Is the mere creation of a cellular structure a detrimental act, and even more so a detrimental act *vis-à-vis* an involuntary creditor? To a non-PCC jurisdiction, it would depend upon all the factors and the attitude of the local judiciary. Obviously if the creditor was an involuntary creditor, a local court may be more sympathetic to its plight. However, for the PCC promoters

Article 13 allows an easy get-out; certainly as regards voluntary creditors. All that is required under Article 13 is that the parties to a contract detrimental to the general body of creditors apply a choice of law clause in favour of a legal system which precludes challenge to the alleged detrimental act. In short apply wherever possible the local law of the PCC jurisdiction, i.e. apply Gibraltar or Malta law.

9.1.10. Article 20 - return and imputation - "the hotch pot rule"

Article 20 is a statutory reiteration of the generally accepted international 'rule of hotch pot'[92], which is sometimes also referred to as, in a national as opposed international context, 'the rule' against double dividends' and is referred to in the EU Regulation as 'return and imputation'. Article 20 states: "*(1) A creditor who, after opening of the proceedings referred to in Article 3(1) obtains by any means, in particular through enforcement, total or partial satisfaction of his claim on the assets belonging to the debtor situated within the territory of another Member State, shall return what he has obtained to the liquidator, subject to Articles 5 and 7. (2) In order to ensure equal treatment of creditors a creditor who has, in the course of insolvency proceedings, obtained a dividend on his claim shall share in distributions made in other proceedings only where creditors of the same ranking or category have, in those other proceedings, obtained an equivalent dividend*". According to, "The EC Regulation on Insolvency Proceedings", a commentary and annotated guide by Gabriel Moss QC, Professor Ian Fletcher and Stuart Isaacs QC, "*The aim of Article 20 is to ensure equal treatment of non-preferential, unsecured creditors throughout all states to which the Regulation applies. The policy of pari passu distribution for all creditors with the same ranking throughout the EU...is one of the fundamental policies of the [EU Insolvency Regulation]*". The Virgos-Schmit Report claims (at paragraph 175): that "*the method of [a hotch pot] calculation is relatively simple. It comprises four rules*". It then goes onto describe these rules in 10 paragraphs: the length of which somewhat belies the alleged simplicity. It is not the intention of this book to discuss the specific hotch pot rules.

How does the hotch pot rule impact upon the cellular structure? This question really revolves around whether the cellular structure and cellular debtors are recognised. The above quotes however seem to argue both ways. The emphasis on the fundamental policy of *pari passu* and equal treatment seems to negate cellular priority. Whereas, the reference to "*creditors of the same ranking*" seems to accommodate cellular priority. If

---

[92] Best enunciated in English law in *Cleaver v Delta American re [2001] 2 AC 328*, PC.

the notion of cellular priority is accepted then the *"relatively simple"* calculations are simply applied to each cell (and indeed the hub) as if each cell (and indeed the hub) were separate *"legal persons"*. However this may not be the case EU-wide. Consequently as some jurisdictions may not accept the separateness of a cell for hotch pot calculation, one creditor could end up with more than another creditor.

9.1.11. Article 26 - public policy

Article 26 states: *"Any Member State may refuse to recognise insolvency proceedings opened in another Member State or to enforce a judgment handed down in the context of such proceedings where the effects of such a recognition or enforcement would be manifestly contrary to that State's public policy, in particular its fundamental principles of constitutional rights and liberties of the individual"*. It is doubtful whether the apparent abandonment of the *pari passu* principle in PCC cellular priority would fall foul of this Article. The Virgos-Schmit Report states (at paragraph 204): *"The public policy exception ought to operate only in exceptional cases. For this reason Article 26 requires recognition or enforcement of the foreign judgment to be 'manifestly' contrary to public policy. Furthermore, Article 26 does not require the compatibility with public policy of the rule or principle applied by the foreign court to be ascertained in the abstract, but that the result of recognition or enforcement of the judgment offends against public policy. Verification of conformity with public policy is directed towards the result of the recognition or enforcement which means that all circumstances peculiar to the case, including the connection with the requested State, are relevant"*. From this it can be seen that voluntary PCC creditors are unlikely to fall within the ambit of Article 26.

The Virgos-Schmit Report continues (at paragraph 206): *"Public policy operates as a general clause as regards recognition and enforcement, covering fundamental principles of both substance and procedure. Public policy may thus protect participants or persons concerned by proceedings against failures to observe due process. Public policy does not involve a general control of the correctness of the procedure followed in another Contracting State, but rather of essential procedural guarantees such as the adequate opportunity to be heard and the rights of participation in the proceedings. Rights of participation and non-discrimination play a special role in the case of plans to reorganise businesses or compositions, in relation to creditors whose participation is hindered or who are the subject of unfounded discrimination"*. Article 26 thus focuses on the rules of natural justice, i.e. 'the right to be heard', 'the absence of partiality', etc. The mere existence therefore of a PCC is unlikely to be a problem under Article 26. This does not mean that a PCC regime *cannot* fall under Article 26; that is if the rules as they relate to creditors rights of audience, etc, abandon natural justice. It is merely that the peculiar PCC priority rules do not founder under Article 26.

9.1.12. Article 32 - exercise of creditor rights

Article 32(1) states: *"Any creditor may lodge his claim in the main proceedings and in any secondary proceedings"*. The Virgos-Schmit Report states (at paragraph 235): *"Pursuant to Article 4(2)(h), the law of the State of the opening of the proceedings [the COMI State] determines the rules governing the lodging of claims. However national law concerning the creditors entitled to lodge claims is replaced by the provision in Article 32(1), which entitles any creditor to lodge his claim in the main proceedings [i.e. the COMI proceedings, which presumably in the case of an EU-registered PCC will be either Gibraltar or Malta] and in any secondary proceedings. The creditor is entitled to lodge claims in the proceedings of his choice, even in several proceedings"*.

Why would a creditor wish to *"lodge his claim in the main proceedings and in any secondary proceedings"*? Because, regardless of any PCC cellular structure, the assets, liabilities and indeed priorities are likely to be different in secondary proceedings. The hotch pot rule may not eradicate these different outcomes. Therefore, Article 32 creates possible conflict between an EU PCC jurisdiction (with its COMI proceedings) and an EU non-PCC jurisdiction (with its secondary proceedings). For instance a Belgian creditor of an EU PCC (with the primary proceedings in either Gibraltar or Malta and secondary proceedings in Belgium) could in the secondary proceedings seek a dividend which he would not otherwise gain under the relevant PCC cellular priority rules, i.e. he was a creditor of cell A and the secondary proceedings related to cell B. This would be because there would be (in Belgium) possible confusion as to who was the debtor (cell A or cell B). Why? Because Belgium law (say) does not ordinarily recognise a PCC cellular structure.

Article 32(2) continues: *"The liquidators in the main and in any secondary proceedings shall lodge in other proceedings claims which have already been lodged in the proceedings for which they were appointed, provided that the interests of the creditors in the latter proceedings are served thereby, subject to the right of creditors to oppose that or to withdraw the lodgement of their claims where the law applicable so provides"*.

There are two provisos to Article 32(2):

(a) re liquidators, *"the interests of the creditors in the latter proceedings [must be] served thereby"*; and

(b) re creditors, *"to oppose that or to withdraw the lodgement of their claims where the law applicable so provides"*.

Both of these provisos could affect PCCs.

As to the liquidator (proviso (a)) the Virgos-Schmit Report states at paragraph 239: *"... if the liquidator finds that the assets to be distributed in other proceedings are so significant that even the ordinary unsecured creditors in his proceedings may receive a dividend, in competition with the ordinary unsecured creditors lodging claims in other proceedings, the lodging of the claim may be useful and will take place"*. This could be the case if the secondary proceedings have not recognised (for whatever reason) the PCC cellular priority structure. Consequently, the creditors represented by this liquidator could have (subject to not achieving more than 100 per cent of their claim) a 'second bite of the cherry' in another secondary proceedings jurisdiction which (for whatever reason) has not recognised the PCC cellular structure. The secondary proceedings liquidator would not (in this case) wish to lodge his claims in the primary COMI proceedings. Why? Because the primary proceedings have recognised the PCC cellular structure.

As to the creditor (proviso (b)) the Virgos-Schmit Report states (at paragraph 239): *"The creditor may have various reasons for opposing the lodging of his claim in proceedings other than those he has selected"*. An obvious reason would be to avoid the negative (as far as this creditor is concerned) impact of PCC cellular priority. The possibility of confusion between normal *pari passu* and cellular *pari passu* principles could be heightened. Or, as the authors suspect, lessened. Why? Because, of Article 32(3) which states: *"the liquidator in the main or secondary proceedings shall be empowered to participate in other proceedings on the same basis as a creditor, in particular by attending creditors meetings"*. Whilst it is possible for a belligerent secondary proceedings liquidator who does not wish to recognise cellular *pari passu* to represent his creditors in the main proceedings, it is also possible vice-versa, i.e. the COMI Liquidator to be represented in the secondary proceedings. Given the greater influence accorded to the main proceedings liquidator it is probable that Article 32(3) will lessen any potential conflict.

9.1.13. National exceptions within the EU

Portugal

Portugal is a full EU Member State and a full signatory to the EU Insolvency Regulation. However: *"The Portuguese Republic indicated in a unilateral statement made at the meeting of the Council of the European Union... that, under the conditions set out in Article 26 [the public policy exemption] Portuguese public policy might be invoked to defend important local interests against the application of Article 37*[93] *which concerns the conversion of territorial proceedings opened before the main proceedings, where those interests are not sufficiently taking into account in such conversion"*. (Virgos-Schmit Report at paragraph 210). What these *"important local interests"* are is unknown. It is thought that they must be by their very nature major security interests, such as energy security, transport and the like. It is unlikely that they would be 'defending local creditors'. Consequently it is believed that this unilateral statement does not bear on the viability of intra-EU PCC enforcement. Thus, for the purposes of PCCs, Portugal should be considered no different from the majority of EU Member States.

Denmark

Denmark is a full EU Member State. However under the Amsterdam treaty, Denmark is exempt from any EU legislative measures adopted via Title IV of the EC Treaty (see consolidated EC Treaty, Article 61(c)) and the EU Regulation was adopted via Title IV. Thus the EU Regulation does not apply to Denmark. When considering the position of Denmark therefore, national Danish law should be considered.

Malta

Malta is a full EU Member State. Importantly Malta possesses one of the two EU PCC regimes. Its PCC regime is considered in detail.

Gibraltar

Gibraltar is part of the EU by virtue of UK membership, but it is not a separate EU Member State. However, it enjoys a position similar to that of a full EU Member State. Thus for the purposes of the EU Insolvency Regulation, Gibraltar should be regarded as a full signatory.

The Virgos-Schmit Report states (at paragraphs 300-301):

"The Convention [i.e. the EU Regulation] has no provisions governing territorial application. Consequently the general rules of public international law, i.e. Article 29 of the 1969 Vienna Convention on the Law of Treaties are applicable...[Thus the EU Insolvency Regulation] applies to the whole territory of the Contracting States. This includes non-European territories which are an integral part of the territory of the States. However, the autonomy of these territories can vary widely. Consequently, the Contracting States may exclude or reserve the application of... [the EU Regulation] to these territories by means of a declaration to that effect. This is the case, for example with the Netherlands in

---

93 *The conversion of earlier proceeding*

relation to the Netherlands Antilles and Aruba". No such declaration has been made by the UK with regards to Gibraltar. In addition to the above, Gibraltar is included within the scope of the EC treaty (see Article 299(4)) and thus the EU Insolvency Regulation undoubtedly covers Gibraltar.

Importantly, Gibraltar possesses one of the two avowedly EU PCC regimes. Its PCC regime is considered below. Finally, but unlike Malta, Gibraltar is covered by the Commonwealth insolvency regime considered in detail elsewhere.

Channel Islands and the Isle of Man

The Channel Islands consists of four separate jurisdictions (Guernsey, Jersey, Alderney and Sark) of which two (Guernsey and Jersey) have PCC regimes: as does the Isle of Man. In addition to paragraphs 300 - 301 of the Virgos-Schmit Report reproduced above, paragraph 302 continues: *"[the EU Regulation] does not apply to those territories whose international relations are assumed by any of the Contracting States, but which are not an integral part of their territory being a separate entity. In principle...[the EU Regulation] does not apply to them, no matter whether they are European or non-European territories... ."* Thus the EU Regulation does not apply to these territories. However the 'Commonwealth insolvency regime' does apply.

The Maltese PCC regime

Malta is officially a bilingual (English and Maltese) Common Law (with Civil Law overtones) jurisdiction. Given its British colonial history many of its statutes will be familiar to the Common Law (particularly English) reader. The Maltese PCC regime has been introduced by amending the existing Companies Act regime. Thus it allows for delegated legislation to create and control the use of PCCs, and the amending legislation often states that the existing Companies Act shall be applied *mutatis mutandis* to each cell. The generic PCC legislation draws heavily on existing legislation and import concepts, such as liquidation from existing company law.

Maltese law allows for multi-class/sub-fund companies[94] and 'cell companies' i.e. PCCs.[95] Whilst multi-class/sub-fund companies share similarities with PCCs, for the purposes of this book, they are not regarded as PCCs. Article 84A(1) states: *"The Minister... acting on advice of*

---

[94] See Article 83 of the Maltese Companies Act (Chapter 386, as amended on the 1 January 1996, the Maltese Companies Act.

[95] See Articles 84 A, B and C of the Maltese Companies Act.

the competent authority under the Insurance Business Act, may make regulations which provide for the formation, constitution, authorisation and regulation of cell companies, make it possible for a company authorised under the Insurance Business Act, to carry on business of insurance, or any other business as may be prescribed, to convert into a cell company, and for all matters that may arise in connection therewith... ."

As can be seen Article 84A focuses on insurance. Further the sole piece of delegated legislation under Article 84A[96] only considers insurance. Consequently as Maltese law currently stands:

(a) the use of Maltese PCCs is limited to insurance PCCs; and

(b) the EU Insolvency Regulation consequently is irrelevant. Why? Because Maltese PCCs will only be governed, within an EU context, by the EU Insolvency Insurance Directive.

Further discussion therefore as to Maltese PCCs is found in the EU Insolvency Insurance Directive noted below.

The Gibraltar PCC regime

Gibraltar has developed its PCC regime (and hence its PCC insolvency regime) by drafting PCC generic primary legislation. Thus PCCs can be used as a platform for a variety of purposes. This is the Protected Cell Companies Act 2001 the ("Gibraltar PCC Act") which covers the formation and possibly insolvency of PCCs. For the purposes of considering intra-EU insolvency, it is supported by the Credit Institutions (Reorganisation and Winding Up) Act 2005 (i.e. the EU Insolvency Banking Directives, which as noted above is not covered in this book) and the Insurers (Reorganisation and Winding Up) Act 2004 which is discussed below. The purpose of this section is to consider both an insolvency overview of the Gibraltar PCC Act and in particular intra-EU enforcement under the EU Regulation. The Gibraltar PCC Act is also considered as an examplar within other chapters of this book. It has been chosen because of the authors' familiarity with the Gibraltar PCC Act. As an example, it is used, when considering comparative jurisdictional attitudes to PCC director liability.

---

96 Subsidiary Legislation 386.10, Companies Act (Cell Business Carrying on Business of Insurance) Regulations.

9.2. Part 1 of the Gibraltar PCC Act of the EU

9.2.1. Section 3 - PCC "Formation and Attributes"

Section 3(2) states: *"For the avoidance of doubt.... (a) a... [PCC] is a single legal person; and (b) the creation by a... [PCC] of a cell does not create, in respect of that cell, a legal person separate from the company"*.

This statement is usual in PCC statutes. It is a complete statement of the novelty of a PCC. Elsewhere we have addressed this novelty. More especially in the context of the EU Regulation and the possible conflict between the "*debtor*" and the "*legal person*" that exists for PCCs within the EU Regulation. But can this novel entity be created from a standard company?

Section 3(1)(b) states: "*... a company may be... converted.... into a... [PCC].*"

Most PCC jurisdictions allow conversion i.e. conversion of an existing standard 'limited' to a PCC. Were a non-PCC jurisdiction to take an antagonistic attitude to PCCs, then conversion, particularly if it affected existing and especially involuntary creditors, would add to that antagonism: the court in the non-PCC State would look to methods to refuse recognition. It is highly improbable however that a Gibraltar PCC conversion would cause intra-EU enforcement difficulties for two reasons:

1. The incorporation and conversion of a PCC requires the consent of the Commissioner or Finance Centre Director, etc (see Section 11(1) and (2)) which is highly unlikely to be given if its conversion (or indeed its establishment) would cause existing creditors difficulties. In that regard Gibraltar follows the principle adhered to in all reputable jurisdictions that one cannot establish an off-the-peg PCC.
2. There would appear to be no particular article of the EU Regulation that would specifically apply to such conversion.

9.2.2. Section 6 – "the position of creditors"

Section 6 describes cellular priority by stating in section 6(2): "*No such creditor shall have any rights other than the rights referred to in this section [and elsewhere within the Act]*". We have seen that if COMI is within Gibraltar, then this cellular priority (certainly as regards "*the main proceedings*") will be accepted. The issues lie with secondary proceedings (which only apply because Gibraltar PCCs can enjoy the benefits of the EU Regulation protection, unavailable to most PCCs) and the section 6(3) claim (usual in most PCC statutes) to extraterritoriality.

Section 6(3) commences: "*There shall be implied (except insofar as the same is expressly excluded in writing) in every transaction entered into by a... [PCC] the following terms*", contained within subsections (a) to (c); as to which see below.

If the transaction in question is subject to Gibraltar law and especially if it is a voluntary transaction (i.e. there are no involuntary creditors) then this aspect of section 6(3) ('the imposition of implied terms') presents little issue. But what if that was not the case? Remember the EU Regulation public policy carve-out (Article 26) is limited to "*fundamental principles or the constitutional rights and liberties of the individual*". Section 6(3) also expressly states: "*except insofar as the same is expressly excluded in writing*". It is therefore open to the parties to contract out of this term. Any party contracting with the PCC would know that there are unusual aspects to a PCC and would have researched the same.

The three terms implied in section 6(3) are:

"*(a) that no party shall seek ...wheresoever... to... attempt to use any cellular assets attributable to any cell of the company to satisfy liability not attributable to that cell;*

(b) that if any party succeeds... wheresoever in using any cellular assets attributable to any cell ... to satisfy a liability not attributable to that cell the party shall be liable to the company to pay a sum equal to the value of the benefit thereby obtained by him; and

(c) that if any party succeeds in seizing... any cellular assets attributable to any cell of the company to satisfy a liability not attributable to that cell, that party shall hold those assets or those proceeds on trust for the company and shall keep those assets... separate".

If the secondary proceedings Liquidator (and his jurisdiction) recognises cellular priority (because it believes the "*debtor*" and "*legal person*", or rather the "*legal identity*" are the same) then no problems will emerge. If, however, this is not the case then obvious problems may occur. Section 6(3)(a)-(c) establish described rights *in rem* and a form of set-off. It should be remembered that there are two exceptions to the universality of the main jurisdiction proceedings (i.e. the COMI proceedings). In the EU Regulation the COMI proceedings would be usually in the case of a PCC the home jurisdictions of either Gibraltar or Malta. These two exceptions are third party rights *in rem* (Article 5) and set-off (Article 6). Thus even if the secondary proceedings liquidator recognised PCC priority, the creditor who enjoyed the *in rem* or set-off rights may exercise his rights. His *in rem* rights may not revolve around a discussion as to whether the "*debtor*" and *"the legal person"* are the same. Why? Because *in rem* rights follow the assets and not the person, legal, natural, or otherwise entity involved; that is, they do not follow the person, i.e. they are not *in personam* rights. Set-off of course is generally debtor specific.

Section 6(6) states in the usual terms, i.e. similar provisions apply worldwide, including Malta: *"... any cellular assets attributable to a cell of a... [PCC] being taken in execution in respect of a liability not attributable to that cell, and insofar as such assets or compensation in respect thereof cannot otherwise be restored to the cell affected, the company shall - (a) cause or procure its auditor, acting as expert and not as an arbitrator, to certify the value of the assets lost by the cell affected; and (b) transfer or pay to the cell affected, from the cellular or non-cellular assets to which the liability was attributable, assets or sum sufficient to restore to the cell affected the value of the assets lost"*. A distinction needs to be drawn between an individual *"acting as an expert"* and an individual acting *"as an arbitrator"*. The distinction is often limited in practice. Nevertheless the *de jure* (i.e. at law) distinction is important. An arbitrator is a quasi-judicial office bound by the rules of natural justice, more particularly the duty to hear both sides equally in the presence of each other.

In short, an Arbitrator acts in accordance with *"fundamental principles or the constitutional rights and liberties of the individual" i.e. Article 26 of the EU Regulation*. An expert is not so necessarily bound. This leads to a major practical difference. An arbitrator as a quasi-judicial officer cannot be sued; judges can never be sued. An expert can be sued. Given that an expert is not strictly bound by natural justice, section 6(a) may run counter to Article 26. However such an impasse is highly unlikely for the following reasons:

1. We are here talking about an insolvency. Not only are these comments specific to insolvency, such a dispute is unlikely to occur other than in an insolvency. Why else would it be necessary for a creditor to seize assets? From a practical perspective it is unlikely that an auditor, who has not been paid, will volunteer his services as an expert in such a controversial area.
2. We are here talking about insolvency which means that an IP will be in place. It is the IP's duty, *inter alia,* to admit and otherwise consider creditor claims; including but not limited to an application to court for directions and declarations. Consequently an IP can usually achieve the desired net result (i.e. sections 6(3)(b) and (c)) without an expert involvement; and

3. Section 14 (*"Disputes as to liability attributable to cells"*) states: *"In the event of any dispute as to... [cellular assets and liabilities] the Court, on the application of the... PCC, and without prejudice to any other right or remedy of any person, may issue a declaration in respect of the matter in dispute"*.

Again, the declaration could take account of the powers noted in sections 6(3) (b) and (c).

Thus intra-EU enforcement of section 6(3)(b) and (c) is easily done without causing difficulties for the EU Regulation. It can be done via either the powers of the Liquidator or of the court.

9.2.3. Section 8 – "Cell shares and share capital"

Section 8 allows for cellular share capital (as do many PCC regimes including Malta), and hence cell shares and cellular dividends. However, the existence of cellular share capital does give rise to a problem; that of whether a cell has all the indices (if not the claim) of being a separate legal person when considered by a non-PCC jurisdiction.

9.2.4. Section 13 – "Liability of cellular assets"

Section 13 (4) (a) importantly states the case of cellular *pari passu*: *"the liabilities ... of the cellular assets attributable to a particular cell...shall abate rateably until the value of the aggregate liabilities equals the value of those assets"*. PCCs do not therefore negate the fundamental principle of *pari passu*. Rather, it can be claimed, they simply amend it to take account of the known (i.e. known to be creditors of the PCC) cellular structure. Thus, save for involuntary creditors, there can be no criticism of a PCC as being antithetical to *pari passu*. Consequently, the PCC regime is consistent with the EU Regulation with regard to *pari passu*.

9.2.5. Section 15 – "Company to inform persons they are dealing with... [PCC]"

At the risk of directorial personal liability, section 15(1) states: a PCC *"shall - (a) inform any person with whom it transacts that it is a... [PCC]; and (b) for the purposes of that transaction, identify or specify the cell in respect of which that person is transacting, unless that transaction is not a transaction in respect of a particular cell"*. Section 15 adds greater weight (with the possible exception of an involuntary creditor) to section 14 if any criticism is offered that the PCC defeats *pari passu*. PCC directorial liability is further analysed below.

9.3. Parts II (sections 19-23) and III (sections 24-28) - Receivership and Administration Orders

9.3.1. Introduction

As noted elsewhere, PCC States have developed their PCC regimes generally along one of three insolvency routes. The 'US model' creates a named individual (usually the Insurance Commissioner for the State) to be responsible for the winding up or insolvency of a PCC. Consequently, it is outside the normal insolvency provisions of (say) the US, whereas the 'usual route' (followed by Gibraltar) and the 'amending route' (followed by Malta) will draw heavily on the jurisdictions existing insolvency provisions. Therefore, the 'usual route' and 'amending route' sit within the normal insolvency provisions of the jurisdiction. Usually the IP is someone who would be qualified to act regardless of whether the company is a PCC or not.

9.3.2. The three insolvency processes under the Gibraltar PCC Act

There are three types of insolvency process (all of which are in some way analogous to a non-PCC Gibraltar company insolvency and to UK insolvency processes) within the Gibraltar PCC Act (Section 18(7)):

"(a) a liquidator... appointed [by the court] to act in respect of the company or the company has passed a resolution for voluntary winding up;

(b) a receivership order.... made in respect of the cell;

(c) an administration order... in respect of the cell [or] the company".

In other words:

(a) a Liquidator proper (i.e. the individual is called a liquidator whereas the term *"Liquidator"* within the EU Regulation describes all insolvency appointments). Such a Liquidator can be a compulsory liquidator (i.e. appointed by the court) or a voluntary liquidator (i.e. appointed by the company by way of a resolution for voluntary winding up). Further a liquidator can only be appointed over the hub, i.e. the PCC itself, and not over an individual cell or cells;

(b) a receiver under a receivership order which can only be made in respect of a cell, or cells, but not over the hub, i.e. the PCC itself; and

(c) an Administrator under an Administration Order, which can be made against a cell or the hub, i.e. the PCC itself. The *"liquidator"* process does not have a specific part within the Gibraltar PCC Act. Rather it is referred to particularly in Part 1 of the Act.

9.3.3. Gibraltar and its relationship to the UK re the EU Insolvency Regulation

We have seen that Gibraltar is an 'integral member' of the EU Regulation. Its legal system, including its insolvency regime, is very much based upon the English (and Common Law) system. However, it is not a separate EU Member State. Consequently, it is not specifically referred to in the EU Regulation Annexes which list the recognised insolvency processes. Rather because of its special relationship with the UK, the insolvency processes noted for the UK in the EU Regulation Annexes apply to Gibraltar. Thus only insolvency processes of the UK noted in the Annexes can be used by Gibraltar under the EU Regulation.

The UK (and Member States, such as Malta and Ireland, which have insolvency regimes based upon English law as well as territories, such as Gibraltar, associated with the UK) is traditionally regarded as a pro-creditor insolvency jurisdiction: that is it asserts the rights of creditors over and above the rights of the debtor (the insolvent company). The US (whilst a Common Law country) is traditionally regarded as a pro-debtor insolvency jurisdiction, in that an insolvent company may seek protection from its creditors through an insolvency process. The UK now has a pro-debtor insolvency process, an Administration Order. Whilst not acting absolutely in tandem, Gibraltar (like other associated territories of the UK) has also followed the UK trend of moving from pro-creditor to pro-debtor. But it must be emphasised that the Gibraltar insolvency regime is not a mirror image of the UK insolvency regime. There are differences. We need to consider whether these differences affect intra-EU enforcement of PCC cellular priority.

Annex A of the EU Regulation (as amended) lists the following relevant UK proceedings (and hence Gibraltar proceedings, where applicable) as recognised *"insolvency proceedings"*:

(a) Winding up by or subject to the supervision of the Court;

(b) Creditors' voluntary winding up (with the confirmation of the Court);

(c) Administration, including appointments made by filing prescribed documents with the court;

(d) Voluntary arrangements under insolvency legislation; and

(e) Bankruptcy or sequestration.

It is imperative for intra-EU enforcement of PCC cellular priority that the relevant PCC insolvency process is recognised under the EU Regulation.

The Virgos-Schmit Report sums it up at paragraph 48: "*Only those proceedings expressly entered in the list will be considered 'insolvency proceedings' as covered by the Convention and will be able to benefit from its provisions. In an area where national laws differ considerably, the lists are aimed at providing legal certainty regarding the proceedings to which the Convention may be applied*".

9.3.4. The Gibraltar liquidator process

Within English-based legal systems, insolvent (as opposed to solvent) liquidation is commonly a process whereby the company terminates (is dissolved) and its assets are distributed to his creditors. It is not normally a rehabilitation or reorganisation procedure.

Annex A of the EU Regulation notes two UK and hence Gibraltar "*liquidation processes*":

(a) Winding up by or subject to the supervision of the court (commonly referred to as 'compulsory liquidation'); and

(b) Creditors' voluntary winding up (commonly referred to as 'voluntary liquidation') with the confirmation of the Court.

'Winding up by or subject to the supervision of the Court', involves two procedures:

1. 'winding up by the Court', which is a common UK process; and
2. 'winding up subject to the supervision of the Court', which was abolished in the UK under the 1986 Insolvency Act. However it still forms part of the Gibraltar insolvency regime. Thus a Gibraltar-only procedure is allowed for under Annex A which refers to UK procedures.

The creditors' voluntary winding up (commonly referred to as "voluntary liquidation" or "CVL") insolvency procedure presented a problem for the UK. The UK (and other jurisdictions which have tended to follow English insolvency law) tend to have a *laissez-faire* attitude of non-Court involvement. Many Civil Law jurisdictions (the majority of EU Member States) sometimes find it disconcerting. A CVL entails minimal court involvement. The company resolves to wind up and thereby call a meeting of creditors. This meeting (usually) confirms the company resolution and appoints (or confirms the appointment) of a liquidator. It is thus very democratic. Having said that, the Court does have power to intervene and to give directions. This absence of major court involvement caused commentators to have concern. It was felt that a CVL may not therefore be "*insolvency proceedings*" within the meaning of Article 2 (a) of the EU Regulation. The UK therefore created a new procedure under rule

7.62 of the Insolvency Rules 1986 (as amended). Under Rules 7.62 a CVL Liquidator can apply to Court for confirmation that his appointment is within the EU Regulation. Commentators have however noted that regardless of this rule, it was always open for a CVL liquidator to so apply. Gibraltar does not have this new procedure. It is recommended that any Gibraltar CVL Liquidator apply to Court for a declaration that he is covered by the EU Regulation. Subject to the above, Annex A presents no problems for intra-EU enforcement of Gibraltar PCC cellular priority.

There is no provision within the Gibraltar PCC Act for the liquidation of a cell. Indeed the Act is quite clear. Section 17 states: "*Notwithstanding... law to the contrary, in the winding up of a ... [PCC] (whether compulsory or voluntary or subject to the supervision of the court and whether solvent or insolvent) –*

(a) the assets forming part of the estate shall only be the non-cellular assets;

(b) the winding up shall not... affect the authority or power, of any officer, receiver, administrator, servant or agent of the ... [PCC] in respect of the cellular assets".

The fact that a PCC liquidator does not have control of cellular assets does not present a problem under the EU Insolvency Regulation. For as the Virgos-Schmit Report states at paragraph 49(c):

"*It should be remembered that partial divestment, whether of his assets or his power of administration, is sufficient. The legal nature that such divestment may take, depending on the national legislation applicable, has no bearing on the application of the Convention to the proceedings in question*".

The relevant remedies for a cell are threefold:

(a) receivership: see below, on the basis that the cell is insolvent;

(b) administration: see below, on the basis that the cell is insolvent; and

(c) cell transfer: on the basis that the cell is solvent and the company and/or other cells are insolvent. As to cell transfer, section 18(7)(a) allows for the transfer of cellular assets from a PCC, by way of court order; "*notwithstanding that a liquidator has been appointed to act in respect of the company or the company has passed a resolution for voluntary winding up*". Such a cell transfer (provided that the relevant cell has not become subject to secondary proceedings elsewhere within the EU) does not seem to present a problem under the EU Regulation. Indeed it seems an admirable solution to prevent the entanglement of non-PCC jurisdictions in a novel area of law with which they may feel some discomfort.

9.3.5. The Gibraltar receiver process

We have seen that the only insolvency processes recognised under the EU Regulation are those noted within the Annex and the term 'receiver' is not listed in the Annex. Thus there is obvious doubt as to whether a cell insolvency, utilising in Gibraltar 'a receiver' constitutes *"insolvency proceedings...listed in the Annexes"* as the term *"liquidator"* does not encompass 'a receiver' in Gibraltar. Three suggestions have been made to overcome this difficulty. The first suggestion is always to use an insolvency process (if that is possible) that is described within the EU Regulation Annexes as an acceptable insolvency process. The problem here is that may strain the definition of the relevant terms. The second suggestion is to change the Annexes to include, for instance, the term 'receiver'. This would require a major legislative change. There is a third alternative, to simply amend the Gibraltar PCC Act so that the term 'receiver' becomes (say) *"liquidator"*. Frankly, this seems the best solution.

How did this issue (of a Gibraltar receiver) come about? We have noted that the UK is a *laissez-faire* pro-creditor jurisdiction. Receivership is a manifestation of that *laissez-faire* pro-creditor attitude. Receivership (more especially Administrative Receivership and a Law of Property Act Receivership) was by way of a unilateral act of appointment by the secured creditor. Thus the receiver looked primarily to realising assets in favour of the appointor. It was therefore not a *"collective insolvency proceeding"* involving the court. Consequently it was excluded from Annex A (more especially the UK section) of the EU Regulation. Manifestly the functions of a 'receiver' within the Gibraltar PCC Act do not constitute 'the mischief' for which the UK receiver was excluded from Annex A. A receiver can only be appointed under the Gibraltar PCC Act by the court making a *"receivership order"* under section 19(1). A *"receivership order"* can only be made (section 19(3)) *"for the purposes of - (a) the orderly winding up of the business of or attributable to the cell; and (b) the distribution of the cellular assets attributable to the cell to those entitled to have recourse thereto"*. A *"receivership order"* is not as its name may initially suggest, a 'self-help remedy' and it is well within the spirit the EU Regulation *"collective insolvency procedure"*. Unfortunately, its name is not within the EU Regulation list of approved insolvency processes.

PCC statute draftsmen have understandably sought to draw a distinction between the insolvency of a cell or cells on the one hand, and the insolvency of the hub or PCC on the other hand. Further, draftsmen have sought to draw a distinction between liquidation proper processes (i.e. non-rehabilitative processes) and rehabilitative processes on the other hand. A PCC receivership order is a quasi-liquidation. It is a non-rehabilitative order over a cell because it provides for *"the orderly winding up of the business of or attributable to the cell"*. In the matrix of cellular versus non-cellular and rehabilitative versus non-rehabilitative insolvency processes, draftsmen have sought to draw distinctions by way of different terminology, i.e. there should be different terms for cellular versus non-cellular (or PCC) insolvency processes, as well as different terms for rehabilitative and non-rehabilitative processes. This was a problem with the original drafting of PCC legislation in Guernsey. The problem was easily solved by using as many insolvency-oriented terms as possible. Hence, the use of the word 'receiver'. There appears to be no reason why the Gibraltar PCC Act cannot be changed so that *"receiver"* is changed to 'liquidator'. However there would need to be another change to indicate that the liquidator was either a liquidator of the PCC or of a cell. Pending that change, if there is any issue of intra-EU enforcement, then the receivership order route is best avoided wherever possible.

9.3.6. The Gibraltar administrator process

As has been noted, the term *"Administrator"* is referred to in Annex A of the EU Insolvency Regulation and is therefore *prima facie* covered by the same. The spirit of a Gibraltar PCC Act Administrator is also well within the EU Insolvency Regulation. The appointment of an Administrator requires an *"Administration Order"* granted by the Court (section 24(1)). It is a rehabilitative process and there are no EU Regulation difficulties in that regard. It is also a 'collective process' because (section 24(4)): *"The purposes for which an administration order may be made are - (a) the survival as a going concern of the cell or (as the case may be) of the company; (b) the more advantageous realisation of the business and assets of or attributable to the cell or (as the case maybe) the business and assets of the company than would be achieved by a receivership of the cell or (as the case may be) by the liquidation of the company"*. Given the difficulties for intra-EU enforcement of a *"Receivership Order"* under the Gibraltar PCC Act, there appears to be no difficulty with granting an *"Administration Order"*, purely to overcome those difficulties. Evidently if a *"Receivership Order"* causes difficulty for intra-EU enforcement of the PCC cellular priority and an *"Administration Order"* does not, then there would be a "*more advantageous realisation of the business and assets of or attributable to the cell... than would be achieved by a receivership of the cell*". English courts have faced similar dilemmas and the issue boils down to, 'would the granting of an Administration Order, as opposed to any other order, be an abuse of process?' This would be an issue for the local court. It would not be an EU Regulation issue. Pending any change to the PCC Gibraltar Act, it provides a neat solution to the problem of intra-EU enforcement of PCC cellular priority.

Administration Orders only came about in the UK as a result of the 1986 Insolvency Act. They were unknown beforehand. Their introduction was seen as a move towards a rehabilitation-orientated insolvency regime with the UK becoming more pro-debtor. The main Gibraltar insolvency regime is contained within the Companies Act. The Gibraltar Companies Act does not make provision for Administration Orders. This does not present a problem for intra-EU enforcement of a Gibraltar PCC under the EU Regulation. It is irrelevant where in the legislation of a jurisdiction it makes reference to the Annex A insolvency procedures.

9.4. THE EU Insurance Insolvency Directive

9.4.1. Background

The EU Insurance Insolvency Directive, because it is a Directive (rather than Regulation) is binding as to the result to be obtained. It leaves the methodology and implementation to the individual Member State. Consequently in order to interpret the Directive, one must always look at national laws. Nevertheless it is helpful in interpreting national laws to consider the text itself. This book will not consider each and every Member State implementation of the EU Insurance Insolvency Directive. Rather it will look at the overview and consequently consider in detail only the text itself of the EU Insurance Insolvency Directive.

Directive 2001/17/EC of the European Parliament and of the Council of 19 March 2001 on the reorganisation and winding-up of insurance undertakings

HAVE ADOPTED THIS DIRECTIVE:

TITLE I SCOPE AND DEFINITIONS

Article 1

Scope

1. This Directive applies to reorganisation measures and winding-up proceedings concerning insurance undertakings.

2. This Directive also applies, to the extent provided for in Article 30, to reorganisation measures and winding-up proceedings concerning branches in the territory of the Community of insurance undertakings having their head office outside the Community.

Article 2

Definitions

For the purpose of this Directive:

(a) "insurance undertaking" means an undertaking which has received official authorisation in accordance with Article 6 of Directive 73/239/EEC or Article 6 of Directive 79/267/EEC;

(b) "branch" means any permanent presence of an insurance undertaking in the territory of a Member State other than the home Member State which carries out insurance business;

(c) "reorganisation measures" means measures involving any intervention by administrative bodies or judicial authorities which are intended to preserve or restore the financial situation of an insurance undertaking and which affect pre-existing rights of parties other than the insurance undertaking itself, including but not limited to measures involving the possibility of a suspension of payments, suspension of enforcement measures or reduction of claims;

(d) "winding-up proceedings" means collective proceedings involving realising the assets of an insurance undertaking and distributing the proceeds among the creditors, shareholders or members as appropriate, which necessarily involve any intervention by the administrative or the judicial authorities of a Member State, including where the collective proceedings are terminated by a composition or other analogous measure, whether or not they are founded on insolvency or are voluntary or compulsory;

(e) "home Member State" means the Member State in which an insurance undertaking has been authorised in accordance with Article 6 of Directive 73/239/EEC or Article 6 of Directive 79/267/EEC;

(f) "host Member State" means the Member State other than the home Member State in which an insurance undertaking has a branch;

(i) "administrator" means any person or body appointed by the competent authorities for the purpose of administering reorganisation measures;

(j) "liquidator" means any person or body appointed by the competent authorities or by the governing bodies of an insurance undertaking, as appropriate, for the purpose of administering winding-up proceedings;

(k) "insurance claims" means any amount which is owed by an insurance undertaking to insured persons, policy holders, beneficiaries or to any injured party having direct right of action against the insurance undertaking and which arises from an insurance contract or from any operation provided for in Article 1(2) and (3), of Directive 79/267/EEC in direct insurance business, including amounts set aside for the aforementioned persons, when some elements of the debt are not yet

known. The premiums owed by an insurance undertaking as a result of the non-conclusion or cancellation of these insurance contracts and operations in accordance with the law applicable to such contracts or operations before the opening of the winding-up proceedings shall also be considered insurance claims.

The purpose of the EU Insurance Insolvency Directive is stated in Recital 9:

"The Directive does not seek to harmonise national legislation concerning reorganisation measures and winding-up proceedings but aims at ensuring mutual recognition of Member States' reorganisation measures and winding-up legislation concerning insurance undertakings as well as the necessary cooperation. Such mutual recognition is implemented in this Directive through the principles of unity, universality, coordination, publicity, equivalent treatment and protection of insurance creditors".

It is this last principle, *"the protection of insurance creditors"* that may cause some difficulties, both generally and specifically as to PCCs. Alternatively, it may be argued that PCCs protect insurance creditors at the expense of non-insurance creditors; or non-insurance creditors are often involuntary creditors who may only enjoy priority with regard to the hub capital. National laws have already often allowed for the 'special protection of insurance creditors', at the expense perhaps of the 'general principle of equivalent treatment of creditors'. Consequently the EU Insurance Insolvency Directive may not alter the substantive law of Member States; but it is permissive and consequently allows for latitude in exploring the priority between 'equivalence' and 'insurance protection'.

9.4.2. The EU Insurance Insolvency Directive and its Recital: its general aims, purpose and ambit

Recital 4 limits the extent of the EU Insolvency Directive: *"This Directive should not regulate the effects of the reorganisation measures and winding-up proceedings vis-à-vis third countries [save for branches of non-EU insurance undertakings]"*. Thus apparently only intra-EU proceedings are within its ambit. It is for this reason that the authors recommend when considering a PCC that a PCC should be based in an EU member jurisdiction.

According to Recital 5: *"This Directive should concern winding-up proceedings whether or not they are founded on insolvency...It should apply to collective proceedings as defined by the home Member States' legislation in accordance with Article 9"*. If the winding-up concerns a solvent entity, the firewalling of a PCC is unlikely to cause difficulties. As to whether a PCC insolvency is a *"collective proceeding"*, reference should be made to the similar discussion concerning the EU Regulation.

Recitals 7, 10 and 11 point to major differences between the EU Insurance Insolvency Directive and the EU Regulation. An insurance company does not have a COMI in the sense of an ordinary company under the EU Regulation. An insurance company needs to be specifically authorised. Consequently it is governed by its authorising body which is part and parcel of the Member State regulations. Within the EU, the insurance undertaking is always governed therefore by its home jurisdiction. Nor are there specific insolvency procedures, such as those found within Annex A of the EU Insolvency Regulation which presupposes the generic "Liquidator". Recital 7 states:

"The definition of [a] branch, in accordance with existing insolvency principles, should take account of the single legal personality of insurance undertaking. The home Member State's legislation should determine the way in which the assets and liabilities held by independent persons who have a permanent authority to act as agent for an insurance undertaking should be treated in the winding-up of an insurance undertaking".

Recital 7 augurs well for the intra-EU recognition of an insurance PCC. The home jurisdiction of a PCC (i.e. Malta and Gibraltar) is paramount.

Recitals 10 and 11 strengthen the home jurisdiction role: *"Only the competent authorities of the home Member State should be empowered to take decisions on winding-up proceedings concerning insurance undertakings (principle of unity). These proceedings should produce their effects throughout the Community and should be recognised by all Member States. All the assets and liabilities of the insurance undertaking should, as a general rule, be taken into consideration in the winding-up proceedings (principle of universality)... The home Member State's law should govern the winding-up decision concerning an insurance undertaking, the winding-up proceedings themselves and their effects, both substantive and procedural... except where the Directive provides otherwise"*. The exceptions are noted within Recital 24 and *"should concern the effects of such reorganisation measures or winding-up proceedings on certain contracts and rights, third parties' rights in rem, reservations of title, set-off, regulated markets, detrimental acts, third party purchasers and lawsuits pending"*. These exceptions are similar to those found within the EU Regulation.

Many jurisdictions have long recognised the special nature of insurance insolvencies. Consequently the normal *pari passu* rules are altered so that insurance claimants are given special priority. Indeed various types of insurance claimant (especially long-tail versus short-tail) are given a special priority within the already prioritised class of insurance claimants.

Recitals 13 and 14 recognise this special position: "*It is of utmost importance that insured persons, policy holders, beneficiaries and any injured party having a direct right of action against the insurance undertaking on a claim arising from insurance operations be protected in winding-up proceedings... In order to achieve this objective Member States should ensure special treatment for insurance creditors according to one of two optional methods provided for in this Directive. Member States may choose between granting insurance claims absolute precedence over any other claim with respect to assets representing the technical provisions or granting insurance claims a special rank which may only be preceded by claims on salaries... [etc]. Neither of these two methods provided for in this Directive impedes a Member State from establishing a ranking between different categories of insurance claims... This Directive should ensure an appropriate balance between the protection of insurance creditors and other privileged creditors protected by the Member State's legislation and not harmonise the different systems of privileged creditors existing in the Member States*".

Given that an insurance PCC is usually designed to provide priority to special classes of insurance creditor within the firewalled cells, Recitals 13 and 14 again augur well for intra-EU insurance PCC recognition.

9.5. The EU Insolvency Insurance Directive: Articles

9.5.1. Article 1

Article 1 states: "*This Directive applies to reorganisation measures and winding-up proceedings concerning insurance undertakings [as more particularly described in Article 2, and] also applies... to reorganisation measures and winding-up proceedings concerning branches in the territory of the Community of insurance undertakings having their head office outside the community*".

Whilst the EU Insurance Insolvency Directive does not have the equivalent of Annex A of the EU Regulation (which lists acceptable insolvency procedures) the accepted general consensus is that a creditor-appointed receiver (i.e. appointed out-of-court) is outside of the Directive: it being neither a 'reorganisation measure' nor a 'winding-up proceeding'. However if a receiver is appointed under the Gibraltar PCC legislation over a cell and this appointment is by way of a court appointment, then given the absence of Annex A limits, such a receiver could fall within the definition of a winding up proceeding.

The accepted consensus is that Article 1 limits the Directive to direct insurance and therefore excludes reinsurance. Given that there is no insolvency Directive yet on reinsurance, if the PCC is a reinsurance company, it may be excluded from the EU Insurance Insolvency Directive. Consequently it may fall under the EU Regulation. Given the nature of a PCC insurance company it may be difficult to ascertain whether it is an insurance or indeed a reinsurance company. This is even more so if some cells are insurance and other cells are reinsurance platforms. The question then may be asked: Is the PCC a group of companies? If so a Pandora's Box of problems may be opened. The problems could include: treating each cell as a separate company; or subjecting the PCC insolvency to both the EU Regulation and the EU Insurance Insolvency Directive simultaneously.

It can be seen that despite Recital 4 (limiting the EU Insolvency Directive to the EU) Article 1 does provide some effect *vis-à-vis* third countries in respect of branches. A branch is defined (in Article 2) as a "*any permanent presence of an insurance undertaking in the territory of a Member State other than the home Member State which carries out insurance business*". It is a different test from the equivalent 'establishment test' ("*any place of operations with the debtor carries out a non-transitory economic activity with human means and goods*") found in the EU Regulation. "*Non-transitory*" seems to equate to "*permanent presence*". There seems to be no good reason for such different wording aimed presumably at a very similar result. One difference could be of importance. The EU Regulation refers to "*debtor*", or "*legal person*", or indeed "*legal identity*" (the impact of which is discussed above) whereas the EU Insurance Insolvency Directive refers to "*insurance undertaking*"; and indeed refers to throughout to "*insurance undertakings*". An "*insurance undertaking*" could refer to a cell, whereas the term "*debtor*" may not because PCC legislation does not regard the cell as a separate legal person. However, the EU Insurance Insolvency Directive would impact upon a non-EU PCC which had a branch (however defined) within the EU. Consequently it is advisable to consider establishing in the first place, an EU-based PCC.

9.5.2. Article 2 - definitions

Other than those definitions noted above, two further definitions are of importance.

Article 2(i) and (j) states: "*'administrator' means any person or body appointed by the competent authorities for the purpose of administering reorganisation measures;...'a liquidator' means any person or body appointed by the competent authorities or by the governing bodies of an insurance undertaking, as appropriate, for the purpose of administering winding-up proceedings"*. This is a permissive definition. Thus it is unlike the EU Insolvency Regulation with its prescriptive Annex A list of acceptable procedures.

9.5.3. Article 4

Article 4 states the elemental principle, with regard to *"reorganisation measures"* (and hence not winding-up procedures), namely: *"Only the competent authorities of the home Member States shall be entitled to decide on the reorganisation measures with respect to an insurance undertaking, including its branches in other Member States... The reorganisation measures shall be governed by the laws, regulations and procedures applicable in the home Member State.... The reorganisation measures shall be fully effective throughout the Community... without any further formalities"*. Article 3 is clear. In respect of a reorganisation measure (in Gibraltar, an Administration Order) then the home jurisdiction (subject to noted exceptions) rules. Thus, a PCC insolvency should be recognised throughout the EU.

9.5.4. Article 9

Article 9 is the equivalent of article 4 in respect of *"winding-up proceedings"*; as opposed to 'reorganisation measures'. Article 9(1) states: *"The decision to open up winding-up proceedings with regard to an insurance undertaking, the winding-up proceedings and their effect shall be governed by the laws, regulations and administrative provisions applicable in its home Member State unless otherwise provided..."*. Article 9(2) then goes on to provide a non-exhaustive list of what: *"The law of the home Member State shall determine in particular... [including] the treatment of assets... the rules governing the distribution of proceeds from the realisation of assets, the ranking of claims [etc]"*. Again, in respect of a winding-up (in Gibraltar, a liquidation, or, for reasons noted above, even a receivership of a cell) then the home jurisdiction (subject to noted exceptions) rules. Thus, again an EU-based PCC insolvency should be recognised throughout the EU.

9.5.5. Article 10

Article 10(1) states: *"Member States shall ensure that insurance claims take precedence over other claims on the insurance undertaking according to one or both of the following methods: (a) insurance claims shall, with respect to assets representing the technical provisions, take absolute precedence over any other claim on the insurance undertaking; (b) insurance claims shall, with respect to the whole of the insurance undertaking's assets, take precedence over any other claim on the insurance undertaking with the possible exception of [employees, taxes and rights in rem]"*. The EU Insurance Insolvency Directive assists PCCs. *Prima facie* Article 10 assists PCCs as it allows for a derogation from the normal *pari passu* principle in that insurance claims are elevated. The reference to *"insurance undertaking"* at first sight is also helpful, for it avoids the debate concerning *"debtor"*. However what is the *"insurance undertaking"*? Is it the PCC, its hub or indeed a relevant cell? Given that Article 10 makes reference to the *"claims on the insurance undertaking"*, it should be assumed that a cell (because that is where the claims will rest primarily) is an *"insurance undertaking"*. An alternative view maybe that given that Article 10(1)(b) refers *"to the whole of the insurance undertaking's assets"*, that may implicitly refer to the PCC itself.

Given the 'EU definition' of insurance which excludes reinsurance, what of reinsurance claims and their priority? A PCC normally works whereby the insured builds up a reserve within a cell; but throughout that process reinsures the risk. This is not a problem peculiar to PCCs; it is a problem for all EU registered insurance undertakings. However a PCC, because of its nature, may be able to overcome the difficulties more easily than any other form of insurance company. It may be possible to create bankruptcy remote cells within a PCC structure whereby a reinsurance priority is elevated.

9.5.6. Articles 19-26: provisions common to reorganisation measures and winding-up proceedings

Some of the exceptions have been noted when considering the EU Regulation. None, in the authors' view impact directly upon PCCs. Article 19 considers *"certain contracts and rights"*, more especially those relating to employment and immovable property. Article 20 refers to *"Third parties' rights in rem"*. Article 21 to *"Reservation of title"*. Article 22, *"Set-off"*. Article 23, *"Regulated markets"*. Article 24, *"Detrimental acts"*. Article 25, *"Protection of third party purchasers"*. And Article 26, *"Lawsuits pending"*.

9.5.7. Article 27 - Administrators and liquidators

Article 27(2) states: *"Administrators and liquidators shall be entitled to exercise within the territory of all Member States all the powers which they are entitled to exercise within the territory of the home Member State. Persons to assist or, where appropriate, represent administrators and liquidators may be appointed, according to the home Member State's legislation, in the course of the reorganisation measure or winding-up proceedings, in particular in host Member States and, specifically, in order to help overcome any difficulties encountered by creditors in the host Member State"*. It is evident therefore that the Administrator or Liquidator so appointed will enforce a PCC priority.

9.5.8. Article 30 – "Branches of third country insurance undertakings"

The EU Insurance Insolvency Regulations consider primarily EU regulated insurance companies. However, Article 30 addresses branches of non-EU insurance companies, namely:

"When an insurance undertaking whose head office is outside the Community has branches established in more than one Member State, each branch shall be treated independently with regard to the application of the Directive. The competent authorities and the supervisory authorities of the Member States shall endeavour to coordinate their actions. Any administrators or liquidators shall likewise endeavour to coordinate their actions...". Branch *"means any permanent presence of an insurance undertaking in the territory of a Member State other than the home member state which carries out its insurance business".*

How could a non-EU insurance PCC have an EU branch? Theoretically, if a cell is sufficiently controlled by the insured then it could be argued that the cell has become a branch of the PCC. The obvious safeguard for this is to leave the management to the professionals offshore.

9.6. The EU Insurance Regulation and the UK

The Insurance Insolvency Directive was implemented in the UK via the Insurers (Reorganisation and Winding-Up) Regulations 2004 (as amended)) (the "UK Insolvency Insurance Regulations") and as to Lloyd's, the Insurers Reorganisation and Winding-Up (Lloyd's) Regulations 2005).

The UK Insurance Insolvency Regulations are considered in detail because London is the EU insurance market place. Consequently if a PCC insurance insolvency (even of an EU insurance undertaking) is to be entangled in any jurisdiction other than its home jurisdiction, it could well be that of the UK. More especially given the separate insolvency jurisdictions by the UK (i.e. Scotland, Northern Ireland and England & Wales), that of England.

Many EU countries, for example Germany, require that insurance companies have their head office in the same place as their registered office. Thus, unlike the EU Regulation, the possibility of an insurance company, being separate from its registered office is far less likely than for an ordinary non-insurance company. However, that possibility exists.

A third country insurer is therefore defined as a: *"person who has permission under [the Financial Services and Markets Act 2000] to effect or carry out contracts of insurance and whose head office is not in the UK or an EEA state [Regulation 48]"*. Regulation 49 goes on the say that "[*in the event of the reorganisation or winding up of a third party insurer] Parts III, IV and V of the Regulations apply*". Most notably Part III allows for a *non-pari passu* priority.

At first sight therefore, PCCs registered in the EEA, may have rights (in the event of an insolvency comes before a UK court), to enforce cellular priority. However, there is still a potential problem. The UK Insolvency Insurance Regulations follow the narrow definition of insurance, by specifically excluding reinsurance. The definition of a UK insurer means any person who has permission under Part IV of the Financial Services and Markets Act 2000 to effect or carry out contracts of insurance but does not include a person who, in accordance with that permission, carries on that activity exclusively in relation to reinsurance contracts.[97] Thus a reinsurer which is not authorised to conduct direct insurance business under the Act will clearly fall outside the definition of a UK insurer. Consequently in that case the EU Regulation (and not the EU Insurance Insolvency Regulations) could theoretically apply.

Part IV of the UK Insolvency Insurance Regulations implements Article 10 of the EU Directive. As such the UK now has a major derogation from normal *pari passu,* because Article 10 gives insurance creditors priority over non-insurance creditors in an insolvency of an insurance company. Specifically, regulation 20 of the UK Insolvency Insurance Regulation states: *"Except [to] the extent of regulation 27, section 175 of the 1986 Act [the UK Insolvency Act 1986] or article 149 of the 1989 order [the Insurance (Northern Ireland) Order 1989] does not apply in the case of a winding-up of a UK insurer, and instead the provisions of Regulation 21 to 26 have effect"*. Section 175 of the Insolvency Act 1986 states that preferential debts (most notably employee liabilities) rank ahead of other creditors.

Depending upon the nature of the insurance company (i.e. long term and general insurance or composite insurance) the exact priority in the event of an insolvency will be changed. But in either event (long term and general insurance or composite insurance) the priority will not be the normal UK *pari passu*.

An EU PCC (i.e. a Gibraltar or Maltese PCC) may not be wound up in the UK (unless in the most unusual of cases). So we need to look at the effect of UK legislation on non-EU insurance PCCs. It is now open to claim to a

[97] See the 'interpretation section' (section 2) of the UK Insolvency Insurance Regulations.

UK court that the non-EU PCC priority rules should be respected. Why? Because the UK Insolvency Insurance Regulations mean the UK is not wedded to a traditional view of *pari passu*. The UK Insolvency Insurance Regulations represent a derogation from the *pari passu* principle. However, the response of the Court could be twofold to a cellular priority claim:

1. 'Yes the UK derogates for insurance companies, but that is it', and you can not say 'extend this derogation to non-insurance companies if the relevant PCC is not an insurance or even a reinsurance company'.
2. 'Well okay there is a derogation for insurance companies and our PCC is an insurance company, not covered by the EU Insurance Insolvency Regulations (for whatever reason). However the specific PCC priority rules do not equate with the relevant priority rules as noted in the UK Insurance Insolvency Regulation'.

The authors consider both of these responses unduly narrow. In both types of insurance companies allowed for in the EU regime (i.e. long term and general insurance or composite insurance), preferential debts are accorded priority over insurance debts. Preferential debts will vary from jurisdiction to jurisdiction. However, they are usually government imposts (e.g. tax, social security, etc) and employee liabilities. The former are involuntary creditors and the latter partly involuntary, i.e. in the event of a redundancy. Consequently preferential debts (the involuntary creditor) often represent the major thorn in cellular priority implementation. It is always open for a PCC Articles of Association to state what will happen in the event of an insolvency. More especially, in an insolvency in a jurisdiction outside of the home jurisdiction of the PCC. The Articles could state that certain involuntary creditors will be paid, at the behest of the local IP/directors, so as to ensure local recognition, as best as possible of the cellular priority, but without effecting inter-cellular creditors integrity. Indeed this may be done without articles, as in the case of contractual PCCs. Many PCC regimes allow directors the allocate liabilities accordingly by apportionment.

The English Courts have proved reluctant to enforce foreign insolvency codes that are not sufficiently aligned with the UK. Two cases are of importance. In *BCCI SA (No. 11) [1997] 1 BCLC 80*, it was held that the English set-off rules were mandatory. Therefore the English liquidator should not remit assets outside the jurisdiction to the principle insolvency jurisdiction (in this case it was Luxembourg, but the case predated the EU Regulation) without first abiding by English set off rules. In *Re Focus*

Insurance Company Limited [1997] BCLC 219, the court refused a request (this time under a section 426 request) from Bermuda, seeking an examination under oath of a bankrupt, who was subject to a UK bankruptcy. This was regardless of the fact that the party seeking the examination was the major creditor and that the company was a Bermudan company, of which the bankrupt was a director. The refusal was because of the incompatibility with UK law of the request. Both of these cases are now over 10 years old. Whilst they suggest that the judiciary are unprepared to assist a PCC liquidator to enforce PCC priority rules, there are some distinctions that can be drawn:

1. The UK has now derogated from the monolithic view of *pari passu* priority – through the UK Insurance Insolvency Regulations.
2. The judiciary will have become aware through the Model Law and the EU Regulation of assisting in the enforcement of foreign insolvency proceedings that are not *"manifestly contrary to public policy"*. But here there is an exception for set off in any event.
3. The UK allows for a priority change of sorts in any event in general insolvencies. R.2.67(3) of the Insolvency Rules 1986 states: *"The court may, in the event of the assets being insufficient to satisfy the liability make an order as to payment out of the assets of the expenses incurred in such order as the court thinks just"*.
4. Save for the involuntary creditor, the creditors knew what they were doing when they contracted with a PCC.

It is unlikely that a cell, or indeed a PCC itself, could ever fall into the trap (if trap it be) of becoming a branch. Why? Because a branch under the UK regulations is defined (and is elsewhere so defined) as having the meaning given by *"article 1(b) of the life insurance directive or the third non life insurance directive"*; and this is defined in the directive as:

"...any permanent presence of an undertaking in the territory of a Member State shall be treated in the same way as an agency or branch, even if that presence does not take the form of a branch or agency, but consists merely of an office managed by the undertaking's own staff or by a person who is independent but has permanent authority to act for the undertaking as an agency would".

10. UNCITRAL MODEL LAW

10.1. Background

On 30 May 1997 the United Nations Commissions on International Trade Law ("UNCITRAL") adopted the Model Law on cross-border insolvency ("Model Law") with a view to assisting States: to manage cross-border insolvencies in a *"Fair and efficient"* manner; encourage *"Cooperation between courts"*; create *"Greater legal certainty"*; *"Protection and maximisation of… the debtors assets"*; and offer *"rescue facilitation"*.[98]

The Model Law has much in common with the EU Regulation, in being an attempt to harmonise international law and in its reference to COMI. Indeed, many clauses of the Model Law are nearly identical to the EU Regulation. The major difference between the two transnational regimes is that in respect of the Model Law it is just that, a model law that States are free to adopt some, but not necessarily all of its elements. Thus in any analysis it needs to be recognised that national deviations from the 'model' will occur. Contrawise EU Member States either accepted the EU Regulation in full or, in the case of Denmark, did not accept it at all. This chapter will therefore look primarily to the Model Law itself. It will only consider 'national deviations' from the Model Law if they are considered material in the context of PCCs. As at the time of writing the following States have adopted the Model Law in its entirety, or with alternations, or in yet to be promulgated legislation:

Australia (2008),
British Virgin Islands ("BVI") (2005),
Colombia (2006),
Eritrea,
Japan (2000),
Mauritius (2009),
Mexico (2000),
Montenegro and Serbia (2002 and 2004, respectively),
New Zealand (2006),
Poland (2003),
Republic of Korea (2006),
Romania (2003),
Slovenia (2007)
South Africa (2000),

98 See the Preamble to Part 1 of the Model Law.

UK (2006), and
USA (2005).

It should also be noted that a substantial number of States have adopted legislation, that whilst not adopting the Model Law, facilitates much of it. An example is Canada, which we will consider in this book.

Of these, four States[99] have only adopted to the extent of reciprocity, i.e. the Model Law will only work within those jurisdictions where the counterparty involved has also adopted the Model Law. Importantly, of the adopting States only the US,[100] Mauritius and the BVI (as noted above, subject to reciprocity) have adopted PCC legislation. Both of the US and BVI have only allowed PCCs for insurance purposes which, as we shall see, are in any event excluded from the Model Law. However, PCCs around the World are not now used exclusively for insurances. Further, unless Model Law adopting States have a reciprocity clause, it is irrelevant as to whether the PCC home jurisdiction is also a Model Law adopting State. Thus a non-insurance PCC incorporated in a non-Model Law adopting State may still get Model Law protection in a Model Law adopting State; that is provided the enacting State has not got a reciprocity clause.

The primary question posed by this chapter is: *Does the existence of the Model Law enhance the international enforceability of PCCs, more especially non-insurance PCCs?* Like the EU Regulation, interpretation of the Model Law may be aided by considering its accompanying interpretation guide. For the Model Law, it is Part 2, or "*Guide to Enactment*" (the "Guide"): Part 1 being the Model Law itself and Part 2 being the Guide. More especially paragraph 19 of the Guide which states that: "*the EU Regulation establishes a cross-border insolvency regime within the EU for cases where* ***the debtor*** *[our emphasis, note not the 'legal person', etc, as in the EU Regulation] has a … [COMI in the EU] the…. [EU] Regulation does not deal with cross-border insolvency matters extending beyond … [the EU]. Thus the Model Law offers to [EU] States … a complimentary regime of considerable practical value that addresses [in a similar way] the many cases of cross-border cooperation not*

[99]The BVI, Mexico, Romania and South Africa

[100]In the following States and Possessions: Arkansas, Delaware, Illinois, Iowa, North and South Carolina, Rhode Island, US Virgin Islands as to the Company Organisation, Management, Securities 290-1 Protected Cell Company Model Act of 1999 (the US PCC Model Act); and in legislation related to the US PCC Model Act, Arizona, Montana, Oklahoma, Texas, Utah, Vermont and West Virginia, but there is no legislation at Federal level.

covered by the .... [EU] Regulation". Can PCC providers and users enjoy the claimed *"Greater legal certainty for trade and investment"* (as claimed in preamble (b)) of the Model Law? In order to answer that question we will consider the material Articles and headings.

10.2. The Title – "Model Law", etc

"The word 'insolvency', as used in the title of the Model Law, refers to various types of collective proceedings against insolvent debtors. The reason is that the Model Law (as pointed out above in paragraphs 23 and 24) covers proceedings concerning different types of debtors and, among those proceedings, deals with proceedings aimed at reorganising the debtor and proceedings leading to a liquidation of the debtor as a commercial entity.... It should be noted that in some jurisdictions the expression 'insolvency proceedings' has a narrow technical meaning in that it may refer, for example, only to collective proceedings involving a company or a similar legal person or only to collective proceedings against a natural person. No such distinction is intended to be drawn by the use of the term 'insolvency' in the title of the Model Law, since the Model Law is designed to be applicable to proceedings regardless of whether they involve a natural person or a legal person as the debtor. If in the enacting State the word 'insolvency' may be misunderstood as referring to one particular type of collective proceeding, another term should be used to refer to the proceedings covered by the Law [paras 51-52 inclusive of the Guide]".

The Model Law appears more flexible than the EU Regulation in that it emphases *"debtor"* insolvency as opposed to (say) *"legal person"* insolvency. Thus the Model Law can possibly therefore accommodate a cellular insolvency, which as we have learned never involves a separate identifiable legal person.

10.3. Article 1 of the Model Law – Scope of Application

Article 1(1)(d) of the Model Law relates to the Scope of Application of the Model Law: and for our purpose, also the concept of *"interested persons"*. *"These laws [i.e. the Model Law as implemented in the relevant State] apply where... (d) Creditors or other interested persons in a foreign State have an interest in requesting the commencement of, or participating in, a proceeding under [identify laws of the enacting State relating to insolvency]"*. The Guide adds little in understanding Article 1 as it applies to PCCs. However, the phrase *"or other interested persons"* may prove important. The classic PCC regime states that creditors should be told at inception that they are creditors of (say) cell X, or cell Y or cell Z and if not so stated, or indeed if specifically stated, they become creditors of the PCC hub. Thus in the event of the insolvency of cell Y, then a creditor of cell X, according to the law of the PCC State, could not claim in the insolvency of cell Y. However, Article 1(d) would allow the cell X creditor surely as an *"interested person"* to state his case in the insolvency of cell Y. The Model Law is thus wider than the EU Regulation in its 'rights of audience'. It may thus allow more argument against the PCC cellular priority in a court of a non-PCC jurisdiction. In most Model Law adopting States, Article 1 has been adopted without alteration and the *"other interested person"* may feature strongly in a PCC insolvency in a non-PCC Model Laws State.

Article 1 covers 'Scope of the Application' and includes excluded economic activities. According to Article 1(2): *"This law does not apply to a proceeding [designate any type of entities; such as banks or insurance companies, that are subject to a special insolvency regime in this State and that this State wishes to exclude them from this Law]."* All Model Law adopting States have excluded certain entities, more especially insurance and banking debtors. The UK also excludes (see the Cross-Border Insolvency Regulations 2006 (the "UK Cross-Border Regulations"). The UK has 13 exclusions (Chapter 1, Article 1 of the Cross-Border Regulations) and interestingly excludes both insurance and reinsurance European Economic Area ("EEA") companies. Given the paramount use of PCCs for insurance (and reinsurance purposes) then it has to be said that the Model Law may have limited impact on the worldwide recognition of PCC insolvencies. However, all is not lost as there remain several other relevant transnational regimes. More especially the EU Insurance Insolvency Regulations governing exclusively institutions based in the EU and EEA. Consequently a PCC should be established within the EU to ensure EU-wide recognition in the event of an insolvency. In the case of the UK, section 426 of the Insolvency Act (the "Commonwealth Insolvency Regime") may mean that a PCC established in various Commonwealth States (the so-called "Designated Territories") would also be recognised widely.

10.4. Article 2 – "Definitions"

10.4.1. Proceedings

According to Article 2(a): "Foreign proceedings" means a: *"collective judicial or administrative proceeding… pursuant to a law relating to insolvency in which proceeding the assets and affairs of the debtor are subject to control or supervision by a foreign court, for the purpose of reorganisation or liquidation"*. Again, the Model Law appears wider in scope than the EU Regulation. The Model Law goes further with the disjunctive *"or administrative proceedings"* which would imply the proceedings need not be collective.

Indeed the apparently very wide ranging ambit of Article 2 is strengthened by paragraph 71 of the Guide which states – *"The definitions of proceedings or persons emanating from foreign jurisdictions avoid the use of expressions that may have different technical meaning in legal systems and instead describe their purpose or function. This technique is used to avoid inadvertently narrowing the range of possible foreign proceedings that might obtain recognition and to avoid unnecessary conflict with terminology used in the laws of the enacting State. As noted in paragraph 52 above, the expression 'insolvency proceedings' may have a technical meaning in some legal systems, but it is intended in sub-paragraph (a) to refer broadly to proceedings involving companies in severe financial distress"*.

According to Article 2(b) – *"Foreign main proceeding means a foreign proceeding taking place in the State where the debtor has ... [its COMI]"*. Further, paragraph 72 of the Guide states: "*The expression ... [COMI] is used also in the [EU Regulation]...*" Consequently reference should be made to the discussions concerning the EU Regulation and COMI.

However, it needs to be remembered that a Model Law adopting State can alter the Model Law. Section 18.6(1) of the Canadian Company Creditors Arrangement Act 1997 (the "CCAA"), now repealed by section 131 of the Wage Earner Protection Program Act, stated that a *"foreign proceeding"* is: *"a judicial or administrative proceeding commenced outside Canada in respect of a debtor under a law relating to bankruptcy or insolvency and dealing with the collective interest of creditors generally"*. It has now been replaced by a new definition of "foreign proceeding" under Section 45(1) to mean "a judicial or an administrative proceeding, including an interim proceeding, in a jurisdiction outside Canada dealing with creditors' collective interests generally under any law relating to bankruptcy or insolvency in which a debtor company's business and financial affairs are subject to control or supervision by a foreign court for the purpose of reorganization".

Thus, even the disjunctive *"administrative proceedings"* needs to be *"collective"*. Further, not only *"collective" but even more emphatically "creditors generally"*. Unfortunately a cellular insolvency that is otherwise a "foreign proceeding" may find that is not a *"foreign proceeding"* within Canada as it may fall foul of this CCAA definition.

The US Bankruptcy Code (the "US Code") is, however, perhaps more helpful. Under the US Code (s.101) the term "foreign proceeding" means: *"collective judicial or administrative proceeding in a foreign country, including an interim proceeding, under a law relating to insolvency or adjustment of debt in which proceeding the assets and affairs of the debtor are subject to control or supervision by a foreign court for the purpose of reorganisation or liquidation."* Previously there had been a long history within the US of considering whether the foreign insolvency process offered 'adequate protection' in 'ancillary proceedings'. This Model Law definition does not refer to all of the assets of the debtor and to debt adjustment; both of which may (with the addition of the reference to *"estate"*) assist in allowing for a purely cellular insolvency to come within the purview of a foreign main proceeding. The apparent dropping of the previous requirement for 'adequate protection' in 'ancillary proceedings' may lead to a threat in the US of litigation that such an absence of 'adequate protection' is unconstitutional. This may augur badly for a US Model Law insolvency of a non-US PCC. Alternatively it must be remembered that the US already has its own PCC legislation.

The term *"establishment"* used in Article 2(f) is also used in the EU Regulation. However, the Model Law does not use the EU Regulation terms of *"territorial"* or *"secondary proceedings"*. Rather the Model Law uses *"foreign non-main proceedings"*, although little seems to turn on this.

10.4.2. Debtor

The term *"debtor"* is used in the Model Law; most Model Law adopting States make the Model Law paramount over other local insolvency law. However, conflict, especially regarding a PCC, may occur as to what the term '*debtor*' does or can cover. The UK Cross-Border Regulations[101] state at section 3(2): *"in the case of any conflict between any provision of ... [UK] insolvency law or of Part 3 of the Insolvency Act 1986,[102] the latter shall prevail"*.

Unfortunately there is no provision within the Insolvency Act or the Insolvency Rules for a "non-natural" debtor that is not a company. It is either a natural or a legal person, Rule 13.8 of the Insolvency Rules 1986 states precisely this dichotomy: *"References to 'the insolvent estate' are (a) in relation to a company insolvency, the company's assets, and (b) in relation to an individual insolvency [with which we are not here concerned], the bankrupt's estate (or as the case may be) the debtor's property"*.

[101] SI 2006/1030

[102] Therefore presumably any rules and other delegated legislation made under the Insolvency Act 1986 such as the Insolvency Rules 1986, the latter [i.e. the Model Law as enacted].

A UK judge could therefore easily avoid the possible conflict caused by recognising a PCC under the Model Law, by stating that a debtor could only apply to a company (or the whole PCC) or a natural person, i.e. an individual; but not therefore a cell. According to the UK Cross-Border Regulations (Schedule 2, Part 1, the definitions section in section 1(1): "*In this Schedule 'relevant company' means a company within the meaning of section 735(1) of the Companies Act 1985 or an unregistered company within the meaning of Part 5 of the 1986 Act which is subject to a requirement imposed by virtue of Section 690A [4], 691(1) or Section 718 of the Companies Act 1985*".

Whilst it may be possible to argue that a cell is an unregistered company within Part 5 of the Insolvency Act 1986, it is hard to argue that the cell may be subject to the noted Companies Act requirements. As to whether a cell (as opposed to a PCC itself) could be an unregistered company, the following criteria are considered identifying factors:

(a) legal character, which may be something more diffuse than legal personality;

(b) status; and

(c) capacity.[103]

Given that the Model Law can be adopted with alterations, States have made alterations to and/or additions to the definitions section. Unlike the confusing and often narrow definition used by the EU Regulation as to when the EU Regulation applies (a "*legal person*" or "*entity*", *et al),* the Model Law simply refers throughout to a "*debtor*". As we have seen a cell can be a "*debtor*" but not a "*legal person*" and this may cause difficulties for a cellular insolvency under the EU Regulation. Not so the term "*debtor*", which can refer to the cell as well as to the PCC itself. However, Model Law adopting States may have specifically defined "*debtor*" so as to create similar problems to those noted with the EU Regulation for cells.

Most States have simply (i.e. as in the UK Cross-Border Regulations) referred to the Model Law in this regard verbatim and thus referred to "*debtor*" without further definition. Not so in the US. Under section 1502(1) Chapter 15 of the US Code states: "*debtor means an entity that is the subject to a foreign proceeding*". The term "*entity*" is further defined within section 101 of the US Code as: "*entity includes [i.e. it is not an exclusion definition] person, estate, trust, governmental unit and US trustee*". The term "*estate*" may be sufficiently wide-ranging to cover a cell. Even if the term

[103] *St James' Club (1852)* 2 DEGM and G

"estate" is not so wide-ranging, the definition is non-exclusive. Thus a structure, such as a cell, which does not fit within any of the terms used, is not thereby automatically excluded. Canada in its enacting statute states *"a 'debtor company'* means *'...an insolvent person'."* As we have seen a cell cannot be a legal person. Consequently Canada may have a problem with accepting a PCC cellular insolvency.

10.5. Article 5 – Foreign Representative

Article 5 allows for an IP to act as a *"foreign representative"* abroad i.e. in say a non-PCC Model Law adopting State. The question is, "What can the foreign representative do in the foreign proceedings?" and this question is answered in Articles 11 and 12.

10.6. Article 6 – Public Policy Exception

Article 6 allows for a *"public policy exception" à la mode* of the EU Regulation. However some Model Law States have extended the public policy exception noted in the Model Law. For instance Serbia and Montenegro, Romania and Japan have omitted the word *"manifestly"* as in *"manifestly contrary to public policy"*. Poland also excludes foreign law where the COMI is Polish. Japan adds the phrase contrary to *"good custom"*. Article 6 may prove problematical for PCC cellular priority transnational enforcement. Why? Because of the divergencies from the Model Law standard wording and:

(i) the propensity of some Model Law States (notably the US) to resort to litigation and constitutional rights;

(ii) the lack of a supervening court (*à la mode* of the EU ECJ under the EU Regulation); and

(iii) the novelty of PCCs.

10.7. Articles 11 and 12 – Foreign Representatives and Proceedings

Articles 11 and 12 provide for the *"foreign representative"* to commence proceedings and to participate in *"foreign proceedings"* respectively. Thus a PCC cell IP may theoretically also act in a non-PCC Model Law adopting State. To that limited extent it may augur favourably for PCCs.

10.8. Article 13 – Creditor Discrimination

Article 13 provides for access for foreign creditors in a Model Law adopting State and the fact that they are foreign creditors will not affect their priority ranking. Consequently it leaves open a PCC priority ranking or rather it does not address the priority ranking of a PCC. To that limited extent it may augur favourably for PCCs.

Article 13 may present a problem for PCCs. Its aim is benign: *"foreign creditors have the same rights... as [local] creditors"*. However, given the unusual priority structure of PCCs, unforeseen problems may occur.

Unlike most of the Model Law, Article 13 of the Model Law allows for alternate wording. Most States have had a history of refusing to enforce foreign tax and social security claims.[104] Of late this attitude has changed somewhat. Article 13(1) states: *"foreign creditors have the same rights regarding commencement of, and participation in, a proceeding [identify laws of the enacting State relating to insolvency] as creditors in this State"*.

Throughout this book, it has been noted that the bugbear of PCCs is the involuntary creditor. The most common involuntary creditor is likely to be a government tax. Let us assume that the Model Law adopting State follows the 'modern route' of enforcing foreign tax and social security claims. In such a case it is open for the involuntary government creditor to argue that the very nature of a PCC means that its claim is invariably subordinated. Consequently, that the PCC cellular priority is open to challenge because, as an involuntary creditor, the government would only have recourse to the hub and not the individual cells. This must be contrasted with the ordinary position of the normal voluntary creditor who has recourse in the first place to the cell assets and then if there is a cellular deficiency, usually to the hub capital.

This Model Law sub-article may allow for, in certain jurisdictions, recognition of PCC cellular priority. *"The court is not restricted unnecessarily in its ability to grant any type of relief that it is available under the law of the enacting State... The proviso 'under the law of this State' reflects the principle underlying the Model Law that recognition of a foreign proceeding does not mean extending the effects of the foreign proceeding as they may be prescribed by the law of the foreign State. Instead, recognition of a foreign proceeding entails attaching consequences envisaged by the law of the enacting state [paragraphs 154 and 159 of the Guide]"*.

10.9. Article 16 – Presumptions Concerning Recognition

Article 16 contains three presumptions, two of which are of possible assistance to a PCC insolvency. Article 16(1) states that a certificate provided by the foreign representative to the effect that the foreign

[104] See *Government of India, Ministry of Finance v Taylor* [1955] AC 491.

proceeding is a proceeding to be presumed valid by the court, i.e. that the foreign representative is appointed to *"administer the reorganisation"*.

As such there would appear to be a presumption that a PCC insolvency, or more particularly a cell insolvency, fell within the definition of a *"foreign proceeding"* as a *"collective judicial or administrative procedure."*[105] This augurs well for PCCs and the enforcement of a PCC priority in the event of insolvency for it avoids the difficulties of the EU Regulation with its prescribed Annex A lists of insolvency proceedings. Article 16(3) states in the same mode as the EU Regulation: *"In the absence of proof to the contrary, the debtor's registered office...is presumed to be the...[debtor's COMI]"*.

Thus the IP of a PCC insolvency or more particularly of a cellular insolvency established anywhere in the world, as against a Model Law adopting State, without a reciprocity clause, would be presumed to fall within the Model Law. Thus its main proceedings would be within the PCC incorporation State. The reference to *"other interested parties"* is supplemented in the UK by: *"at the hearing of the application, the applicant [i.e. the 'foreign representative'] and any of the following... may appear ... [j] with the permission of the court, any other person who appears to have an interest justifying his appearance"*.[106]

Model Law adopting States have enacted their own procedural laws to implement the Model Law. These procedural laws may cause difficulties for a foreign representative i.e. a foreign IP of a PCC and/or a PCC cell. For instance the Cross-Border Regulations demands that any application for *"foreign representative"* relief (i.e. Article 21): *"must be supported by an affidavit sworn by the foreign representative stating... (e) whether to the best of his knowledge and belief ... the interest of the debtors creditors ... and* ***any other interested parties*** *[our emphasis, more especially in the case of PCC creditors, creditors who are not creditors of the relevant cell insolvency]... will be adequately protected."*[107]

Model Law adopting States tend to have similar procedural rules. A *"foreign representative"* PCC IP or PCC cellular IP should (especially in the case of an ex parte hearing) disclose at length the nature of a PCC. The *"foreign representative"* IP should go further in appropriate circumstances.

---

[105] See Article 2(a) of the Model Law.

[106] Cross-Border Regulations , Schedule 2, Part 6, Section 25(1)

[107] UK Cross-Border Regulations, Schedule 2, Part 3, Section 7.

He may invite a representative of any local creditor affected by the PCC (whether of the hub or of another cell) to attend the hearing to argue against the concept of a PCC viz the priority rules of a PCC. Inevitably this will lead to a general discussion as to whether a PCC insolvency:

(i) falls within the Model Law as a *"collective insolvency"* or

(ii) is *"manifestly contrary to public policy"; or*

(iii) local creditors are "adequately protected" (however defined).

Nevertheless in a spirit of "*cooperation between the court*" noted in the Model Law preamble, this exercise should be considered. If there is not a full account of the PCC concept given at such an application, there is always the danger that the *"foreign representatives"* IP being called to account later. For instance, a UK court could impose personal liability if the *"foreign representatives"* has for instance *"misapplied... money... of the debtor"*[108] i.e. even placing monies in the appropriate cell and thereby disregarding normal *pari passu*.

Where possible, for Model Law purposes, a PCC should be established in a State which has a separate and specific insolvency code and that code covers, often by *mutatis mutandis* amendments, PCC and PCC cell insolvencies. It should also be noted that some Model Law States have extended the insolvency definition. For instance, the US, via Section 101(23) of the US Code: *"under a law relating to insolvency or adjustment of debt"*.

The article 16(3) presumption that *"the debtors office is presumed to be the... [debtors COMI]"* was tested in a US case involving a PCC: *re SPhinX Ltd, et al, Debtors in Foreign Proceedings, chapter 15, case number 06 -- 11760 - US bankruptcy Court for the Southern District of New York ("re SPhinX").*

Re SPhinX appears to be the first case under Chapter 15 of the US Bankruptcy Code (which implements the UNCITRAL Model Law) to consider COMI. Importantly, PCCs were also tangentially involved. The Cayman Islands SPhinX Funds were in liquidation in the Cayman Islands. The SPhinX Funds were subject to US litigation concerning a preference. In order to stymie this litigation, the Cayman Islands liquidators petitioned for US recognition that the Cayman Islands liquidation was the *"main proceedings"*, i.e. the SPhinX Funds had a Cayman Islands COMI. The US Court refused to recognize the Cayman Islands proceedings as the *"main proceedings"*. But this, however, was not

[108] UK Cross-Border Regulations , Schedule 2, Part 8, Section 29(3)

on the basis that COMI was elsewhere, i.e. for instance in the US. The court refusal to recognize the Cayman Islands proceedings was on the ground that: *"[A] primary basis for the Petition and the investors' tacit consent to the Cayman Islands proceedings as foreign main proceedings, is improper…This litigation strategy appears to be the only reason for the request for recognition of the Cayman Islands proceedings as a foreign main proceedings"*. In short the decision turned on 'abuse of process'.

Despite the failure of the *re SPhinX* judgment to address the issue of COMI head on it remains one of the few reported cases worldwide involving a PCC and insolvency. For that reason it is worth quoting extensively from the court report:[109]

"Facts… the SPhinX Funds Business and Contacts with the Cayman Islands. Each of the SPhinX Funds is either a 'limited liability company' or a 'segregated portfolio company' [i.e. a PCC] incorporated and registered in the Cayman Islands…The SPhinX Funds were established as offshore entities apparently to attract non-US and US tax exempt investors in light of favourable Cayman Islands tax benefits and regulations (with the… [PCCs] subject to more regulation than the other SPhinX Funds)… [The] SPhinX Funds did not conduct a trade or business in the Cayman Islands. They had no employees and no physical offices in the Cayman Islands (or elsewhere, for that matter). The SPhinX Funds were prohibited as "exempted companies" from engaging in business in the Cayman Islands… [under the] …Companies Law (2004 Revision) of the Cayman Islands… Indeed except for corporation books and records… required to be maintained under the Cayman Islands Law… they have acknowledged instead that "substantially all" of the Debtors assets are in the US… From… inception, their hedge fund business was actually conducted under a fully discretionary investment management contract by PlusFunds… a Delaware corporation located in New York City…The SPhinX Funds auditors were… an international accounting firm, with a Cayman Islands address... It is not clear how much work the auditors actually performed in the Cayman Islands... None of the directors resided in the Cayman Islands… [and no] board meeting… took place there... Until recently, the stock of… the Debtors was traded on the Irish stock exchange."

The authors' mantra is, 'keep everything generally within the PCC jurisdiction'. Here the Cayman Islands segregated portfolio company (or PCC), as an exempted company, was prohibited from engaging in business in the Cayman Islands except in furtherance of their business

[109] Available in http://www.nysb.uscourts.gov/opinions/rdd/150507_30_opinion.pdf

carried on outside of the Cayman Islands. Most commentators consider that the COMI of the SPhinX Funds was not in the Cayman Islands. It was probably in the US. If COMI had been found to be (or more importantly was fully argued to be) in the US then a US *"main proceedings"* insolvency would have followed. Such a case would have been of greater assistance to the authors; more especially in ascertaining how a foreign jurisdiction would view an alien PCC. Even then, however, it would have been of limited assistance. Remember the US is a PCC jurisdiction. Despite the court not finding the COMI to be in the Cayman Islands, it followed that the *"non-main proceedings"* in the Cayman Islands continued. (It is to be noted that the Cayman Liquidators appealed the decision to the United States District Court for Southern District of New York. On July 2007 the District Court upheld the decision of the Bankruptcy Court and declined to recognise the proceedings as foreign non-main proceedings).

The authors do not consider the judgment as providing an important judicial insight into PCCs. Nevertheless it has some value, because the judgment tangentially touched on areas of concern. These areas of concern are noted below.

(A) *"It is far from clear whether under US law, the investors in the SPhinX Funds would be viewed in such capacity as creditors and whether claims that they might assert arising from the purchase or sale of their interests in the Debtors would be treated on same priority as creditor claims".* This is an acknowledgement of a radically different priority. It is surprising that it was not taken further. It is a doubtful as to whether this statement constitutes *obiter dictum*. However it does seem to constitute a tacit acceptance of a priority shift.

(B) *"[Xs]... joint objection to the Petition asserted that the SPhinX Funds may be solvent;... [the liquidators] disagree, but,... the court determined that it was unnecessary to address the issue at this time".* The issue of what constitutes a debtor (i.e. is it a cell or the whole PCC entity) and therefore whether some cells may be or may not be solvent, was not addressed. This issue has been addressed extensively in this book.

(C) The judgment noted: *"Because their money is ultimately at stake, one generally should defer, therefore, to the creditors acquiescence in or support of a proposed COMI".* Consequently, certainly as to voluntary creditors, PCC directors should get creditors' written agreement, at the inception of the creditor relationship, that they will support *"main proceedings"* in the home jurisdiction. This can be by way of a simple signed acknowledgement that they (the creditors) recognize the COMI of the PCC to be within the PCC jurisdiction.

(D) The judge noted the pragmatism of allowing the Cayman Islands liquidator to continue in office as was: *"And the Court notes that no one, including the objectors, has questioned the...[Cayman Island liquidators] ability to wind up the Debtors or that the Cayman Court would supervise the foreign proceedings fairly"*. Two issues appeared to be raised here. First it can be seen that the issues may not have been fully argued by the parties in *re SPhinX*. Viewed from one perspective, it should be possible to claim (if not to prove) that a PCC priority is unfair. Second, the judge obviously considered that as far as the Cayman Islands liquidation itself was concerned, matters were progressing reasonably. Consequently PCC promoters should seek a jurisdiction with an adequate insolvency infrastructure.

(E) *"[The liquidators] argued that Cayman Islands Law has specific winding up requirements... with respect to... [PCCs]"*. The judgment seems to acknowledge something more than the above noted pragmatism. The judgment, in not rejecting outright the liquidator's argument, seems to suggest something further; that if a jurisdiction has specific PCC insolvency legislation, then other jurisdictions should leave the PCC insolvency to that jurisdiction. All PCC jurisdictions provide for PCC insolvency legislation. Obviously such a judicial thought process can only augur well for the international recognition of a PCC priority in a PCC insolvency. The US is of course a PCC jurisdiction. However, its PCC regime is limited to insurance. The SPhinX Funds were not insurance funds. Consequently the US PCC regime could not be used.

(F) As noted there was little, *"disputing the Cayman Islands liquidators... satisfaction of Chapter 15 requirements"*. The judgment then went on to say: *"In any event, the Cayman Islands proceedings under which the SPhinX Funds are being wound up subject to the supervision of the... [Cayman Islands] Court in collective proceedings... are 'foreign proceedings' under the Bankruptcy Code"*. This statement was made on the basis that US courts had previously found; *"court supervised Cayman Islands winding up proceedings... foreign proceedings"*. Contrariwise, the judgment noted that a voluntary Cayman Islands winding up proceedings that was not subject to the supervision by the Cayman Islands Court, was not so recognized. Thus there was not a discussion as to whether a PCC insolvency (regardless of court supervision) was *"collective"* in its nature. Again this issue is addressed in this book.

(G) The PCC structure seems to have not been questioned in the judgment. Was this because it was not sufficiently argued? Or was it because the US is a PCC jurisdiction? Or was it because the fact that the insolvent entity was the PCC was irrelevant to the issues facing the court? For whatever reason, it appears that the presence of a PCC structure was not considered a problem. The court stated its position: *"Thus it does not appear that the commencement of... [the Cayman Islands liquidations of these]... entities, all of which are registered in the Cayman Islands and several of which, as... [PCCs]... are subject to additional Cayman Islands regulation, would be "manifestly contrary to the public policy of the United States" [being a reason under the UNCITRAL Model Law for not recognizing a foreign proceeding]".*

(H) Given the above, there was obviously no discussion as to what constitutes a debtor under the UNCITRAL Model Law, i.e. is it the cell or the hub? This was despite the apparent multiplicity of debtors within the SPhinX Funds.

(I) Shareholders (at a cellular level) have a greater interest in the insolvency outcome of a PCC than shareholders in an ordinary limited liability company. Thus PCC promoters will note with interest the judgment comments: *"It is reasonable to assume that the... shareholders, if they have in proper economic stake in the proceeding... can, absent an improper purpose, best determine how to maximise the efficiency of a liquidation".*

What conclusions if any can be drawn from this?

(1) At the risk of being repetitive, follow the mantra, 'keep things local'. The issue of COMI is paramount. It would appear that the SPhinX Funds COMI was not in the Cayman Islands.

(2) Certainly in the US, an international PCC insolvency is not greeted with immediate opprobrium. However, the US is a PCC jurisdiction.

The Cayman Islands liquidators have set up a very comprehensive website http://www.sphinxfunds.com (the "Website") for the purpose of providing *"investors and creditors of the [Sphinx] Companies and other interested parties with copies of press releases and other relevant information pertaining to the official liquidation of the Companies."*

It would seem from the information publicly available that substantive arguments relating to the nature of the cellular structure were aired before the United States Court of Appeals for the Second Circuit ("the Court of Appeals") in a separate action by the Sphinx Liquidator (the "Liquidator") and investors *In Refco Inc, et al, (case number 06-5786-bk (L)).*

According to the court judgment the facts giving rise to the appeal were[110]:

"[it was alleged] Sphinx's excess margin cash [was] invested in accounts at its affiliate Refco Capital Markets Ltd ("Refco"], the debtor in the underlying bankruptcy proceedings. On October 12, 2005, five days before Refco, Inc ("Refco") filed for bankruptcy protection under Chapter 11… a total of US$312,046,266.23 was transferred, from the Sphinx accounts at RCM to its affiliates Refco, LLC, and ultimately to accounts held on behalf of the cells at [financial institution]. [The Official Committee of Refco] commenced … proceeding on behalf of RCM seeking avoidance and recovery of the transfer made to the cells …. [on the basis] that the transfer was preferential. … On April 20, 2006 … the Committee and Sphinx agreed to a settlement whereby Sphinx, on behalf of the cells, would return US$263 million to the RCM estate (the "Settlement"] … After hearing the arguments from all parties, including Investors, the bankruptcy court approved the Settlement as being in the best interests of the debtors, their estate and creditors… Investors appealed the approval to the district court…. The district court rejected … Investors' arguments [and they appealed to the Court of Appeals]."

The Liquidator submitted with their brief, detailed legal arguments from UK counsel. The court document[111] dated 4 March 2007 (the "Court Document") has been made public in the Website and gives a very valuable insight into the legal (and practical) issues arising from the nature of an SPC (PCC). From the Court Document counsel was asked to opine *"on (i) the nature and limitations of Sphinx SPC's segregated portfolio company (SPC) structure under Cayman Islands law; (ii) whether it was lawful under the laws of the Cayman Islands for Sphinx SPC to meet the alleged liability arising from the Preference Action by releasing funds at … the account; (iii) whether the Settlement Agreement, which is the subject of the appeal, is unlawful under Cayman Islands law; and (iv) whether the former directors of Sphinx SPC at the time of the Settlement Agreement…had authority under the Articles of Association and relevant Cayman Islands law to enter into the Settlement Agreement."* All the issues were closely linked to the statutory segregation of assets and liabilities in the cellular structure.

---

[110]http://www.ca2.uscourts.gov/decisions/isysquery/2ef6d767-291d-4bad-93a2-a67e8bda8a1a/1/doc/06-5786-bk_opn.pdf#xml=http://www.ca2.uscourts.gov/decisions/isysquery/2ef6d767-291d-4bad-93a2-a67e8bda8a1a/1/hilite/

[111]http://www.sphinxfunds.com/files/Pages%2069%20-%2098%20-%20Affidavit%20T%20%20Lowe.pdf

The Court of Appeals upheld the Settlement but side-stepped these issues. Again back to the court report:

"In an SPC, each investor's assets and liabilities are held in a particular portfolio, or 'cell', managed by the company. According to the parties, the SPC structure permits a company to segregate the assets and liabilities it holds on behalf of a particular investor from the assets and liabilities it holds on behalf of other investors, and from the general assets of the company itself. While an SPC is a single legal entity, the individual cells within it are not. Sphinx manages fifteen separate cells...According to Investors, directors of an SPC are required by law to keep each cell's assets segregated and separately identifiable from the others. Where a particular cell incurs liability in excess of its assets, the creditor may be paid first from the assets of the liable cell, and then from the SPC's general assets, if permitted by the articles of association and only to the extent that the company's general assets exceed any minimum capital amounts required by Cayman regulatory law. In no case may the assets of one cell be permitted to satisfy the liabilities of another. Investors allege that RAI placed the cells' funds in unsegregated accounts at RCM. By contrast, Appellees – the Official Committee of Unsecured Creditors of Refco Incorporated and its affiliated debtors and debtors-in-possession ("Committee") – assert that Investors' funds were held in separate accounts in the name of each of the cells while at RCM. The record establishes that Sphinx is a single legal entity, and that the individual cells are not legally separate entities from Sphinx. By investing in Sphinx, Investors placed control of their funds entirely within the hands of the Sphinx directors (or managers acting on behalf of the directors).

Only Sphinx, not individual Investors, or even Investors as a group, could assert a claim against the Refco estate, and only Sphinx was permitted to negotiate a settlement with the Committee. Investors maintain a financial "interest" in Sphinx, but they are not a "party in interest" within the meaning of the Bankruptcy Code. The party in interest in the bankruptcy sense, representing the Investors' financial interest, is Sphinx... But one cannot avoid the conclusion that the bankruptcy court is not the appropriate forum in which to resolve Investors' disputes with the Sphinx board.... That issue, however, is not for the bankruptcy court. Bankruptcy courts are primarily courts of equity, but they are not empowered to address any equitable claim tangentially related to the bankruptcy proceeding. Bankruptcy court is a forum where creditors and debtors can settle their disputes with each other. Any internal dispute between a creditor and that creditor's investors belongs elsewhere....[The Liquidators] may only bring an action on behalf of the company that the company could have brought itself... Sphinx consented to the Settlement. Indeed, without Sphinx's consent, the Settlement Agreement would never have been presented to the bankruptcy court for approval. Having consented to the Settlement below, Sphinx is bound by it on appeal...Clearly, as a party to the Settlement, Sphinx is precluded from appealing the bankruptcy court's order."

From the judgment there is no suggestion that the court failed to understand the nature of an SPC (or PCC). Nor is there any suggestion of the court rejecting the statutory ring-fencing within the cellular structure on grounds that segregation was contrary to public policy or offensive to local law. Nevertheless, by deciding that the bankruptcy court was not the appropriate forum in which to resolve investors' (shareholder) dispute with the Sphinx board and that the bankruptcy court approval of the Settlement Agreement, consented to by Sphinx, precluded Sphinx from appealing the court's order, the Court of Appeals avoided having to deal with of the substantive issues put forward by the Appellants.

One of the most interesting aspects of the arguments put forward under Cayman Islands law in challenging the Settlement Agreement was the view expressed by counsel with regards to trust law and the nature of the cellular assets. This is set out in the Court Document. The advice received by the Liquidators is also summarized in the Third Interim Report[112] of the Liquidators dated 7 May 2007 (available from the Website). According to the Liquidators, the legal advice received was effectively that the SPC is a trust company, with each cell having the characteristic of trust funds, managed separately and discretely by the SPC. Further, the beneficiaries of each trust are not just the investors (shareholders) in a cell but also the creditors of the cell and the Liquidators must manage them as trust property. The Third Interim Report acknowledged the profound implications for the Liquidator, who if the legal analysis was correct, had stepped into the shoes of the board of directors of a trust company!

Commentators have disagreed with this trust analysis. It has also been suggested that the Liquidation Committee obtained its own opinion from another UK counsel[113]. Looked at from one level, a cell does have *some* characteristics of a trust. A trust (like a cell) is not a separate legal entity. Trust assets must be kept separate from the trustee's estate or the assets of any other trust. But a cell is not a trust nor is a PCC a trust company. PCC legislation provides its own separate statutory rules which apply to PCCs whether in or out of liquidation.

---

[112] http://www.sphinxfunds.com/files/Third%20Interim%20Report%20of%20the%20JOLs%20-%20May%207,%202007.pdf

[113] See article in http://www.mondaq.com/article.asp?articleid=58214

It would appear that a Global Settlement has now been reached with sanction from the Caymans Courts concerning the preference dispute. It also appears that the issue of the trust will not be tested in the Cayman Courts as the Liquidators and Liquidation Committee seek to discuss a potential scheme of arrangement.

Interestingly, in the recent decision *In re Saad Investments Finance Company (No 5) Limited,* the US Bankruptcy Court for the District of Delaware granted Chapter 15 relief in connection with liquidation proceedings in the Cayman Islands of an exempted company. In granting the Third Revised Order Recognising Foreign Proceeding dated 3 February 2010[114], the court found that the Cayman proceedings were foreign proceeding and were entitled to recognition as a foreign main proceeding, the company had its COMI in the Cayman Islands, and that such recognition *"is necessary and appropriate, in the interest of public and international comity, consistent with the public policy of the United States and the objectives of Chapter 15..."* Although the company was not a PCC, it was an investment company whose assets consisted primarily of interests in fifty seven private equity funds and one hedge fund and therefore in essence a Fund of Funds. The decision is significant in that the Delaware Court did not deny or limit the availability of Chapter 15 protection to a Cayman exempted company. In fact, based on the facts of the case, there is no reason to believe that the decision would have been any different if the company had been constituted as a SPC. Factors that appear to have supported the finding of a Cayman COMI were that the majority of the investments were in Cayman funds (i.e. Cayman Islands assets) and that one of the equity holders (another Cayman company) was itself in liquidation proceedings in the Cayman Islands.

10.10. Article 17 – Recognition and Relief Re Foreign Proceedings

Articles 17 is core to the Model Law and provides for the recognition of the *"foreign proceedings"*, more especially as to whether it is a main (i.e. COMI-based) or *"non-main [or in the words of the EU Regulation, 'secondary' or 'territorial'] proceedings"*. It is thus core to the general question posed: 'does the Model Law assist in the international recognition of PCC priority rankings in an insolvency?' The question may be answered by

[114] http://www.kineticpartners.com/public/kyfunds/docs/ThirdRevisedOrderRecognizingForeignProceeding.pdf

looking at the relief available. And: "*The relief flowing from recognition may depend upon the category into which a foreign proceeding falls. For example, recognition of a 'main' proceeding triggers an automatic stay of individual creditor actions or executions concerning the assets of the debtor (article 20, subparagraph 1(c))' [paragraph 126 of the Guide]*".

Article 17 is designed to be permissive. Recognition will be automatic if certain procedural safeguards are noted and the "*foreign proceeding*" is not "*manifestly contrary to public policy*". Consequently there is no requirement to consider whether the "*foreign proceedings*" are sufficiently akin to the local legal and insolvency proceeding. It is hoped that in the US at least, adoption of the Model Law will preclude lengthy comparative analysis. However, not all the Model Law States have been so liberal in their Model Law adoption. For instance Japan defines "*foreign proceedings*" as: "*foreign insolvency proceeding means a proceeding taking place in a foreign State that corresponds to a bankruptcy proceeding, a civil rehabilitation proceeding, a corporate reorganisation proceeding or a special liquidation proceeding [Article 2(1) of the Law on the Recognition of Foreign Proceedings]*". The obvious question is; 'would the novelty of a PCC insolvency, more especially a cellular insolvency, so correspond to any Japanese proceeding'?

10.11. Articles 21 and 22 – relief granted and creditor protection

"*Article 21 – relief that may be granted upon recognition of a foreign proceeding –*

Upon recognition of a foreign proceeding, whether main or non-main, where necessary to protect the assets of the debtor or the interests of the creditors, the court may, at the request of the foreign representative, grant any appropriate relief, including [but not limited to]: (a) Staying … proceedings … (b) Staying execution … (c) Suspending the right to transfer … assets … (d) Providing for the examination of witnesses … (e) Entrusting the administration or realisation of all or part of the debtors assets located in this State to the foreign representative or another person designated by the court".

Consequently a PCC liquidator is, if granted 'turnover of the assets', able to enforce PCC priority worldwide.

Article 21(2) states: "*Upon recognition of a foreign proceeding … the court may … entrust the distribution … of the debtor's assets … to the foreign representative … provided that the court is satisfied that the interests of creditors … are adequately protected*". According to para 157 of the Guide: "*The 'turnover' of assets to the foreign representative (or another person), as envisaged in paragraph 2, is discretionary. It should be noted that the Model Law contains several safeguards designed to ensure the protection of local interests before assets are turned over to the foreign representative. Those safeguards include the following: the general statement of the principle of protection of local interests in article 22, paragraph 1; the provision in article 21, paragraph 2, that the court should not authorise the turnover of assets until it is assured that the local creditors' interests are protected; and article 22, paragraph 2, according to which the court may subject the relief that it grants to conditions it considers appropriate".*

However, the above is tempered by Article 22 (*"Protection of creditors and other interested persons"*): *"In granting or denying relief… or in modifying or terminating relief… the court must be satisfied that the interests of the creditors and other interested persons, including the debtor are adequately protected."* According to [paragraph 161 of] the Guide: *"The idea underlying article 22 is that there should be a balance between relief that may be granted to the foreign representative and the interests of the persons that may be affected by such relief. This balance is essential to achieve the objectives of cross-border insolvency legislation."* So, imagine an unsympathetic judge in a non-PCC non-main proceedings jurisdiction confronted by the PCC's cellular priority apparent breach of *pari passu*. He could circumvent the high hurdle of the *"manifestly contrary to public policy"*, and reject a PCC IP *"turnover of assets"*, because the *"interests of creditors"* and importantly *"other persons"* (i.e. PCC creditors but not a creditor of the particular debtor cell) are not adequately protected by the PCC structure.

Article 21(g) states that *"upon recognition"* of a *"foreign proceeding"*, relief may include: *"Granting any additional relief that may be available to [a local IP] under the [local] laws of this [Model Law adopting] State"* i.e. in the UK a foreign IP could be granted relief that could be granted a UK IP.

The Guide at paragraph 159 states:

"The proviso 'under the law of this State' reflects the principle underlying the Model Law that recognition of a foreign proceeding does not mean extending the effects of the foreign proceeding as they may be prescribed by the law of the foreign State. Instead, recognition of a foreign proceeding entails attaching… consequences envisaged by the law of the enacting State".

Article 21(1)(g) does not mean that foreign insolvency law has extra-territorial effect: nor does it stop the local courts from giving effect to foreign insolvency law under their local conflict of laws rules. Thus a UK court could 'enforce' foreign antecedent transaction laws, if it was considered that the UK law was insufficient. For instance, if a creditor preference occurred but was outside the pre-insolvency time limits imposed by the UK.

Article 21(2) allows the court to grant the foreign representative the power to distribute local assets in line with foreign insolvency law, provided the court is satisfied that the interests of local creditors are *"adequately protected"*. Thus, as in the first instance decision in *Re HIH Casualty and General Insurance* (*"HIH"*) (a section 426 of the Insolvency Act 1986, application to a UK Court) it may mean that a UK version of *pari passu* must always be followed. But, the role of the *pari passu* principle has often been misunderstood and exaggerated. The Court of Appeal in *Re HIH* rejected the first instance courts reasoning. The Court held that English assets may be transferred to a foreign insolvency holder. This was even though the consequence of such a transfer is to disapply English law.

The Court of Appeal rejected this pre-Cross-Border Regulations first instance outright assault on internationalism thus:

"There may be circumstances in which it is for the benefit of the creditors that a transfer should be made, notwithstanding that their interests in the liquidation in England, when viewed in isolation, would be adversely effected. For example, the savings in cost by avoiding duplication may offset any reduction in prospective dividend. Similarly a loss of priority may be sufficiently offset by an increase in the pool available for distribution to those whose priority was changed. The admission of further creditors may be offset by an increase in the assets available for distribution to that class of creditor".

The Court of Appeal nevertheless decided that the jurisdiction should not be exercised, because the outcome for some creditors would be worse than if the English assets were distributed according to English law. The case then went on appeal to the House of Lords (now the Supreme Court). In allowing the appeal whereby assets were ordered to be remitted to Australia, Lord Hoffman ([2008] 3 ALL ER 869):

"The primary rule of private international law which seems to me applicable to this case is the principle of (modified) universalism, which has been the golden thread running through English cross-border insolvency law since the eighteenth century. That principle requires that English courts should, so far as is consistent with justice and UK public policy, co-operate with the courts in the country of the principal liquidation to ensure that all the company's assets are distributed to its creditors under a single system of distribution. That is the

purpose of the power to direct remittal. [Paragraph 30] In the present case I do not see that it would offend against any principle of justice for the assets to be remitted to Australia. In some cases there may be some doubt about how to determine the appropriate jurisdiction which should be regarded as the seat of the principal liquidation. I have spoken in a rather old-fashioned way of the company's domicile because that is the term used in the old cases, but I do not claim it is necessarily the best one. Usually it means the place where the company is incorporated but that may be some offshore island with which the company's business has no real connection. The Council Regulation on insolvency proceedings ((EC) No 1346/2000 of 29 May 2000) uses the concept of the "centre of a debtor's main interests" as a test, with a presumption that it is the place where the registered office is situated: see article 3.1. That may be more appropriate. But in this case it does not matter because on any view, these are Australian companies. They are incorporated in Australia, their central management has been in Australia and the overwhelming majority of their assets and liabilities are situated in Australia [Paragraph 31] ".

The House of Lords' reasoning in *HIH* will no doubt influence the UK's attitude to Article 21(2) of the Model Law and the UK Cross-Border Regulations[115].

Article 21(2) will not probably supersede the rights of UK secured creditors (paragraphs 70-73 of Schedule B1 to the Insolvency Act 1986) as they are currently enjoyed. However, this does give rise to a question considered elsewhere: 'does a creditor's right to enjoy cellular priority amount to a right *in rem* and if so, could, or indeed, should Article 21(2) overwrite that *in rem* right?'

Article 21(3) states that the relief granted to a representative of a foreign non-main proceeding must relate to assets that, under the local law, should be administered in the foreign non-main proceeding. Thus, the PCC's assets should be held in the PCC's home jurisdiction.

Thus Article 21(1)(g) may at first sight negate extraterritoriality, more specifically the extraterritoriality of a PCC insolvency. However, two angles are of importance:

1. some enacting States have specifically allowed for extraterritoriality; subject to at least the public policy exception; and

[115] See also decision of Court of Appeal (Ontario) in Cravell Insurance Co, Re 2006 (Docket C43657) where the court upheld recognition of a UK order *"in an age where the rules of private international law are evolving to accommodate the increasingly transnational nature of commerce"*.

2. some enacting States via Article 21(1)(g) and their conflict of law rules allow for effective extraterritoriality.

Amongst the first category of the Model Law adopting States, Serbia is unique. Article 175 paragraph 1 of the new Serbian Bankruptcy Act states: *"unless otherwise stipulated in the law, the substantial law of the [say PCC] State where the proceedings are commenced [presumably the COMI state] shall govern the insolvency proceedings"*.

Romania's Model Law adoption is the same as Serbia, but with the cut-out clauses similar to the EU Regulation for retention of title ('ROT'), setoff, employee rights *et al* and is of some assistance in establishing PCC ranking. Why? Because the cut-out clauses tend to refer to items which are unlikely to be found relevant in most PCCs.

As to the second category, there is discussion as to whether a PCC priority rule is procedural or substantive. UK law has previously applied foreign law in an insolvency. It has done so by applying English choice of law clauses which through conflict of law rules, allows for foreign law. Article 21(1)(g) can only encourage that practice. Article 21(2) allows the court to grant the *"foreign representative"* the power to distribute local assets in accordance with foreign insolvency law, subject to *"adequate protection"*. The UK has threatened abandonment of *pari passu* (admittedly in insurance insolvency with its consequent novelties) in the *HIH* case. Consequently the UK judiciary may feel more comfortable in applying foreign common law (the *"Designated States"* under section 426 of the UK Insolvency Act 1986 are all former colonies of the UK) than (say) a non-EU Civil Law State.

The UK has an interesting derogation from Articles 19-21 (from the perspective of PCCs especially insurance PCCs). Under Schedule 1, Chapter 1, Article 1, paragraph 5 of the UK Cross-Border Regulations *"Where a foreign proceeding regarding a debtor who is insured in accordance with the provision of the Third Parties (Rights against Insurers) Act 1930 [the "Third Parties Act"] is recognised*[116] *under this law, any stay and suspension referred to in article 20(1) and any relief granted by the court under article 19 or 21 shall not apply to or effect – (a) any transfer of rights of the debtor under that Act; (b) any claim, action, cause or proceeding by a third party against an insurer under or in respect of rights of the debtor transferred under that Act"*.

---

[116] i.e. cut through provisions whereby the 'victim' of an insured can claim directly against the insurance or reinsurance policy of the insured, as opposed to being an otherwise unsecured creditor of the insured.

At first sight this may present difficulties for a PCC whereby cells act as self insurance or reinsurance vehicles; especially bearing in mind the primary use of PCCs has traditionally been that of insurance. However, the effect of the Third Parties Act exclusion is likely to be minimal. This is given the UK's exclusion of both insurance and reinsurance companies from its adoption of the Model Law. It has to be remembered that the UK Cross-Border Regulations exclude both insurance and reinsurance providers.

10.12. Articles 25 and 27 – Cooperation and Direct Communication

Articles 25 and 27 create a duty of *"cooperation and direct communication between local and foreign IPs and/or Courts"*. However, this cooperation would not mean a recognition of a PCC priority ranking *per se*. For PCCs, therefore, it would mean that even an unsympathetic non-PCC jurisdiction should begrudgingly cooperate with the PCC jurisdiction. However, it should be noted that the phrase is (in the UK Cross-Border Regulations and most other Model Law adopting States) *"the court may cooperate to the maximum extent"* and not the UNCITRAL *"shall"* cooperate.

10.13. Article 32 – "Hotch pot"

Article 32 – *"Rule of payment in concurrent proceedings"* or 'Hotch pot Rule'[117] states: *"Without prejudice to secured claims or rights in rem a creditor who has received part payment in respect of its claim in a proceeding pursuant to a law relating to insolvency in a foreign State may not receive a payment for the same claim ... [the local law and insolvency] regarding the same debtor so long as the payment to the other creditors of the same class is proportionately less than the payment the creditor has already received"*.

According to the Guide (paragraph 199): *"Article 32 does not affect the ranking of claims as established by the law of the enacting State"* and (paragraph 200) *"The words 'secured claims' are used to refer generally to claims guaranteed by particular assets, whilst the words 'rights in rem' are intended to indicate rights relating to a particular property that are enforceable also against third parties. A given right may fall within the ambit of both expressions, depending on the classification and terminology of the applicable law. The enacting State may use another term or terms for expressing those concepts"*.

---

[117] See similar rules in the EU Regulation and under the Model Law paragraph 200 of the Guide.

However, some PCC jurisdictions ensure that the cell will always be treated as owned by the stakeholder, who therefore enjoys, it is submitted, an *in rem* right. Witness the Anguillan Protected Cell Companies Act 2004, section 16(9): *"An account owner's or counterparty's beneficial interest in a protected cell account is personal property notwithstanding the nature of the property of the protected cell account".*

Article 32 of the Model Law, together with the Guide are of greater assistance than the equivalent hotch pot Article 20 of the EU Regulation and accompanying Virgos Schmit Report in enforcing PCC insolvency priority. This is for a variety of reasons:

1. The Model Law refers to *"debtor"* and avoids the difficulties (especially in respect of cellular as opposed to PCC hub insolvency) of the *"legal person"* references in the EU Regulation. Indeed the particular reference to *"same debtor"* may go further. In any cellular insolvency there are usually two *'debtors'*; the cell and the hub to the extent that the cell deficiency makes a call upon the hub capital. Consequently the term *"same debtor"* may allow for PCC priority (as opposed to *"the debtor"*, which implies a *'single debtor'*). This may be reinforced by the similar reference to *"same class"*.
2. The Guide's definition of 'secured creditor' is more helpful than the Virgos-Schmit Report, 'leaving it to the EU Member States'. A cell's creditor rights to a particular cell's assets could 'fall within the ambit of both expressions'. So PCC cellular priority is, theoretically, guaranteed by way of a claim to security. It is more helpful because if a cell stakeholders interest in a cell is an *in rem* secured right, most, if not all jurisdictions will allow priority. The priority is justified by it being a security, not because of a PCC's claim to a non-*pari passu* distribution. Having said that, many Model Law-adopting States may have already defined 'secured creditor'. In the UK, the Cross-Border Regulations, Schedule 1 Article 2 ("definitions section") state in England and Wales 'security' means: *"any mortgage, charge, lien or [given that a cell is unlikely per se to fall within the previous three definitions] other security"*.

11. THE COMMONWEALTH INSOLVENCY REGIME AND OTHER UK MATTERS

11.1. Section 426 of the Insolvency Act 1986

11.1.1. Section 426: an introduction

Section 426 provides for mutual assistance between the constituent parts of the United Kingdom (Northern Ireland, Scotland, and England & Wales) and designated non-UK territories. It, therefore, places the UK's courts on par with these foreign-designated courts. This on par placement indicates the theoretical importance of this section. These foreign courts are always Commonwealth courts, which is why section 426 is sometimes referred to as the 'Commonwealth Insolvency Regime'. Section 426(4) states: "*The courts having jurisdiction in relation to insolvency law in any part of the UK shall assist the courts having the corresponding jurisdiction in any other part of the UK or any other relevant country or territory*".

The authors make no apology for concentrating on this 'non-transnational insolvency regime'. It is considered along with other transnational and international regimes such as the EU Regulation and the Model Law, for a variety of reasons:

1. the UK is a major trading nation and PCCs may hold assets within the UK. This is despite the general precaution that a PCC should hold all of its assets within the PCC jurisdiction itself. Given the trading status, it is possible that liabilities may also arise within the UK;
2. English 'choice of law' clauses are commonplace;
3. many PCC jurisdictions are Commonwealth States and are therefore possibly covered by this Commonwealth Insolvency Regime; and
4. section 426 is an important adjunct to the EU Regulation and the Model Law itself in that it can operate when those regimes cannot.

11.1.2. What Commonwealth Jurisdictions are covered by Section 426 and have PCC legislation?

The chart below shows that the major international PCC centres are included (i.e. they are "Designated Territories"). It is worth noting that other Commonwealth countries have similar legislation. For example, Australia's section 29 of its Bankruptcy Act, in which the similarly designated territories include two PCC jurisdictions, Jersey (as in the Channel Islands) and the USA.

SECTION 425 – DESIGNATED TERRITORIES

Territory	UK Statutory Ref	PCC Legislation	Notes
Guernsey	S426 (11) Insolvency Act 1986	The Protected Cell Companies Ordinance 1997 (as amended)	(C)
Jersey	S426 (11) Insolvency Act 1986	Companies (Jersey) Law 1991 (as amended)	
Isle of Man	S426 (11) Insolvency Act 1986	Companies Act 2006 and the Protected Cell Companies Act 2004	(C)
Anguilla	Cooperation of Insolvency Courts (Designation of Relevant Countries and Territories) Order 1986 SI 1986/2123	Protected Cell Companies Act 2004	
The Bahamas	Cooperation of Insolvency Courts (Designation of Relevant Countries and Territories) Order 1986 SI 1986/2123	Segregated Accounts Companies Act 2004	(C)
Bermuda	Cooperation of Insolvency Courts (Designation of Relevant Countries and Territories) Order 1986 SI 1986/2123	Segregated Accounts Companies Act 2002 (Amendment)	(C)
The Cayman Islands	Cooperation of Insolvency Courts (Designation of Relevant Countries and Territories) Order 1986 SI 1986/2123	Companies Law (2009) Revision	
Gibraltar	Cooperation of Insolvency Courts (Designation of Relevant Countries and Territories) Order 1986 SI 1986/2123	Protected Cell Companies Act 2001	(B)
The Turks and Caicos Islands	S426 (11) Insolvency Act 1986	Protected Cell Ordinance 2006	

Territory	UK Statutory Ref	PCC Legislation	Notes
The British Virgin Islands	S426 (11) Insolvency Act 1986	Insurance (Amendment) Act 2002, amending the Insurance Act 1994	(A) (C)
Notes: - (A) Model Law enacting State, but with reciprocity; (B) 'EU Member State', covered by the EU Regulation; (C) PCC legislation mainly, if not exclusively insurance only.			
The other non-PCC states covered by section 426 or its delegated legislation are Australia, Botswana, Canada, the Falkland Islands, Hong Kong, the Republic of Ireland, Montserrat, New Zealand, St Helana, South Africa, Tuvalu and Malaysia. As can be seen a number of PCC Commonwealth jurisdictions are excluded, most notably the independent Caribbean and Indian Ocean OFCs, such as Barbados and Mauritius respectively.			

11.1.3. Interaction between Section 426, and the Model Law and the EU Regulation

As far as the UK is concerned, this trio of regimes can act in concert and can provide a variety of solutions, especially for PCCs. For example, both the Model Law and the EU Regulation exclude insurance. Insurance is still a major force behind PCC development; section 426 does not exclude insurance, indeed some of its more important cases concerns recognition of foreign insurance regimes.[118] Second, as to the Model Law, if a *"foreign proceeding"* was commenced using a *"presence of asset"* or *"sufficient connection"* as a jurisdictional basis, but the debtor had no COMI or *"establishment"* in the *"foreign proceeding"* jurisdiction, then UK Model Law recognition (via the UK Cross-Border Regulations) would not be available. Not so with section 426, provided the *"foreign proceeding"* was commenced in a jurisdiction covered by section 426. If the nature of the 'insolvency appointment' was such that it fell outside of the Model Law definition of insolvency or the EU prescribed insolvency processes, such as a 'receiver', more especially a receiver of a PCC cell; then section 426 could still assist.

By way of example in the case of the EU Regulation, the only EU jurisdiction which is also a Designated Territory within section 426 is Gibraltar. Gibraltar is also one of the two EU PCC States, the other being

[118] See notably Re HIH Casualty and General Insurance Limited [2005] EWHC 2125; [2006] 2 All ER 671.

Malta. The Gibraltar PCC statute allows for the appointment of a 'receiver' over a PCC cell. A 'receiver' is not an insolvency procedure noted with Annex A of the EU Regulation. Further, a 'receiver' may not be within the collective definition of insolvency noted within the Model Law. A 'receiver' would however be included under section 426.

11.1.4. What is the "insolvency law" within section 426

Section 426(10)(a) states that *"insolvency law"* means specific UK Acts as section 426 relates to intra-UK court assistance. However, *"insolvency law"* means: *"in relation to any relevant country or territory*[119] *so much of the law of that country or territory as corresponds to provisions falling within"* UK insolvency statutes. So, *"insolvency law"* as it relates to Designated Territories may be wider than the corresponding definition within the Model Law. It would thus assist with the enforcement of PCC cellular priority in the event of a PCC insolvency.

11.1.5. Court Cooperation

The Model Law (and also as adopted by the UK in its Cross-Border Regulations) states that courts *"may cooperate"*. As can be seen from the above, section 426(4) imposes a mandatory *"shall assist"*. It should be remembered that Designated Territories are placed on par with intra-UK court assistance. Therefore, a PCC IP would seek judicial assistance (provided he was from a Designated Territory) under section 426. Section 426(4) is supplemented by section 426(5) which states: *"For the purposes of subsection (4), a request made to a court in any part of the UK... or in a [Designated Territory] ... is authority for the court to which the request is made to apply, in relation to any matters specified in the request, the insolvency law which is applicable by either [i.e. maybe it includes the PCC law of the Designated Territory] in relation to comparable matters falling within its jurisdiction. In exercising its discretion... a court shall have regard in particular to the rules of private international law"*.

11.1.6. Given a section 426 application by a PCC IP from a Designated Territory, how could a UK court react?

Section 426(5) is initially clear and ends in doubt. The reference is to the insolvency law applicable to *"either court"*, i.e. a court in the PCC jurisdiction and UK court. But that the insolvency law of the PCC jurisdiction *"corresponds"* to UK insolvency law. Given it *"corresponds"*

---

[119] i.e. Designated Territories, that is non-UK jurisdictions, more especially non-UK PCC Designated Territory jurisdictions, noted on the "Section 425 – Designated Territories" chart on the previous page.

which (and why) of two systems should be applied? Four questions need to be asked, and these are dealt with below.

1. Have novel insolvency concepts, not ordinarily equally recognised in both courts (i.e. the UK and the Designated Territory) been recognised under section 426 and thus, will the novelty of a PCC or PCC cellular insolvency be so recognised?

The answer is "yes". However, the request traffic has tended to be one way with the UK essentially exporting its insolvency systems to the Designated Territories. Examples include:

(a) *Re Television Trade Rentals [2002] EWHC 211*, where a Manx company became subject to a UK Company Voluntary Arrangement ("CVA") although the CVA insolvency procedure did not exist under Manx law; and

(b) *Re BCCI SA (No. 9) [1994] 1 WLR 708* where the UK 'wrongful and fraudulent trading provisions' of the Insolvency Act 1986, was used as against a Cayman Islands insolvency. They were used at a time when there were no similar provisions within Cayman Islands law.

Given this degree of latitude there would appear to be no reason why a UK court would not regard a PCC insolvency as corresponding to UK insolvency law. This is stated on the basis that the UK has quite happily exported insolvency procedures that do not directly equate with the local laws of the Designated Territory jurisdiction. It would seem therefore not unnatural that the situation be reversed. Unfortunately, there is no case law yet to support this presumption.

2. Has section 426 been used to change the normally perceived *pari passu* principles of UK traditional insolvency law?

The answer is again, probably "yes". This brings us back to *Re HIH Casualty and General Insurance* ["*HIH*"].

HIH involved an Australian (hence the Designated Territory status within section 426) insurance company (hence outside the Model Law) liquidation. The Australian insurance insolvency law dictated a deviation from the normal *pari passu* distribution. This deviation was in a manner not dissimilar to the EU Insurance Insolvency Directive to which the UK now adheres. The Australian liquidator sought the remission of UK assets to Australia. This was so that they may be distributed according to Australian insolvency law, more especially Australian insurance insolvency law. The High Court and the Court of Appeal declined the request. Failing such remission, the UK assets would be distributed in the

UK according to UK *pari passu* principles under UK insolvency law. The Court of Appeal concluded that the Australian distribution process was not "*substantially similar*" to the UK process. That decision, however, was overturned by the House of Lords (now the Supreme Court). The following quotes from Lord Hoffman sums up the court's approach on the matter:

"It is true that Australian law would treat insurance creditors better and non-insurance creditors worse than English law did at the relevant time. But that seems to me no reason for saying that the Australian law offends against English principles of justice. As it happens, since the appointment of the provisional liquidators, English law has itself adopted a regime for the winding up of insurance companies which gives preference to insurance creditors: see regulation 21(2) of the Insurers (Reorganisation and Winding Up) Regulations 2004 (SI 2004/353), giving effect to the European Parliament and Council Directive 2001/17/EC on the reorganisation and winding up of insurance companies. So English courts are hardly in a position to say that an exception to the pari passu rule for insurance creditors offends against basic principles of justice. [Paragraph 32].

Furthermore, it seems to me that the application of Australian law to the distribution of all the assets is more likely to give effect to the expectations of creditors as a whole, than the distribution of some of the assets according to English law. Policy holders and other creditors dealing with an Australian insurance company are likely, so far as they think about the matter at all to expect that in the event of insolvency their rights will be determined by Australian law. Indeed, the preference given to insurance creditors may have been seen as an advantage of a policy with an Australian company. [Paragraph 33]

In my opinion, therefore, this is a case in which it is appropriate to give the principle of universalism full rein. There are no grounds of justice or policy which require this country to insist upon distributing an Australian company's assets according to its own system of priorities only because they happen to have been situated in this country at the time of the appointment of the provisional liquidators." [Paragraph 36]

This seems to encapsulate the principle that where insolvency proceedings are commenced in the home jurisdiction by a principal liquidator, the UK courts should remit assets to that liquidator in order to ensure distribution under a single system. As such, the same should apply to UK assets of a cell; they should be distributed to the PCC liquidator and dealt with in accordance with PCC law.

3. Has a PCC ever been subject to section 426?

The answer is "no". A PCC has never been subject to section 426, but it has got close. One of the very few cases reported worldwide, involving a PCC and insolvency is Messenger Insurance PCC Limited (in administration) ("the Messenger Insolvency") in Guernsey, which has partially answered the question, albeit indirectly. Given that the Messenger Insolvency is one of the very few worldwide reported PCC insolvencies, it is worth noting in detail its background by quoting from publicly available records:

"The [Guernsey] legislation which governs protected cell companies is the Protected Cell Companies Ordinance, 1997 as amended ["the Ordinance]). This litigation [the Messenger Insolvency litigation before the Guernsey Court] is the first in this jurisdiction in which that legislation will be considered. It is also to be noted that the Ordinance provides for the appointment of an administrator. The power to appoint an administrator was innovative[120] *in legislation governing Guernsey companies. The Companies (Guernsey) Law 1994 … does not make provision for the appointment of an administrator"* – paragraph 6 of the approved text of the Judgment of Bailiff Roland.[121] This and other judgments involving the same or similar parties are referred to as the "Messenger Guernsey Litigation":

"It is not necessary to review in great detail the problems confronting the Applicant [Messenger] which gave rise to the Guernsey Freezing Order [granted prior to the Guernsey Administration Order] or the application for an [Guernsey] Administration Order to be made. Suffice it to record that Cable and Wireless/Pender contend that five employees of Cable and Wireless, in breach of their fiduciary and other duties, devised and carried out a dishonest scheme to pass insurance premiums received by Pender to a vehicle which they secretly owned namely the Applicant… It is claimed that the amount of premium paid to or for the benefit of the Applicant was approximately £85.4 million. Cable and Wireless/Pender's claim is against the entirety of the Applicant and they are advancing a proprietary claim to the monies held by the Applicant (without limitation). It is not a claim limited to any particular Cell or part of the Applicant [Messenger] which is a…[PCC], incorporated under Guernsey Law." (Paragraph 5 of the Messenger Guernsey Litigation).

---

[120] At the relevant time, the situation in Guernsey was similar to that of Gibraltar in that an administration order was not provided within the insolvency code but only specifically to PCCs.

[121] *Messenger Insurance PCC Ltd (in administration) ("the Applicant") v. Cable and Wireless plc and Five others, 16th August 2005 Guernsey Law Reports 2005-06 GLR 206*

It can be seen, therefore, that this is not a normal insolvency of a trading loss. But rather an insolvency following alleged fraud. Further, the claim is not to any cell. Rather it is against the entirety of the operation, because of the alleged fraud.

Following the allegation of fraud, but before the Administration Order: *"...the English High Court had made an unlimited [i.e. and more especially not limited to a particular cell] freezing order against the entirety of the Applicant and later that same day the Court made an unlimited [i.e. and more especially not limited to a particular cell] freezing order against the Applicant in Guernsey"*: Paragraph 7 of the Messenger Guernsey Litigation.

The English Court was not therefore asked to consider a section 426 Application by the Administrator. The English Court was seized with the question of the 'proprietary claim', which would preclude the question of whether the English Court should address the PCC priority issue. Further: *"The [Guernsey] Court also relied on Mr Justice Morison's [an English Judge] observations in his judgment... [wherein] He stated that he expected that the rights or wrongs of the proprietary claim would be fully argued in the Cable and Wireless/Pender litigation in the English High Court."* (Paragraph 67 of the Messenger Guernsey Litigation).

As can be seen, therefore, the issue of enforcing the PCC cellular priority in England via section 426 was not addressed. Further, the English Court did not at any time object to the cellular structure of the Messenger Insolvency. The real importance of the Messenger Insolvency is not section 426. Rather it is the analysis of the practical problems which may face an IP when he considers his fees and expenses.

4. How can a PCC draftsman or IP create structures that may assist with a section 426 application?

It is submitted that a UK Scheme of Arrangement is a suitable structure and the same is explained below.

11.1.7. Schemes of Arrangement: Section 427 and alternative statutory approach to *pari passu*

A Scheme of Arrangement is a procedure in the UK (and other UK influenced jurisdictions) , endorsed by statute, whereby different classes of stakeholder (i.e. creditors and shareholders) can have a forced alteration of their rights (provided the majority of the class agree). The fact that creditors can be divided into classes (and thereby have different priorities) possibly gives rise to a *de facto* PCC.

Most PCC Designated Territories have Schemes of Arrangement provisions. A Scheme of Arrangement falls under section 425 of the UK Companies Act (as amended). The relevant self-explanatory sections are section 425(1) and (2) and (6).

*"**425(1) [Court may order meeting]** Where a compromise or arrangement is proposed between a company and its creditors, or any class of them, or between the company and its members, or any class of them, the court may on the application of the company or any creditor or member of it, or in the case of a company being wound up [or [in administration], of the liquidator or administrator], order a meeting of the creditors or class of creditors, or of the members of the company or class of members (as the case may be), to be summoned in such manner as the court directs.*

***425(2) [Three-fourths majority binding]** If a majority in number representing three-fourths in value of the creditors or class of creditors or members or class of members (as the case may be), present and voting either in person or by proxy at the meeting, agree to any compromise or arrangement, the compromise or arrangement, if sanctioned by the court, is binding on all creditors or the class of creditors or on the members or class of members (as the case may be), and also on the company or, in the case of a company in the course of being wound up, on the liquidator and contributories of the company.*

***425[6] [Definitions]** In this section and the next (a) "company" means any company liable to be wound up under this Act, and (b) "arrangement" includes a reorganisation of the company's share capital by the consolidation of shares of different classes or by the division of shares into shares of different classes, or by both of those methods".*

As can be seen, a Scheme of Arrangement (by arranging creditors or members into classes) can therefore abandon *pari passu*. However, this abandonment requires a 75% approval for any given class. Obviously, a class can correspond to a cell and/or a hub.

Although obviously comparable with a UK Scheme of Arrangement under section 425, both the UK and the Irish Scheme of Arrangement provisions are not contained within the insolvency law proper. Rather they are contained within the respective Companies Act. Consequently, therefore, they are outside of the EU Regulations and possibly the Model Law.

The UK courts first applied the insolvency law of a Designated Territory in *Re Business City Express Limited [1997] 2 BCLC 510*. In this case an already approved Irish Scheme of Arrangement was made binding on the company's UK creditors. A Scheme of Arrangement has obvious advantages to a PCC re-organisation. Each cell (and where applicable) its shareholders can be regarded as a *"class of creditors or members"* within section 425(1). The solution, therefore, for an IP considering a PCC insolvency in a Designated Territory with UK assets and liabilities is to consider a Scheme of Arrangement. Most PCC Designated Territories have Scheme of Arrangement legislation based on the UK's, i.e. section 86 onwards of the Cayman Islands' Companies Act 2004 (as amended). However, can the PCC draftsman go one stage further? Can the PCC promoter draft the PCC constitution in such as way that a Scheme of Arrangement would inevitably occur if it was required for re-organisation purposes? Methods could include in addition to a contractual PCC:

1. Articles of Association identifying classes of creditors and members should a Scheme of Arrangement occur; and
2. the creation of Powers of Attorney between creditors and/or officers of the PCC which can only be used for voting purposes in a Scheme of Arrangement.

11.1.8. Concluding thoughts

Some tentative conclusions can be drawn. First, the UK now has a changed priority ranking (i.e. non- *pari passu*) for insurance insolvencies (*HIH* was an insurance insolvency) in the form of the EU Insurance Insolvency Regulations. Consequently, there is a directly comparable UK insolvency procedure for an insurance company from normal *pari passu*. As to the UK, this procedure is now inter alia contained within Insurers (Reorganisation and Winding Up) Regulations 2004. Thus, even if one was to adopt the narrow interpretation of what constitutes insolvency law (i.e. it must be contained within a specifically insolvency-orientated law) when dealing with the Designated Territory the Insurers (Reorganisation of Winding Up) Regulations 2004 would be acceptable. Alternatively, would the court say, following the introduction of the EU Insurance Insolvency Regulations, that there is a similar procedure within the UK. Second, would the court conclude regardless of the House of Lords (now the Supreme Court) decision in *HIH* that the majority of a PCC's creditors are presumably voluntary creditors and they knew what they had let themselves in for. As for involuntary creditors, and the hub capital, they do share *pari passu* with cell deficiency creditors? Indeed, in some jurisdictions they may have a super priority, over and above cell deficiencies. Third, the very nature of a PCC insolvency may well mean that there are *"savings in costs by avoiding duplication"* and/or *"the pool available for distribution"*[122] increases. One cannot overlook the facts on the ground. Fourth, most PCC statutes stipulate that any creditor who supplants the PCC priority rules would either:

(a) have that asset set off against their liability; or

(b) become a creditor for that amount and be pursued by the IP for that amount; or

(c) hold the asset on trust for the company. Thus costs would probably be increased, but the pool not so increased. By way of an example:

"If any party succeeds by any means whatsoever or wheresoever in establishing any interest in or recourse against any asset linked to any segregated account [i.e. protected cell] of the company in respect of a liability not linked to that segregated account, that party shall be liable to the company to pay a sum equal to the value of the benefit thereby obtained by him... and if any party shall succeed in seizing ... any assets ... in respect of a liability not linked to that segregated account [i.e. protected cell] that party shall hold those assets... on trust [section 17B Bermuda Segregated Account Companies Amendment Act 2004]".

Consequently, it is unlikely that the *"pool available for distribution"* to UK creditors would improve. Commentators have claimed that *HIH* will also frame the UK judiciary's response to Article 21(2) of the Model Law.

11.2. Part V of the UK Insolvency Act 1986 ("Part V")

11.2.1. Introduction

The UK has a claim to extraterritoriality via Part V of the Insolvency Act 1986. It includes the claimed right to liquidate foreign (i.e. non-UK) companies. According to section 220 of the Insolvency Act 1986 an *"'unregistered company' includes... any association and any company, with the [exception of] ... a company registered in ... the UK".*

In short, an unregistered company is a foreign registered company or association. The term *"association"* has been held to mean only associations formed for gain and profit.[123] Plainly, therefore, a PCC (being a company) and a cell (being a profit-making association) could fall within the section 220 definition. So could a foreign PCC be wound up in the UK? What would be the consequences?

[122] As postulated in the Court of Appeal *HIH* decision.

[123] *Re St James's Club (1852) 2 De GM & G 383 at 386*

If the COMI of the PCC is elsewhere within the EU, then according to the EU Regulation, the exclusive jurisdiction to open main insolvency proceedings would be the COMI State; presumably Gibraltar or Malta. Only, at best, "*secondary*" and "*territorial*" proceedings would be opened within the UK. To that extent it is probable that Gibraltar and Maltese PCCs are immune from liquidation via Part V of the Insolvency Act 1986. A similar logic applies under the Model Law but perhaps with more opportunities to utilise Part V: the reason being that within the Model Law there is less prescription in its application.

As to connection with the UK, the current Part V position is as stated in *Re Real Estate Development Company [1991] BCLC 210* as a three-fold "*core requirement*":

1. That there must be a sufficient connection with England and Wales which may, but does not necessarily have to, consist of assets within the jurisdiction.
2. That there must be a reasonable possibility if a winding-up order is made of benefit to those applying for the winding-up order.
3. One or more persons interested in the distribution of assets of the company must be persons over whom the Court can exercise jurisdiction.

Re Compania Merabello San Nicholas SA [1973] 1 Ch 75 involved a Panamanian company which had never carried on a UK business. However, its sole remaining asset was a 'UK reinsurance claim'. This was held to be sufficient nexus. Such a scenario is possible for a non-EU PCC. In which case, the question the UK liquidator would ask is: Which rule of priority applies? Thus the general advice of many PCC professionals of 'keep your assets and liabilities local to the PCC jurisdiction', whilst important is not fail-safe.

11.2.2. Part V grounds to "wind up"

Given that we have established that a non-EU PCC having little connection with the UK, could be wound up in the UK, in what circumstances would Part V apply? The grounds for winding up are contained within section 221(5) of the Insolvency Act, namely as relevant:

"*(b) if the company [or association] is unable to pay its debts; [and/or]...*

(c) if the court is of the opinion that it would be just and equitable that the company should be wound up".

Sub-paragraph (5) contains both a cashflow and a balance sheet test and contains interesting problems were a creditor to wind up a PCC and/or cell under Part V. The Court may well become involved in analysing the priority structure when determining whether an insolvency had occurred under either test. For example, assuming a hub creditor were to bring a Part V action, it may well argue that the hub was insolvent because it could not take into account cellular assets; indeed had to make good cellular deficiencies. Would the fact that the petitioning creditor calculated insolvency via this route, amount to an acknowledgment of cellular priority? Alternatively, if a creditor of either the hub or of a cell bundled all of the assets and liabilities together, and said: 'look overall, this organisation is insolvent', and his argument was accepted at the petition stage, would this mean that a court denied the validity of the priority structure?

The *"just and equitable ground"* presents possible interesting outcomes. It is improbable that a voluntary creditor could argue that the PCC structure was, of itself, *"unjust and inequitable"*, to such an extent that he should not be bound by it: thus consequently, the Court should exercise its discretion and wind up the entity (presumably a non-EU PCC) in the UK. However, it could be open for an involuntary creditor to so argue.

The Part V potential PCC pitfalls are not peculiar to the UK. Similar wording exists elsewhere e.g. Australia (The Winding Up Act Rules of the Supreme Court 1985 CW-11, as amended), Canada (Part 5.7 of the CDDA and France (i.e. Articles 14 and 15 of the Civil Law Code).

Some comfort is given by section 221(1) which states: "*Subject to the provision of this Part [Part V] any unregistered company may be wound up...and all the provisions of this...[Insolvency Act] and the Companies Act about winding-up apply to an unregistered company with the exception and additions mentioned...*". None of these exceptions and additions are directly pertinent to PCCs. Section 221, however, does have a *mutatis mutandis* approach to unregistered companies. The question is, "is it sufficient to override the express reference to 'formed under the Companies Act'?"

11.3. Part V and limited liability

Section 226 of the Insolvency Act 1986 ("Contributees in a winding up of an unregistered company") may present problems for a PCC insolvency

11.3.1. PCC jurisdictions and their claims to extraterritoriality

Section 226 (1) states:

"[Deemed contributory]. In the event of an unregistered company being wound up, every person is deemed a contributory who is liable to pay or contribute to the payment of any debt or liability of the company, or to pay or contribute to the payment of any sum for the adjustment of the rights of members among themselves, or to pay or contribute to the payment of the expenses of the winding up of the company".

Section 226 (2) [liability for contributions] states:

"Every contributory is liable to contribute to the company's assets all sums due from him in respect of such liability as is mentioned above." But under whose law is the contributory deemed a contributory?

Section 79 states:

"In this Act and the Companies Act, the expression "contributory" means every person liable to contribute to the assets of a company in the event of its being wound up, and for the purposes of all proceedings for determining, and all proceedings prior to the final determination of, the persons who are to be deemed contributories, includes any person alleged to be a contributory".

Section 74 further states:

"When a company is wound up, every present and past member is liable to contribute to its assets to any amount sufficient for payment of its debts and liabilities, and the expenses of the winding up, and for the adjustment of the rights of the contributories among themselves.... [but] This is subject as follows ... (d) in the case of a company limited by shares, no contribution is required from any member exceeding the amount (if any) unpaid on the shares in respect of which he is liable as a present or past member". There is a similar provision for companies 'limited by guarantee'. No mention is made understandably of companies 'limited by cells'?

Several unpleasant theoretical possibilities exist for a PCC wound up under Part V. One possibility is that cell members of a solvent cell X, are required to 'contribute' to the extent of the 'unpaid capital' to meet deficiencies of other insolvent cells or even of an insolvent hub. The court simply says 'you are shareholders with unpaid capital and the whole PCC entity is insolvent'. Alternatively, at the very least, cell shareholders of an insolvent cell would have to pay up.

Another possibility is as follows. Section 74 of the Insolvency Act 1986, which limits shareholder liability is not contained within Part V of the Insolvency Act, but Part IV. Further, section 74 is prefaced and circumscribed by section 73 which states that a company (i.e. not an unregistered company) means: *"a company formed and regulated under this Act [the Companies Act 1985, as amended, more especially section 735] or an existing company [which means] ... a company formed and regulated under the former Companies Act"*. Thus theoretically there is no limitation on members in the event of a winding-up under Part V of the Insolvency Act? To date, this line of reasoning has only been advanced by academics. But given the peculiarities of PCCs and the fact that involuntary creditors may feel especially aggrieved, such an approach may be greeted sympathetically by a Court.

Given that Part V can create problems for PCCs, how can it be avoided? As we have seen the effect of Part V may in any event have been limited due to the introduction of the EU insolvency regimes (both the EU Regulation and the EU Insurance Insolvency Regulations) and of the UNCITRAL Model Law. Part V could be said to have become irrelevant internationally. But alternatively we have also seen that the UK connection need only be tenuous. A reinsurance claim suffices and London is an international insurance centre. Therefore, in addition to the normal PCC mantra 'keep the assets, contracts and the management local', we should add the following warning: 'if it is necessary to have any dealings outside of the home jurisdiction do so via a bankruptcy-remote SPV'. Thus, if a cell needs to have dealings outside of the local PCC jurisdiction it should do so via an SPV. There is nothing to stop a PCC and/or in respect of a cell owning a separate company. If this separate company (i.e. the SPV) becomes insolvent, its effects will then be minimised.

11.3.2. UK Company Directors Disqualification Act 1986 ("CDDA") and Similar Provisions

The CDDA provides a regime to disqualify directors from further acting as such, usually following upon an insolvency; that is if their conduct was sufficiently serious to warrant disqualification. Similar regimes exist throughout the world. Given that a PCC will not be a UK corporation, does the CDDA apply to non-UK corporations? The answer is 'yes'. Section 22(2) of the CDDA states: *"The expression "company" – (a) in section 11, [referring bankrupts] includes an unregistered company and a company incorporated outside Great Britain which has an established place of business in Great Britain and (b) [the much wider] elsewhere, includes any company which may be wound up under Part V of the Insolvency Act"*.

We have seen that Part V of the UK Insolvency Act 1986 is especially expansive. Foreign (i.e. non-UK companies) have proved to be within the

CDDA in *Re Eurostem Maritime Limited [1987] PCC 190* and *Official Receiver v Brady [1999] BCC 258.* A cell may be an *"association"* under section 220(1) Insolvency Act and consequently could fall within section 22(2)(b) CDDA. However, section 22(1) (section 22 is the CDDA interpretation section) may preclude this: *"This section has effect with respect to the meaning of expressions used in this... [CDDA] Act, and applies unless the context otherwise requires"*.

A PCC proper would always be classed as a company for the purposes of the CDDA. Having established that CDDA applies to foreign corporations and thus PCCs and/or possibly its cells, are there any territorial limits to the CDDA, other than those imposed by Part V case law? The core section within the CDDA is section 6(1): *"The court shall make a disqualification order against a person in any case where, on an application under this section, if it is satisfied – (a) that he is or has been a director of a company which has... become insolvent and (b) that his conduct as a director of that company (either taken alone or taken together with his conduct as a director of any other company or companies) makes him unfit"*.

Section 6 thus contains no territorial restriction. It may be applied to persons of any nationality anywhere. Although the court has a discretion not to order that the proceedings be served out of the jurisdiction.[124] In this case proceedings were issued in Alderney, part of the Bailiwick of Guernsey, a PCC jurisdiction. Section 6 creates the theoretical possibility of multiple CDDA guilt prosecutions or evidence taken from multiple failures in the *"or taken together"* reference. A PCC insolvency could have multiple cellular insolvencies. Thus if each insolvency is taken as a company insolvency, the apparent guilt may be perceived as greater. On the other hand, if there is only one cellular insolvency (and thus potentially one PCC hub insolvency as well) with the remaining cells continuing as solvent entities, a director may argue that the existence of the 'other successful companies' is evidence of his fitness to continue as a director.[125]

---

[124] *Re Seagull Manufacturing Company Limited [1994] 2 WLR 453*

[125] *Re DJ Matthews (Joinery Design) Limited [1988] BCC 513 and Re Burnham Marketing Services Limited [1993] BCC 518.*

12. DIRECTOR LIABILITY and PCC INSOLVENCIES

12.1. Director liability – notification and segregation liabilities

12.1.1. Introduction

In addition to the normal insolvency-led director liability (i.e. personal and civil liability for antecedent transactions, wrongful trading, etc) we have seen that a director in the UK, may also face a quasi-criminal liability under the Company Directors Disqualification Act 1986 ("CDDA"). Therefore, it must be assumed so would a director of a PCC wound-up in the UK under Part V of the Insolvency Act 1986 as an unregistered company. Similar provisions exist elsewhere throughout the world. All of the above are liabilities that a director of any company could face. The fact that the company was a PCC makes for a greater or different CDDA risk.

That additional PCC risk stems from failures associated with PCCs and may be categorised as threefold:

(a) a failure to notify PCC creditors (however defined) that they are dealing with a PCC and hence that liability was further limited (i.e. limited to cells) as is recourse to assets (the "notification liability");

(b) a failure to correctly segregate intercellular assets and liabilities (the "segregation liability"); and

(c) a failure of the PCC to be internationally recognised as such (the "non-recognition liability") in a non-PCC jurisdiction.

All three such liabilities are considered below. It is assumed that directorial liability will incur primarily consequent to PCC insolvency.

12.1.2. Notification liability

Notification liability can come in two ways:

(i) 'PCC and/or hub notification', i.e. notification that the legal entity is itself a PCC, as opposed to (say) a GmbH; and/or

(ii) 'cellular notification', i.e. that liability falls to a cell, or indeed the hub. The notification liability can be simply put by quoting (the relatively standardised wording of) Article 105(1) and (2) of the Qatar Financial Centre Regulation No 2 of 2005 ("QFC"). Part IV of which deals with PCCs.

"(1) *A PCC shall:*

(A) *inform any person with whom it transacts that it is a PCC; and*

(B) *for the purposes of that transaction, identify or specify the Cell in respect of which that person is transacting, unless that transaction is not a transaction in respect of a particular Cell.*

(2) *If, in contravention of Article 105(1), a PCC:*

(A) *fails to inform a person that he is transacting with a PCC, and that person is otherwise unaware that, and has no reasonable grounds to believe that, he is transacting with a PCC; or*

(B) *fails to identify or specify the Cell in respect of which a person is transacting, and that person is otherwise unaware of, and has no reasonable basis of knowing, which Cell he is transacting with;*

then, in either such case:

(C) *the directors shall (notwithstanding any provision to the contrary in the PCC's articles of association or in any contract with the PCC or otherwise) incur personal liability to that person in respect of the transaction; and*

(D) *the directors shall have a right of indemnity against the Non-Cellular Assets of the PCC, unless they were fraudulent, reckless or negligent, or acted in bad faith."*

To what extent is any such test satisfied by the usual statement requirement, exemplified in article 100(1) QFC: *"The name of a PCC shall end in the expression 'Protected Cell Company','PCC' ..."*? Certainly in many jurisdictions mere failure to abide by section 100(1) or a similar requirement leads to a notification liability. Witness 100(4) of the QFC: *"Unless and until a PCC has complied with the provisions of this Article 100, it shall be deemed not to be a PCC"*. Many jurisdictions have similar provisions to the QFC (i.e. they are notification presumptive in that the law requires specific reference to a PCC). No jurisdiction appears to have the positive reverse, i.e. the mere non-reference to a PCC of itself leads to personal liability. Many jurisdictions are vague: the term PCC should be used, but personal liability does not automatically follow if it is not used. However, even the notification-presumptive states like Qatar, allow a get-out clause, see clause 105(3):

(3) *Notwithstanding the provisions of Article 105(2)(1), the Tribunal may relieve a director of all or part of his personal liability thereunder if he satisfies the Tribunal that he ought to be so relieved because:*

(A) *he was not aware of the circumstances giving rise to his liability and, in being not aware, he was neither fraudulent, reckless or negligent, nor acted in bad faith; or*

(B) *he expressly objected, and exercised such rights as he had as a director, whether by way of voting power or otherwise, so as to try to prevent the circumstances giving rise to his liability.*

What constitutes notification? At the very least, guidance should be taken from standard historical corporate structures, i.e. companies and limited liability partnerships. In those cases, the mere reference to a limited liability entity (by way of (say) reference to the abbreviated "Ltd" when referring to a company) has historically meant that the creditor is on notice that the entity is of limited liability. But the question should be asked if the issue of liability is raised in a non-PCC State: Given the novelty of a PCC structure, should notification go further than a mere repetition of the term 'PCC' in corporate documentation?

First, look at the initial consideration of the notification liability: it comes at two levels, hub/PCC and cellular notification. Both must be considered. A statutory example being article 105(1) (see above) of the QFC PCC regime. If a creditor is notified of the fact that he is dealing with a cell, is that sufficient notification of the PCC's novelty?

Second, undoubtedly compliance with article 105(1) (or similar provision) is sufficient notification within PCC jurisdictions. But what of a non-PCC jurisdiction and especially involving an involuntary creditor? An involuntary creditor will usually receive a sympathetic hearing in a local non-PCC court. In an insurance-based PCC, particularly an insurance-based OFC PCC who are the involuntary creditors? They are usually the taxman and the victim claiming on an insurance policy with the contractual or statutory cut-through provision. Even an OFC PCC may well be faced with onshore imposts and taxes.

Most PCC regimes have fairly standard notification directorial sanctions. A standard PCC regime statute is section 13 of the Protected Cell Companies Act Belize 2000:

"(1) A protected cell company shall: (a) inform any person with whom it conducts business transactions that it is a protected cell company; and (b) for the purpose of such business transactions identify, or specify the cell in respect of which that person is transacting, unless such business transaction is not a transaction in respect of a particular cell of a protected cell company.

(2) If, in contravention... a [PCC]:

(a) fails to inform any person that he is transacting with a [PCC], and that person is otherwise unaware and has no reasonable grounds to believe that he is transacting with a [PCC]; or

(b) fails to identify or specify the cell..., and that person is otherwise unaware of, and has no reasonable basis of knowing..

then in either case:

(i) the directors of the [PCC] shall... incur personal liability...; and

(ii) the directors of the [PCC] shall have a right of indemnity against the non-cellular assets of the [PCC], unless they acted fraudulently, recklessly, negligently or in bad faith."

However, not all statutes are so demanding. The Protected Cell Companies Act 2004 of Anguilla does not provide for a personal liability sanction for directors. The main reference is in section 6 which is, it should be said, relatively standard throughout PCC regimes, which states:

"A protected cell company or any person associated with it shall—

(a) inform any person with whom it enters into a transaction that it is a protected cell company;

(b) where the transaction relates to a protected cell account, for the purposes of that transaction, identify or specify that protected cell account; and

(c) include a reference to the fact that the company is registered under the PCC Act on its letterhead and contracts."

Failure to comply with this requirement, however, constitutes a criminal offence under section 29 of the Anguillan regime.

The Jersey PCC regime goes one stage further. It has a subjective, rather than an objective test. As can be seen, the directors need not simply and objectively ensure by notification on company records, etc, that the third party creditor is aware he is dealing with a PCC and/or a cell; the directors must subjectively make the third party creditor aware by whatever means.

"(1) *A director of a protected cell company must exercise his or her powers and must discharge his or her duties in such a way as shall best ensure that –*

(a) the cellular assets of the company are kept separate and are separately identifiable from the non-cellular assets of the company; and

(b) the cellular assets attributable to each cell of the company are kept separate and are separately identifiable from the cellular assets attributable to other cells of the company.

(2) A director of a protected cell company must ensure, when the company enters into an agreement in respect of a cell or the company –

(a) that the other party to the transaction knows or ought reasonably to know that the cell company is acting in respect of a particular cell; and

(b) that the minutes of any meeting of directors held with regard to the agreement clearly record the fact that the company was entering into the agreement in respect of the cell and that the obligation imposed by sub-paragraph (a) was or will be complied with.

(3) A director who fails to comply with the requirements of paragraph (1) or paragraph (2) shall be guilty of an offence.

(4) The duties of a director of a protected cell company under this Article are in addition to those under Article 74."[126]

Jersey is unusual in a further effect. Each cell must have a name (as opposed to mere attribution in the internal accounts of the PCC). Also, Jersey (presumably when contracting with third parties) requires the cell's name to end in 'PC', see Article 127YS(3):

"(3) A protected cell company must assign a distinctive name to each of its cells that-

(a) distinguishes the cell from any other cell of the company; and

(b) ends with the words 'Protected Cell' or with the abbreviation 'PC'"

12.2. Segregation liability - background

When considering directorial segregation liability, the following factors need to be considered:

(a) Does the directorial liability extend to the loss suffered by the mis-segregation or are the directors merely fined. Under the Isle of Man Protected Cell Companies Act 2004 section 6(1) and section 7: "*A PCC may create one or more cells for the purposes of segregating and protecting cellular assets in the manner provided by this Act…Section 7(1) It is the duty of the directors of a PCC – (a) to keep the cellular assets separate and separately identifiable from the non-cellular assets and (b) to keep the assets attributable to each cell separate and separately identifiable from the cellular*

[126] The Jersey PCC regime (Companies Amendment No. 8) (Jersey) Law 2005, Article 127YR

assets attributable to the other cells...7(4) if default is made in complying with sub-section 1, the directors are liable to a default fine". This should be contrasted with the BVI code (the Insurance (Amendment) Act 2002). Section 30F(2a) – *"the Directors shall, notwithstanding any provision to the contrary in the Company's Articles, or in any contract with such company or otherwise, incur personal liability for the liabilities of the company and the segregated portfolio under the act, matter, deed, agreement, contract, instrument or arrangement that was executed"*. However, there is a statutory indemnity (subject to fraud, recklessness and a bad faith test) noted in section 30F(2)(b).

(b) Can the directors, or more properly a director, claim a defence that the mis-segregation was not his fault. For example, the Cayman Islands Companies Law (2009 Revision) section 218(3) states: *"...the Court may relieve a director of his personal liability thereunder if he satisfies the Court that he ought to be relieved because (a) he was not aware... (b) he expressly objected."*

(c) If the directors (or more properly a director) have a defence, is the burden of proof reversed, i.e. does the director need to prove it was not his fault? A fine (as in the Manx example) being a quasi-criminal penalty, lays the burden with the prosecutor, whereas the burden is reversed in the Cayman Islands case. Some PCC regimes do not consider this issue at all. They leave it to the common law or contract by way of a tangential reference. For example, see the Bermudan Segregated Accounts Companies Act 2000, (as amended) section 18(15). *"(15) To the extent that, at law or in equity, a segregated accounts company or manager has duties (including fiduciary duties) and liabilities relating to segregated account or to a beneficial owner or to a counterparty: - (a) that company or manager acting under a governing instrument is not liable to the segregated account or to any beneficial owner or counterparty for the company's good faith reliance on the provisions of that governing instrument; and (b) the company's or manager's duties and liabilities may be expanded or restricted by provisions in a governing instrument. (16) The provisions of this section and section 11 operate to the exclusion of any law relating to trusts treating with the same subject matter, and no rule of law relating to trusts may be pleaded by any person to augment or modify the operation of this Act, but nothing in this section shall be construed to deny the remedy of tracing in law and in equity the assets or the proceeds of the assets of any segregated account where such assets or proceeds have been commingled."*

It is recommended that in such circumstances a health warning be considered, i.e. a notification on its headed notepaper that 'ABC PCC is a company constituted under the laws of XYZ with liability restricted to individual cells'. The greater the health warning, the less the moral objection that can be raised in the court of a non-PCC jurisdiction. The segregation liability is the duty, more especially described in QFC Article 95(2).

"(2) *It shall be the duty of the directors of a PCC:*

(A) *to keep Cellular Assets separate and separately identifiable from Non-Cellular Assets; and*

(B) *to keep Cellular Assets attributable to each Cell separate and separately identifiable from Cellular Assets attributable to other Cells"*

Naturally any failure to segregate adequately will become an issue upon insolvency.

What potential liabilities exist? The relevant PCC code may establish an intercellular/hub dispute resolution procedure. This is all the more so because many jurisdictions have restrictions on the use of a PCC and/or require authorisation for their creation and/or management. For instance QFC Article 104(1):

"(1) *In the event of any dispute as to:*

(A) *whether any right is or is not in respect of a particular Cell;*

(B) *whether any creditor is or is not a creditor in respect of a particular Cell;*

(C) *whether any liability is or is not attributable to a particular Cell; or*

(D) *the amount to which any liability is limited*

the Tribunal, on the application of the PCC, and without prejudice to any other right or remedy of any person, may issue a declaration in respect of the matter in dispute."

Such a provision would matter if any (for example) article 104(2)(D) declaration is adhered to by the relevant parties:

"(2) *The Tribunal, on hearing an application for a declaration under Article 104(1) may:*

(A) *direct that any person shall be heard on the application;*

(B) *make an interim declaration, or adjourn the hearing, conditionally or unconditionally;*

(C) *make the declaration subject to such terms and conditions as it thinks fit; or*

(D) *direct that the declaration shall be binding upon such persons as may be specified."*

But if (as is often the case) the assets and the creditors are situated in a non-PCC jurisdiction, it comes down to international recognition of the PCC as a concept. This issue is discussed elsewhere.

The PCC code may establish a statutory liability (as opposed to just a duty) upon the directors. But even if just a duty is imposed, it must certainly be supplemented by remedies, such as breach of statutory duty, breach of fiduciary duty and/or negligence.

In all three cases (breach of statutory duty, breach of fiduciary duty and negligence) who will take the remedy? Is there a viable victim? This goes to the heart of the nature of a PCC. In the event of a collapse of an ordinary corporation (i.e. with the historical perspective of *pari passu*) victims come forth i.e; the creditors and shareholders. It is generally accepted that the creditors will get their money back from the estate and the shareholders may have a right of action against the directors. But a PCC stands this logic on its head as there are competing shareholder classes. The individual cells, whether separately capitalised or not, can be regarded as individual shareholder classes. Not only do the individual cells compete, but they compete with the true shareholder class, the hub shareholders.

12.2.1. Segregation Duties: Directors and IPs: a Case of Conflict of Interest

Despite the fundamental that a cell is not a separate legal entity (*cf* Jersey ICCs), invariably PCC codes allow for separate insolvency procedures for individual cell(s) and/or the hub: see QFC Article 109(1) and (2):

"(1) *Notwithstanding any statutory provision or rule of law to the contrary, an administrator may be appointed under the Insolvency Regulations in respect of a PCC or in respect of one or more Cells of a PCC.*

(2) *Where an administrator is appointed under the Insolvency Regulations in respect of one or more Cells of a PCC, the relevant provisions of the Insolvency Regulations shall apply as if references therein to a Company were to be interpreted as references to a Cell."*

The majority of non-US PCC jurisdictions follow the Common Law model of appointing an independent IP over an entity (i.e. an administrator or liquidator). The US model tends to be a 'debtor-in-possession' (i.e. incumbent management) model. We suggest that the PCC's uniqueness (i.e. it is a platform for disparate interests) means that the debtor-in-the-possession model is less appropriate to a PCC insolvency. However, a PCC's uniqueness poses difficulties for the independent IP model. These difficulties are particularly focused in any discussion as to the segregation liability. In group insolvencies there is always going to be a pay-off between costs and the conflicts of interests involved in having a group appointment (i.e. a single IP appointed over each company within the group). Not only is there the segregation liability concern, but see QFC Article 103(5): *"For the avoidance of doubt, a PCC may enter into arm's length transactions in respect of two or more of its Cells giving rise to reciprocal liabilities attributable to such Cells."* In an insolvency the most obvious argument for a PCC-based jurisdiction IP to face when seeking international recognition in a potentially unsympathetic non-PCC jurisdiction is: 'that the PCC is shown in reality to be a series of companies and consequently that the PCC regime itself is a sham'. This will especially be the case if there are individual cell shareholders, who will need to be separately represented.

Who represents whom and who is the victim in cell-segregated insolvency? It will be no different to any other insolvency (group or otherwise) regardless of whether a plea is to a Court or to a specially constituted PCC tribunal (see QFC article 104 above). As to whether the plea should be submitted to a tribunal or a Court, a preference would be for a court. Provided the PCC jurisdiction has a mutual recognition treaty with the non-PCC jurisdiction, then it is probable that the treaty would only allow for the recognition of courts. It may not allow for the recognition of tribunals. Further such treaties/conventions would not allow for the recognition ordinarily of an insolvency. Insolvency, along with probate is usually excluded from such mutual recognition treaties and conventions.[127] Thus, a court ordered segregation declaration is obviously preferable. Additionally, if the court ordered segregation declaration is recognised this may add some weight (in order to avoid inconsistency) to the non-PCC jurisdiction, recognising the validity of the IP appointment over the PCC. Hence such recognition may lead to the breaking of the normal *pari passu* priority.

[127] e.g. the Brussels and Lugarno Conventions

12.2.2. Non-Recognition Liability

Whilst the issue of non-recognition itself is addressed separately here, in large part the issues that flow from non-recognition are covered elsewhere. The non-recognition liability that is addressed here is the liability that adheres to the directors from the mere non-recognition of the PCC concept. The specific question therefore is: If a PCC is not recognised in the non-PCC jurisdiction will any actions of the directors, especially those in abiding by the duties of the PCC jurisdiction, cause potential liability to the PCC directors in a non-PCC jurisdiction? There will be a clash between two concepts: the rules of the cellular priority and then normal *pari passu* principle. The forceful claim of PCC priority is put thus in QFC Article 103(1)(A) and (5) and (6) which states:

"(1) *Subject to the provisions of Article 103(2) and save to the extent that the PCC may have agreed that a liability shall be the liability solely of the PCC's Non-Cellular Assets, or of the Cellular Assets attributable to a particular Cell of the PCC, where any liability arises which is attributable to a particular Cell of a PCC:*

(A) *the Cellular Assets attributable to that Cell shall be primarily used to satisfy the liability…*

(5) *For the avoidance of doubt, a PCC may enter into arm's length transactions in respect of two or more of its Cells giving rise to reciprocal liabilities attributable to such Cells.*

(6) *This Article 103 shall apply to the assets of the PCC wherever situated."*

QFC Article 103, quoted above, is an apparent cast-iron repudiation of *pari passu,* to which the director must acceed. Its sanction applies *"wherever [assets are] situated"*. The directors of a QFC PCC must apply cellular priority which clashes with *pari passu*. Conversely section 239 of the UK Insolvency Act states in support of the *pari passu* principle: *"where the company has…given a preference… the court shall…order as it thinks fit [and] a company gives a preference…if the company does anything or suffers anything [i.e. it abides by the PCC regime cellular priority and segregation?] …which has the effect of putting that person into a position which…will be better."*

Let us imagine a possible scenario. A UK-based insured creates a non-UK PCC ("ABC PCC" of Jersey) with UK-based assets. A catastrophe occurs and some cells become highly insolvent; some cells become marginally insolvent and some cells marginally solvent. Viewed as a whole the PCC is either a marginally solvent or marginally insolvent. Third parties who could benefit from the Rights of Third Parties Act 1932 (whereby third parties would be paid direct the insurance without their claim being rateably reduced) petition for the company's (i.e. ABC PCC) liquidation under section 5 of the UK Insolvency Act 1986[128]. In short the company faces both UK and Jersey insolvencies. Presumably section 425 of the Insolvency Act (the mutual recognition of Jersey) applies. So the first question either court faces is, what is the added benefit of a second insolvency process where a first insolvency has occurred in either jurisdiction? The answer is 'to enforce their view of priority' and especially for the Jersey directors (presumably they are there) to prove Jersey's supremacy. Presumably the Jersey equivalent of the Rights of Third Parties Act 1932 (The Third Parties Rights Against Insurers (Jersey) Law 1948) does not apply, it having been specifically amended to take account of PCCs. Thus the involuntary creditor (the claimant victim under a Rights of Third Parties Act) has no interest in the Jersey insolvency. ABC PCC's directors in accordance with Jersey law maintain strict segregation, at the expense of the involuntary creditor. In short, the directors show a possible preference. The preference is to the possibly connected (i.e. insured) creditor looking at it from the perspective of UK preference law. Why? Because it is possible (if not probable) that the insured creditors will be connected. Thus under UK law a preference has occurred. The director's possible sole defence is his motivation. English law requires not just that the preference occurred, but that he was motivated by a desire to prefer. The director's defence could be that he was merely acting in accordance with (say) Jersey law and not by a personal desire to prefer. Not all jurisdictions have 'intent provisions' within their 'detrimental act regimes'.

The court's sympathy would be even more tested if the relevant PCC regime had statutory non-recourse to the hub as in the case of say Jersey PCCs. Thus in the insolvency of ABC PCC, the Jersey hub remains unscathed. But involuntary UK creditors with potentially easy access to UK-based assets (including those of the hub possibly) remain unpaid. Directorial personal liability as a result of non-recognition of the PCC concept in a non-PCC jurisdiction for antecedent transactions is a possibility. The obvious answers are to avoid having assets and liabilities in non-PCC jurisdictions. Failing that an adequate Directors and Officers ("D and O") insurance policy is recommended. Further a D and O policy that specifically covers PCC issues.

Traditionally director insolvency liability fell into:

[128] Though, remember the UK Insolvency Act cannot apply to EU insurance companies.

1. antecedent transactions (such as a preference) whereby the *pari passu* principle was allegedly overturned;
2. trading whilst insolvent (such as wrongful trading) whereby the position of the company was made worse;
3. quasi-criminal liability (such as in the UK, the CDDA) whereby directors are disqualified from taking advantage of limited liability henceforth;
4. criminal liability proper (such as theft, which is not addressed in this book); and
5. negligence, or breach of fiduciary duty.

It is improbable that insurance and investment PCCs would be trading companies, save for the possible exception of funds, taking short positions i.e. the typical hedge fund, as opposed to being a passive investor.

Thus, trading whilst insolvent actions are unlikely; this regardless of whether international recognition of the PCC occurs. The cellular shareholders could argue, in a non-PCC jurisdiction, that mere shareholding was being dissipated at the expense of the hub shareholding. This especially is the case in statutory non-recourse jurisdictions, such as Jersey PCCs. However, even an unsympathetic non-PCC court should give short shrift to such a claim. The cellular shareholders know what they were doing after all. Ditto with a negligence claim. It is possible for a CDDA action to apply to a non-UK company wound up under section 5 of the Insolvency Act. However it is perhaps improbable that by itself, acting in accordance with the PCC view of priority, would lead to censure.

This situation may be different if a successful preference claim was mounted. Interestingly, the CDDA draws a distinction between the standard director (who is judged by an objective standard) and an educated director such as the usual OFC PCC director. The OFC director is often a lawyer or accountant. He is therefore judged by a subjective (and thus higher) standard. Reverting to our Anglo-Jersey example; whether a PCC director who is a doubly-qualified English solicitor and Jersey advocate (and hence bound by both regimes) would be separately viewed under English law, under presumably a higher subjective standard, is to say the least, moot.

12.2.3. What Constitutes a Director?

The CDDA notes several times that the term *"director"* includes *"shadow director"*. Section 22(4) of the CDDA states a "director" *"includes any person occupying the position of director, by whatever name called"*. Further section 22(5) states a *"shadow director"* means *"in relation to a company [which includes a company capable of being wound up under Part V of the Insolvency Act 1986] means a person in accordance with whose directions or instructions the directors of the company are accustomed to act (but so that a person is not deemed to be a shadow director by reason only that the director acts on advice given by him in a professional capacity"*).

'Cell owners' may well be shadow directors (i.e. *de facto* directors) if not *de jure* directors of the cell. Indeed, many PCC regimes allow for cellular capitalisation as well as cell directors. Thus, a PCC may have several sets of directors. Further, given that they will invariably direct the PCC *de jure* directors (i.e. the hub directors) as to how the PCC should act *vis-à-vis* the cell, these cellular directors may well become shadow directors of the hub. This is despite the fact that the direction given by the cellular directors may well be limited to matters pertaining to their cell. Thus if a PCC insolvency occurs with some cells remaining solvent, even directors or shadow directors of the solvent cell, may well become shadow directors of the hub in the insolvency. In short, whilst the cellular directors are not directly connected with any insolvency of the hub, or indeed of any of the other cells within the PCC, they could become liable.

Some jurisdictions have sought to preclude this possibility. For instance the Bermudan Segregated Accounts Companies Act 2000 (as amended) states: s.18(4) *"Except to the extent otherwise provided in the governing instrument but subject to subsection 7(b), neither the power to give directions to the segregated accounts company or other persons nor the exercise thereof by any person (including a beneficial owner) shall cause the person giving directions to be a trustee or officer of the company.*

Other jurisdictions have sought to avoid the matrix noted above. This is done by requiring that directors of the cells have to be directors also of the hub. For instance Article 127YD of the Companies (Jersey) Law 1991 (as amended to incorporate Jersey's PCC regime):

"(1) A cell of an incorporated cell company –

(a) is created on the day specified in the certificate of incorporation in relation to the cell to be the date of incorporation of the cell; and

(b) is, in accordance with this Law, a company from that day.

(2) A cell of a protected cell company is created on the day specified in the certificate of recognition in relation to the cell to be the date on which the cell was created.

(3) *A cell of a protected cell company shall not be a company but it shall, except as otherwise provided by this Part, be treated as a company registered under this Law for the purpose of the application to it of this Law.*

(4) *In accordance with paragraph (3), except as otherwise provided by this Part, this Law shall apply to a cell of a protected cell company as if a reference in this Law –*

(a) *to a company were a reference to the cell;*

(b) *to the directors of a company were a reference to the directors of the cell;*

(c) *to the memorandum or articles of a company were a reference to the memorandum or articles of the cell;*

(d) *to incorporation were a reference to the creation of the cell;*

(e) *to a certificate of incorporation were a reference to a certificate of recognition;*

(f) *to members of a company were a reference to the members of the cell;*

(g) *to shares in a company were a reference to shares in the cell;*

(h) *to assets and liabilities of a company were a reference to the assets and liabilities of the cell; and*

(i) *to the share capital of a company were a reference to the share capital of the cell.*

(5) *Despite Article 2 –*

(a) *a cell of a protected cell company is not, by virtue only of being such a cell of the company, a subsidiary or wholly owned subsidiary of the company; and*

(b) *a cell of an incorporated cell company is a company that is not a subsidiary or wholly owned subsidiary of the cell company."*

The Jersey approach is sensible. As it avoids the matrix problem noted above of multiple directors. Further, the absence of separate directors may be considered by a non-PCC jurisdiction as not indicating that a PCC is in reality of series of companies. The Anguillan approach is again different. Its PCC regime creates a 'cell protector role', which can be regarded as a shadow director. The Anguillan PCC Act s.7 states: *"A [PCC]... shall appoint and maintain a ... [PCC] representative in Anguilla who shall be a person approved by the Commission as a protected cell account representative of the company"*. The duties imposed on this representative are akin to a normal director's duties. Specific penalties follow under the regime for breach of representative duties. Given that the representative is *de facto* a director, perhaps the Jersey approach is correct; the Anguillan cell representative should be made *de jure* director.

12.2.4. What constitutes a Shadow Director?

The answer is not clear and will depend upon the facts. At one end of the spectrum the board is a merely 'puppet board'. It should be remembered that the 'nominee director' is often found in OFCs that have PCC regimes. The 'nominee director' may well be regarded as a puppet. It has been suggested that a holding company that exercises sufficient 'downstream' control could be a shadow director. Perversely in a PCC, the cells (which could be analogised as subsidiaries to the PCC hub or holding company) may exercise the opposite, i.e. 'upstream control'. *In Hydrodam (Corby) Limited [1994] BCC 161*, it was stated: *"what is needed is, first, a board of directors claiming and purporting to act as such; and secondly, a pattern of behaviour in which the board did not exercise any discretion or judgment of its own, but acted in accordance with the directions of others"*. This should be contrasted with *Secretary of State for Trade and Industry v Becker [2002] EWHC 2200 (Ch)* where it was held that it was insufficient that a sole director had acted upon an alleged directors control on one occasion only.

The terms *"shadow director"* and *"director"* it is claimed, do not usually overlap, i.e. they are mutually exclusive. Given the peculiarities of the PCC cellular structure, it is necessary to consider the definition of a *de facto* director in detail. According to Miller J in *Re Hydrodan (above): "A de facto director is a person who assumes to act as a director. He is held out as a director by the company and claims and purports to be a director, although never actually or wholly validly appointed as such. To establish that a person was a de facto director of a company, it is necessary to plead and prove that he undertook functions in relation to the company which could properly be discharged only by a director. It is not sufficient to show that he was concerned with the management of the company's affairs and undertook tasks in relation to its business which can be properly performed by a manager below board level"*.

The current *de facto* director UK position is as stated in *Secretary of State for Trade and Industry v Deverell [2001] Ch 340*:

(a) the term is to be construed in the normal way and not more strictly because it may have penal consequences;

(b) it is not necessary that the person's influence should be exercised over the whole field of the company's activities and could therefore relate to just one cell;

(c) whether any particular communication is to be construed as a direction or instruction is to be objectively ascertained by the Court:

the parties own understanding or description of its nature may be relevant but cannot be conclusive;

(d) the concepts of 'direction' and 'instruction' do not exclude the concept of 'advice', more especially non-professional advice;

(e) it is not necessary (though probably sufficient) to show that the properly appointed directors or some of them cast themselves in a subservient role or surrendered their own directions.

It should be remembered that the majority of PCC jurisdiction have their CDDA equivalents.

12.2.5. What constitutes behaviour serious to warrant CDDA Prosecution?

The CDDA lists non-exclusive factors, including Schedule 1 Part II: "6. *The extent of the directors responsibility for the causes of the company becoming insolvent …8. The extent of the directors responsibility for the company entering into any transaction… (a) liable to be set aside … [as a preference or a transaction at an undervalue]*".

Strangely, it is not the actual setting aside that is important but its potentiality to be set aside (i.e. "*liable to be set aside*") which is reinforced by the reference in Scotland to sub-section 8 as "*challengeable*".

The difficulty here is the conflict between the PCC priority structure and the traditional *pari passu* notion. It is noted that acting on professional advice has a long judicial acceptance of being a CDDA defence.[129] It is presumed that all directors will take such advice. From this it can be seen that the risks of a CDDA action are limited. Against this, however, has been a line of juridical reasoning that has said that failure to set aside sufficient monies for involuntary government debts is perhaps more culpable that any other form of failure to so set aside. This is on the basis that government debts are a quasi-trust.[130]

International regimes sit uncomfortably with the CDDA and similar acts in their own jurisdictions. We have seen that the Model Law (Article 23) and EU regimes (both the EU Regulation (Article 13) and the EU Insurance Insolvency Regulations (Article 30) state that antecedent transaction litigation should rest with the "*main proceeding*". However, a

---

[129] See *Re Bath Glass Limited [1988] 4 BCC 130, Re McNulty's Interchange Limited [1989] 4 BCC 533; Re Douglas Construction Services Limited [1988] 4 BCC 553; Re CU Fittings Ltd [1989] 5 BCC 210; Re Gladrose Limited [1994] BCC 11;* and *Re Brad Crowns Limited [2001] 1 BCC 547.*

[130] *Re Wedgecroft Limited* unreported of 7 March 1986

CDDA prosecution does not fall within these regime's definition of antecedent transactions; CDDA prosecutions do not of themselves reverse a transaction to ensure the originally envisaged *pari passu* which is the rationale of antecedent transaction. Rather CDDA actions are quasi-criminal in nature. They do not benefit the creditors at large or increase the assets due to the estate. Consequently, it seems that they can be prosecuted in *"secondary"* (i.e. under the EU Regulation) or *"non-main proceedings"* (i.e. Model Law) States, i.e. in non-PCC states where secondary or non-main proceedings occur. However, the likelihoods of such prosecutions are remote. This is for several reasons. First many PCC regimes already have CDDA type statutes. It is doubtful whether a *"secondary"* or *"non-main"* proceeding State (i.e. the non-PCC state) would take action as a creditor[131] if the individual faced action back home under a similar regime. Second, resources for such prosecutions are limited. Local authorities tend to go for 'low hanging fruit' without the legal and procedural obstacles that a first PCC CDDA prosecution would entail. Third, in the nature of a PCC, creditors are often stakeholders, certainly stakeholders in the cell and they may well lose out in the event of insolvency. Case law has indicated that a personal loss as a creditor (i.e. of the director's company for which we can class a cell stakeholder to be) weighs heavily with the Court. Remote as these negative consequences may be, prudent measures should be undertaken by those who utilise PCCs. Such measures would include:

(a) act always on written professional advice if there is any danger of insolvency;

(b) leave the management of the PCC and its cells to local professionals; and

(c) especially if an onshore individual must become involved, get the best D&O insurance cover available.

12.2.6. Corporate directors

The use of corporate directorships is common, especially in OFCs. They are often used to ensure that the company is regarded for tax purposes as managed offshore as the corporate director is a company formed in that jurisdiction. This is especially the case for PCCs. Stakeholders in individual cells want to be directors of those cells. However they also want those cells to be considered offshore for tax purposes. However, they should not be regarded as circumventing CDDA type legislation.

---

[131] Especially if the relevant alleged director resided abroad.

Invariably, those that direct the corporate director will be classed as shadow directors. There can be no escape. However, in considering a choice of PCC jurisdiction regard should be had to whether corporate directorships are allowed. The Jersey[132] regime states:

"A body corporate shall not be a director of a company unless –

(a) the body corporate is a company that is permitted under the terms of its registration under the Financial Services (Jersey) Law 1999 to act as, or fulfil the requirements of, a director; and

(b) the body corporate has no director that is a body corporate."

[132] See Article 73 of the Companies (Jersey) Law 1991 (as amended)

13. PIERCING THE CORPORATE VEIL

13.1. Introduction

The veil of incorporation is the veil which separates the company from its shareholders. In this section we consider under what circumstances the introduction of a PCC might lead to the piercing of that veil. English law commentators have noted that the corporate veil will be pierced possibly by and through:

(1) agency

(2) fraud or sham

(3) trust

(4) enemy connection

(5) specific legislation.

It is improbable that an agency-principal relationship can be found between the cell and the hub. This is because the hub and cells constitute one legal person and the agency-principal relationship requires two persons. As to agency between cell shareholders and stakeholders and cell, then that falls to the general law unrelated to PCCs. The courts have been loath to find an agency relationship between the shareholders and a separate company. The challenge therefore, is to establish what the legal identity of PCC is. The problem for the PCC draftsman is to ride two horses at the same time: that is, the cell is not a separate *de jure* legal identity but has all the *de facto* aspects of a legal identity.

As to 'riding two horses', witness Article 127YP of the Companies (Jersey) Law 1991 (introduced by the Companies (Amendment No. 8) (Jersey) Law 2005):

"(1) A cell of a protected cell company is not a body corporate and has no legal identity separate from that of its cell company [being the standard PCC position].

(2) However, a cell of a protected cell company may enter into an agreement with its cell company or with another cell of the company that shall be enforceable as if each cell of the company were a body corporate that had a legal identity separate from that of its cell company [this subsection encapsulates the *de facto* versus *de jure* tension].

(3) Where a protected cell company is liable for any criminal penalty, under this Law or otherwise, due to the act or default of a cell of the company or of an officer of a cell of the company, the penalty –

> (a) *may only be met by the company from the cellular assets of the cell; and*
>
> (b) *shall not be enforceable in any way against any other assets of the company, whether cellular or non-cellular."*

The obviousness of a cell being a *de facto* company is highlighted further with the Jersey regime at s.127YD (*'status of cells'*):

"(1) A cell of an incorporated cell company –

(a) is created on the day specified in the certificate of incorporation in relation to the cell to be the date of incorporation of the cell; and

(b) is, in accordance with this Law, a company from that day.

(2) A cell of a protected cell company is created on the day specified in the certificate of recognition in relation to the cell to be the date on which the cell was created.

(3) A cell of a protected cell company shall not be a company but it shall, except as otherwise provided by this Part, be treated as a company registered under this Law for the purpose of the application to it of this Law.

(4) In accordance with paragraph (3), except as otherwise provided by this Part, this Law shall apply to a cell of a protected cell company as if a reference in this Law –

(a) to a company were a reference to the cell;

(b) to the directors of a company were a reference to the directors of the cell;

(c) to the memorandum or articles of a company were a reference to the memorandum or articles of the cell;

(d) to incorporation were a reference to the creation of the cell;

(e) to a certificate of incorporation were a reference to a certificate of recognition;

(f) to members of a company were a reference to the members of the cell;

(g) to shares in a company were a reference to shares in the cell;

(h) to assets and liabilities of a company were a reference to the assets and liabilities of the cell; and

(i) to the share capital of a company were a reference to the share capital of the cell.

(5) Despite Article 2 –

(a) *a cell of a protected cell company is not, by virtue only of being such a cell of the company, a subsidiary or wholly owned subsidiary of the company; and*

(b) *a cell of an incorporated cell company is a company that is not a subsidiary or wholly owned subsidiary of the cell company."*

13.2. Insurance and third parties

Tort presents a problem for PCCs. The normal tortious issue with 'piercing the corporate veil' is closely related to sham or fraud. In order to defeat restraints, such as 'restraint of trade clauses', an individual often incorporates[133] and the tortious act that surrounds such an incorporation, is inducing breach of contract, etc.

Moreover the Third Parties (Rights Against Insurers) Act 1930[134] (with its equivalent in most English influenced PCC offshore financial centres) is of importance. This Act is significant for PCCs and its main elements are reproduced below:-

"1. Rights of third parties against insurers on bankruptcy etc, of the insured

1(1) Where under any contract of insurance a person (hereinafter referred to as the insured) is insured against liabilities to third parties which he may incur, then –

(a) .....

(b) in the case of the insured being a company, ... [becoming insolvent under the Insolvency Act 1986] ....;

if, either before or after that event, any such liability as aforesaid is incurred by the insured, his rights against the insurer under the contract in respect of the liability shall, notwithstanding anything in any Act or rule of law to the contrary, be transferred to and vest in the third party to whom the liability was so incurred."

Moreover:-

"2 Duty to give necessary information to third parties

2(1) In the event of ... a winding-up order being made, or a resolution for a voluntary winding-up being passed, with respect to any company or of the company entering administration or of a receiver or manager of the company's business or undertaking being duly appointed or of

---

[133] See *Gilford Motor Company Limited v. Horne* [1993] *1 Ch 935*

[134] There is a bill to replace the Act currently having its second reading before the UK House of Lords.

possession being taken by or on behalf of the holders of any debentures secured by a floating charge of any property comprised in or subject to the charge it shall be the duty of the ... liquidator, administrator, receiver or manager, or person in possession of the property to give at the request of any person claiming that the ... company is under a liability to him such information as may reasonably be required by him for the purpose of ascertaining whether any rights have been transferred to and vested in him by this Act and for the purpose of enforcing such rights, if any, and any contract of insurance, in so far as it purports, whether directly or indirectly, to avoid the contract or to alter the rights of the parties thereunder upon the giving of any such information in the events aforesaid or otherwise to prohibit or prevent the giving thereof in the said events shall be of no effect.

2(2) If the information given to any person in pursuance of subsection (1) of this section discloses reasonable ground for supposing that there have or may have been transferred to him under this Act rights against any particular insurer, that insurer shall be subject to the same duty as is imposed by the said subsection on the persons therein mentioned.

2(3) The duty to give information imposed by this section shall include a duty to allow all contracts of insurance, receipts for premiums, and other relevant documents in the possession or power of the person on whom the duty is so imposed to be inspected and copies thereof to be taken.

3 Settlement between insurers and insured persons

3(1) Where ... in the case of the insured being a company, a winding-up order or an administration order has been made or a resolution for a voluntary winding-up had been passed, with respect to the Company, no agreement made between the insurer and the insured after liability has been incurred to a third party and after the commencement of the ... winding-up or the day of the making of the administration order, as the case may be, nor any waiver, assignment or other disposition made by, or payment made to the insured after the commencement or day aforesaid shall be effective to defeat or affect the rights transferred to the third party under this Act, but those rights shall be the same as if no such agreement, waiver, assignment, disposition or payment has been made."

It should be noted that the UK Insolvency Act appears to cover an unregistered company wound up under Part V of the Insolvency Act 1986. The third party victim is usually a victim of a tortious act. Plainly this Act is a *prima facie* breach of cellular priority. However, can the cellular breach be widened? If a company is wound up and its cells, or some of its cells are not, does the Act apply to the solvent cells, and if so, to what consequence? Most PCC legislation in offshore jurisdictions postdates the local equivalent of this Third Parties Act. Therefore, could the local equivalent be said to be overruled, if it has not already been amended to take account of PCCs?

13.2.1. Sham: generally

The real question in 'lifting the corporate veil' in respect of a PCC is, 'Is the whole PCC construct a sham?' The US Model Law assists here tangently via Section 6E – *"in no event shall the establishment of one or more protected cells alone constitute or be deemed to be a fraudulent conveyance, an intent by the protected cell company to defraud creditors, or the carrying out of business by the......[PCC] for another fraudulent purpose"*. This neatly amplifies the presumed English Law position noted by Lord Cooke in his first Hamlyn lecture (when considering the English law sham doctrine): *"the sham transaction is not simply the act of incorporation, but the legal obligations undertaken by the entity thereafter"*.

Thus, two of the world's major jurisdictions (the US and the UK) would be unlikely to find that the mere creating of a PCC itself is a sham or a fraud. This, however, could be subject to one caveat: 'PCC conversion'. Most PCC regimes allow for an existing non PCC corporation to convert. However, usually only after permission is granted, i.e. it is rare for there to be an automatic right to convert. However, if there is a risk, it is the risk that a non-PCC captive will convert to a PCC and place bad risks into different cells from good risk. The steps usually required to arrange for a PCC conversion, should ensure that mere conversion would not present difficulties *per se*.

13.2.2. US Shams: an introduction

US law perhaps is one of the most developed common law jurisdictions when it comes to analysing what constitutes a sham.

US law has sought to lift the corporate veil in sham or alter ego situations, and has looked to the following factors:

(i) 'corporate shareholders';

(ii) 'closely held corporations';

(iii) 'significant involuntary creditors'; and

(iv) 'under-capitalisation'.

Commentators have referred to the 'totality of circumstances', behind these factors such as:

(a) failure to observe corporate formality;

(b) non payment of dividends;

(c) the siphoning of funds;

(d) non-functioning officers;

(e) non-existent separate records; and

(f) the intermingling of funds.

But what is an alter ego? Is it the hub for the cell or the cell's shareholders for the cell? It is presumed that if the PCC structure is recognised, it can not be the hub for the cell, because they are the same legal person and consequently alter ego does not apply. If it is the cell shareholders for the cell, then those involved with PCCs should avoid the 'totality of circumstances' noted above.

13.3. Cell migration

A bigger problem than PCC conversion could be cell migration. A cell can often migrate under PCC regimes at any time; even after a PCC insolvency. The ability to control a cell in this manner by the shareholders certainly adds 'to the totality of circumstances'.

A statutory example of cell migration is found in Jersey PCC regime at Article 127YI (*'Transfer of cell'*) of the Companies (Jersey) Law 1991 (as amended):

"(1) A cell of a cell company may become a cell of another cell company by being transferred from the former to the latter.

(2) The companies shall enter into a written agreement (the "transfer agreement") that sets out the terms of the transfer.

(3) A transfer of a cell is provisionally approved if –

(a) the directors of the cell company from which the cell is to be transferred have approved the transfer agreement;

(b) the agreement is approved by a special resolution of the cell company to which the cell is being transferred; and

(c) any of the following occur –

(i) the transfer agreement is sanctioned by the court as an arrangement in accordance with Article 125,

(ii) the transfer agreement is consented to by all the members of the cell being transferred and all the creditors (if any) of that cell,

(iii) where the agreement of all the creditors of the cell cannot be obtained, the transfer is authorized by a special resolution of

the cell and sanctioned by the court on it being satisfied that no creditor of the cell will be materially prejudiced by the transfer.

(4) *A director of a cell who has approved a transfer agreement under which the cell shall be transferred to another cell company shall, as soon as practicable after the transfer has been provisionally approved in accordance with paragraph (3) –*

(a) *sign a declaration stating that the director believes on reasonable grounds that –*

(i) *the cell is able to discharge its liabilities as they fall due, and*

(ii) *the transfer has been provisionally approved in accordance with paragraph (3); and*

(b) *ensure that a copy of the declaration is delivered to the cell company to which the cell is to be transferred.*

(5) *A director who makes a declaration under paragraph (4) without having reasonable grounds to do so is guilty of an offence.*

(6) *The cell company to which the cell is to be transferred shall, within 21 days of receiving the declaration required to be delivered to the cell company under paragraph (4)(b), deliver to the registrar –*

(a) *a copy of the special resolution of the cell company provisionally approving the transfer agreement;*

(b) *a copy of the transfer agreement;*

(c) *a copy of the memorandum and the articles that it is intended the cell being transferred shall have when it is transferred; and*

(d) *a copy of the declaration delivered to the cell company under paragraph (4)(b).*

(7) *If a cell company fails to deliver to the registrar the documents mentioned in paragraph (6) within the period specified in that paragraph, the company, and every officer of it who is in default, is guilty of an offence.*

(8) *If a cell company delivers to the registrar, within the period specified in paragraph (6), the special resolution of that company provisionally approving the transfer agreement, the company shall be taken to have complied with the requirements of Article 100(1) in relation to that resolution.*

(9) *The registrar may, after receiving the documents referred to in paragraph (6) in relation to the transfer of a cell –*

(a) *if the requirements of this Article have been complied with, approve the transfer of the cell; or*

(b) if the requirements of this Article have not been complied with, refuse to approve the transfer of the cell.

(10) The registrar may not approve the transfer of a cell under paragraph (9) if the transfer would be inconsistent with the memorandum or articles of the cell, the cell company transferring the cell or the cell company to which it is to be transferred.

(11) If the registrar approves the transfer of the cell –

(a) the cell is transferred to the cell company specified in the transfer agreement in relation to the cell to be the cell company to which it is to be transferred;

(b) the cell ceases to be a cell of the cell company that transferred it;

(c) the cell becomes a cell of the company to which it has been transferred;

(d) the registrar shall register the transfer of the cell, and the memorandum and articles, delivered to the registrar under paragraph (6);

(e) the registrar shall, in the case of –

(i) the transfer of a cell to an incorporated cell company, issue a certificate of incorporation of the cell under Article 9 as if he or she had received an application for the creation of the cell under Article 127YA, or

(ii) the transfer of a cell to a protected cell company, issue a certificate of recognition of the cell under Article 9 as if he or she had received an application for the creation of the cell under Article 127YA and Article 127YC(10) applied in relation to the cell; and

(f) the registrar shall record that the cell has ceased to be a cell of the company that transferred the cell.

(12) If a cell that was a cell of an incorporated cell company is transferred under paragraph (11)(a) –

(a) all property and rights to which the cell was entitled immediately before the transfer shall –

(i) if the transfer is to an incorporated cell company, remain the property and rights of the cell, or

(ii) if the transfer is to a protected cell company, become the property and rights of that company in respect of the cell;

(b) the liabilities, and all contracts, debts and other obligations to which the cell was subject immediately before the transfer shall –

(i) if the transfer is to an incorporated cell company, remain the liabilities, contracts, debts and other obligations of the cell, or

(ii) if the transfer is to a protected cell company, become the liabilities, contracts, debts and other obligations of that company in respect of the cell; and

(c) all actions and other legal proceedings which, immediately before the transfer were pending by or against the cell may –

(i) if the transfer is to an incorporated cell company, be continued by or against the cell, or

(ii) if the transfer is to a protected cell company, be continued by or against that company in respect of the cell.

(13) If a cell that was a cell of a protected cell company is transferred under paragraph (11)(a) –

(a) all property and rights of that company in respect of the cell immediately before the transfer shall –

(i) if the transfer is to an incorporated cell company, become the property and rights of the cell, or

(ii) if the transfer is to a protected cell company, become the property and rights of that company in respect of that cell;

(b) all liabilities, contracts, debts and other obligations of that company in respect of the cell, to which the protected cell company was subject immediately before the transfer shall –

(i) if the transfer is to an incorporated cell company, become the liabilities, contracts, debts and other obligations of the cell, or

(ii) if the transfer is to a protected cell company, become the liabilities, contracts, debts and other obligations of that company in respect of the cell; and

(c) all actions and other legal proceedings that, immediately before the transfer, were pending by or against the protected cell company in respect of the cell may –

(i) if the transfer is to an incorporated cell company, be continued by or against the cell, or

(ii) if the transfer is to a protected cell company, be continued by or against that company is respect of the cell.

(14) The operation of paragraphs (11), (12) and (13) shall not be regarded –

(a) as a breach of contract or confidence or otherwise as a civil wrong;

(b) *as a breach of any contractual provision prohibiting, restricting or regulating the assignment or transfer of rights or liabilities; or*

(c) *as giving rise to any remedy by a party to a contract or other instrument, as an event of default under any contract or other instrument or as causing or permitting the termination of any contract or other instrument, or of any obligation or relationship."*

From a post-insolvency perspective, what is more problematic is the 'forced migration' of a cell as in s.127YJ:

"(1) *Where a cell company with one or more cells is being wound up under Part 21 the company shall not be taken to have no assets and no liabilities while the company continues to have any such cell.*

(2) *Accordingly, in the course of the winding up of the company each cell of the company must -*

(a) *be transferred to another cell company;*

(b) *be wound up;*

(c) *be continued as a body corporate or cell under the law of another jurisdiction;*

(d) *be incorporated independently of the cell company; or*

(e) *be merged with another company."*

Surely a post-insolvency cell migration could fall under the 'totality of circumstances'. Admittedly the Jersey provision has many safeguards. But the safeguards tend to the protection of the cell creditor; not the creditors of all of the PCC.

13.4. International factors influencing 'piercing the corporate veil'.

Corporate limited-liability is accepted worldwide, but most jurisdictions have some exceptions to that rule. This section will not look at specific statutory exceptions. It will look at the general factors that have influenced courts worldwide, but particularly US courts, in 'piercing the corporate veil', more especially in a PCC context. In piercing the corporate veil, courts will have to balance the economic and social aspects of limited-liability, against the perceived injustice of limited liability abuse.

The judiciary have tended to look to a 'totality of the circumstances' test. Circumstances which may give rise to piercing the corporate veil include, without limitation:

1. the failure to observe corporate formalities being an implicit recognition that the entity is not in reality separate from either the group or its owners, i.e. its alter ego;
2. the degree of support offered by shareholders, which again points to an alter ego;
3. the non-functioning of officers which may indicate control by an alter ego or shadow director(s); and
4. intermingling of monies between the corporate entity and its shareholders.

All of the above present obvious difficulties for PCCs.

13.4.1. Groups

There is often a reluctance of courts to adhere to the doctrine of strict limited liability with groups. Thus, a group should not be perceived as casting away a member of the group that has become insolvent. There are a number of reasons why courts are not so reluctant to pierce the corporate veil with group companies. The most obvious is that piercing the corporate veil of group companies is not a direct attack on limited liability. The liability is still limited, but the limit is merely that of the parent or of the group. The judiciary have felt able, in the past, to pierce the group corporate veil because managers would otherwise not be averse to putting their riskier adventures in one group company. This would be done knowing that in a worse case scenario, job security, etc, would be offered by the rest of the group. Consequently risk is not fairly shared amongst the group.

In the event of a cellular insolvency, would the judiciary require the insured group company which was the beneficiary of the insolvent cell, to make good the losses? The most obvious question the judiciary must ask is: Is a cell within a PCC, a group company such that I may employ any accepted judicial line of reasoning which allows me to pierce the corporate veil in groups situations? This question is also considered elsewhere within this book, i.e. can and/or should a company consolidate a cell within its group accounts? Regardless of accounting logic, a judge will probably look at the practical situation and consider the following factors:

(a) is the cell separately capitalised with a separate shareholding;

(b) what degree of control does the group exercise over the cell; and then

(c) was limited liability, in this case cellular limited-liability, abused?

The existence of cellular limited liability, as opposed general limited liability, is not likely to affect the judicial attitude of piercing the corporate veil in 'group situations'. However, the fact that a cellular structure is novel may mean an initial judicial uncertainty in exercising any powers to pierce the corporate veil.

Some jurisdictions address this issue head on. For instance the Jersey regime (Companies (Jersey) Law 1991, as amended) Article 127YD(5)) states: *"Despite Article 2,*[135] *(a) a cell of a cell company is not, by virtue only of being such a cell of the company, a subsidiary or wholly owned subsidiary of the company."* To what extent a non-PCC jurisdiction confronted with a piercing of the corporate veil argument revolving around groups would pay heed to this statutory exposition is unknown.

13.4.2. Alter-ego

If the limited-liability company merely reflects an individual (i.e. it is its alter ego) then the judiciary are more likely to intervene and pierce the corporate veil; that is if it is proven that the limited-liability has been abused. The smaller the number of shareholders, the more forceful the alter ego argument becomes. Given that control of the cell will ultimately be in the hands of the hub, it is submitted that an 'alter ego attack on corporate limited-liability' could be successful in respect of a PCC cell. In this context the cellular assets can be thought of as 'blind trust' assets; the hub controlling the use of the assets. Consequently and more especially given the novelty of the structure, and hence the resultant judicial uncertainty, PCCs may successfully be used as 'asset protection trusts' ("APTs"). It is submitted that the 'alter ego argument' is unlikely to feature highly in any attack upon cellular limited liability. This is especially if the individual cell is not individually capitalised with cellular shareholdings.

13.4.3. Involuntary versus voluntary creditors

Obviously the judiciary are more sympathetic to the position of an involuntary creditor when he complains of limited liability, than of a voluntary creditor. The voluntary creditor must have been aware that he was contracting, or otherwise entering into legal relations, with a limited liability entity. The sheer novelty of a cell within a PCC may also influence the judiciary in offering greater sympathy to the involuntary creditor. Against that must be put the regular requirement of most PCC

---

[135] Which defines the meaning of "*subsidiary*" as "*A body corporate is a subsidiary of another body corporate if the second body – (a) holds a majority of voting rights in the first body...*".

statutes to inform individuals that they are dealing with the cellular structure and that liability is limited to the cell. However, this cannot work normally with involuntary creditors. Tax and similar authorities can be informed upfront: to that extent the mischief of involuntariness can be minimised. Whether the tax authorities will take cognisance of the cellular structure, particularly in a non-PCC jurisdiction however is open to doubt. The most obvious involuntary creditor within a PCC will be victims of tortious actions who can claim under an insurance policy. Given that many such victims are protected by statutory cut-through proceedings, it may be improbable that involuntary creditors will be able to mount a successful attack (by reason only of their involuntary status) against PCC cellular limited-liability.

13.4.4. Under-capitalisation

The risk/reward ratio for equity in an under-capitalised vehicle may well be judicially unacceptable. If the vehicle loses money then the owners lose little. But if the entity makes money, the owners have a proportionately larger gain. Most PCC jurisdictions often require a special level of authorisation to create a PCC (usually by way of permission from a senior government official). Further in the case of 'captive insurance PCCs', also certain insolvency thresholds; under-capitalisation of itself is therefore unlikely to feature largely in any attack upon PCC limited liability. Unfortunately under-capitalisation is a double-edged sword. Many PCC regimes allow cells to be individually capitalised with individual cellular shareholdings. These individual cellular shareholdings are often intended to beef-up capital. However, whilst the shareholdings may beef-up capital, they also provide more of a direct link to the end beneficiary, the insured. Consequently they are more likely to give rise to the cell being classified as part of a group, or the alter ego of its shareholders.

13.5. Financial centres and/or OFCs

The fact that PCCs may well be situated in 'financial centres' may mean a greater or lesser likelihood of piercing the corporate veil for a variety of reasons. Obviously the home jurisdiction of a PCC is less likely to pierce the corporate veil as it will regard the nature of a PCC as less novel than (say) a non-PCC jurisdiction. Onshore non-PCC jurisdictions may unfortunately be suspicious and unsympathetic to the peculiar claims of a PCC. However, professionals in OFCs will be well-versed in adhering to procedural peculiarities. Consequently to the outside world there is less of a risk of a 'failure to adhere to corporate formalities indicating the separateness of the PCC and/or cell from (say) its shareholders'.

13.6. PCC conversion

PCCs may give rise to one peculiar set of circumstances allowing a piercing of the corporate veil. Most PCC regimes allow for the conversion of a non-PCC company to a PCC. Such a conversion possibly could give rise to difficulties. If a mutual insurance captive wished to convert to a PCC then the mere 'initial allocation of assets and liabilities to individual PCC cells, out of the original non-PCC company' is an exercise requiring great control. Such an element of control could well come within an *alter ego* framework. Further if the demutualisation occurred because some mutual members were considered more risky than others and the less risky members were not prepared any longer to share risk with the more risky members, then the court's sympathy would not be with the PCC.

As to conversion of an ordinary company to a PCC, additional safeguards can be built in, such as the Cayman Islands (Companies Law (2009 revision)) section 214(4): *"A director who makes a declaration… [as to the solvency of a company wishing to convert to a PCC] without reasonable grounds… is guilty of an offence…".* Further, notice to existing creditors is often required. For instance, the Cayman Islands section 214(1)(a)(v) *"that each creditor of the company has consented in writing to the transfer of assets and liabilities into the segregated portfolio".*

13.7. Minimising measures

The following measures should be adopted by PCCs to minimise corporate veil piercing claims:

1. Minimise its dealings with a non-PCC jurisdiction. Thus all assets, liabilities contracts, etc, should be situated in and/or subject to the laws of a PCC jurisdiction, ideally a home jurisdiction of a PCC. This is a commonsense policy and its benefits are not limited to any piercing of the corporate veil danger.
2. Ensure corporate formalities adherence. Keep capitalisation, where possible, at the hub as opposed to the cellular level. Capitalisation at the cellular level may well lead to a conclusion that the cell is a subsidiary and more connected to the insured than is desirable.
3. Utilise a PCC which has an extended audit and compliance committee's functions. The audit committee has a function of both controlling directors and liaising with the auditors. In PCCs it is often given an extended function of protecting cellular firewalling although this is best done via a compliance committee. If such an audit committee exists then insured's should feel a lesser desire to appoint their own "*shadow directors*" within the PCC, either at a hub

of cellular level, to protect their interests. The appointment or control over PCC directors (control equalling "*shadow directors*") imputes circumstances that could give rise to a valid corporate veil piercing.

13.8. Antecedent transactions and detrimental acts

As noted elsewhere antecedent transactions (in the Insolvency Act 1986, "*adjustment of prior transactions*" or, in the Model Law and the EU Regulation, "*detrimental acts*") are transactions occurring in the run-up to formal insolvency; but which, more importantly, may disturb the normal *pari passu* principle by assisting a third party over the general body of creditors. Such provisions exist throughout the world. For the purposes of this book we will concentrate on the English provisions, namely section 239 Preferences (i.e. "*where the company…gives a preference to any person*") and section 238 Transactions and Undervalue (i.e. " *where the company has entered into a transaction with any person at an undervalue*"). The importance of the English provisions stems from Part V of the Insolvency Act 1986. Further, such provisions are replicated throughout most insolvency regimes, especially regimes based upon English law. Part V, section 221(1) notes that the English antecedent legislation applies to unregistered company insolvencies.

The mere operation of a PCC and its segregation do not automatically create antecedent transactions "*as to a transaction at an undervalue*"; that is unless they also create a preference. However, "*a preference*" does appear to be formed by the very act of segregation. It is well established that directors must segregate assets and liabilities under all PCC Acts under pain of either a fine or personal liability, or indeed both. And it naturally follows that a preference, therefore, could occur as some creditors will benefit by being "*posted*" (or in the language of many, PCC Acts), "*attributed*" to the more solvent of cells within the PCC. However, it is a defence to an attack of preference, for the director to say: 'I had to segregate under the local PCC laws, despite the fact that consequently a creditor seemed to be preferred'. Similar defences exist worldwide in the form of section 239(5) of the Insolvency Act which states: "*The court shall not make an order… in respect of a preference… unless the company… was influenced… by a desire [to prefer].*"

The preference was usually made by a desire on the behalf of the directors not to incur sanction; rather than by way of a desire genuinely to prefer one creditor over another. This logic goes well beyond Part V (which we have noted may have limited impact in a post the EU

Regulation and Model Law) given that the three transactional regimes[136] all specifically refer to antecedent transactions. For instance: Article 4(2)(m) of the EU Regulation states, *"The law of the state of the opening of proceedings shall determine... in particular.... the rules relating to the voidness, voidability or unenforceability of legal acts detrimental to all the creditors"*. This Article is far reaching for, as the Virgos-Schmit Report notes at paragraph 91(m); *"This paragraph is to be taken in conjunction with Article 13..... In the case of secondary proceedings the local rules on invalidation of a detrimental act shall be applicable only insofar as damage has been caused to the debtors estate which are in this State (e.g. to the estate of the secondary proceedings."*

Further, Article 9 of the EU Insurance Insolvency Directive states: *"The decision to open up proceedings with regard to an insurance undertaking, the winding-up proceedings and their effects shall be governed by the laws, regulations and administrative provisions applicable in its home member state.... The law of the home member state shall determine in particular... (l)The rules relating to the voidness, voidability or enforceability of legal acts detrimental to all creditors."*

Article 23(2) *"Actions to avoid acts detrimental to creditors"* – of the Model Law is clear:-

"When the foreign proceeding is a foreign non-main proceeding[137] the court must be satisfied that the action relates to assets that, under the law of the state, should be administered in the foreign main proceedings."

As noted elsewhere, the Model Law does not have the mandatory effect of the EU regimes. The UK judiciary, therefore, still has the scope to apply UK insolvency proceedings, more especially antecedent transaction law, but it is contended that this scope is limited. It is open for the foreign representative to contend that the home antecedent transaction legislation would apply. This would obviously mean that, merely because of the PCC, there would be no antecedent transaction, i.e. the mere establishment of the PCC does not give rise to a (say) fraudulent conveyance.

Some PCC states attempt to minimise the threat of *"detrimental acts"* litigation against directors by specific statutory statements. We have seen that the US PCC Model Law states that the mere creation of a PCC is not a *"fraudulent conveyance"*. Whilst the US protects at inception, Jersey

---

[136] EU Regulation, EU Insurance Insolvency Regulation and Model Law.

[137] i.e. we assume the COMI is the home PCC incorporation jurisdiction

protects at the close, for cell migration *"shall not be regarded [as of itself] a civil wrong"*.

In conclusion, the risk to directors of antecedent transaction regulation purely from acting in accordance with the home PCC legislation is limited.

PCC directors can manage the danger of an inter-cellular *"antecedent transaction"* or *"detrimental act"*, whilst still hopefully segregating, cell assets collectively. Nevertheless, extreme care must be used at all times by directors in exercising their segregation duties. Some PCC regimes have actually spelt-out in statute the possibility of an inter-cellular *"antecedent transaction"* or *"detrimental act"*. An example is section 14 of the Anguillan Protected Cell Companies Act 2004:

Internal transactions

14. (1) Notwithstanding any enactment or rule of law to the contrary –

(a) a protected cell company acting in respect of the general account may enter into transactions with the company acting in respect of one or more protected cell accounts; and

(b) a protected cell company acting in respect of a protected cell account may enter into transactions with the company acting in respect of one or more other protected cell accounts.

(2) For the avoidance of doubt –

(a) a transaction referred to in subsection (1);...

Shall have effect or otherwise (as the case may be) as the transaction would have done under the general law if the transaction had been entered into between the company and a third party, and without restricting the generality of the foregoing –

(c) such a transaction shall be void, voidable, illegal or reversible at the instance of any creditor of the company in respect of the relevant protected cell account or at the instance of the company itself in respect of the relevant protected cell account or at the instance of any other person if the transaction would have been void, voidable, illegal, or reversible (as the case may be) by such person under any rule of law which would have applied to the transaction if the transaction had been entered into between the company and a third party in the same circumstances; and

(d) an account owner, counterparty, or receiver of any given protected cell account shall have standing to pursue, on behalf

> *of the relevant protected cell account, any rights of action (including recourse to arbitration under subsection (4)) available to... the protected cell account pursuant to this section.*

Indeed some regimes go further such as the Manx section 19(4): *"All sums recovered by a PCC as a result of a trust [created through the unauthorised seizure or attachment] will be credited against any concurrent liability".*

Given that these dangers are ever present, the PCC creator director should ensure excellent D&O cover. Further, he should create strong audit and compliance committees. Finally, as ever, he should keep the actions of the PCC as far as possible within the home jurisdiction.

14. PCC CELLS: AN ASSET IN AN INSOLVENCY?

14.1. The PCC as an Asset Protection Trust (APT) and "Antecedent Transactions" generally: The non-traditional uses of PCCs

The APT has been vigorously marketed over the years. Essentially it is a device whereby an individual (that is the 'settler' and it may not be a natural person) places assets into a trust. This is so that should a calamity occur to the beneficiary, the beneficiary may still enjoy the trust assets. The calamity is often expected to be some insolvency event. APTs have been used by HNWIs entering into marriage with low net value individuals and it is felt (as is often the case) that a prenuptial agreement lacks validity. The process can also obviously be used post-marriage when it looks a 'little rocky'. Practitioners in high litigation areas (the anecdotal Californian obstetrician) who face the continued threat of predatory litigation and the consequent ever-present threat of bankruptcy, also avail themselves of APTs.

The problem with a trust as an anti-bankruptcy device is the Statutes of Elizabeth, from which the majority of Common Law jurisdictions derive their antecedent transaction legislation. In this context an antecedent transaction is a transaction occurring before formal insolvency, which is reversible after insolvency, i.e. usually a gift by the now bankrupt entity (whether a natural person or a corporation) within a prescribed period before the bankruptcy. APT jurisdictions have tended to reduce this prescribed period.

A full list of APT regimes is listed within *Asset Protection Trusts*[138]. By reducing the prescribed pre-insolvency periods and other hindrances caused by the Statutes of Elizabeth (as substantially very much amended over the centuries) the APT jurisdiction claims that the potentially bankrupt settler is safe to enjoy his APT asset post-insolvency. However, this is untrue if, as is most often the case, the APT assets are still located within the bankrupt's home jurisdiction. The bankruptcy court usually simply ignores the trust and orders that the assets be part of the debtor's estate. This is always assuming that the local court is made aware of the assets. There are further problems with APTs. First, many jurisdictions

---

[138] by Grundy, Briggs and Field, published by Key Haven Publications Plc

have tax laws for trusts, especially offshore trusts and consequently the settlement itself may give rise to financially detrimental consequences. Second, the settler has transferred his property to a third party, in a far away jurisdiction over which, despite recent innovations like a 'trust deed protector' he has little or no control. To overcome these problems, practitioners have offered more innovative corporate structures, notably the Nevisian Custodial Company, in which shareholdings can be arbitrarily changed by the custodian director or automatically lost and reassigned upon individual shareholder bankruptcy. The novelty of a Nevisian Custodial Company augured badly for their widespread acceptance. Further, the obvious flaw is that the automatic reassignment on bankruptcy would mean that under most Statutes of Elizabeth-based prescribed time limits, the reassignment would be an antecedent transaction, and did not help i.e. the automatic reassignment but would be within the prescribed pre-bankruptcy period. Having noted these criticisms such a transfer may work. The question is: Could a PCC be used to create a similar structure? According to s.127YB of the Companies (Jersey) Law 1991 (as amended) it can: "*The memorandum or articles of a cell may [...] provide that the cell shall be wound up and dissolved on – (a) the bankruptcy ... of any cellular member of the cell.*"

Thus the first stage of the process appears to be provided for in statute. There would appear to be nothing stopping a resolution onto the second stage, i.e. automatic assignment.

Estate planners are now considering PCCs as an APT device, because a PCC appears to create a *de facto* APT without the APT's problems. First, PCCs do not purport to create a trust of the cells. Indeed, some jurisdictions go further and statutorily state, "*and the ... [PCC] may not be, or may not hold itself out to be, a trustee with respect to those protected cell assets of that protected cell account [South Carolina Protected Cell Companies Code of Law section 38-10-30C, 'Establishment of protected cells'].*" It should be emphasised that South Carolina limits its PCCs to insurance and thus, its PCC codes cannot be used as an attempt to be a quasi-APT.

PCCs have been sold as an anti-bankruptcy device (both personal and corporate). To quote an unnamed OFC practitioner: "*It is the structure of the entity itself. Think of a house with a locked front door and rooms inside, each with their own key. PCCs have, in concert with other entities, been used to construct what has been a wall against creditors and prying eyes. Whilst these claims can only be tested by time, the novel use of a PCC for privacy is an interesting approach and a valuable piece of intellectual property.*"

What is the relationship between the hub and the cell, and can it defeat bankruptcy, i.e. can the cellular structure become an alternative to the APT structure noted above? In order to answer this question we need to consider other questions. For instance: Is the relationship between the cell and the hub that of agent and principal? If so, can that relationship act as an APT? It seems improbable that an agent principal relationship exists, given that the cells do not have a separate legal identity from the hub. The agent principal relationship requires two parties. Most PCC statutes are at pain to point out that the PCC is a single legal entity. For instance the Isle of Man Protected Cell Companies Act 2004 section 2 states:

"Fundamental nature of a... [PCC] – section 2(1) A [PCC]... is a single legal person (2) The creation by a PCC of a cell does not create, in respect of that cell, a legal person separate from the company."

Even if an agency-principal arrangement exists, that, of itself, would not defeat the claims of the bankrupt's estate. Is the cell hub arrangement that of a secured creditor, i.e. the stakeholder in the cell, having a prior right to the assets enjoys an *in rem* relationship? The *in rem* relationship is by way of the PCC setting aside some of its funds (more especially the funds and assets contained within the cell) for the benefit of the particular creditor or, more especially, cell stakeholder. This is a possible description of the relationship. However, it does not preclude the formation of specific *in rem* rights over and above the cell stakeholder viz that particular cell.

A PCC of itself is unlikely to be an alternative to an APT. It could be an alternative in combination with other structures. Most PCC legislation allows for this. For the Isle of Man explicitly states: *"section 6(1) [Protected Cells Companies Act 2004]: A PCC may create one or more cells for the purpose of segregating and protecting cellular assets ... [but the duty to segregate under section 7(1)] does not prevent the directors arranging the cellular assets and non-cellular assets to be held – (a) by or through a trustee, custodian or nominee."*

If one regards an APT as an abuse, then the best defence to the abuses of a PCC is the fact that most PCC jurisdictions heavily regulate the incorporation of PCCs. For instance, the Mauritius Protected Cell Companies (Amendment of Schedule) Regulations 2005 Schedule (section 4): the *"Permissible activities by PCCs"* are:

a. the ubiquitous *"Insurance business"*;

b. specialised *"Collective investment schemes"* and *"close-ended funds"*, which may be too unwieldy for APT purposes;

c. *"collective investment schemes"* and *"close-ended funds"*, likewise may be too unwieldy for APT purposes;

d. *"Structured finance business"*, being *"principally for the purpose of issuing bonds"*, again possibly too unwieldy for APT purposes; and

e. *"Asset holding"*, and here is the rub, for the purposes of *"holding and managing assets (or portfolios of assets) in different cells for such class of beneficial owners, high net worth individuals and institutional investors as may be defined by the ... [Mauritius Commission]."*

See also the Segregated Accounts Companies Act 2004 of Bahamas, Section 37 – *"to the extent that, at law or in equity, a segregated accounts company or manager has duties (including fiduciary duties) and liabilities related to a segregated account or to a beneficial owner...."*

14.2. Comparative PCC insolvency priorities

14.2.1. Introduction

A PCC segregates assets and liabilities into cells ('segregated accounts') and hub (or core): this is the *raison d'être* of a PCC. It can be illustrated by reference to the general rule noted in most PCC regimes: 'the director must allocate a liability to a particular cell and if they do not, then it is allocated to the hub and/or the director's personal liability'.

This segregation duty is supported by director liability if a failure to segregate does occur. This can be illustrated by reference to: *"If a segregated portfolio company [i.e. a PCC] is in breach ... [of the duty to segregate] the directors shall (notwithstanding any provisions to the contrary in the company's articles or in any contract with such company or otherwise) incur personal liability...."*[139]

Further, if a creditor defeats cellular priority, action is taken against the creditor and this can be illustrated by reference to: *"if any party succeeds by any means ... in using any cellular assets attributable to any cell ... to satisfy a liability not attributable to what cell, that party shall be liable to the company to pay a sum equal to the value of the benefit thereby obtained."*[140]

However, the above does not preclude the sharing of costs amongst cells and even with the hub. However, in the event of an insolvency this may lead to contention and as illustrated by reference to: *"There is no default ...*

---

[139] *The Cayman Islands Companies Law (2009) Revision s.218(2)*

[140] *Gibraltar Protected Cell Companies Act 2001 s.6(3)(b)*

[in the duty to segregate] if cellular assets or non-cellular assets, or a combination of both, are ...collectively invested or collectively managed."[141]

PCC statutes tend to follow similar wordings and concepts. The above quotes could have been taken from a number of jurisdictions. They present a simple template for any IP to follow in any insolvency. However it is in practice, rather than in theory, that the difficulties are likely to occur. These difficulties were only tangentially addressed in the Messenger Insolvency.

14.2.2. Different priorities

PCC statutes diverge in their treatment of inter-cellular priority and various paths are discernible; all revolving around priorities concerning the hub. Usually, but not always, hub capital is available to meet cell deficiencies. So, in the event of a cell insolvency, the cell can lay claim to the hub capital. Consequently, in any PCC insolvency, there will usually be two debtors; the cell and, to the extent of the cell deficiency making the hub insolvent, the hub. The various paths diverge as to the priority of the cell deficiency in the hub insolvency. These divergences can be shown by asking questions:

(A) Does the PCC regime provide for 'cross-stream accounting liability', whereby individual cells are liable upon the insolvency of other cells? Usually specifically as regards an individual PCC, 'has there been an agreed intercellular assumption of liability'? Thus, for example, did cells X and Y, agree to meet the deficiency of cell Z, in the event of the insolvency of cell Z? Given that the *raison d'être* of a PCC is intercellular firewalling, such an intercellular liability assumption would be unusual. Thus this cross-stream accounting liability usually arises from agreement. Many PCC regimes specifically allow for an agreed (and in the case of insolvency only perhaps, a non-agreed in the sense of cost sharing upon insolvency) cross-stream accounting liability. This cross-stream accounting liability comes in many guises: (a) including, but not limited to IP fees, a matter discussed elsewhere; (b) intercellular set off; and (c) a statutory allowance, if it is indeed needed, for stakeholders to agree amongst themselves for cross-stream accounting liability. Virtually all PCC regimes allow for (b) and (c). As such cross-stream accounting liability will not be considered as an exception and analysed as such. Suffice it to say that the Anguillan PCC regime is

[141] *Manx Protected Cell Companies Act 2004 s.7(3)*

an example. As regards intercellular set off the Anguillan PCC section 16(5) states: *"A... [PCC] may... (c) exercise the same rights of set off (if any) as between accounts [i.e. cells] as apply under the general law in respect of companies, including, on an insolvent liquidation"*. Section 13 of the Anguillan PCC Act describes the Anguillan PCC priority rules. As regards an intercellular allowance to cross-stream accounting liability the Anguillan PCC section 13(5) states the permissive: *"Unless otherwise expressly agreed in writing by the affected parties"*.

(B) Does the PCC regime provide for 'down-stream accounting liability', whereby cells are required to meet any deficiency of the hub? Thus if the hub is insolvent, can the hub call on cells of the hub to meet its deficiency: and if so in what proportions (and by what methodology are the proportions calculated) are the cells liable? For instance, are all cells called to account equally for the deficiency, regardless of their own position? Alternatively, are the cells called to account ratably, depending upon their size; and if so, how is the size established? Or again alternatively, are only cell surpluses available to meet any hub deficiency; and if so, how are the surpluses calculated? An example of such a regime, discussed below, is the US Model Law PCC Act.

(C) Does the PCC regime provide for 'up-stream accounting liability', whereby the hub is required to meet the deficiency of cells? Thus if a cell is insolvent, can the cell call on the hub to meet the deficiency: and if so, if there are several cells insolvent, in what proportions (and by what methodology are the proportions calculated) does the hub meet the deficiencies, more especially if it itself thereby becomes insolvent through this process? Up-stream accounting liability is perhaps the default position of most PCC regimes. As such up-stream accounting liability will not be considered as an exception and analysed as such. Suffice it to say that the Barbadian PCC regime is an example. Section 356.33(1) of the Barbados Companies Act 1985 (as amended) states: *"where any liability arises which is attributable to a particular cell of a ... [PCC]- (a) the cellular assets attributable to that cell shall be primarily used to satisfy the liability; (b) the company's non-cellular assets [i.e. the hub assets] shall be secondarily used to satisfy the liability, provided that the cellular assets attributable to the relevant cell have been exhausted"*.

(D) Does the PCC regime provide for no cross-stream, down-stream, or indeed up-stream accounting liability? Thus, at all times, hub and cellular firewalling remains integral. An example of such a regime, discussed below, is that of the Jersey PCC Act.

(E) Does the PCC regime make provision for who owns any surpluses arising in either the hub or any other cells? Or put another way, who owns the surpluses? An example of a PCC regime which addresses this question is the Anguillan PCC Act 2004, section 16(9): *"An account owner ... interest in a... cell... is personal property".*

(F) What provision does the PCC regime make for priority within the cell in the event of insolvency? This is not a question of cross-stream, down-stream, or indeed up-stream accounting liability. Rather a question of what priority rules apply within the cell. For instance, does the PCC regime provide for preferential or priority creditors of the cell to be paid in priority to ordinary creditors; and if so, how does the PCC regime define preferential or priority creditors? Alternatively, does the PCC regime provide for what may be called, 'deferred creditors'? Such deferred creditors are usually connected party creditors. If any provision is made for such creditors, it is usual that they are deferred to ordinary non-connected creditors. Further, how does the PCC regime define such a creditor? This is an important question for PCCs as the division between what is an investor and what is a creditor can become blurred. Finally, what specific provisions, if any, are made for the registration of *in rem* creditors as against a specific cell? These various, but connected issues are discussed throughout this book.

The above questions pose many sub-questions. PCC regime priority variants should be viewed as spectrum. It would be impossible to consider all of the posed sub-questions, without inviting further sub-questions. The current purpose is merely an overview: to look at, as it were, the primary colours in the spectrum. Also it should be remembered that it is possible to superimpose a contractual PCC on to a statutory PCC framework. Further it should also be remembered that virtually all PCC regimes allow stakeholders to depart, at least in part and always provided it is consensual, from the statutory PCC priority rules. In short, statutory regimes virtually always allow for contractual regimes. Even the Jersey PCC Act, (which is described in detail below as rigid) allows for some consensual deviation. Finally, a note of caution: the evolution of the PCC is still in its infancy. Many of the sub-questions posed cannot be answered with certainty. This is especially the case for methods of calculation of liability for any deficiency. The answers do not yet exist in many evolving PCC regimes. The PCC statutes have often failed to address these issues. Given the paucity of PCC insolvency case law, there is little judicial guidance. The answers are often found within the articles and memorandum of association of the PCC. It is these internal constitutions of PCCs that provide the methods of calculation; often simply by way of directorial attribution. To what extent such directorial attribution based upon the internal constitution of a PCC, would be recognized internationally, is a moot issue.

In the authors' opinion, some courts in non-PCC jurisdictions may be sympathetic (when enforcing cellular priority in a non-PCC jurisdiction) to the hub creditors enjoying hub priority. This is because involuntary creditors will almost always be hub creditors. As involuntary creditors, the directors cannot easily allocate them a cell and hence by default they default to the hub. Not all PCC statutes state this obvious consequence. The Manx PCC Act 2004, section 17(7) does: *"Any liability not attributable to a particular cell of a PCC will be the liability solely of the company's non-cellular assets."* Stating the obvious has clarity for the directors and offers some comfort. Alternatively, the voluntary creditors ('who knew what they were doing anyhow') get (or may get) 'two bites of the cherry'; that is if accorded equal hub ranking following the cellular deficiency:

1. In the cellular insolvency to the exclusion of others in that they enjoy cellular priority.
2. Rateably, in the hub to the extent of the cellular deficiency with other hub creditors.

This will be perceived as all the worse if the local non-PCC jurisdiction accords (as is often the case) preferential treatment to government debts (i.e. taxes, social security, etc) which are likely to be the most common form of involuntary creditor.

In some jurisdictions a form of 'equitable subordination' occurs whereby those associated with the cell have their claims demoted to third party creditors. Section 31(1) of the Bahamas Segregated Accounts Companies Act 2004 states: *"In the event that a segregated account [i.e. a cell] has insufficient assets ... the priority ... shall... be determined by terms of the governing instrument [i.e. the articles] and any contracts ... and any ambiguity ... shall be resolved as follows: (a) the claims of the creditors shall rank ahead of the claims of account owners; (b) the claims of the creditors amongst themselves ... equally; and (c) the claims of the account owners amongst themselves ... equally"*. In countries which have 'equitable subordination' (i.e. Germany) in their general insolvency law then such a ranking may be greeted favourably.

Many jurisdictions have a broad 'super prioritisation'. An example being the Manx PCC regime section 17(4) – *"in the case of loss or damage which is attributable to a particular cell of a PCC and which is caused by fraud, the loss or damage shall be the liability solely of the company's non-cellular [i.e. hub or core] assets"*. Such a provision is highly commendable if the hub acts as a quasi-agent of the cell.

14.2.3. The Jersey Difference

The Jersey PCC Regime (introduced by the Companies (Amendment No. 8) (Jersey) Law 2005), potentially bars any cellular claim against the hub. In short, not only are cellular assets firewalled from inter-cellular claims, but so is the hub from any cellular claims whatsoever. As can seen from section 127YT, reproduced below, the Jersey statutory priority is dictated very much by the articles of association of the PCC:

"(1) Where a protected cell company -

(a) enters into a transaction in respect of a particular cell of the company; or

(b) incurs a liability arising from an activity or asset of a particular cell,

a claim by any person in connection with the transaction or liability extends only to the cellular assets of the cell.

(2) Where a protected cell company -

(a) enters into a transaction in its own right and not in respect of any of its cells;

(b) incurs a liability arising from an activity of the company in its own right and not in respect of any of its cells; or

(c) incurs a liability arising from an asset held by the company in its own right and not in respect of any of its cells,

a claim by any person in connection with the transaction or liability extends only to the non-cellular assets of the company.

(3) Except as provided by paragraphs (4) and (6), a protected cell company has no power [to upstream or downstream liability, that is] -

(a) to meet any liability attributable to a particular cell of the company from the non-cellular assets of the company; or

(b) to meet any liability, whether attributable to a particular cell or not, from the cellular assets of another cell of the company.

(4) If -

(a) *a protected cell company is permitted to do so under its articles; and*

(b) *the requirement set out in paragraph (5) is satisfied,*

the company may meet any liability attributable to a particular cell of the company from the company's non-cellular assets.

(5) *The requirement mentioned in paragraph (4)(b) is that prior to the protected cell company meeting any liability attributable to the particular cell from the company's non-cellular assets the directors who are to authorise the liability being met in such a way must make a statement that, having made full enquiry into the affairs and prospects of the company, they have formed the opinion -*

(a) *that, immediately following the date on which the liability is proposed to be met by the non-cellular assets of the company, the company will be able to discharge its liabilities as they fall due; and*

(b) *that, having regard to the prospects of the company and to the intentions of the directors with respect to the management of the company's business and to the amount and character of the financial resources that will in their view be available to the company, the company will be able to continue to carry on business and will be able to discharge its non-cellular liabilities as they fall due until the expiry of the period of one year immediately following the date on which the liability is proposed to be met by the non-cellular assets of the company or until the company is dissolved under Article 150, whichever first occurs.*

(6) *A protected cell company may meet any liability, whether attributable to a particular cell or not, from the cellular assets of another cell if –*

(a) *it is permitted to do so by the articles of that other cell; and*

(b) *the requirement set out in paragraph (7) is satisfied.*

(7) *The requirement mentioned in paragraph (6)(b) is that prior to the protected cell company meeting any liability from the cellular assets of that other cell the directors who are to authorise the liability being met in such a way must make a statement that, having made full enquiry into the affairs and prospects of that cell, they have formed the opinion-*

(a) *that, immediately following the date on which the liability is proposed to be met by the cellular assets of the cell, the cell will be able to discharge its liabilities as they fall due; and*

(b) *that, having regard to the prospects of the cell and to the intentions of the directors with respect to the management of the cell's business and to the amount and character of the financial resources that will in their view be available to the cell, the cell will be able to continue to carry on business and will be able to discharge its liabilities as they fall due until the expiry of the period of one year immediately following the date on which the liability is proposed to be met by the cellular assets of the cell or until the cell is dissolved, as if it were a company, under Article 150, whichever first occurs.*

(8) *A director who makes a statement under paragraph (5) or paragraph (7) without having reasonable grounds for the opinion expressed in the statement is guilty of an offence."*

14.2.4. The US Difference

Most PCC regimes tend to pre-suppose some upstream accounting, however limited, i.e. cell creditors may have access in the event of a cellular deficiency to the hub or core capital. All PCC regimes, subject to limited exceptions with regards to IP fees and the like, guarantee cellular integrity. Very few PCC regimes appear to allow for downstream liability, i.e. the hub creditors having access to the cells assets. The US model PCC regime does. The US PCC Model Code is a generic statute that can be adopted with or without amendment by US states. Section 6 of the US PCC model law ("*Reach of Creditors and Other Claimants*") albeit in language only found in the US PCC code, starts in the usual PCC fashion: "*Protected cell assets shall be available to the creditors of the … [PCC] that are creditors in respect of the protected cell and shall be entitled … to have recourse to the protected cell asset attributable to that cell … Creditors with respect to a protected cell shall not be entitled to have recourse against the protected cell assets of other protected cells*". So far, so good. It continues: "*…of other protected cells or the assets of the PCCs general account*", thus, apparently barring upstream liability (i.e. cellular recourse to the hub or the core) of any kind. Such an absolute bar is unusual. Certainly in its clarity it is unusual but perhaps not unique. What follows apparently in respect of 'downstream accounting' is most unusual: "*Protected cell assets shall only be available to creditors of a … [PCC, i.e. the hub] after all protected cell liabilities have been extinguished or otherwise provided for …*". This downstream accounting maintains cellular integrity *vis-à-vis* its liabilities, i.e. all the cellular liabilities must have been met. However it apparently allows unmet hub liabilities to eat into cellular assets and, therefore stands out. The danger of a solvent cell being swamped is limited. In most PCC priorities, a cellular deficiency is met by the hub. If the hub can then 'downstream account' to solvent cells, cellular creditor integrity would be lost. The US system can only work because of its stark preclusion of 'upstream accounting' i.e. cellular deficiencies are not met by the hub.

14.2.5. The Bermudan Difference

The Bermudan PCC priority was initially an even greater departure from the *pari passu* norm. As noted in the introduction, the collective notion of insolvency, negates chronological priority. So, at the point of formal insolvency, all creditors within a class share are pro-rated as to a dividend. However, the pre-amended Bermudan Segregated Accounts Companies Act 2000, section 17(7) states: "*The order and priority of the paying out of funds from a segregated account taken together, and failing a sufficient statement of particulars governing the priority of those payments, they shall be made in the order of the dates of the respective transactions, so that the first in time shall be first to be paid*". It was unlikely that such a statute would be enforced outside Bermuda. It appears that this concern has been recognised in the Segregated Accounts Companies Act 2002 and the new section 17(7) which lays down the following acceptable priority: "*without prejudice to the rights of any parties holding valid security interest... and any valid preferential claims... priority rights shall be ... (a)... claims of creditors... ahead of claims of account owners (b) the claims of creditors inter se shall rank pari passu and (c) the claims of account owners inter se shall rank pari passu*". This is an amending Act. It is uncertain whether companies formed prior to the amending act would be governed by the old chronological priority.

14.2.6. Preferential Liabilities and PCCs

Some non-EU jurisdictions have followed one of the two EU methods of non *pari passu* priority for insurance PCCs, i.e. the same methodology as the EU, save for the additional cellular priority. They even allow for prefential creditors. Such creditors are often involuntary. But even some go further and remove preferential creditors that are connected and thus possibly not voluntary. A notable example is the St. Kitts Captive Insurance Companies Act 2006, which allows for PCCs. Section 22(3)(d) states that "*Officers and directors shall not be entitled to... this [employee priority]*".

14.2.7. Shareholder Liabilities

"A beneficial owner's beneficial interest in a segregated account is personal property, notwithstanding the nature of the property of the segregated account" – section 18(11) Segregated Accounts Companies Act 2000 of Bermuda.

In this case *'beneficial owner'* means any person who is – *"identified in or by reference to a governing instrument as having a legal or beneficial interest in a segregated account (b) the registered holder of any security linked to a segregated account; or (c) designated as having a beneficial interest in a segregated account in the records of a segregated accounts company.* [Section 2(1)]".

Very few PCC regimes address the limited liability of 'cell owners'. Given that they are not trading companies, this is perhaps appropriate. Nevertheless one of the few categorical statements is the Bermudan Segregated Accounts Companies Act 2000, which states: *"Except to the extent otherwise provided in the governing instrument, the account owners are entitled to the same limitation of personal liability as is enjoyed by members of companies limited by shares... [Section 18(5)"*. It is possible to create an unlimited PCC, but with many of the attributes of a limited company. Some jurisdictions have sought to shift the burden of risk onto the cellular shareholders. The Mauritius PCC Act section 18 states: *"Where the liabilities of the company exceed the assets of the company, the [relevant authorities] may require the company to furnish such guarantees...to the shareholders of each of the cells."* According to Article 3I of the Companies (Jersey) Law 1991 (introduced by the Companies (Amendment No. 8) (Jersey) Law 2005) a PCC may be an unlimited company. However, given the Jersey PCC regime allows for a bar on upstream accounting liability there can be no chance of the hub being called on to meet a cellular deficiency. Thus it is difficult (but not impossible) for hub to become insolvent. Given this absence of risk, the presence of an unlimited PCC may be considered of merit.

14.3. Expenses in a PCC insolvency

14.3.1. IP expenses and priority allocation in a PCC or PCC cellular insolvency

PCC jurisdictions have tended not to address this issue in statute and appear to have made two assumptions. The first assumption is that the IP will allocate his fees and disbursements fairly regardless of statutory prescription. Such an allocation could be by way of a time cost basis per estate, i.e. each cell and/or hub with disbursements pro-rated accordingly, either as to time cost or value. The assumption of allocating fairly stems from a *mutatis mutandis* basis taking, by way of analogy, a group insolvency. The second assumption is that there would be heavy court involvement with fees and expenses.

14.3.2. The Messenger Insolvency

Both of these assumptions were tested in one of the few reported cases worldwide in which a PCC insolvency was addressed, the Messenger Insolvency Litigation. It is therefore appropriate to reproduce a relevant quote[142]:

"It was ordered that … the remuneration of the Administrators and the expenses properly incurred by them shall be payable from the assets of the Applicant as follows and in the following shares or proportions:-

(i) The Administrators' remuneration and legal or other proper expenses and disbursements relating to the [X] litigation… [pertaining to cell 123]… including the costs of further investigation of the financial position on the Cell… [123] contracts of reinsurance… shall be funded wholly from the assets of cell … [123].

(ii) The Administrators' remuneration and legal and other proper expenses and disbursements relating to the [Y] arbitration… [pertaining to cell 456]… including the cost of further investigation of the financial position on the Cell… [456] contracts of reinsurance with [Y]… shall be funded wholly from the assets of … [cell 456].

(iii) The Administrators' remuneration and legal and other proper expenses and disbursements relating to the claim commenced by … [z] in the Royal Court of Guernsey shall be funded wholly from the assets of … [cell 456].

(iv) On an interim basis only, and subject to any adjustment, if necessary, at a final determination of the Administration Order or final ascertainment by the Court or Administrators of the liabilities attributable to each and any of the cells, and with such order deemed to be in compliance with the … Ordinance, with such compliance to be confirmed upon final determination of the Administration Order, the Administrators' remuneration and legal and other proper expenses and disbursements attributable to … [cell 789] shall be funded (to the extent that the assets of … [cell 7889] are insufficient) wholly from the assets of … [cell 456].

(v) On an interim basis only, and subject to any adjustment, if necessary, at a final determination of the Administration Order or final ascertainment by the Court or Administrators of the liabilities attributable to each and any of the cells, and … with such order deemed to be in compliance with the

---

142 Guernsey Law Reports 2005-06 GLR 206

... Ordinance, with such compliance to be confirmed upon final determination of the Administration Order, the Administrators' remuneration and legal and other proper expenses and disbursements attributable to the Core, or not specifically attributable to individual cells, shall be funded by the Core, and then re-charged by the Core as general costs of the Administration to ... [cell 456] and ... [x] 50% to each.

(4) *All alleged security and proprietary claims over the assets of the Core or of any Cell of the Applicant... and any expenses properly incurred by them in the conduct of the Administration... [But] For the avoidance of doubt nothing in this Order shall otherwise affect the relative priorities of any liabilities of the Applicant [i.e. Messenger, the PCC itself] or its Cells. [Paragraph 3 of the Messenger Guernsey litigation]".*

It should be noted that in the Messenger case: "*The Administrators... emphasised that the Applicant [i.e. Messenger, the PCC itself] had no substantial non-cellular assets [paragraph 22 of the Messenger insolvency litigation].*"

Thus, the problem faced by the Administrators was: "*The Applicant and all Respondents (save for ...)... were of the view that if the Administration Order were to continue and the Court were to continue to permit creditors to advance their claims then the Administrators should be sufficiently funded both to investigate the claims... and to take appropriate steps for the time being to preserve the Applicant's position in the face of various claims. [Paragraph 30 of the Messenger Guernsey litigation]*"

14.3.3. How do PCC regimes address IP costs?

As mentioned, the Messenger Insolvency involved fraud, which complicated the issue, but the question remains: How do PCC Regimes address IP costs? Unfortunately, PCC codes tend to avoid this issue and do not detail an answer. Like Guernsey, most jurisdictions leave it to the Court. The Court may well feel on sure ground with such an interventionalist approach to fees because the establishment of a PCC often requires special regulatory approval: "*A...[PCC] cannot be incorporated except under the authority and in accordance with ... written consent given by the Commission [paragraph 8 of the Messenger Guernsey litigation]*". A PCC IP appointment also requires consent and "*Notice of an application to the Court for an administration order in respect of a ... [PCC] must be served on the Commission. [paragraph 8 of the Guernsey Messenger Insolvency Litigation]*").

However, leaving matters to the court also induces uncertainty. There appears to be no good reason why the situation cannot be clarified by the introduction of a provision similar to the UK Insolvency Rules 1986 and thereby introduce an expenses priority regime. The UK Insolvency Rules even provide for a priority regime amongst competing expenses. However, such a regime would only solve some of the problems. What happens if some cells, or indeed the hub (as in the Messenger Insolvency) have no assets, either no assets *per se*, or no free or recoverable assets, and the creditors (or at least all save for one) are not so amenable to the Administrators? The Guernsey courts solve the problem by: *"On an interim basis only, and subject to any adjustment, if necessary, at the final determination..."*. Thus they allowed for the potentially dipping in from one cell to fund another. This may be justifiable if allegations of fraud are involved (especially intercellular fraud), but difficult otherwise to justify. A PCC's *raison d'être* is cellular integrity and cellular integrity should even extend to IPs.

14.3.4. Proprietary claims versus IP fees

As has been emphasised, the Messenger Insolvency involved fraud and the assertion of a 'proprietary claim'. It seems implicit from the Messenger Insolvency Litigation report that a distinction was drawn between a 'proprietary' claim stemming from (for instance) fraud and the 'normal' claim of a cell creditor to the assets of a cell.

14.3.5. If PCC statues address IP fees, how do they do it?

A distinction in PCC regimes is often drawn between receivers or liquidators (IPs appointed over cellular insolvencies usually) and administrators (IPs appointed over the PCC itself usually). Treatment of receivers remuneration and expenses where they have been appointed only over the cell varies between PCC regimes. The Vanuatu Protected Cell Companies Act 2005 section 24 (*"Remuneration of receiver")* states: *"The remuneration of a receiver and any expenses he or she properly incurs are payable, in priority to all claims, from: (a) the cellular assets attributable to the cell for which the receiver was appointed; and (b) if these are insufficient, the non-cellular assets of the ... [PCC]."* This should be contrasted with the Cayman Islands Companies Law (2009 Revision) section 228, where despite the court appointing and supervising the receiver, *"The remuneration of a receiver and any expenses properly incurred by him shall be payable, in priority to all other claims, from the segregated portfolio [i.e. cellular] assets attributable to the segregated portfolio [i.e. the cell] in respect of which the receiver was appointed but not from any other assets of the segregated portfolio company."* The classic fraudster's route is to leave insufficient assets within the vehicle for creditors, which makes it difficult to appoint an IP to investigate; this is especially the case if there is no public funding available within the jurisdiction. Consequently the Vanuatuan regime has some merit in this regard versus the Cayman Islands regime.

The Mauritius example may be of some use:

Section 23 [Protected Cell Companies Act 1999 as amended] – *"the remuneration of an administrator and any expenses properly incurred by him, shall be payable in priority to all other claims – (a) in the case of the administration of a cell, from – (i) the cellular assets attributable to the cell; and (ii) to the extent that these may be insufficient, the non-cellular assets of the … [PCC]; and (b) in the case of an administration of a [PCC] from (i) the non-cellular assets of the company and (ii) to the extent that these may be insufficient, the cellular assets, in such shares or proportions as the Court may direct."*

In some cases it would appear that the hub account is absolutely protected. Take section 13(5) of the Anguillan Protected Cells Companies Act 2004: *"Unless otherwise expressly agreed in writing… where a liability … in respect of or attributable of a particular protected cell … that liability shall (c) extend only to … assets linked to that … cell … (d) not extend to … assets linked to any other cell … and (e) not extend to … the general account [i.e. the hub or core]."*

A similar result is achieved in Jersey under the Jersey PCC regime Companies (Jersey) Law 1991 Article 127YD, a cell is to be treated as a company for most purposes (including liquidation) and under Article 152:

"A liquidator appointed under Article 149 is entitled to receive from the company the remuneration –

(a) agreed between the liquidator and the company before his or her appointment;
(b) subsequently approved by the company in general meeting; or
(c) subsequent determined by the court."

However statutory uncertainty is sometimes introduced, for example the liquidator under the Anguillan regime (section 23(2) – *"The remuneration to be paid by the liquidator shall be apportioned by the liquidator to each … cell … and the general account [i.e. the hub] in such amounts as would best reflect the duties performed by the liquidator and approved by the court."*

The authors' forsee some difficulty ahead in the world of insolvent PCCs and IPs fees. IPs should tread gingerly.

14.4. Cellular structures and *in rem* or secured rights

14.4.1. Proprietary Claims – the issue of subordination

What is the exact nature of a cell owner's claim to the assets of the cell? It may be ownership. If it is not who could have a better claim? The issue of 'proprietary claims' was addressed in the Messenger Insolvency Litigation.

"It was common ground that a court had a limited discretion, which it could exercise... where a proprietary claim had been advanced... It followed that if the Applicant was to benefit from the limited discretion that the Court might exercise the Applicant must show an arguable case for denying that they belong to the claimant... As Gee states ... – "Where there are assets which may belong to the claimant, the Court will not allow these funds to be used for legal costs until the defendant has shown by 'proper evidence' that he has no other assets which can be used for the purposes. If there are such funds, then the defendant must use these funds first before any question arises of his having access to funds which are the subject of the proprietary claim. But once it is shown there are no other assets except those subject to a proprietary claim, the court must make a difficult decision in the exercise of its discretion as to what is to be done." [paragraphs 53-56 the Messenger Insolvency Litigation].

A direct proprietary claim (as in the Messenger Insolvency Litigation) over cell assets is of a superior ranking to a claim of another cell creditor who merely has his claim met from cellular assets. To that extent, the issue of 'subordination' noted in Messenger may well be of limited impact to non-fraud insolvency. However, as noted above, many PCC jurisdictions go further.

Section 16(9) of the Anguilan PCC Act states: *"An account owner's or counterparty's beneficial interest in a protected cell account is personal property notwithstanding the nature of the property of the protected cell account."* Surely this is a right *in rem,* which defeats or ranks ahead of all other claims.

14.4.2. Conflict of law: substance and procedure

Private international law and conflict of laws (and for the purposes of this analysis we will concentrate on English law) often recognises a distinction between procedural and substantive law. Local law may enforce a foreign substantive law but not a foreign procedural law. The logic of this distinction is that procedure goes to the manner of how the local court (i.e. the English court) addresses the issue in the first place. Thus the obvious question is: If a PCC insolvency is enforced in an English court, will the Court view the cellular firewalling as procedural or substantive in nature? This distinction may be difficult to draw in practice when reviewing the foreign PCC legislation. It would be helpful if the PCC legislation expresses the situation explicitly. For instance the PCC regime stated: 'this matter is substantive'. It is to be assumed that an English court would take this legislative statement at face value and accept the same. Even so, there is still room for debate. Any such legislative statement would have to refer specifically to the item under consideration. A blanket statement that all matters are substantive may well be impossible to defend.

This distinction between substantive and procedural may be difficult to draw in practice when reviewing the foreign PCC legislation. For instance, if the PCC legislation states that 'cell X creditors shall have no remedy against cells Y and Z', then that may well be regarded as procedural. The remedy would ordinarily exist against cells Y and Z, but there is a procedural bar. Alternatively, if the PCC legislation states that 'cell X creditors shall only have a remedy against cell X assets', then that may well be regarded as substantial. Such a legislative statement changes the nature of the legal remedy by saying that no such remedy exists; rather than that the remedy is barred. Based upon this analysis, a creditor could feel justifiably that it is a 'distinction without a difference'. His outcome depends upon whether the legislation is raised in the negative ('he can't have a remedy against the other cells') or the positive ('he can only have a remedy against the one cell'). The matter may well be further complicated by how English law has traditionally looked at company liability. Rights and liabilities of company shareholders *vis-à-vis* third parties have tended under English law to be governed by the law of incorporation and hence of the PCC jurisdiction.

There is little English case law which can be applied to the PCC scenario. Two old cases have been noted as providing some possible guidance. In *Melan v The Duke de Fitzjames (1797) 1 Bos and Pul 138*, the debtor (the Duke) entered into a French non-recourse mortgage, i.e. under French law the debt fell only on the property and in the event of a deficiency there was no personal liability to the debtor. The creditor sued in England for bankruptcy at the time and, therefore, imprisonment. The court distinguished between *"the nature of the contract"* (i.e. the substance governed by French law) of the contract, as against the procedural enforcement in England. If a similar agreement had been reached in England, then there could have been *"recourse to the Duke and not just the property"*: consequently, bankruptcy, and thus imprisonment, would have been an available remedy. French law precluded the same. Consequently the procedural remedy was not available. The logic of *Melan v The Duke de*

Fitzjames (1797) (there being a distinction between substance and procedure) was accepted in *De La Vega against Vianna (1830) 1B & Ad 284,* but with a different outcome. A Portuguese creditor and a Spanish debtor both resided in England and the debt arose under Portuguese law. The Spanish debtor sued for arrest in England, a remedy unavailable in Portugal. The court granted the arrest remedy apparently concluding that the remedy was not procedural in nature. This case has been cited in subsequent cases. Why are these cases of importance? First, as already noted, they draw the distinction between substance and procedure in enforcing a debt. Second, there is the difficulty in practice of drawing that distinction. Third, whether a liability can be restricted to certain assets if that liability is governed by a foreign law, i.e. could a foreign PCC cellular firewalling be enforced within England. Fourth, they indicate the lack of substantive judicial authority in this area.

14.4.3. *In rem* v *in personam* liability

Regardless of whether the liability arises within a PCC jurisdiction, does the fact that the creditor is secured (*in rem*) or unsecured (*in personam*) matter from the perspective of both the hub, its cells, or of any individual creditor? The question raises several possibilities, depending on the factors involved: secured versus unsecured: PCC jurisdiction v non-PCC jurisdiction; and asset v liability. Let us start with the easiest. It has to be assumed that if the assets and liabilities are in a PCC jurisdiction, then from the perspective of the PCC there can be little of concern. PCC codes attempt to enforce PCC priority rules vigorously for example: see QFC article 96(3)(A)-(C)(4): *"There shall be implied...in every transaction entered into by a PCC the following terms: (A) that no party shall seek...to use any Cellular Assets attributable to any cell...to satisfy a liability not attributable to that cell; (B) that if any party succeeds...that party shall be liable to the PCC...; and (C) that, if any party succeeds in seizing [such assets]...that party shall hold those assets...as trust property"*. Would the relatively standard (it is seen in other PCC regimes) article 96 (3)(A)-(C) be recognised internationally? The answer is not known but can be answered at several levels. If the creditor is purely unsecured, then the question is: Can the unsecured creditor petition locally for the insolvency of the PCC itself or obtain its execution against the PCC's assets? The creditor would face as a first issue, 'a defence that the creditor knew of the PCC and its cellular structure'; there would be much discussion as to the facts of the case. Arguably, if the court acknowledges that the creditor was aware of the structure, then there must be some partial recognition of the existence of the structure. The second issue is even if it is accepted that the creditor has recourse to a particular cells assets and not to the hub, or indeed the whole of ABC PCC it will be for ABC PCC to prove that the relevant assets over which execution is sought, belong to cell Y as opposed to cell Z of ABC PCC. This may well be present evidential difficulties.

14.5. A consideration of UK cases and *pari passu*

Two UK cases are of relevance: *HIH* (as previously analysed) and *Re Collins and Aikman Europe SA and Others [2007] 1 BCLC 182 ("Collins and Aikman")*.

Collins and Aikman involved an Administration Order over a pan-European business with a UK COMI. The IPs were concerned to avoid "secondary proceedings" in local jurisdictions and thus gave assurances at meetings of creditors and creditors committees that if no "secondary proceedings" were commenced in other jurisdictions, the creditors position under their local law would be respected, as far as possible, in the English administration. In order to honour these assurances, the administrators wished to make distributions in the EU jurisdictions according to the local law. The administrators accordingly applied to the court for directions that they be permitted to make distributions according to the local law. The question, therefore, revolved around whether a distribution could be made under the English Administration order to creditors that were preferential creditors within the relevant EU jurisdictions. However, they were not preferential creditors according to English insolvency law. Thus the application to Court was not to defeat ordinarily understood English *pari passu*. Rather, the application to Court was to defeat English priority rules. Nevertheless the case offers some guidance as to whether a UK court would accept a derogation from English *pari passu*.

Reproduced below is an extract from the Court Report (*[2007] 1 BCLC 182)*:

"The administrators contended that they were entitled to make distributions according to local law under paras 65[143] *or 66*[144] *of Sch. B1 to the Insolvency*

---

[143] *65(1) - The administrator of a company may make a distribution to wake creditor of the company. 65(2) Section 175 shall apply in relation to a distribution under this paragraph as it applies in relation to winding up.*
65(3) A payment may not be made by way of distribution under this paragraph to a creditor of the company who is neither a secured not preferential unless the court gives permission.

[144] *Paragraph 66 - the administrator of a company may make a payment otherwise than in accordance with paragraph 65 or paragraph 13 of schedule 1 [of the Insolvency Act 1986, which states,*

Act 1986 or alternatively the court could authorise such distributions either under the rule in Ex p James, which enabled the court to direct administrators, as officers of the court, to fulfil an obligation of conscience even if that meant overriding the rights of others who were entitled to rely on the strict rules of law and equity, or under the inherent jurisdiction [of the court]. Under para 65 of Sch. B1 an administrator had power to make a distribution to creditors but that power was subject to s.175 of the... [Insolvency Act 1986][145]*,... and was also subject to permission of the court being obtained for a distribution to creditors who were neither secured or preferential. Under para 66 of Sch.B1 an administrator could make a payment otherwise than in accordance with para 65 or para 13 of Sch. 1 (which referred to payments which were necessary or incidental to the performance of the administrator's functions) if he thought it likely to assist achievement of the purpose of administration."*

As to para 65 of schedule B1 of the Insolvency Act 1986 it was held -

"It was doubtful whether the administrators could rely on para 65 of Sch. B1 to the 1986 Act to make distributions according to local law, because the reference to s.175 of the Act and consequent implied reference to preferential debts appeared to require any distribution under para 65 to be made on the basis that those creditors who would be characterised under English law as preferential creditors be paid, or provision for their payment be made, before any general distribution was made."

The above statement does not therefore preclude a distribution of ordinary unsecured (more particularly non-preferential) creditors according to a relevant PCC priority. To that limited extent it is helpful.

As to para 66 of schedule B1 of the Insolvency Act 1986 it was held -

"However, given that para 66 of Sch.B1, on the other hand, contained no limit requiring payment of secured or preferential creditors in priority to other creditors and that the term 'payments' in para 66 was wide enough to include 'distributions' by an administrator, the payments could be regarded as being properly made if the administrators reasonably thought them to be 'likely to assist achievement of the purpose of administration' within para 66. Moreover, having regard to the intention of the legislation, other than in very exceptional circumstances, no distinction was to be made either between the giving of an

---

"Powers Of [an] Administrator... [includes the] Power to make any payment which is necessary or incidental to the performance of his functions.

145 *Which states - "175 (1) [payment in priority] In a winding up the company's preferential debts shall be paid in priority to all other debts".*

assurance of payment and the performance of that assurance. Nor, other than in very exceptional cases, was any distinction to be made between assurances given in enforceable contractual form and those that were not since administrators were expected to behave honourably, a failure to honour non-contractual assurances would be likely to lead to costly and time-consuming misrepresentation claims by creditors who relied on the assurances, and the process of administration would be brought into disrepute if the confidence and trust between administrators and creditors on which the process depended was undermined. On the facts, there was no doubt that, at the time they gave the assurances that the position of creditors under local law would be respected in the English administration, the administrators thought that the giving of such assurances, would be likely to assist the achievement of the purpose of the administration and that sufficed, firstly, to enable the administrators without impropriety to propose under para 66 that the assured payments should be paid and, secondly, for them to seek directions to that effect under para 63 of Sch.B1. It followed that the court had jurisdiction to give the administrators directions to give effect to the assurances which they had given and to depart from the application of ordinary provisions of English law as the law of the main proceedings."

This quote offers potential considerable support for a derogation from UK *pari passu* principles in favour of a PCC cellular priority. For it is possible *"to depart from the application of ordinary provisions of English law as the law of the main proceedings"* if *"the payments could be regarded as ...likely to assist achievement of the purpose of administration."* There can be three purposes for an Administration Order: (*"[s.8(3) Insolvency Act 1986 as amended by s.248 of the Enterprise Act 2002 -]... (a) rescuing the company as a going concern; (b) achieving a better result for the company's creditors as a whole than would be likely if the company were wound up (without first being in administration); or. (c) realising property in order to make a distribution to one or more secured or preferential creditors."*). Whatever the purpose it is submitted that adherence to the PCC cellular priority would be more likely to achieve any of these objectives. Failure to abide by PCC cellular priority would have the following negative consequences:

1. There would be considerable and costly litigation which would preclude all the possible purposes for an Administration Order.
2. Cells would migrate and consequently purpose (a) ("the survival of the company") would be unlikely.
3. There would be considerable unhealthy competition between the alleged primary insolvency (i.e. if applicable the COMI insolvency) and alleged secondary (or if applicable non-main) proceedings. This competition would again result in self-defeating litigation.

Collins and Aikman may have looked to preferential creditors and not ordinary unsecured creditors. Nevertheless the logic (as it was applied to preferential creditors) is equally applicable to ordinary unsecured creditors; this is so, regardless whether the ordinary unsecured creditor is a creditor of a PCC.

This quote also addresses another issue, that of the "assurance of payment" given by the Administrator. In an international PCC insolvency an Administrator could, in order to achieve the purpose of the administration, give assurances that as far as practicable he will, wherever, abide by PCC cellular priority. If he gave such assurances, it appears that an English court would back up those assurances.

15. TAX TREATMENT OF A PCC

15.1. Tax creditors

Governments may become an extraneous creditor of a PCC in respect of tax. A distinction needs to be drawn between the possible tax treatment by tax authorities within the jurisdiction where the PCC is incorporated and foreign/federal tax authorities. The former would be naturally bound by PCC legislation in any tax claim brought against the company; for the purposes of segregating the assets and liabilities of cells, 'liabilities' would obviously include any tax. Therefore, the legal position would be that income attributable to individual cells would be chargeable to tax separately in respect of each cell for the purposes of the applicable local tax legislation. On the other hand, in the absence of court, tax or legislative guidance, we cannot be certain how other jurisdictions would treat a PCC, namely whether they will treat the PCC as a single taxpayer on the basis that the cells do not have separate legal existence, or alternatively treat each cell as separate entities *for tax purposes*. The former treatment would require the PCC to submit a single tax return for all cells.

15.2. Local v Foreign; State v Federal tax Treatment of a PCC

In a decision dated 9 January 2009 of the Income Tax Appellate Tribunal in India, the Tribunal had to consider the tax treatment of a Mauritian PCC (*Nicholas Applegate South East Asia Fund Ltd v Assistant Director of Income Tax 11 I.T.L. Rep. 630*). The facts were:

"The taxpayer was a Mauritian investment company, divided under Mauritian legislation into four protected cells, each of which engaged in share dealing in India. The company filed four tax returns in respect of the four cells. The returns were filed simultaneously with the same assessing officer by the date required. Subsequently the company realised that it should file a single return and filed a return which consolidated the four cell returns, coming to the same total figures and claiming losses and exemptions. The assessing officer declared the cell returns invalid, refused to accept the late consolidated return and disallowed the claims. The taxpayer appealed arguing that it was entitled to the benefit of s.292B of the Income Tax Act 1961 which provided that errors did not invalidate a return provided the substance and purpose of the Act was complied with. One member of the ITAT agreed with this argument but the other considered that no return had been filed by the taxpayer in time and so it was not entitled to

protection in respect of errors made in a return. The matter was referred to the President of the ITAT Bench."

Finding in favour of the taxpayer the Tribunal held that:

"The object of s.292B was to prevent injustice by reason of a technical default. Taking too narrow a view of the section defeated its object. By filing four returns in which in aggregate the total loss of the taxpayer was disclosed, the taxpayer had complied with the intent and purpose of the Act. All the relevant and correct information had been filed by the time required so that an assessment could be made after proper scrutiny. The four cell returns had been filed bona fide and disclosed the total loss. No prejudice had been caused to the Revenue and it was incorrect to hold that the four returns had been invalid."

The issue in this case was whether the obligation to file a tax return had been satisfied if each cell of a Mauritian PCC submitted a separate return, or whether the PCC had to file a single consolidated return. The conclusion of the Tribunal was that the separate returns disclosed the required information, and satisfied the statutory obligation.

The Indian tax authorities considered the legal status of a PCC and argued:

(1) 'Persons' could file the tax return. A 'company' was one of the persons mentioned in the section, which has to file the return.

(2) The cells could not be considered to be a 'company' and therefore, these cells could neither file the returns independently, nor could returns filed by them be revised by applicable statute.

(3) Since the loss was incurred by the assessee company, the return could be filed only by the assessee company.

(4) Consequently, four returns filed by these cells could not be considered as valid.

The PCC had mistakenly argued that its four cells had separate legal existence. Of course, they did not.

The Tribunal held that this was a *"very narrow view of statutory provisions"* and that the four cells of the assessee, by filing four returns, in which the total loss claimed by the assessee was disclosed, did comply in substance and in effect with the intent and purpose of the Act.

This was a fair and practical way of dealing with the issue in a manner that did not prejudice either the taxpayer or the tax authorities whilst preserving the integrity of the PCC structure, but leaving open the question: if the separate tax returns for the cells showed a loss for say two cells and a profit for the other two cells, but with a tax liability on a consolidated basis, would tax assessments have been issued individually in respect of each cell or one consolidated return? If the former, it would be consistent with PCC legislation, namely, the tax claim would be enforced only against the corresponding cell assets. If a consolidated tax assessment was made, it could be highly prejudicial to the cellular structure.

There can be no doubt that the tax assessment would be in the name of the PCC, not the individual cells. But the tax authorities could equally raise separate tax assessments against the company in respect of each individual cell, thereby recognising that the PCC does not constitute a single business for tax purposes. An English law trust, for example, does not have separate legal personality as such and where a person (and this includes a company) acts as trustee, for tax purposes he would be expected to submit two separate tax returns: one in respect of his personal income and another in respect of the trust. The position of a PCC should not be any different. Further, this tax treatment would look at the economic substance (namely, each cell as a separate and distinct economic entity) and not just the legal form of the PCC (namely, a single entity for juridical purposes).[146]In the absence of a tax avoidance motivation, this should not prejudice any of the parties: the taxpayer does not suffer a foreign tax treament which is commercially and economically fundamentally different to what he had intended and expected as a matter of PCC law, but this is no less favourable to the foreign tax authority.

The taxation position of US entities is also noteworthy in this discussion. This is because of the potential different tax classification for Federal and State tax purposes.

In a captive situation it is usual to speak of transfer of risk, not just in order for the transaction to constitute 'insurance', but also because the corporate insured would typically be required to demonstrate such 'risk transfer' in order to obtain deductibility of insurance premiums. The first tax question in a cell captive is, has there been a transfer of risk?

In its first official guidance on the subject of protected cell companies, the US Internal Revenue Service (IRS) provided examples of situations in which US companies can and cannot take tax deductions for premiums

---

[146] The approach to tax laws whereby a transaction is characterised otherwise than in accordance with their legal form is not new ('substance over form').

paid in cell captive insurance arrangements. In Revenue Ruling 2008-8, the IRS has provided two examples of cell arrangements. In the case of a parent-subsidiary insurance relationship, the premiums would not be tax-deductible for federal income tax purposes; in the case of insurance between an insurance subsidiary and other subsidiaries of the same parent, they would be. The status of the insurer as a PCC was not relevant to the tax analysis.

More specifically, the IRS has said that it will treat a captive cell arrangement as insurance for income tax purposes if the cell insures several different subsidiaries of the corporation that owns control of the cell. They will not treat the captive cell arrangement as insurance if the cell simply covers the corporation directly.

Simultaneously with Revenue Ruling 2008-8[147], the IRS also released Notice 2008-19 requesting comments on proposed guidance with respect to the entity classification issues related to cells and PCCs.

The Notice requests comment on the proposed guidance *"In order to ensure that entity classification and federal tax elections for Protected Cell Companies are both legally correct and administrable in all cases"*. Further it *"also requests comments on what guidance, if any, would be appropriate concerning similar segregated arrangements that do not involve insurance"*[148].

The proposed guidance would treat a cell of a PCC as a separate entity for tax purposes if:

"(a) the assets and liabilities of the cell are segregated from the assets and liabilities of any other cell and from the assets and liabilities of the Protected Cell Company such that no creditor of any other cell or of the Protected Cell Company may look to the assets of the cell for the satisfaction of any liabilities, including insurance claims (except to the extent that any other cell or the Protected Cell Company has a direct creditor claim against such cell); and

[147] See also IRS private letter ruling of the 11 December 2009 in response to a taxpayer's question as to whether its business as a captive reinsurer was "insurance" for tax purposes. (The facts also included a reinsurer segregated cell company).

[148] See the American Bar Association (Section of Taxation) response to the IRS dated 5 January 2009 to Notice 2008-19 addressing segregated arrangements that do not involve insurance; available in http://www.hro.com/files/file/publications/Article-ABA-Section-Taxation-Comments.pdf

(b) based on all the facts and circumstances, the arrangements and other activities of the cell, if conducted by a corporation, would result in its being classified as an insurance company ...."

Treating each cell as an insurance company appears sensible, preserves the integrity of the cell structure and also has the benefit of easing the tax administration.

The approach seems consistent with the long-standing IRS treatment[149] of series trusts whereby each series in a series trust is treated as a separate and distinct entity. The IRS has also confirmed[150] that each LLC portfolio of a "Series LLC" that held multiple asset portfolios was to be treated as a separate entity under the federal income tax.

The New York State Bar Association Tax Section in response to *Notice 2008-19 and Protected Cell Companies Outside of the Insurance Arena* has made submisions (May 2, 2008) to the IRS and Treasury proposing a safe harbour that would determine whether a cell of a PCC should be treated as a separate entity for tax purposes, namely (1) the PCC is formed under the statute of a state or foreign sovereign jurisdiction and (2) the statute provides for unambiguous separateness of assets and liabilities of the PCC and permits beneficial ownership to be held on a cell by cell basis[151].

15.3. International Taxation and the PCC

Most countries contain provision for the taxation of non-resident companies established by certain resident companies in low tax countries, known as Controlled Foreign Company ("CFC") rules, which look to subject the profits to tax through deeming provisions if the subsidiary does not distribute substantially all of its income. The exemptions to such rules are difficult to apply in practice and are subject to close scrutiny by the tax authorities. The UK, for instance, has CFC legislation and was one of the first countries to introduce such legislation. The majority of offshore insurance captives with UK parents are likely to be treated as CFCs. The parent company would pay tax in the UK in respect of its

149 This is in the form of private letter rulings (PLR); for a thorough discussion of PLRs see 'Check-the-Box' Classification of Series Entities By H. Karl Zeswitz JR. and William R. Pauls, BNA, Vol. 9, No 12 January 2009. Also see National Securities Series-Industrial Stock v. CLR 13 TC 884 (1949)

150 LTR 200803004

151 Available in http://www.nysba.org/AM/Template.cfm?Section=TaxSection_Reports_2008&CONTENTID=28863&TEMPLATE=/CM/ContentDisplay.cfm

subsidiary (CFC's) profits; likewise for investment companies. The UK authorities, however, have not issued any guidance on how they will seek to tax PCCs under CFC rules.[152]

If a single cell within a PCC were not caught by the CFC regime, this may create a tax planning opportunity because of the absence of control by the very nature of the cell structure. For example, with companies established for structured finance and controlled by offshore charitable trusts, single purpose cells within a PCC have permitted banks to capitalise individual cells without assuming 'control' of the company but allowing them to participate in the profits (via the cell).

The use of PCCs in tax planning has been less common in practice than would have been expected; perhaps due to the commercial considerations of giving up 'control' and/or the questions around segregation of cell assets in foreign proceedings.

One of the few jurisdictions to have issued guidance on the tax treatment of a PCC is the Australian Government Tax Office (ATO Interpretative Decision ID 2008/23 of 25 January 2008).

The issue in question was:

"Will an individual 'cell' in a protected cell company incorporated under Guernsey law, in respect of which a taxpayer subscribes for redeemable preference shares (RPS), be a controlled foreign company (CFC) for the purposes of section 340 of the Income Tax Assessment Act 1936 (ITAA 1936)?"

The facts were simple and typical of a PCC:

"An Australian resident taxpayer subscribes for redeemable preference shares (RPS) in respect of a relevant individual cell in a Guernsey protected cell company (protected cell company).

The protected cell company is a limited liability company incorporated under Guernsey's Protected Cell Companies Ordinance 1997 (as amended by Ordinance No.V of 1997; by No. XV of 1998; by No. XXI of 2005) (the PCC Ordinance) and registered under the provisions of The Companies (Guernsey) Law 1994 (as amended).

The protected cell company may form one or more cells."

---

[152] The Revenue has issued guidance in other context – see *"IPT anti-avoidance measure concerning protected cell companies and higher rate IPT"* (*HMRC Reference: BN CE 19/03*) and *HMRC Tax Bulletin Issue 73* (*"Finance Act 2004 – Offshore Funds Legislation"*).

The answer to the issue at stake was: "*No. An individual cell in a Guernsey protected cell company, in respect of which a taxpayer subscribes for RPS, will not be a CFC for the purposes of section 340 of the ITAA 1936.*"

The reasons for the decision were straightforward and the applicable law did not allow for a different decision. Thus:

"Section 340 of the ITAA 1936 provides that a company is a CFC at a particular time if, at that time, the company is a resident of a listed country or of an unlisted country and satisfies one of the three control tests contained therein.

Whether a cell in a protected cell company is a CFC for the purposes of section 340 of the ITAA 1936 requires the determination of whether a cell in a protected cell company constitutes a company.

The term 'company' is defined in subsection 995-1(1) of the Income Tax Assessment Act 1997 (ITAA 1997) to mean:

(a) a body corporate; or

(b) any other unincorporated association or body of persons;

*but does not include a *partnership or a *non-entity joint venture.*

**denotes a term defined in subsection 995-1(1) of the ITAA 1997*

The term 'body corporate' is not defined in the ITAA 1936 or the ITAA 1997.

The Commissioner has considered the meaning of the term 'body corporate' in Miscellaneous Taxation MT 2006/1 - The New Tax System: the meaning of entity carrying on an enterprise for the purposes of entitlement to an Australian business number (ABN).

Paragraph 30 of MT 2006/1 states that the term 'body corporate' has the following meaning:

'Body Corporate' is not a defined term. The term takes its meaning from the general law. 'Body corporate' is a general term to describe an artificial entity having separate legal existence. A body corporate has the ability to continue in existence indefinitely and to keep its identity regardless of changes to its membership. It also has the power to act, hold property, enter into legal contract, sue and be sued in its own name, just as a natural person can.

The protected cell company is incorporated under the PCC Ordinance and registered under the provisions of the Companies (Guernsey) Law 1994 (as amended).

By virtue of section 1(2) of the PCC Ordinance, the protected cell company itself is a legal person and is therefore a 'body corporate' for the purposes of paragraph (a) of the definition of 'company' in subsection 995-1(1) of the ITAA 1997.

The taxpayer will become a shareholder in the protected cell company by subscribing for RPS in respect of a particular cell in the protected cell company, and therefore becomes a member of a 'body corporate'. The taxpayer will not become a member of any other 'company', as that term is defined in subsection 995-1(1) of the ITAA 1997, within the protected cell company through the subscription of RPS in the protected cell company.

Accordingly, the protected cell company itself is a 'company' as that term is defined in subsection 995-1(1) of the ITAA 1997.

Each individual cell in the protected cell company is not a company under subsection 995-1(1) of the ITAA 1997 and therefore cannot be a CFC for the purposes of section 340 of the ITAA 1936."

Clearly, if the cells themselves were separate legal entities (e.g. in the case of an ICC), the decision would have gone the other way[153].

Similarly, with a PCC established as a single corporate entity and individual cells not having separate legal existence, it was, until the UK Budget changes in 2008, difficult to see how the UK CFC rules could have applied where the core controlling shares were independently owned by a non-UK parent (for example, a captive manager). This is because UK legislation did not look to individual cells for the purposes of the CFC rules.

Here the changes introduced to the definition of 'control' in the 2008 Budget should be noted:

(3) In section 755D (meaning of control)— (a) after subsection (1) insert—

"(1A) For the purposes of this Chapter a person also controls a company if the person possesses, or is entitled to acquire, such rights as would— (a) if the whole of the income of the company were distributed, entitle the person to receive the greater part of the amount so distributed, (b) if the whole of the company's share capital were disposed of, entitle the person to receive the greater part of the proceeds of the disposal, or (c) in the event of the winding-up of the company or in any other circumstances, entitle the person to receive the greater part of the assets of the company which would then be available for distribution.", and in subsection (2), after "above" insert "or satisfy subsection (1A) above"[154].

Essentially, this definition of 'control' applies substance over form. Control exercised by income and asset rights, in addition to control by

---

153 Since then the Australian Government has released a consultation paper entitled: *Reform of the Controlled Foreign Company Rules* (5 January 2010) to modernize CFC rules.

154 Finance Act 2008, section 64, amending ICTA 1988.

voting rights would be caught by the amendments to the CFC rules. It would therefore seem to be sufficiently wide to catch a PCC where there are only a few cells and one cell has a disprortionate entitlement to the profits of the company as a whole. This could therefore potentially impact on foreign owned protected cell companies. Consider the following hypothetical scenario:

The 'core' (non-cellular voting) shares in a Guernsey PCC are owned by a non-UK entity. It has a few cells. Each cell has a separate cell shareholder without voting rights attaching to those shares. The new UK CFC definition of 'control' creates a potential problem for the cell users since it seems to disregard the legal form of the structure. This may have been an unintended consequence and one which has raised concerns within the securitisation industry in particular in the context of orphan vehicles since it could result in the taxation of income of a cell for taxpayers who had no interest in it or ability to share in its profits. It was less of a concern for insurers if they could rely on one of the exemptions available e.g. local business substance.

More recently, in its 2010 Budget the South African Government announced changes to the way a PCC is to be taxed. In a National Treasury Budget review document[155] and under the heading *"Closure of Sophisticated Tax Loopholes"* it was noted that *"Taxpayers had sought to bypass CFC legislation through the use of Protected Cell Companies"* on the basis that *"Investors typically have full control over the cell, but fail to satisfy the requisite CFC ownership requirements in the foreign entity overall"*. It is therefore *"proposed to treat each cell as a deemed separate company with the ownership requirements measured separately."* By treating a cell as a separate company for taxation purposes at shareholder level, equally the same tax treatment at cell company level should follow.

Some countries have similar tax provisions for individuals that, for example, in the case of the UK, will attribute any capital gains of a foreign company to its resident shareholders. But opportunities for tax planning still exist in the UK under the Taxation of Chargeable Gains Act 1992 section 13, where individual shareholders have less than 10 per cent of the shares in the company. A cell of a PCC is therefore an ideal structure for investment holding purposes if the company has more than 10 shareholders.

---

[155]http://www.treasury.gov.za/documents/national%20budget/2010/review/Annexure%20c.pdf

SPVs owned by charitable trusts have existed for many years.[156] The use of trusts in common law jurisdictions is unimpeachable and whether a trust will fail as a sham will depend on a number of circumstances. The fact that a special purpose vehicle is set up by a charitable trust to support an underlying business transaction (e.g. securitisation), connected to the business needs and for the principal benefit of a financial institution, is not a reason to set aside the trust if the trust is entitled to receive the residual value of the SPV (even if nominal)[157] on it being wound-up.

The typical form of trust deed will contain the following provisions:

1. It will exclude from any entitlement to benefit from the trust (as "Excluded Persons") any person who directly or indirectly provides funds or property to be held by the Trustees as part of the Trust Fund.
2. It will clearly state the charitable nature of the trust by defining who the potential beneficiaries are, subject to the exercise of discretion by the trustees with regards to the appointment of beneficiaries and distribution of trust property.
3. Following the establishment of the SPV, the trust property will comprise the entire issued shares in the company. Typically the trust deed will therefore contain a restrictive clause as follows: *"subject to any and every exercise of the powers contained in this trust deed, the Trustees shall exercise or refrain from exercising all voting rights attaching to the shares described in the Schedule in such manner as they shall think fit provided that they shall not exercise their voting rights to wind up the Company unless and until they have received written confirmation from the Directors that the Company does not intend to carry on further business."*

It would also be advisable to include provision to the effect that:

(1) *"without prejudice to the proper exercise of their powers as members of the Company, the Trustees shall not be required or permitted to interfere in the management or conduct of the Company or the business of the Company"*; and

(2) *"The Trustees shall not be bound or required to interfere in the conduct of any company in any part of the capital of which the Trustees shall have invested or hold an investment or of any business of any such company (and whether or not the Trustees shall have power to control any such company or business) and*

[156] They were the subject to negative attention from The Guardian on 5 December 2007 in an article entitled *"Revealed: how UK banks exploit charity tax laws"*.

[157] For example, in a securitisation, the trust will receive the paid up share capital when the last note matures and the SPV is wound-up.

the Trustees shall be at liberty to leave the conduct of its business (including the payment or non-payment of dividends) wholly to the directors."

The PCC fund structure also offers flexibility for international tax planning that other corporate structures may not. Giving an example of this Freddie White and Adrian Hogg of Grant Thornton Fund Administration Limited (a fund administration company) told the co-author of this book: *"Where US and non-US investors wish to invest in the same strategy (US investors for this purpose being US Persons as defined by Rule 902 of Regulation S under the Securities Act 1933), it is possible to establish what is commonly referred to as a master-feeder fund structure. In such a structure, three separate entities are established: the first that caters for non-US investors (usually referred to as the 'Offshore Feeder'), a second that caters for US investors (the 'Onshore Feeder') and a third that aggregates the assets in the Offshore Feeder and the Onshore Feeder (the 'Master Fund')."*

By using this structure the assets of the Offshore Feeder and the assets of the Onshore Feeder are invested in the Master Fund. The Master Fund then invests the combined assets according to the investment strategy. This strategy allows for separate record keeping reporting for US investors (Onshore Feeder) and non-US investors (Offshore Feeder). This is of particular importance in order for a fund structure to appeal to US investors since the Onshore Feeder (for US investors) would elect to be treated as a "partnership" for US tax purposes. As such, the master-feeder fund structure should enable US investors to prepare accounts and records (in the Onshore Feeder) in order to ensure compliance with US tax reporting requirements. It also keeps non-US investors in the Offshore Feeder separate. As far as the promoter of the structure is concerned it allows its investment strategy to be available to non-US investors and US investors in a tax compliant manner.[158]

The PCC allows the traditional master-feeder fund structure to be taken to the next level. Establishing a master-feeder fund can be a time consuming and costly exercise as instead of one fund being formed three are required (the Onshore Feeder, Offshore Feeder and the Master Fund). However, once established the PCC master-feeder fund structure could be used time and again whereby a regular company structure would generally only have a single use. For example, a promoter could establish

---

[158]It is essential that any such structure obtains appropriate US professional advice (including tax and securities advice) prior to execution. The above is included in this book for illustration purposes only. It does not purport to offer tax advice.

a PCC master-feeder fund structure and adopt a strategy of investment in real estate and designate Cell A in each of the Onshore Feeder, the Offshore Feeder and Master Fund for such a purpose. The promoter could then create a derivative and commodity investment strategy and designate Cell B in each of the Onshore Feeder, the Offshore Feeder and Master Fund for the purpose. By final example the same promoter could create a distressed debt investment strategy and designate Cell C in each of the Onshore Feeder, the Offshore Feeder and Master Fund for the purpose. As Freddie White and Adrian Hogg conclude: *"Had a traditional company been used the promoter would have had to establish three separate master-feeder fund structures for substantial time and cost consideration. With the PCC the possibilities for the promoter, under the guidance of their professional advisors, are endless. In this respect the PCC clearly outperforms the traditional regular company."*

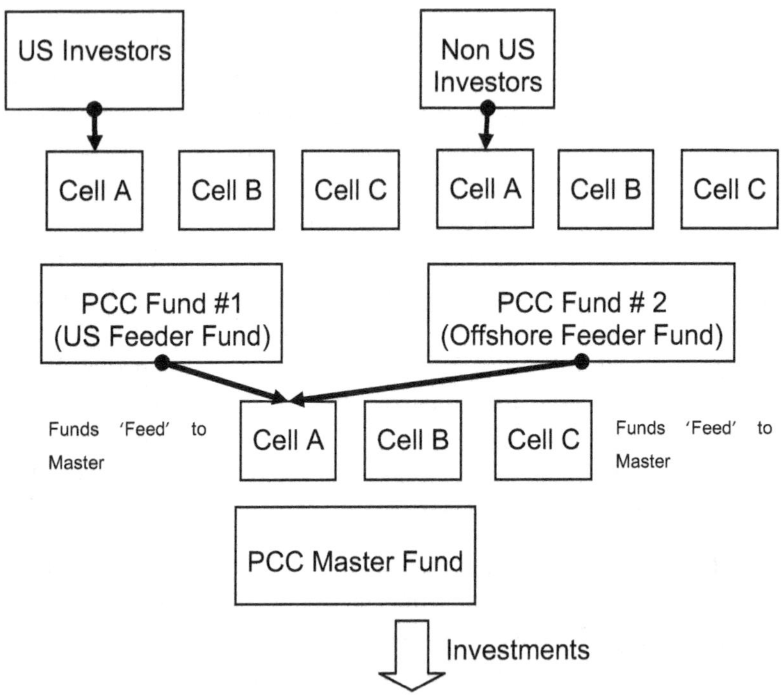

Diagram 9: A PCC Master Feeder Fund

As far as insurance is concerned, the purpose behind the establishment of an insurance company is, of course, not tax avoidance (as distinct from any tax planning considerations behind where it is set up or how it is structured). In the case of a CFC captive, tax considerations are obviously even more remote. The same is also largely true for investment funds and indeed repackaging (or securitisation). As such these would not normally be viewed as tax driven structures.

But there is no reason why the PCC cannot be used in legitimate tax structures like any other type of company.

Taxation is notoriously difficult (some would argue impossible) to harmonise internationally. This therefore creates opportunities for tax arbitrage; namely, taking advantage of differences in tax treatment between different jurisdictions. A very simple example of tax arbitrage is the use of financial instruments to exploit the distinction between capital and income or interest and equity for tax purposes in different tax systems (e.g. country of issuer and investor). All large international banks are involved in structuring such products.

Where a PCC is used in any tax related transaction involving structured products, care must be taken to ensure not only that the company is managed and controlled from the home jurisdiction as we have seen, but that the proposed transaction is supported by tax opinions[159] (based on a disclosure of the full facts) from competent law firms covering all the jurisdictions involved and all parties concerned. Further, at no point should the PCC be involved in the marketing of any tax related product or offering any advice whatsoever to investors or counterparties.

A couple of examples can be given by way of illustration of what a PCC should avoid in a tax context. One, it should not enter into a cell transaction whereby its (the cell's) solvency depends on a successful claim for a tax refund (eg a VAT refund scheme[160]). That would put the cell structure at risk. Similarly, a tax driven cellular transaction that relies on a particular tax treatment (i.e. no liability to tax) should ideally be agreed in advance with the tax authorities[161] or the relevant cell should be funded to meet any potential tax liability. It would certainly be too risky to proceed with a transaction simply on the assumption of 'no tax'.

---

[159] 'Should' level opinions.

[160] For example, a WHA type VAT scheme, where the judicial pendulum for and against entitlement to the refund may swing one way and the other as the case goes on appeal through the Courts, would be inappropriate for a cell within a PCC.

[161] Some jurisdictions allow for advance or post-transaction tax rulings e.g. the UK has the procedure in the Code of Practice 10 for non-business customers, and guidance for non-statutory clearances for businesses on in the HMRC website: http://www.hmrc.gov.uk/cap/links-dec07.htm

A detailed analysis around tax issues is (naturally) outside the scope of this book. The point to make is that a PCC is not a tax driven structure *per se*, but it can be applied in a tax context just like any other type of company. Any tax planning involving the use of a PCC (indeed involving any entity) must work in 'law' and proceed on the assumption of full disclosure to the tax authorities, and not on the latter not being expected to ask too many questions. Many jurisdictions will attack a transaction on the basis that there is no real economic purpose other than tax avoidance, of substance over form and/or abuse of law principles. On the other hand, this has to be weighed up against a taxpayer's right to structure business activities in most tax-efficient manner and a PCC can fulfill any number of business functions with real economic purpose.

We conclude this discussion by citing three judicial observations:

First, the judgment of the European Court in *Gemeente Leusden and Holin Groep* (a VAT case), paragraph 79:[162]

"... under the law of a Member State, a taxpayer cannot be censured for taking advantage of a provision or a lacuna in the legislation which, without constituting an abuse, has allowed him to pay less tax ..."

Second, the reasoning in Edinburgh VAT Tribunal in the case of *RBS Property Developments Limited (VTD 17789)*:

"A taxpayer is entitled so to construct his activities as to obtain favourable taxation consequences. To suggest otherwise, apart from calling in question the wisdom of Lord Hoffman in the cases above cited could create a concept of a duty on a taxpayer not to minimise but to maximise his tax liability by seeing to it that he paid any tax which might on any view of the situation be due. Persons do not conduct their business with a view to providing finance to the authorities. It is arguable that the correct economic activity for a trader is to retain as much of the funds he has earned for his own or shareholders benefit as he legitimately can."

Third, the judgment of the European Court in *Cadbury Schweppes plc, Cadbury Schweppes Overseas Ltd v Commissioners of Inland Revenue*, paragraph 55:[163]

---

[162] Joined Cases C-487/01 and C-7/02

[163] Case C-196/04

"It follows that, in order for a restriction on the freedom of establishment to be justified on the ground of prevention of abusive practices, the specific objective of such a restriction must be to prevent conduct involving the creation of wholly artificial arrangements which do not reflect economic reality, with a view to escaping the tax normally due on the profits generated by activities carried out on national territory."

15.4. Tax issues Regarding a Cell Captive

Whilst it may not be possible to review the tax legislation of every jurisdiction in which a PCC underwrites risk, the directors must ensure at all times that the company is managed and controlled from the home jurisdiction.

The composition of the Board of Directors and place where Board meetings are held will obviously be important in making the determination of where the company's business is managed. In principle, it should not be of concern that certain directors of the insurer are non-residents; this as long as their actions as directors take place in the home jurisdiction at properly convened and held Board meetings.

Under most tax systems, should a tax authority in a foreign jurisdiction be able to demonstrate that the management and control was being exercised in its territory, the company would be treated as tax resident. Corporate tax would accordingly be chargeable on its profits.

The key points to bear in mind with regards to management and control are:

- The directors of the insurance company must take an active involvement in the transactions and the business of the company.
- Policy decisions (e.g. principally in respect of underwriting, claims and investments) must actually be made at board meetings in the home jurisdiction.
- An effective decision as to whether to sign the documents/pass a resolution is required – i.e. there must be active discussion by the directors. This requires some minimum level of information, so that decisions are made on an informed basis.

The mere physical acts of signing documents and resolutions would not be considered enough to constitute actual management and control.

Clearly the key functions to be performed by the Board of an insurance company are: underwriting (including policy issuance), claims handling, pricing and investment. These are functions that demonstrate 'mind and management'. Each insurance company would therefore need to be able to provide such evidence in support (typically but not exclusively through Board papers and properly recorded minutes).

In this context, non-executive directors have an important role to play, namely challenging the executive management (particularly with regards to performance) and meeting business plan objectives and contributing to overall strategy. For a PCC, the experience and expertise of non-executive directors will provide reassurance to cell shareholders about operational compliance.

At main board level, the following are likely to be items for inclusion at each Board Meeting:

1. Review minutes of previous meeting and matters arising.
2. Review latest management accounts.
3. Review underwriting and approve new products and/or rates.
4. Review financial solvency.
5. Review management performance.
6. Review of third party service providers.
7. Review claims performance.
8. Complaints report.
9. Compliance report.
10. Risk log review.
11. Review of investment performance.
12. Audit committee report.
13. Consideration of legislative, tax or regulatory changes.

15.5. Concluding remarks

Taxation is a significant potential area of risk for a PCC. In particular, if the company has tax liabilities in a foreign jurisdiction in respect of business attributable to a cell (e.g. it has a branch and therefore a tax presence there), the tax authorities in that jurisdiction may well attempt to claim against the entire or any assets of the company to satisfy those liabilities. Assuming that the sole business establishment of the PCC (and sole tax residence) is in the jurisdiction of incorporation and the cells have no unsatisfied tax liabilities, this should not be a concern. The best advice possible is therefore to ensure that the affairs of the PCC are managed solely from within its domicile. This is the mantra of this book.

16. WHAT ARE THE GROUP ACCOUNTING ISSUES?

The Group accounting issues revolve around one question: Should the cell be incorporated into the consolidated accounts of its stakeholder?

16.1. Group protected cell companies - accounting considerations under International Financial Reporting Standards

What aspects of International Financial Reporting Standards (IFRS) would need to be considered by a stakeholder in a PCC?

There is no guidance issued by either the International Accounting Standards Board (IASB) or its interpretive body the International Financial Reporting Interpretations Committee (IFRIC) that deals specifically with PCCs. Accordingly, a 'first principles' approach will be required having regard to the general principles of IFRS. It follows that there can be no generic accounting solutions for the accounting by stakeholders in PCCs. Accordingly a stakeholder will need to consider carefully the exact facts and circumstances that surround each situation before any accounting conclusions can be drawn. This consideration should be in conjunction with the appropriate professional advice.

Given the potential diverse applications of PCCs, IFRS could generate many different accounting answers depending on use. Further, IFRS might produce different results for different entities. This would depend upon whether they subscribe to the hub (or core) capital of a PCC (for example sponsors) or are entities that subscribe for capital or otherwise utilise just specific cells of a PCC.

The following discussion considers some of the general IFRS considerations that might commonly apply to an entity that makes use of a particular cell of a PCC ("a Cell Investor").

What general IFRS considerations should a Cell Investor consider? Take a simple example in which a Cell Investor subscribes for shares issued by a cell of a PCC. As consideration for those shares the Cell Investor transfers to the PCC certain financial assets – a small holding of equity shares in a third party listed company for example.

The obvious question the Cell Investor will need to consider is one of consolidation and, if so, how much of the PCC should be consolidated – one cell, several cells, or the whole PCC?

16.2. Group consolidation considerations

16.2.1. Group general considerations

The general requirement of IFRS is that a parent is required to consolidate its subsidiaries. Accordingly there is a question of whether a PCC, in part or in whole, would be considered to be a subsidiary of a Cell Investor.

The applicable IFRS standard is IAS 27 Consolidated and Separate Financial Statements. IAS 27 defines a subsidiary as an entity that is "controlled" by another entity (the parent). So the key question is whether the Cell Investor *controls* the PCC and to what extent.

IAS 27 defines "control" as the power to govern the financial and operating policies of an entity so as to obtain benefits from its activities. It is worth noting that this does not necessarily require a conventional share interest. The standard explains that normally "control" is presumed to exist when the parent owns more than half of the voting power of another entity; that is unless in exceptional circumstances such ownership does not constitute control. Further, IAS 27 explains that control also exists when the parent owns less than half of the voting power of another entity but can nevertheless control the entity. Control can be through other means such as a power to appoint the majority of controlling board members or power to govern the financial and operating policies under an agreement.

But how do governance considerations apply to an interest in a PCC? For example, if in this illustration the PCC is structured such that each cell can issue its own discrete share capital, distinct from the share capital issued from other cells and the core, then to what extent does the Cell Investor "govern" all or part of the PCC? Do governance considerations apply just to a particular cell or more widely? And how do the governance rights of our cell investor interact with governance rights of other Cell Investors of their cells and the governance rights of the sponsor of the PCC that holds any core shares? Do such rights amount to a veto of control? Or are such rights potentially minority interests? Obviously complicated scenarios could present themselves.

However, an important question is whether, in a particular situation, the normal governance-based criteria of IAS 27 (i.e. voting and board decisions) are in fact the appropriate tests of control because, in certain situations, governance based criteria become difficult to apply sensibly. This is normally the case when an interest in an entity is actually an interest in a special purpose entity ("SPE", the term used in IFRS).

Therefore a cell investor would need to consider whether an investment in a cell of a PCC is actually an interest in a special purpose entity (SPE).

16.2.2. Group special purpose entities

An SPE is an entity that is created to accomplish a narrow and well-defined objective. It is often the case that such entities are subject to arrangements that impose limits on the ability of their management to make decisions concerning the financial and operating policies of the entity. As such, the normal governance considerations of IAS 27 of voting power and board decisions are difficult, if not meaningless, to apply to an interest in a SPE.

It is quite possible that an analysis of the facts and circumstances could lead to the conclusion that a PCC, or at least a cell of a PCC, is in fact an SPE. In our example, this might be the case if the nature of the cells of the PCC is merely storage facilities for assets – effectively a collection of silos for cell investors to store financial assets until they are needed. Let us assume that this is the case and that each cell is set up on 'auto-pilot' to hold assets and no variation from course is permitted. As such there are no real commercial decisions to be made during the life of the cell. At this point our example runs into trouble because, as an 'auto-pilot' entity it has no reason or need to make commercial decisions about its future. Accordingly, an analysis of board control and voting rights becomes inconclusive.

So if the normal IAS 27 governance tests of control break down when applied to a SPE, how should an entity approach the question of consolidation of such an entity? IFRS guidance here is provided by SIC-12 Consolidation – Special Purpose Entities. SIC-12 is an interpretation of IAS 27 which seeks to explain how the concept of control is applied to a SPE and the circumstances in which a SPE should be consolidated by an entity. SIC-12 achieves this by describing certain additional indicators of control by an entity over a SPE beyond those set out in IAS 27:

In substance

1) the activities of the SPE are being conducted on behalf of the entity according to its specific business needs so that the entity obtains benefits from the SPE's operation;
2) the entity has the decision-making powers to obtain the majority of the benefits of the activities of the SPE or, by setting up an "autopilot" mechanism, the entity has delegated those decision-making powers;

3) the entity has rights to obtain the majority of the benefits of the SPE and therefore may be exposed to the risks incident to the activities of the SPE; or

4) the entity retains the majority of the residual or ownership risks related to the SPE or its assets in order to obtain benefits from its activities.

Looking at the above tests, it is apparent that emphasis is placed on the 'substance' of the investment; that is, the economic reality of the arrangement is considered rather than merely its legal form.

This is particularly apparent from tests 3 and 4. Test 3 is effectively asking the question as to whether an entity enjoys the benefits of the assets contained within the SPE (for example if the assets held are listed equity shares then the benefits of any increase in share price accrue to the entity). Or whether the entity is exposed to the risk associated with those assets (for example the risk of value of investments falling). Where an entity is exposed to the 'majority' of such risk and reward then that entity is likely to be identified as the parent of the SPE under the guidance of SIC-12, but this is subject to an assessment of the wider facts and circumstances of the particular case for any evidence that could contradict such a conclusion.

Test 4 is essentially an articulation of the risk and rewards of ownership to which the holder of an equity share in a non-SPE entity is exposed; that is the residual interest in assets after the deduction of liabilities. Accordingly, when an entity is economically exposed to the majority of the same residual risk and reward to which an entity investing in a 'normal', non-SPE entity would be then that entity is likely to be identified by SIC-12 as the parent of the SPE. Again this is subject to an assessment of the wider facts and circumstances of the particular case for evidence that could contradict such a conclusion. Test 4 is a good example of applying 'substance' rather than legal form because it shows that an entity can be required to consolidate a SPE even if it does not hold share capital in the SPE.

So, how might the tests of SIC-12 be applied in the context of a PCC that is a SPE? In particular how does the fact that there may be several cells in existence each with their own assets and each with their own Cell Investors? Should the tests of SIC-12 be applied to just the cells in which our cell investor has invested directly or should the tests be applied to the PCC more widely?

It is likely that the precise structure of the PCC would be an important consideration in the application of the SIC-12 tests. For example, as noted above, tests 3 and 4 are based on an assessment of exposure to risk and reward. Therefore it would be necessary to have an understanding of the extent to which any risks or benefits are pooled or cross-collateralised within the PCC; either from other cells or from the core. Where such cross-collateralisation exists then it may be appropriate that the SIC-12 tests are applied to a PCC beyond consideration of a single cell since the risk to which a cell investor is exposed is not limited to a single cell.

However, where the PCC operates such that a cell investor retains risk with regard to the assets that it transfers into a particular cell, and those assets are not cross collateralised with other assets in the PCC structure, then the cell investor would most likely evaluate risk and benefits only of those assets that it has transferred to that ring-fenced cell. Depending on an assessment of all facts and circumstances, this might have the effect that such 'ring-fenced' cells are consolidated by the cell investor.

16.2.3. Group summary

As can be seen, there is a lack of specific IFRS accounting guidance for investing in PCCs. However, the existing IFRS guidance such as that discussed above that considers consolidation matters provide principles that can be drawn upon.

The key question for a cell investor would be to determine whether its interest in a PCC amounts to an interest in a SPE or not; and if so, whether that interest is limited to a particular cell or the PCC more widely.

Obviously in the event that the cell into which a cell investor transfers assets is consolidated, the group accounts of the cell investor will effectively continue to recognise those transferred assets as if no transfer had taken place. For the same reason the cell investors consolidated income statement would continue to recognise gains and losses that arise on those transferred assets.

There can be no generic accounting solutions for investments in PCCs given the variety of applications they can potentially be used for – each situation should be considered in the light of its specific facts and circumstances in conjunction with professional advice as necessary. For that reason this book limits accounting discussions to high level general IFRS issues that a cell investor would need to consider rather than any specific scenarios.

17. WHAT ARE THE PCC and CELLULAR ACCOUNTING ISSUES?

The PCC cellular accounting issues revolve around the extent to which the cells, as opposed to the PCC itself need to prepare and submit accounts. Several issues are raised:

1. to what extent is the cell treated as a *de facto* company for accounts purposes, i.e. does it have to prepare separate accounts or can it rely on mere 'attribution'?
2. if separate accounts have to be prepared, need they be filed and to what extent need they be filed?
3. what directorial sanctions exist for failure to abide by accounting requirements?

A statutory example being Jersey under the Companies (Jersey) Law 1991 (as amended) which considers these three issues below.

17.1. Article 127 YE - Annual return in respect of cells

(1) *Article 71(1) (which requires a company to deliver an annual return to the registrar) shall not apply to a cell of a cell company.*

(2) *However, the cell company must –*

(a) *include in its annual return the information required by Article 71 in respect of each cell of the company; and*

(b) *in respect of each of its cells – deliver to the registrar a copy of so much of its annual return as relates to the cell.*

(3) *If a cell company fails to comply with paragraph (2) it is guilty of an offence.*

(4) *A cell of a cell company shall provide all relevant information to the cell company in sufficient time to enable the cell company to comply with the requirements of paragraph (2) in relation to the cell company.*

(5) *If a cell fails to comply with paragraph (4), the cell, and, where the cell is a public company, every officer of the cell who is in default, is guilty of an offence.*

17.2. Article 127YF of the Law is repealed.

17.3. Article 127YG Accounts of cell companies

(1) *Nothing in Article 104 shall be taken to require a cell company to prepare the accounts in relation to a cell of the company that are required to be prepared in relation to the cell.*

(2) *Subject to any provision to the contrary in the articles of a cell of a cell company or of the company, a member of the cell company who is not a member of the cell shall only be entitled to be provided by the cell with so much of the accounts of the cell as is necessary in order for the cell company to comply with the requirements of Article 127YE(2) in relation to the cell company.*

(3) *Nothing in this Article shall require the preparation, in relation to a cell of a cell company, of accounts in relation to the affairs of the cell that occurred before this Article came into operation.*

18. CONCLUSIONS

18.1. Insolvency conclusions

As to insolvency, can some conclusions be made at to the best PCC structure and method of managing the same. The authors offer the following advice –

1. A statutory PCC can coexist with a contractual PCC, i.e. a PCC formed according to a PCC statute can coexist with a contractual PCC whereby cellular stakeholders contract with each other so as to effect a cellular structure. Thus, cell owners should always try the belt and braces approach of a statutory PCC coexisting with a contractual PCC.
2. Choose a PCC jurisdiction that enjoys maximum international insolvency protection. It is submitted that EU membership offers the greatest transnational insolvency regime. Consequently the leading PCC jurisdictions are Gibraltar and Malta.
3. Consider a regime that has multi-lateral insolvency assistance. Unfortunately the European (more especially the Council of Europe), the Nordic, the Latin American and North American (NAFTA) "conventions" have had little or no impact. However, the Commonwealth regime (as manifested in the UK under section 426) has had some impact. Consideration should therefore be given to Designated Territory PCCs .
4. Minimise all PCC dealings outside of the PCC jurisdiction. If services (or goods) cannot be purchased in the home PCC jurisdiction (say reinsurance) purchase the same in a PCC jurisdiction and/or through an SPV controlled by the PCC and/or through a cell. Failure to do so may result in a Part V or similar insolvency proceedings. Keep it local.
5. Manage the affairs of the PCC in the PCC jurisdiction, so that the PCC COMI can never be regarded as being anywhere else other than in the PCC home jurisdiction. Again, keep it local.
6. Consider a PCC jurisdiction that creates the maximum directorial sanction in the event of mis-segregation. More especially that the director(s) is/are liable for the loss stemming from mis-segregation and not merely a fine. Further that if a director is to avoid sanction, the burden of proof is reversed, i.e. the director has to prove that he should not be made culpable for mis-segregation. In this regard careful consideration should be given as to the advisability of limited

liability corporate directors. The use of corporate directors (i.e. instead of natural persons as directors) may be of use. For instance if the corporate director is incorporated locally, this can assist in maintaining COMI being within the PCC direction. However, a corporate director has limited liability and hence there is less of a remedy against that director in the event of mis-segregation.

7. Print the maximum health warnings possible everywhere in every respect to do with the PCC. For instance that 'this company is a PCC incorporated under the laws of (X) and that the liability is limited to certain cells/hubs/central capital/etc'. The reference should extend beyond what is required by statute to (say) the website, cheques, brochures, *et al*.
8. Ensure that all creditors/suppliers etc sign a supply agreement (i.e. do more than simply advise or notify suppliers of a PCC existence); wherein liability is noted and to which cell or hub is liable. Ensure that all parties have written proof of notification of cellular liability.
9. Consider the selective use of trusts, i.e. the hub is named as the trustee of the cell. Trust relationships tend to be recognised as not forming part of an insolvent's estate and consequently if for any reason cellular segregation fails, the PCC priority rules may well be saved by the existence of a trust. Whilst certain PCC regimes may state a trust relationship does not automatically exist between hub and cell, there is little to stop the creation. This is save for one possible theoretical objection: the cell and the hub are the same legal person. However, a non-PCC jurisdiction may find a trust relationship easier to accept than the PCC.
10. Consider cell shareholders taking security over cells. Again security relationships tend to be recognised as an exception to the *pari passu* principle.
11. Consider the use of cell shareholdings. If a PCC has cell shareholdings then the cell itself is more likely, in some jurisdictions to be treated as a separate company and/or the alter ego of its shareholders. The former may be a good result, the latter however will usually be a bad result.
12. Always use professional independent staff to ensue that records, etc are fully maintained so that the alter ego analysis never becomes a problem.
13. Consider the priority structure of the PCC, i.e. is the hub to be made liable and if so, to what extent for any cell deficiency?

14. As far as possible minimise involuntary creditors, by keeping the affairs of the company within the PCC jurisdiction. Thus taxation and government imposts, whilst involuntary, are likely to be less of a problem. Employees should also be minimised because redundancy and similar provisions can be classed as involuntary creditors so use contractors. The use of an SPV for trading purposes should minimise direct involuntary creditor involvement, such as tortious and environmental claims.
15. Be careful upon converting an ordinary company into a PCC so that no single cell becomes a 'dump cell' as this (even in its home jurisdiction) could give rise to a possible antecedent transaction claim.
16. Does the PCC regime claim extraterritoriality explicitly, as implicitly may be insufficient?
17. Does the PCC regime allow for cellular migration, especially post-formal insolvency?
18. Does the PCC regime make adequate provisions for insolvency (i.e. creating a statutory insolvency regime) within either its insolvency code (wherein it is perhaps more likely to be recognised) or in its company code (wherein it is perhaps less likely to be recognised). The difference in outcome is, however, marginal. Of more importance is a developed insolvency infrastructure, consisting of local professionals well versed in insolvency.

18.2. General Conclusion and Summary

As we have seen, cell transactions take place across many jurisdictions around the world including Europe and the US, the two leading trading blocs. A court decision that holds against the ring-fence (or internal shield) within a PCC would have a significant impact on thousands of cross border cell transactions and contracting parties will be faced with a consequence which neither they nor PCC legislation had intended. It would be a mistake for a court to look at the PCC narrowly in terms of legislation that only exists in some 'offshore islands'. Many States in the US have PCC legislation. Also, and more importantly, legislation and business forms in many jurisdictions perform a similar function. Some are difficult to distinguish from cell legislation in what they are intended to achieve, such as the US Series LLC, the Italian regime (*'dedicated assets to a specified activity'* and *'financing allocated to a specific business activity'*), the Luxembourg SICAV and securitisation regimes, the Irish Investment Fund and the French FCC (among others). They are all intended to segregate assets and liabilities for specific business transactions. Even outside these legislative regimes, there are other legal concepts that have been used to achieve the same purpose over many years and in very many commercial transactions including the use of the trusts and security arrangements (such as the collateralised contract). Deliberately disregarding the law of the jurisdiction of the PCC's incorporation and thereby the statutory ring-fence on the basis that a local court can only apply national law, would not only be an outright attack on internationalisation and principles of comity, but also disrupt cross border trade (perhaps, too, inward investment) and constitute an indirect challenge of specific rules and concepts that exist across legal systems and numerous other jurisdictions. This is so even for an involuntary creditor. It is therefore not a decision that a judge sitting in a local court room can take easily or lightly.

Appendix 1:

Specimen Articles and Memorandum for an insurance PCC

Note: The name "ABC" in the text of the documents is used for fictitious purposes. The documents in these Appendices are intended as guidance only and legal advice should be obtained in all cases based on the facts and proposed structure in question. No resemblance to any company or entity is intended nor should be inferred from any documentation. Due to the uniformity of PCC laws around the world, these documents can be amended and adapted for use locally where appropriate and in accordance with local professional advice. This is not produced, and cannot be used, for the purposes of marketing or recommending any matters addressed herein.

THE GIBRALTAR COMPANIES ACT

and

THE PROTECTED CELL COMPANIES ACT

COMPANY LIMITED BY SHARES

MEMORANDUM AND ARTICLES OF ASSOCIATION

of

ABC INSURANCE PCC LIMITED

1. The name of the Company is "**ABC INSURANCE PCC LIMITED**".

2. The Registered Office of the Company will be situated in Gibraltar.

3. The Company is a Protected Cell Company for the purposes of the Protected Cell Companies Act. The objects of the Company are:

    (1) (a) To undertake carry on and transact all classes of insurance and re-insurance business to acquire or extinguish or otherwise deal with any insurance or reinsurance made with the Company and to re-insure and co-insure all or any risks and to undertake all kinds of re-insurance and co-insurance.

(b) To undertake and carry on the business of accident, employer's liability, fidelity guarantee, third party, burglary or theft, fire, life, aircraft, marine, storm, motor vehicle, plate glass and mortgage or other investment insurance, or any of them and to transact all or any other kinds of insurances and carry on all or any class of assurance business.

(c) To carry on business as an insurance company for the purpose of insuring the members of the Company and/or any company which is a subsidiary or holding company of any member of the Company or a subsidiary of any such holding company and/or any director and/or officer and/or employee and/or agent of any member of the Company or any other such other company against risk arising from the business activities of any such insured person. To re-insure such risks or any of them in whole or in part and on such terms as the Company decides.

(2) To carry on business as an investment company.

(3) To purchase or acquire for any estate or interest and hold use deal or trade in whether with a view to profit or not and by any means property and rights of all kinds real or personal movable or immovable legal or equitable and to hold any such property and rights in the name of the Company or its nominees and to exercise and enforce all rights and powers as owners and to develop any such property or rights.

(4) To prepare any property of the Company for building or other purposes and to construct alter demolish and improve buildings and lands and to enter into contracts and arrangements of any kind with any person.

(5) To advance deposit or lend money securities and property to any person on any terms.

(6) To borrow or raise money in any manner and to secure the repayment of any money borrowed raised or owing by assignment charge hypothecation pledge or mortgage

on all or any of the property or rights of the Company present future vested or contingent including uncalled capital.

(7) To guarantee assure or become liable for or to indemnify against any loss damage or obligation of any person whether or not connected or associated in any manner with the Company (including without limitation any holding or subsidiary company of the Company and any subsidiary of any such holding company) and whether for direct or indirect consideration benefit or advantage and in connection with or support of such arrangements to assign charge hypothecate mortgage or pledge all or any of the undertaking and property of the Company (including uncalled capital) and to enter into any contracts or other transactions in relation to any such arrangements.

(8) To accept payment for any property right or undertaking sold or disposed of or dealt with by the Company either in cash or in shares or other securities whether with or without deferred or preferred rights or in debenture securities or mortgages or in any other manner.

(9) To issue and deposit any shares or securities which the Company may issue by way of charge hypothecation pledge or mortgage to secure any sum less than the nominal amount of such shares or securities and also by way of security for the performance of any obligations or liabilities of the Company or any person whether or not the Company has an interest in such person or his business.

(10) To accumulate capital for any of the purposes of the Company and to appropriate any property or rights for specific purposes conditionally or unconditionally and to allow any person having dealings with the Company to share in the Company's profits or any other advantages or benefits.

(11) To pay all or any expenses incurred in connection with formation and promotion of the Company or to contract with any other person to pay the same and to pay commissions to brokers and others for underwriting

placing selling or guaranteeing the subscription of any shares or securities of the Company or any other entity promoted by the Company.

(12) To enter into arrangements with any state government or authority national local or otherwise and to obtain therefrom all rights concessions or privileges conducive to the Company's objects and to oppose the grant to any other person or similar rights concessions and privileges.

(13) To make gifts to any persons in such circumstances and whether of cash or other property or rights as may be considered directly or indirectly conducive to any of the Company's objects and to oppose the grant to any other person of similar rights concessions and privileges.

(14) To subscribe or guarantee money for charitable or benevolent objects and to aid in the establishment and support of association for the benefit of person at any time employed by or having dealings with the Company or the dependants or families of such person and to establish and support association institutions funds and trusts to benefit employees (including directors) and their respective dependants and families at any time and to grant pensions and allowances and to make payments towards insurances for the purpose of indemnifying the Company in respect of claims for any risks or accidents to any officers or employees of the Company whether in the course of their respective employment or not and to pay premiums on any such insurances including against illness accident or death or for any other purpose.

(15) To draw make accept endorse issue discount and execute deeds agreements arrangements cheques promissory notes bills of exchange and lading warrants securities debentures and all other negotiable and transferable instruments or transactions whatsoever.

(16) To enter into any joint ventures or arrangements or agreements for sharing profits with any persons.

(17) To distribute in specie among the members by way of dividend or bonus or on a return of capital any property or rights of the Company or any proceeds of sale.

(18) To effect insurances and re-insurances against risks of every description whether for the Company or any other person.

(19) To amalgamate with any other company whose objects are or include similar to those of the Company whether by sate or by purchase (for full or partly paid shares or otherwise) of the undertaking or by sale or purchase (for full or partly paid shares or otherwise) of all or controlling interest in the shares of the Company or any such other company or partnership or any arrangement in the nature of partnership or in any other manner.

(20) To procure the Company to be recognised or registered anywhere and to carry on all or any part of the Company's business anywhere whether or not the Company has established an office or is so recognised or registered and as principals agents constructors trustees nominees or otherwise and by or through such persons and either alone or in conjunction with others.

(21) To do all such other things as the Company may think incidental to or connected with any of the above objects or conducive to their attainment or otherwise likely in any respect to be advantageous to the Company.

And it is hereby declared that the word "person" in this Memorandum (except in reference to the Company) shall include any individual partnership or other body of persons whether incorporated or not and any government state or authority and further that the objects specified in each paragraph shall be treated as independent and accordingly in no way limited or restricted by reference to or inference from any other paragraph or from the name of the Company and may be carried out as fully and construed as widely as if each paragraph defined the objects of a separate and independent company.

4. The liability of the members is limited to the amount (if any) for the time being unpaid on the shares held by each of them respectively.

5. The share capital of the Company is £[•] divided into [•] Core Shares of £1 each and [•] Unclassified Shares of £0.01 each. Unclassified Shares may be issued as Nominal Shares or as

Insurance Shares designated by reference to different cells for the purposes of The Protected Cell Companies Act as amended from time to time.

(1) The Company has power to increase or reduce its share capital and to attach to any shares in the initial or increased or reduce capital any preferred deferred qualified or special rights privileges and conditions or to subject the same to any restrictions or limitations and to consolidate or sub-divide all or any of its shares into shares of a larger or smaller denomination.

(2) The rights for the time being attached to any shares in the initial capital and to any shares having preferred deferred qualified or special rights privileges and conditions may be altered or dealt with in accordance with the Articles of Association.

6. The shares shall be paid for according to the terms of allotment or otherwise by calls as the Board of Directors shall think fit.

THE GIBRALTAR COMPANIES ACT

and

THE PROTECTED CELL COMPANIES ACT

COMPANY LIMITED BY SHARES

ARTICLES OF ASSOCIATION

of

ABC INSURANCE PCC LIMITED

DEFINITIONS

1. In these Articles the words standing in the first column of the Table next hereinafter contained shall bear the meanings set opposite to them respectively in the second column thereof, if not inconsistent with the subject or context.

Words	**Meanings**
Accounting Date	The date on which ends the financial year of the Company each year and shall be 31 December or as shall be determined by the Directors.
Annual General Meeting	The general meeting held each year pursuant to Article 50.
Article	An article in these Articles of Association.
Auditors	The auditors of the Company appointed pursuant to the provisions of the Companies Law.
Cell	A cell created by the company for the purpose of protecting Cellular Assets.
Regulatory Authority	The Gibraltar Financial Services Commission or such other body for the time being exercising regulatory responsibility for insurance companies in Gibraltar in accordance with the Insurance Companies Act of Gibraltar (as amended from time to time).
Companies Laws	The Companies Act of Gibraltar as from time to time amended supplemented, consolidated or replaced.
Directors	The directors of the Company and "Board" shall be construed accordingly.

Extraordinary General Meeting	Shall have the meaning ascribed to it by Article 53.
Insurance Share	An Unclassified Share issued as a redeemable preference share and termed an Insurance Share pursuant to Article 14.
Core Fund	The fund established pursuant to Article 10.2.
Core Share	A Core Share forming part of the initial authorised capital pursuant to Article 4 or forming part of any increase in authorised capital pursuant to Article 5.
Manager	The insurance manager licensed as such by the Financial Services Commission and appointed pursuant to Article 3.
Member	A holder of Shares.
Net Asset Value	The amount determined in respect of any Cell on any particular day as being the Net Asset Value of the Cell.
Nominal Share	An Unclassified Share issued as a Nominal Share pursuant to Article 12.
Ordinary Resolution	A resolution of the Company passed at a duly convened meeting by a show of hands or on a poll by a simple majority of the votes cast.
Protected Cell Act	The Protected Cell Companies Act as amended, supplemented, re-enacted or replaced from time to time.
Redemption Price	The amount payable on the redemption of any Insurance Share determined in accordance with Article 16.
Seal	The Common Seal (if any) of the Company.
Secretary	The secretary of the Company so appointed by the Directors.
Share	A Core Share, an Insurance Share or an Unclassified Share or any or all of them (as the case may be).
Special Resolution	Shall have the meaning ascribed thereto by the Companies Laws.
Unclassified Share	An Unclassified Share forming part of the initial authorised capital pursuant to Article 4 or forming part of any increase in authorised capital pursuant to Article 5.

2(1). In these Articles unless there be something in the subject or context inconsistent with such construction:-

(a) words importing the singular number shall be deemed to include the plural number and vice versa;

(b) words importing the masculine gender only shall include the feminine gender;

(c) words importing persons shall include companies or associations or bodies of persons, whether corporate or not;

(d) the words:-

(i) "may" shall be construed as permissive;

(ii) "shall" shall be construed as imperative;

(e) references to a class or type of Insurance Share or similar references at any time when all Insurance Shares in issue constitute a single class or type shall be construed as referring to that single class or type and the relevant provision shall be applied accordingly;

(f) subject to the foregoing provisions of this Article, any words defined in the Companies Laws, the Protected Cell Act, or the Interpretation and General Clauses Act shall bear the same meaning in these Articles.

2(2) The Regulations in Table A being the First Schedule in the Companies Laws shall not apply to the Company.

2(3) The Company is a Private Company within the meaning of the Companies Laws and accordingly the following provisions shall have effect, namely:-

(a) The right to transfer and transmit the shares of the Company is restricted in manner hereinafter provided.

(b) The number of Members of the Company (exclusive of persons who are in the employment of the Company and of persons who have been formerly in the employment of the Company who were, while in such employment and have continued after the determination of such employment to be, Members of the Company) is limited to fifty, provided that where two or more persons hold one or more Shares in the Company jointly, they shall for the purpose of this Article be treated as a Single Member.

(c) Any invitation to the public to subscribe for any shares or debentures or debenture stock of the Company is hereby prohibited.

(d) The Company shall not have power to issue Share Warrants to bearer.

MANAGEMENT

3. The Directors may appoint a Manager and may entrust to and confer upon the Manager so appointed any of the powers exercisable by them as Directors in relation to each cell other than the power to make calls or forfeit Shares upon such terms and conditions (including remuneration of the Manager) and with such restrictions as they think fit and either collaterally with or to the exclusion of their own powers.

SHARE CAPITAL

4. The authorised share capital of the Company is £[•] divided into:-

(a) [•] Core Shares of £1 each;

(b) [•] Unclassified Shares of £0.01 each;

each having attached the rights herein contained including without limitation as to votes (Article 61) as to dividends (Article 118) and upon a winding-up (Article 137).

VARIATION OF SHARE CAPITAL

5.1. The Company may from time to time by Ordinary Resolution increase its authorised capital by such sum to be divided into Shares of such amounts as the Ordinary Resolution shall prescribe. All new Shares shall be subject to the provisions of the Articles with reference to payment lien transfer transmission and otherwise.

5.2. Subject to the provisions of the Companies Laws the Company may by Special Resolution from time to time reduce its share capital in any way and in particular without prejudice to the generality of the foregoing power may:-

(a) extinguish or reduce the liability on any of its Shares in respect of share capital not paid up; or

(b) with or without extinguishing or reducing liability on any of its Shares:-

(i) cancel any paid up share capital which is lost or which is not represented by available assets; or

(ii) pay off any paid-up share capital which is in excess of the requirements of the Company

and may if and so far as is necessary alter its Memorandum of Association and Articles of Association by reducing the amount of its share capital and of its Shares accordingly.

6. The Company may from time to time by Ordinary Resolution:-

(a) consolidate and divide all or any of its share capital into Shares of larger amount than its existing Shares; and

(b) sub-divide its Shares or any of them into Shares of smaller amount than its existing Shares so however that in the sub-division the proportion between the amount paid and the amount if any unpaid on each reduced Share shall be the same as it was in the case of the Share from which the reduced Share is derived.

7. The Company may also from time to time by Ordinary Resolution cancel any Shares which at the date of the passing of the Ordinary Resolution have not been taken or agreed to be taken by any person and may diminish the amount of its share capital by the same amount of the Shares so cancelled.

ISSUE OF SHARES

8. Subject to the Companies Laws and as herein provided, any Shares in the Company for the time being unissued shall be under the control of the Directors who may allot and dispose of or grant options over the same or fractions thereof to such persons, on such terms and in such manner as they think fit and without prejudice to any special rights for the time being conferred on the holders of any Shares or class of Shares (which special rights shall not be varied or abrogated except with such consent or sanction as is provided by Article 21) any Shares in the Company may be issued with or have attached thereto such preferred, deferred or other special rights or such restrictions whether in regard to dividend, return of capital, voting or otherwise as the Company may from time to time by Special Resolution determine. Provided always that where at any time Insurance Shares of the Company in issue are divided into separate classes no class of Insurance Shares may be issued other than to or for the benefit of a single holder (other than with the consent of the holders for the time being of the

majority in nominal value of the Core Shares) and no further issues of Insurance Shares of that class may be issued other than to the existing member or members of that class.

9. The Company may on any issue of Shares pay such commission or brokerage as the Directors shall from time to time determine and as may be lawful.

CORE SHARES

10.1 Core Shares shall be issued at par or at a premium at such time and for such consideration as the Directors think fit.

10.2 The Directors shall establish a separate fund for the proceeds from allotment and issue of Core Shares and shall maintain all the assets, income, earnings, liabilities, expenses and costs of such fund segregated and separate from all other assets, income, earnings, liabilities, expenses and costs of each Cell as non-cellular assets of the Company.

UNCLASSIFIED SHARES

11. Unclassified Shares may be issued as Insurance Shares or Nominal Shares.

NOMINAL SHARES

12. Nominal Shares shall be issued only at par and only for the purpose of providing funds for the redemption of Insurance Shares. In a winding up a holder of Nominal Shares shall only be entitled to participate to the extent provided by Article 138(b). Where fractions of Insurance Shares are to be redeemed, equivalent fractions of Nominal Shares shall be issued.

13. Subject to the provisions of the Companies Laws the Company may from time to time redeem at par all or any of the Nominal Shares for the time being issued and outstanding out of any monies which may lawfully be applied for the purpose upon giving to the holders of the Nominal Shares to be redeemed not less than one month's notice provided that the holder may waive that notice.

INSURANCE SHARES

Issue

14. The Directors may from time to time determine that Insurance Shares shall be divided into separate classes. Each class of Insurance Share shall be constituted as a separate cell for the

purposes of the Protected Cell Act. In a winding up a holder of Insurance Shares shall only be entitled to participate in the assets of the Cell constituted in respect of the relevant class of Insurance Share.

15. The terms upon which and the price per share at which the first issue of Insurance Shares of any class shall be effected and the time of such issue shall be determined by the Directors.

Redemption

16.1. Insurance Shares shall be redeemed subject to the provisions of the Companies Laws and upon and subject to the following terms and conditions:

16.2. The Company shall have the right, at any time after the date of the allotment of any Insurance Share (provided it is fully paid) and with the prior written consent of the Regulatory Authority to redeem such number of Insurance Shares as it shall in, its sole discretion decide at the Net Asset Value therefor applying at the date of such redemption (or at such other value as may from time to time be agreed between the Directors and the holder or holders of such Insurance Shares) and in the case of partial redemption proportionately in respect of each holding of Insurance Shares. Not less than two weeks notice of the intention of the Company to redeem shall be given to the holders of the Insurance Shares to be redeemed. The notice shall be in writing and shall fix the time and place for such redemption.

16.3. Subject to the prior written consent of the Regulatory Authority a holder of Insurance Shares shall have the right, at any time after the date of allotment of any Insurance Share (provided it is fully paid) to redeem such number of his Insurance Shares as he may decide and as may be lawful at the Net Asset Value therefor applying at the date of such redemption (or at such other value as may from time to time be agreed between the Directors and the holder or holders of such Insurance Shares). Not less than two weeks notice of such holder's intention to redeem shall be given to the Company which shall by notice in writing to such holder set a time and place for such redemption.

16.4. At the time and place so fixed the registered holders of the Insurance Shares to be redeemed shall be bound to deliver up to the Company the relative certificates for cancellation, and the Company shall pay to them the redemption money in respect of such Insurance Shares.

16.5. At the date fixed for redemption of any of the Insurance Shares dividends shall cease to accrue on such Insurance Shares except in respect of any Insurance Shares in respect of which, on due presentation of the certificate or certificates (or an indemnity in respect thereof in form reasonably satisfactory to the Company) payment due at such redemption was refused.

16.6. If any holder of Insurance Shares shall fail or refuse to surrender the certificate or certificates for such Insurance Shares or shall fail or refuse to accept the redemption money payable in respect of them such money shall be retained and held by the Company in trust for such holder but without interest or further obligation whatever.

16.7. The Net Asset Value for each class of Insurance Shares shall be determined separately by reference to the Cell appertaining to that class of Insurance Shares and to each such determination the following provisions shall apply:-

(1) The Net Asset Value shall be determined as at such date as is, in the opinion of the Directors, the nearest practicable date to the date in relation to which and the purposes for which such valuation is to apply (the "Valuation Point").

(2) The Net Asset Value of each Cell shall be equal to the value determined by the Directors in their absolute discretion as at the Valuation Point of all the assets, less all the liabilities (actual, contingent and prospective so far as the same can be quantified), of the Company attributable to the relevant Cell as at such Valuation Point.

(3) The value of the assets of a Cell shall be determined at what the Directors in their opinion is a fair value therefor.

(4) The liabilities of a Cell shall be deemed to include all the liabilities (including such amount as the Directors determined to provide in respect of contingent or prospective liabilities) of whatsoever kind and nature

attributable to the Cell except liabilities represented by Insurance Shares. In determining the amount of such liabilities the Directors may calculate any liabilities on an estimated figure for yearly or other periods in advance and accrue the same in equal proportions over any such period.

17. Subject to any legal regulatory or administrative issues being resolved and in accordance with the relevant provsions of the Companies Laws, the nominal amounts paid up on Insurance Shares of any class shall be redeemed out of the proceeds arising from the issue of an equal number of Nominal Shares and the premium (if any) received by the Company on the issue of such Insurance Shares shall be paid from the relevant share premium account provided always that at the discretion of the Directors the nominal amounts paid up on such Insurance Shares and any such premium may be redeemed out of the profits of the Company which would otherwise have been available for dividend upon Insurance Shares of the class in question.

18. Upon the redemption of an Insurance Share of any class being effected pursuant to these Articles the Applicant shall cease to be entitled to any rights in respect thereof (excepting always to the right to receive a dividend which has become due and payable in respect thereof prior to such redemption being effected and to receive the proceeds of such redemption) and accordingly his name shall be removed from the Register with respect thereto and the Insurance Share be available for re-issue and until re-issue shall form part of the unissued share capital of the Company as an unclassified share.

Cells

19. The Directors may establish Cells (with or without share capital) and shall establish a Cell for each class of Insurance Share in issue and each Cell shall constitute a cell for the purposes of the Protected Cell Act and the Directors shall maintain all the assets, income, earnings, liabilities, expenses and costs of each Cell segregated and separate from all other assets, income, earnings, liabilities, expenses and costs of the Company and of each other Cell, and the following provisions shall apply thereto:

(a) any consideration received on, or proceeds from, the allotment and issue of a class of Insurance Shares shall be applied to the Cell established for that class of Insurance Shares, and the assets and liabilities and income and expenditure attributable thereto shall be applied only to that Cell subject to the following sub-paragraphs of this Article and on a redemption of any Insurance Share of a particular class the assets of the fund established for that class shall be reduced by the amount of the Redemption Price;

(b) for each Cell the Company shall keep separate books in which all transactions relating to that Cell shall be recorded;

(c) any asset derived from any other asset or assets (whether cash or otherwise) attributable to a Cell shall be applied in the books of the Company to the same Cell as the asset or assets from which it was derived and any increase or diminution in the value of an asset attributable to a Cell shall be applied to that Cell;

(d) in the event that there is any asset of the Company (not being proceeds received on the subscription for Core or Nominal Shares or assets derived from such proceeds for Core Shares) which the Directors do not consider readily attributable to a particular Cell or Cells the Directors shall allocate such asset to and among any one or more of the Cells in such manner and on such basis as they in their discretion deem fair and equitable and the Directors shall have the power to and may at any time and from time to time vary such basis in respect of any asset not previously allocated to one or more Cells;

(e) each Cell shall be charged with the liabilities expenses costs charges or reserves of the Company (or the appropriate proportion thereof) that are in the absolute discretion of the Directors attributable to such Cell and any liabilities, expenses, costs, charges or reserves of the Company not so attributable to any particular Cell or Cells shall be allocated and charged by the Directors between one or more Cells in such manner and on such basis as the Directors in their discretion deem fair and equitable and the Directors shall have the power to and may at any time and from time to time vary such basis including where circumstances so permit the subsequent re-allocation of such liabilities, expenses, costs, charges and reserves;

(f) where the assets of the Company attributable to the Nominal Shares give rise to any net profits, the Directors may allocate assets representing such net profits to such Cell or Cells as they deem appropriate. Where the assets of the Company attributable to the Core Shares give rise to any net profits the Directors shall allocate assets representing such net profit to the Core Fund;

(g) subject as otherwise provided in these Articles the assets held for a Cell established in respect of a class of Insurance Shares shall be applied solely in respect of Insurance Shares of the class to which that Cell was established and in the case of the fund established pursuant to Clause 10.2, the Core Shares and Articles 118 to 124 (Dividends) Article 125 (Reserve Fund) Article 126 (Capital Appreciations) Articles 127 and 128 (Capitalisation) and Articles 137 to 139 (Winding Up) shall be construed accordingly;

(h) the provisions of the Protected Cell Act shall apply to each Cell.

RESTRICTION ON FURTHER ISSUES

20. The unissued share capital shall be at the disposal of the Board which may allot grant options over or otherwise dispose of them to such persons on such terms and conditions and at such times as the Board determines.

MODIFICATION OF RIGHTS

21. Subject to the provisions of the Companies Laws, all or any of the special rights and privileges for the time being attached to any class of Shares for the time being issued may from time to time (whether or not the Company is being wound up) be altered or abrogated with the consent in writing of the holders of not less than three-fourths of the issued Shares of that class or with the sanction of a resolution passed at a separate class meeting of the holders of the Shares of that class by a majority of three-fourths of the votes cast at such meeting. For such

purposes the Directors may, with the approval of the Auditors, treat all the classes of Shares as forming one class if they consider that all such classes would be affected in the same way by the proposals under consideration, but in any other case shall treat them as separate classes.

22. The special rights and privileges attached to any class of Shares shall be deemed to be varied by:
   (a) any amendment to this Article to Article 8 or to Article 21;
   (b) by any reduction of issued share capital (excluding any redemption of Insurance Shares and excluding any reduction of cell share capital of any Cell other than the Cell established for that class of Shares);
   (c) by any merger, reconstruction or amalgamation affecting the Company or its share capital;
   (d) by any discontinuance of or change in the nature of the business of the Company.

23. Subject to Article 22 the special rights attached to any Shares or class of Shares having preferential rights (unless otherwise expressly provided by the conditions of issue of such shares) shall be deemed not to be varied by:-
   (a) the issue or redemption of any Insurance Shares in accordance with these Articles;
   (b) a reduction of issued share capital of any Cell established for any other class of Shares;
   (c) the exercise by the Directors of any discretion under these Articles or, if the Company should be wound up, the exercise by the liquidator of their powers under Article 19;
   (d) the payment of a dividend on Core Shares where the dividend is paid out of non-cellular assets; or
   (e) the removal and appointment of the Manager.

CALLS ON SHARES

24. The Directors may from time to time make calls upon the Members in respect of any moneys unpaid on their Shares (whether on account of the nominal amount of the Shares or by way of premium) and each Member shall (subject to being given at least fifteen days notice specifying the time or times and place of payment) pay to the Company at the time or times

and place so specified the amount called on his Shares. A call may be made payable by instalments. A call may be revoked or postponed as the Directors may determine.

25. A call shall be deemed to have been made at the time when the resolution of the Directors authorising the call was passed.

26. The joint holders of a Share shall be jointly and severally liable to pay all calls and other moneys due in respect thereof.

27. If a sum called in respect of a Share is not paid before or on the day appointed for payment thereof the person from whom the sum is due shall pay interest on the sum from the day appointed for payment thereof to the time of actual payment at such rate as the Directors may determine but the Directors shall be at liberty to waive payment of such interest wholly or in part.

28. Any sum which by the terms of issue of a Share becomes payable upon allotment or at any fixed date whether on account of the nominal value of the Share or by way of premium shall for all the purposes of these Articles be deemed to be a call duly made and payable on the date on which by the terms of issue the same becomes payable and in the case of non-payment all the relevant provisions of these Articles as to payment of interest forfeiture or otherwise shall apply as if such sum had become payable by virtue of a call duly made and notified.

29. The Directors may make arrangements on the issue of Shares for a difference between the holders of such Shares in the amount of calls to be paid and in the times of payment.

30. The Directors may if they think fit receive from any Member willing to advance the same all or any part of the money uncalled and unpaid upon the Shares held by him beyond the sums actually called up thereon as a payment and such payment in advance of calls shall extinguish so far as the same shall extend the liability upon the Shares in respect of which it is advanced and the Company may (until the same would but for such advance become presently payable) pay interest at such rate as the Directors shall think fit upon the money so received or so much thereof as from time to time exceeds the amount of the calls then made upon the Shares in respect of which it has been received provided always any amount paid

up in advance of calls shall not entitle the holder of the Shares upon which such amount is paid to participate in respect thereof in any dividend until the same would but for such advance become payable.

FORFEITURE OF SHARES

31. If a Member fails to pay any call or instalment of a call on the day appointed for payment thereof the Directors may at any time thereafter during such time as any part of such call or instalment remains unpaid serve a notice on him requiring payment of so much of the call or instalment as is unpaid together with any accrued interest and any costs charges and expenses incurred by the Company by reason of such non-payment.

32. The notice shall name a further day (not earlier than fourteen days from the date of serving thereof) on or before which, and the place where, the payment required by the notice is to be made and shall state that in the event of non-payment at or before the time and the place appointed the Shares on which the call was made will be liable to be forfeited.

33. If the requirements of any such notice as aforesaid are not complied with any Share in respect of which such notice has been given may at any time thereafter before payment of all calls instalments interest costs charges and expenses due in respect thereof has been made be forfeited by a resolution of the Directors to that effect and such forfeiture shall include all dividends which shall have been declared on the forfeited Shares and not actually paid before forfeiture.

34. A forfeited Share shall become the property of the Company and may be sold re-allotted or otherwise disposed of either to the person who was before forfeiture the holder thereof or entitled thereto or to any other person upon such terms and in such manner as the Directors shall think fit and whether with or without all or any part of the amount previously paid up on the Share or credited as so paid up and at any time before a sale re-allotment or disposition the forfeiture may be cancelled on such terms as the Directors think fit. The Directors may if necessary authorise some person to transfer a forfeited Share to any other person as aforesaid.

35. A person whose Shares have been forfeited shall cease to be a Member in respect of the forfeited Shares but shall notwithstanding the forfeiture remain liable to pay to the Company all moneys which at the date of forfeiture were presently payable by him to the Company in respect of the Shares with interest thereon from the date of forfeiture until payment at such rate as the Directors may determine and the Directors may enforce payment without any allowance for the value of the Shares at the time of forfeiture.

36. A record in the minute book of the Company that a Share has been duly forfeited in pursuance of these Articles and stating the time when it was forfeited shall be conclusive evidence of the facts therein stated as against all persons claiming to be entitled to the Share adversely to the forfeiture thereof and such record and the receipt of the Company for the consideration (if any) given for the Share on a sale re-allotment or disposal thereof together with the certificate (if issued) for the Share delivered to the purchaser or allottee thereof shall (subject to the execution of a transfer if the same be so required) constitute a good title to the Share.

37. The person to whom the Share is sold re-allotted or disposed of in accordance with the immediately preceding Article hereto shall be registered as the holder of the Share and not be bound to see to the application of the consideration (if any) nor shall his title to the Share be affected by any irregularity or invalidity in the proceedings in reference to the forfeiture sale re-allotment or disposal of the Share.

38. The provisions of these Articles as to forfeiture shall apply in the case of non-payment of any sums which by the terms of issue of a Share become payable at a fixed time whether on account of the nominal amount of the Share or by way of premium as if the same had been payable by virtue of a call duly made and notified.

LIEN

39. Without prejudice to the provisions of Articles 31 to 38 and in addition thereto the Company shall have a first and paramount lien and charge on all the Shares registered in the name of a Member (whether solely or jointly with others) for his debts liabilities and engagements (either alone or jointly with any

other person and whether a Member or not) to or with the Company whether the period for payment or discharge thereof shall have actually arrived or not. Such lien shall extend to all dividends from time to time declared in respect of such Shares. Unless otherwise agreed the registration of a transfer of Shares shall operate as a waiver of the Company's lien (if any) on such Shares.

40. For the purpose of enforcing such lien the Company may sell (in such manner as the Directors think fit) any Shares on which the Company has a lien but no sale shall be made unless some sum in respect of which the lien exists is presently payable nor until the expiration of fourteen days after a notice in writing stating and demanding payment of the sum presently payable and giving notice of intention to sell in default shall have been served on the holder for the time being of the Shares or the person entitled by reason of his death or bankruptcy to the Shares. For the purposes of giving effect to any such sale the Directors may authorise some person to transfer to the purchaser thereof the Shares so sold.

41. The net proceeds of such sale after payment of the cost of such sale shall be applied in or towards payment or satisfaction of the debt or liability in respect whereof the lien exists so far as the same is presently payable and any residue shall (subject to a like lien for debts or liabilities not presently payable as existed upon the Shares prior to the sale) be paid to the person entitled to the Shares at the time of the sale. The purchaser shall be registered as the holder of the Share transferred and he shall not be bound to see to the application of the purchase money nor shall his title to the Shares be affected by any irregularity or invalidity in the proceedings in reference to the sale.

TRANSFER AND TRANSMISSION OF SHARES

42. All transfers of shares may be effected by transfer in writing in any form as the Board may accept. Any instrument of transfer shall be signed by or on behalf of the transferor who shall be deemed to remain the holder until the name of the transferee is entered in the Register.

43. Every instrument of transfer shall be left at the Registered Office or such other place as the Board may prescribe with the certificate of every share to be transferred and such other

evidence as the Board may reasonably require to prove the title of the transferor or his right to transfer the shares; and the transfer and certificate shall remain in the custody of the Board but shall be at all reasonable times produced at the request and expense of the transferor or transferee or their respective representatives. A new certificate shall be delivered to the transferee after the transfer is completed and registered on his application and when necessary a balance certificate shall be delivered if required by him in writing. A fee determined by the Board may be charged for each transfer and also for the registration of every probate notice power of attorney or document tendered for registration and shall be paid before registration.

44. Subject as hereinafter provided, no transfer of any share in the capital of the Company shall be made or registered without the previous consent of the Board which may in its absolute discretion and without assigning any reason therefor, decline to register any transfer of any share whether or not it is a fully paid share. The Board shall not give such consent unless the shares to be transferred have been offered for transfer to the existing shareholders of the same class for a price not exceeding the nominal value and the other shareholders have declined in writing to the Board such offer.

45. Subject to any requirement from time to time imposed by the Board, any member being a body corporate (the "Original Member") shall be entitled to transfer all of its shares to any other body corporate which is for the time being its holding or subsidiary company or another subsidiary of its holding company (each such body corporate being hereinafter referred to as a "Group Company") but if a Group Company whilst it is a member shall cease to be a Group Company in relation to the Original Member it shall within 21 days of so ceasing transfer the shares held by it to the Original Member or any Group Company of the Original Member.

46. Subject to any requirement from time to time imposed by the Board, any member may transfer shares to a nominee or trustee for that member alone and any nominee or trustee of any person or persons may at any time transfer any shares to that other person or persons or to another nominee or trustee for

that other person or persons provided always no beneficial interest in such shares passes by reason of such transfer.

47. The Company shall keep the Register in accordance with the Companies Laws.

48. On the death of a member the survivors where the deceased was a joint holder and the executors of the deceased where he was a sole holder shall be the only persons recognised by the Company as having any title to or interest in his shares; but nothing herein shall release the estate of a deceased joint holder from any liability in respect of any share jointly held.

49. A person entitled to shares in consequence of death disability or insolvency shall not be entitled to receive notice of or attend or to vote at any meeting or (save as regards the receipt of such dividends as the Board shall not elect to retain) to exercise any of the rights of a holder unless and until he shall have been registered as holder.

GENERAL MEETINGS

50. The Company shall in each year hold a general meeting as its Annual General Meeting in addition to any other meeting in that year. Annual General Meetings shall be held at such time and place in Gibraltar as may be determined by the Directors.

51. Notices of every general meeting shall be given in any manner herein authorised to every Member and to:-

(a) each Director and Alternate Director of the Company;

(b) the Auditors;

(c) the Manager; and

(d) such other person(s) as the Directors shall at any time and from time to time determine.

52. Any Member present either personally or by proxy at any meeting of the Company shall for all purposes be deemed to have received due notice of such meetings and where requisite of the purposes for which such meeting was convened.

53. All general meetings (other than Annual General Meetings) shall be called Extraordinary General Meetings, may be convened whenever the Directors think fit and such meetings must be held in Gibraltar.

54. The number of Members entitled to requisition a meeting, the number forming a quorum and the number entitled to demand a poll shall be as stated in the Companies Laws provided that in the case of any class meeting the numbers therein referred to shall be calculated by reference to the issued Shares of the class in question and not by reference to the issued Shares of the Company.

55. All business shall be deemed special that is transacted at an Extraordinary General Meeting, and also all business that is transacted at an Annual General Meeting with the exception of declaring or approving the payment of dividends the consideration of the accounts and reports of the Directors, the Manager and Auditors the election of Directors and Auditors in place of those retiring and the appointment and the fixing of the remuneration of the Directors and the Auditors.

56. If a poll is validly demanded it shall be taken in such a manner and at such place as the chairman of the meeting may direct (including the use of ballot or voting papers or tickets) and the result of a poll shall be deemed to be a resolution of the meeting at which the poll was demanded.

57. The chairman of the meeting may in the event of a poll appoint scrutineers and may adjourn the meeting to some place and time fixed by him for the purpose of declaring the result of the poll.

58. A poll demanded on any question other than the election of a chairman of the meeting or an adjournment shall be taken at such time and place as the chairman of the meeting directs not being more than thirty days from the day of the meeting or adjourned meeting at which the poll was demanded.

59. The demand for a poll shall not prevent the continuance of a meeting for the transaction of any business other than the question on which the poll was demanded.

60. A demand for a poll may be withdrawn and no notice need be given of a poll not taken immediately.

<u>VOTES OF MEMBERS</u>

61. Subject to any special rights or restrictions for the time being attached to any class of Shares, at general meetings of the Company:-

(a) holders of Nominal Shares shall not be entitled to vote in respect thereof;

(b) holders of Core Shares shall be entitled

(i) on a show of hands (if present in person) to one vote;

(ii) on a poll (if present in person or by proxy) to one vote in respect of each Core Share held by him.

(c) holders of Insurance Shares shall not be entitled to vote at General Meetings except at separate class Meetings of the holders of Insurance Shares or any class of Insurance Shares.

62. In the case of joint holders of a Share such persons shall not have the right of voting individually but shall elect one of their number to represent them and vote in their names in default of which the vote of the first-named who tenders a vote whether in person or by proxy shall be accepted to the exclusion of the votes of the other joint holders and for this purpose "first-named" shall be determined by the order in which the names stand in the Register in respect of the Shares.

63. Guardians in the names of their wards and attornies in the names of their principals may vote at General Meetings and this provision shall be deemed also to apply mutatis mutandis to persons exercising the functions or similar functions being appointed under the laws of any other jurisdiction provided always such evidence as the Directors may require of the authority of the person claiming to vote whether under this Article shall have been deposited at the registered office of the Company not less than forty-eight hours before the time of holding the meeting or adjourned meeting at which such person claims to vote.

64. No Member shall unless the Directors otherwise determine be entitled to vote at any general meeting either personally or by proxy or to exercise any privileges as a Member unless all calls and other sums presently payable by him in respect of Shares in the Company of which he is the holder or one of the joint holders have been paid.

65. No objection shall be raised to the qualification of any voter except at the meeting or adjourned meeting at which the vote objected to is given or tendered and every vote not disallowed

at such meeting shall be valid for all purposes. Any such objection made in due time shall be referred to the chairman of the meeting whose decision shall be final and conclusive.

66. Any instrument appointing a proxy shall be in writing under the hand of the appointor or of his attorney duly authorised in writing or if the appointor is a corporation either under its common seal or under the hand of an officer or attorney so authorised.

67. Any person (whether a Member of the Company or not) may be appointed to act as proxy. A Member may appoint more than one proxy to attend on the same occasion.

68. The instrument appointing a proxy and the power of attorney or other authority (if any) under which it is signed or a notarially certified copy of such power or authority shall be deposited at the registered office of the Company or at such other place as is specified for that purpose in the notice of meeting or in the instrument of proxy issued by the Company not less than forty-eight hours before the time appointed for holding the meeting at which the person named in the instrument proposes to vote and in default the instrument of proxy shall not be treated as valid. No instrument appointing a proxy shall be valid after the expiration of twelve months from the date named in it as the date of its execution except at an adjourned meeting or on a poll demanded at a meeting or an adjourned meeting in cases where the meeting was originally held within twelve months from such date.

69. An instrument of proxy shall be in the usual common form or such other form as the Directors may approve.

70. The Directors may at the expense of the Company send by post or otherwise to the Members instruments of proxy (with or without prepaid postage for their return) for use at any general meeting or any meeting of any class of Members of the Company either in blank or nominating in the alternative any one or more of the Directors or any other persons. If for the purpose of any meeting invitations to appoint a proxy or person or one of a number of persons specified in the invitations are issued at the expense of the Company such invitations shall be issued to all (and not to some only) of the

Members entitled to be sent a notice of the meeting and to vote thereat by proxy.

71. A vote given in accordance with the terms of an instrument of proxy shall be valid notwithstanding the death or insanity of the principal or the revocation of the instrument of proxy or of the authority under which the instrument of proxy was executed or of the transfer of the Share in respect of which the instrument of proxy is given provided always no intimation in writing of such death insanity revocation or transfer shall have been received by the Company at its registered office before the commencement of the meeting or adjourned meeting at which the instrument of proxy is used.

72. Any corporation which is a Member of the Company may by resolution of its Directors or other governing body or officers authorised by such body authorise such person as it thinks fit to act as its representative at any meeting of the Company or at any meeting of any class of Members of the Company and the person so authorised shall be entitled to exercise the same power on behalf of the corporation which he represents as that corporation could exercise if it were an individual Member of the Company.

DIRECTORS

73. Unless otherwise determined by the Members by Ordinary Resolution in general meeting the number of Directors shall not be less than two and if there are only two they shall both be residents of Gibraltar. The first Directors shall be appointed in writing by the subscribers to the Memorandum of Association. Furthermore, the Board of Directors shall comprise such number of Gibraltar residents as shall constitute a majority. They shall hold office until they resign or are disqualified in accordance with Article 84 hereof.

74. Subject to the provisions of Article 84 the Directors shall have power at any time and from time to time to appoint any person to be a Director either to fill a casual vacancy or as an addition to the existing Directors. Any Director so appointed shall hold office only until the next following Annual General Meeting and shall then be eligible for re-election. The holders of the majority in nominal value of the Core Shares for the time being in issue shall have the right by notice in writing to the

Company to appoint additional Directors or to remove any Director from office.

75. The Directors shall be entitled to such remuneration as may be voted to them by the Company in general meeting. Such remuneration shall be deemed to accrue from day to day. The Directors may also be paid all travelling hotel and other expenses properly incurred by them in attending and returning from meetings of the Directors or any committee of the Directors or general meetings of the Company or in connection with the business of the Company.

76. The Directors may grant special remuneration to any Director who, being so called upon, shall be willing to render any special or extra services to the Company. Such special remuneration may be made payable to such Director in addition to or in substitution for his ordinary remuneration as a Director, and may be made payable by a lump sum or by way of salary or commission or by any or all of those modes or otherwise.

77. A Director need not be a Member of the Company.

ALTERNATE DIRECTORS

78. Each Director shall have the power to nominate another Director or any other person to act as an Alternate Director and at his discretion to remove such Alternate Director and on such appointment being made the Alternate Director may in the absence or incapacity of the Director he represents attend any meeting of Directors and exercise and discharge all the functions powers and duties of a Director of the Company. A Director who is resident of Gibraltar may not appoint an Alternate who is not also a resident of Gibraltar.

79. Any Director of the Company who is appointed as Alternate Director shall be entitled at a Meeting of the Directors to cast a vote of his appointor in addition to the vote to which he is entitled in his own capacity as a Director of the Company and for quorum purposes shall count as a separate and additional Director present but not so that less than two individuals shall be capable of constituting a quorum.

80. Any person appointed as an Alternate Director shall vacate such office as such Alternate Director if and when the Director for whom he has been appointed vacates his office as Director.

81. The remuneration of such an Alternate Director shall be payable out of the remuneration payable to the Director appointing him and the proportion thereof shall be agreed between them.

82. Every instrument appointing an Alternate Director shall be in such form as the Directors may determine.

83. The appointment of an Alternate Director and any revocation thereof shall take effect when lodged at the registered office of the Company.

DISQUALIFICATION AND RETIREMENT OF DIRECTORS

84. The office of a Director shall be vacated in any of the following events namely if:-

(a) he resigns his office by notice in writing by him and left at the registered office of the Company;

(b) he becomes bankrupt or makes any arrangements or composition with his creditors generally;

(c) he becomes of unsound mind;

(d) he is absent from Meetings of the Directors for four successive meetings without leave expressed by a resolution of the board and the Directors resolve that he vacate his office;

(e) he be requested by all the other Directors (not being less than three in number) to vacate his office; or

(f) he is removed from office by Resolution of the holders of Core Shares at any class meeting of such holders or by writing in accordance with Article 74.

85. The Directors holding office at the date of the adoption of these Articles shall continue to hold office subject to Article 84.

86. At least seven days' previous notice in writing shall be given to the Company of the intention of any Member to propose any person other than a retiring Director for election to the office of Director and the willingness of such person to be so elected provided always if the Members present at a general meeting unanimously consent the chairman of such meeting may waive the said notice and submit to the meeting the name of any person so nominated.

TRANSACTIONS WITH DIRECTORS

87. A Director may hold any other office or place of profit under the Company (other than the office of Auditor) in conjunction with his office of Director on such terms as to tenure of office or otherwise as the Directors may determine.

88. No Director or intending Director shall be disqualified by his office from contracting with the Company as vendor purchaser or otherwise nor shall any such contract or any contract or arrangement entered into by or on behalf of the Company in which any Director is in any way interested render the Director liable to account to the Company for any profit realised by any such contract or arrangement by reason of such Director holding that office or of the fiduciary relationship thereby established but the nature of his interest must be declared by him at the meeting of the Directors at which the question of entering into the contract or agreement is first taken into consideration or if the Director was not at the date of that meeting interested in the proposed contract or arrangement then at the next meeting of the Directors held after he becomes so interested. A general notice in writing given to the Directors by any Director to the effect that he is a member of any specified company or firm and is to be regarded as interested in any contract or arrangement which may thereafter be made with that company or firm shall (if the Director shall give the same at a meeting of the Directors or shall take reasonable steps to procure that the same is brought up and read at the next meeting of the Directors after it is given) be deemed a sufficient declaration of interest in relation to any contract or arrangement so made.

89. Save as in these Articles provided, a Director shall not vote in respect of any contract or arrangement or any other proposal whatsoever in which he has any material interest otherwise than by virtue of his interest in Shares or debentures or other securities of or otherwise through the Company or by virtue of his employment by or shareholding in a company associated with the Company. A Director shall not be counted in the quorum at a meeting in relation to any resolution on which he is debarred from voting.

90. A Director shall (in the absence of some other material interest than is indicated below) be entitled to vote (and be counted in the quorum) in respect of any resolution concerning any of the following matters namely:-

(a) the giving of any security or indemnity to him in respect of money lent or obligations incurred by him at the request of or for the benefit of the Company or any of its subsidiaries;

(b) the giving of any security or indemnity to a third party in respect of a debt or obligation of the Company or any of its subsidiaries for which he himself has assumed responsibility in whole or in part under a guarantee or indemnity or by the giving of security;

(c) any proposal concerning an offer of Shares or debentures or other securities of or by the Company or any of its subsidiaries for subscription or purchase in which offer he is or is to be interested as a participant in the underwriting or sub-underwriting thereof;

(d) any proposal concerning any other company in which he is interested, directly or indirectly and whether as an officer or shareholder or otherwise howsoever, provided that he is not the holder of or beneficially interested in one per cent, or more of the issued Shares of such company (or of any third company through which his interest is derived) or of the voting rights available to Members of the relevant company (any such interest being deemed for the purpose of this Article to be a material interest in all circumstances).

91. Where proposals are under consideration concerning the appointment (including fixing or varying the terms of appointment) of two or more Directors to offices or employment with the Company or any company in which the Company is interested such proposals may be divided and considered in relation to each Director separately and in such case each of the Directors concerned (if not debarred from voting under the provisions of Article 90(d)) shall be entitled to vote (and be counted in the quorum) in respect of each resolution except that concerning his own appointment.

92. If any question shall arise at any meeting as to the materiality of a Directors interest or as to the entitlement of any Director to vote and such question is not resolved by his voluntarily agreeing to abstain from voting, such question shall be referred to the chairman of the meeting and his ruling in relation to any other Director shall be final and conclusive except in a case where the nature or extent of the interests of the Director concerned have not been fairly disclosed.

93. The Company may by Ordinary Resolution suspend or relax the provisions of Articles 88 and 89 to any extent or ratify any transaction not duly authorised by reason of a contravention of any of the said paragraphs.

94. Any Director may act by himself or his firm in a professional capacity for the Company and he or his firm shall be entitled to remuneration for professional services as if he were not a Director provided always nothing herein contained shall authorise a Director or his firm to act as Auditor to the Company.

95. Any Director may continue to be or become director managing director manager or other officer or member of any company in which the Company may be interested and (unless otherwise agreed) no such Director shall be accountable for any remuneration or other benefits received by him as a Director managing director manager or other officer or member of any such other company.

96. The Directors may exercise the voting power conferred by the share in any other company held or owned by the Company or exercisable by them as directors of such other company in such manner in all respect as they think fit (including the exercise thereof in favour of any resolution appointing themselves or any of them director managing director managers or other officer of such company or voting or providing for the payment or remuneration to the directors managing director Manager or other officer of such company).

POWERS OF DIRECTORS

97.1. The business of the Company shall be managed in Gibraltar by the Directors who may exercise all the powers of the Company as are not by the Companies Laws or these Articles required to be exercised by the Company in general meeting subject nevertheless to any relevant provisions of the Companies Laws and these Articles and to such regulations as may be prescribed by the Company in general meeting but no regulations made by the Company in general meeting shall invalidate any prior act of the Directors which would have been valid if such regulations had not been made.

97.2. In all transactions with third parties the Directors shall inform such third party that the Company is a Protected Cell Company, and unless the transaction is not in respect of any particular Cell identify or specify the Cell in respect of which the third party is transacting.

98. The Directors may from time to time and at any time by power of attorney attested by any person duly authorised in that regard appoint any company firm or person or any fluctuating body of persons whether nominated directly or indirectly by the Directors to be the attorney or attorneys of the Company for such purposes and with such powers authorities and discretion (not exceeding those vested in or exercisable by the Directors under these Articles) and for such period and subject to such conditions as they may think fit and any such other power of attorney may contain such provisions for the protection and convenience of persons dealing with any such attorneys as the Directors may think fit and may also authorise any such attorney to sub-delegate all or any of the powers authorities and discretions vested in him.

99. (1) All cheques, promissory notes, drafts bills of exchange and other negotiable or transferable instruments and all receipts for moneys paid to the Company shall be signed drawn accepted endorsed or otherwise executed as the case may be in such manner as the Directors shall from time to time by resolution determine.

(2) The Directors shall ensure that at all times cellular assets are kept separate from and separately identifiable from non-cellular assets and that assets attributable to each Cell are separate and separately identifiable from cellular assets attributable to other Cells.

(3) The Directors shall identify or specify the Cell in respect of which or with which any third party is transacting and

inform such third party accordingly unless a third party is transacting otherwise than with a specified Cell.

(4) The Board may from time to time appoint and remove an investment manager or investment managers for the purpose of managing the Company's investments.

PROCEEDINGS OF DIRECTORS

100. The Directors shall meet together in Gibraltar for the dispatch of business adjourn and otherwise regulate their meetings as they think fit. Questions arising at any meeting shall be determined by a majority of votes. In case of an equality of votes the chairman shall have a second or casting vote. A Director may and the Secretary on the requisition of a Director shall at any time summon a meeting of the Directors.

101. The quorum necessary for the transaction of business of the Directors may be fixed by the Directors and unless so fixed at any other number shall be two, provided that where there are only two such directors at any meeting forming a quorum each such director must be resident in Gibraltar.

102. The continuing Directors or a sole continuing Director may act notwithstanding any vacancies in their number but if and so long as the number of Directors is reduced below the minimum number fixed by or in accordance with these Articles the continuing Directors or Director may act for the purpose of filling up vacancies in their number or of summoning general meetings of the Company, but not for any other purpose. If there be no Directors or Director able or willing to act, then any two Members may summon a general meeting for the purposes of appointing Directors.

103. The Directors may from time to time elect and remove a chairman and if they think fit a deputy chairman of the board of Directors and determine the period for which they respectively are to hold office. The chairman or failing him the deputy chairman shall preside at all meetings of the Directors but if there be no chairman or deputy chairman or if at any meeting the chairman or deputy chairman be not present within five minutes after the time appointed for holding the same the Directors present may choose one of their number to be chairman of the Meeting.

104. A resolution in writing signed by all the directors shall not be as valid and effectual as a resolution passed at a meeting of the Directors duly convened.

105. A meeting of Directors or of a committee may not be validly held if the Directors are not in the same place in Gibraltar.

106. A meeting of the Directors for the time being at which a quorum is present shall be competent to exercise all powers and discretions for the time being exercisable by the Directors.

107. The Directors may delegate any of their powers to committees consisting of such of their body as they think fit. Any committee so formed shall in the exercise of the powers so delegated conform to any regulations that may be imposed on them by the Directors.

108. The meetings and proceedings of any such committee consisting of two or more Directors shall be governed by quorum and other provisions of these Articles regulating the meetings and proceedings of the Directors so far as the same are applicable and are not superseded by any regulations made by the Directors under the last preceding Article.

109. All acts done by any meeting of Directors or of a committee of Directors in Gibraltar or by any person acting as a Director shall notwithstanding that it be afterwards discovered that there was some defect in the appointment of any such Director or person acting as aforesaid or that they or any of them were disqualified or had vacated office or were not entitled to vote be as valid as if every such person had been duly appointed and was qualified and had continued to be a Director and had been entitled to vote.

BORROWING POWERS

110. Subject as hereinafter provided the Directors may exercise all the powers of the Company to borrow or raise money and secure any debt or obligation of or binding on the Company in any manner including by the issue of debentures (perpetual or otherwise) and to secure the repayment of any money borrowed raised or owing by mortgage charge pledge or lien upon the whole or any part of the property or assets (whether present or future) of the Company and also by a similar mortgage charge pledge or lien to secure and guarantee the

performance of any obligation or liability undertaken by the Company or any third party provided always that no money shall be borrowed by or on behalf of any Cell without the consent in writing of the holders of a majority of the Insurance Shares of that Cell in issue. Cellular assets may not be used to guarantee or secure the repayment of any borrowing save in respect of borrowing made for the benefit of that Cell.

MANAGING DIRECTORS

111. The Directors may from time to time appoint one or more of their body to be a managing director of the Company and may fix his or their remuneration, provided that any such person must be resident only in Gibraltar.

112. Every managing director shall be liable to be dismissed or removed by the board of Directors at any time. The board may however enter into an agreement with any person who is or is about to become a managing director with regard to the length and terms of his employment but so that the remedy of any such person for any breach of such agreement shall be in damages only and he shall have no right or claim to continuance in such office contrary to the will of the Directors or of the Company in general meeting.

113. Should the Articles be amended so as to require retirement of Directors by rotation a managing director shall not while he continues to hold that office be liable to retire by rotation and he shall not be taken into account in determining the rotation in which the other Directors shall retire (except for the purpose of fixing the number to retire in each year) but he shall be subject to the same provisions as to removal and disqualification as the other Directors and if for any reason he ceases to hold the office of Director he shall ipso facto cease to be a managing director.

114. The Directors may from time to time entrust to and confer upon the managing director or managing directors all or any of the powers of the Directors (not including the power to make calls forfeit Shares borrow money or issue debentures) that they may think fit but the exercise of all powers by the managing director or managing directors shall be subject to all such regulations and restrictions as the Directors may from time to time make and impose and the said powers may at any time be withdrawn revoked or varied.

SECRETARY

115. The Directors shall appoint a Secretary and may also appoint an assistant secretary, provided that any such person must be resident only in Gibraltar. Anything required or authorised to be done by or in the presence of the Secretary may if the office is vacant or the Secretary is absent or incapable of acting be done by or in the presence of any assistant secretary or if there is no assistant secretary present or capable of acting by or in the presence of any officer of the Company authorised generally or specially in that behalf by the Directors and any such assistant secretary or officer shall in such circumstances be a Secretary of the Company for the purposes of the Company Law provided that any provisions of these Articles requiring or authorising a thing to be done by or to a Director and the Secretary shall not be satisfied by its being done by or to the same person acting both as Director and as or in the place of the Secretary.

116. No person shall be appointed to hold office as Secretary who is:-

(a) the sole Director of the Company; or

(b) a corporation the sole Director of which is the sole Director of the Company; or

(c) the sole Director of a corporation which is the sole Director of the Company; or

(d) not a resident of Gibraltar.

THE SEAL

117. If the Directors resolve to adopt a Seal then the Directors shall provide for the safe custody of the Seal and the Seal shall never be used except by the authority of a resolution of the Directors or of a committee of the Directors authorised by the Directors in that behalf. The Directors may from time to time make such regulations as they see fit (subject to the provisions of these Articles relating to share certificates) determining the persons and the number of such persons in whose presence the Seal shall be used and (subject as aforesaid) until otherwise determined the Seal shall be affixed in the presence of two Directors or of one Director and the Secretary or some other persons duly authorised by the Directors.

DIVIDENDS

118. No dividends shall be paid on Nominal Shares. Notwithstanding any provision of these Articles, the Insurance Shares shall be undated and non-cumulative.

119. The Company may at a separate meeting of the holders of a class of Insurance Shares or of the holders of the Core Shares by Ordinary Resolution declare dividends on such class of Insurance Shares or Core Shares (as the case may be) but no dividend shall exceed the amount recommended by the Directors. The Directors may from time to time pay such interim dividends as appear to the board of Directors to be justified by the profits of the Company. No dividend shall be declared or paid other than from the profits or gains resulting from the Company's business.

120. If at any time the Insurance Shares in issue are divided into separate classes different amounts of dividends may be payable in respect of the separate classes.

121 Subject to the provisions of Article 119 all Insurance Shares of any class in issue and all Core Shares in issue at the date of the declaration of a dividend shall rank for such dividend in proportion to the amount paid up on such shares (otherwise than in advance of calls) respectively and (unless otherwise determined by the Directors) shall rank for dividend from the beginning of the Accounting Period in which they are issued.

122. The Directors may deduct from any dividend or other moneys payable to any Member on or in respect of an Insurance Share or a Core Share (as the case may be) all sums of money (if any) presently payable by him to the Company on account of calls or otherwise in relation to the Insurance Shares or the Core Shares (as the case may be) of the Company.

123. All unclaimed dividends may be invested or otherwise made use of by the Directors for the benefit of the Company until claimed. No dividends shall bear interest against the Company. The payment by the Directors of any unclaimed dividend or other moneys payable on or in respect of a Insurance Share or on or in respect of a Core Share into a separate account shall not constitute the Company a trustee in respect thereof and any

dividend unclaimed after a period of six years from the date of declaration shall be forfeited and shall revert to the Company.

124. Any resolution declaring a dividend on the Insurance Shares or the Core Shares whether a resolution of the Company in general meeting or a resolution of the Directors, or any resolution of the Directors for the payment of a fixed dividend on the date prescribed for the payment thereof, may specify that the same shall be payable to the persons registered as the holders of such Insurance Shares or Core Shares (as the case may be) at the close of business on a particular date, notwithstanding that it may be a date prior to that on which the resolution is passed (or, as the case may be, that prescribed for payment of a fixed dividend), and thereupon the dividend shall be payable to them in accordance with their respective holdings so registered, but without prejudice to the rights inter se in respect of such dividend of transferors and transferees of any Shares.

RESERVE FUND

125. Before the declaration of a dividend in respect of any Cell the Directors may set aside any part of the net profits attributable to that Cell to create a reserve fund for that Cell and may apply the same either by employing it in the business of the Company or by investing it in such manner as they think fit. Such reserve fund may be applied for the purpose of maintaining assets of the Cell replacing wasting assets meeting contingencies forming an insurance fund or for any other purpose for which the net profits attributable to that Cell may be lawfully used and until the same shall be applied it shall be deemed to remain undivided profits. The Directors may also carry forward to the accounts of the succeeding year or years any balance of profits which they shall not think fit either to divide or to place to reserve.

CAPITAL APPRECIATIONS

126. All appreciations or surpluses (other than appreciations or surpluses which the Directors shall resolve to distribute by way of dividend) realised upon or derived from the sale, realisation or payment-off of property or investments, or from any variation or transposition of property or investments, or other realisations of capital assets, and any other sums (other than

appreciations or surpluses which the Directors shall resolve to distribute by way of dividend) which in the opinion of the Directors are of a capital nature shall be applied within the relevant Cell in accordance with the Insurance Companies Act.

CAPITALISATION

127. The Company may at a separate meeting of the holders of a class of Insurance Shares in the case of a resolution affecting a Cell or the holders of Core Shares in the case of a resolution affecting the Core Fund by Ordinary Resolution but only upon the recommendation of the Directors resolve that it is desirable to capitalise and set free any part of the amount:-

(a) standing to the credit of any of the reserve accounts of that Cell or the Core Fund as the case may be (excluding the share premium account but including capital reserve);

(b) standing to the credit of the profit and loss account of that Cell or the Core Fund as the case may be; or

(c) which is otherwise available for distribution from that Cell or the Core Fund as the case may be but is not required for the payment of any dividend on that class of Insurance Shares or Core Shares (as the case may be) with a preferential right to dividend

and accordingly that this sum or these sums be set free for distribution amongst the holders of the relevant class of Insurance Shares or Core Shares (as the case may be) who would have been entitled thereto if it had been distributed by way of dividend and in the same proportion on condition that the same be not paid in cash but be applied either in or towards paying up any amounts for the time being unpaid on any such Insurance Shares or Core Shares (as the case may be) or in paying up in full unissued Insurance Shares of the relevant class or Core Shares (as the case may be) to be allotted and distributed (credited as fully paid up) to and amongst the holders of such Insurance Shares or Core Shares (as the case may be) in the proportion aforesaid or partly in one way and party in the other.

128. Whenever such a resolution as aforesaid shall have been passed the Directors shall make all appropriations and applications of the undivided profits resolved to be capitalised thereby and all

allotments and issues of fully paid Insurance Shares (if any) or Core Shares (as the case may be) and generally shall do all acts and things required to give effect thereto with full power to the Directors to authorise any person to enter on behalf of all the Members entitled thereto into an agreement with the Company providing for the allotment to them respectively (credited as fully paid up) of any further Insurance Shares to which they may be entitled upon such capitalisation or (as the case may require) for the payment up by the Company on their behalf by the application thereto of their respective proportions of the profits resolved to be capitalised of the amounts or any part of the amounts remaining unpaid on their Insurance Shares or Core Shares (as the case may be) and any agreement made under such authority shall be effective and binding on all such Members.

ACCOUNTS

129. The Directors shall cause to be kept in Gibraltar proper accounts with respect to:-

(a) all sums of money received and expended by the Company and the matters in respect of which such receipts and expenditure take place; and

(b) all sales and purchases by the Company; and

(c) the assets and liabilities of the Company;

in order to enable the accounts of the Company and accounts in respect of each Class Fund to be prepared.

130. The books of account shall be kept at the Registered Office or at such other place in Gibraltar as the Directors think fit and shall always be open to inspection by the Directors.

131. No Member (other than a Director) shall have any right to inspect any account or book or document of the Company except as conferred by the Companies Laws or authorised by the Directors or by the Company in General Meeting.

132. A balance sheet of the Company shall be made out as at each Accounting Date and laid before the Company at its Annual General Meeting in each year, and such balance sheet shall contain a general summary of the assets and liabilities of the Company. The balance sheet shall be accompanied by a report of the Directors as to the state and condition of the Company,

and the amount (if any) which they have carried or propose to carry to reserve, together with a revenue account and balance sheet in respect of each Cell. The balance sheet in respect of each Cell shall be signed on behalf of the Directors by at least two of the Directors of the Company. The Auditors' report shall be attached to the balance sheet of the Company, or there shall be inserted at the foot of the balance sheet of the Company a reference to the report. The Auditors' report shall be read at the Annual General Meeting.

133. A printed copy of every balance sheet of the Company and of all documents annexed thereto, including the reports of the Directors and the Auditors and the revenue accounts and balance sheets in respect of each Cell and such other information and reports as may from time to time be required by the Companies Laws, shall not less than twenty-one days previous to the Meeting be delivered or sent by ordinary post to the registered address of every person entitled to receive notices in accordance with Article 51 hereof provided always this Article shall not require a copy of these documents to be sent to more than one of the joint holders of any Shares and provided further that this Article shall not require revenue accounts and balance sheets of any Cell to be sent to anyone other than a holder of Insurance Shares of the class attributable to that Cell.

AUDITORS

134. (a) The Company shall at each Annual General Meeting appoint an Auditor or Auditors to hold office from the conclusion of that meeting until the conclusion of the next Annual General Meeting.

(b) The first Auditors of the Company shall be appointed by the Directors at any time before the first Annual General Meeting of the Company and the Auditors so appointed shall hold office until the conclusion of that Meeting.

(c) The Directors may fill any casual vacancy in the office of Auditors but while any such vacancy continues the surviving or continuing Auditors if any may act.

The remuneration of any Auditors appointed by the Directors shall be fixed by the Directors and of any Auditors appointed by the Company shall be fixed by the Company at the Annual

General Meeting at which such appointment shall be made or in such manner as such Meeting may determine.

NOTICES

135. Any notice or document may be served by the Company on any Member either personally or by sending it through the post as a prepaid letter addressed to such Member at his address as appearing in the Register. In the case of joint holders of Shares notice shall only be given to that one of the joint holders whose name stands first in the Register in respect of the joint holding and notice so given shall be sufficient notice to all the joint holders.

136. Any notice or document delivered or sent by post to or left at the registered address of any Member shall notwithstanding that such Member be then dead or insolvent and whether or not the Company has notice of his death or insolvency be deemed to have been duly served in respect of any Shares registered in the name of such Member as sole or joint holder unless his name at the time of the service of the notice or document shall have been removed from the Register as the holder of the Shares in question and such service shall for all purposes be deemed a sufficient service of such notice or document on all persons interested (whether jointly with or as claiming through or under him) in the Share.

WINDING UP

137. If the Company shall be wound up the Liquidator shall apply the assets of the Company in satisfaction of creditors' claims in conformity with the provisions of the Protected Cell Act.

138. The assets available for distribution in each Cell in respect of which Insurance Shares of a particular class have been issued shall be distributed among the Members entitled to participate in such class in the following priority:-

(a) First, in the payment of the holders of the Insurance Shares of that class of a sum equal to the nominal amount of the Insurance Shares of such class held by such holders respectively provided that there are sufficient assets available in the relevant Cell to enable such payment to be made. In the event that, as regards any class of Insurance Shares, there are insufficient assets available in the relevant cell to enable such payment to be made, no recourse shall be had to any non-cellular assets nor to the assets of any other Cell;

(b) Secondly, in the payment to the holders of the Nominal Shares of that class of sums up to the nominal amount paid up thereon provided always if there are insufficient assets as aforesaid to enable such payment in full to be made, no recourse shall be had to any non cellular assets nor to the assets of any other Cell.

(c) Thirdly, in the payment to the holders of the Insurance Shares of each class of any balance then remaining in the relevant Cell, such payment being made in proportion to the number of Insurance Shares of the relevant class held.

139. If the Company shall be wound up the liquidator may with the authority of a Special Resolution divide among the Members holding Insurance Shares of the Cell in specie the whole or any part of the cellular assets of the Cell and whether or not the assets shall consist of property of a single kind and may for such purposes set such value as he deems fair upon any asset or classes of assets and may determine how such division shall be carried out as between the Members holding Insurance Shares of that cell. The liquidator may with the like authority vest any part of the assets in trustees upon such trusts for the benefit of Members holding Insurance Shares of that cell as the liquidator with the like authority shall think fit and the liquidation of the Company may be closed and the Company dissolved but so that no Member shall be compelled to accept any shares in respect of which there is liability.

INDEMNITY

140. Save as otherwise provided by the Companies Laws and Protected Cell Act every Director Secretary Manager and other officer or servant of the Company shall be indemnified by the Company against and it shall be the duty of the Directors out of the non-cellular assets of the Company to pay all costs losses and expenses which any such officer or servant may incur or become liable to by reason of any contract entered into or in any way in discharge of his duties including legal expenses and the amount for which such indemnity is provided shall immediately attach as a lien on the property of the Company

and have priority as between the Members over all other claims.

141. Save as otherwise provided by the Companies Laws and Protected Cell Act no Director Secretary Manager or other officer or servant of the Company shall be liable for the acts receipt neglects or defaults of any other person or for joining in any receipt or other act for conformity or for any loss or expense happening to the Company through the insufficiency or deficiency of title to any property acquired by order of the Directors for or on behalf of the Company or for the insufficiency or deficiency of any security in or upon which any of the moneys of the Company shall be invested or for any loss or damage arising from the bankruptcy insolvency or tortuous act of any person with whom any moneys securities or effects shall be deposited or for any loss damage or misfortune whatsoever which shall happen in the execution of the duties of his respective office or in relation thereto unless the same happen through his own wilful breach of duty or failure to exercise due care.

142. The directors may exercise all the powers of the Company to purchase and maintain for any director, auditor or other officer (including former directors and other officers) or any other person insurance against any liability for negligence, default, breach of duty or breach of trust or any other liability which may lawfully be insured against.

PROHIBITION ON DIVIDENDS AND OTHER DISTRIBUTIONS

143. Notwithstanding any provision of these Articles, no payment shall be declared or made by the Company by way of dividend or other distribution, purchase, redemption, reduction or return of shares or capital or by addition to or repayment of any dividend reserve without the consent of the Regulatory Authority. Subject to the consent of the Regulatory Authority, no dividends or other distributions payable in respect of Shares, whether pursuant to the provisions of these Articles or otherwise shall constitute a debt enforceable against the Company.

Appendix 2:
Specimen Articles of Contractual Cell Company

THE GIBRALTAR COMPANIES ACT

COMPANY LIMITED BY SHARES

ARTICLES OF ASSOCIATION

"ABC CONTRACTUAL CELL COMPANY"

DEFINITIONS

1. In these Articles the words standing in the first column of the Table next hereinafter contained shall bear the meanings set opposite to them respectively in the second column thereof, if not inconsistent with the subject or context.

Words	**Mean**
Accounting Date	The date on which ends the financial year of the Company each year and shall be the last day in December.
Annual General Meeting	The general meeting held each year pursuant to these Articles.
Article	An article in these Articles of Association.
Auditors	The auditors of the Company.
Class B Shares	Shares issued pursuant to Article 3(b), and "B Shares" and Class B Preferred Shareholder shall be construed accordingly.
Companies Act	The Companies Act and every Act for the time being in force in Gibraltar concerning companies with limited liability necessarily affecting this Company and "the Act" shall be construed accordingly.
Directors	The directors of the Company and "Board" shall be construed accordingly.
Extraordinary General Meeting	Shall have the meaning ascribed to it in these Articles.
Manager	Any Manager of the Company for the time being so appointed.

Member	A holder of Shares.
Net Asset Value	The amount determined for any Class Fund on any particular day as being the Net Asset Value of such class of B Share as at the day concerned pursuant to Article 15.4.
Nominal Share	Shares issued pursuant to Article 11.
Ordinary Shares	Shall mean Shares in the capital of the Company of £1 nominal value each, issued subject to and in accordance with the provisions of the Act and these Articles and having the rights provided under these Articles with respect to such Shares.
Ordinary Resolution	A resolution of the Company passed at a duly convened meeting by a show of hands or on poll by a simple majority of the votes cast.
Class B Preference Shareholder's Fund	A fund within the Company's insurance business, the assets and income of which are applied for the purposes of or are invested in connection with the insurance business conducted by the Company and maintained in accordance with the agreement entered into by the Company with the holder of the Class B Share which shall be segregated and represented by a separate class of Preferred Share, and "Class Fund" shall be construed accordingly.
Preferred Share	Shall mean all or any of the_redeemable preferred shares allotted to a single Member and issued subject to and in accordance with the provisions of the Act and these Articles and having the rights provided under these Articles with respect to such shares.
Redemption Price	The amount payable on the redemption of any Preferred Share which in respect of each Class of B Share shall equal in amount to the Net Asset Value of the Class Fund.

Seal	The seal of the Company from time to time approved and adopted by the Directors.
Secretary	The secretary of the Company so appointed by the Directors.
Shares	The shares, Preferred or otherwise, from time to time in the capital of the Company.
Shareholder's Agreement	The agreement to be entered into by each Class B Preferred Shareholder and the Company.
Insurance Policy	The insurance policy which the Company intends to issue to each Class B Preferred Shareholder immediately following the entering into the Shareholder's Agreement.

2.1. In these Articles unless there be something in the subject or context inconsistent with such construction:-

2.1.1. words importing the singular number shall be deemed to include the plural number and vice versa,

2.1.2. words importing the masculine gender only shall include the feminine gender;

2.1.3. words importing persons shall include companies or associations or bodies of persons, whether corporate or not;

2.1.4. the words: -

2.1.4.1. "may" shall be construed as permissive

2.1.4.2. "shall" shall be construed as imperative

2.1.5. references to a class or type of Preferred Share or similar references at any time when all Preferred Shares in issue constitute a single class or type shall be construed as referring to that single class or type and the relevant provision shall be applied accordingly.

2.2 The Regulations in Table "A", being the First Schedule in the Act, shall not apply to the Company.

2.3. The Company is a public company within the meaning of the Act.

SHARE CAPITAL

3. The Classes and maximum number of Shares the Company is authorised to issue are:

(a) [•] shares at par value of £1 each to be designated Ordinary Shares.

(b) [•] shares at par value of £1 each, with each such share to be designated a separate class of non-voting, non-dividend entitlement, redeemable preferred share, each share numbered consecutively B1 to B[•] and treated as a separate class of share (collectively "the Class B Shares"). Each Class B Share shall carry no right to dividend, but shall entitle the holders to participate in the profits or assets of the Company on redemption and winding-up thereof subject to and in accordance to these Articles.

(c) [•] shares at par value of £1 each, to be designated Nominal Shares and to be issued pursuant to clause 11.

VARIATION OF SHARE CAPITAL

4. The Company may from time to time by Ordinary Resolution increase its authorised capital by such sum to be divided into Shares of such amounts as the Ordinary Resolution shall prescribe. All new Shares shall be subject to the provisions of the Articles with reference to payment lien transfer transmission and otherwise.

5. Subject to the provisions of the Companies Act, the Company may by Special Resolution from time to time reduce its share capital in any way and may if and so far as is necessary alter its Memorandum of Association and Articles of Association by reducing the amount of its share capital and of its Shares accordingly.

6. Subject to the provisions of the Companies Act, the Company may from time to time by Ordinary Resolution:-

   6.1 consolidate and divide all or any of its share capital into Shares of larger amount than its existing Shares; and

   6.2 sub-divide its Shares or any of them into Shares of smaller amount than its existing Shares so however that in the sub-division the proportion between the amount paid and the amount if any unpaid on each reduced Share shall be the same as it was in the case of the Share from which the reduced Share is derived.

7. The Company may also from time to time by Ordinary Resolution cancel any Shares which at the date of the passing of the Ordinary

Resolution have not been taken or agreed to be taken by any person and may diminish the amount of its share capital by the same amount of the Shares so cancelled.

ISSUE OF SHARES

8. Subject to the Companies Act and as herein provided, any Shares in the Company for the time being unissued shall be under the control of the Directors who may allot and dispose of or grant options over the same or fractions thereof to such persons, on such terms and in such manner as they think fit and without prejudice to any special rights for the time being conferred on the holders of any Shares or class of Shares, any Shares in the Company may be issued with or have attached thereto such preferred, deferred or other special rights or such restrictions whether in regard to dividend, return of capital, voting or otherwise as the Company may from time to time determine.

9.1 Subject to the provisions of the Companies Act, the Company may on any issue of Shares pay such commission or brokerage as the Directors shall from time to time determine.

9.2 The Directors shall have the power to impose such restrictions as they may think necessary for the purpose of ensuring that no Preferred Shares in the Company are acquired or held by any person in breach of the laws or requirements of any country or governmental authority.

9.3 No person shall be recognised by the Company as holding any Share upon any trust and the Company shall not be bound by or recognise (even when having notice thereof) any equitable contingent future or partial interest in any Share or (except only as by these Articles otherwise provided or as by law required) any other right in respect of any Share except an absolute right thereto in the registered holder.

ORDINARY SHARES

10. The Ordinary Shares shall only be issued for cash at par value and the Directors shall allocate the proceeds from allotment and issue of the Ordinary Shares to a segregated fund.

NOMINAL SHARES

11. Nominal Shares may be issued but shall be issued only at par and only for the purpose of providing funds for the redemption of Preferred Shares. Where fractions of Preferred Shares are to be redeemed, equivalent fractions of Nominal Shares shall be issued.

12. Subject to the provisions of the Companies Act, the Company may from time to time redeem at par all or any of the Nominal Shares for the time being issued and outstanding out of any monies which may lawfully be applied for the purpose upon giving to the holders of the Nominal Shares to be redeemed not less than one month's notice provided that the holder may waive that notice.

PREFERRED SHARES

13. The rights, preferences and limitations of the Preferred Shares are as follows:-

    (a) If any Preferred Shares shall be redeemed or otherwise retired, it shall return to the status of an authorised but unissued Preferred Share of such class.

    (b) Each outstanding Class B Share shall entitle the registered holder of record of the Preferred Share to participation in earnings with respect to the Class Fund in accordance with the Shareholder's Agreement entered into by the Company with the registered holder of that Class of B Share.

    (c) The holders of B Shares shall not be entitled to vote at General Meetings of the Company.

    (d) The amount payable by the holder of any B Share upon the issue of such Share shall be the aggregate of the nominal value of such Share and such premium as the Board in its Discretion shall decide.

14. The terms upon which and the price per share at which the issue of Class B Shares shall be effected and the time of such issue shall be determined by the Directors provided that these shall only be issued by the Company to Preferred Shareholders who have executed a Shareholder's Agreement and whose identity has been approved by the Board.

REDEMPTION AND TRANSFER OF PREFERRED SHARES

15.1 Subject to the Shareholder's Agreement to be entered into by the Company with each Class B Shareholder and to any legal, regulatory and administrative issues being resolved, the Directors shall proceed to seek the redemption of the Class B Share in accordance with Article 16 and at not less than the Redemption Price, following the expiry of the Insurance Policy attributable to each holder of a B Share provided that the redemption of each

Preferred Share shall be effective on the date to be designated in the Company's notice to the holder of the Preferred Share ("the Redemption Date") and in any event, no earlier than the expiry of the Insurance Policy of such Class B Preferred Shareholder.

15.2. At the time and place fixed for redemption the registered holders of the B Share to be redeemed shall be bound to deliver up to the Company the relative certificate for cancellation, and the Company shall pay to them the redemption proceeds in respect of such Preferred Share.

15.3 If any holder of a B Share shall fail or refuse to surrender the certificate for such B Share or shall fail or refuse to accept the redemption money payable in respect of it such money shall be retained and held by the Company in trust for such holder but without interest or further obligation whatever.

15.4 The Net Asset Value for each Class B Share shall be determined separately by reference to the Class Fund appertaining to that Class B Share and to each such determination, subject always to the Shareholder's Agreement entered into by the Company with each such Class B Preferred Shareholder, the following provisions apply.

15.4.1 The Net Asset Value shall be determined as at such date as is in the opinion of the Directors the nearest practicable date to the date in relation to which and the purposes for which such valuation is to apply ("the Valuation Point").

15.4.2 The Net Asset Value of each Class Fund shall be equal to the value determined by the Directors in their absolute discretion as at the Valuation Point of all the assets, less all the liabilities (actual, contingent and prospective so far as the same can be quantified), comprised within the relevant Class Fund as at such Valuation Point in accordance with each Shareholder's Agreement entered into by the Company with the holder of that class of B Share.

15.4.3 The value of assets of the Class Fund shall be determined at what the Directors in their opinion consider is a fair value therefor.

16. Subject to any legal regulatory or administrative issues being resolved and in accordance with the provisions of the Companies Act, the nominal amounts paid up on any Class B Share shall be redeemed out of the proceeds arising from the issue of a Nominal

Share and the premium (if any) payable by the Company shall be paid from the relevant share premium account or at the discretion of the Directors the nominal amount paid up on such B Share and any such premium may be redeemed out of the profits of the appropriate Class Fund or partly in one way and partly in the other, and for this purpose the Net Asset Value (if any) in respect of any such share shall be transferred from the Class Fund to the general assets of the Company before the share is redeemed.

16.1 No Preferred Shareholder may dispose of its Preferred Share in the Company at any time except in accordance with the provisions of these Articles.

16.2 For the purpose of this Article "dispose" or "disposal" shall refer to any sale, exchange, redemption, realisation, transfer, alienation, disposal, donation, pledge or encumbrance of any right to or interest in a share in the Company or any offer made in relation thereto.

16.3 The Company shall not be obliged to register any transfer made in breach of these Articles and the Preferred Shares comprised in any transfer so made shall, carry no rights whatsoever, unless and until, in each case, the breach is rectified to the absolute satisfaction of the Company.

16.4 In those circumstances determined pursuant to the Shareholder's Agreement entered into by the Company with any holder of a Class of B Share, the Company may require the redemption of such a Preferred Share, in which case the relevant provisions of these Articles relating to the procedure for redemption shall apply to such redemption of the Preferred Share.

16.5 If it shall come to the notice of the Board that any Preferred Share is owned directly or beneficially either by any person in breach of any law or requirement of any country or governmental authority or as may cause any restriction to or withdrawal of the Company's authorisation from the Financial Services Commission to carry on insurance business, then the Board may give notice to such person requiring him to transfer such share to a person who is qualified or entitled to own the same or the Board may notwithstanding any other provision in these Articles redeem such share.

16.6 The proceeds of any redemption effected pursuant to this Article will be deposited by the Company in a bank for payment to any person against surrender of the certificate representing the Preferred Share previously held by such person or the proffering of such other evidence as to title as the Directors may require. Upon the deposit of such proceeds of redemption as aforesaid, such person shall have no further interest in such Preferred Share or any claim against the Company in respect thereof except the right to receive the proceeds of redemption so deposited (without interest) upon surrender of the said certificate.

16.7 The exercise by the Board of the power conferred by sub-paragraph 6 of this Article shall not be questioned or invalidated in any case on the ground that there was insufficient evidence of ownership of the Preferred Share by any person or that the true ownership of any Preferred Share was otherwise than appeared to the Board at the relevant date provided that the said powers shall have been exercised in good faith.

16.8 If it shall come to the notice of the Board that any Preferred Share is owned directly or beneficially by any person such that the status, standing or tax residence of the Company is or may be prejudiced or the Company may suffer any pecuniary disadvantage which it would not otherwise have suffered the Board may resolve to give notice in writing in accordance with sub-paragraph 5 of this Article to any such person requiring him to transfer such share or the Board may notwithstanding any other provision of these Articles redeem such share.

16.9 The Directors may at any time and from time to time call upon any holder of a Preferred Share by notice in writing to provide the Directors with such information and evidence as they shall require upon any matter connected with or in relation to such holder of a Preferred Share in order to satisfy themselves upon any matter concerning in their opinion the status, standing, or tax residence of the Company.

17. Upon the redemption of a Preferred Share of any class being effected pursuant to these Articles the applicant shall cease to be entitled to any rights in respect thereof and accordingly his name shall be removed from the Register with respect thereto and the Preferred Share be available for re-issue and until re-issue shall form part of the unissued share capital of the Company.

CLASS FUND

18. The Directors shall establish a segregated fund within its insurance business for each Class B Share in issue into which the consideration received by the Company upon the issuance of that particular class of share will be allocated and each such fund shall constitute a separate fund for the purposes of the insurance business underwritten by the Company in accordance with the Shareholder's Agreement to which it is a party and the directors shall maintain all the assets, income, earnings, liabilities, expenses and costs attributable to each such fund segregated and separate from all other assets, income, earnings, liabilities, expenses and costs of any other fund, and subject always to the Shareholder's Agreement entered into by the Company with such Preferred Shareholder, the following provisions shall apply thereto.

18.1 any consideration received on or proceeds from the allotment and issue of a Class B Share and all sums payable by the Preferred Shareholder in his capacity as annuitant under the Insurance Policy shall be applied to the fund established for that Class B Share, and the assets and liabilities and income and expenditure attributable thereto shall be applied only to that fund and on a redemption of the Class B Share the assets of the fund established for that class shall be reduced by the amount of the Redemption Price;

18.2 for each fund the Company shall keep a record of all transactions relating to that fund;

18.3 any asset derived from any other asset or assets (whether cash or otherwise) comprised in any fund shall be applied in the books of the Company to the same fund as the asset or assets from which it was derived and any increase or diminution in the value of an asset comprised in a fund shall be applied to that fund;

18.4 in the event that there is any asset of the Company (not being proceeds received on the subscription for Ordinary or Nominal Shares or assets derived from such proceeds) which the Directors do not consider readily attributable to a particular fund or funds the Directors shall allocate such asset to and among any one or more of the funds in such manner and on such basis as they in their absolute discretion deem appropriate and the Directors shall have the power to and may at any time and from time to time vary such basis in respect of any asset not previously allocated to one or more funds;

18.5 each fund shall be charged with the liabilities expenses costs charges or reserves of the Company (or the appropriate proportion thereof) that are in the absolute discretion of the Directors attributable to such fund and any liabilities, expenses, costs, charges or reserves of the Company not so attributable to any particular fund or funds shall be allocated and charged by the Directors between one or more funds in such manner and on such basis as the Directors in their discretion deem appropriate and the Directors shall have the power to and may at any time and from time to time vary such basis including where circumstances so permit the subsequent re-allocation of such liabilities, expenses, costs, charges and reserves;

18.6 if as a result of a creditor proceeding against certain of the assets of the Company or otherwise a liability expense, cost, charge or reserve would have been borne in a different manner from that in which it would have been borne under the preceding sub paragraph of this Article the Directors may transfer in the books and records of the Company any assets to and from any of the funds to achieve the position had the preceding paragraph of this Article applied;

18.7 subject as provided in these Articles, the assets attributable to each Class Fund shall be applied solely in respect of the Class B Share for which each such fund was established;

18.8 before any Class B Share is redeemed, the Company shall transfer the Net Asset Value of the Class Fund (if any) to the general assets of the Company, and the Redemption Price in respect of such share shall equal in amount to the Net Asset Value (subject to the reduction of any tax which may be payable).

RESTRICTION ON FURTHER ISSUES

19. The unissued share capital shall be at the disposal of the Board which may allot grant options over or otherwise dispose of them to such persons on such terms and conditions and at such times as the Board in its absolute discretion determines.

MODIFICATION OF RIGHTS

20. In respect of Ordinary Shares, and subject to the provisions of the Companies Act, all or any of the special rights and privileges for the time being attached to any such class of Shares for the time being issued may from time to time (whether or not the Company is being wound up) be altered or abrogated with the consent in writing of the holders of not less than three-fourths of the issued Shares of that class or with the sanction of a resolution passed at a meeting of the holders of the Shares of that class by a majority of three-fourths of the votes cast at such meeting.

21. In respect of all other classes of Shares, and subject to the Companies Act, the Directors shall in their absolute discretion be entitled from time to time to vary or abrogate the rights and privileges attached to any such class of Shares.

22. The special rights and privileges attached to any class of Shares shall be deemed to be varied by:

    22.1. any amendment to this Article, to Article 8 or to Article 20;

    22.2. by any reduction of issued share capital (excluding any redemption of Preferred Shares);

    22.3 by any merger, reconstruction or amalgamation affecting the Company or its share capital;

    22.4 by any discontinuance of or change in the nature of the business of the Company.

23. Subject to Article 22, the special rights attached to any Shares or class of Shares having preferential rights (unless otherwise expressly provided by the conditions of issue of such Shares) shall be deemed not to be varied by:

    23.1 the issue or redemption of any Preferred Shares in accordance with these Articles; or

    23.2. the exercise by the Directors of any discretion under these Articles or, if the Company should be wound up, the exercise by the liquidator of their powers.

CALLS ON SHARES

24. The Directors may from time to time make calls upon any Member in respect of any moneys unpaid on their Shares (whether on account of the nominal amount of the Shares or by way of premium)

and each Member shall (subject to being given at least fifteen days written notice specifying the time or times and place of payment) pay to the Company at the time or times and place so specified the amount called on his Shares. A call may be made payable by instalments. A call may be revoked or postponed as the Directors may determine in their absolute discretion.

25. A call shall be deemed to have been made at the time when the resolution of the Directors authorising the call was passed.

26. The joint holders of a Share shall be jointly and severally liable to pay all calls and other moneys due in respect thereof.

27. If a sum called in respect of a Share is not paid before or on the day appointed for payment thereof (time being of the essence) the person from whom the sum is due shall pay interest on the sum from the day appointed for payment thereof to the time of actual payment at such rate as the Directors may determine but the Directors shall be at liberty to waive payment of such interest wholly or in part.

28. Any sum which by the terms of issue of a Share becomes payable upon allotment or at any fixed date whether on account of the nominal value of the Share or by way of premium shall for all the purposes of these Articles be deemed to be a call duly made and payable on the date on which by the terms of issue the same becomes payable and in the case of non payment all the relevant provisions of these Articles as to payment of interest forfeiture or otherwise shall apply as if such sum had become payable by virtue of a call duly made and notified.

29. The Directors may make arrangements on the issue of Shares for a difference between the holders of such Shares in the amount of calls to be paid and in the times of payment.

30. The Directors may if they think fit receive from any Member willing to advance the same all or any part of the money uncalled and unpaid upon the Shares held by him beyond the sums actually called up thereon as a payment and such payment in advance of calls shall extinguish so far as the same shall extend the liability upon the Shares in respect of which it is advanced and the Company may (until the same would but for such advance become presently payable) pay interest at such rate as the Directors shall think fit upon the money so received or so much thereof as from time to time exceeds the amount of the calls then made upon the Shares in respect

of which it has been received provided that any amount paid up in advance of calls shall not entitle the holder of the Shares upon which such amount is paid to participate in respect thereof in any dividend until the same would but for such advance become payable.

FORFEITURE OF SHARES

31. If a Member fails to pay any call or instalment of a call on the day appointed for payment thereof (time being of the essence) the Directors may at any time thereafter during such time as any part of such call or instalment remains unpaid serve a notice on him requiring payment of so much of the call or instalment as is unpaid together with any accrued interest and any costs charges and expenses incurred by the Company by reason of such non-payment.

32. The notice shall name a further day (not earlier than fourteen days from the date of serving thereof) on or before which and the place where the payment required by the notice is to be made and shall state that in the event of non-payment at or before the time and the place appointed the Shares on which the call was made will be liable to be forfeited.

33. If the requirements of any such notice as aforesaid are not complied with any Share in respect of which such notice has been given may at any time thereafter before payment of all calls instalments interest costs charges and expenses due in respect thereof has been made be forfeited by a resolution of the Directors to that effect and such forfeiture shall include all dividends which shall have been declared on the forfeited Shares and not actually paid before forfeiture.

34. A forfeited Share shall become the property of the Company and may be sold re-allotted or otherwise disposed of either to the person who was before forfeiture the holder thereof or entitled thereto or to any other person upon such terms and in such manner as the Directors shall think fit and whether with or without all or any part of the amount previously paid up on the Share or credited as so paid up and at any time before a sale re-allotment or disposition the forfeiture may be cancelled on such terms as the Directors think fit. The Directors may if necessary authorise some person to transfer a forfeited Share to any other person as aforesaid.

35. A person whose Shares have been forfeited shall cease to be a Member in respect of the forfeited Shares but shall notwithstanding the forfeiture remain liable to pay to the Company all moneys which

at the date of forfeiture were presently payable by him to the Company in respect of the Shares with interest thereon from the date of forfeiture until payment at such rate as the Directors may determine and the Directors may enforce payment without any allowance for the value of the Shares at the time of forfeiture.

36. A record in the minute book of the Company that a Share has been duly forfeited in pursuance of these Articles and stating the time when it was forfeited shall be conclusive evidence of the facts therein stated as against all persons claiming to be entitled to the Share adversely to the forfeiture thereof and such record and the receipt of the Company for the consideration (if any) given for the Share on a sale re-allotment or disposal thereof together with the certificate (if issued) for the Share delivered to the purchaser or allottee thereof shall (subject to the execution of a transfer if the same be so required) constitute a good title to the Share.

37. The person to whom the Share is sold re-allotted or disposed of in accordance with the immediately preceding Article hereto shall be registered as the holder of the Share and not be bound to see to the application of the consideration (if any) nor shall his title to the Share be affected by any irregularity or invalidity in the proceedings in reference to the forfeiture sale re allotment or disposal of the Share.

38. The provisions of these Articles as to forfeiture shall apply in the case of non-payment of any sums which by the terms of issue of a Share become payable at a fixed time whether on account of the nominal amount of the Share or by way of premium as if the same had been payable by virtue of a call duly made and notified.

LIEN

39. Without prejudice to the provisions of these Articles and in addition thereto the Company shall have a first and paramount lien and charge on all the Shares registered in the name of a Member (whether solely or jointly with others) for his debts liabilities and engagements (either alone or jointly with any other person and whether a Member or not) to or with the Company whether the period for payment or discharge thereof shall have actually arrived or not. Such lien shall extend to all dividends from time to time declared in respect of such Shares. Unless otherwise agreed in writing the registration of a transfer of Shares shall operate as a waiver of the Company's lien (if any) on such Shares.

40. For the purpose of enforcing such lien the Company may sell (in such manner as the Directors think fit) any Shares on which the Company has a lien but no sale shall be made unless some sum in respect of which the lien exists is presently payable nor until the expiration of fourteen days after a notice in writing stating and demanding payment of the sum presently payable and giving notice of intention to sell in default shall have been served on the holder for the time being of the Shares or the person entitled by reason of his death or bankruptcy to the Shares. For the purposes of giving effect to any such sale the Directors may authorise some person to transfer to the purchaser thereof the Shares so sold.

41. The net proceeds of such sale after payment of the cost of such sale shall be applied in or towards payment or satisfaction of the debt or liability in respect whereof the lien exists so far as the same is presently payable and any residue shall (subject to a like lien for debts or liabilities not presently payable as existed upon the Shares prior to the sale) be paid to the person entitled to the Shares at the time of the sale. The purchaser shall be registered as the holder of the Share transferred and he shall not be bound to see to the application of the purchase money nor shall his title to the Shares be affected by any irregularity or invalidity in the proceedings in reference to the sale.

TRANSFER AND TRANSMISSION OF ORDINARY SHARES

42. All transfers of Ordinary Shares may be effected by transfer in writing in any form as the Board may accept. Any instrument of transfer shall be signed by or on behalf of the transferor who shall be deemed to remain the holder until the name of the transferee is entered in the Register.

43. Every instrument of transfer shall be left at the Registered Office or such other place as the Board may prescribe with the certificate of every Ordinary Share to be transferred and such other evidence as the Board may reasonably require to prove the title of the transferor or his right to transfer the shares, and the transfer and certificate shall remain in the custody of the Board but shall be at all reasonable times produced at the request and expense of the transferor or transferee or their respective representatives. A new certificate shall be delivered to the transferee after the transfer is completed and registered on his application and when necessary a balance certificate shall be delivered if required by him in writing. A fee

determined by the Board may be charged for each transfer and also for the registration of every probate notice power of attorney or document tendered for registration and shall be paid before registration.

44. Subject as hereinafter provided, no transfer of any Ordinary Share in the capital of the Company shall be made or registered without the previous sanction of the Board which may in its absolute discretion and without assigning any reason therefor, decline to register any transfer of any such share whether or not it is a fully paid share provided that the Board shall sanction any transfer made in accordance with the provisions of these Articles unless the registration thereof would permit the registration of a transfer of shares on which the Company has a lien. In the event of disposition to a third party, the transferor shall be obligated to transfer to the Company such information concerning the business of the transferee as the Company may request.

45. Subject to any requirement from time to time imposed by the Board, the holder of Ordinary Shares being a body corporate (the "Original Member") shall be entitled to transfer all of its shares to any other body corporate which is for the time being its holding or subsidiary company or another subsidiary of its holding company (each such body corporate being hereinafter referred to as a "Group Company") but if a Group Company whilst it is a member shall cease to be a Group Company in relation to the Original Member it shall within 21 days of so ceasing transfer the shares held by it to the Original Member or any Group Company of the Original Member.

46. Subject to any requirement from time to time imposed by the Board, the holder of Ordinary Shares may transfer its shares to a nominee or trustee for that member alone and any nominee or trustee of any person or persons may at any time transfer any shares to that other person or persons or to another nominee or trustee for that other person or persons.

47. The Company shall keep the Register in accordance with the Companies Act.

DEATH DISABILITY OR INSOLVENCY

48. On the death of a member the survivors where the deceased was a joint holder and the executors of the deceased where he was a sole holder shall be the only persons recognised by the Company as

having any title to or interest in his Shares; but nothing herein shall release the estate of a deceased joint holder from any liability in respect of any share jointly held.

49. A person entitled to Shares in consequence of death disability or insolvency shall not be entitled to receive notice of or attend or to vote at any meeting or (save as regards the receipt of such dividends as the Board shall not elect to retain) to exercise any of the rights of a holder unless and until he shall have been registered as holder.

GENERAL MEETINGS

50. The Company shall in each year hold in Gibraltar a general meeting as its Annual General Meeting in addition to any other meeting in that year. Annual General Meetings shall be held at such time and place as may be determined by the Directors.

51. Notices of every general meeting shall be given in any manner herein authorised to every Member and to:-

    51.1. each Director and Alternate Director of the Company;

    51.2. the Auditors;

    51.3. the Manager; and

    51.4. such other person(s) as the Directors shall at any time and from time to time determine.

52. Any Member present either personally or by proxy at any meeting of the Company shall for all purposes be deemed to have received due notice of such meetings and where requisite of the purposes for which such meeting was convened.

53. All general meetings (other than Annual General Meetings) shall be called Extraordinary General Meetings, may be convened whenever the Directors think fit and may be held at any place whether in Gibraltar or elsewhere.

54. Such Meeting shall also be convened by such requisitionists as provided by the Companies Act. If at any time there are not within Gibraltar sufficient Directors capable of acting to form a quorum, any Director or any two members of the Company may convene an Extraordinary General Meeting in the same manner as that in which meetings may be convened by the Directors, provided that in the case of any class meeting, the numbers of members entitled to requisition a meeting shall be calculated by reference to the issued

Shares of the class in question and not by reference to the issued Shares of the Company.

55. All business shall be deemed special that is transacted at an Extraordinary General Meeting, and also all business that is transacted at an Annual General Meeting with the exception of declaring or approving the payment of dividends the consideration of the accounts and reports of the Directors, the Manager and Auditors the election of Directors and Auditors in place of those retiring and the appointment and the fixing of the remuneration of the Directors and the Auditors.

56. At any General Meeting, a resolution put to the vote of the meeting shall be decided on a show of hands unless a poll is demanded (before or on the declaration of the result of the show of hands) by one member present or by proxy and entitled to vote in which case it shall be taken in such a manner and at such place as the chairman of the meeting may direct (including the use of ballot or voting papers or tickets) and the result of a poll shall be deemed to be a resolution of the meeting at which the poll was demanded.

57. The chairman of the meeting may in the event of a poll appoint scrutineers and may adjourn the meeting to some place and time fixed by him for the purpose of declaring the result of the poll.

58. A poll demanded on any question other than the election of a chairman of the meeting or an adjournment shall be taken at such time and place as the chairman of the meeting directs not being more than thirty days from the day of the meeting or adjourned meeting at which the poll was demanded.

59. The demand for a poll shall not prevent the continuance of a meeting for the transaction of any business other than the question on which the poll was demanded.

60. A demand for a poll may be withdrawn and no notice need be given of a poll not taken immediately.

VOTES OF MEMBERS

61. Subject to any special rights or restrictions for the time being attached to any class of Shares, at General Meetings of the Company:-

    61.1. holders of Nominal Shares shall not be entitled to vote in respect thereof,

61.2. holders of Ordinary Shares shall be entitled

61.2.1 on a show of hands (if present in person) to one vote,

61.2.2. on a poll (if present in person or by proxy) to one vote in respect of each Ordinary Share held by him.

61.3 holders of Class B Shares shall not be entitled to vote at General Meetings. The holders of Class B Shares shall be entitled to attend and speak (but not vote) at General Meetings.

62. In the case of joint holders of a share such persons shall not have the right of voting individually but shall elect one of their number to represent them and vote in their names in default of which the vote of the first-named who tenders a vote whether in person or by proxy shall be accepted to the exclusion of the votes of the other joint holders and for this purpose "first-named" shall be determined by the order in which the names stand in the Register in respect of the Shares.

63. No member shall unless the Directors otherwise determine be entitled to vote at any general meeting either personally or by proxy or to exercise any privileges as a member unless all calls and other sums presently payable by him in respect of shares in the Company of which he is the holder or one of the joint holders have been paid.

64. No objection shall be raised to the qualification of any voter except at the meeting or adjourned meeting at which the vote objected to is given or tendered and every vote not disallowed at such meeting shall be valid for all purposes. Any such objection made in due time shall be referred to the chairman of the meeting whose decision shall be final and conclusive.

65. Any instrument appointing a proxy shall be in writing under the hand of the appointor or of his attorney duly authorised in writing or if the appointor is a corporation either under its common seal or under the hand of an officer or attorney so authorised.

66. Any person (whether a member of the Company or not) may be appointed to act as proxy. A member may appoint more than one proxy to attend on the same occasion, but where a member appoints more than one proxy only one such proxy may vote on a show of hands.

67. The instrument appointing a proxy and the power of attorney or other authority (if any) under which it is signed or a notarially

certified copy of such power or authority shall be deposited at the registered office of the Company or at such other place as is specified for that purpose in the notice of meeting or in the instrument of proxy issued by the Company not less than forty-eight hours before the time appointed for holding the meeting at which the person named in the instrument proposes to vote and in default the instrument of proxy shall not be treated as valid. No instrument appointing a proxy shall be valid after the expiration of twelve months from the date named in it as the date of its execution except at an adjourned meeting or on a poll demanded at a meeting or an adjourned meeting in cases where the meeting was originally held within twelve months from such date.

68. An instrument of proxy shall be in the usual common form or such other form as the Directors may approve.

69. The Directors may at the expense of the Company send by post or otherwise to the members instruments of proxy (with or without prepaid postage for their return) for use at any general meeting or any meeting of any class of members of the Company

70. A vote given in accordance with the terms of an instrument of proxy shall be valid notwithstanding the death or insanity of the principal or the revocation of the instrument of proxy or of the authority under which the instrument of proxy was executed or of the transfer of the share in respect of which the instrument of proxy is given provided that no intimation in writing of such death insanity revocation or transfer shall have been received by the Company at its Registered Office before the commencement of the meeting or adjourned meeting at which the instrument of proxy is used.

71. Any corporation which is a member of the Company may by resolution of its Directors or other governing body or officers authorised by such body authorise such person as it thinks fit to act as its representative at any meeting of the Company and the person so authorised shall be entitled to exercise the same power on behalf of the corporation which he represents as that corporation could exercise if it were an individual member of the Company.

DIRECTORS

72. Unless otherwise determined by the Company in General Meeting the number of Directors shall not be less than two. The first Directors shall be appointed in writing by the subscribers to the

Memorandum of Association. They shall hold office until they resign or are disqualified in accordance with Article 83 hereof.

73. Subject to the provisions of these Articles the Directors shall have power at any time and from time to time to appoint any person to be a Director either to fill a casual vacancy or as an addition to the existing Directors. Any Director so appointed shall hold office only until the next following Annual General Meeting and shall then be eligible for re-election. The holders of the majority in nominal value of the Ordinary Shares for the time being in issue shall have the right by notice in writing to the Company to appoint additional Directors or to remove any Director from office.

74. The Directors shall be entitled to such remuneration as may be voted to them by the Company in General Meeting. Such remuneration shall be deemed to accrue from day to day. The Directors may also be paid all travelling subsistence hotel and other expenses properly incurred by them in attending and returning from meetings of the Directors or any committee of the Directors or general meetings of the Company or in connection with the business of the Company.

75. The Directors may grant special remuneration to any Director who, being so called upon, shall be willing to render any special or extra services to the Company. Such special remuneration may be made payable to such Director in addition to or in substitution for his ordinary remuneration as a Director, and may be made payable by a lump sum or by way of salary or commission or by any or all of those modes or otherwise.

76. A Director need not be a member of the Company.

ALTERNATE DIRECTORS

77. Each Director shall have the power to nominate another Director or any other person to act as an Alternate Director and at his discretion to remove such Alternate Director and on such appointment being made the Alternate Director may in the absence or incapacity of the Director he represents attend any meeting of Directors and exercise and discharge all the functions powers and duties of a Director of the Company. An Alternative Director must be a resident of Gibraltar

78. Any Director of the Company who is appointed as Alternate Director shall be entitled at a Meeting of the Directors to cast a vote of his appointor in addition to the vote to which he is entitled in his own capacity as a Director of the Company and for quorum

purposes shall count as a separate and additional Director present but not so less than two individuals shall be capable of constituting a quorum.

79. Any person appointed as an Alternate Director shall vacate such office as such Alternate Director if and when the Director for whom he has been appointed vacates his office as Director.

80. The remuneration of such an Alternate Director shall be payable out of the remuneration payable to the Director appointing him and the proportion thereof shall be agreed between them.

81. Every instrument appointing an Alternate Director shall be in such form as the Directors may determine.

82. The appointment of an Alternate Director and any revocation thereof shall take effect when lodged at the registered office of the Company.

DISQUALIFICATION AND RETIREMENT OF DIRECTORS

83. The office of a Director shall be vacated in any of the following events namely if:

(a) he resigns his office by notice in writing by him and left at the registered office of the Company;

(b) he becomes bankrupt or makes any arrangements or composition with his creditors generally;

(c) he becomes of unsound mind;

(d) he is absent from Meetings of the Directors for four successive meetings without leave expressed by a resolution of the board and the Directors resolve that he vacate his office;

(e) he be requested by all the other Directors (not being less than two in number) to vacate his office;

(f) he becomes resident in the UK; or

(g) he is removed from office by Resolution of the holders of Ordinary Shares or by writing in accordance with these Articles.

84. The Directors nominated by the subscribers to the Memorandum of Association of the Company shall continue to hold office subject to Article 83.

85. At least seven days' previous notice in writing shall be given to the Company of the intention of any member to propose any person

other than a retiring Director for election to the office of Director and the willingness of such person to be so elected provided that if the members present at a general meeting unanimously consent the chairman of such meeting may waive the said notice and submit to the meeting the name of any person so nominated.

TRANSACTIONS WITH DIRECTORS

86. A Director may hold any other office or place of profit under the Company (other than the office of Auditor) in conjunction with his office of Director on such terms as to tenure of office or otherwise as the Directors may determine.

87. No Director or intending Director shall be disqualified by his office from contracting with the Company as vendor purchaser or otherwise nor shall any such contract or any contract or arrangement entered into by or on behalf of the Company in which any Director is in any way interested render the Director liable to account to the Company for any profit realised by any such contract or arrangement by reason of such Director holding that office or of the fiduciary relationship thereby established but the nature of his interest must be declared by him at the meeting of the Directors at which the question of entering into the contract or agreement is first taken into consideration or if the Director was not at the date of that meeting interested in the proposed contract or arrangement then at the next meeting of the Directors held after he becomes so interested. A general notice in writing given to the Directors by any Director to the effect that he is a member of any specified company or firm and is to be regarded as interested in any contract or arrangement which may thereafter be made with that company or firm shall (if the Director shall give the same at a meeting of the Directors or shall take reasonable steps to procure that the same is brought up and read at the next meeting of the Directors after it is given) be deemed a sufficient declaration of interest in relation to any contract or arrangement so made.

88. Save as in these Articles provided, a Director shall not vote in respect of any contract or arrangement or any other proposal whatsoever in which he has any material interest otherwise than by virtue of his interest in Shares or debentures or other securities of or otherwise through the Company. A Director shall not be counted in the quorum at a meeting in relation to any resolution on which he is debarred from voting.

89. A Director shall (in the absence of some other material interest than is indicated below) be entitled to vote (and be counted in the quorum) in respect of any resolution concerning any of the following matters namely:-

(a) the giving of any security or indemnity to him in respect of money lent or obligations incurred by him at the request of or for the benefit of the Company or any of its subsidiaries;

(b) the giving of any security or indemnity to a third party in respect of a debt or obligation of the Company or any of its subsidiaries for which he himself has assumed responsibility in whole or in part under a guarantee or indemnity or by the giving of security;

(c) any proposal concerning an offer of Shares or debentures or other securities of or by the Company or any of its subsidiaries for subscription or purchase in which offer he is or is to be interested as a participant in the underwriting or sub-underwriting thereof,

(d) any proposal concerning any other company in which he is interested, directly or indirectly and whether as an officer or shareholder or otherwise howsoever, provided that he is not the holder of or beneficially interested in one per cent or more of the issued Shares of such company (or of any third company through which his interest is derived) or of the voting rights available to members of the relevant company (any such interest being deemed for the purpose of this Article to be a material interest in all circumstances).

90. Where proposals are under consideration concerning the appointment (including fixing or varying the terms of appointment) of two or more Directors to offices or employment with the Company or any company in which the Company is interested such proposals may be divided and considered in relation to each Director separately and in such case each of the Directors concerned (if not debarred from voting) shall be entitled to vote (and be counted in the quorum) in respect of each resolution except that concerning his own appointment.

91. If any question shall arise at any meeting as to the materiality of a Director's interest or as to the entitlement of any Director to vote and such question is not resolved by his voluntarily agreeing to abstain from voting, such question shall be referred to the chairman of the

meeting and his ruling in relation to any other Director shall be final and conclusive except in a case where the nature or extent of the interests of the Director concerned have not been fairly disclosed.

92. The Company may by Ordinary Resolution suspend or relax the provisions of Articles 87 and 88 to any extent or ratify any transaction not duly authorised by reason of a contravention of any of the said paragraphs.

93. Any Director may act by himself or his firm in a professional capacity for the Company and he or his firm shall be entitled to remuneration for professional services as if he were not a Director provided that nothing herein contained shall authorise a Director or his firm to act as Auditor to the Company.

94. Any Director may continue to be or become director managing director manager or other officer or member of any company in which the Company may be interested and (unless otherwise agreed) no such Director shall be accountable for any remuneration or other benefits received by him as a Director managing director manager or other officer or member of any such other company.

95. Subject as in these Articles provided, the Directors may exercise the voting power conferred by the share in any other company held or owned by the Company or exercisable by them as directors of such other company in such manner in all respect as they think fit (including the exercise thereof in favour of any resolution appointing themselves or any of them director managing director managers or other officer of such company or voting or providing for the payment or remuneration to the directors managing director Manager or other officer of such company).

POWERS OF DIRECTORS

96. The business of the Company shall be managed in Gibraltar by the Directors who may exercise all the powers of the Company as are not by the Companies Act or these Articles required to be exercised by the Company in general meeting subject nevertheless to any relevant provisions of the Companies Act and these Articles and to such regulations being not inconsistent thereto as may be prescribed by the Company in general meeting but no regulations made by the Company in general meeting shall invalidate any prior act of the Directors which would have been valid if such regulations had not been made.

97. The Directors may from time to time and at any time by power of attorney under the Seal appoint any company firm or person or any fluctuating body of persons whether nominated directly or indirectly by the Directors to be the attorney or attorneys of the Company for such purposes and with such powers authorities and discretion (not exceeding those vested in or exercisable by the Directors under these Articles) and for such period and subject to such conditions as they may think fit and any such other power of attorney may contain such provisions for the protection and convenience of persons dealing with any such attorneys as the Directors may think fit and may also authorise any such attorney to sub-delegate all or any of the powers authorities and discretions vested in him.

98. All cheques promissory notes drafts bills of exchange and other negotiable or transferable instruments and all receipts for moneys paid to the Company shall be signed drawn accepted endorsed or otherwise executed as the case may be in such manner as the Directors shall from time to time by resolution determine.

PROCEEDINGS OF DIRECTORS

99. The Directors may meet together for the dispatch of business adjourn and otherwise regulate their meetings as they think fit. No meetings of Directors shall be held otherwise than in Gibraltar and any meeting held outside Gibraltar and any resolution purporting to be approved at a meeting of the Directors held outside Gibraltar shall be invalid. The Directors shall ensure that the Company is considered as resident in Gibraltar by the relevant local tax authorities. Questions arising at any meeting shall be determined by a majority of votes. In case of an equality of votes the chairman shall have a second or casting vote. A Director may and the Secretary on the requisition of a Director shall at any time summon a meeting of the Directors.

100. The quorum necessary for the transaction of business of the Directors shall be two Directors, provided that where there are only two such directors at any meeting forming a quorum each such director must be resident in Gibraltar.

101. The continuing Directors or a sole continuing Director may act notwithstanding any vacancies in their number but if and so long as the number of Directors is reduced below the minimum number fixed by or in accordance with these Articles the continuing Directors or Director may act for the purpose of filling up vacancies

in their number or of summoning general meetings of the Company, but not for any other purpose. If there be no Directors or Director able or willing to act, then any two Members may summon a general meeting for the purposes of appointing Directors.

102. The Directors may from time to time elect and remove a chairman and if they think fit a deputy chairman of the board of Directors and determine the period for which they respectively are to hold office. The chairman or failing him the deputy chairman shall preside at all meetings of the Directors but if there be no chairman or deputy chairman or if at any meeting the chairman or deputy chairman be not present within five minutes after the time appointed for holding the same the Directors present may choose one of their number to be chairman of the Meeting

103. A resolution in writing signed in Gibraltar by all the Directors for the time being entitled to receive a notice of a meeting of the Directors shall be as valid and effectual as a resolution passed at a meeting of the Directors duly convened and held and may consist of several documents in the like form each signed by one or more of the Directors.

104. Members of the Board of Directors or of any committee thereof may participate in a meeting of the Board or of such committee by means of conference telephone or similar communications equipment by means of which all persons participating in the meeting can hear each other provided that each participant is in Gibraltar. Participation in a meeting pursuant to this provision shall constitute presence in person at such meeting.

105. A meeting of the Directors for the time being at which a quorum is present shall be competent to exercise all powers and discretions for the time being exercisable by the Directors.

106. The Directors may delegate any of their powers to committees consisting of such of their body as they think fit. Any committee so formed shall in the exercise of the powers so delegated conform to any regulations that may be imposed on them by the Directors.

107. The meetings and proceedings of any such committee consisting of two or more Directors shall be governed by quorum and other provisions of these Articles regulating the meetings and proceedings of the Directors so far as the same are applicable and

are not superseded by any regulations made by the Directors under the last preceding Article.

108. All acts done by any meeting in Gibraltar of Directors or of a committee of Directors or by any person acting as a Director shall notwithstanding that it be afterwards discovered that there was some defect in the appointment of any such Director or person acting as aforesaid or that they or any of them were disqualified or had vacated office or were not entitled to vote be as valid as if every such person had been duly appointed and was qualified and had continued to be a Director and had been entitled to vote.

BORROWING POWERS

109. Subject as hereinafter provided the Directors may exercise all the powers of the Company to borrow or raise money and secure any debt or obligation of or binding on the Company in any manner including by the issue of debentures (perpetual or otherwise) and to secure the repayment of any money borrowed raised or owing by mortgage charge pledge or lien upon the whole or any part of the property or assets (whether present or future) of the Company and also by a similar mortgage charge pledge or lien to secure and guarantee the performance of any obligation or liability undertaken by the Company or any third party. Money may be borrowed so long as the bank charges and interest are at no greater rate than is, in accordance with normal banking practice, the commercial rate for a loan of the size of a loan in question negotiated at arm's length.

MANAGING DIRECTORS

110. The Directors may from time to time appoint one or more of their body to be a managing director of the Company and may fix his or their remuneration, provided that any such person must be resident only in Gibraltar.

111. Every managing director shall be liable to be dismissed or removed by the board of Directors at any time. The board may however enter into an agreement with any person who is or is about to become a managing director with regard to the length and terms of his employment but so that the remedy of any such person for any breach of such agreement shall be in damages only and he shall have no right or claim to continuance in such office contrary to the will of the Directors or of the Company in general meeting.

112. Should the Articles be amended so as to require retirement of Directors by rotation a managing director shall not while he continues to hold that office be liable to retire by rotation and he shall not be taken into account in determining the rotation in which the other Directors shall retire (except for the purpose of fixing the number to retire in each year) but he shall be subject to the same provisions as to removal and disqualification as the other Directors and if for any reason he ceases to hold the office of Director he shall ipso facto cease to be a managing director.

113. The Directors may from time to time entrust to and confer upon the managing director or managing directors all or any of the powers of the Directors (not including the power to make calls forfeit Shares borrow money or issue debentures) that they may think fit but the exercise of all powers by the managing director or managing directors shall be subject to all such regulations and restrictions as the Directors may from time to time make and impose and the said powers may at any time be withdrawn revoked or varied.

SECRETARY

114. The Directors shall appoint a Secretary and may also appoint an assistant secretary, provided that any such person must be resident only in Gibraltar. Anything required or authorised to be done by or in the presence of the Secretary may if the office is vacant or the Secretary is absent or incapable of acting be done by or in the presence of any assistant secretary or if there is no assistant secretary present or capable of acting by or in the presence of any officer of the Company authorised generally or specially in that behalf by the Directors and any such assistant secretary or officer shall in such circumstances be a Secretary of the Company for the purposes of the Companies Act provided that any provisions of these Articles requiring or authorising a thing to be done by or to a Director and the Secretary shall not be satisfied by its being done by or to the same person acting both as Director and as or in the place of the Secretary.

115. No person shall be appointed to hold office as Secretary who is:-

(a) the sole Director of the Company, or

(b) a corporation the sole Director of which is the sole Director of the Company, or

(c) the sole Director of a corporation which is the sole Director of the Company; or

(d) not resident only in Gibraltar.

THE SEAL

116. The Directors shall provide for the safe custody of the Seal and the Seal shall never be used except by the authority of a resolution of the Directors or of a committee of the Directors authorised by the Directors in that behalf. The Directors may from time to time make such regulations as they see fit (subject to the provisions of these Articles relating to share certificates) determining the persons and the number of such persons in whose presence the Seal shall be used and (subject as aforesaid) until otherwise determined the Seal shall be affixed in the presence of two Directors or of one Director and the Secretary or some other persons duly authorised by the Directors.

DIVIDENDS

117. No dividends shall be paid on Nominal Shares or Class B Shares.

118. Subject to the statutory and regulatory requirements concerning solvency margins and reserves, the Board may from time to time declare dividends to be paid to the Ordinary Shareholders according to their rights and interests in the profits, including such interim dividends as appear to the board of Directors to be justified by the profits of the Company. Dividends shall be declared and payable only if the Company will have, after giving effect to the dividend, sufficient net assets to meet the relevant solvency margin prescribed by Gibraltar law.

119. No dividend shall be declared or paid other than from the profits or gains resulting from the Company's business and in any event no dividend shall be paid out of funds attributable to any Class Fund.

120. Subject to the rights of persons entitled to Shares with special rights as to dividends, all dividends shall be declared and paid according to the amounts paid on the shares, but if and so long as nothing is paid up on any of the Shares in the Company, dividends may be declared and paid according to the amounts of the Shares and (unless otherwise determined by the Directors) shall rank for dividend from the beginning of the Accounting Period in which they are issued.

121. The Directors may deduct from any dividend or other moneys payable to any Member all sums of money (if any) presently payable by him to the Company on account of calls or otherwise in relation to the Ordinary Shares (as the case may be) of the Company.

122. All unclaimed dividends may be invested or otherwise made use of by the Directors for the benefit of the Company until claimed. No dividends shall bear interest against the Company. The payment by the Directors of any unclaimed dividend or other moneys payable on or in respect of a Share allocated to a segregated fund shall not constitute the Company a trustee in respect thereof and any dividend unclaimed after a period of six years from the date of declaration shall be forfeited and shall revert to the Company.

123. Any resolution declaring a dividend on any Share, or any resolution of the Directors for the payment of a fixed dividend on the date prescribed for the payment thereof, may specify that the same shall be payable to the persons registered as the holders of such Shares at the close of business on a particular date, notwithstanding that it may be a date prior to that on which the resolution is passed (or, as the case may be, that prescribed for payment of a fixed dividend), and thereupon the dividend shall be payable to them in accordance with their respective holdings so registered, but without prejudice to the rights inter se in respect of such dividend of transferors and transferees of any Shares.

RESERVE FUND

124. Before the declaration of a dividend, the Directors may set aside any part of the net profits not attributable to any Class Fund to create a reserve fund and may apply the same either by employing it in the business of the Company or by investing it in such manner as they think fit. Such reserve fund may if so determined by the Board be applied for the purpose of maintaining assets of the Company replacing wasting assets meeting contingencies forming an insurance fund or for any other purpose for which the net profits of the Company may be lawfully used and until the same shall be applied it shall be deemed to remain undivided profits. The Directors may also carry forward to the accounts of the succeeding year or years any balance of profits which they shall not think fit either to divide or to place to reserve.

CAPITAL APPRECIATIONS

125. All appreciations or surpluses in respect of a particular Class Fund realised upon or derived from the sale, realisation or payment-off of property or investments, or from any variation or transposition of property or investments, or other realisations of capital assets, and any other sums which in the opinion of the Directors are of a capital nature shall be applied in respect of the relevant Class Fund in accordance with the Insurance Companies Act.

CAPITALISATION

126. The Company may upon the recommendation of the Directors resolve that it is desirable to capitalise and set free any part of the amount:-

(a) standing to the credit of any of the Company's reserve accounts (excluding the share premium account but including capital reserve),

(b) standing to the credit of the profit and loss account , or

(c) which is otherwise available for distribution but is not required for the payment of any dividend and accordingly that this sum or these sums be set free for distribution amongst the Members who would have been entitled thereto if it had been distributed by way of dividend and in the same proportion on condition that the same be not paid in cash but be applied either in or towards paying up any amounts for the time being unpaid on any Shares held by such Members respectively or in paying up in full unissued Shares to be allotted and distributed (credited as fully paid up) to and amongst such Members in the proportion aforesaid or partly in one way and partly in the other, and the Directors shall give effect to such resolution.

127. Whenever such a resolution as aforesaid shall have been passed the Directors shall make all appropriations and applications of the undivided profits resolved to be capitalised thereby and all allotments and issues of fully paid Shares and generally shall do all acts and things required to give effect thereto with full power to the Directors to authorise any person to enter on behalf of all the Members entitled thereto into an agreement with the Company providing for the allotment to them respectively (credited as fully paid up) of any further Shares to which they may be entitled upon such capitalisation or (as the case may require) for the payment up

by the Company on their behalf by the application thereto of their respective proportions of the profits resolved to be capitalised of the amounts or any part of the amounts remaining unpaid on their existing Shares and any agreement made under such authority shall be effective and binding on all such Members.

ACCOUNTS

128. The Directors shall cause to be kept in Gibraltar proper books of accounts with respect to:-

(a) all sums of money received and expended by the Company and the matters in respect of which such receipts and expenditure take place; and

(b) all sales and purchases by the Company;

(c) the assets and liabilities of the Company; and

(d) separate underwriting and capital accounts for each Class B Shareholder in accordance with the Shareholder's Agreement to which it is a party.

129. The books of account shall be kept at the Registered Office or at such other place in Gibraltar as the Directors think fit and shall always be open to inspection by the Directors and the Manager.

130. No Member (other than a Director) shall have any right to inspect any account or book or document of the Company except as conferred by the Companies Act or authorised by the Directors or by the Company in General Meeting.

131. A balance sheet of the Company shall be made out as at each Accounting Date and laid before the Company at its Annual General Meeting in each year, and such balance sheet shall contain a general summary of the assets and liabilities of the Company. The balance sheet shall be accompanied by a report of the Directors as to the state and condition of the Company, and the amount (if any) which they have carried or propose to carry to reserve. The Auditors' report shall be attached to the balance sheet of the Company, or there shall be inserted at the foot of the balance sheet of the Company a reference to the report. The Auditors' report shall be read at the Annual General Meeting.

132. A printed copy of every balance sheet of the Company and of all documents annexed thereto, including the reports of the Directors and the Auditors and such other information and reports as may from time to time be required by the Companies Act, shall not less

than twenty-one days previous to the Annual General Meeting be delivered or sent by ordinary post to the registered address of every person entitled to receive notices in accordance with these Articles provided that this Article shall not require a copy of these documents to be sent to more than one of the joint holders of any Shares.

AUDITORS

133. (a) The Company shall at each Annual General Meeting appoint an Auditor or Auditors to hold office from the conclusion of that meeting until the conclusion of the next Annual General Meeting.

(b) The first Auditors of the Company shall be appointed by the Directors at any time before the first Annual General Meeting of the Company and the Auditors so appointed shall hold office until the conclusion of that Meeting.

(c) The Directors may fill any casual vacancy in the office of Auditors but while any such vacancy continues the surviving or continuing Auditors if any may act.

The remuneration of any Auditor or Auditors appointed by the Directors shall be fixed by the Directors and of any Auditor or Auditors appointed by the Company shall be fixed by the Company at the Annual General Meeting at which such appointment shall be made or in such manner as such Meeting may determine.

NOTICES

134. Any notice or document may be served by the Company on any Member either personally or by sending it through the post as a prepaid letter addressed to such Member at his address as appearing in the Register. In the case of joint holders of Shares notice shall only be given to that one of the joint holders whose name stands first in the Register in respect of the joint holding and notice so given shall be sufficient notice to all the joint holders.

135. Any notice or document delivered or sent by post to or left at the registered address of any Member shall notwithstanding that such Member be then dead or insolvent and whether or not the Company has notice of his death or insolvency be deemed to have been duly served in respect of any Shares registered in the name of such Member as sole or joint holder unless his name at the time of

the service of the notice or document shall have been removed from the Register as the holder of the Shares in question and such service shall for all purposes be deemed a sufficient service of such notice or document on all persons interested (whether jointly with or as claiming through or under him) in the Share.

WINDING UP

136. In the event of any voluntary or involuntary liquidation, dissolution or winding up of the affairs of the Company, after payment of all liabilities of the Company, each holder of a Class B Share shall be entitled to receive that amount determined pursuant to the Shareholder's Agreement entered into by the Company with that holder of the Preferred Share plus the return of the capital (including share premium) on its Preferred Share before any distribution of the assets of the Company shall be made to the holders of the Ordinary Shares or Nominal Shares. After such payment(s) shall have been made in full to the holders of the outstanding Class B Shares, or funds necessary for such payment shall have been set aside in trust for the account of the holders of the outstanding Class B Shares so as to be available therefor, the holders of the outstanding Class B Shares shall be entitled to no further participation in the distribution of the assets of the Company, and the remaining assets of the Company, if any, shall be divided and distributed among the holders of the Ordinary Shares and Nominal Shares then outstanding, based on their respective Shares in the following order and manner of priority. First, the Ordinary Shares shall receive a return of its capital (including share premium) and any amount of unpaid cumulative dividends. Then, the capital with respect to the Nominal Shares shall be repaid. Finally, any amount of net income remaining in the Company shall be divided among the holders of Ordinary Shares in such manner and on such basis as they in their absolute discretion deem fair and equitable.

137. If the Company shall be wound up the liquidator may with the authority of a Special Resolution of the Company and any other sanction required by the Companies Act divide among the Members in specie or kind the whole or any part of the assets of the Company and whether or not the assets shall consist of property of a single kind and may for such purposes set such value as he deems fair upon any asset to be divided as aforesaid and may determine how such division shall be carried out as between the

Members or different classes of Members. The liquidator may with the like authority vest any part of the assets in trustees upon such trusts for the benefit of Members as the liquidator with the like authority shall think fit and the liquidation of the Company may be closed and the Company dissolved but so that no Member shall be compelled to accept any Shares in respect of which there is any liability.

INDEMNITY

138. Every director, secretary, manager and other officer or servant of the Company shall be indemnified by the Company against and it shall be the duty of the Directors to pay all costs losses and expenses which any such officer or servant may incur or become liable to by reason of any contract entered into or in any way in discharge of his duties including legal expenses and the amount for which such indemnity is provided shall immediately attach as a lien on the property of the Company and have priority as between the Members over all other claims.

139. No director, secretary, manager or other officer or servant of the Company shall be liable for the acts receipt neglects or defaults of any other person or for joining in any receipt or other act for conformity or for any loss or expense happening to the Company through the insufficiency or deficiency of title to any property acquired by order of the Directors for or on behalf of the Company or for the insufficiency or deficiency of any security in or upon which any of the moneys of the Company shall be invested or for any loss or damage arising from the bankruptcy insolvency or tortuous act of any person with whom any moneys securities or effects shall be deposited or for any loss damage or misfortune whatsoever which shall happen in the execution of the duties of his respective office or in relation thereto unless the same happen through his own wilful breach of duty or failure to exercise due care.

PROTECTED CELL COMPANY

140. The Company shall, subject to applicable law, have power to convert into a Protected Cell Company.

Appendix 3: Specimen Memorandum and Articles of Association of a PCC Umbrella Fund

THE GIBRALTAR COMPANIES ACT

THE GIBRALTAR PROTECTED CELL COMPANIES ACT

COMPANY LIMITED BY SHARES

MEMORANDUM OF ASSOCIATION

of

ABC PCC LIMITED

1. The name of the Company is '**ABC PCC LIMITED**'.

2. The Registered Office of the Company will be situated in Gibraltar.

3. The Company is established as a Protected Cell Company for the purposes of the Protected Cell Companies Act, 2001 (as amended).

4. The objects for which the Company is established are:

   (1) a) To carry on the business of an investment company and for that purpose to acquire and hold either in the name of the Company or in that of any nominee cash, property, equity and derivative instruments, including (without limitation) futures and/or forwards on any security, commodity and/or derivative instrument, commercial interest rate, currency, stock or indices or on any non-ferrous and precious metals, options to dispose of any security, commodity, interest rate, currency, index, swap on non-ferrous and precious metal, options on futures or options on options; contracts for differences, including index contracts and swaps and all ancillary transactions to any of the above, including margined and/or collateralised transactions and off-exchange contracts anywhere in the world ('Investments').

   b) To exercise and enforce all rights and powers conferred by or incident to the ownership of any such Investments including without prejudice to the generality of the foregoing all such powers of veto or control as may be conferred by virtue of the holdings of the Company of some special proportion of the issued or nominal amount thereof.

c) To carry on business as a general commercial company.

(2) To acquire such Investments by original subscription, syndicate participation, tender, purchase, exchange or otherwise, and to guarantee the subscription thereof; and to exercise and enforce all rights and powers conferred by or incidental to the ownership thereof.

(3) To deposit money in any currency with such persons and on such terms as may seem expedient and to discount, buy and sell bills, notes, coupons and other negotiable or transferable securities or documents.

(4) To employ or otherwise engage experts for the purpose of all or any of the objects of the Company and with limiting the generality of the foregoing to investigate and examine into the condition, prospects, value, character, and circumstances of any business concern or undertaking, or of any assets, properties or rights.

(5) To borrow or raise money for the account of the Company and to secure or discharge any debt or obligation of or binding on the Company in such manner as may be thought fit.

(6) To accumulate in any class for any of the purposes of that class, and to appropriate any of the assets of any class to specific purposes, either conditionally or unconditionally, and to admit any of those who have dealings with any class to any share in the profits thereof, or to any other special rights, privileges, advantages or benefits.

(7) To pay commission to any individual, body corporate, association or company in consideration of the subscription or any agreement to subscribe, whether absolutely or conditionally, for any shares in this Company or any other company in which this Company may be, or may be about to be, interested or in consideration of the procuring of an agreement to procure subscriptions, whether absolute or conditional, for any shares in this Company or in any such other company as aforesaid.

(8) To carry on anywhere as a trading trust finance agency and manufacturing company and generally to undertake all kinds of investment trading manufacturing and other operations.

(9) To act as trustees liquidators executors administrators managers receivers fiduciaries directors secretaries officers attorneys or agents anywhere.

(10) To purchase or acquire for any estate or interest and hold use deal or trade in whether with a view to profit or not and by any means property and rights of all kinds real or personal movable or immovable legal or equitable and to hold any such property and rights in the name of the Company or its nominees and to exercise and enforce all rights and powers as owners and to develop any such property rights.

(11) To prepare any property of the Company for building or other purposes and to construct alter demolish and improve buildings and lands and to enter into contracts and arrangements of any kind with any person and to undertake the management of property buildings and lands whether belonging to the Company or otherwise.

(12) To advance deposit or lend money securities and property to any person on any terms and to hire lease or sell goods of every description whether under hire purchase or on deferred payment or any terms.

(13) To borrow or raise money in any manner and to secure the repayment of any money borrowed raised or owing by assignment charge hypothecation pledge or mortgage on all or any of the property or rights of the company present future vested or contingent including uncalled capital.

(14) To guarantee assure or become liable for or to indemnify against any loss damage or obligation of any person whether or not connected or associated in any manner with the Company (including without limitation any holding or subsidiary company of the Company and any subsidiary of any such holding company) and whether for direct or indirect consideration benefit or advantage and in connection with or support of such arrangements to assign charge hypothecate mortgage or pledge all or any of the undertakings and property of the Company (including uncalled capital) and to enter into any contracts or other transactions in relation to any such arrangements.

(15) To accept payment for any property right or undertaking sold or disposed of or dealt with by the company either in cash or in shares or other securities whether with or without deferred or preferred rights or in debenture securities or mortgages or in any other manner.

(16) To issue and deposit any shares or securities which the Company may issue by way of charge hypothecation pledge or mortgage to secure any sum less than the nominal amount of such shares or securities and also by way of security for the performance of any obligations or liabilities of the Company or any person whether or not the Company has an interest in such person or his business.

(17) To accumulate capital for any of the purposes of the Company and to appropriate any property or rights for specific purposes conditionally or unconditionally and to allow any person having dealings with the Company to share in the Company's profits or any other advantages or benefits.

(18) To pay all or any expenses incurred in connection with formation and promotion of the Company or to contract with any other person to pay the same and to pay commissions to brokers and others for underwriting placing selling or guaranteeing the subscription of any shares or securities of the Company or any other entity promoted by the Company.

(19) To enter into arrangements with any state government or authority national local or otherwise and to obtain therefrom all rights concessions or privileges conducive to the Company's objects and to oppose the grant to any other person or similar rights concessions and privileges.

(20) To subscribe or guarantee money for charitable or benevolent objects and to aid in the establishment and support of association for the benefit of person at any time employed by or having dealings with the Company or the dependants or families of such person and to establish and support association institutions funds and trusts to benefit employees (including directors) and their respective dependants and families at any time and to grant pensions and allowances and to make payments towards insurances for the purpose of indemnifying the Company in respect of claims for any risks or accidents to any officers or employees of the Company whether in the course of their respective employment or not and to pay

premiums on any such insurances including against illness accident or death or for any other purpose.

(21) To draw make accept endorse issue discount and execute deeds agreements arrangements cheques promissory notes bills of exchange and all other negotiable and transferable instruments or transactions whatsoever.

(22) To enter into any joint ventures or arrangements or agreements for sharing profits with any persons.

(23) To distribute in specie among the Members by way of dividend or bonus or on a return of capital any property or rights of the Company or any proceeds of sale.

(24) To effect insurances and re-insurances against risks of every description whether for the Company or any other person.

(25) To amalgamate with any other company whose objects are or include similar to those of the Company whether by sale or by purchase (for full or partly paid shares or otherwise) of the undertaking or by sale or purchase (for full or partly paid shares or otherwise) of all or controlling interest in the shares of the Company or any such other company or partnership or any arrangement in the nature of partnership or in any other manner.

(26) To procure the Company to be recognised or registered anywhere and to carry on all or any part of the Company's business anywhere whether or not the Company has established an office or is so recognised or registered and as principals agents constructors trustees nominees or otherwise and by or through such persons and either alone or in conjunction with others.

(27) To do all such other things as the Company may think incidental to or connected with any of the above objects or conducive to their attainment or otherwise likely in any respect to be advantageous to the Company.

And it is hereby declared that the word 'person' in this Memorandum (except in reference to the Company) shall include any individual partnership or other body of persons whether incorporated or not and any government state or authority and further that the objects specified in each paragraph shall be treated as independent and accordingly in no way limited or restricted by reference to or inference from any other paragraph or from the name of the

Company and may be carried out as fully and construed as widely as if each paragraph defined the objects of a separate and independent company.

5. The liability of the Members is limited to the amount (if any) for the time being unpaid on the shares held by each of them respectively.

6. The Company has an authorised capital of £[•], US$[•] CHF [•] and €[•] divided into:

   a) [•] ordinary shares having a nominal value of £1.00 per share which may be issued as Founder Shares;

   b) [•] redeemable preference shares having a nominal value of £0.0001 per share which may be issued as separate classes of Participation Shares or as Nominal Shares;

   c) [•] redeemable preference shares having a nominal value of US$0.0001 per share which may be issued as separate classes of Participation Shares or as Nominal Shares;

   d) [•] redeemable preference shares having a nominal value of 0.0001 CHF per share which may be issued as separate classes of Participation Shares or as Nominal Shares; and

   e) [•] redeemable preference shares having a nominal value of €0.0001 per share which may be issued as separate classes of Participation Shares or as Nominal Shares.

The Participation Shares and Nominal Shares shall be issued as redeemable preference shares.

7. The Company, provided it is a collective investment scheme licensed, authorized or otherwise regulated under the Financial Services (Investment and Fiduciary Services) Act 1989 or the Financial Services (Collective Investment Schemes) Act 2005, is hereby authorised to issue fractions of a share as the Directors may by resolution determine and each such fractional share shall have the corresponding fractional rights, obligations, designations, powers, preferences, qualifications, limitations and liabilities of a whole share of the same class.

8. We, the several persons whose names addresses and descriptions are hereto subscribed are desirous of being formed into a company in pursuance of this memorandum of association, and we respectively agree to take the number of shares in the capital of the company set opposite our names.

A

THE GIBRALTAR COMPANIES ACT
THE GIBRALTAR PROTECTED CELL COMPANIES ACT

COMPANY LIMITED BY SHARES

ARTICLES OF ASSOCIATION

of

ABC PCC LIMITED

DEFINITIONS

1. In these Articles the words standing in the first column of the Table next hereinafter contained shall bear the meanings set opposite to them respectively in the second column thereof, if not inconsistent with the subject or context.

Words	**Meanings**
£	The lawful currency of the United Kingdom of Great Britain and Northern Ireland.
Accounting Date	31st December in each year or such other date as determined by the Directors from time to time.
Administrator	Any company appointed and for the time being acting as administrator of the Company pursuant to these Articles.
Administration Fee	The administrator fee payable by the Company to the Administrator, pursuant to the Administration Agreement.
Administration Agreement	Any agreement for the time being subsisting between the Company and the Administrator and relating to the appointment and duties of the Administrator.
Annual General Meeting	The general meeting held each year pursuant to these Articles.

Article	An article in these Articles of Association.
Articles	The Articles of Association of the Company.
Auditors	The auditors of the Company appointed pursuant to the provisions of the Companies Act.
Base Currency	Currency in which the accounts of the Company or a Cell are drawn up and in which Shares in the capital of the Company or a Cell are denominated.
Broker	Any company appointed and for the time being acting a broker of the Company pursuant to these Articles.
Brokerage Fee	The brokerage fee payable by the Company to the Broker, pursuant to the Brokerage Agreement.
Brokerage Agreement	Any agreement for the time being subsisting between the Company and the Broker and relating to the appointment and duties of the Broker.
Business Day	Any day on which banks in Gibraltar are open for business, excluding Saturdays and Sundays.
Cell	A cell created by the Company for the purpose of protecting and segregating cellular assets in the manner provided for by the PCC Act and represented by a class of Participation Share and, if in issue, Nominal Share, of the Company, formed and constituted in accordance with these Articles.
CHF	The lawful currency of Switzerland.
Clearer	Any company appointed and for the time being acting a clearer of the Company pursuant to these Articles.
Clearing Fee	The clearing fee payable by the Company to the Clearer, pursuant to the Clearing

	Agreement, for the services of the Clearer.
Clearing Agreement	Any agreement for the time being subsisting between the Company and the Clearer and relating to the appointment and duties of the Clearer.
Companies Act	Gibraltar's Companies Act, 1930 as from time to time amended or replaced.
Company	ABC PCC LIMITED
Continuing Offer	The continuing offer of Participation Shares not subscribed during the Initial Offer Period to be issued at the discretion of the Directors.
Continuing Offer Period	Such period, as determined by the Directors in their absolute discretion, during which subscriptions for Participation Shares in a particular Cell under the Continuing Offer may be made.
Custodian	Any company appointed and for the time being acting as custodian of the Company pursuant to these Articles.
Custodian Fee	The custodian fee payable by the Company to the Custodian, pursuant to the Custodian Agreement, for the services of the Custodian.
Custodian Agreement	Any agreement for the time being subsisting between the Company and the Custodian and relating to the appointment and duties of the Custodian.
Dealing Days	Such Business Day or Days as the Directors may from time to time, in their absolute discretion, determine.
Directors	The members of the board of directors of the Company appointed pursuant to the provisions of the Companies Act and EIF Regulations.
EIF Regulations	Financial Services (Experienced Investor Funds) Regulations 2005 as from time to time

	amended or replaced.
Eligible Person	An Experienced Investor.
Experienced Investor	A person or body who, as defined in the EIF Regulations, at the time of the investment, falls into one of the following categories: (a) a person or partnership whose ordinary business or professional activity includes, or it is reasonable to expect that it includes, acquiring, underwriting, managing, holding or disposing of investments, whether as principal or agent, or the giving of advice concerning investments; (b) a body corporate which has net assets in excess of €1,000,000 or which is part of a group which has net assets in excess of €1,000,000; (c) an unincorporated association which has net assets in excess of €1,000,000; (d) the trustee of a trust where the aggregate value of the cash and investments which form part of the trust's assets in excess of €1,000,000; (e) an individual whose net worth, or joint net worth with that person's spouse, is greater than €1,000,000, excluding that person's principal place of residence; or (f) a participant who invests a minimum of €100,000 in the Company.
Euro and/or €	The lawful currency of the participating member states of the European Union which have adopted the single currency in accordance with the EC Treaty of Rome dated 25th March 1957 (as amended by the Maastricht Treaty dated 7th February 1992).
Extraordinary General Meeting	Shall have the meaning ascribed to it by these Articles.

Founder Share	A share in the capital of the Company issued as an ordinary share with a nominal value of £1.00, designated at the time of issuance as a Founder Share and representing the non-cellular assets of the Company.
Gross Assets	The total value of all investments held by the Company or by any Cell, as the context may require, before deducting any liabilities, including borrowings.
Initial Offer	The offer of Participation Shares during the Initial Offer Period.
Initial Offer Period	Such period, as determined by the Directors in their absolute discretion, during which subscriptions for Participation Shares in a particular Cell under the Initial Offer may be made.
Initial Offer Price	The price of the Participation Shares issued at the Initial Offer as determined by the Directors in their absolute discretion.
International Financial Reporting Standards	International Financial Reporting Standards as adopted by the International Accounting Standards Board.
Investment	Property, cash, equity and derivative instruments, including (without limitation) futures and/or forwards on any security, commodity, interest rate, currency, stock or indices or on any non-ferrous and precious metals, options on futures or options on options; contracts for differences, including index contracts and swaps and all ancillary transactions to any of the above, including margined and/or collateralised transactions and off-exchange contracts.
Investment Manager	Any person, firm or corporation appointed and for the time being to invest the assets acting as Investment Manager of the Company pursuant to these Articles and

	designated as the Investment Manager.
Investment Management Fee	The investment management fee payable by the Company to the Investment Manager, pursuant to the Investment Management Agreement for the services of the Investment Manager.
Investment Management Agreement	Any agreement for the time being subsisting between the Company and the Investment Manager and relating to the appointment and duties of the Investment Manager.
Member	A person who is registered as the holder of Founder Shares, Nominal Shares, or Participation Shares in the Register of Members.
Net Asset Value or NAV	The amount determined in respect of any Cell in different Base Currencies, as the context may require, as being the Net Asset Value of the Cell and as described in the 'Determination of the NAV per Participation Share' section of these Articles.
NAV per Participation Share	The Net Asset Value for each class of Participation Share determined separately by reference to the Cell appertaining to that class of Participation Share and in respect of which the provisions under 'Determination of the NAV per Participation Share' section of these Articles shall apply.
Nominal Share	A share issued in the capital of the Company as a redeemable preference share pursuant to these Articles and termed a Nominal Share.
Participation Share	A share issued in the capital of the Company as a redeemable preference share and which will include any Nominal Share that is converted to a Participation Share.
Paying Bank	Any company appointed and for the time being acting as a paying bank of the Company pursuant to these Articles.
Paying Bank Fee	The paying bank fee payable by the Company to the Paying Bank, pursuant to the Paying Bank

	Agreement, for the services of the Paying Bank.
Paying Bank Agreement	Any agreement for the time being subsisting between the Company and the Paying Bank and relating to the appointment and duties of the Paying Bank.
PCC Act	Gibraltar's Protected Cell Company Act 2001 as from time to time amended or replaced.
Offering Memorandum	Any document (including any Private Information Memorandum) by which the Company offers or invites offers for its Participation Shares as it may be amended from time to time.
Offer Price	The price for a Participation Share offered for subscription during the Continuing Offer Period.
Ordinary Resolution	A resolution of the Company passed at a duly convened meeting by a show of hands or on a poll by a simple majority of votes cast.
Redemption Date	The Dealing Day as determined by the Offering Memorandum in each Cell and/or any other date or dates as the Directors may from time to time determine.
Redemption Price	The price at which any Participation Share shall be redeemed, calculated in accordance with these Articles.
Redemption Request	A written request to redeem one or more Participation Shares, signed by the registered holder or holders thereof, in the form specified in the applicable Private Information Memorandum or in such other form as the Directors may from time to time determine.
Register of Members or Register	The list of Members holding legal title to Shares, such list being is kept at the registered office of the Company.
Reporting Period	The time period, as determined by the Private Information Memorandum, for the preparation of the NAV in each Cell or any other date or dates as the Directors may from time to time

	determine.
Seal	The Common Seal (if any) of the Company.
Secretary	The Secretary of the Company so appointed by the Directors.
Securities Act 1933	The United States Securities Act of 1933 as from time to time amended or replaced.
Share	Any Founder Share, A Nominal Share or Participation Share.
Share Premium Account	The account of this name directed to be established pursuant to these Articles.
Share Transfer Request	A written request to transfer one or more Participation Shares, signed by the registered holder or holders thereof, in the form specified in the applicable Private Information Memorandum or in such other form as the Directors may from time to time determine.
Special Resolution	Shall have the meaning ascribed thereto by the Companies Act.
Performance Fee	The Performance fee payable by the Company to the Investment Manager pursuant to the Investment Management Agreement.
US Dollars, US$ and/or $	The lawful currency of the United States of America.
United States or U.S.	United States of America
U.S. Person	A U.S. Person as defined by Rule 902 of Regulation S under the Securities Act 1933
Valuation Day	The last Business Day as defined in Part B to the Private Information Memorandum pertaining to each Cell or such other day as the directors may from time to time determine.

2. (1) In these Articles unless there be something in the subject or context inconsistent with such construction:

(a) words importing the singular number shall be deemed to include the plural number and vice versa;

(b) words importing the masculine gender only shall include the feminine gender.

(c) words importing persons shall include companies or associations or bodies of persons, whether corporate or not;

(d) the words:

(i) 'may' shall be construed as permissive;

(ii) 'shall' shall be construed as imperative

(e) subject to the foregoing provisions of this Article, any words defined in the Companies Act or the Interpretation and General Clauses Act shall bear the same meaning in these Articles.

(2) The regulations in Table A being the First Schedule in the Companies Act shall not apply to the Company.

(3) The Company is a Private Company within the meaning of the Companies Act as well as an Experienced Investor Fund within the meaning of the EIF Regulations formed as a Protected Cell Company within the meaning of the PCC Act and accordingly the following provisions shall have effect, namely:-

(a) the right to transfer and transmit the Shares of the Company is restricted in the manner hereinafter provided;

(b) any invitation to the public to subscribe for any Shares of the Company is prohibited unless they fall within the definition of an Experienced Investor as defined by the EIF Regulations;

(d) any purchase of shares by a person who does not fall within the definition of Experienced Investor as defined in the EIF Regulations to subscribe for any Participation Shares of the Company is hereby prohibited;

(e) the Company shall not have power to issue Share Warrants to bearer; and

(f) the Company does not keep and is prohibited from keeping its Register of Shares outside Gibraltar.

SHARE CAPITAL AND CLASSES OF SHARES

3. The Company has an authorised capital of £[•], US$[•], CHF [•] and €[•] divided into:

   (a) [•] ordinary shares having a nominal value of £1.00 per share which may be issued as Founder Shares each which shall have voting rights but shall not participate in any profit or distribution of the Company that is attributable to the Cells.

   (b) [•] redeemable preference shares having a nominal value of £0.0001 per share which may be issued as separate classes of Participation Shares or as Nominal Shares;

   (c) [•] redeemable preference shares having a nominal value of US$0.0001 per share which may be issued as separate classes of Participation Shares or as Nominal Shares;

   (d) [•] redeemable preference shares having a nominal value of 0.0001 CHF per share which may be issued as separate classes of Participation Shares or as Nominal Shares;

   (e) [•] redeemable preference shares having a nominal value of €0.0001 per share which may be issued as separate classes of Participation Shares or as Nominal Shares;

   each having attached the rights herein contained.

   (1) The Founder Shares carry no right to any dividend. The Founder Shares carry the right to receive notice of and attend and vote at General Meetings. Consequently references to Special Resolutions and Ordinary Resolutions are to such resolutions passed by holders of the Founder Shares. Founder Shares may not be redeemed.

   (2) Nominal Shares shall have no voting rights and shall not participate in any profit or distribution of the Company (except the repayment of the amount paid up on the Nominal Shares).

(3) Participation Shares shall not be entitled to vote at General Meetings except at separate class Meetings of the holders of Participation Shares of any class of Participation Shares provided that the holders of the Founder Shares also have the right to attend and vote at such meetings.

(4) If at any time the Participation Shares in issue are divided into separate classes different amounts of dividends may be payable in respect of the separate classes. No dividends shall be declared or paid other than from the profits or gains of the relevant Cell.

(5) Each class of Participation Share, and their respective Nominal Shares if in issue, shall be constituted as a separate Cell for the purposes of the PCC Act. In the event of a winding-up, each Participation Share carries an entitlement, with respect to the assets of the Cell constituted in respect of the relevant class of Participation Share, to a return of the nominal capital paid up in respect of each share in priority to the repayment of the nominal capital paid up on Nominal Shares of that Cell. Only Participation Shares carry the right to participate in the assets of the Cell after the return of the nominal capital paid up on Nominal Shares.

(6) All shares are, when issued, fully paid and non-assessable, and Members have no personal liability for the debts of the Company. The shares have no pre-emptive, conversion, exchange or other rights or privileges save as set out in the Memorandum and Articles of Association of the Company.

(7) The Company shall keep a Register of Members and file allotments, redemptions and transfers of Shares at the Gibraltar Registry of Companies in accordance with the requirements of the Companies Act.

VARIATION OF SHARE CAPITAL

4. (1) The Company may from time to time by Ordinary Resolution increase its authorised capital by such sum to be divided into Shares of such amounts as the Ordinary Resolution shall prescribe. All new Shares shall be

subject to the provisions of the Articles with reference to payment lien transfer transmission and otherwise.

(2) Subject to the provisions of the Companies Act the Company may by Special Resolution from time to time reduce its unissued share capital in any way and in particular without prejudice to the generality of the foregoing power may:

(a) extinguish or reduce the liability on any of its Shares in respect of share capital not paid up; or

(b) with or without extinguishing or reducing liability on any of its Shares:

(i) cancel any paid up share capital which is lost or which is not represented by available assets; or

(ii) pay off any paid-up share capital which is in excess of the requirements of the Company.

and may if and so far as is necessary alter its Memorandum of Association and Articles of Association by reducing the amount of its share capital and of its Shares accordingly.

5. The Company may from time to time by Ordinary Resolution:

(a) consolidate and divide all or any of its share capital into Shares of larger amount than its existing Shares; and

(b) sub-divide its Shares or any of them into Shares of smaller amount than its existing Shares so however that in the sub-division the proportion between the amount paid and the amount if any unpaid on each reduced Share shall be the same as it was in the case of the Share from which the reduced Share is derived.

6. The Company may also from time to time by Ordinary Resolution cancel any Shares which at the date of the passing of the Ordinary Resolution have not been taken or agreed to be taken by any person and may diminish the amount of its share capital by the same amount of the Shares so cancelled.

ISSUE OF SHARES

7. (1) Subject to the Companies Act and as herein provided any Shares in the Company for the time being unissued shall be under the control of the Directors who may allot them to such persons, on such terms and in such manner as they think fit.

(2) The Company may issue Participation Shares which may to be redeemed or are liable to be redeemed at the option of the Company and all Participation Shares shall be redeemable in accordance with the provisions of these Articles.

(3) The Company, provided it is a collective investment scheme licensed, authorized or otherwise regulated under the Financial Services (Investment and Fiduciary Services) Act 1989 or the Financial Services (Collective Investment Schemes) Act 2005, is hereby authorised to issue fractions of a share as the Directors may by resolution determine and each such fractional share shall have the corresponding fractional rights, obligations, designations, powers, preferences, qualifications, limitations and liabilities of a whole share of the same class. Fractional Shares shall be issued to three (3) decimal places. If the fourth (4th) decimal is a number equal to or greater than five (5), the third decimal place shall be rounded up to the nearest whole number. If the fourth (4th) decimal is a number less than five (5), the third decimal place shall be rounded down to the nearest whole number.

8. The Company may on any issue of Shares pay such commission or brokerage as the Directors shall from time to time determine and as may be lawful.

ISSUE OF FOUNDER SHARES

9. Founder Shares shall be issued only for cash at par value. The Directors shall establish a separate fund for the proceeds from allotment and issue of Founder Shares and shall maintain all the assets, income, earnings, liabilities, expenses and costs of such fund segregated and separate from all other assets, income,

earnings, liabilities, expenses and costs of each Cell as non cellular assets of the Company.

ISSUE OF PARTICIPATION SHARES

10. (1) Subject as hereinafter provided, on receipt by the Company's Administrator of:

(a) an application in writing in the form specified in the applicable Offering Memorandum or in such other form as the Directors may from time to time determine (an 'Application'), and

(b) the additional information and declarations specified in the applicable Offering Memorandum (or such additional information and declarations (if any) as the Directors may from time to time determine);

from any Eligible Person or Eligible Persons (the 'Applicant'), the Company may, subject to the terms of the applicable Offering Memorandum and the provisions of this Article, issue to the Applicant the Participation Shares requested to be issued in the Application.

(2) Under the Continuing Offer Directors may issue Participation Shares on each Dealing Day at the prevailing NAV per Participation Share, of the particular class of Participation Shares being issued, at their absolute discretion.

Participation Shares will be issued, at the Directors' sole discretion, at the NAV per Participation Share at the close of business on the Valuation Day immediately preceding the relevant Dealing Day.

All monies payable on or in respect of a Participation Share of a class shall be paid in the currency of denomination of the Cell to which such Participation Share is attributable or in such other currency as the Directors may determine either generally or in relation to a particular class of Participation Share or in any specific case.

Unless otherwise permitted by the Directors, applications for Participation Shares during the Continuing Offer must be received at least three (3) Business Days before the Valuation Day and payment for such subscriptions must be received in cleared funds by 5:00 p.m. (Gibraltar Time) on each Valuation Day in order for Participation Shares to be issued on the following Dealing Day. If an application is received late it will be dealt with on the next Dealing Day at the NAV per Participation Share at the close of business on the Valuation Day preceding the next Dealing Day.

(3) The Directors may, in their absolute discretion and without giving any reason, refuse any application for Participation Shares, and may (but shall not be under any duty to do so) impose such restrictions as they may think necessary for the purpose of ensuring that no Participation Shares are acquired or held by or transferred to any person in breach of any law or requirement of any country or governmental or regulatory authority or in circumstances which in the opinion of the Directors might result in the Company incurring any liability to taxation or suffering any pecuniary or other disadvantage which the Company might not otherwise have incurred or suffered or may cause the Company to be classified as an investment company under the United States Company Act of 1940 or any other U.S. rules and regulations.

(4) Participation Shares issued during the Initial Offer Period shall be issued, at the Directors' sole discretion, at an Initial Offer Price per Participation Share.

(5) Any premium paid on each issue of Participation Shares shall be transferred to the Share Premium Account.

(6) No Participation Shares may be issued during any period when the determination of the NAV per Participation Share is suspended pursuant to the terms hereof.

(7) During any period of suspension an applicant may revoke an application for Participation Shares at any time prior to the termination of the period of suspension.

(8) Unless otherwise permitted by the Directors, no Participation Share may be issued other than as fully

paid and the Company shall decline to allot Participation Shares to satisfy any Application unless cleared funds in full payment of the Participation Shares to which an Application relates have been received by the Company by close of business in such place and on such date as is specified in the applicable Offering Memorandum.

(9) Except as the Directors may permit, the Company shall not issue certificated Shares and Shares will be issued in registered form.

REDEMPTION OF PARTICIPATION SHARES

11. Holders of Participation Shares wishing to redeem all or any of their Participation Shares must serve a Redemption Request in writing in the form specified in the applicable Offering Memorandum or in such other form as the Directors may from time to time determine.

The Redemption Request shall include such information and declarations specified in the applicable Offering Memorandum or such additional information and declarations (if any) as the Directors may from time to time determine.

The Redemption Request must be delivered to at the Company's Administrator.

Subject to the terms of these Articles, the Company shall, upon receipt of a Redemption Request, redeem the Participation Shares requested to be redeemed in the Redemption Request at the Redemption Price of those Participation Shares on such Redemption Date following receipt of the Redemption Request as is provided in the applicable Offering Memorandum and otherwise in accordance with the provisions of these Articles.

Subject to the discretion of the Directors, Redemption Requests must be received at least three (3) Business Days before a Valuation Day in order for Participation Shares to be redeemed on the following Redemption Date. If an application is received late it will be dealt with on the next Redemption Date at the NAV per Participation Share at the close of business on the Valuation Day preceding the next Redemption Date to which the Redemption Request relates.

12. Where certificates have been issued to a Member in respect of any Participation Shares the subject of a Redemption Request, that Redemption Request shall not be valid in relation to those Participation Shares unless the Redemption Request is accompanied by the relevant certificates or shall be valid only when such certificates have been received by the Company.

13. The Company, its directors and agents may rely upon any Redemption Request believed by them in good faith to be genuine.

14. The price at which any Participation Share shall be redeemed pursuant to a Redemption Request shall be the NAV per Participation Share of that Participation Share as of the close of business on the Redemption Date.

15. Subject to the discretion of the Directors, on any redemption:

    (a) Any Redemption Request received after 5:00 p.m. (Gibraltar time) on a Business Day or received on a day other than a Business Day may be deemed by the Directors to be received on the next following Business Day;

    (b) On redemption of only part of the Participation Shares comprised in a certificate, the Directors may at the request of the Member procure a balance certificate in respect of such Participation Shares as are not redeemed to be sent free of charge to the Member or as he shall direct;

    (c) Under normal circumstances the proceeds of a redemption of Participation Shares shall be paid by telegraphic transfer in the Base Currency of the Shares being redeemed within ten (10) Business Days of the applicable Redemption Date.

    The Directors reserve the right, at their absolute discretion, to delay the payment and/or make stage payments in relation to a Redemption Request to correspond with the time when liquid funds are available to fund the redemption.

    The Directors reserve the right, at their absolute discretion, to delay the payment and/or make stage payments in relation to a Redemption Request if, as determined by the Directors, the preparation of the NAV of a Cell to which a redemption relates is delayed or to be delayed beyond the normal Reporting Period.

(d) The Directors may dispense with the production of any lost or destroyed certificate if a Member makes application to the Company for the replacement of a lost or destroyed certificate in accordance with these Articles prior to submitting a Redemption Request;

(e) Subject to Sub-Article (f), a Member shall not be entitled to withdraw a Redemption Request.

(f) If the determination of the NAV per Participation Share is suspended beyond the day on which it would normally occur, the right of the Member to have his Participation Shares redeemed shall be similarly suspended and during the period of suspension he may withdraw his Redemption Request. Any withdrawal of a Redemption Request under the provisions of this Article shall be made in writing and shall be effective only if actually received by the Company's Administrator before termination of the period of suspension. If the Redemption Request is not so withdrawn the Participation Shares the subject of the Redemption Request shall be redeemed on the Redemption Date next following the termination of the suspension;

(g) The nominal value of Participation Shares shall be redeemed either out of the proceeds arising from a fresh issue of shares made for the purpose of the redemption or out of profits of the Company which would otherwise be available for dividend in respect of the Participation Shares requested to be redeemed. The premium (if any) shall be paid either from the Share Premium Account or out of profits available for dividend in respect of the Participation Shares requested to be redeemed.

(h) If a redemption would otherwise result in a Member having a residual holding of Participation Shares valued at less that €100,000 in respect of any Cell, the Directors may deem the relevant Redemption Request to have been made in respect of all the Participation Shares of that Cell held by that Member.

16. Subject to the provisions of the Companies Act and subject as hereinafter provided the Company may at any time, by giving thirty (30) days prior written notice to a Member, redeem all or any of that Member's Participation Shares on the first Redemption Date next following the expiry of the thirty (30) day notice period (the 'Compulsory Redemption Date').

17. The price at which any Participation Share shall be compulsorily redeemed shall be the NAV per Participation Share of that Participation Share as of the close of business on the Valuation Day prior to the Compulsory Redemption Date, and:

    (1) shall be payable on the Compulsory Redemption Date;

    (2) shall be paid in the Base Currency of the Cell being redeemed or, at the option of the Directors, in any other currency or in specie.

18. All costs incurred in a compulsory redemption of Participation Shares shall be for the account of the Member thereof and may be withheld from the proceeds of the redemption.

19. The Company shall have no responsibility in effecting a compulsory redemption of Participation Shares other to act in good faith and in a commercially reasonable manner.

20. The procedure for determining which Participation Shares will be compulsorily redeemed in any particular case is subject to change at the discretion of the Directors. In exercising discretion and in making determinations as to whether to compulsorily redeem Participation Shares, and in determining which Members shall be subject to compulsory redemption, the Directors may act upon the basis of such information as may be known to it, without any obligation to make special inquiries, and may rely upon the advice of counsel. In no event shall the Company or the Investment Manager be liable to any Member for any consequence of exercising any discretion or making any determination with respect to such compulsory redemption.

21. A Member shall cease for all purposes to be a Member of the Company on the applicable Redemption Date or Compulsory Redemption Date.

ISSUE OF NOMINAL SHARES

22. The Directors may issue Nominal Shares at the times and at the value that they, in their absolute discretion, determine.

23. Nominal Share may be issued at the Directors' absolute discretion, for the purposes of funding a redemption of Participation Shares, or for any other purpose as the Directors, in their absolute discretion, see fit.

24. Any premium paid on each issue of Nominal Shares shall be transferred to the Share Premium Account.

REDEMPTION OF NOMINAL SHARES

25. The Directors shall redeem Nominal Shares at the times that they, in their absolute discretion, determine.

26. Subject to the provisions of the Companies Act, the Company may from time to time redeem Nominal Shares at the same value of which they were issued out of any monies which may lawfully be applied for the purpose.

27. Subject to Articles 54 to 57 hereof Nominal Shares may at the Directors absolute discretion be converted into Participation Shares of the class of its issuance at an amount equal to the Offer Price of the Participation Shares in issue. The conversion of Nominal Shares to Participation Shares will be subject to the holder of the Nominal Shares being an Eligible Person at the time of conversion.

TRANSFERS AND TRANSMISSION OF SHARES

28. All transfers of Shares may be effected by transfer in writing in any form as the Directors may accept. Any instrument of transfer shall be signed by or on behalf of the transferee and the transferor who shall be deemed to remain the holder until the name of the transferee is entered in the Register.

29. Every instrument of transfer shall be left at such place as the Directors may prescribe and such other evidence as the Directors may reasonably require to prove the title of the transferor or his right to transfer the Shares; and the transfer shall remain in the custody of the Directors but shall be at all reasonable times produced at the request and expense of the transferor or transferee or their respective representatives. Share certificates

representing Shares transferred will be issued in accordance with the requirements of the Companies Act. A fee determined by the Directors may be charged for each transfer and also for the registration of every probate notice power of attorney or document tendered for registration and shall be paid before registration.

30. Subject as hereinafter provided, no transfer of any Share in the capital of the Company shall be made or registered without the previous sanction of the Directors who may in their absolute discretion and without assigning any reason therefore, decline to register any transfer of any Share whether or not it is a fully paid Share.

31. Any transferee will be required to provide the same information, which would be required in connection with a direct subscription in order for a transfer application to be considered by the Administrator. Violation of applicable ownership and transfer restrictions may at the discretion of the Directors result in compulsory redemption of the relevant Participation Shares.

32. Subject to any requirement from time to time imposed by the Directors, any Member may transfer Shares to a nominee or trustee for that Member alone and any nominee or trustee of any person or persons may at any time transfer any Shares to that other person or persons or to another nominee or trustee for that other person or persons PROVIDED THAT no beneficial interest in such Shares passes to the trustee or any other person by reason of such transfer.

33. The Company shall keep the Register in accordance with the Companies Act.

34. On the death of a Member the survivors where the deceased was a joint holder and the personal representative of the deceased where he was a sole holder shall be the only person recognised by the Company as having any title to or interest in his Shares; but nothing herein shall release the estate of a deceased joint holder from any liability in respect of any Share jointly held.

35. A person entitled to Shares in consequence of death disability or insolvency shall not be entitled to receive notice of or attend or to vote at any meeting or (save as regards the receipt of such dividends as the Directors shall not elect to retain) to exercise any

of the rights of a holder unless and until he shall have been registered as a holder.

DETERMINATION OF THE NAV PER PARTICIPATION SHARE

36. The NAV per Participation Share of each Cell shall be calculated by the Administrator on an accruals basis of accounting as at the close of business on each Valuation Day or at other such times as the Directors may determine.

37. The value of the assets and liabilities attributable to each Cell and the method of valuation of such assets and liabilities shall be determined by the Directors (which may consult with and rely on the advice of the Investment Manager or the Administrator).

38. Subject to the discretion of the Directors, the NAV per Participation Share of any Cell shall be calculated by:

(1) Ascertaining the NAV of such Cell as at each Valuation Day or at other such time as the Directors may determine;

(2) Dividing the resulting NAV by the number of issued Participation Shares in respect of such Cell outstanding (including the Participation Shares (if any) being redeemed but excluding Participation Shares to be issued on the Dealing Day following such Valuation Day and the effect of Nominal Shares) and;

(3) Rounding the resulting NAV per Participation Share to the nearest whole Cent (for Euro and US$), Centimes (for CHF) and Pence (for £), and in the case of fractions of 0.005 and more, rounding up.

39. On any particular date the NAV of a Cell shall be equal to the value on that date of the assets of the Cell less all liabilities so attributable at that time.

40. If there is more than one Cell within the Company then separate Cell accounts shall be established in the books of the Company for each Cell.

The assets and liabilities and income and expenses attributable to each Cell shall be allocated to each Cell, and included within each Cells accounts, in accordance with the requirements of the PCC Act.

41. The determination of the NAV per Participation Share made during any accounting period of the Company shall be examined and reported thereon by the Company's auditors as part of the audit of the Company's affairs for that accounting period and as of the Company's Accounting Date. The Company's accounts, presenting all assets, liabilities, income and expenses of the Company, shall be made available at the registered office of the Administrator as soon as possible after each Accounting Date. In the event that there is a disagreement between the Directors and the Auditors regarding any such determination and the Directors and the Auditors are unable to reach agreement, the final determination shall be made by the Directors. In such a case, the Auditors shall express any differing opinion in their report.

42. In determining the amount of liabilities, expenses, costs, charges or reserves of the Company (or the appropriate proportion thereof) that are in the absolute discretion of the Directors attributable to each cell and any liabilities, expenses, costs, charges or reserves of the Company not so attributable to any particular cell or cells, shall be allocated and charged between one or more cells in such manner and on such basis as the Directors, in their absolute discretion, deem fair and equitable and the Directors have the power to and may at any time, and from time to time, vary such basis including where circumstances so permit the subsequent re-allocation of such liabilities, expenses, costs, charges and reserves.

43. The Company shall recognise a financial asset or a financial liability on its balance sheet when, and only when, the entity becomes a party to the contractual provisions of the instrument.

44. An entity shall remove a financial asset or liability (or part of a financial asset or liability) from its balance sheet when, and only when, it is extinguished (i.e. when the obligation specified in the contract is discharged or cancelled or expires).

45. When a financial asset or financial liability is recognised initially it shall be measured at its fair value.

46. Financial assets and financial liabilities after initial recognition will be categorised and recognised as financial assets or financial liabilities at fair value through profit or loss which shall be measured at their fair values, without any deduction for

transaction costs it may incur on sale or other disposal, unless applicable accounting standards require otherwise.

47. A gain or loss on a financial asset or financial liability classified, in accordance with International Financial Reporting Standards, as "fair value through profit or loss" shall be recognised in the profit or loss account.

48. The value of the Company's financial instruments will be determined as follows:

(a) Each financial asset and/or financial liabilities (including spot, forward or derivative contracts) which are traded on a Recognised Exchange (other than a financial asset and/or financial liability which, in the opinion of the Directors or the Administrator as their delegate, falls to be valued under (c) (iii) below) will be valued on the Recognised Exchange or, if traded on more than one Recognised Exchange, on the Recognised Exchange which the Directors, or the Administrator as their delegate, determine provides the fairest criterion of value for such financial asset and/or financial liability, by reference to the last traded price on the relevant Recognised Exchange as at the Valuation Day or, if no such last traded price is available, or is unrepresentative in the opinion of the Directors or the Administrator as their delegate, such financial asset and/or financial liability shall be valued at the middle market quotation or if the last middle market quotation is unavailable, or is unrepresentative in the opinion of the Directors or the Administrator as their delegate, such financial asset and/or financial liability shall be valued at the probable realisation value as certified by a competent person approved for that purpose by the Administrator; or at such other value as the Directors or the Administrator as their delegate, with the approval of the Directors or the Administrator as their delegate consider in the circumstances to be fair.

(b) The value of any financial asset and/or financial liability which is not traded on a Recognised Exchange (other than an financial asset and/or financial liability which, in the opinion of the Directors or the Administrator as their delegate, falls to be valued under (c) (iii) below) shall be the probable realisation value of the financial asset and/or financial liability determined in good faith by the Directors and the Administrator.

(c) The prices of over-the-counter spot contracts, forwards and option contracts shall be valued as follows:

(i) spot contracts shall be valued at the mid-exchange rate as determined the Directors or the Administrator as their delegate as of the relevant Valuation Day;

(ii) forward contracts shall be valued in the same manner as spot contracts referred to in paragraph (a) above as adjusted for the mid-price premium or discounts as determined the Directors or the Administrator as their delegate or on the basis of the latest available quotation provided by the relevant counterparty to the Administrator as of the relevant Valuation Day; and

(iii) other over-the-counter contracts will be valued as determined by the Directors or the Administrator as their delegate on the basis of the latest available quotation provided by the relevant counterparty to the Directors or the Administrator as their delegate as of the relevant Valuation Day.

(d) Cash deposits and similar liquid Investments will be valued at their nominal value together with all accrued interest thereon to the relevant Valuation Day.

(e) Treasury bills and bills of exchange shall be valued with reference to prices ruling in the appropriate markets for such instruments of like maturity, amount and credit risk as of the relevant Valuation Day.

49. The Directors, in consultation with the Administrator, shall be entitled to adopt an alternative method of valuation in relation to any particular asset or liability if the Directors consider, on the advice of the Investment Manager and/or the Administrator, that the method of valuation otherwise provided for in the Articles of Association does not provide a fair valuation of that asset.

50. In determining the liabilities of any class:

(a) in the event any net amount payable in respect of any such liability is not payable until some future time after the relevant Valuation Day, the Directors (which may consult with and rely on the advice of the Investment Manager and/or the Administrator) shall make such allowance as is considered appropriate to reflect the true current value of that liability;

(b) the Directors may calculate administrative and other expenses of a regular or recurring nature as well as accrued assets on an estimated figure for yearly or other periods in advance and accrue the same in equal proportions over any such period.

51. Except as provided in these Articles, in determining the NAV per Participation Share , the value of the assets and liabilities of the Cell shall be determined on the basis of generally accepted accounting principles.

52. In determining the NAV for each class of Participation Shares the following provisions shall apply:

(a) the price per Participation Share of any Participation Share of that class to be issued for which application has been made to the Company (less commissions, if any, and less any other duties and charges payable by the Company in connection with the issuance thereof) shall be deemed to be an asset attributable to that class on the Dealing Day;

(b) the price per Participation Share of any Participation Share of that class for which a Redemption Request has been received shall from the close of business on the Redemption Date on which that Participation Share is actually redeemed and until the Redemption Price is paid shall be deemed to be a liability attributable to the class in respect of which that Participation Share has been issued;

(c) financial assets and financial liabilities, cash balances and other assets shall be valued and liabilities shall be calculated in Pounds Sterling and if not initially expressed in Pounds Sterling, shall be valued at the exchange rate in effect on the relevant Valuation Day.

53. Valuations are made by the Directors or at their discretion in accordance with fair value principles and/or applicable generally accepted accounting principles, including provisions for proper accruals and reserves.

SUSPENSION OF THE DETERMINATION OF NET ASSET VALUE AND THE REDEMPTION AND RE-PURCHASE RIGHTS OF MEMBERS

54. The Directors may, in their sole discretion, suspend the calculation of the NAV per Participation Share in relation to the Participation Shares issued in respect of a particular class of the Company (the 'Suspended Class')

(a) during any period when any stock exchange or over-the-counter market on which any of the assets of that Suspended Class are quoted, traded or dealt in is closed, other than for ordinary holidays and weekends, or during periods in which dealings are restricted or suspended;

(b) when as a result of political, economic, military or monetary events or any circumstances outside the control, responsibility and power of the Company, disposal of assets or liabilities by the Suspended Class would not be reasonably practicable or would be seriously prejudicial to the Members of the Suspended Class;

(c) during any breakdown in the means of communication normally employed in determining the price or value of any of the assets or liabilities of that Suspended Class, or of current prices in any stock market as aforesaid, or when for any other reason the prices or values of the assets or liabilities of that Suspended Class cannot reasonably be promptly and accurately ascertained; or

(d) during any period when the transfer of funds involved in the realisation or acquisition of any assets or disposal of any liabilities cannot, in the opinion of the Directors, be effected at normal rates of exchange;

(e) upon the decision to liquidate and dissolve the Company.

55. Any such suspension shall take effect at such time as the Directors shall declare but not later than the close of business on the Business Day next following the declaration and thereafter there shall be no determination of the NAV per Participation Share in relation to the class in question until the Directors shall, in their sole discretion, declare the suspension to be at an end except that the suspension shall terminate in any event on the first Business Day on which:

(a) the condition giving rise to the suspension shall have ceased to exist; and

(b) no other condition under which suspension is authorised under these Articles shall exist.

56. Each declaration by the Directors suspending determination of the NAV per Participation Share in relation to any particular class shall be consistent with such official rules and regulations (if any) relating to the subject matter thereof as shall have been promulgated by any authority having jurisdiction over the Company as shall be in effect at the time. To the extent not inconsistent with such official rules and regulations, the determination of the Directors shall be conclusive.

57. Whenever the Directors shall declare a suspension of the determination of the NAV per Participation Share in relation to any particular class, the Directors shall publish that suspension in such manner as the Directors deem appropriate to any Member likely to be affected thereby.

LIEN

58. Without prejudice to anything in these Articles the Company shall have a first and paramount lien and charge on all the Shares registered in the name of a Member (whether solely or jointly with others) for his debts liabilities and engagements (either alone or jointly with any other person and whether a Member or not) to or with the Company whether the period of payment or discharge thereof shall have actually arrived or not. Such lien shall extend to all dividends from time to time declared in respect of such Shares. Unless otherwise agreed the registration of a transfer of Shares shall operate as a waiver of the Company's lien (if any) on such Shares.

59. For the purpose of enforcing such lien the Company may sell (in such manner as the Directors think fit) any Shares on which the Company has a lien but no sale shall be made unless some sum in respect of which the lien exists is presently payable nor until the expiration of twenty (20) days after a notice in writing stating and demanding payment of the sum presently payable and giving notice of intention to sell in default shall have been served on the holder for the time being of the Shares or the person entitled by reason of his death or bankruptcy to the Shares. For the purposes of giving effect to any such sale the Directors may authorise some person to transfer to the purchaser thereof the Shares so sold.

60. The net proceeds of such sale after payment of the cost of such sale shall be applied in or towards payment or satisfaction of the debt or liability in respect whereof the lien exists so far as the same is presently payable and any residue shall (subject to a like lien for debts or liabilities not presently payable as existed upon the Shares prior to the sale) be paid to the person entitled to the Shares at the time of the sale. The purchaser shall be registered as the holder of the Share transferred and he shall not be bound to see to the application of the purchase money nor shall his title to the Shares be affected by any irregularity or invalidity in the proceedings in reference to the sale.

GENERAL MEETINGS

61. The Company shall in each year hold a general meeting as its Annual General Meeting in addition to any other meeting in that year. Annual General Meetings shall be held at such time and place as may be determined by the Directors.

62. Notices of every general meeting shall be given in any manner herein authorised to every Member entitled to vote at such a meeting and to:

(a) each Director and Alternate Director of the Company;

(b) the Auditors;

(c) the Investment Manager; and

(d) such other person(s) as the Director shall at any time and from time to time determine.

63. Any Member present either personally or by proxy at any meeting of the Company shall for all purposes be deemed to have

received due notice of such meetings and where requisite of the purposes for which such meeting was convened.

64. All general meetings (other than Annual General Meetings) shall be called Extraordinary General Meetings, may be convened whenever the Directors think fit and such meetings must be held in Gibraltar.

65. The number of Members entitled to requisition a meeting, the number forming a quorum and the number entitled to demand a poll shall be as stated in the Companies Act provided that in the case of any class meeting the numbers therein referred to shall be calculated by reference to the issued Shares of the class in question and not by reference to the issued Shares of the Company.

66. All business shall be deemed special that is transacted at an Extraordinary General Meeting, and also all business that is transacted at an Annual General Meeting with the exception of declaring or approving the payment of dividends the consideration of the accounts and reports of the Directors, the Investment Manager and Auditors the election of Directors and Auditors in place of those retiring and the appointment and the fixing of the remuneration of the Directors and the Auditors.

67. If a poll is validly demanded it shall be taken in such a manner and at such place as the chairman of the meeting may direct (including the use of a ballot or voting papers or tickets) and the result of a poll shall be deemed to be a resolution of the Meeting at which the poll was demanded.

68. The chairman of the meeting may in the event of a poll appoint scrutineers and may adjourn the meeting to some place and time fixed by him for the purpose of declaring the result of the poll.

69. A poll demanded on any question other than the election of a chairman of the meeting or an adjournment shall be taken at such time and place as the chairman of the meeting directs not being more than thirty days from the day of the meeting or adjourned meeting at which the poll was demanded.

70. The demand for a poll shall not prevent the continuance of a meeting for the transaction of any business other than the question on which the poll was demanded.

71. A demand for a poll may be withdrawn and no notice need be given of a poll not taken immediately.

VOTE OF MEMBERS

72. Subject to any special rights or restrictions for the time being attached to any class of Shares, at any general meetings of the Company:

(a) holders of Participation Shares shall not be entitled to vote in respect thereof except as may be required by the Companies Act;

(b) holders of Founder Shares shall be entitled

(i) on a show of hands (if present in person) to one vote;

(ii) on a poll (if present in person or by proxy) to one vote in respect of each Founder Share held by him.

73 In the case of joint holders of a Share such persons shall not have the right of voting individually but shall elect one of their number to represent them and vote in their names in default of which the vote of the first-named who tenders a vote whether in person or by proxy shall be accepted to the exclusion of the votes of the other joint holders and for this purpose 'first-named' shall be determined by the order in which the names stand in the Register in respect of the Shares.

74. Guardians in the names of their wards and attorneys in the names of their principals may vote at general meetings and this provision shall be deemed also to apply mutates mutandis to persons exercising the functions or similar functions being appointed under the laws of any other jurisdiction PROVIDED THAT such evidence as the Directors may require of the authority of the person claiming to vote whether under this Article shall have been deposited at the registered office of the Company not less than forty-eight hours before the time of holding the meeting or adjourned meeting at which such person claims to vote.

75. No Member shall unless the Directors otherwise determine be entitled to vote at any general meeting either personally or by proxy or to exercise any privileges as a Member unless all calls and other sums presently payable by him in respect of Shares in

the Company of which he is the holder or one of the joint holders have been paid.

76. No objection shall be raised to the qualification of any voter except at the meeting or adjourned meeting at which the vote objected to is given or tendered and every vote not disallowed at such meeting shall be valid for all purposes. Any such objection made in due time shall be referred to the chairman of the meeting whose decision shall be final and conclusive.

77. Any instrument appointing a proxy shall be in writing under the hand of the appointor or of his attorney duly authorised in writing or if the appointor is a corporation either under its common seal or under the hand of an officer or attorney so authorised.

78. Any person (whether a Member of the Company or not) may be appointed to act as proxy. A Member may appoint more than one proxy to attend on the same occasion.

79. The instrument appointing a proxy and the power of attorney or other authority (if any) under which it is signed or a copy certified by a Notary Public of such power or authority shall be deposited at the registered office of the Company or at such other place as is specified for that purpose in the notice of meeting or in the instrument of proxy issued by the Company not less than forty-eight hours before the time appointed for holding the meeting at which the person named in the instrument proposes to vote and in default the instrument of proxy shall not be treated as valid. No instrument appointing a proxy shall be valid after the expiration of twelve months from the date named in it as the date of its execution except at an adjourned meeting or on a poll demanded at a meeting or an adjourned meeting in cases where the meeting was originally held within twelve months from such date.

80. An instrument of proxy shall be in the usual common form or such other form as the Directors may approve.

81. The Directors may at the expense of the Company send by post or otherwise to the Members instruments of proxy (with or without prepaid postage for their return) for use at any general meeting or any meeting of any class of Members of the Company either in blank or nominating in the alternative any one or more

of the Directors or any other persons. If for the purpose of any meeting invitations to appoint a proxy or person or one of a number of persons specified in the invitations are issued at the expense of the Company such invitations shall be issued to all (and not to some only) of the Members entitled to be sent a notice of the meeting and to vote thereat by proxy.

82. A vote given in accordance with the terms of an instrument of proxy shall be valid notwithstanding the death or insanity of the principal or the revocation of the instrument of proxy or of the authority under which the instrument of proxy was executed or of the transfer of the Share in respect of which the instrument of proxy is given PROVIDED THAT no intimation in writing of such death insanity revocation or transfer shall have been received by the Company at its registered office before the commencement of the meeting or adjourned meeting at which the instrument of proxy is used.

83. Any corporation which is a Member of the Company may by resolution of its Directors or other governing body or officers authorised by such body authorise such person as it thinks fit to act as its representative at any meeting of the Company or at any meeting of any class of Members of the Company and the person so authorised shall be entitled to exercise the same power on behalf of the corporation which he represents as that corporation could exercise if it were an individual Member of the Company.

DIRECTORS

84. Unless otherwise determined by the Members by Ordinary Resolution in general meeting the number of Directors shall not be less than two. The first Directors shall be appointed in writing by the Subscribers to the Memorandum of Association. They shall hold office until they resign or are disqualified in accordance with these Articles.

85 If so required by the EIF Regulations from time to time, a minimum of two Directors of the Company shall be authorised by the Financial Services Commission to act as the directors of an experienced investor fund.

86. Subject to the provisions of these Articles the Directors shall have power at any time and from time to time to appoint any person to be a Director either to fill a casual vacancy or as an addition to the

existing Directors. Any Director so appointed shall hold office only until the next following Annual General Meeting and shall then be eligible for re-election.

87. The Directors shall be entitled to such remuneration as may be voted to them by the Company in general meeting. Such remuneration shall be deemed to accrue from day to day. The Directors may also be paid all travelling hotel and other expenses properly incurred by them in attending and returning from meetings of the Directors or any committee of the Directors or general meetings of the Company or in connection with the business of the Company.

88. The Directors may grant special remuneration to any Director who, being so called upon, shall be willing to render any special or extra services to the Company. Such special remuneration may be made payable to such Director in addition to or in substitution for his ordinary remuneration as a Director, and may be made payable by a lump sum or by way of salary or commission or by any or all of those modes or otherwise.

89. A Director need not be a Member of the Company but all Directors must be eligible to act as a Director, pursuant to the Companies Act.

ALTERNATE DIRECTORS

90. Each Director, except stated in these Articles, shall have the power to nominate another Director or any other person to act as an Alternate Director and at his discretion to remove such Alternate Director and on such appointment being made the Alternate Director may in the absence or incapacity of the Director he represents attend any meeting of Directors and exercise and discharge all the functions powers and duties of a Director of the Company.

91 Directors that have been authorised by the Financial Services Commission to act as a director for experienced investor funds that have been appointed in such capacity to act as a Director of the Company do not have the power to nominate another Director or any other person to act as an Alternate Director.

92. Any Director of the Company who is appointed as Alternate Director shall be entitled at a Meeting of the Directors to cast a vote of his appointor in addition to the vote to which he is

entitled in his own capacity as a Director of the Company and for quorum purposes shall count as a separate and additional Director present but not so that less than two individuals shall be capable of constituting a quorum.

93. Any person appointed as an Alternate Director shall vacate such office as such Alternate Director if and when the Director for whom he has been appointed vacates his office as Director.

94. The remuneration of such an Alternate Director shall be payable out of the remuneration payable to the Director appointing him and the proportion thereof shall be agreed between them.

95. Every instrument appointing an Alternate Director shall be in such form as the Directors may determine.

96. The appointment of an Alternate Director and any revocation thereof shall take effect when lodged at the registered office of the Company.

DISQUALIFICATION AND RETIREMENT OF DIRECTORS

97. The office of a Director shall be vacated in any of the following events namely if:

(a) he resigns his office by notice in writing by him and left at the registered office of the Company;

(b) he becomes bankrupt or makes any arrangements or composition with his creditors generally;

(c) he becomes of unsound mind;

(d) he is absent from Meetings of the Directors for four successive meetings without leave expressed by a resolution of the Directors and the Directors resolve that he vacate his office;

(e) he is no longer approved by the Financial Services Commission to act as a director for an experienced investor fund when he has been appointed in such capacity as a Director for the Company;

(f) he be requested by all the other Directors (not being less than three in number) to vacate his office; or

(g) he is removed from office by Resolution of the holders of Founder Shares at any meeting of such holders or by writing in accordance with these Articles.

98. The Directors holding office at the date of the adoption of these Articles shall continue to hold office subject to these Articles.

99. At least seven days' previous notice in writing shall be given to the Company of the intention of any Member to propose any person other than a retiring Director or existing Director for election to the office of Director and the willingness of such person to be so elected PROVIDED THAT if the Members present at a general meeting unanimously consent the chairman of such meeting may waive the said notice and submit to the meeting the name of any person so nominated.

TRANSACTIONS WITH DIRECTORS

100. A Director may hold any other office or place of profit under the Company (other than the office of Auditor) in conjunction with his office of Director on such terms as to tenure of office or otherwise as the Directors may determine.

101. No Director or intending Director shall be disqualified by his office from contracting with the Company as vendor purchaser or otherwise nor shall any such contract or any contract or arrangement entered into by or on behalf of the Company in which any Director is in any way interested render the Director liable to account to the Company for any profit realised by any such contract or arrangement by reason of such Director holding that office or of the fiduciary relationship thereby established but the nature of his interest must be declared by him at the meeting of the Directors at which the question of entering into the contract or agreement is first taken into consideration or if the Director was not at the date of that meeting interested in the proposed contract or arrangement then at the next meeting of the Directors held after he becomes so interested. A general notice in writing given to the Directors by any Director to the effect that he is a member of any specified company or firm and is to be regarded as interested in any contract or arrangement which may thereafter be made with that company or firm shall (if the Director shall give the same at a meeting of the Directors or shall take reasonable steps to procure that the same is brought up and read at the next meeting of the Directors after it is given) be deemed a sufficient declaration of interest in relation to any contract or arrangement so made.

102. Save as in these Articles provided, a Director shall not vote in respect of any contract or arrangement or any other proposal whatsoever in which he has any material interest otherwise than by virtue of his interest in Shares or other securities of or otherwise through the Company or by virtue of his employment by or shareholding in a company associated with the Company. A Director shall not be counted in the quorum at a meeting in relation to any resolution on which he is debarred from voting.

103. A Director shall (in the absence of some other material interest than is indicated below) be entitled to vote (and be counted in the quorum) in respect of any resolution concerning any of the following matters namely:

(a) the giving of any security or indemnity to him in respect of money lent or obligations incurred by him at the request of or for the benefit of the Company or any of its subsidiaries;

(b) the giving of any security or indemnity to a third party in respect of a debt or obligation of the Company or any of its subsidiaries for which he himself has assumed responsibility in whole or in part under a guarantee or indemnity or by the giving of security;

(c) any proposal concerning an offer of Shares or other securities of or by the Company or any of its subsidiaries for subscription or purchase in which offer he is or is to be interested as a participant in the underwriting or sub-underwriting thereof;

(d) any proposal concerning any other company in which he is interested, directly or indirectly and whether as an officer or shareholder or otherwise howsoever, provided that he is not the holder of or beneficially interested in one per cent, or more of the issued Shares of such company (or of any third company through which his interest is derived) or of the voting rights available to members of the relevant company (any such interest being deemed for the purpose of this Article to be a material interest in all circumstances).

104. Where proposals are under consideration concerning the appointment (including fixing or varying the terms of appointment) of two or more Directors to offices or employment

with the Company or any company in which the Company is interested such proposals may be divided and considered in relation to each Director separately and in such case each of the Directors concerned (if not debarred from voting under the provisions of these Articles shall be entitled to vote (and be counted in the quorum) in respect of each resolution except that concerning his own appointment.

105. If any question shall arise at any meeting as to the materiality of a Directors interest or as to the entitlement of any Director to vote and such question is not resolved by his voluntarily agreeing to abstain from voting, such question shall be referred to the chairman of the meeting and his ruling in relation to any other Director shall be final and conclusive except in a case where the nature or extent of the interests of the Director concerned have not been fairly disclosed.

106. The Company may by Ordinary Resolution suspend or relax the provisions of these Articles to any extent or ratify any transaction not duly authorised by reason of a contravention of any of the said paragraphs.

107. Any Director may act by himself or his firm in a professional capacity for the Company and he or his firm shall be entitled to remuneration for professional services as if he were not a Director PROVIDED THAT nothing herein contained shall authorise a Director or his firm to act as Auditor of the Company.

108. Any Director may continue to be or become director managing director manager or other officer or member of any company in which the Company may be interested and (unless otherwise agreed) no such Director shall be accountable for any remuneration or other benefits received by him as a director managing director manager or other officer or member of any such other company.

109. The Directors may exercise the voting power conferred by the share in any other company held or owned by the Company or exercisable by them as directors or such other company in such manner in all respects as they think fit (including the exercise thereof in favour of any resolution appointing themselves or any of them director managing director managers or other officer of such company or voting or providing for the payment or

remuneration to the directors managing director manager or other officer of such company).

POWERS OF DIRECTORS

110. The business of the Company shall be managed by the Directors who may exercise all the powers of the Company as are not by the Companies Act or these Articles required to be exercised by the Company in general meeting subject nevertheless to any relevant provisions of the Companies Act and these Articles and to such regulations as may be prescribed by the Company in general meeting but no regulations made by the Company in general meeting shall invalidate any prior act of the Directors which would have been valid if such regulations had not been made.

111. In all transactions with third parties the Directors shall inform such third party that the Company is a Protected Cell Company and unless the transaction is not in respect of any particular Cell, identify or specify the Cell in respect of which the third party is transacting.

112. The Directors may from time to time and at any time by power of attorney attested by any person duly authorised in that regard appoint any company firm or person or any fluctuating body of persons whether nominated directly or indirectly by the Directors to be the attorney or attorneys of the Company for such purposes and with such powers authorities and discretion (not exceeding those vested in or exercisable by the Directors under these Articles) and for such period and subject to such conditions as they may think fit and any such other power of attorney may contain such provisions for the protection and convenience of persons dealing with any such attorneys as the Directors may think fit and may also authorise any such attorney to sub-delegate all or any of the powers authorities and discretions vested in him.

113. The Directors shall ensure that at all times cellular assets are kept separate from and separately identifiable from non-cellular assets and that assets attributable to each Cell are separate and separately identifiable from cellular assets attributable to other Cells.

114 All cheques promissory notes drafts bills of exchange and other negotiable or transferable instruments and all receipts for moneys paid to the Company shall be signed drawn accepted endorsed or otherwise executed as the case may be in such manner as the Directors shall from time to time by resolution determine.

115. The Directors shall identify or specify the Cell in respect of which or with which any third party is transacting and inform such third party accordingly unless a third party is transacting otherwise than with a specified Cell.

PROCEEDINGS OF DIRECTORS

116. The Directors may meet together for the dispatch of business adjourn and otherwise regulate their meetings as they think fit. Questions arising at any meeting shall be determined by a majority of votes. In case of an equality of votes the chairman shall have a second or casting vote. A Director may and the Secretary on the requisition of a Director shall at any time summon a meeting of the Directors.

117. The quorum necessary for the transaction of business of the Directors may be fixed by the Directors and unless so fixed at any other number shall be two.

118. The continuing Directors may act notwithstanding any vacancies in their number but if and so long as the number of Directors is reduced below the minimum number fixed by or in accordance with these Articles the continuing Directors or Director may act for the purpose of filling up vacancies in their number or of summoning general meetings of the Company, but not for any other purpose. If there be no Directors or Director able or willing to act, then any two Members may summon a general meeting for the purposes of appointing Directors.

119. The Directors may from time to time elect and remove a chairman and if they think fit a deputy chairman of the Board of Directors and determine the period for which they respectively are to hold office. The chairman or failing him the deputy chairman shall preside at all meetings of the Directors but if there be no chairman or deputy chairman or if at any meeting the chairman or deputy chairman be not present within five minutes after the time appointed for holding the same the Directors

present may choose one of their number to be chairman of the Meeting.

120. A resolution in writing signed by all the Directors for the time being entitled to receive a notice of a meeting of the Directors shall be as valid and effectual as a resolution passed at a meeting of the Directors duly convened and held, and may consist of several documents in the like form each signed by one or more of the Directors PROVIDED THAT such resolution shall not be valid unless a majority of the signatories are resident in and/or have given their signatures in Gibraltar.

121. Subject to the required quorum a meeting of Directors or of a committee may be validly held notwithstanding that such Directors may not be in the same place provided that:

(a) they are in constant communication with each other throughout by telephone, television or other form of communication; and

(b) all Directors entitled to attend such meeting so agree.

122. A meeting of the Directors for the time being at which a quorum is present shall be competent to exercise all powers and discretions for the time being exercisable by the Directors.

123. The Directors may delegate any of their powers to committees consisting of such of their body as they think fit. Any committee so formed shall in the exercise of the powers so delegated conform to any regulations that may be imposed on them by the Directors.

124. The meetings and proceedings of any such committee consisting of two or more Directors shall be governed by quorum and other provisions of these Articles regulating the meetings and proceedings of the Directors so far as the same are applicable and are not superseded by any regulations made by the Directors under the last preceding Article.

125. All acts done by any meeting of Directors or of a committee of Directors or by any person acting as a Director shall notwithstanding that it be afterwards discovered that there was some defect in the appointment of any such Director or person acting as aforesaid or that they or any of them were disqualified or had vacated office or were not entitled to vote be as valid as if

every such person had been duly appointed and was qualified and had continued to be a Director and had been entitled to vote.

BORROWING POWERS

126. Subject as hereinafter provided the Directors may exercise all the powers of the Company to borrow or raise money and secure any debt or obligation of or binding on the Company in any manner and to secure the repayment of any money borrowed raised or owing by mortgage charge pledge or lien upon the whole or any part of the property or assets (whether present or future) of the Company and also by a similar mortgage charge pledge or lien to secure and guarantee the performance of any obligation or liability undertaken by the Company or any third party.

MANAGING DIRECTORS

127. The Directors may from time to time appoint one or more of their body to be a managing director of the Company and may fix his or their remuneration.

128. Every managing director shall be liable to be dismissed or removed by the Directors at any time. The Directors may however enter into an agreement with any person who is or is about to become a managing director with regard to the length and terms of his employment but so that the remedy of any such person for any breach of such agreement shall be in damages only and he shall have no right or claim to continuance in such office contrary to the will of the Directors of the Company in general meeting.

129. Should the Articles be amended so as to require retirement of Directors by rotation a managing director shall not while he continues to hold that office be liable to retire by rotation and he shall not be taken into account in determining the rotation in which the other Directors shall retire (except for the purpose of fixing the number to retire in each year) but he shall be subject to the same provisions as to removal and disqualification as the other Directors and if for any reason he ceases to hold the office of Director he shall ipso facto cease to be a managing director.

130. The Directors may from time to time entrust to and confer upon the managing director or managing directors all or any of the powers of the Directors (not including the power to make calls forfeit Shares borrow money) that they may think fit but the

exercise of all powers by the managing director or managing directors shall be subject to all such regulations and restrictions as the Directors may from time to time make and impose and the said powers may at any time be withdrawn revoked or varied.

SECRETARY

131. The Directors shall appoint a Secretary and may also appoint an assistant secretary. Anything required or authorised to be done by or in the presence of the Secretary may if the office is vacant or the Secretary is absent or incapable of acting be done by or in the presence of any assistant secretary or if there is no assistant secretary present or capable of acting by or in the presence of any officer of the Company authorised generally or specially in that behalf by the Directors and any such assistant secretary or officer shall in such circumstances be a Secretary of the Company for the purposes of Company Law PROVIDED THAT any provisions of these Articles requiring or authorising a thing to be done by or to a Director and the Secretary shall not be satisfied by its being done by or to the same person acting both as Director and as or in the place of the Secretary.

THE SEAL

132. If the Directors resolve to adopt a Seal then the Directors shall provide for the safe custody of the Seal and the Seal shall never be used except by the authority of a resolution of the Directors or of a committee of the Directors authorised by the Directors in that behalf. The Directors may from time to time make such regulations as they see fit (subject to the provisions of these Articles relating to Participation Shares) determining the persons and the number of such persons in whose presence the Seal shall be used and (subject as aforesaid) until otherwise determined the Seal shall be affixed in the presence of two Directors or of one Director and the Secretary or some other persons duly authorised by the Directors.

DIVIDENDS

133. Subject to the provisions of the Companies Act, the Company in General Meeting may declare dividends on Participation Shares, but no dividend shall exceed the amount recommended by the Directors. The Directors may from time to time if they think fit pay such interim dividends on Participation Shares as appear to

the Directors to be justified by the profits of the class in respect of which the Participation Shares have been issued. No dividends shall be paid on Nominal Shares or Founder Shares.

134. No dividend shall be payable except out of such funds as may be lawfully distributed as dividend.

135. Subject to the following provisions of this Article all dividends declared and paid to the holders of Participation Shares shall be in proportion to the amounts paid up on such Participation Shares held by them respectively. The Participation Shares unless otherwise determined by the Directors rank for dividend as from the beginning of the accounting period in which they are issued.

136. All unclaimed dividends may be invested or otherwise made use of by the Directors for the benefit of the Company until claimed. No dividend shall bear interest against the Company. The payment by the Directors of any unclaimed dividend or other monies payable on or in respect of a Participation Share into a separate account shall not constitute the Company a trustee in respect thereof and any dividend unclaimed after a period of twelve years from the date of declaration of such dividend shall be forfeited and shall revert to the Company and be credited to the class in respect of which the dividend or other monies were paid.

137. Any dividend, redemption monies payable on liquidation or other monies payable on or in respect of a Share may be paid by cheque or sent through the post to the registered address of the Member or person entitled thereto and in the case of joint holders to that one whose name stands first on the Register of Members in respect of their joint holding. Every such cheque shall be made payable to the order of the person to whom it is sent, and payment of the cheque shall be a good discharge to the Company. Every such cheque shall be sent at the risk of the person entitled to the money represented thereby.

138. If several persons are registered as joint holders of any Share, any one of them may give effectual receipts for any dividend or other monies payable on or in respect of the Share.

SHARE PREMIUM AND RESERVE ACCOUNTS

139. The Directors shall establish an account to be called the Share Premium Account and shall carry to the credit of such account from time to time a sum equal to the amount or value of the premium paid on the issue of any Share. If the Company issues Participation Shares in relation to a particular class, a separate Share Premium Account shall be established for that class (to be called a Class Share Premium Account) to the credit of which shall be carried a sum equal to the amount or value of the premium paid in respect of Participation Shares issued in relation that class.

140. There shall be debited to the Share Premium Account on the redemption of a Share the difference between the nominal value of such Share redeemed and the Redemption Price (which difference shall be called the Redemption Premium) PROVIDED ALWAYS that at the discretion of the Directors the Redemption Premium may be paid out of the profits of the Company available for dividend. If the Company has issued Participation Shares in relation to a particular class, no Redemption Premium may be debited to the Class Share Premium Account of that class or be paid out of the profits of the Company attributable to that class other than the Redemption Premium paid in respect of Participation Shares issued in relation to that class.

141. The Company shall at all times comply with the provisions of the Companies Act in relation to the Share Premium Account and the premiums attaching to Participation Shares and in relation to the redemption of the Participation Shares.

142. The Directors may set aside out of the profits of the Company and carry to the credit of any reserve account such sums as they think proper which shall at the discretion of the Directors be applicable for any purpose to which the profits or reserves may be properly applied and pending such application may at the like discretion either be employed in the business of the Company or be invested in such investments as the Directors may from time to time think fit. The Directors may also carry forward to the accounts of the succeeding year or years any balance of profits which they shall think fit to place on reserve. If the Company has issued Participation Shares in relation to a particular class, a separate reserve account or accounts shall be established for that

class (to be called a Class Reserve Account) to the credit of which shall be carried a sum equal to the amount or value of the premium paid in respect of Participation Shares issued in relation that class.

ACCOUNTS

143. The Directors shall cause to be kept proper accounts with respect to:

(a) all sums of money received and expended by the Company and the matters in respect of which such receipt and expenditure take place, and

(b) all sales and purchases by the Company, and

(c) the assets and liabilities of the Company;

(d) each class created by the Company

144. The books of account shall be kept at the Registered Office or at such other place as the Directors think fit, and shall always be open to inspection by the Directors.

145. The Directors shall from time to time cause to be prepared and to be laid before the Company in General Meeting Profit and Loss Accounts and Balance Sheets made up to the Accounting Date in each year or such other date and for the Cell, Cells and/or the Company as the Directors may from time to time decide. The financial statements shall be prepared in accordance with International Financial Reporting Standards.

146. A printed copy of the Directors' Report and Auditors' Report accompanied by the Balance Sheet and Profit and Loss Account of the Company shall not less than twenty-one days previous to such General Meeting be delivered or sent by post to the registered address of every Member of the Company entitled to receive notices in accordance with these Articles and to the Auditors PROVIDED THAT this Article shall not require a copy of these documents to be sent to more than one of the joint holders of any Shares.

147. Every account of the Directors when audited and approved by any General Meeting shall be conclusive, except as regards any error discovered therein within three months next after the approval thereof. Whenever such an error is discovered within

that period the account shall forthwith be corrected and thereupon shall be conclusive.

AUDITORS

148. (a) The Company shall at each Annual General Meeting appoint an Auditor or Auditors to hold office from the conclusion of that meeting until the conclusion of the next Annual General Meeting.

(b) The first Auditors of the Company shall be appointed by the Directors at any time before the first Annual General Meeting of the Company and the Auditors so appointed shall hold office until the conclusion of that Meeting.

(c) The Directors may fill any casual vacancy in the office of Auditors but while any such vacancy continues the surviving or continuing Auditors if any may act.

149. The remuneration of any Auditors appointed by the Directors shall be fixed by the Directors and of any Auditors appointed by the Company shall be fixed by the Company at the Annual General Meeting at which such appointment shall be made or in such manner as such Meeting may determine.

NOTICES

150. Any notices or document may be served by the Company on any Member either personally or by sending it through the post as a prepaid letter addressed to such Member at his address as appearing in the Register. In the case of joint holders of Shares notice shall only be given to that one of the joint holders whose name stands first in the Register in respect of the joint holding and notice so given shall be sufficient notice to all the joint holders.

151. Any notice or document delivered or sent by post to or left at the address of any Member as stated in the Register shall notwithstanding that such Member be then dead or insolvent and whether or not the Company has notice of his death or insolvency be deemed to have been duly served in respect of any Shares registered in the name of such Member as sole or joint holder unless his name at the time of the service of the notice or document shall have been removed from the Register as a holder of the Shares in question and such service shall for all purposes be deemed a sufficient service of such notice or document on all

persons interested (whether jointly with or as claiming through or under him) in the Share.

WINDING UP

152. If the Company shall be wound up the Liquidator shall apply the assets of the Company in satisfaction of creditors' claims in conformity with the provisions of the PCC Act.

153 (1). The assets available for distribution in each Cell in respect of which Participation Shares of a particular class have been issued shall be distributed among the members entitled to participate in such class in the following priority:-

(a) First, in the payment of the holders of the Participation Shares of that class of a sum equal to the nominal amount of the Participation Shares of such class held by such holders respectively provided that there are sufficient assets available in the relevant Cell to enable such payment to be made. In the event that, as regards any class of Participation Shares, there are insufficient assets available in the relevant cell to enable such payment to be made, no recourse shall be had to any non-cellular assets nor to the assets of any other Cell;

(b) Secondly, in the payment to the holders of the Nominal Shares of that class of sums up to the nominal amount paid up thereon provided that if there are insufficient assets as aforesaid to enable such payment in full to be made, no recourse shall be had to any non-cellular assets nor to the assets of any other Cell.

(c) Thirdly, in the payment to the holders of the Participation Shares of each class of any balance then remaining in the relevant Cell, such payment being made in proportion to the number of Participation Shares of the relevant class held.

(2) The assets available for distribution in respect of the non-cellular assets shall subject to and after payment in full of the claims of creditors in accordance with Article 152 be distributed to the holders of Founder Shares in payment of an amount equal to the nominal amount for the time being paid up on such shares and as to the balance then remaining to the holders of the Founder Shares pro rata in proportion to the number of Founder Shares

held by them. In the event that there are insufficient non-cellular assets available to enable such payment to be made, no recourse shall be had to any cellular assets.

154. If the Company shall be wound up the liquidator may with the authority of a Special Resolution divide among the members holding Participation Shares of the Cell in specie the whole or any part of the cellular assets of the Cell and whether or not the assets shall consist of property of a single kind and may for such purposes set such value as he deems fair upon any asset or classes of assets and may determine how such division shall be carried out as between the members holding Participation Shares of that Cell. The liquidator may with the like authority vest any part of the assets in trustees upon such trusts for the benefit of members holding Participation Shares of that cell as the liquidator with the like authority shall think fit and the liquidation of the Company may be closed and the Company dissolved but so that no member shall be compelled to accept any shares in respect of which there is liability.

INDEMNITY

155. Save as otherwise provided by the Companies Act and PCC Act, every Director Secretary Manager and other officer or servant of the Company shall be indemnified by the Company against and it shall be the duty of the Directors out of the assets of the Company to pay all costs losses and expenses which any such officer or servant may incur or become liable to by reason of any contract entered into or in any way in discharge of his duties including legal expenses and the amount for which such indemnity is provided shall immediately attach as a lien on the property of the Company and have priority as between the Members over all other claims.

156. Save as otherwise provided by the Companies Act and PCC Act, no Director Secretary Manager or other officer or servant of the Company shall be liable for the acts receipt neglects or defaults of any other person or for joining in any receipt or other act for conformity or for any loss or expense happening to the Company through the insufficiency or deficiency of title to any property acquired by order of the Directors for or on behalf of the Company or for the insufficiency or deficiency of any security in or upon which any of the moneys of the Company shall be

invested or for any loss or damage arising from the bankruptcy insolvency or tortuous act of any person with whom any moneys securities or effects shall be deposited or for any loss damage or misfortune whatsoever which shall happen in the execution of the duties of his respective office or in relation thereto unless the same happen through his own wilful breach of duty or failure to exercise due care.

157. Further or in the alternative to indemnify and hold harmless the every Director Secretary Manager and other officer or servant of the Company from all liability incurred by him in defending any proceedings, whether civil or criminal, in which judgment is given in his favour or which he is acquitted or in connection with any application under section 378 of the Companies Act (or its equivalent) in which relief is granted to it by the court.

158. The aforementioned indemnities are separate and distinct indemnities and if for any reason one of them is held to be void or unenforceable, it shall not affect the validity or enforceability of the others.

159. The Directors may exercise all the powers of the Company to purchase and maintain for any director, auditor or other officer (including former directors and other officers) or any other person insurance against any liability for negligence, default, breach of duty or breach of trust or any other liability which may lawfully be insured against.

Appendix 4:

Specimen Private Information Memorandum of a PCC Umbrella Fund

Reliance on this Private Information Memorandum and the Part B/Cell A Private Information Memorandum for the purpose of buying shares in the [•] Property Fund may expose an individual to a significant risk of losing all of the property or other assets invested

[•] PCC LIMITED

A Gibraltar Protected Cell Company Experienced Investor Fund

[•] 2010

PRIVATE INFORMATION MEMORANDUM

Issued by [•] PCC Limited (the "Company") and approved by [•] Limited who is authorised and regulated by the Financial Services Authority in the UK in connection with the promotion of the [•] Property Fund, a Cell of the Company. [•] Limited is not otherwise involved in the promotion of the [•] Property Fund. The Company is incorporated in Gibraltar under the Companies Act of Gibraltar and is established as a protected cell company pursuant to the Protected Cell Companies Act 2001. The [•] Property Fund is a cell of the Company (also known as Cell A) which has been created for the purposes set out in Part B of this Private Information Memorandum. In the UK, the Company is classed as an unregulated collective investment scheme.

This Private Information Memorandum and its Part B/Cell A Private Information Memorandum are exempt from the restrictions on the promotion of unregulated schemes (in section 238 of the Financial Services and Markets Act 2000) and should be disregarded by members of the public because they are aimed solely at Professional Investors, Certified Sophisticated Investors, Certified High Net Worth Individuals and High Net Worth Companies and any other persons as permitted by law (the Financial Services and Markets Act (Promotion of Collective Investments scheme) Exemptions) Order 2001 (SI 2001/1060) and relevant regulations (COBS 4.12 of the Handbook of the Financial Services Authority in the UK).

A High Net Worth Individual has an annual income in excess of £100,000 or net assets in excess of £250,000 (excluding his main residence, pension and insurance policies). A Certified High Net Worth Individual is a person who has been certified within the past 12 months by an authorised person as sufficiently knowledgeable to understand the risks associated with participating in unregulated schemes. A High Net Worth Company normally has net assets in excess of £5 million.

Please note that an investment in the Company is a high risk investment designed for sophisticated investors who can afford to lose all of their investment. If you have any doubts or queries, you should consult an authorised person specialising in advising on unregulated collective property schemes. The value of any investment may go down and you may not get back your original investment. Due to the level of borrowing that may be undertaken, it should be noted that in a falling property market, such borrowing may accelerate substantially the rate of losses that may be incurred. Investors may not be able to make any claims under the Financial Services Compensation Scheme or under the Financial services Ombudsman Scheme. Reliance on this promotion for the purpose of buying shares in the [•] Property Fund may expose an individual to a significant risk of losing all of the property or other assets invested.

It is not expected that investors will realise any value until the expiry of the [•] Property Fund. Any investor wishing to dispose of shares before then may find it difficult to dispose of the shares at a reasonable price or at any price. Investors may be obliged to hold shares until expiry of the [•] Property Fund when the assets will be sold and any liabilities including any borrowing will be repaid. Full details of the investment risks are set out on pages 14 to 17 of this Private Information Memorandum and pages 20 to 28 of its Part B/Cell A Private Information Memorandum.

THIS PRIVATE INFORMATION MEMORANDUM IS TO BE READ IN CONJUCTION WITH PART B/CELL A PRIVATE INFORMATION MEMORANDUM AND TOGETHER THEY FORM A SINGLE DOCUMENT AND SHOULD BE READ AS ONE DOCUMENT

The Directors of the Company whose names appear on page [ ] of this Private Information Memorandum have taken all reasonable care to ensure that the facts stated in this document are true and accurate in all material respects, and that there are no other facts the omission of which would make misleading any statement in the document, whether of facts or of opinion. The Directors accept responsibility accordingly.

INVESTMENT WARNING

[•] PCC LIMITED (the "Company") has been established in Gibraltar as an Experienced Investor Fund. It is suitable only for those who fall within the definition of "Experienced Investor" contained in the Financial Services (Experienced Investor Funds) Regulations, 2005.

Requirements which may be deemed necessary for the protection of retail or non-Experienced Investors, do not apply to Experienced Investor Funds. By acknowledging this statement you are expressly agreeing that you fall within the definition of an "Experienced Investor" and accept the reduced requirements accordingly.

You are wholly responsible for ensuring that all aspects of this Company are acceptable to you. Investment in Experienced Investor Funds may involve special risks that could lead to a loss of all or a substantial portion of such investment. Unless you fully understand and accept the nature of this Company and the potential risks inherent in this Company you should not invest in this Company.

Further information in relation to the regulatory treatment of Experienced Investor Funds in Gibraltar may be obtained from the Gibraltar Financial Services Commission.

APPENDIX 4

ABOUT THIS PRIVATE INFORMATION MEMORANDUM

GENERAL

This Private Information Memorandum which contains certain information about the Company and invites selected individuals, to apply for Participation Shares (as defined herein) in the Company. It has been approved by the Controller and Administrator of the Company on the advice of legal counsel ("Controller" is defined in the Financial Services (Experienced Investor Funds) Regulations, 2005 as a person or persons responsible for the management and control of an Experienced Investor Fund).

Prospective investors should, however, not construe the contents of this Private Information Memorandum as legal, tax or financial advice. Each prospective investor should consult his own professional advisors as to (a) the legal requirements within the country of his residence for the purchase, holding or disposal of Participation Shares in the Company, (b) any foreign exchange restrictions that may be relevant to him and the income and other tax consequences that may be relevant to the purchase, holding or disposal of those shares.

Additionally the Company's portfolio is subject to normal market fluctuations as well as the risks inherent in the investment instruments described below under "Investment Objectives and Policy", "Investment Guidelines and Restrictions" and "Risk Factors" and there can be no assurance that appreciation of the Company's assets will occur or that losses will not be realised. Consequently, the value of Participation Shares may be subject to volatile movements and may fall as well as rise. Investment in Participation Shares should be considered speculative and suitable only for persons who can assume the risk of losing their entire investment.

EXPERIENCED INVESTORS

This Private Information Memorandum invites Experienced Investors as defined in the Financial Services (Experienced Investor Funds) Regulations, 2005 to apply for Participation Shares in the Company. It does not constitute a general offer or invitation to the public to subscribe for shares or securities in the Company other than Experienced Investors as so defined. An Experienced Investor is a person or body who, at the time of the investment, falls into one of the following categories:

(a) a person or partnership whose ordinary business or professional activity includes, or it is reasonable to expect that it includes, acquiring, underwriting, managing, holding or disposing of investments, whether as principal or agent, or the giving of advice concerning investments;

(b) a body corporate which has net assets in excess of €1,000,000 or which is part of a group which has net assets in excess of €1,000,000;

(c) an unincorporated association which has net assets in excess of €1,000,000;

(d) the trustee of a trust where the aggregate value of the cash and investments which form part of the trust's assets in excess of €1,000,000;

(e) an individual whose net worth, or joint net worth with that person's spouse, is greater than €1,000,000, excluding that person's principal place of residence; or

(f) a participant who invests a minimum of €100,000 in the fund.

The Company's Administrator, have notified the Gibraltar Financial Services Commission, the Authority regulating collective investment schemes in Gibraltar, of the establishment of the Company. A copy of this Private Information Memorandum together with an Opinion from the Company's lawyer that the Company complies with the Financial Services (Collective Investment Schemes) Act 2005 and the Financial Services (Experienced Investor Funds) Regulations, 2005 has been filed with the Gibraltar Financial Services Commission. Further information in relation to the regulatory treatment of Experienced Investor Funds in Gibraltar may be obtained from the Gibraltar Financial Services Commission.

The minimum investment for an Experienced Investor who does not fall within paragraphs (a) to (e) above is €100,000 or its foreign currency equivalent.

RESTRICTIONS ON DISTRIBUTION

THE DISTRIBUTION OF THIS DOCUMENT AND THE OFFERING OF THE PARTICIPATION SHARES IN CERTAIN JURISDICTIONS MAY BE RESTRICTED. ACCORDINGLY THIS DOCUMENT MAY NOT BE USED FOR THE PURPOSE OF AND DOES NOT CONSTITUTE, AN OFFER OR SOLICITATION BY ANYONE IN ANY JURISDICTION OR IN ANY CIRCUMSTANCES IN WHICH SUCH SOLICITATION IS NOT AUTHORISED OR TO ANY PERSON TO WHOM IT IS UNLAWFUL TO MAKE SUCH OFFER OR SOLICITATION.

No person is authorised to issue any advertisement, give any information or make any representation in connection with the offering, subscription or sale of Participation Shares if it is not contained in this document. Any advertisement so issued or information or representation not so contained must not be relied upon as having been authorised by or on behalf of the Company. The delivery of this document at any time and the allocation of Participation Shares do not imply that information contained in this document is correct at any time subsequent to its date.

Persons into whose possession this Private Information Memorandum comes are required by the Company to inform themselves about and to observe any such restrictions. This Private Information Memorandum does not constitute, and may not be used for the purpose of, an offer or solicitation to anyone in any jurisdiction in which such offer or solicitation is not authorised or to any person to whom it is unlawful to make such offer or solicitation.

RESTRICTIONS WITHIN THE U.S.

THE PARTICIPATION SHARES OF THE COMPANY HAVE NOT BEEN REGISTERED UNDER THE U.S. SECURITIES ACT OF 1933 AND THE COMPANY HAS NOT BEEN REGISTERED UNDER THE U.S. INVESTMENT COMPANY ACT OF 1940. PARTICIPATION SHARES MAY NOT BE AND WILL NOT BE OFFERED FOR SALE OR SOLD, TRANSFERRED OR DELIVERED, DIRECTLY OR INDIRECTLY, IN THE UNITED STATES, ITS TERRITORIES OR POSSESSIONS, OR TO A U.S. PERSON (AS DEFINED HEREIN).

Accordingly, the Participation Shares may not be offered, sold or delivered, directly or indirectly, in the United States, or to any resident thereof (including any corporation, partnership or other entity organised or created under the laws of the United States or any political subdivision thereof) or to any estate or trust the income of which is subject to United States Federal Income Taxation, regardless of its source or to any person, corporation, partnership or other entity qualifying as a "U.S. Person" as defined under the Securities Act from time to time EXCEPT FOR any person falling within any relevant exemption under the Securities Act 1933 (each such prohibited person being a "U.S. Person").

For your information, the definition of U.S. Person is contained in Rule 902 of Regulation S under the Securities Act 1933 which reads:

a. U.S. person.

1. "U.S. person" means:

   i. Any natural person resident in the United States;

   ii. Any partnership or corporation organized or incorporated under the laws of the United States;

   iii. Any estate of which any executor or administrator is a U.S. person;

   iv. Any trust of which any trustee is a U.S. person;

   v. Any agency or branch of a foreign entity located in the United States;

   vi. Any non-discretionary account or similar account (other than an estate or trust) held by a dealer or other fiduciary for the benefit or account of a U.S. person;

   vii. Any discretionary account or similar account (other than an estate or trust) held by a dealer or other fiduciary organized, incorporated, or (if an individual) resident in the United States; and

   viii. Any partnership or corporation if:

      A. Organized or incorporated under the laws of any foreign jurisdiction; and

      B. Formed by a U.S. person principally for the purpose of investing in securities not registered under the Act, unless it is organized or incorporated, and owned, by accredited investors (as defined in Rule 501(a)) who are not natural persons, estates or trusts.

RESTRICTIONS WITHIN THE UNITED KINGDOM

The Company is a collective investment scheme whose promotion in the United Kingdom is restricted by Section 238 of the Financial Services and Markets Act 2000 (the "FSMA"). Participation Shares may not be offered or sold in the UK other than to persons who are already participants in the Company or persons who have been, in the last 30 months, participants in the Company and persons for whom an authorized person to carry on investment business under the FSMA has taken reasonable steps to ensure that investment in the Company is suitable and who is an established or newly accepted customer. Participation Shares may not be offered or sold by an authorised person in the United Kingdom other than to persons authorised to carry on investment business under the FSMA and persons whose ordinary business involves the acquisition and disposal of property of the same kind as the property or a substantial part of the property in which the Company invests and persons permitted to receive this document under the Financial Services (Promotion of Unregulated Schemes) Regulations 1991. Except as described above, no document, including this document, issued in connection with the Participation Shares in the United Kingdom may be passed on to any person, unless that person is of a kind described in Article 11 (3) of the Financial Services (Investment Advertisements) (Exemptions) Order 1996 (as amended) or is a person to whom this document may be otherwise lawfully be issued or passed on.

This Private Information Memorandum is intended solely for the person to whom it has been delivered by the Company for the purpose of evaluating a possible investment by the recipient in the Participation Shares, and it is not to be reproduced or distributed to any other persons (other than professional advisers of the prospective investor receiving this document from the Company).

The undersigned being Directors of the Company authorise the issue of this Private Information Memorandum.

[•]

[•]

[•]

APPENDIX 4

CONTENTS

APPENDIX H
CERTIFICATE OF EMPLOYER OF ACCOUNTANT RELATING TO HIGH NET WORTH INDIVIDUALS (FOR UK PURPOSES ONLY)

APPENDIX I
PAYMENT INSTRUCTIONS

APPENDIX J
REDEMPTION REQUESTS

SECTION 1

DIRECTORY

DIRECTORS OF THE COMPANY

[•]

REGISTERED OFFICE

[•]

ADMINISTRATOR

[•]

PAYING BANK

[•]

AUDITOR

[•]

LEGAL ADVISORS

[•]

SECRETARY

[•]

SECTION 2

SUMMARY

This Summary should be read in conjunction with and is qualified in its entirety by reference to the information appearing in the main text of this Private Information Memorandum (as may be amended from time to time) and the documents described herein.

THE COMPANY	Is a protected cell company with registered number [•] incorporated in Gibraltar on [•]. The Company's legal status means that the Directors may create separate classes of shares with differing investment objectives and to which specific assets are attributed (the "Cells").
THE CELLS	Each Cell shall constitute a separate cell with one or more separate classes of shares (a "Cell") for the purposes of the Protected Cell Companies Act 2001 (the "PCC Act") in Gibraltar. Participation Shares, as defined below, may be issued and redeemed by the Company based on the underlying net value of a Cell's assets. Specific information relating to each Cell is detailed in Part B of this Private Information Memorandum.
FINANCIAL REPORTING DATE	31 December in each year or such other time as determined by the Directors for time to time.
BASE CURRENCY	The Base Currency of the Company is the Sterling ("Sterling" or "£"). The Base Currency of the Cells of the Company may be in currencies other than Sterling (£).
BUSINESS DAY	Any day on which the banks of Gibraltar are open for business, excluding Saturdays and Sundays.
VALUATION DAY	The last Business Day as defined in Part B of this Private Information Memorandum pertaining to each Cell or such other day as Directors may from time to time determine.

INVESTMENT

The investment objective for each Cell are more specifically detailed in Part B of this Private Information Memorandum.

ELIGIBLE INVESTORS

Shares in the Company may only be subscribed to those investors who are not restricted to invest in the Company as defined in this Private Information Memorandum.

The Company will not accept any subscription from an investor or permit the sale or transfer of Participation Shares, if in the reasonable opinion of Directors of the Company (who may seek legal counsel's opinion to support their presumption), such transaction would cause the Company to be deemed a "controlled foreign corporation" under Subpart F of the Internal Revenue Code of 1986.

Participation Shares may be subscribed to only by Experienced Investors as defined under the Financial Services (Experienced Investor Funds) Regulations, 2005. Experienced Investors are generally persons or entities whose business or profession includes dealing with investments or who have a net worth in excess of €1,000,000 or who invest a minimum of €100,000 in the Company.

For the purposes of this Private Information Memorandum the words shareholder and investor shall be deemed to be interchangeable.

SUBSCRIPTIONS

The Company is offering redeemable preference shares for subscription in each Cell on terms specified in Part B of this Private Information Memorandum for each Cell. The redeemable preference shares being issued as Participation Shares. The closing dates for receipt of initial subscription payments and details of the continuing offer for each Cell are listed in Part B of this Private Information Memorandum.

The minimum initial investments and additional minimum investments are detailed in Part B of this Private Information Memorandum. The Board of Directors reserves the right to vary any of the subscription requirements of the Company.

REDEMPTION AND TRANSFER OF SHARES

Participation Shares can be redeemed in each Cell on terms specified in Part B of this Private Information Memorandum. In the event that a shareholder wishes to sell or transfer shares to someone who is not an existing shareholder, then the purchaser must first be approved by the Board of Directors.

INITIAL ORGANISATION COSTS

The Company will be responsible for paying its preliminary expenses including expenses relating to the establishment of the Company in Gibraltar, the negotiation and preparation of the contracts to which it is party, the fees and expenses of its professional advisers in establishing the Company (the "Initial Organisation Costs"), The Initial Organisation Costs are estimated not to exceed £200,000 and will be paid by the Company and amortised over a period of 60 months. The Company will levy such costs to each Cell in proportion to the assets of each Cell.

The Company will pay the Administrator on a basis points fee system based on the Net Asset Value of the Company. All company secretarial services will be provided on a time spent basis at standard terms and conditions.

If the Company appoints a custodian (the "Custodian"), the Company would pay the Custodian fees on a basis points fee system based on the Net Asset Value of the Company.

The Company will pay its own company advisory, legal, audit and other expenses and will then levy such expenses that are not attributable to a particular cell or cells to be allocated and charged between one or more cells in such manner and on such basis as the Directors, in their absolute discretion, deem fair and equitable and the Directors have the power to and may at any time, and from time to time, vary such basis including where circumstances so permit the subsequent re-allocation of such liabilities, expenses, costs, charges and reserves.

The Company will pay the Investment Manager (if appointed) a Management Fee and Performance Fee. The Management Fees and Performance Fees are payable at the rates and based on the terms and conditions as detailed in Part B of this Private Information Memorandum.

The Investment Committee (if appointed) will be paid fees at the rates and based on the terms and conditions as detailed in Part B of this Private Information Memorandum.

DIRECTORS

[•] (the "Directors" and/or the "Board of Directors") have been appointed Directors of the Company pursuant to the terms and conditions of the Directorship Agreements dated [•].

The directors shall hereafter be referred to collectively as the "Directors" and/or the "Board of Directors".

INVESTMENT MANAGER

The Directors have not appointed an investment manager and/or investment managers to act for the Company (the "Investment Manager" and/or "Investment Managers"). The Directors may, at their discretion, appoint an Investment Manager and/or Investment Managers to act for Cells of the Company that may be formed from time to time. If the Directors appoint an Investment

Manager and/or Investment Managers to act for a Cell of the Company the terms and conditions of their appointment will be detailed in each and every respective Part B Private Information Memorandum.

INVESTMENT COMMITTEE The Board of Directors may appoint a committee from time to time to assist the Board of Directors with the management of the investments of a Cell of the Company.

ADMINISTRATOR [•] Limited (the "Administrator") has been appointed as Administrator of the Company pursuant to the terms and conditions of an Administration Agreement dated [•]

PAYING BANK [•] (the "Paying Bank") has been appointed by the Company as its Paying Bank.

AUDITOR [•] has accepted the appointment as the Company's auditor (the "Auditor").

SECRETARY [•] Limited has accepted the appointment as the Company's secretary (the "Secretary"). The Secretary is appointed and may be replaced pursuant to the Company Management Agreement between the Company and the Secretary dated 20 August 2009.

DIVIDEND POLICY Dividend policy in relation to each Cell are set out in Part B of this Private Information Memorandum.

CHANGES TO THE PRIVATE INFORMATION MEMORANDUM This Private Information Memorandum (and any and all Part B Private Information Memorandum's) may be amended to take into account any material changes from time to time and any such amendment will be notified in advance to the Financial Services Commission and thereafter to the Shareholders of the Company. Neither the delivery of this document, nor the offer, issue or sale of Shares in the Company shall under any circumstances constitute a representation that the affairs of the Company have not changed since the date hereof.

TAXATION

The Company shall apply to the Commissioner of Income Tax for a certificate of exemption from Gibraltar income tax under the Income Tax (Allowances, Deductions and Exemptions) Rules, 1992.

EACH SHAREHOLDER SHOULD CONSULT HIS OR HER TAX ADVISOR AS TO HIS OR HER OWN TAX POSITION.

SECTION 3

INVESTMENT OBJECTIVES, INVESTMENT STRATEGY AND RISK FACTORS

[•] PCC LIMITED was incorporated on [•] with registration number [•] and is registered under the laws of Gibraltar as a private company. It has its registered office at [•], Gibraltar. The Company is an Experienced Investor Fund under the Financial Services (Experienced Investor Funds) Regulations, 2005. The Company is also a protected cell company for the purposes of the Protected Cell Companies Act 2001 (the "PCC Act") which means that under Gibraltar law the Directors may create separate and statutorily segregated classes of shares with differing investment objectives and to which specific assets are attributed (the "Cells").

One or more Cells will constitute separate Cells whose assets will be kept separate and separately identifiable from assets not attributable to that Cell. Under Gibraltar law, provided the requirements of the PCC Act are complied with, the assets attributable to each Cell will only be available to the creditors of the Company who are creditors in respect of that Cell and shall be protected from creditors of the Company who are not creditors in respect of that Cell.

3.1 INVESTMENT OBJECTIVES

The Directors may create separate Cells, each with differing investment objectives and the particulars of which are more specifically detailed in the respective Part B of this Private Information Memorandum for each of the Cells as and when they are created.

3.2 INVESTMENT STRATEGY

The investment strategy for each Cell created is more specifically detailed in the respective Part B of this Private Information Memorandum.

3.3 RISK FACTORS

Investments in the Participation Shares will involve certain risks associated with investments and there can be no assurance that the investment objectives of the Company will be achieved.

Investors will not have an opportunity to select or value any of the investments of each Cell. The Directors of the Company may delegate the selection of investments to an Investment Manager. The likelihood that Investors will realise income or gain will depend on the skill and expertise of the Directors of the Company and the Investment Manager (if appointed from time to time) and the legal structure and operations it has created.

Investment in Participation Shares of the Company is intended only for, and limited to, the professional or sophisticated investor who can afford the risks inherent in this type of investment.

There may be a change in government regulation or policies which materially adversely affects the Company's activities. This is true with respect both to the regulation and policies of the Government of Gibraltar as well as that of the governments of any countries where the Company invests.

Prospective investors are recommended to review this Private Information Memorandum in its entirety in conjunction with Part B of the relevant Cell before deciding whether to invest in Participation Shares and should consider those specific risks associated with each Cell as detailed in Part B of this Private Information Memorandum and the more general risks associated with investment in the Company which are as follows:

3.3.1 LIQUIDITY

Certain investments held by a Cell of the Company may be relatively illiquid making it difficult to acquire or dispose of them at the fair value of the investments as there may be little or no market for such investments. Accordingly the Cell's ability to respond to movements in the market may be impaired and settlement of transactions subject to delay. It may not always be possible for the Cell to sell an investment at the desired price or to liquidate an open position due to market conditions. In some cases it may be impossible for the Cell to liquidate its positions and expose it to losses. There can be no assurance that an investor will be able to realise his investment before the Cell is wound up and the capital is returned to the shareholders.

3.3.2 EXCHANGE RATE

The Company accepts subscriptions, pays redemptions and computes Net Asset Values in the base currency of each Cell. However, many or all of the investments held by a Cell of the Company may be denominated in currencies other than in the base currency of the Cell. Accordingly, currency exchange rates could play an important role in the Cell's return to investors. A change in the value of currencies against the base currency of a Cell will result in a corresponding change in base currency value of the Cell's assets denominated in these currencies.

3.3.3 LEVERAGE

A Cell may use leverage in its investment programme when deemed appropriate by the Board of Directors and/or Investment Manager. Leverage is the use of borrowed funds for investment. The amount of leverage employed by the Cells of the Company will be determined in each and every Cell as detailed in the relevant Part B of this Private Information Memorandum. While the use of leverage can substantially improve the return on invested capital, it may also substantially increase the adverse impact to which an investment portfolio may be subject.

3.3.4 REGULATORY SUPERVISION

The investments of the Cells of the Company will not be monitored or supervised by any regulatory body although the Company and its Administrator are subject to the authority of the Financial Services Commission of Gibraltar (the "FSC"). As an Experienced Investor Fund, the Company will provide annual audited financial statements to the FSC. As an Experienced Investor Fund the Company is registered under the Financial Services (Collective Investment Schemes) Act 2005. Further information in relation to the regulatory treatment of Experienced Investor Funds in Gibraltar may be obtained from the Gibraltar Financial Services Commission.

3.3.5 RELIANCE UPON DIRECTORS

The success of the Company and its Cells will be dependent to a large extent upon the efforts and skills of the Directors, their associates and/or advisors (including the Investment Manager if appointed from time to time, depending on the investment strategy of each Cell).

3.3.6 LACK OF OPERATING HISTORY

The Company is recently formed and has no operating history.

3.3.7 EXPENSES

The Company and the Cells must pay various fees and other costs regardless of whether it is profitable. The Company and the Cells thus must generate net investment income in order to break even.

3.3.8 PROTECTED CELL COMPANY

The Company is a protected cell company for the purposes of the PCC Act which means that under Gibraltar law, provided the conditions laid down in the PCC Act are complied with, assets attributable to each Cell of the Company shall only be available to creditors in respect of that Cell and the assets of that Cell shall be protected from creditors of the Company who are not creditors in respect of that Cell. Potential investors should be aware that the segregation of assets and liabilities in this manner under Gibraltar law might not necessarily be recognised in jurisdictions where the Company's assets are located.

3.3.9 CROSS LIABILITY BETWEEN CELLS

3.3.9.1 NO RECOURSE TO THE ASSETS OF ANY OTHER CELL

Each separate Cell will maintain separate accounting books and records. A holder of shares issued in a given Cell shall be entitled to look solely to the assets of that Cell in respect of all payments (including dividends, if applicable) due in respect of the shares held by that holder which are issued in that Cell. If the realised net assets of the relevant Cell are insufficient to pay any amounts due on the relevant shares, the holder of those shares shall have no further right of payment in respect of those shares nor any claim against or recourse to any of the assets of any other Cell or any of the other non-cellular assets of the Company.

3.3.9.2 ALLOCATION OF LIABILITIES BETWEEN CELLS

The Company may from time to time incur liabilities which are not attributable to a single given Cell, but which may relate to or inure to the general benefit of more than one Cell. In such circumstances the Directors shall allocate to each relevant Cell a proportion of such liabilities *pro-rata* to the Cell or on such other basis as the Directors, after consultation with the Investment Adviser, may determine having regard to what the Directors consider in their discretion to be fair and reasonable in the circumstances.

3.3.9.3 ALLOCATION OF LIABILITIES AMONG ALL SHAREHLDERS IN THE EVENT OF NON-RECOGNITION OF PROTECTED CELL STATUS

The Company expects from time to time to make issues of shares in different Cells. Each Cell is not a separate legal entity. The Company as a whole is one legal entity. A protected cell company is a company whose principal feature is that each cell has its own distinct assets which are not available to creditors of other cells or of the company as a whole. Whilst the Company intends at all times to comply with the stipulation in the PCC Act that the Company identifies the specific Cell in respect of which it is transacting from time to time, and whilst the PCC Act seeks to protect the assets of cells of protected cell companies from the claims of creditors of other cells or of the Company as a whole, as a matter of

Gibraltar law, it is possible that the law of another jurisdiction may not recognise the nature of protected cell companies as intended under the PCC Act. The protected cell company structure has not, so far as the Directors are aware, been tested in any courts. Accordingly, if the assets of the Company are situated in a jurisdiction other than Gibraltar, or legal proceedings are brought in respect of the Company outside Gibraltar, it is not known whether courts in other jurisdictions would recognise the protected cell structure and the integrity of Cells. As such, it is possible that a judgment in a jurisdiction other than Gibraltar may deem the assets of other Cells to be available to meet the claims of creditors of a given Cell or of the Company as a whole. Similarly, it is conceivable that a creditor of one Cell or of the Company as a whole may, in taking action against the Company in respect of that Cell or of the Company as a whole, occasion the transpiration of what may be deemed to be an insolvency, termination or like event insofar as the contractual relations of one or more of the Company's other Cells are concerned (whether in respect of any property developments investments or otherwise), thereby causing such other Cell or Cells or the Company as a whole to be in default of their contractual obligations or otherwise adversely impacting upon their respective contractual standing. However, the Company will wherever possible endeavour to transact with all counterparties in accordance with the PCC Act of Gibraltar and otherwise on a limited recourse basis with the intention of legislating that claims against the Company would be restricted to the assets of the relevant Cell in respect of which the transaction or transactions giving rise to the claim were entered into. Under the PCC Act, creditors of a particular Cell may, pursuant to a recourse agreement, have recourse to the non-cellular assets of the Company to the extent that the assets of that particular Cell are insufficient to meet the liability in question. As at the date of this Private Information Memorandum, the Directors are not aware of any such existing recourse agreement or any other existing or contingent liability.

3.3.9.4 CONSEQUENCES OF WINDING-UP PROCEEDINGS

If the Company fails for any reason to meet the obligations of any one or more of its Cells or any of its non-cellular obligations, or is unable to pay its debts or those attributable, in accordance with the PCC Act, to any of its Cells, a creditor may be entitled to make an application for the winding up of the Company. The commencement of such proceedings may entitle creditors to terminate contracts with the Company and claim damages for any loss arising from such early termination. The commencement of such proceedings may result in the Company being dissolved at a time prior to the relevant scheduled Redemption Date and the assets of its Cells being realised and applied to pay off the liabilities attributable to those Cells respectively. Notably, it is possible that such proceedings may be issued as a consequence of only one Cell failing to have sufficient assets to meet the obligations of the Company entered into in respect of that Cell, while the other Cells continue to have sufficient assets to enable the Company to discharge their respective liabilities. In other words, notwithstanding the separatist provisions of the PCC Act and the endeavours of the Company and the Directors to ensure that the Company transacts on a limited recourse basis in respect of transactions entered into with respect to its particular Cells from time to time, any difficulties the Company may experience in respect of discharging the obligations of one Cell may conceivably have an adverse impact on the position of other Cells which are otherwise solvent and performing as intended in the event winding-up proceedings are commenced.

In the event that the Company becomes subject to winding-up proceedings, the liquidator of the Company will be bound by the PCC Act to keep cellular assets separate and separately identifiable from other cellular assets and from non-cellular assets and to discharge the claims of creditors in conformity with the provisions of the PCC Act.

In the event of winding-up proceedings being commenced, the Company may not be able to pay the full redemption monies due and any amount of dividends and any other or alternative amounts (if any) anticipated in respect of the Shares of any Cell.

3.3.10 CONCENTRATION OF INVESTMENTS

The Cells of the Company may at times hold relatively few investments. The Cells of the Company could be subject to significant losses if it holds a large position in a particular investment that decreases in value.

3.3.11 EFFECT OF REDEMPTION

If significant redemptions of Participation Shares are requested it may not be possible for the Cells of the Company to liquidate its investments at the time the request for redemption is received at the fair value of the investments resulting in a decreased value of the investments.

There may be specific additional Risk Factors in relation to a particular Cell. Please see Part B of this Private Information in relation to each and every Cell of the Company.

SECTION 4

MANAGEMENT, SERVICE PROVIDERS AND AUDITOR

4.1 BOARD OF DIRECTORS

The function of the Directors is to conduct the Company's business operations and review and be responsible for the activities of the Company pursuant to Directorship Agreements between the Directors and the Company.

The members of the Board of Directors are elected and may be removed by the holders of the majority in nominal value of the Founder Shares of the Company (herein defined) to serve for an indefinite term. The Directors will serve until their resignation, incapacity or removal. The Directors also have the power to appoint any person to be a Director either to fill a casual vacancy or as an addition to the existing Directors. The members of the Board of Directors will serve until their resignation, incapacity, death or removal.

The Directors will hold a board meeting of the Company at least quarterly to review the investment and administrative affairs of the Company.

The Board of Directors of the Company currently consists of the following:

[•]

[•]

[•]

4.2 INVESTMENT MANAGER

The Directors have not appointed an Investment Manager and/or Investment Managers to act for the Company.

The Directors may, at their discretion, appoint an Investment Manager and/or Investment Managers to act for Cells of the Company that may be formed from time to time.

If the Directors appoint an Investment Manager and/or Investment Managers to act for a Cell of the Company the details of the terms and conditions of their appointment will be detailed in each respective Part B of this Private Information Memorandum.

4.3 INVESTMENT COMMITTEE

The Directors may appoint a committee to assist the Board of Directors with the management of the investments of a Cell of the Company. If such a committee is formed, the details of the terms and conditions of their appointment will be detailed in each respective Part B of this Private Information Memorandum.

4.4 ADMINISTRATOR

The Company has appointed [•] Limited (the "Administrator") as the administrator of the Company.

The Administrator is appointed and may be replaced pursuant to an Administration Agreement between the Company and the Administrator dated [•]. In accordance with the terms of the Administration Agreement the Administrator will be responsible, among other things, for the following matters, under the general supervision of the Board of Directors:

- Communicating with shareholders;
- Maintaining the Company's share register;
- Processing subscriptions and redemptions;
- Maintaining the Company's financial and accounting records;
- Preparing financial statements;
- Dealing with the Company's auditor; and
- Arranging for the provision of accounting, clerical and administrative services.

4.5 CUSTODIAN AND/OR PAYING BANK

[•] (the "Paying Bank") has been appointed by the Company as its Paying Bank. The Paying Bank, as appointed, will not provide any other services or perform any functions except that of a regular commercial bank and the usual administrative matters relating such services, and will have no other duties or responsibilities relating to the Company, for example the Paying Bank will not provide safe custody of assets, advisory services or asset management services nor will it monitor investment management activities or investment strategies of the Company.

The Paying Bank has not warranted the contents of this Private Information Memorandum or Part B of this Private Information

Memorandum nor will it be involved in the management, administration or Net Asset Value calculation of the Company.

The Paying Bank will not act as sponsor or promoter of the Company. Therefore, the Paying Bank will not assume any liability for negligent or wilful misconduct of the Company's Investment Manager, Trustee (or corresponding hierarchical level) or Administrator and potential investors should not rely upon the Paying Bank in deciding whether or not to invest in the Company.

If the Company appoints a Custodian, which may be appointed from time to time by the Board of Directors in respect of any Cell of the Company, the Custodian would be appointed on behalf of and pursuant to an agreement that would be entered into between the Custodian and the respective Cell and/or the Company.

The Custodian, if appointed, would not provide any other services or perform any other functions except safekeeping and the usual administrative matters relating to the safe custody of the assets of the Company, and would have no other duties or responsibilities relating to the Company, for example the Custodian would not provide advisory services or asset management services nor would it monitor investment management activities or investment strategies of the Company.

The Custodian, if appointed, would not supervise or control the activities of the Investment Manager or the Administrator of the Company. The Custodian, if appointed, would not warrant the contents of this Private Information Memorandum or its Part B nor would it be involved in the management, administration or Net Asset Value calculation of the Company.

The Custodian, if appointed, would not act as sponsor or promoter of the Company. Therefore, the Custodian would not assume any liability for negligent or wilful misconduct of the Company's Investment Manager or Administrator and potential investors should not rely upon the Custodian, if appointed, in deciding whether or not to invest in the Company.

4.6 AUDITOR

[•] Limited have accepted appointment as Auditor of the Company.

The Company shall at each Annual General Meeting appoint an Auditor or Auditors to hold office from the conclusion of that meeting until the conclusion of the next Annual General Meeting.

The first Auditor of the Company shall be appointed by the Directors at any time before the first Annual General Meeting of the Company and the Auditor so appointed shall hold office until the conclusion of that Meeting.

The Directors may fill any casual vacancy in the office of Auditor but while any such vacancy continues the surviving or continuing Auditor if any may act.

SECTION 5

FEES AND EXPENSES

5.1 INITIAL ORGANISATION COSTS

Costs and expenses associated with the initial organisation of the Company, including government, incorporation charges and professional fees and expenses in connection with the preparation of the Company's information documents, legal and fiscal advice, and the preparation of its corporate documents and contracts, are expected not to exceed £[•] and are paid by the Company out of the initial proceeds of the offering of the Participation Shares. Such organisational costs and expenses will be amortised by the Company over a period of 60 months. It is important to note that under International Financial Reporting Standards the amortisation of such costs are not allowed and in accordance with International Financial Reporting Standards such costs may be expensed in full in the audited financial statements of the Company in order for the financial statements to be prepared in accordance with International Financial Reporting Standards. The Directors acknowledge that amortising such costs are in line with industry practice.

5.2 FEES OF THE DIRECTORS

The Directors are paid a fee of £[•] per annum. The Company will also pay the reasonable expenses of the Directors incurred in carrying out their duties.

5.3 FEES OF THE INVESTMENT MANAGER

If the Directors appoint an Investment Manager and/or Investment Managers to manage a Cell of the Company the Investment Manger would be paid a Management and Performance Fee pursuant to the agreement between the Company and the Investment Manager and/or Investment Managers that would be payable at the rates and based on the terms and conditions as detailed in Part B of this Private Information Memorandum.

5.4 FEES OF THE INVESTMENT COMMITTEE

The Investment Committee (if appointed) will be paid fees at the rates and based on the terms and conditions as detailed in Part B of this Private Information Memorandum.

5.5 FEES OF THE ADMINISTRATOR

Pursuant to the Administration Agreement dated [•], the Administrator will receive from the Company remuneration for services rendered on a basis points fee system based on the Net Asset Value of the Company subject to a minimum fee. The terms and conditions regarding the calculation and payment of the Administration Fees are detailed in Part B to this Private Information Memorandum.

5.6 FEES OF THE CUSTODIAN AND/OR PAYING BANK

The Company will pay commercial rates and charges to its Paying Bank.

If appointed, the Company would pay charges at commercial rates to its Custodian as detailed in Part B of this Private Information Memorandum.

5.7 OTHER OPERATING EXPENSES

The Company will bear all other expenses incidental to its operations and business, including:

- Registered office;
- Banking charges;
- Fees and expenses of the Company's legal advisors and the auditor;
- Any income tax, withholding taxes, transfer taxes and other governmental charges and duties occurring for the Company; and
- The costs of printing and distributing any prospectuses and reports as well as notices to the shareholders.

The Company will levy such expenses to each Cell in the discretion of the Directors either as relates to each Cell or, if not specifically attributable to a Cell or Cells shall be allocated and charged between one or more cells in such manner and on such basis as the Directors, in their absolute discretion, deem fair and equitable and the Directors have the power to and may at any time, and from time to time, vary such basis including where circumstances so permit the subsequent re-allocation of such liabilities, expenses, costs, charges and reserves.

SECTION 6

THE COMPANY

6.1 SHARE CAPITAL

The Company has an authorised capital of GBP£[•], €[•], US$[•] and, CHF [•] divided into:

(a) [•] ordinary shares having a nominal value of £1.00 per share which may be issued as Founder Shares each which shall have voting rights but shall not participate in any profit or distribution of the Company that is attributable to the Cells.

(b) [•] redeemable preference shares having a nominal value of £0.0001 per share which may be issued as separate classes of Participation Shares or as Nominal Shares;

(c) [•] redeemable preference shares having a nominal value of €0.0001 per share which may be issued as separate classes of Participation Shares or as Nominal Shares;

(d) [•] redeemable preference shares having a nominal value of US$0.0001 per share which may be issued as separate classes of Participation Shares or as Nominal Shares;

(e) [•] redeemable preference shares having a nominal value of 0.0001 CHF per share which may be issued as separate classes of Participation Shares or as Nominal Shares.

Nominal Shares shall have no voting rights and shall not participate in any profit or distribution of the Company (except the repayment of the amount paid up on the Nominal Shares). Nominal Shares may be issued in respect of a Cell for the purposes of funding a redemption of Participation Shares, or for any other purpose as the Directors, in their absolute discretion, see fit.

Participation Shares shall not be entitled to vote at General Meetings except at separate class Meetings of the holders of Participation Shares of any class of Participation Shares provided that the holders of the Founder Shares also have the right to attend and vote at such meetings.

If at any time the Participation Shares in issue are divided into separate Cells different amounts of dividends may be payable in respect of the each Cell. No dividends shall be declared or paid other than from the profits or gains of the relevant Cell.

One or more classes of Participation Share, and Nominal Shares if in issue, shall be constituted as a separate Cell for the purposes of the PCC Act. In the event of a winding-up, each Participation Share carries an entitlement to a return of the nominal capital paid up in respect of each share in priority to the repayment of the nominal capital paid up on Nominal Shares and Founder Shares. Only Participation Shares carry the right to share in surplus assets after the return of the nominal capital paid up on Nominal Shares and Founder Shares.

All shares are, when issued, fully paid and non-assessable, and shareholders have no personal liability for the debts of the Company. The shares have no pre-emptive, conversion, exchange or other rights or privileges save as set out in the Memorandum and Articles of Association of the Company.

The Company shall in each year hold a general meeting as its Annual General Meeting in addition to any other meeting in that year. Such meetings may be held at such time and place as may be determined by the Directors. A meeting may also be convened by such requisitions as provided by the Companies Act.

The Directors may at any time convene a separate meeting of any class of holders of shares. A separate meeting of any class may also be convened by such requisition as is provided in accordance with the Companies Act. Notices of every general meeting of the Company shall be given in the manner authorised in the Articles of Association to every Member. At any general meeting of the Company, a resolution put to the vote of the meeting shall be decided on a show of hands of those entitled to vote unless a poll is demanded. The Articles of Association of the Company provide further details of the manner in which meetings of the Company will be held.

6.2 GIBRALTAR LEGAL REQUIREMENTS AND ANTI-MONEY LAUNDERING

As part of the Company's responsibility for the prevention of money laundering, the Company may require a detailed verification of an investor's identity. An individual shall be required to produce a copy of a passport or national identity card with photograph, together with one form of proof of residence, and copies of these shall be certified as true copies by a lawyer, accountant, banker or other such responsible individual. The Company may require that such documents be certified by a Notary Public and or affixed with an Apostille.

In the case of corporate applicants, they may be required to produce a certified copy of the certificate of incorporation (and any change of name), memorandum and articles of association (or equivalent), the names, occupations, dates of birth and residential and or business addresses of all directors, and or beneficial owners, along with certified copy of a passport or national identity card with photograph together with one form of proof of residence, and these shall be certified by a lawyer, accountant or banker. The Company may require that such documents be certified by a Notary Public and or affixed with an Apostille. The Company may require that the directors and or beneficial owners be required to provide details of their name and address of employer or business, their position with the Employer or Business, origin of assets, estimated total income and assets.

Each investor will be required to produce a letter of reference from a banker, lawyer or accountant in the attached format in the Appendices, or in any other such form as the Directors of the Company may from time to time accept.

The Company reserves the right to request such information as is necessary to verify the identity of an applicant. In the event of delay or failure by the applicant to produce any information required for verification purposes, the Company may refuse to accept the application and the subscription moneys relating thereto.

Each subscriber and shareholder shall be required to make such representations to the Company as the Company, the Administrator or the Investment Manager shall require in connection with applicable anti-money laundering procedures, including, without limitation, representations to the Company such subscriber or shareholder is not a prohibited country, territory, individual or entity listed on the US Department of Treasury's Office of Foreign Assets Control ("OFAC") website, an that it is not directly or indirectly affiliated with any country, territory, individual or entity named on an OFAC list or prohibited by any OFAC sanctions programmes. Such subscriber or shareholder shall also represent to the Company that amounts contributed by it to the Company were not directly or indirectly derived from activities that may contravene US Federal, state or international laws and regulations, including, without limitation, any applicable anti-money laundering laws and regulations.

The Administrator may disclose information regarding investors to such parties (for example, its affiliates, attorneys, auditors, administrators or regulators) as it deems necessary or advisable to facilitate the transfer of shares, including, but not limited to, in connection with anti-money laundering and similar laws. The Administrator or other service providers may also release information if compelled to do so by law or by any regulatory (including self-regulatory) organisation or pursuant to any investigation related to anti-money laundering or other laws or regulations.

Additional requirements may be imposed from time to time to comply with all applicable anti-money laundering laws, including the United States Patriot Act.

6.3 REGISTRATION AND TRANSFER OF SHARES

Except as the Directors may permit, the Company shall not issue certificated Shares and Shares will be issued in registered form.

The Company maintains a current list of the registered names and addresses of the Company's shareholders at the registered office of the Company in Gibraltar.

Transfers of shares can only take effect by serving upon the Company in the manner prescribed by law, an instrument of transfer signed by or on behalf of the transferor and the transferee. In the event that any share certificates have been issued in respect of shares which are transferred those share certificates must be endorsed by the shareholder and returned to the Company.

Any transferee will be required to provide the same information which would be required in connection with a direct subscription in order for a transfer application to be considered by the Directors. Violation of applicable ownership and transfer restrictions may, at the discretion of the Directors, result in compulsory redemption of the relevant Participation shares.

The Shares of the Company are not listed on any securities exchange. As of the date of this Private Information Memorandum there is not any secondary market for trading in the Shares of the Company.

Shares may not be transferred to any U. S. Person as defined herein.

6.4 NET ASSET VALUATIONS

Net asset valuations will be determined by the Administrator on the Valuation Day (the last Business Day as defined in Part B to this Private Information Memorandum pertaining to each Cell or such other day as the Directors may from time to time determine). The Board of Directors may determine any other date as being the Valuation Day.

Net Asset Value calculations are determined in the following manner:

6.4.1 NET ASSET VALUE

The Net Asset Value in respect of each Cell at a particular Valuation Day is calculated by the Administrator on an accruals basis of accounting by subtracting from the total value of the assets attributable to the Cell an amount equal to all liabilities and contingencies attributable to the respective Cell for which the Administrator determines should be made.

6.4.2 NET ASSET VALUE PER PARTICIPATION SHARE

The Net Asset Value per Participation Share on any Valuation Day is equal to the Net Asset Value of a particular Cell divided by the total number of Participation Shares outstanding on Valuation Day (including the Participation Shares (if any) being redeemed but excluding Participation Shares to be issued on the Business Day following the Valuation Day and the effect of Nominal Shares). The Net Asset Value per Participation Share will be rounded to two decimal places (a number equal to or greater than five (5) shall be rounded up to the nearest whole number, a number less than five (5) shall be rounded down to the nearest whole number).

6.4.3 VALUATION

Valuations are made by the Directors or the Administrator as their delegate in accordance with International Financial Reporting Standards, including provision for proper accruals and reserves. Full details of valuation techniques will be detailed in Part B of this Private Information Memorandum pertaining to each Cell or such other value as the Directors may from time to time determine.

6.4.4 FOREIGN EXCHANGE RATES

The Company's financial statements are maintained in Great Britain Pounds ("GBP", or "£") and the accounts for each of the Cells are maintained in the base currency of that Cell. Assets and liabilities denominated in other currencies are translated at the rate of exchange in effect at the relevant Valuation Day and translation adjustments are reflected in the results of operations. Portfolio transactions and income and expenses are translated at the rates of exchange in effect at the time of each transaction.

6.5 INVESTOR SUITABILITY

6.5.1 EXPERIENCED INVESTORS

The Company is an Experienced Investor Fund as defined under the Financial Services (Experienced Investor Funds) Regulations, 2005. Participation Shares may be subscribed to only by Experienced Investors as defined under the Financial Services (Experienced Investor Funds) Regulations, 2005. An Experienced Investor is generally:

(a) a person or partnership whose ordinary business or professional activity includes, or it is reasonable to expect that it includes, acquiring, underwriting, managing, holding or disposing of investments, whether as principal or agent, or the giving of advice concerning investments;

(b) a body corporate which has net assets in excess of €1,000,000 or equivalent or which is part of a group which has net assets in excess of €1,000,000 or equivalent;

(c) an unincorporated association which has net assets in excess of €1,000,000 or equivalent;

(d) the trustee of a trust where the aggregate value of the cash and investments which form part of the trust's assets is in excess of €1,000,000 or equivalent;

(e) an individual whose net worth, or joint net worth with that person's spouse, is greater than €1,000,000 or equivalent, excluding that person's principal place of residence; or

(f) a participant who invests a minimum of €100,000 or equivalent in the Company.

6.5.2 NON U.S. PERSON

Each prospective investor will be required to certify that the Participation Shares are not being acquired directly or indirectly for the account or benefit of a U.S. Person as defined above.

SECTION 7

TAXATION

7.1 THE COMPANY

The following is a summary of Gibraltar's tax position which is in effect on the date of this Private Information Memorandum. Please note that there is always a risk that the current tax legislation may be changed or its interpretation may come into effect after such date.

The Company is established as an Experienced Investor Fund and pursuant to Rule 3(17) of the Income Tax (Allowances, Deductions and Exemptions) Rules 1992 (the "Rules"), the investment income of the Company shall be exempted from tax. The Company will apply for a certificate of exemption from the Commissioner of Income Tax under the Rules.

Under the current Gibraltar law, there is no withholding tax on dividend payments to shareholders not resident in Gibraltar for Gibraltar income tax purposes.

No death duties, capital gains tax, gift, inheritance or capital transfer taxes are levied in Gibraltar.

Income derived from the underlying investments of the Company and/or any of its Cells may be subject to local taxation in the country where those investments are situated.

7.2. THE SHAREHOLDERS

The summary in paragraph 20 above does not purport to be a comprehensive description of all the tax considerations that may be relevant to the decision to purchase, own or dispose of the Participation Shares in the Company. Prospective investors of the Participation Shares should inform consult their tax advisers on any tax consequences in particular to their circumstances arising in the jurisdiction in which they are resident or domiciled for tax purposes in connection with the acquisition, ownership, redemption or disposition of the Participation Shares.

EACH SHAREHOLDER SHOULD CONSULT A TAX ADVISER AS TO HIS OR HER OWN TAX POSITION.

SECTION 8

MATERIAL CONTRACTS AND CONFLICTS OF INTEREST

8.1 MATERIAL CONTRACTS

The following contracts have been entered into by the Company (other than in the ordinary course of business) since incorporation and are, or may be, material.

Directorship Agreements (as amended from time to time) between the Company and the Directors specifies the terms whereby the Directors agree to act as Directors of the Company. These agreements will continue in force subject to the termination provisions contained in them. The Directors are empowered under the agreements to delegate their functions, powers, discretions, privileges and duties, as permitted by law, as they deem appropriate as long as the delegation of functions, powers, discretions, privileges and duties are not in conflict with the requirements of the Financial Services (Experienced Investor Funds) Regulations, 2005. The agreements contain an indemnity to the Directors in respect of actions brought against them provided such actions are not in respect of expense, loss, liability or damage which was caused by the Directors' own negligence, default, breach of duty or breach of trust.

Administration Agreement (as amended from time to time) between the Company and the Administrator specifies the terms whereby the Administrator agrees to act as administrator for the Company. This agreement shall continue in effect until terminated at any time by either party without the payment of any penalty, upon not less than 90 days written notice to the other party, except that this agreement may be terminated immediately by either party if the other shall commit any breach of its obligations under it subject to a 30 day remedy period, or appoint a liquidator or receiver or become insolvent and unable to pay its debts as they fall due. The agreement contains an indemnity from the Administrator to the Company in respect of all liabilities, losses, damages, actions, proceedings and claims which may be brought against, suffered or incurred by the Company to the extent that they are directly attributable to the gross negligence, fraud or wilful misconduct on the part of the Administrator in the performance of its duties.

Custodian Agreement, a Custodian, which may be appointed from time to time by the Board of Directors in respect of any Cell of the Company, would enter into an agreement with the Company which would specify the terms whereby the Custodian agrees to act as Custodian for the Company. Such Agreement would continue in force until determined by either party giving written notice as will be provided for in the respective agreements. Custodian agreements may contain an indemnity to the Custodian in respect of actions brought against it provided such actions are not in respect of expense, loss, liability or damage which was caused by the Custodian's gross negligence, fraud and/or wilful default.

Company Management Agreement (as amended from time to time) between the Company and the Secretary shall specify the terms whereby the Secretary agrees to act as secretary for the Company. This agreement shall continue in effect until terminated at any time by either party without the payment of any penalty, upon not less than 30 days written notice to the other party, except that this agreement may be terminated upon not less than 14 days notice to the other party of either party if the other shall commit any breach of its obligations, or appoint a liquidator or receiver or become insolvent and unable to pay its debts as they fall due. The agreement provides for a limitation of the Secretary's liability for any losses whether in contract, tort or otherwise, for any losses whatsoever and howsoever caused arising from or in any way connected with the agreement.

8.2. CONFLICTS OF INTEREST

There may arise instances where the interest of the Directors or their affiliates and service providers of the Company conflict with interests of the Company and its shareholders. Such conflicts include, but are not limited to the following:

a) The Directors may be engaged in other substantial activities apart from the activities with respect to the Company and may devote to the Company only as much time as is reasonably necessary, in their judgement, for its management.

b) The Founder Shares of the Company are currently held by one of the directors of the Company, [•]. Holding of the Founder Shares entitles the holder, among other things, to appoint and remove the Directors and other service providers of the Company. In the event of a conflict of interest between his duties and office as shareholder in, and director of, the Company the Directors' duty to act in the interests of the shareholders of the Company shall prevail.

c) One or more of the Directors my be a director of other companies that trade similar instruments and/or invest in similar assets to that traded by the Company and/or any of its Cells.

SECTION 9

ADDITIONAL INFORMATION

9.1 REPORTING

The Company will provide annual audited financial statements to the shareholders of the Cell within 6 months of the end of each Financial Reporting Date of the Company. The first Financial Reporting Date of the Company will be [•]. Thereafter, the Financial Reporting Date will occur annually on 31 December.

While the Directors of the Company will endeavour to provide audited financial statements within the time deadlines stated, the Director and/the Company shall not be held liable for any delays in providing the relevant reports and/or publishing the relevant information which result from unexpected contingencies, such as delays in receiving necessary information from which to prepare such reports or information; equipment failure; fire or other physical damage to office or equipment; power failures or acts of God.

Distribution of annual reports will be effected after the finalisation of the audit of the financial statements. A copy of the Company's latest audited financial statements can be obtained by the Company's shareholders free of charge at the offices of the Administrator at [•], Gibraltar.

All notices to the shareholders will be sent by the Administrator to the registered shareholders of the Company.

9.2 RELEVANT DOCUMENTATION

This Private Information Memorandum and its Part B pertaining to any Cell created is not intended to provide a complete description of the Company's Memorandum and Articles of Association or the agreements with the Directors and other service providers. Copies of all such documents are available for inspection by shareholders during normal business hours at the office of the Administrator. Shareholders may inspect copies of the annual audited report and accounts, when available, and the register of shareholders of the Company at the offices of the Administrator. The Memorandum and Articles of Association of the Company are available for inspection at the office of the Administrator during normal business hours and [•], Gibraltar.

9.3 ENQUIRIES

Enquiries concerning the Company and its shares (including information concerning subscription and valuation of the Participation Shares) should be directed to:

The Board of Directors

[•] PCC LIMITED

[•]

Gibraltar

9.4 GOVERNING LAW

The Company is governed by the law of Gibraltar and any dispute relating to the Company shall be submitted in first instance to the competent court of Gibraltar.

APPENDIX A

SUBSCRIPTION CHECK LIST

All or any of following documents or such additional or other documents as the Company may require for purposes of compliance must be faxed and then sent to the Company:

For a suscription to be accepted by the Company the following documents, or such additional or other documents as the Directors may in their absolute discretion require, must be sent to the Administrator (contact details as per Appendix F) in original form bearing an original signature of the Subscriber or an authorised signatory thereof. Subscription Requests should be sent by courier ONLY. Subscription Requests should not be sent by post or any other alternative means.

All investors

☐ completed and signed Subscription Agreement (Appendix B)

☐ completed and signed schedule of Subscription Information (Appendix C)

Individual investors

☐ certified copy of a passport or identification card

☐ certified copy of one utility bill (no more than three months old)

☐ letters of reference from one professional (banker, lawyer or accountant) in the form set out in Appendix D or other form as the Directors may from time to time accept.

Institutional investors, companies listed on a recognised exchange and regulated entities approved by the Company

☐ details of licensing authority/regulatory body that has authorised the institutional investor

Corporate investors (except for institutional investors, companies listed on a recognized exchange and regulated entities approved by the Company)

☐ certified copy of a passport or identification card for each director, shareholder (if their shareholding is in excess of 25% + 1 share) and beneficial owners (if their shareholding is in excess of 25% + 1 share)

- ☐ certified copy of one utility bill (no more than three months old) for each individual as stated above
- ☐ letters of reference from one professional (banker, lawyer or accountant) in the form set out in Appendix E for each individual as stated above
- ☐ certified copy of certificate of incorporation
- ☐ certified copy of memorandum and articles of association (or equivalent)

Trusts (except for registered charities)

- ☐ certified copy of a passport or identification card in respect of any individual who is trustee, named beneficiary/object or settlor
- ☐ certified copy of one utility bill (no more than three months old) in respect of any individual who is trustee, named beneficiary/object or settlor
- ☐ letters of reference from one professional (banker, lawyer or accountant) in the form set out in Appendix B in respect of any individual who is trustee, named beneficiary/object or settlor.
- ☐ (*any company that is trustee, named beneficiary/object or settlor except for companies listed on a recognized exchange*) - documents required of a corporate investor

APPENDIX B

SUBSCRIPTION AGREEMENT

The Board of Directors

[•] PCC LIMITED

[•]

Gibraltar

Dear Sirs

The undersigned (the "Shareholder" and/or the "Subscriber") acknowledges having received the Private Information Memorandum dated [•] and the Part B/Cell A Private Information Memorandum for the offering of redeemable preference shares (the "Participation Shares") of the [•] PROPERTY FUND (the "Company") pursuant to the terms of the Private Information Memorandum and its Part B/Cell A Private Information Memorandum and subject to the provisions of the Memorandum and Articles of Association of the Company.

The Shareholder further acknowledges that it has read the Private Information Memorandum in conjunction with Part B/Cell A Private Information Memorandum and understood the investment warning required by the Financial Services (Experienced Investor Funds) Regulations, 2005 (the "Regulations") as contained within the Private Information Memorandum and its Part B/Cell A Private Information Memorandum.

The Subscriber represents and warrants that:

1) it will not disclose the information contained in the Private Information and its Part B/Cell A Private Information Memorandum to any third parties and the information therein is used solely for its own purpose;

2) the Participation Shares are not being purchased with a view to immediate resale or active trading;

3) all consents required to be obtained and all regulatory or legal requirements necessary to be complied with or observed in order for this Agreement or the issuance of the Participation Shares to be lawful and valid under the laws of any jurisdiction to which the

Subscriber is subject to have been obtained, complied with or observed;

4) none of the Participation Shares (nor any interest therein) are being acquired or will at any time be held, directly or indirectly, for the account or benefit of a Politically Exposed Person ("PEP") such as a senior political figure or the spouse or associate of a senior political figure;

5) none of the Participation Shares (nor any interest therein) are being acquired or will at any time be held, directly or indirectly, for the account or benefit of a person on any Swiss or UK Foreign Office Money Laundering or Terrorism "Watch List";

6) the Subscriber has not relied on any representations or other information purported to be given on behalf of the Company except as set forth in the Private Information Memorandum and Part B/Cell A Private Information Memorandum, any documents referred to therein or the published financial statements of the Company;

7) none of the Participation Shares (nor any interest therein) are being acquired or will at any time be held, directly or indirectly, for the account or benefit of a U.S. Person and none of the Participation Shares will be transferred to any person who has failed to supply a similar representation. "U.S. Person" means:

   i. Any natural person resident in the United States of America, its territories and possessions, any State of the United States, and the District of Columbia (the "United States")
   ii. Any partnership or corporation organized or incorporated under the laws of the United States;
   iii. Any estate of which any executor or administrator is a U.S. person;
   iv. Any trust of which any trustee is a U.S. person;
   v. Any agency or branch of a foreign entity located in the United States;
   vi. Any non-discretionary account or similar account (other than an estate or trust) held by a dealer or other fiduciary for the benefit or account of a U.S. person;
   vii. Any discretionary account or similar account (other than an estate or trust) held by a dealer or other fiduciary organized, incorporated, or (if an individual) resident in the United States; and

viii. Any partnership or corporation if:

a) Organized or incorporated under the laws of any foreign jurisdiction; and

b) Formed by a U.S. person principally for the purpose of investing in securities not registered under the United States Securities Act of 1933, as amended, (the "Securities Act"), unless it is organized or incorporated, and owned, by accredited investors (as defined in Rule 501(a) of the Securities Act) who are not natural persons, estates or trusts.

8) The Shareholder is an Experienced Investor within the meaning specified in regulation 3 of the Financial Services (Experienced Investor Funds) Regulations, 2005.

9) The Subscriber will promptly inform the Company of any changes to the information disclosed, or to any of the above representations.

The Subscriber agrees to indemnify and hold harmless the Company, its Directors and officers and each other person or entity, if any, who controls it, against any and all loss, liability, claim, damage, costs and expense whatsoever (including but not limited to any and all expenses whatsoever reasonably incurred in investigating preparing or defending against any litigation commenced or threatened or any claim whatsoever) arising out of or based upon any false representation or warranty or breach or failure by the Subscriber to comply with the covenant or agreement made by the Subscriber herein or in any other document in connection with this transaction.

The Subscriber acknowledges that there can be no assurance that appreciation of the Company's assets will occur or that losses will not be realised and that the value of Participation Shares may be subject to volatile movements and may fall as well as rise.

This Agreement shall be governed by and interpreted in accordance with the laws of Gibraltar and the exclusive jurisdiction of the courts of Gibraltar, which the Subscriber hereby admits.

Name/For and on behalf of:

Date:

Signature:

APPENDIX C

SUBSCRIPTION INFORMATION

Date of Subscription:...

Name & Address for Share Registration:

....

....

Postal Address (if other than address of registration):

....

....

Telephone:..

Fax:...

E-mail:...

Name of Cell for which the Subscription pertains:

....

Amount of Subscription (Currency, Amount in Numbers and in Words):

....

In currency:

☐ *USD*____________________

☐ *EUR*____________________

☐ *CHF*____________________

☐ *GBP*____________________

Other than cash (full details):

Details of account and Name & Address of Remitting Bank:

Bank Name & Address: ....

Swift Code: ....

Account name & number: ....

IBAN: ....

Details of Bank account for transfers and payments of Redemptions in case of redemption (if different from above):

Bank Name & Address: ....

Swift Code: ....

Account name & number: ....

IBAN: ....

Physical Share Certificate Required?

☐ *YES*

☐ *NO (recommended)*

Is the subscriber the exclusive beneficial owner of the assets?

☐ *YES*

☐ *NO (if no, please provide full details of beneficial owner)*

Is the subscriber a politically exposed person?

☐ *YES*

☐ *NO*

Is the subscriber a U.S. Person?

☐ *YES*

☐ *NO*

Source of wealth of assets deposited with the bank (please tick)

☐ *Sale of business*

☐ *Investment profits*

- ☐ *Life time earnings/salary*
- ☐ *Gift/inheritance*
- ☐ *Sale of real estate*
- ☐ *Other (please specify)*

Signed: ....

Date: ....

Name: ....

Entity (if corporate investor): ....

Position of signatory: ....

Company's use only

Accepted and confirmed:

- ☐ *YES*
- ☐ *Name of Cell* ____________________________________
- ☐ *Number of shares issued* ______________________________
- ☐ *Issue price of shares issued* ____________________________
- ☐ *NO (please specify)*

Signed: ....

Date: ....

Name: ....

APPENDIX D

INDIVIDUAL INVESTOR

FORM OF LETTER TO BE PROVIDED FOR EACH INDIVIDUAL INVESTOR

[Letterhead of banker/lawyer/accountant]

[Date]

Dear Sir

This letter is to confirm that ____________ of _______________ [insert Residential Address] has been known to me/us for ____ years [must be minimum of two years] and to confirm that during that time he has always proved reliable, honest and trustworthy in his financial and business dealings.

Yours faithfully

[MUST BE SIGNED BY A BANKER, LAWYER OR ACCOUNTANT]

APPENDIX E

CORPORATE INVESTOR

FORM OF LETTER TO BE PROVIDED FOR EACH OF THE BENEFICIAL OWNERS AND SHAREHOLDERS (IF THEIR SHAREHOLDING IS IN EXCESS OF 25% + 1 SHARE) AND DIRECTORS OF EACH CORPORATE INVESTOR

(EXCEPT FOR INSTITUTIONAL INVESTORS, COMPANIES LISTED ON A RECOGNISED EXCHANGE AND REGULATED ENTITIES APPROVED BY THE COMPANY)

[Letterhead of banker/lawyer/accountant]

[Date]

Dear Sir

This letter is to confirm that ______________ of ________________ [insert Residential Address] has been known to me/us for ____ years [must be minimum of two years] and to confirm that during that time he has always proved reliable, honest and trustworthy in his financial and business dealings.

Yours faithfully

[MUST BE SIGNED BY A BANKER, LAWYER OR ACCOUNTANT]

APPENDIX F

SOPHISTICATED INVESTOR

(FOR UK PURPOSES ONLY)

The [•] Property Fund or Cell A is a cell of [•] PCC Limited, incorporated in Gibraltar. In the UK, it is classed as an unregulated collective investment scheme, the details of which may not be promoted to the general public. Certain restricted categories of individual are exempt from the restriction on the promotion of unregulated schemes' (in section 238 of the Financial Services and Markets Act 2000), including but not limited to Certified Sophisticated Investors, as defined in the certificate set out below. There is set out below a declaration and a certificate in the form required under the Financial Services and Markets Act 2000 (Promotion for Collective Investment Schemes) (Exemptions) Order 2001.

Please note that if you are a Certified Sophisticated Investor the purchase of shares in the [•] Property Fund may expose you to a significant risk of losing all of the property invested. If you have any doubts about such investment, you should consult an authorised person specialising on participation in unregulated property schemes.

APPENDIX 4

Declaration by Individual

Name

Address

Date

I make this statement so that I can receive promotions which are exempt from the restriction on promotion of unregulated schemes in the Financial Services and Markets Act 2000. The exemption relates to certified sophisticated investors and I declare that I qualify as such. I accept that the [•] Property Fund is not authorised or recognised for the purposes of that Act. I accept that I may not be able to make any claims under the Financial Services Compensation Scheme or under the Financial Services Ombudsman Scheme. I am aware that it is open to me to seek advice from an authorised person who specialises in advising on this kind of investment.

Signature

APPENDIX G

HIGH NET WORTH INDIVIDUALS

(FOR UK PURPOSES ONLY)

High Net Worth Individuals

The [•] Property Fund or Cell A is a cell of [•] PCC Limited incorporated in Gibraltar. It is classified in the UK as an unregulated collective investment scheme, the details of which may not be promoted to the general public. Certain restricted categories of individual are exempt from the restriction on the promotion of unregulated schemes (in section 238 of the Financial Services and Markets Act 2000), including but not limited to High Net Worth Individuals (as defined in the certificate set out below) provided that they sign a declaration that they qualify as such and in addition have been certified as such by an employer or an accountant. There is set out below a declaration and a certificate in the form required under the Financial Services and Markets Act 2000 (Promotion of Collective Investment Schemes) (Exemptions) Order 2001.

Please note that if you are a High Net Worth Individual the purchase of shares in the [•] Property Fund may expose you to a significant risk of losing all of the property invested. If you have any doubts about such investment, you should consult an authorised person specialising in advising on participation in unregulated property schemes.

APPENDIX 4

Declaration by Individual

Name:

Address:

Date:

I make this statement so that I am able to receive promotions of units in unregulated collective investment schemes where such promotions are exempt from the restriction in section 238 of the Financial Services and Markets Act 2000. The exemption relates to certified high net worth individuals and I declare that I qualify as such. I accept that the [•] Property Fund to which the promotions will relate are not authorised or recognised for the purposes of that Act. I accept that I may not be able to make any claims under the Financial Services Compensation Scheme or under the Financial Services Ombudsman Scheme. I am aware that it is open to me to seek advice from an authorised person who specialises in advising on this kind of investment.

Signature:

APPENDIX H

CERTIFICATE OF EMPLOYER OR ACCOUNTANT RELATING TO HIGH NET WORTH INDIVIDUALS (FOR UK PURPOSES ONLY)

Name of individual
providing the certificate:

Name of employer
or accountant:

Address of employer
or accountant:

Confirmation of status
(employer or accountant):

Date:

This certificate relates to:
[name]

of
[address].

In my opinion, the individual to whom this certificate relates either:

(i) had, during the financial year immediately preceding the date on which the certificate is signed, an annual income of not less than £100,000; or

(ii) held, throughout the financial year immediately preceding the date on which the certificate is signed, net assets to the value of not less than £250,000.

APPENDIX 4

I note that in determining an individual's "net assets", no account is to be taken of:

(a) the property which is her/her primary residence or of an any loan secured on that residence;

(b) any rights under a qualifying contract of insurance; or

(c) any benefits (in the form of pensions or otherwise) which are payable on the termination of his/her service or on his/her death or retirement and to which he is (or his dependents are), or may be, entitled.

Signed:

APPENDIX I

PAYMENT INSTRUCTIONS

Once the Subscription Documents been filled in and faxed and then sent to the Company, subscription funds should be sent to the Company at the following address:

Account Name: [•] PCC LIMITED

Account number:

IBAN:

Swift Code:

Sort Code:

Bank:

Currency:

☐ *USD (amount)* ____________________

☐ *EUR (amount)* ____________________

☐ *CHF (amount)* ____________________

☐ *GBP (amount)* ____________________

Reference:

☐ *Subscribers Name:*____________________

☐ *Name of Cell for which the Subscription pertains:* ________________

Please remember to add the name of the Subscriber as a reference on the fund wiring instructions to ensure proper crediting of funds.

Please also advise the Administrator that the funds have been sent. Please contact the Administrator if you are having difficulty sending funds:

[•] Limited

[•], Gibraltar

Tel: (350) [•], Fax: (350) [•], E-mail: [•]

APPENDIX J

REDEMPTION REQUESTS

Shareholders wishing to redeem all or any of their shareholding must serve a Redemption Request to the Administrator of the Company at the following address:

[•] Limited

[•]

Gibraltar

Tel: (350) [•]

Fax: (350) [•]

E-mail: [•]

A Redemption Request so given shall be in writing signed by the shareholder or an authorised signatory thereof and shall include full details of the shareholding including the name(s) and address(es) of the shareholder, the number of shares held and the number of shares being redeemed.

If a redemption would otherwise result in a shareholder having a residual holding of Participation Shares valued at less than €100,000 in any Cell, the Directors, at their absolute discretion, may deem the Redemption Request to have been made in respect of all the Participation Shares of that Cell held by that shareholder.

A Redemption Request should be sent to the Administrator of the Company. The Redemption Request be sent to the Administrator in the form of a letter (including the following information).

For a Redemption Request to be effective must be sent to the Administrator in original form bearing an original signature of the shareholder or an authorised signatory thereof. Redemption Requests should be sent by courier ONLY. Redemption Requests should not be sent by post or any other alternative means.

Details of Redemption Request:

☐ *Subscribers Name:* ______________________________

☐ *Name of Cell for which the Redemption Request pertains:*

____

☐ *Number of shares being requested to be Redeemed:* ____________

☐ *Number of shares remaining in the Cell after the Redemption Request:*

____

Signed: ....

Date: ....

Name: ....

Entity (if corporate investor):..

Position of signatory (if corporate investor):..

Appendix 5:

The Reinsurance Assignment Agreement

THIS DEED OF ASSIGNMENT OF REINSURANCE AGREEMENT is made on the day of 2010

BETWEEN:

ABC INSURANCE PCC LIMITED, a Protected Cell Company incorporated under the laws of Gibraltar with registered office situate at [•] (the "Assignor") in respect of Cell [•]; and

[•], a limited liability company incorporated in [•] with its registered office at [•] registered with [•] under company no [•] (the "Assignee"), for itself and as agent for the companies listed in Schedule Two (collectively referred to hereunder as the "Insured Persons").

WHEREAS:

(a) The Assignor is a Protected Cell Company under the laws of Gibraltar pursuant to the Protected Cell Companies Act 2001 (as amended).

(b) The Assignor has entered into a policy of insurance (hereinafter referred to as the "Cell Policy") which it has issued with No [•] to the Insured Persons and has entered into a reinsurance agreement pursuant to which it has reinsured its liability under the Cell Policy.

(c) The Assignor has set up the protected cell within the Assignor (such cell to be known as the "Cell [•]") for the sole purpose of reinsuring the Cell Policy;

(d) The Assignor, in order to further protect the Insured Persons' rights and interests in the Cell Policy, has agreed to enter into this Assignment of Reinsurance Agreement in favour of the Insured.

IT IS AGREED as follows:

1. **DEFINITIONS AND INTERPRETATION**

(1) In this Agreement the following expressions shall, except where the context otherwise requires, have the following meanings:

"Acknowledgement" means an acknowledgement substantially in the form set out in Schedule 1 to this Agreement;

"Encumbrance" means any mortgage, pledge, lien, charge, assignment, hypothecation, security interest, title retention, preferential right or trust arrangement and any other security agreement or arrangement;

"Assignor's Obligations" means all amounts and obligations which may at any time and from time to time hereafter be due, owing, or payable or be expressed to be due, owing, or payable, by the Assignor to the Insured Persons under or pursuant to the Cell Policy.
"this Agreement" means this Deed of Assignment of Reinsurance Agreement together with the Recitals hereof and the Schedules hereto, as the same may be amended, modified, varied, restated, novated or supplemented from time to time.

2. ASSIGNMENT

(1) By way of continuing security for the Assignor's Obligations, the Assignor hereby as beneficial owner assigns and agrees to assign absolutely to [•] all of its present and future right, title and interest in and to the benefits and recoveries (including, but not limited to, the proceeds) in respect of the Policy and/or cover notes (including all claims of whatsoever nature thereunder except for returns of premiums in respect thereof). For the avoidance of doubt, this Agreement constitutes an absolute assignment of the benefit, rights, title, interest and proceeds of the Policy by way of security subject to (2) below.

(2) Subject to the terms of this Agreement, upon all of the Assignor's Obligations being irrevocably discharged in full the property assigned pursuant to Clause 2(1) shall be reassigned to the Assignor without recourse to or warranty by the Insured Persons' other than a warranty that such property shall be free of any Encumbrance created by the Insured Persons' and the Insured Persons' shall, at the cost of the Assignor, execute such documents as the Assignor may reasonably require to effect or confirm such reassignment. Upon payment and discharge of all the Assignor's Obligations in full, the Insured Persons' shall pay the (remaining) proceeds (if any) of the Policy received by it, after the date of such payment, to the Assignor on demand for the benefit of the Cell [•].

3. REPRESENTATIONS AND WARRANTIES

The Assignor hereby represents and warrants to Assignee for the benefit of the Insured Persons' that:

(a) the Assignor is a company that has been duly formed and is validly existing under the laws of Gibraltar;

(b) the Assignor has full power, authority and legal right to enter into, execute and perform, and has taken all necessary action duly to authorise the entry into, execution, performance and delivery of, this Agreement, the creation of the security hereunder and the carrying out of its obligations hereunder;

(c) the Assignor has, where required by the terms of the Policy or by any relevant law or regulation, obtained or is obtaining the prior written consent of any relevant reinsurer to this Assignment; for the avoidance of doubt, the obtaining of the Acknowledgement shall be deemed to satisfy this requirement;

(d) this Agreement has been duly executed and constitutes all its legal, valid and binding obligations enforceable in accordance with its terms;

(e) the execution and performance by it of this Agreement, the assignment hereunder and the performance and observance by it of its obligations hereunder do not and will not:

(i) conflict with any law, rule or regulation or judicial, administrative or governmental order, judgment, injunction, determination or award applicable to it; or

(ii) conflict with any provision of its constitutive documents; or

(iii) conflict with, or result in any breach of, any of the terms or provisions of, or constitute a default under, any mortgage, deed, agreement or other instrument, arrangement, obligation or duty to which it is a party or is subject or by which any of its assets is bound; or

(iv) cause the exceeding of any limitation (whether imposed by law, statute, decree, rule, regulation, agreement, its constitutive documents or otherwise howsoever) on any of its powers or on any right or ability of its directors to exercise such powers or cause the exceeding of any other limit affecting it;

(f) other than the assignment hereby constituted, the Assignor has not created and there does not subsist any Encumbrance over the Policy, any part thereof or any of the rights, title or interests referred to in Clause 2(1) nor has the Assignor agreed to create any such Encumbrance;

(g) the assignment hereby constituted is legal, valid and binding and will constitute upon the service of the notice referred to in Clause 4(a) of this Agreement an absolute assignment by way of first specific legal charge and ranks and will rank ahead of any other Encumbrance (save for any Encumbrance preferred by law and not by contract) on or over the Policy or any part thereof and is not liable to avoidance on liquidation or bankruptcy, composition or any other similar insolvency proceedings; and

(h) save for registration of details of this Agreement with the Gibraltar Registrar of Companies no other filings are required to be made with any public or governmental office in Gibraltar to ensure the validity, enforceability or admissibility in evidence of this Agreement.

The Assignor hereby covenants with Assignee for the benefit of the Insured Persons' that each of the above representations and warranties will be correct in all respects at all times during the continuance of the security hereby constituted and as long as any Secured Obligations are outstanding as if repeated each day by reference to the then existing circumstances.

4. COVENANTS

The Assignor covenants that it shall:

(a) immediately following execution of this Agreement, give notice of this Agreement and the assignment herein contained to each reinsurance company through which the Policy is effected and maintained and in addition, promptly after any change in any such reinsurance company, or the identity of the re-insurers, as the case may be, give such notice to the new, replacement or additional re-insurers, each such notice to be in the form of Schedule Two hereto, and shall procure and deliver to the Agent an acknowledgement of each such notice by the relevant reinsurance company, as the case may be, in the form of the Acknowledgement;

(b) procure that a note of the interest of the Insured Persons' is endorsed upon the Policy; and

(c) not, save as provided in this Agreement, assign, pledge or charge, or create or permit to subsist any Encumbrance on or over, its right, title and interest in and to the Policy any proceeds thereof or any of the rights, title or interests referred to in Clause 2(1).

5. FURTHER ASSURANCE

The Assignor covenants that it will from time to time at the request of the Insured Persons' do or execute any further things, assurances and documents as may be required by law or as the Insured Persons' may reasonably consider necessary to establish, maintain and protect the rights of the Insured Persons' hereunder.

6. **POWER OF ATTORNEY**

(1) The Assignor hereby, by way of security for the performance of its obligations hereunder, irrevocably appoints the Insured Persons' (jointly and each severally) as its attorneys for and on its behalf and in its name or otherwise, at such time and in such manner as the attorneys may think fit:

(a) to execute and do any assurance, act or thing which the Assignor is required to do under this Agreement; and/or

(b) generally in its name and on its behalf to exercise all or any of the rights in relation to the enforcement of this Agreement conferred upon the Agent under this Agreement.

(2) The Assignor hereby ratifies and confirms and agrees to ratify and confirm whatever any such attorneys shall do or purport to do in the exercise or purported exercise of the power of attorney in Sub-Clause 6(1) except where such actions constitute gross negligence or wilful misconduct.

7. **APPLICATION OF INSURANCE PROCEEDS**

(1) All proceeds of the Policy received by the Assignor shall be dealt with and applied in the following order:

(a) first, in or towards payment of all costs, charges and expenses paid or incurred by the Insured Persons' in connection with or incidental to the exercise or performance by the Insured Persons' of any of the rights, powers or remedies hereby conferred or conferred by applicable law, or in connection with or incidental to the enforcement or realisation of the security hereby constituted;

(b) second, in or towards payment to the Insured Persons' in satisfaction of the Assignor's Obligations;

(c) third, the surplus, if any, shall be paid to the Assignor for the benefit of Cell [•].

8. **SUCCESSORS IN TITLE**

(1) The obligations on the part of the Assignor contained herein shall bind it and its successors and assigns and shall inure to the benefit of the Insured Persons' and their successors and assigns whether so expressed or not. Each of the Insured Persons shall be entitled to enforce the provisions of this Agreement against the Assignor directly. Assignee holds its rights under this Agreement on trust for the Insured Persons.

9. CONTINUING AND INDEPENDENT SECURITY

(1) This Agreement and the security hereby constituted shall remain in full force and effect by way of continuing security and shall not be affected in any way by any settlement of account or by:

(a) any other security, guarantee or insurance now or hereafter held by the Insured Persons' or any other person in respect of the Assignor's Obligations, any of them or any other liabilities; or

(b) the release of or any amendment to any security, guarantee or insurance (including, except to the extent of the relevant release or amendment, the security hereby constituted); or

(c) the enforcement or absence of enforcement of any security, guarantee or insurance (including the security hereby constituted); or

(d) any time, indulgence, waiver or consent given to the Assignor or any other person whether by the Insured Persons' or any other person; or

(e) the making or absence of any demand for payment of any liabilities made on the Assignor or any other person whether by the Insured Persons' or any other person; or

(f) the bankruptcy, insolvency, administration, appointment of a receiver or examinee or winding-up of the Assignor or Cell [•], the Insured Persons' or any other person; or

(g) the illegality, invalidity or unenforceability of or any defect in any provision of the Cell Policy;

(h) any agreement, security, guarantee, insurance, payment or other transaction which is capable of being avoided under or affected by any law relating to bankruptcy, insolvency, administration, examination or winding-up or any release, settlement or discharge given or made by the Insured Persons' on the faith of any such agreement, security, guarantee, insurance, payment or other transaction, and any such release, settlement or discharge shall be deemed to be limited accordingly.

(2) The Insured Persons' need not before exercising any of the rights, powers or remedies conferred upon it by this Agreement or by law (a) take action or obtain judgment against the Assignor or any other person in any court, (b) make or file claim or proof in a winding-up, examination or liquidation of the Assignor or Cell [•] or any other

person, or (c) enforce or seek to enforce the recovery of the Assignor's Obligations.

(3) This Agreement shall not be in any way discharged or impaired by reason of any other circumstance which might (but for this provision) constitute a legal or equitable discharge of this Agreement or any of its provisions.

(4) The Insured Persons' shall not be liable:

(a) by reason of the Insured Persons' entering into possession of the Policy or of any payments thereunder, to account as mortgagee in possession thereof for anything except actual receipts; or;

(b) for any loss upon realisation or for any default or omission for which a mortgagee in possession might be liable unless such loss is caused by the fraud or negligence or wilful misconduct of the Insured Persons'.

(5) The Insured Persons' accept, agree and acknowledge that (a) the Assignor is a "Protected Cell Company" under the laws of Gibraltar; (b) the obligations of the Assignor hereunder are obligations in respect of Cell [•] and not in respect of any of its other cellular assets; (c) the assets and undertakings in respect of Cell [•] are separate to and independent of all other assets and undertakings which are attributable to other cells which may exist from time to time; (d) the Assignor provides this security on the express understanding that for the satisfaction of its obligations and liabilities arising under or pursuant to this agreement, the Assignee may have recourse only to the assets attributable to Cell [•], and no recourse shall be had to the assets of any other cell, notwithstanding any provision of any agreement between the Assignor and the Assignee that would purport to extend the liability of the Assignor beyond that contemplated in this clause.

10. NOTICES

All notices, requests, demands or other communications provided for herein shall be in writing, shall be delivered by hand or by first-class mail, postage prepaid and shall be addressed to the parties hereto at their respective addresses listed below or to such other persons or addresses as the relevant party shall designate as to itself from time-to-time in a writing delivered in like manner:

If to **the Assignor**, to it at:

Attn:

If to the **Insured Persons'**, to them at:

Attn:

11. SEVERABILITY

If at any time any provision hereof becomes invalid, illegal or unenforceable in respect of the laws of any jurisdiction, the validity, legality or enforceability in respect of the remaining provisions hereof shall not in any way be affected or impaired thereby and such invalidity, illegality or unenforceability shall not affect the validity, legality or enforceability of such provision in any other jurisdiction.

12. COUNTERPARTS

This Agreement may be executed in any number of counterparts and by different parties on separate counterparts and all such counterparts together shall constitute one and the same instrument.

13. GOVERNING LAW AND JURISDICTION

(1) This Agreement is governed by, and shall be construed in accordance with, the laws of Gibraltar.

(2) (a) The Assignor agrees that all disputes howsoever arising under, from or in connection with, this Agreement shall be governed exclusively by, and shall be determined in accordance with, the laws of Gibraltar in the Gibraltar Courts.

(b) The Assignor irrevocably waives any objection which it may have now or in the future to the laying of the venue of the proceedings in any such court and any claim that any such proceedings have been brought in an inconvenient forum and irrevocably agrees that a judgment in any proceedings brought in the Courts of Gibraltar shall be conclusive and binding upon it and may be enforced in the courts of any other jurisdiction.

IN WITNESS whereof this Agreement has been executed and delivered as a Deed on the date which appears first on page 1.

SCHEDULE 1

NOTICE OF COMPLETION DATE IN RESPECT OF DEED OF ASSIGNMENT OF REINSURANCE AGREEMENT

To: [•]

Deed of Assignment of Reinsurance Agreement dated [•], 2010 (the "Assignment of Reinsurance") in favour of [•] in respect of Insurance Policy Nunmber [•] (the "Policy")

We refer to the deed of assignment of reinsurance agreement between ourselves and [•] on behalf of the Insured Persons' dated[•], 2010 (the "Assignment of Reinsurance").

Please take notice that by the Assignment of Reinsurance the Assignor assigned to [•] on behalf of the Insured Persons' (details of which are attached to this Notice) by way of security all of the Assignor's present and future right, title and interest in and to the benefits in respect of the Policy (including all claims of whatsoever nature thereunder and except for returns of premiums in respect thereof).

All proceeds of the Policy to which the Assignor is entitled shall be paid, subject to the terms of such policy, in accordance with the provisions of the Assignment of Reinsurance.

Please acknowledge receipt of this notice by signing and returning the acknowledgement on the enclosed copy of this notice.

This notice shall be governed by and construed in accordance with Gibraltar law.

Dated this day of , 2010

....

ABC INSURANCE PCC LIMITED

APPENDIX 5

ACKNOWLEDGEMENT

To: ABC Insurance PCC Limited ("Assignor")

We hereby acknowledge receipt of an executed copy of the Assignment of Reinsurance and we hereby (i) acknowledge that the Completion Date is [•], 2010; (ii) again confirm our consent and agreement to the assignment referred to in the Assignment of Reinsurance (iii) confirm our agreement to be bound thereby (iv) confirm that, save for the notice of assignment dated [•] , 2010 delivered to us by the Assignor in respect of the Policy, we have not previously received any notice of any other assignment of the interest of the Assignor or any other party in the Policy or sums from time to time becoming due thereunder to which the Assignor or any other party is entitled and (iv) agree to endorse the interest of the Insured Persons' and the on the Policy.

Dated: , 2010

....

For and on behalf of

SCHEDULE 2

[•]

EXECUTED AS A DEED by

the duly authorised signatory of)
ABC INSURANCE)
PCC LIMITED)
)
in the presence of:)

Signed: ....

Name and address of witness: ....

SIGNED by)
for and on behalf of)
[•])
)
in the presence of:)

Witness..

Name

Address

Index

FSC
www.fsc.org
MIX
Papier | Fördert gute Waldnutzung
FSC® C083411

Kolibri 360 GmbH
Ferdinand-Jühlke-Straße 7
99095 Erfurt, Deutschland
produktsicherheit@kolibri360.de